P9-EMO-265

TAKING SIDES

Clashing Views in

Science, Technology, and Society

TENTH EDITION, EXPANDED

TAKING SIDES

Clashing Views in

Science, Technology, and Society

TENTH EDITION, EXPANDED

Selected, Edited, and with Introductions by

Thomas A. Easton
Thomas College

The McGraw·Hill Companies

Connect
Learn
Succeed™

TAKING SIDES: CLASHING VIEWS IN SCIENCE, TECHNOLOGY AND SOCIETY, TENTH
EDITION, EXPANDED

1 2 3 4 5 6 7 8 9 0 DOC/DOC 1 0 9 8 7 6 5 4 3 2

MHID: 0-07-8050456
ISBN: 978-0-07-8050459
ISSN: 1552-4477

Managing Editor: *Larry Loeppke*
Marketing Director: *Adam Kloza*
Marketing Manager: *Nathan Edwards*
Senior Developmental Editor: *Debra A. Henricks*
Content Licensing Specialist: *Rita Hingtgen*
Project Manager: *Jessica Portz*
Cover Designer: *Studio Montage, St. Louis, MO*
Buyer: *Jennifer Pickel*
Media Project Manager: *Sridevi Palani*

Compositor: MPS Limited
Cover Image: © Blend Images LLC/ RF

Editors/Academic Advisory Board

Members of the Academic Advisory Board are instrumental in the final selection of articles for each edition of TAKING SIDES. Their review of articles for content, level, and appropriateness provides critical direction to the editors and staff. We think that you will find their careful consideration well reflected in this volume.

TAKING SIDES: Clashing Views in Science, Technology, and Society

Tenth Edition, Expanded

EDITOR

Thomas A. Easton
Thomas College

ACADEMIC ADVISORY BOARD MEMBERS

Preface

Those who must deal with scientific and technological issues—scientists, politicians, sociologists, business managers, and anyone who is concerned about energy policy, genetically modified foods, government intrusiveness, expensive space programs, or the morality of medical research, among many other issues—must be able to consider, evaluate, and choose among alternatives. Making choices is an essential aspect of the scientific method. It is also an inescapable feature of every public debate over a scientific or technological issue, for there can be no debate if there are no alternatives.

The ability to evaluate and to select among alternatives—as well as to know when the data do not permit selection—is called critical thinking. It is essential not only in science and technology but in every other aspect of life as well. *Taking Sides: Clashing Views in Science, Technology, and Society* is designed to stimulate and cultivate this ability by holding up for consideration 22 issues that have provoked substantial debate. Each of these issues has at least two sides, usually more. However, each issue is expressed in terms of a single question in order to draw the lines of debate more clearly. The ideas and answers that emerge from the clash of opposing points of view should be more complex than those offered by the students before the reading assignment.

The issues in this book were chosen because they are currently of particular concern to both science and society. They touch on the nature of science and research, the relationship between science and society, the uses of technology, and the potential threats that technological advances can pose to human survival. And they come from a variety of fields, including computer and space science, biology, environmentalism, law enforcement, and public health. I wish to thank Jeff Hecht for sharing his memories of the dawn of the modern computer age.

Organization of the book For each issue, I have provided an *issue introduction*, which provides some historical background and discusses why the issue is important. I then present two selections, one pro and one con, in which the authors make their cases. Each issue concludes with a *exploring the issue* that brings the issue up to date and adds other voices and viewpoints. I have also provided relevant Internet site addresses (URLs) both in the text and on the *Internet References* page that accompanies each part opener. At the back of the book is a listing of all the *contributors to this volume*, which gives information on the scientists, technicians, professors, and social critics whose views are debated here.

Which answer to the issue question—yes or no—is the correct answer? Perhaps neither. Perhaps both. Students should read, think about, and discuss the readings and then come to their own conclusions without letting my or their instructor's opinions (which sometimes show!) dictate theirs. The additional readings mentioned in both the introductions and the exploring the

issue should prove helpful. It is worth stressing that the issues covered in this book are all *live* issues; that is, the debates they represent are active and ongoing. In fact, they are so active and ongoing that when I teach this course, it often feels like a current events course!

Changes to this edition   This tenth edition represents a considerable revision of its predecessor. There are five completely new issues: "Should the Public Have to Pay to See the Results of Federally Funded Research?" (Issue 1); "Is America Ready for the Electric Car?" (Issue 6); "Can Infectious Animal Diseases Be Studied Safely in Kansas?" (Issue 10); "Does Endorsing Open Source Software Fail to Respect Intellectual Property?" (Issue 17); and "Should We Reject the 'Transhumanist' Goal of the Genetically, Electronically, and Mechanically Enhanced Human?" (Issue 19). Four issues have been renamed and given one new essay: "Is It Time to Think Seriously about 'Climate Engineering'?" (Issue 4); "Are We Doing Enough to Protect the Earth from Asteroid and Comet Impacts?" (Issue 12); "Do Humans Belong in Space?" (Issue 14); and "Do Government Internet Surveillance Efforts Threaten Privacy and Civil Rights?" (Issue 16). Three bonus issues: Should Society Impose a Moratorium on the Use and Release of "Synthetic Biology" Organisms? (Issue 20); Is Cyber-War or Cyber-Terrorism a Genuine Threat? (Issue 21); and Will Robots Take Your Job? (Issue 22) have been included in this expanded edition.

In addition, for four of the issues retained from the previous edition, one or both readings have been replaced to bring the debate up to date: "Should the Internet Be Neutral?" (Issue 3); "Is It Time to Revive Nuclear Power?" (Issue 5); "Do Falling Birth Rates Pose a Threat to Human Welfare?" (Issue 7); and "Is There Sufficient Evidence to Conclude That Cell Phones Cause Cancer?" (Issue 8). In all, there are 22 issues. The book's *Introduction* and the issue introductions and exploring the issue in the retained issues have been revised and updated where necessary.

A word to the instructor   An *Instructor's Resource Guide with Test Questions* (multiple-choice and essay) is available through the publisher for the instructor using *Taking Sides* in the classroom. It includes suggestions for stimulating in-class discussion for each issue. A general guidebook, *Using Taking Sides in the Classroom*, which discusses methods and techniques for integrating the pro-con approach into any classroom setting, is also available. An online version of *Using Taking Sides in the Classroom* and a correspondence service for *Taking Sides* adopters can be found at www.mhhe.com/cls.

Taking Sides: Clashing Views in Science, Technology, and Society is only one title in the Taking Sides series. If you are interested in seeing the table of contents for any of the other titles, please visit the Taking Sides Web site at www.mhhe.com/cls.

Thomas A. Easton
Thomas College

Contents in Brief

UNIT 7   Bonus Issues   375

Contents

Attorney and past Register of Copyrights Ralph Oman contends that "If
the NIH [National Institutes of Health] succeeds in putting all of the NIH-
related peer-reviewed articles on its online database for free within one
year of publication, the private publishers will be hard-pressed to survive."
Allowing private publishers to continue to profit by publishing the results of
publically funded research is the best way to ensure public benefit.
Heather Dalterio Joseph argues that permitting public access to NIH-
funded research results does not threaten the viability of journal
publishers. In addition, immediate online access to research results is
invaluable to the public.

Professor J. Scott Turner argues that the real issue is whether the world is
purposeful. Intelligent design can in fact be usefully taught, and doing so
avoids intrusions on academic freedom. The National Academy of
Sciences and Institute of Medicine of the National Academies argue that
evolution is so firmly ensconced in the foundations of modern science
that nonscientific alternatives to evolution such as creationism (including
intelligent design) have no place in the public school science curriculum.

FCC Chairman Julius Genachowski argues that we must preserve the openness and freedom of the Internet to ensure that the Internet continues to support innovation, opportunity, economic growth, and democracy in the twenty-first century. Kyle McSlarrow, president and chief executive officer of the National Cable & Telecommunications Association, argues that "net neutrality" mandates would interfere with the ability of broadband providers to improve Internet access and thus would ultimately undermine consumer choice and welfare.

UNIT 2   ENERGY AND THE ENVIRONMENT   55

Kevin Bullis, energy editor of *Technology Review*, reviews the latest thinking about "geoengineering" as a solution to the global warming problem, and concludes that despite potential side effects and the risk of unknown impacts on the environment, it may be time to consider technologies that can offset global warming. James R. Fleming, professor of science, technology, and society, argues that climate engineers fail to consider both the risks of unintended consequences to human life and political relationships and the ethics of the human relationship with nature.

Allison MacFarlane argues that although nuclear power poses serious problems to be overcome, it "offers a potential avenue to significantly mitigate carbon dioxide emissions while still providing baseload power required in today's world." However, it will take many years to build the necessary number of new nuclear power plants. Professor Kristin Shrader-Frechette argues that nuclear power is one of the most impractical and risky of energy sources. Renewable energy sources such as wind and solar are a sounder choice.

Michael Horn argues that the technology already exists to replace gasoline-burning cars with electric cars and thereby save money, reduce dependence on foreign oil sources, and reduce pollution. All we need is organization and determination. Rick Newman argues that because electric car technology is still new, expensive, and unreliable, it will be at least a decade before consumers are willing to shift from gas burners to electric cars.

UNIT 3   HUMAN HEALTH AND WELFARE   111

Michael Meyer argues that when world population begins to decline after about 2050, economies will no longer continue to grow, government benefits will decline, young people will have to support an elderly population, and despite some environmental benefits, quality of life will suffer. Writer Julia Whitty argues that even though the topic of overpopulation has become unpopular, it is clear that we are already using the Earth's resources faster than they can be replenished, and the only answer is to slow and eventually reverse population growth.

Olga V. Naidenko argues that even though past research into the link between cell phones and cancer has produced ambiguous results, more recent research on people who have used cell phones for many years has produced more worrisome results. More research is needed, but concern is already amply justified, especially in connection with children's exposure to cell phone emissions of radio waves. Linda S. Erdreich argues that independent scientific organizations have reviewed the research to date on the supposed link between cell phones and cancer and concluded that current evidence does not demonstrate that wireless phones cause cancer or have other adverse health effects.

Anne Platt McGinn, a senior researcher at the Worldwatch Institute, argues that although DDT is still used to fight malaria, there are other more effective and less environmentally harmful methods. She maintains that DDT should be banned or reserved for emergency use. Donald R. Roberts argues that the scientific evidence regarding the environmental hazards of DDT has been seriously misrepresented by antipesticide activists. The hazards of malaria are much greater and, properly used, DDT can prevent them and save lives.

Bruce Knight argues that although the U.S. Department of Agriculture's research facility at Plum Island, New York, has served well since it was built over half a century ago, modern technology is capable of ensuring safety at a mainland facility, which would also be cheaper to operate, more easily accessible, and more responsive to potential disease threats. Ray L. Wulf argues that an island location is much more effective at containing infectious diseases such as foot-and-mouth disease. A mainland research facility would permit unhampered spread of such diseases throughout the continental United States, with devastating consequences for the agricultural economy. Modern technology is not adequate to ensure safety, and federal, state, and local authorities are not prepared to deal with an outbreak.

Henry I. Miller and Gregory Conko of the Hoover Institution argue that genetically modified (GM) crops are safer for the consumer and better for the environment than non-GM crops. Jeffrey M. Smith, director of the Institute for Responsible Technology and the Campaign for Healthier Eating in America, argues that GM foods are dangerous to health and should be removed from the marketplace.

UNIT 5   THE COMPUTER REVOLUTION   265

Christof Koch and Giulio Tononi argue that because consciousness is a natural phenomenon, it will eventually be artificially created. To test for such consciousness, however, will require something other than the classic Turing test. John Horgan argues that no one has the foggiest idea of what consciousness really is, and it seems highly unlikely that we will ever be able to create an artificial consciousness. "Engineers and scientists should be helping us face the world's problems and find solutions to them, rather than indulging in escapist, pseudoscientific fantasies like the singularity."

James A. Lewis of the Center for Strategic and International Studies argues that proposed legislation, The Cybersecurity Act of 2009, which calls for Internet surveillance without regard to other legal restrictions, is needed "to bring law to the Wild West" of the Internet and enhance Internet security. Amitai Etzioni argues that new technologies such as those that enable Internet monitoring pose new threats, in particular to privacy. If there must be government surveillance programs, there must also be mechanisms for oversight and accountability. However, the mechanisms of accountability must not lie solely in the hands of government.

The International Intellectual Property Alliance (IIPA) argues that Indonesia should be put on the United States Trade Representative's "Special 301" watchlist because, in part, Indonesia's attempt to promote open source solutions "encourages a mindset that does not give due consideration to the value of intellectual creations." Michael Tiemann of Open Source Initiative objects strenuously, arguing that open source software is just as much an intellectual creation as proprietary software, it depends just as much on copyright protections, and because open source preferences have been promoted in several states, as well as portions of the federal government, the IIPA's position amounts to an attack on the United States itself.

UNIT 6 ETHICS 325

UNIT 7 BONUS ISSUES 375

Jim Thomas, Eric Hoffman, and Jaydee Hanson, representing the Civil Society on the Environmental and Societal Implications of Synthetic Biology, argue that the risks posed by synthetic biology to human health, the environment, and natural ecosystems are so great that Congress should declare an immediate moratorium on releases to the environment and commercial uses of synthetic organisms and require comprehensive environmental and social impact reviews of all federally funded synthetic biology research. Gregory E. Kaebnick of the Hastings Center argues that although synthetic biology is surrounded by genuine ethical and moral concerns—including risks to health and environment—which warrant discussion, the potential benefits are too great to call for a general moratorium.

Mike McConnell argues that the United States is already under attack by cyber-warriors, and we are losing. We need to upgrade cyber-defenses and be prepared to counter-attack. This may include requiring the private sector to share more information with government agencies. Maura Conway argues that even though various cyber-based attacks have been called "cyber-war" and "cyber-terrorism," definitions are crucial. In particular, "cyber-terrorism" fails to qualify as terrorism because it lacks the spectacular public impact of destroying buildings with airliners. "Cyberterrorism . . . is not in our near future."

Marshall Brain argues that by the middle of the twenty-first century, robots will be able to perform nearly any normal job that a human performs today. They will eliminate a huge portion of the jobs currently held by humans. Those humans will be unemployed and—if welfare systems cannot keep up with need—destitute. He insists that "It is time to start rethinking our economy." Peter Gorle and Andrew Clive argue that robots are not a threat to human employment. Historically, increases in the use of automation almost always increase both productivity and employment. Over the next few years, the use of robotics will generate 700,000–1,000,000 new jobs.

Topic Guide

T his topic guide suggests how the selections in this book relate to the subjects covered in your course. You may want to use the topics listed on these pages to search the Web more easily. On the following pages a number of websites have been gathered specifically for this book. They are arranged to reflect the units of this Taking Sides edition. You can link to these sites by going to www.mhhe .com/cls.

All the articles that relate to each topic are listed below the bold-faced term.

Artificial Intelligence

15. Can Machines Be Conscious?
19. Should We Reject the "Transhumanist" Goal of the Genetically, Electronically, and Mechanically Enhanced Human Being?
22. Will Robots Take Your Job?

Business

3. Should the Internet Be Neutral?
6. Is America Ready for the Electric Car?
17. Does Endorsing Open Source Software Fail to Respect Intellectual Property?
20. Should Society Impose a Moratorium on the Use and Release of "Synthetic Biology" Organisms?
22. Will Robots Take Your Job?

Crime

18. Is "Animal Rights" Just Another Excuse for Terrorism?
21. Is Cyber-War or Cyber-Terrorism a Genuine Threat?

Education

1. Should the Public Have to Pay to See the Results of Federally Funded Research?
2. Should "Intelligent Design" Be Taught in Public Schools?

Emerging Applications

6. Is America Ready for the Electric Car?
15. Can Machines Be Conscious?
16. Do Government Internet Surveillance Efforts Threaten Privacy and Civil Rights?

19. Should We Reject the "Transhumanist" Goal of the Genetically, Electronically, and Mechanically Enhanced Human Being?
20. Should Society Impose a Moratorium on the Use and Release of "Synthetic Biology" Organisms?
22. Will Robots Take Your Job?

Energy Options

4. Is It Time to Think Seriously about "Climate Engineering"?
5. Is It Time to Revive Nuclear Power?
6. Is America Ready for the Electric Car?

Environment

4. Is It Time to Think Seriously about "Climate Engineering"?
5. Is It Time to Revive Nuclear Power?
9. Should DDT Be Banned Worldwide?
10. Can Infectious Animal Diseases Be Studied Safely in Kansas?
11. Are Genetically Modified Foods Safe to Eat?
20. Should Society Impose a Moratorium on the Use and Release of "Synthetic Biology" Organisms?

Hardware and Software Design

8. Is There Sufficient Scientific Evidence to Conclude That Cell Phones Cause Cancer?
15. Can Machines Be Conscious?
17. Does Endorsing Open Source Software Fail to Respect Intellectual Property?
21. Is Cyber-War or Cyber-Terrorism a Genuine Threat?
22. Will Robots Take Your Job?

Health

7. Do Falling Birth Rates Pose a Threat to Human Welfare?
8. Is There Sufficient Scientific Evidence to Conclude that Cell Phones Cause Cancer?
9. Should DDT Be Banned Worldwide?
10. Can Infectious Animal Diseases Be Studied Safely in Kansas?
11. Are Genetically Modified Foods Safe to Eat?

Legal and Regulatory Issues

8. Is There Sufficient Scientific Evidence to Conclude that Cell Phones Cause Cancer?
9. Should DDT Be Banned Worldwide?
10. Can Infectious Animal Diseases Be Studied Safely in Kansas?
11. Are Genetically Modified Foods Safe to Eat?
17. Does Endorsing Open Source Software Fail to Respect Intellectual Property?
18. Is "Animal Rights" Just Another Excuse for Terrorism?
20. Should Society Impose a Moratorium on the Use and Release of "Synthetic Biology" Organisms?

Philosophical/Historical/Cultural Issues

2. Should "Intelligent Design" Be Taught in Public Schools?
15. Can Machines Be Conscious?
17. Does Endorsing Open Source Software Fail to Respect Intellectual Property?
19. Should We Reject the "Transhumanist" Goal of the Genetically, Electronically, and Mechanically Enhanced Human Being?
20. Should Society Impose a Moratorium on the Use and Release of "Synthetic Biology" Organisms?
22. Will Robots Take Your Job?

Politics

1. Should the Public Have to Pay to See the Results of Federally Funded Research?
4. Is It Time to Think Seriously about "Climate Engineering"?
10. Can Infectious Animal Diseases Be Studied Safely in Kansas?

14. Is "Manned Space Travel" a Delusion?
16. Do Government Internet Surveillance Efforts Threaten Privacy and Civil Rights?
17. Does Endorsing Open Source Software Fail to Respect Intellectual Property?
19. Should We Reject the "Transhumanist" Goal of the Genetically, Electronically, and Mechanically Enhanced Human Being?
21. Is Cyber-War or Cyber-Terrorism a Genuine Threat?
22. Will Robots Take Your Job?

Population

7. Do Falling Birth Rates Pose a Threat to Human Welfare?
8. Is There Sufficient Scientific Evidence to Conclude That Cell Phones Cause Cancer?
9. Should DDT Be Banned Worldwide?
11. Are Genetically Modified Foods Safe to Eat?
19. Should We Reject the "Transhumanist" Goal of the Genetically, Eectronically, and Mechanically Enhanced Human Being?

Privacy

1. Should the Public Have to Pay to See the Results of Federally Funded Research?
16. Do Government Internet Surveillance Efforts Threaten Privacy and Civil Rights?

Space Technology

4. Is It Time to Think Seriously about "Climate Engineering"?
12. Is NASA Doing Enough to Protect the Earth from Asteroid and Comet Impacts?
13. Will the Search for Extraterrestrial Life Ever Succeed?
14. Do Humans Belong in Space?

Youth

2. Should "Intelligent Design" Be Taught in Public Schools?
7. Do Falling Birth Rates Pose a Threat to Human Welfare?

Introduction

Analyzing Issues in Science and Technology

In his 2008 inaugural address, President Barack Obama said, "We will build the roads and bridges, the electric grids, and digital lines that feed our commerce and bind us together. We will restore science to its rightful place and wield technology's wonders to raise health care's quality and lower its costs." At the 2010 meeting of the American Association for the Advancement of Science, Eric Lander, co-chair of the President's Council of Advisors on Science and Technology, asked, "What is the rightful place of science?" and answered that it belongs "in the president's cabinet and policy-making, in the nation's classrooms; as an engine to propel the American economy; as a critical investment in the federal budget, even in times of austerity; as a tool for diplomacy and international understanding and as an organizing principle for space exploration." (See Eric S. Lander, "Obama Advisor Weighs 'The Rightful Place of Science'," *Science News* (June 5, 2010); the question is also discussed in Daniel Sarewitz, "The Rightful Place of Science," *Issues in Science and Technology* (Summer 2009).) However, John Marburger, science advisor to President George W. Bush, notes in "Science's Uncertain Authority in Policy," *Issues in Science and Technology* (Summer 2010), that policymakers often ignore science in favor of preference, prejudice, and expedience.

The discussion of "the rightful place of science" is important for several reasons. One is simply that previous administrations have often made decisions based less on evidence than on politics and ideology. The other is that a great many of the issues that the United States and the world face today cannot be properly understood without a solid grounding in climatology, ecology, physics, and engineering (among other areas). This is not going to change. In the twenty-first century, we cannot escape science and technology. Their fruits—the clothes we wear, the foods we eat, the tools we use—surround us. They also fill us with both hope and dread for the future, for although new discoveries promise us cures for diseases and other problems, new insights into the wonders of nature, new gadgets, new industries, and new jobs (among other things), the past has taught us that technological developments can have unforeseen and terrible consequences.

Those consequences do *not* belong to science, for science is nothing more (or less) than a systematic approach to gaining knowledge about the world. Technology is the application of knowledge (including scientific knowledge) to accomplish things we otherwise could not. It is not just devices such as hammers and computers and jet aircraft, but also management systems and

institutions and even political philosophies. And it is of course such *uses* of knowledge that affect our lives for good and ill.

We cannot say, "for good *or* ill." Technology is neither an unalloyed blessing nor an unmitigated curse. Every new technology offers both new benefits and new problems, and the two sorts of consequences cannot be separated from each other. Automobiles provide rapid, convenient personal transportation, but precisely because of that benefit, they also create suburbs, urban sprawl, crowded highways, and air pollution, and even contribute to global climate change.

Optimists Vs. Pessimists

The inescapable pairing of good and bad consequences helps to account for why so many issues of science and technology stir debate in our society. Optimists focus on the benefits of technology and are confident that we will be able to cope with any problems that arise. Pessimists fear the problems and are sure their costs will outweigh any possible benefits.

Sometimes the costs of new technologies are immediate and tangible. When new devices—steamship boilers or space shuttles—fail or new drugs prove to have unforeseen side effects, people die. Sometimes the costs are less obvious.

The proponents of technology answer that if a machine fails, it needs to be fixed, not banned. If a drug has side effects, it may need to be refined or its permitted recipients may have to be better defined (the banned tranquilizer thalidomide is famous for causing birth defects when taken early in pregnancy; it is apparently quite safe for men and nonpregnant women).

Certainty Vs. Uncertainty

Another root for the debates over science and technology is uncertainty. Science is by its very nature uncertain. Its truths are provisional, open to revision.

Unfortunately, most people are told by politicians, religious leaders, and newspaper columnists that truth is certain. They therefore believe that if someone admits uncertainty, their position is weak and they need not be heeded. This is, of course, an open invitation for demagogues to prey upon fears of disaster or side-effects or upon the wish to be told that the omens of greenhouse warming and ozone holes (etc.) are mere figments of the scientific imagination. Businesses may try to emphasize uncertainty to forestall government regulations; see David Michaels, *Doubt Is Their Product: How Industry's Assault on Science Threatens Your Health* (Oxford University Press, 2008).

Is Science Just Another Religion?

Science and technology have come to play a huge role in human culture, largely because they have led to vast improvements in nutrition, health care, comfort, communication, transportation, and humanity's ability to affect the world. However, science has also enhanced understanding of human behavior and of how the universe works, and in this it frequently contradicts

what people have long thought they knew. Furthermore, it actively rejects any role of God in scientific explanation.

Many people therefore reject what science tells us. They see science as just another way of explaining how the world and humanity came to be; in this view, science is no truer than religious accounts. Indeed, some say science is just another religion, with less claim on followers' allegiance than other religions that have been divinely sanctioned and hallowed by longer traditions. Certainly, they see little significant difference between the scientist's faith in reason, evidence, and skepticism as the best way to achieve truth about the world and the religious believer's faith in revelation and scripture. This becomes very explicit in connection with the debates between creationists and evolutionists. Even religious people who do not favor creationism may reject science because they see it as denying both the existence of God and the importance of "human values" (meaning behaviors that are affirmed by traditional religion). This leads to a basic antipathy between science and religion, especially conservative religion, and especially in areas—such as human origins—where science and scripture seem to be talking about the same things but are contradicting each other. This point can be illustrated by mentioning the Italian physicist Galileo Galilei (1564–1642), who in 1616 was attacked by the Roman Catholic Church for teaching Copernican astronomy and thus contradicting the teachings of the Church. Another example arose when evolutionary theorist Charles Darwin first published *On the Origin of Species by Means of Natural Selection* in 1859. Mano Singham notes in "The Science and Religion Wars," *Phi Delta Kappan* (February 2000), that "In the triangle formed by science, mainstream religion, and fringe beliefs, it is the conflict between science and fringe beliefs that is usually the source of the most heated, acrimonious, and public debate." Michael Ruse takes a more measured tone when he asks "Is Evolution a Secular Religion?" *Science* (March 7, 2003); his answer is that "Today's professional evolutionism is no more a secular religion than is industrial chemistry" but there is also a "popular evolutionism" that treads on religious ground and must be carefully distinguished. In recent years, efforts to counter "evolutionism" by mandating the teaching of creationism or "intelligent design" (ID) in public schools have made frequent appearances in the news, but so have the defeats of those efforts. One of the most recent defeats was in Dover, Pennsylvania, where the judge declared that "ID is not science." See Jeffrey Mervis, "Judge Jones Defines Science—And Why Intelligent Design Isn't," *Science* (January 6, 2006), and Sid Perkins, "Evolution in Action," *Science News* (February 25, 2006).

Even if religion does not enter the debate, some people reject new developments in science and technology (and in other areas) because they seem "unnatural." For most people, "natural" seems to mean any device or procedure to which they have become accustomed. Very few realize how "unnatural" are such ordinary things as circumcision and horseshoes and baseball.

Yet new ideas are inevitable. The search for and the application of knowledge is perhaps the human species' single most defining characteristic. Other creatures also use tools, communicate, love, play, and reason. Only humans have embraced change. We are forever creating variations on our religions,

languages, politics, and tools. Innovation is as natural to us as building dams is to a beaver.

Efforts to encourage innovation are a perennial topic in discussions of how nations can deal with problems and stimulate their economies (see David H. Guston, "Innovation Policy: Not Just a Jumbo Shrimp," *Nature* (August 21, 2008)). India has a National Innovation Foundation, and a similar government agency has been suggested for the United States (see Robert Atkinson and Howard Wial, "Creating a National Innovation Foundation," *Issues in Science and Technology* (Fall 2008); see also Robert Atkinson and Howard Wial, *Boosting Productivity, Innovation, and Growth through a National Innovation Foundation* (Washington, DC: Brookings Institution and Information Technology and Innovation Foundation, 2008), available online at www.brookings.edu/~/media/Files/rc/reports/2008/04_federal_role_atkinson_wial/NIF%20Report.pdf or www.itif.org/files/NIF.pdf). The closest we have come so far is the Defense Advanced Research Projects Agency (DARPA; www.darpa.mil/), famous for its initiation of Internet technology, and ARPA-Energy (http://arpa-e.energy.gov/), launched in 2007 with hopes for equally impressive results in the field of energy.

Voodoo Science

Public confusion over science and technology is increased by several factors. One is the failure of public education. In 2002, the Committee on Technological Literacy of the National Academy of Engineering and the National Research Council published a report (*Technically Speaking: Why All Americans Need to Know More About Technology*) that said that although the United States is defined by and dependent on science and technology, "its citizens are not equipped to make well-considered decisions or to think critically about technology. As a society, we are not even fully aware of or conversant with the technologies we use every day."

A second factor is the willingness of some to mislead. Alarmists stress awful possible consequences of new technology without paying attention to actual evidence, they demand certainty when it is impossible, and they reject the new because it is untraditional or even "unthinkable." And then there are the marketers, hypesters, fraudsters, activists, and even legitimate scientists and critics who oversell their claims. Robert L. Park, author of *Voodoo Science: The Road from Foolishness to Fraud* (Oxford University Press, 2002), lists seven warning signs "that a scientific claim lies well outside the bounds of rational scientific discourse" and should be viewed warily:

- The discoverer pitches his claim directly to the media, without permitting peer review.
- The discoverer says that a powerful establishment is trying to suppress his or her work.
- The scientific effect involved is always at the very limit of detection.
- Evidence for a discovery is only anecdotal.
- The discoverer says a belief is credible because it has endured for centuries.
- The discoverer has worked in isolation.

- The discoverer must propose new laws of nature to explain an observation.

The Soul of Science

The standard picture of science—a world of observations and hypotheses, experiments and theories, a world of sterile white coats and laboratories and cold, unfeeling logic—is a myth of our times. It has more to do with the way science is presented by both scientists and the media than with the way scientists actually do their work. In practice, scientists are often less orderly, less logical, and more prone to very human conflicts of personality than most people suspect.

The myth remains because it helps to organize science. It provides labels and a framework for what a scientist does; it may thus be especially valuable to student scientists who are still learning the ropes. In addition, it embodies certain important ideals of scientific thought. It is these ideals that make the scientific approach the most powerful and reliable guide to truth about the world that human beings have yet devised.

The Ideals of Science: Skepticism, Communication, and Reproducibility

The soul of science is a very simple idea: *Check it out.* Scholars used to think that all they had to do to do their duty by the truth was to say "According to . . ." some ancient authority such as Aristotle or the Bible. If someone with a suitably illustrious reputation had once said something was so, it was so. Arguing with authority or holy writ could get you charged with heresy and imprisoned or burned at the stake.

This attitude is the opposite of everything that modern science stands for. As Carl Sagan says in *The Demon-Haunted World: Science as a Candle in the Dark* (Random House, 1995, p. 28), "One of the great commandments of science is, 'Mistrust arguments from authority'." Scientific knowledge is based not on authority but on reality itself. Scientists take nothing on faith. They are *skeptical.* When they want to know something, they do not look it up in the library or take others' word for it. They go into the laboratory, the forest, the desert—wherever they can find the phenomena they wish to know about—and they ask those phenomena directly. They look for answers in the book of nature. And if they think they know the answer already, it is not of books that they ask, "Are we right?" but of nature. This is the point of "scientific experiments"—they are how scientists ask nature whether their ideas check out.

This "check it out" ideal is, however, an ideal. No one can possibly check everything out for himself or herself. Even scientists, in practice, look things up in books. They too rely on authorities. But the authorities they rely on are other scientists who have studied nature and reported what they learned. In principle, everything those authorities report can be checked. Observations in the lab or in the field can be repeated. New theoretical or computer models can be designed. What is in the books can be confirmed.

In fact, a good part of the official "scientific method" is designed to make it possible for any scientist's findings or conclusions to be confirmed. Scientists do not say, "Vitamin D is essential for strong bones. Believe me. I know." They say, "I know that vitamin D is essential for proper bone formation because I raised rats without vitamin D in their diet, and their bones turned out soft and crooked. When I gave them vitamin D, their bones hardened and straightened. Here is the kind of rat I used, the kind of food I fed them, the amount of vitamin D I gave them. Go thou and do likewise, and you will see what I saw."

Communication is therefore an essential part of modern science. That is, in order to function as a scientist, you must not keep secrets. You must tell others not just what you have learned by studying nature, but how you learned it. You must spell out your methods in enough detail to let others repeat your work.

Scientific knowledge is thus *reproducible* knowledge. Strictly speaking, if a person says "I can see it, but you can't," that person is not a scientist. Scientific knowledge exists for everyone. Anyone who takes the time to learn the proper techniques can confirm it. They don't have to believe in it first.

As an exercise, devise a way to convince a red-green colorblind person, who sees no difference between red and green, that such a difference really exists. That is, show that a knowledge of colors is reproducible, and therefore scientific, knowledge, rather than something more like belief in ghosts or telepathy.

Here's a hint: Photographic light meters respond to light hitting a sensor. Photographic filters permit light of only a single color to pass through.

The Standard Model of the Scientific Method

As it is usually presented, the scientific method has five major components. They include *observation, generalization* (identifying a pattern), stating a *hypothesis* (a tentative extension of the pattern or explanation for why the pattern exists), and *experimentation* (testing that explanation). The results of the tests are then *communicated* to other members of the scientific community, usually by publishing the findings. How each of these components contributes to the scientific method is discussed briefly below.

Observation

The basic units of science—and the only real facts the scientist knows—are the individual *observations*. Using them, we look for patterns, suggest explanations, and devise tests for our ideas. Our observations can be casual, as when we notice a black van parked in front of the fire hydrant on our block. They may also be more deliberate, as what a police detective notices when he or she sets out to find clues to who has been burglarizing apartments in our neighborhood.

Generalization

After we have made many observations, we try to discern a pattern among them. A statement of such a pattern is a *generalization*. We might form a generalization if we realized that every time there was a burglary on the block, that black van was parked by the hydrant.

Cautious experimenters do not jump to conclusions. When they think they see a pattern, they often make a few more observations just to be sure the pattern holds up. This practice of strengthening or confirming findings by *replicating* them is a very important part of the scientific process. In our example, the police would wait for the van to show up again and for another burglary to happen. Only then might they descend on the alleged villains. Is there loot in the van? Burglary tools?

The Hypothesis

A tentative explanation suggesting why a particular pattern exists is called a *hypothesis*. In our example, the hypothesis that comes to mind is obvious: The burglars drive to work in that black van.

The mark of a good hypothesis is that it is *testable*. The best hypotheses are *predictive*. Can you devise a predictive test for the "burglars use the black van" hypothesis?

Unfortunately, tests can fail even when the hypothesis is perfectly correct. How might that happen with our example?

Many philosophers of science insist on *falsification* as a crucial aspect of the scientific method. That is, when a test of a hypothesis shows the hypothesis to be false, the hypothesis must be rejected and replaced with another.

The Experiment

The *experiment* is the most formal part of the scientific process. The concept, however, is very simple: An experiment is nothing more than a test of a hypothesis. It is what a scientist—or a detective—does to check an idea out.

If the experiment does not falsify the hypothesis, that does not mean the hypothesis is true. It simply means that the scientist has not yet come up with the test that falsifies it. The more times and the more different ways that falsification fails, the more probable it is that the hypothesis is true. Unfortunately, because it is impossible to do all the possible tests of a hypothesis, the scientist can never *prove* it is true.

Consider the hypothesis that all cats are black. If you see a black cat, you don't really know anything at all about all cats. If you see a white cat, though, you certainly know that not all cats are black. You would have to look at every cat on Earth to prove the hypothesis. It takes just one to disprove it.

This is why philosophers of science say that *science is the art of disproving,* not proving. If a hypothesis withstands many attempts to disprove it, then it may be a good explanation of what is going on. If it fails just one test, it is clearly wrong and must be replaced with a new hypothesis.

However, researchers who study what scientists actually do point out that the truth is a little different. Almost all scientists, when they come up with what strikes them as a good explanation of a phenomenon or pattern, do *not* try to disprove their hypothesis. Instead, they design experiments to *confirm* it. If an experiment fails to confirm the hypothesis, the researcher tries another experiment, not another hypothesis.

Police detectives may do the same thing. Think of the one who found no evidence of wrongdoing in the black van but arrested the suspects anyway. Armed with a search warrant, he later searched their apartments. He was saying, in effect, "I *know* they're guilty. I just have to find the evidence to prove it."

The logical weakness in this approach is obvious, but that does not keep researchers (or detectives) from falling in love with their ideas and holding onto them as long as possible. Sometimes they hold on so long, even without confirmation of their hypothesis, that they wind up looking ridiculous. Sometimes the confirmations add up over the years and whatever attempts are made to disprove the hypothesis fail to do so. The hypothesis may then be elevated to the rank of a *theory, principle,* or *law.* Theories are explanations of how things work (the theory of evolution *by means of* natural selection). Principles and laws tend to be statements of things that happen, such as the law of gravity (masses attract each other, or what goes up comes down) or the gas law (if you increase the pressure on an enclosed gas, the volume will decrease and the temperature will increase).

Communication

Each scientist is obligated to share her or his hypotheses, methods, and findings with the rest of the scientific community. This sharing serves two purposes. First, it supports the basic ideal of skepticism by making it possible for others to say, "Oh, yeah? Let me check that." It tells those others where to see what the scientist saw, what techniques to use, and what tools to use.

Second, it gets the word out so that others can use what has been discovered. This is essential because science is a cooperative endeavor. People who work thousands of miles apart build with and upon each other's discoveries, and some of the most exciting discoveries have involved bringing together information from very different fields, as when geochemistry, paleontology, and astronomy came together to reveal that what killed off the dinosaurs 65 million years ago was apparently the impact of a massive comet or asteroid with the Earth.

Scientific cooperation stretches across time as well. Every generation of scientists both uses and adds to what previous generations have discovered. As Isaac Newton said, "If I have seen further than [other men], it is by standing upon the shoulders of Giants" (Letter to Robert Hooke, February 5, 1675/6).

The communication of science begins with a process called "peer review," which typically has three stages. The first occurs when a scientist seeks funding—from government agencies, foundations, or other sources—to carry out a research program. He or she must prepare a report describing the intended work, laying out background, hypotheses, planned experiments, expected results, and even the broader impacts on other fields. Committees of

other scientists then go over the report to see whether the scientist knows his or her area, has the necessary abilities, and is realistic in his or her plans.

Once the scientist has the needed funding, has done the work, and has written a report of the results, that report will go to a scientific journal. Before publishing the report, the journal's editors will show it to other workers in the same or related fields and ask whether the work was done adequately, the conclusions are justified, and the report should be published.

The third stage of peer review happens after publication, when the broader scientific community gets to see and judge the work.

This three-stage quality-control filter can, of course, be short-circuited. Any scientist with independent wealth can avoid the first stage quite easily, but such scientists are much, much rarer today than they were a century or so ago. Those who remain are the object of envy. Surely it is fair to say that they are not frowned upon as are those who avoid the later two stages of the "peer review" mechanism by using vanity presses and press conferences.

On the other hand, it is certainly possible for the standard peer review mechanisms to fail. By their nature, these mechanisms are more likely to approve ideas that do not contradict what the reviewers think they already know. Yet unconventional ideas are not necessarily wrong, as Alfred Wegener proved when he tried to gain acceptance for the idea of continental drift in the early twentieth century. At the time, geologists believed the crust of the Earth—which was solid rock, after all—did not behave like liquid. Yet Wegener was proposing that the continents floated about like icebergs in the sea, bumping into each other, tearing apart (to produce matching profiles like those of South America and Africa), and bumping again. It was not until the 1960s that most geologists accepted his ideas as genuine insights instead of hare-brained delusions.

The Need for Controls

Many years ago, I read a description of a wish machine. It consisted of an ordinary stereo amplifier with two unusual attachments. The wires that would normally be connected to a microphone were connected instead to a pair of copper plates. The wires that would normally be connected to a speaker were connected instead to a whip antenna of the sort we usually see on cars.

To use this device, one put a picture of some desired item between the copper plates. It could be a photo of a person with whom one wanted a date, a lottery ticket, a college, anything. One test case used a photo of a pest-infested cornfield. One then wished fervently for the date, a winning ticket, a college acceptance, or whatever else one craved. In the test case, that meant wishing that all the cornfield pests should drop dead.

Supposedly the wish would be picked up by the copper plates, amplified by the stereo amplifier, and then sent via the whip antenna wherever wish-orders have to go. Whoever or whatever fills those orders would get the message, and then. . . . Well, in the test case, the result was that when the testers checked the cornfield, there was no longer any sign of pests.

What's more, the process worked equally well whether the amplifier was plugged in or not.

I'm willing to bet that you are now feeling very much like a scientist—skeptical. The true, dedicated scientist, however, does not stop with saying, "Oh, yeah? Tell me another one!" Instead, he or she says something like, "Mmm. I wonder. Let's check this out." (Must we, really? After all, we can be quite sure that the wish machine does not work because if it did, it would be on the market. Casinos would then be unable to make a profit for their backers. Deadly diseases would not be deadly. And so on.)

Where must the scientist begin? The standard model of the scientific method says the first step is observation. Here, our observations (as well as our necessary generalization) are simply the description of the wish machine and the claims for its effectiveness. Perhaps we even have an example of the physical device itself.

What is our hypothesis? We have two choices, one consistent with the claims for the device, one denying those claims: The wish machine always works, or the wish machine never works. Both are equally testable, but perhaps one is more easily falsifiable. (Which one?)

How do we test the hypothesis? Set up the wish machine, and perform the experiment of making a wish. If the wish comes true, the device works. If it does not, it doesn't.

Can it really be that simple? In essence, yes. But in fact, no.

Even if you don't believe that wishing can make something happen, sometimes wishes do come true by sheer coincidence. Therefore, if the wish machine is as nonsensical as most people think it is, sometimes it will *seem* to work. We therefore need a way to shield against the misleading effects of coincidence. We need a way to *control* the possibilities of error.

Coincidence is not, of course, the only source of error we need to watch out for. For instance, there is a very human tendency to interpret events in such a way as to agree with our preexisting beliefs, our prejudices. If we believe in wishes, we therefore need a way to guard against our willingness to interpret near misses as not quite misses at all. There is also a human tendency not to look for mistakes when the results agree with our prejudices. That cornfield, for instance, might not have been as badly infested as the testers said it was, or a farmer might have sprayed it with pesticide whether the testers had wished or not, or the field they checked might have been the wrong one.

We would also like to check whether the wish machine does indeed work equally well plugged in or not, and then we must guard against the tendency to wish harder when we know it's plugged in. We would like to know whether the photo between the copper plates makes any difference, and then we must guard against the tendency to wish harder when we know the wish matches the photo.

Coincidence is easy to protect against. All that is necessary is to repeat the experiment enough times to be sure we are not seeing flukes. This is one major purpose of replication.

Our willingness to shade the results in our favor can be defeated by having someone else judge the results of our wishing experiments. Our eagerness to overlook "favorable" errors can be defeated by taking great care to avoid any errors at all; peer reviewers also help by pointing out such problems.

The other sources of error are harder to avoid, but scientists have developed a number of helpful *control* techniques. One is "blinding." In essence, it means setting things up so the scientist does not know what he or she is doing.

In the pharmaceutical industry, this technique is used whenever a new drug must be tested. A group of patients are selected. Half of them—chosen randomly to avoid any unconscious bias that might put sicker, taller, shorter, male, female, homosexual, black, or white patients in one group instead of the other—are given the drug. The others are given a dummy pill, or a sugar pill, also known as a placebo. In all other respects, the two groups are treated exactly the same. Drug (and other) researchers take great pains to be sure groups of experimental subjects are alike in every way but the one way being tested. Here that means the only difference between the groups should be which one gets the drug and which one gets the placebo.

Unfortunately, placebos can have real medical effects, apparently because we *believe* our doctors when they tell us that a pill will cure what ails us. We have faith in them, and our minds do their best to bring our bodies into line. This mind-over-body "placebo effect" seems to be akin to faith healing.

Single Blind.   The researchers therefore do not tell the patients what pill they are getting. The patients are "blinded" to what is going on. Both placebo and drug then gain equal advantage from the placebo effect. If the drug seems to work better or worse than the placebo, then the researchers can be sure of a real difference between the two.

Double Blind.   Or can they? Unfortunately, if the researchers know what pill they are handing out, they can give subtle, unconscious cues. Or they may interpret any changes in symptoms in favor of the drug. It is therefore best to keep the researchers in the dark too; since both researchers and patients are now blind to the truth, the experiment is said to be "double blind." Drug trials often use pills that differ only in color or in the number on the bottle, and the code is not broken until all the results are in. This way nobody knows who gets what until the knowledge can no longer make a difference.

Obviously, the double-blind approach can work only when there are human beings on both sides of the experiment, as experimenter and as experimental subject. When the object of the experiment is an inanimate object such as a wish machine, only the single-blind approach is possible.

With suitable precautions against coincidence, self-delusion, wishful thinking, bias, and other sources of error, the wish machine could be convincingly tested. Yet it cannot be perfectly tested, for perhaps it works only sometimes, when the aurora glows green over Copenhagen, in months without an "r," or when certain people use it. It is impossible to rule out all the possibilities, although we can rule out enough to be pretty confident as we call the gadget nonsense.

Very similar precautions are essential in every scientific field, for the same sources of error lie in wait wherever experiments are done, and they serve very much the same function. However, we must stress that no controls and no peer review system, no matter how elaborate, can completely protect a scientist—or science—from error.

Here, as well as in the logical impossibility of proof (experiments only fail to disprove) and science's dependence on the progressive growth of knowledge (its requirement that each scientist make his or her discoveries while standing on the shoulders of the giants who went before, if you will) lies the uncertainty that is the hallmark of science. Yet it is also a hallmark of science that its methods guarantee that uncertainty will be reduced (not eliminated). Frauds and errors will be detected and corrected. Limited understandings of truth will be extended.

Those who bear this in mind will be better equipped to deal with issues of certainty and risk.

Something else to bear in mind is that argument is an inevitable part of science. The combination of communication and skepticism very frequently leads scientists into debates with each other. The scientist's willingness to be skeptical about and hence to challenge received wisdom leads to debates with everyone else. A book like this one is an unrealistic portrayal of science only because it covers such a small fraction of all the arguments available.

Is Science Worth It?

What scientists do as they apply their methods is called *research*. Scientists who perform *basic or fundamental research* seek no specific result. Basic research is motivated essentially by curiosity. It is the study of some intriguing aspect of nature for its own sake. Basic researchers have revealed vast amounts of detail about the chemistry and function of genes, explored the behavior of electrons in semiconductors, revealed the structure of the atom, discovered radioactivity, and opened our minds to the immensity in both time and space of the universe in which we live.

Applied or strategic research is more mission-oriented. Applied scientists turn basic discoveries into devices and processes, such as transistors, computers, antibiotics, vaccines, nuclear weapons and power plants, and communications and weather satellites. There are thousands of such examples, all of which are answers to specific problems or needs, and many of which were quite surprising to the basic researchers who first gained the raw knowledge that led to these developments.

It is easy to see what drives the effort to put science to work. Society has a host of problems that cry out for immediate solutions. Yet there is also a need for research that is not tied to explicit need because such research undeniably supplies a great many of the ideas, facts, and techniques that problem-solving researchers then use in solving society's problems. Basic researchers, of course, use the same ideas, facts, and techniques as they continue their probings into the way nature works.

In 1945—after the scientific and technological successes of World War II—Vannevar Bush argued in *Science, the Endless Frontier* (National Science Foundation, 1990) that science would continue to benefit society best if it were supported with generous funding but not controlled by society. On the record, he was quite right, for the next half-century saw an unprecedented degree of progress in medicine, transportation, computers, communications, weapons, and a great deal more.

There have been and will continue to be problems that emerge from science and its applications in technology. Some people respond like Bill Joy, who argues in "Why the Future Doesn't Need Us," *Wired* (April 2000), that some technologies—notably robotics, genetic engineering, and nanotechnology—are so hazardous that we should refrain from developing them. On the whole, however, argue those like George Conrades ("Basic Research: Long-Term Problems Facing a Long-Term Investment," *Vital Speeches of the Day* (May 15, 1999)), the value of the opportunities greatly outweighs the hazards of the problems. Others are less sanguine. David H. Guston and Kenneth Keniston ("Updating the Social Contract for Science," *Technology Review* (November/December 1994)) argue that despite the obvious successes of science and technology, public attitudes toward scientific research also depend on the vast expense of the scientific enterprise and the perceived risks. As a result, the public should not be "excluded from decision making about science." That is, decisions should not be left to the experts alone.

Conflict also arises over the function of science in our society. Traditionally, scientists have seen themselves as engaged in the disinterested pursuit of knowledge, solving the puzzles set before them by nature with little concern for whether the solutions to these puzzles might prove helpful to human enterprises such as war, health care, and commerce, among many more. Yet again and again the solutions found by scientists have proved useful. They have founded industries. And scientists love to quote Michael Faraday, who, when asked by politicians what good the new electricity might be, replied: "Someday, sir, you will tax it."

Not surprisingly, society has come to expect science to be useful. When asked to fund research, it feels it has the right to target research on issues of social concern, to demand results of immediate value, to forbid research it deems dangerous or disruptive, and to control access to research results that might be misused by terrorists or others (the issue of "unclassified but sensitive" research was included in the 8th edition of this book; see also Donald Kennedy, "Science and Security, Again," *Science* (August 22, 2008)).

Private interests such as corporations often feel that they have similar rights in regard to research they have funded. For instance, tobacco companies have displayed a strong tendency to fund research that shows tobacco to be safe and to cancel funding for studies that come up with other results, which might interfere with profits.

One argument for public funding is that it avoids such conflict-of-interest issues. Yet politicians have their own interests, and their control of the purse strings—just like a corporation's—can give their demands a certain undeniable persuasiveness.

Public Policy

The question of targeting research is only one way in which science and technology intersect the broader realm of public policy. Here the question becomes how society should allocate its resources in general: toward education

or prisons; health care or welfare; research or trade; and encouraging new technologies or cleaning up after old ones?

The problem is that money is finite. Faced with competing worthy goals, we must make choices. We must also run the risk that our choices will turn out, in hindsight, to have been wrong.

The Purpose of This Book

Is there any prospect that the debates over the proper function of science, the acceptability of new technologies, or the truth of forecasts of disaster will soon fall quiet? Surely not, for some of the old issues will forever refuse to die (think of evolution versus creationism), and there will always be new issues to debate afresh. Some of the new issues will strut upon the stage of history only briefly, but they will in their existence reflect something significant about the way human beings view science and technology. Some will remain controversial as long as has evolution or the population explosion (which has been debated ever since Thomas Malthus' 1798 "Essay on the Principle of Population"). Some will flourish and fade and return to prominence; early editions of this book included the debate over whether the last stocks of smallpox virus should be destroyed; they were not, and the war on terrorism has brought awareness of the virus and the need for smallpox vaccine back onto the public stage. The loss of the space shuttle *Columbia* reawakened the debate over whether space should be explored by people or machines. Some issues will remain live but change their form, as has the debate over government interception of electronic communications. And there will always be more issues than can be squeezed into a book like this one—think, for instance, of the debate over whether elections should use electronic voting machines (discussed by Steve Ditlea, "Hack the Vote," *Popular Mechanics* (November 2004)).

Since almost all of these science and technology issues can or will affect the conditions of our daily lives, we should know something about them. We can begin by examining the nature of science and a few of the current controversies over issues in science and technology. After all, if one does not know what science, the scientific mode of thought, and their strengths and limitations are, one cannot think critically and constructively about any issue with a scientific or technological component. Nor can one hope to make informed choices among competing scientific, technological, or political and social priorities.

Internet References . . .

SavetheInternet.Com

The SavetheInternet.com Coalition believes that the Internet is a crucial engine for economic growth and free speech and lobbies to preserve network neutrality.

www.savetheinternet.com

Discovery Institute

The Discovery Institute's Center for Science and Culture questions the validity of evolutionary theory and promotes the teaching of intelligent design.

http://discovery.org/csc/aboutCSC.php/

National Center for Science Education

The National Center for Science Education provides information and advice to keep evolution in the science classroom and "scientific creationism" out.

www.ncse.com

Directory of Open Access Journals

The Directory of Open Access Journals lists almost 4000 free, full-text, quality-controlled scientific and scholarly journals, a third of which can be searched at the article level.

www.doaj.org/

BioMed Central—Open Access Charter

BioMed Central calls itself the "open access publisher." It defines open access publishing as making materials "universally and freely accessible via the Internet, in an easily readable format . . . immediately upon publication" and commits itself to maintaining an open access policy.

www.biomedcentral.com/info/about/charter/

The Place of Science and Technology in Society

T he partnership between human society and science and technology is an uneasy one. Science and technology offer undoubted benefits, in both the short and long term, but they also challenge received wisdom and political ideology. The issues in this section deal with whether public access to publicly funded research should take precedence over the right of private interests to make money, whether religion should supplant science in the public schools, and whether commerce or freedom is a better foundation for regulation.

- Should the Public Have to Pay to See the Results of Federally Funded Research?
- Should "Intelligent Design" Be Taught in Public Schools?
- Should the Internet Be Neutral?

ISSUE 1

Should the Public Have to Pay to See the Results of Federally Funded Research?

YES: Ralph Oman, from testimony regarding H.R 6845, the Fair Copyright in Research Works Act, before the Subcommittee on Courts, the Internet, and Intellectual Property of the Committee on the Judiciary (September 11, 2008)

NO: Heather Dalterio Joseph, from testimony regarding H.R 6845, the Fair Copyright in Research Works Act, before the Subcommittee on Courts, the Internet, and Intellectual Property of the Committee on the Judiciary (September 11, 2008)

Learning Outcomes

After studying this issue, students will be able to explain:

1. How peer review helps to ensure the quality of scientific publications.
2. Why peer review and open access can coexist.
3. Why university and college libraries favor open access publishing.
4. The role of profit in academic publishing.

ISSUE SUMMARY

YES: Attorney and past Register of Copyrights Ralph Oman contends that "If the NIH [National Institutes of Health] succeeds in putting all of the NIH-related peer-reviewed articles on its online database for free within one year of publication, the private publishers will be hard-pressed to survive." Allowing private publishers to continue to profit by publishing the results of publically funded research is the best way to ensure public benefit.

NO: Heather Dalterio Joseph argues that permitting public access to NIH-funded research results does not threaten the viability of

journal publishers. In addition, immediate online access to research results is invaluable to the public.

According to Peter Suber's "Open Access Overview" (www.earlham.edu/~peters/fos/overview.htm), "open access" refers to the broad-based movement to put peer-reviewed research articles online, free of charge, and without most copyright and licensing restrictions. According to his "Timeline of the Open Access Movement" (www.earlham.edu/~peters/fos/timeline.htm), the movement has roots in the 1960s, well before the Internet came to exist as we know it today. Project Gutenberg (www.gutenberg.org/wiki/Main_Page), which makes public-domain novels and other books freely available, was launched in 1971. For many years, the open access movement was no threat to the standard modes of scientific publishing, but by 2004 it was clear that scientific (and other) journals were becoming so expensive that university and college libraries were being forced to cut back on the number of journals they could subscribe to. Pressure was rising to do something about the problem, and open access looked like a possible solution, as exemplified by the Public Library of Science (PLoS) (see Theodora Bloom, et al., "PLoS Biology at 5: The Future Is Open Access," *PLoS Biology* (October 2008)). In response to a report from the House Appropriations Committee urging the National Institutes of Health (NIH) to require NIH-funded research reports to be deposited in NIH's Internet archive, PubMed Central, NIH director Elias Zerhouni convened meetings with representatives of academic publishers, and others. Publishers expressed concern that making reports freely available would threaten their continued existence (see Jocelyn Kaiser, "House Weighs Proposal to Block Mandatory 'Open Access,'" *Science* (September 19, 2008)).

According to Walt Crawford, "Open Access: It's Never Simple," *Online* (July/August 2008), one major objection to the traditional mode of scholarly publication—meaning that university and college libraries pay to subscribe to a journal—is that subscriptions have become remarkably expensive. Springer-Verlag's journal prices for 2010 can be seen at http://www.springer.com/librarians/price+lists?SGWID=0-40585-0-0-0; seven of those journals are priced at more than $10,000 a year. The prices of Elsevier's titles are listed at http://www.elsevier.com/wps/find/subscriptionpricelist.cws_home/2010subscrippricelistlibr/description; *Life Sciences* cost a library $7095 for 2010 compared with $4031 a year in 2000 and $2325 in 1995. Subscription prices for print journals have grown about 10 percent per year, with electronic access and mixed access being priced even higher. Aggregated (multijournal) electronic-access packages appeared in 2001 to help stabilize prices; see Frances L. Chen, Paul Wrynn, and Judith L. Rieke, "Electronic Journal Access: How Does It Affect the Print Subscription Price?" *Bulletin of the Medical Library Association* (October 2001).

Today aggregated packages (such as Ebsco) are commonplace, with many academic libraries using them to replace paper subscriptions. But even these can be expensive. It is no surprise that libraries are among the strongest backers of the open access movement in the United States and elsewhere (for a

Canadian view, see Heather Morrison and Andrew Waller, "Open Access and Evolving Scholarly Communication," *C&RL News* (September 2008)). Some researchers are addressing the concern that open access journals are somehow inferior to subscription journals in terms of quality control by studying their "impact factor" (how often papers are cited); K. A. Clauson et al., "Open-Access Publishing for Pharmacy-Focused Journals," *American Journal of Health-System Pharmacy* (August 15, 2008), find that impact factors are actually greater for journals with some form of open access. In 2009, five of the most cited papers were open access; see Devon Greyson, Heather Morrison, and Andrew Waller, "Open Access in Canada: A Strong Beginning," *Feliciter* (vol. 56, no. 2, 2010), who call open access "a growing and evolving movement." However, Philip M. Davis, "Author-Choice Open-Access Publishing in the Biological and Medical Literature: A Citation Analysis," *Journal of the American Society for Information Science & Technology* (January 2009), finds that the open access advantage is declining. See also Ji-Hong Park, "Motivations for Web-Based Scholarly Publishing: Do Scientists Recognize Open Availability as an Advantage?" *Journal of Scholarly Publishing* (June 2009).

The pressure for open access does not come only from government agencies such as NIH. Some see open access as a movement to democratize what has until recently been an elite resource; see Ron Miller, "Open Access Battles to Democratize Academic Publishing," *EContent* (April 2009). Leslie Chan, Subbiah Arunachalam, and Barbara Kirsop, "Open Access: A Giant Leap Towards Bridging Health Inequities," *Bulletin of the World Health Organization* (August 2009), argue that only through open access publishing can the latest research results reach those who need them. Harvard University's arts and sciences faculty "has directly challenged the authority of academic journals to control access to research results" by voting to put faculty work in a free online repository, following similar moves by the Howard Hughes Medical Institute and the Wellcome Trust in London. A comment by Patricia Schroeder of the Association of American Publishers that "Publishers may not be as quite as excited to take articles from Harvard" seems more than a little wishful, considering Harvard's reputation; see Andrew Lawler, "Harvard Faculty Votes to Make Open Access Its Default Mode," *Science* (February 22, 2008). In December 2009, Robin Peek, "OAW [Open Access Week] 2009 Exceeds Expectations," *Information Today*, noted that 100 universities have now announced plans to require researchers to deposit research information in open access repositories. The Obama administration has opened discussions over whether to broaden open access beyond the NIH program; see Jocelyn Kaiser, "White House Mulls Plan to Broaden Access to Published Papers," *Science* (January 15, 2010). In July 2010, the Information Policy, Census, and National Archives Subcommittee of the House Committee on Oversight and Government Reform held a hearing to discuss the open access debate, touching on two bills, one that would extend the NIH policy to 11 other research agencies and shorten the 12-month delay before depositing papers in an open archive to just 6 months, and one that would revise copyright law to forbid the practice entirely. Testimony recapitulated many of the points mentioned here; see Jocelyn Kaiser, "House Hearing Explores Debate Over Free Access to Journal Articles," *ScienceInsider* (July 30, 2010).

Are print journals actually threatened by the open access movement? Many commentators remark that journals offer much more than just research reports. However, they may not prove able to sustain high subscription prices. They will be obliged to adapt, as many are already doing, according to Jennifer Howard, "Scholarly Presses Discuss How They're Adapting to a Brave New E-World," *The Chronicle of Higher Education* (July 11, 2008). One such adaptation is publishing books that can be freely downloaded in hope that actual book sales will follow; see John Murphy, "New Entry Tries New Publishing Model," *Research Information* (December 2008). Charles Oppenheim, "Electronic Scholarly Publishing and Open Access," *Journal of Information Science* (vol. 34, no. 4, 2008), expects pressure for open access publishing to continue. On the other hand, no one really expects open access publishing to completely displace the traditional mode; see Jocelyn Kaiser, "Free Journals Grow Amid Ongoing Debate," *Science* (August 20, 2010).

In 2007, legislation mandated that federally funded research reports be given to PubMed Central. The resulting public access policy is described in Robin Peek, "Coming to Grips with the NIH Policy," *Information Today* (September 2008); see also Robin Peek, "The Battle over PubMed Central Continues," *Information Today* (November 2008). Thanks to lobbying by publishers, on September 9, 2008, HR 6845, the Fair Copyright in Research Works Act, was introduced to reverse NIH's policy and forbid other federal agencies from implementing similar policies. The bill was promptly referred to the House Judiciary Committee. It did not come to a vote before that session of Congress ended, but it was reintroduced in 2009. The bill may be moot because in 2009 President Obama signed the Consolidated Appropriations Act, which included a provision making NIH's Public Access Policy permanent; see Robin Peek, "The Tide Has Changed; Get Over It," *Information Today* (May 2009).

A hearing on the bill was held on September 11, 2008. Publisher representatives such as Martin Frank, executive director of the American Physiological Society, supported the bill arguing, "By protecting copyright for research works, [it] will continue to provide incentives for private-sector investment in the peer review process which helps ensure the quality and integrity of scientific research." In the following selections, attorney and past Register of Copyrights Ralph Oman contends in his testimony that "If the NIH [National Institutes of Health] succeeds in putting all of the NIH-related peer-reviewed articles on its online database for free within one year of publication, the private publishers will be hard-pressed to survive." Allowing private publishers to continue to profit by publishing the results of publically funded research is the best way to ensure public benefit. Heather Dalterio Joseph, executive director of the Scholarly Publishing and Academic Resources Coalition Committee, testifies that permitting public access to NIH-funded research results does not threaten the viability of journal publishers. In addition, immediate online access to research results is invaluable to the public.

YES

Ralph Oman

The Fair Copyright in Research Works Act

Mr. Chairman and members of the Subcommittee. It is a great honor to appear again before this distinguished panel. It has been a few years since my last appearance.

Thank you for the opportunity to testify on this matter of importance to copyright generally, and to the public, to the research community, to the authors of scientific, technical, and medical articles, and to the publishers of STM journals. I would like to focus on the larger policy issues that undergird the American copyright system and discuss the proposal of the National Institutes of Health that requires recipients of NIH research grants to effectively renounce copyright in their peer-reviewed article manuscripts just 12 months after publication. I will also briefly mention the bill introduced by Chairman Conyers that seeks to moderate the impact of the NIH proposal in a way that will encourage the broadest possible dissemination of high quality, peer-reviewed articles without running roughshod over the rights of authors and copyright owners.

This hearing is important on another level. The language in the appropriations bill that has given rise to this controversy was never vetted by the Judiciary Committee—the committee with intellectual property expertise. With your scrutiny today, the Subcommittee puts this narrow dispute in the larger context of the constitutional mandate—to promote the progress of science for the public interest. Other than celebrating the Judiciary Committee's involvement, I will not comment on the wisdom of legislating on appropriations bills. Into that Serbonian Bog I will not wade.

Instead, I simply applaud your decision, Mr. Chairman, to give a full airing of these issues before your expert Subcommittee. They bear directly on the copyright policies of our government and the incentives to authorship and publication under U.S. copyright law. For reasons I will discuss, the NIH proposal seems short-sighted, counterproductive, damaging to U.S. creativity, which this subcommittee fosters and safeguards, and contrary to the NIH's own interests in encouraging broad public dissemination of peer-reviewed learned articles. The Appropriations Committee, to its credit, sensed that the NIH proposal ventured into sensitive territory and added a very important proviso. That proviso directed the NIH to "implement the public access policy in a manner consistent with copyright law." In my opinion, the NIH has fallen

The U.S. House of Representatives, September 11, 2008.

short of that dictate in several respects, and, with this committee's expert guidance, they should refine their proposal in ways that are true to both the letter and spirit of the copyright law, and the essential policies behind it.

In this debate, three key questions must be answered. First, what policy will result in the broadest dissemination of high quality, peer-reviewed scholarly articles? Second, is it fair for the U.S. government to appropriate the value-added contributions of the private STM publishers? And, third, is the NIH correct in its assumption that the STM publishers will continue to publish their journals even if they lose 50 percent of their paid subscriptions?

Many of my colleagues in academia recognize that the STM publishers perform many vital functions in bringing these articles into the public forum. For one thing, they make substantial investments in the peer-review process. While they do not as a general rule pay the reviewers, the publishers hire in-house teams to support outside specialists. These teams arrange and coordinate effective distribution, stay close to the academic experts in the discipline personally and professionally, follow the literature, and engage in on-going communications with the authors about the reviewers' comments and the incorporation of those comments into the manuscript.

In addition to the peer-review process, the publishers make judgments about which of the manuscripts to publish, depending on their quality and the level of interest in the research itself. They also edit the manuscripts and make them presentable for publication.

My basic concern about the NIH proposal is that it will, sooner rather than later, destroy the commercial market for these scientific, technical, and medical journals. If this dark prophesy comes to pass, who, I wonder, will handle all of these expensive and sensitive administrative details? Some of my academic colleagues are confident that this change in the mechanics of scientific publishing will have little or no impact on the private sector, and that it will remain as robust as ever, even if the NIH freely publishes all of the NIH peer-reviewed article manuscripts shortly after private publication. Some claim that they have "evidence" that STM publishing will continue to flourish. I have not seen that evidence. To me, it suggests an element of wishful thinking. In my experience, Congress is normally reluctant to hang major legislative change in copyright policy on the thin reed of wishful thinking. With the prospect of free copies available in the near term, who in the face of experience and reality can reasonably expect that subscribers to STM journals, faced with their own budgetary constraints and needs, will not look with real favor on alternative free sources? I can't. It is belied by common sense. Certainly, many university and industry librarians will cancel their subscriptions to these learned journals, with some estimates of a cancellation rate approaching 50 percent. With plummeting sales, how could the STM publishers stay in business? This is a critical point, and one that this committee has a special sensitivity to. It really goes to the heart of the matter, in terms of public policy.

It is a basic premise of copyright that the law is designed to benefit the public, not reward authors or publishers. But, as James Madison wrote in the Federalist Papers, "the public good fully coincides" with the rights of authors and copyright owners. With that admonition, we consider the NIH proposal.

It seems clear that Congress would not want the NIH free access policy to cause many or all of the private STM publishers to fade away. Of course, if fair market competition, or a change in the culture of academic publishing, or costly overhead were eventually to drive the private publishers out of business, so be it. It is one thing that they should suffer demise because of changes in the marketplace, and it is another to be brought down by an ill-considered governmental fiat. The NIH does not intend to perform any of the vetting, selection, and editing functions now performed by the learned societies, by the professional organizations, and by the STM publishers, and I doubt if Congress wants to increase their budget so they can take on these additional responsibilities. So the question occurs: who is going to do it? I do not see replacements for the publishers raising their hands to volunteer. For this reason alone, I question the wisdom of the NIH provision. And there are larger issues as well. Experience teaches that as a general rule Congress prefers to keep the hairy snout of the federal government out of the peer-review and manuscript selection process. We live in an open society, and, with a weather eye on the First Amendment, we try to keep the government at arms length from these delicate publication decisions, so as not to skew the process.

That being said, the NIH provision brings back vivid memories of the debate we had in 1980 with the Small Business and University Patent Procedure Act. In that debate, Senator Russell Long, Chairman of the Senate Finance Committee, following the script written by Admiral Rickover, the father of the nuclear submarine, argued in favor of existing government policy—that patents developed with government research money belong to the taxpayers who subsidize the research. Senator Bayh and Senator Dole reasoned that the taxpayers would get a far greater return on their investment if we instead facilitated private sector ownership and commercialization of the inventions, putting these inventions to work for the people. We are about to celebrate the 30th anniversary of Bayh/Dole, and no one is arguing for its repeal.

The same policy arguments apply in the NIH case. If the NIH succeeds in putting all of the NIH-related peer-reviewed articles on its online database for free within one year of publication, the private publishers will be hard-pressed to survive. To me, it seems far more likely that the U.S. taxpayer will achieve the desired objective—the broadest possible dissemination of the peer-reviewed article manuscripts—under the current system. With the private STM publishers running the peer-review process, selecting the articles, and aggressively marketing their journals to libraries and other research institutions, both foreign and domestic, the current system lets the publishers bring their professional judgment and expertise into the process and ensures high quality scholarship. Paid subscriptions keep the current system perking along, without intrusive government involvement, and without an infusion of funds from the government fisc. If the NIH provision is fully implemented, it will almost certainly end this self-policing and self-financing system and get the federal government deeply into the STM publishing business.

Finally, Mr. Chairman, I would like to mention a few related issues. First, I wonder if any of the manuscript articles that the NIH will publish contain preexisting materials that the NIH researcher did not create and therefore does

not own. Here, I am thinking of charts, diagrams, photographs, and illustrations. Will the NIH commandeer the rights of those creators as well, or will it require the NIH researcher to clear all of those ancillary rights as part of the "contract." Today, of course, the publishers often help the author clear these rights, including electronic distribution rights. Will the NIH undertake this task if the publishers drop out of the picture?

Second, I wonder if the NIH proposal really serves our international interests. Our trade negotiators are constantly fighting for strong intellectual property protection, which is under siege in many countries around the world. I assume that some of the authors (or at least co-authors) are foreign nationals, and would fall under the protection of the Berne Convention. And I assume some of the impacted publisher/copyright owners are foreign as well. As I will note in a moment, the NIH policy will seriously threaten the protection of American authored and published works in foreign countries. This government edict from the NIH, not promulgated "in a manner consistent with copyright law," has a crippling effect on the value of the copyright in these works. Some of my academic colleagues argue that the Berne Convention has no relevance to the NIH policy. They see it as a simple contract matter, and they note that the researchers get very valuable consideration for their assignment of copyright to the NIH under the contract. Granted, the researchers do receive a generous stipend, averaging $400,000, but that fact also makes the whole arrangement suspect. To a serious researcher, an NIH grant is a matter of life and death professionally. To claim that the assignment of the reproduction right is "voluntary"—the product of a free market negotiation—strikes me as disingenuous.

In fact, the government involvement puts the NIH "contract" in a suspect category in the Berne and TRIPs context. It is not a private contract between commercial interests. Let me draw a hypothetical. The U.S. motion picture industry is now permitted to exhibit theatrically only 10 or so films per year in China. Suppose the government of China were to offer the American film producers a deal: "If you sign a contract waiving your reproduction right, we will allow you to exhibit 100 films a year." The producers would crunch the numbers and calculate the bottom line, even while complaining bitterly that the deal is outrageous and clearly a violation of the spirit of copyright and the Berne Convention. Nonetheless, they might conclude that on balance they would make more money with the proffered deal than they now make with limited access to the huge Chinese market. So, in the end, they might sign on the dotted line. Could the United States take that "contract" to the WTO and press a claim under TRIPs that China is not complying with its treaty obligations? I think so. The ensuing mass piracy of American films in China would be a direct result of this unwaivering government action that diminishes copyright, disguised as a "contract." In any case, the NIH free access policy is an unfortunate international precedent for a country like the United States, whose great strength is intellectual property.

The NIH should reconsider the long term consequences of its proposal. The dedicated researchers who benefit from the NIH grants take great professional pride in being published in prestigious learned journals, all of which

constitute a valuable and reliable resource for future research. The NIH itself recognizes that "publication in peer-reviewed journals is a major factor in determining the professional standing of scientists; institutions use publication in peer-reviewed journals in making hiring, promotion, and tenure decisions."

Despite some grumbling about high subscription prices, very few researchers, academics, or librarians are suggesting that the journals have outlived their usefulness. The STM publishers should be given the right to compete fairly in a changing marketplace, in which they will innovate and have the opportunity to flourish on their own merits, as long as their copyrights are protected. Congress should require the NIH to demonstrate convincingly that their free access policy will not jeopardize the existence of the STM publishers and the indispensable role they play in vetting and selecting peer-reviewed articles. Absent that proof, the NIH should rethink their current policy of involuntary assignment. Current law gives the NIH some discretion in implementing their open access policy in a manner consistent with copyright. If the NIH do not amend their policy, Congress should direct them to do so. The Chairman's bill will allow the publishers to continue publishing. It will preserve the STM journals as valuable professional tools for scientific research, thereby promoting the progress of science. By restoring the status quo ante, the Chairman's bill will give the evolving free market a chance to come to grips with the new online technologies without undercutting the incentives that publishers have relied on for two hundred years. I would urge its enactment.

Heather Dalterio Joseph  **NO**

The Fair Copyright in Research Works Act

I am here today because SPARC, ARL, and ATA represent a large number of the users who currently rely on and directly benefit from access to the works that would be affected by this proposed legislation. I am also here having spent fifteen years as a publisher in both not-for-profit and commercial publishing organizations. And finally, I am here as a mother and as a member of the public, with a deep and abiding interest in the results of the research that my tax dollars help to support.

I would like to express my serious reservations about this legislation, and particularly about the negative impact it would have on the advancement of scientific research and on the availability of vital health care information for millions of Americans by overturning the crucially important National Institutes of Health's Public Access Policy.

SPARC, a membership organization of more than 225 college and university libraries in the United States, is dedicated to working collaboratively to expand the dissemination of the results of scholarly research by leveraging the vast new opportunities presented to the academic community in the networked digital environment. ARL represents 123 research libraries in North America. As academic and research libraries, we represent the customer base of the journal publishing industry, providing the majority of the subscription income received by these publishers.

SPARC also serves as the coordinating organization for the Alliance for Taxpayer Access, an alliance of more than 80 libraries, universities, patients advocacy groups, consumer groups, and student organizations who are dedicated to ensuring that a specific subset of scholarly research—specifically the results of research that has been funded using taxpayer dollars—is made freely and rapidly accessible to the public.

U.S. taxpayers underwrite tens of billions of dollars of research each year, and the widespread sharing of the results of this research is an essential component of our government's investment in science. It is only through the **use** of these findings that funders—and, by extension, taxpayers—obtain value from their investment. Faster and wider sharing of knowledge fuels the advancement of science and accordingly, the return of health, economic, and social benefits back to the public. This is why 33 Nobel Laureates have written

The U.S. House of Representatives, September 11, 2008.

in strong support of the NIH Public Access Policy. That letter is included in my written statement.

Yet, despite the fact that the public has paid for this research, colleges, patients, physicians, researchers, and other members of the public frequently cannot access taxpayer-funded research findings because they simply cannot afford to subscribe to all of the journals in which these findings are published.

As the Executive Director of SPARC, I see libraries face this access issue on a daily basis. Even the most well-funded, private university libraries can not afford to subscribe to all of the journals they would like to provide their students. This situation is exacerbated by the continued rapid escalation in price of journal subscriptions, which puts libraries in the position of having to cancel subscriptions. Libraries now routinely find themselves in the position of paying more and more money only to be able to provide their patrons—students, faculty, researchers—with access to less and less.

This is why the organizations that I represent today have enthusiastically supported efforts such as the NIH's which are designed to break this logjam. The NIH Public Access Policy is a simple, effective, and carefully balanced policy. It requires that all investigators funded by the agency submit an electronic version of their final peer-reviewed manuscripts to PubMed Central (PMC), the online archive of the National Library of Medicine, to be made publicly available within twelve months of publication, and in a manner consistent with copyright law.

The policy is designed to create a broadly accessible, permanent archive of the results of NIH-funded research in order to advance the conduct of science and enhance the agency's accountability to the public. In short, this policy ensures that the U.S. taxpayers are able to benefit fully from the research that they have underwritten.

During the extensive public comment periods and discussions that have taken place over the past four years, opponents of the policy have expressed a variety of concerns. Chief among them has been the fear that the policy would create a resource that is competitive with journals, and would ultimately damage publisher revenues. The concern is that their primary customer—academic libraries—will view the availability of an author's manuscript in PubMed Central as an adequate substitute for subscribing to a journal, and will, as result, cancel subscriptions in large numbers. There are several reasons why this fear is unfounded.

First, the current NIH Public Access Policy is a compromise policy that contains safeguards against this happening. Authors who receive NIH funding are required to deposit only their final accepted, peer-reviewed manuscript—the raw, word-processing file—into PubMed Central, rather than the final, copyedited, formatted, enhanced—and copyrighted—version that will ultimately appear in the journal. The final articles with these value-added features remain solely the publishers to distribute and sell as they choose.

Second, the NIH Policy allows an embargo period of up to one year before a manuscript becomes publicly available. In the realm of the extremely fast-moving, crucial biomedical research funded by the NIH, information, after

one year, is already old. The value in the articles resulting from this research lies largely in their immediacy.

Finally, there are very few, if any, journals that publish only research articles that have resulted from NIH funding. The vast majority of journals publish articles resulting from other funding sources, along with review articles, editorial material, commentary, and other value-added material.

The findings of recent studies have supported the use of these safeguards. In a 2006 report commissioned by a publishing organization, the Association of Learned and Professional Society Publishers (ALSP) surveyed librarians to determine what factors would prompt them to cancel journal subscriptions.[1] The report concluded that "availability of content via delayed open access was not an important factor in journal cancellations." Specifically, they noted that for availability of material in an archive such as PubMed Central to become a factor in subscription cancellation:

1. The embargo has to be very short. 82% of librarians surveyed noted it had to be 3 months or less, and for 92% it had to be 6 months or less;
2. The raw manuscript, or preprint, is not a substitute for the journal— only 9% saw access to a preprint as an adequate substitute; and
3. Completeness counts—75% of librarians said the archive would have to contain over 90% of a given journal's content before it became a factor in considering cancellation.

The library community does not view this policy as a chance to save money by cutting subscriptions to biomedical journals—but rather as an important opportunity to supplement our journal collections by providing access to additional material that we would not otherwise be able to provide to our patrons. And importantly, libraries strongly support NIH's role in preserving this biomedical literature for future generations of users.

As a publisher, I have seen first hand that the experience of organizations who have voluntarily participated in depositing materials into PubMed Central supports this survey. As a direct example: The American Society for Cell Biology (ASCB), where I served as Publishing Director, has made the research articles from its journal, *Molecular Biology of the Cell*, available on PubMed Central just two months after their publication since 2001. Additionally, the society puts all of the journal's content into the database, not just the fraction supported by NIH funding. Despite this, the revenue generated by *Molecular Biology of the Cell* has increased steadily since 2001. Participation in PubMed Central actually resulted in an increase in the number of articles downloaded from the society's website, increasing the visibility of the journal and the papers published there.

The ASCB is not alone in this experience. There are several hundred other journals also voluntarily depositing content into PubMed Central. . . . None of these would do so if it threatened their core business in any way.

Finally, as a mother and member of the general public, the NIH Public Access Policy addresses the public's rising interest in self-education on health matters and need to see the results of their extensive investments. The information

we are talking about today is, after all, generated by a public agency tasked with protecting and improving the public health. The information contained in PubMed Central is not esoteric research of interest only to elite scholars. It is crucial, health-related information that can make a life-or-death difference in the lives of the American public. As of today, the NIH database contains more than 27,500 articles on malaria, 50,000 on AIDS, 41,000 on HIV, 5,000 on health disparities, 2,000 on disadvantaged populations and more than 77,000 on diabetes research. This is a vital resource for individuals looking for health care information at any time of the day, from anywhere, any day of the week.

When my five-year-old son was diagnosed just nine weeks ago, with autoimmune, insulin-dependent Type 1 Diabetes, I did what every member of the patients advocacy groups I represent today predicted I would. I got online and looked for every piece of current information I could get my hands on. I did this from home, at 3 in the morning the night we got home from the hospital, desperate for information that could reassure me that there was something else I could do besides wake my child up twice a night to check his blood sugar for signs of hypoglycemia. I found a 2008 study of continuous glucose monitors, rating parent and patient satisfaction in the prevention of night-time instances of low blood sugar.[2] Notably, what was available to me was the authors' final manuscript, posted just one month before, available solely because of the NIH Public Access Policy. It was worth the world to me.

Besides serving the interest of the public as just described, the NIH policy also strikes a careful balance between increasing access to the literature and respecting the concerns of publishers, by operating within the current copyright structure. As noted by 45 of law professors who specialize in copyright law, the NIH policy in no way conflicts with U.S. copyright law. The agency receives a non-exclusive license from the researchers they fund, who retain their copyright and are free to enter into traditional publication agreements with journals or to assign these rights to anyone they want, subject to the standard federal purpose license.

Unfortunately, the Fair Copyright in Research Works Act would effectively overturn this important and much needed policy. By prohibiting agencies from making the results of the research they fund public in the manner that they choose, this bill would significantly inhibit our ability to advance scientific discovery. This legislation is not in the best interest of the taxpayers who fund the research nor the scientific community and the public that rely upon it.

References

1. "ALPSP Survey of Librarians on Factors in Journal Cancellation" Mark Ware Consulting Ltd . . .

2. Weinzimer, Stuart MD, c/o DirecNet Coordinating Center, Jaeb Center for Health Research, FreeStyle Navigator™ Continuous Glucose Monitoring System Use in Children with Type 1 Diabetes Using Glargine-based Multiple Daily Dose Regimens: Results of a Pilot Trial," . . .

EXPLORING THE ISSUE

Should the Public Have to Pay to See the Results of Federally Funded Research?

Critical Thinking and Reflection

1. How does peer review help to ensure the quality of scientific publications?
2. Are "open access" and "peer review" mutually contradictory concepts?
3. Why can university libraries not subscribe to all available high-quality academic journals?
4. Should academic publishing be profit oriented?

Is There Common Ground?

At the core of the debate lie two points: the right of academic publishers to make a profit and the right of the public to have access to the fruits of scientific research. High journal prices favor the former while impeding the latter. In one form, open access publishing says the academic publishers can make a profit for a limited time before articles get put into open access archives. On the other hand, no one really expects open access publishing to completely displace the traditional mode; see Jocelyn Kaiser, "Free Journals Grow Amid Ongoing Debate," *Science* (August 20, 2010).

1. Is this form of open access publishing a viable compromise?
2. Some areas of science have long circulated preprints of articles to give other scientists and even the public a first look at reports. Journals later publish edited, peer-reviewed versions of the reports. Is this a viable compromise?
3. Would the lack of peer reviewing make preprints less than satisfactory?
4. If we reject the idea that academic publishing should be profit oriented, how can the publishers remain in business? Should academic publishing be run by the government?

ISSUE 2

Should "Intelligent Design" Be Taught in Public Schools?

YES: **J. Scott Turner,** from "Signs of Design," *The Christian Century* (June 12, 2007)

NO: **National Academy of Sciences and Institute of Medicine of the National Academies,** from *Science, Evolution, and Creationism* (National Academies Press, 2008)

Learning Outcomes

After studying this issue, students will be able to explain:

1. How the Creationist position excludes non-Christians.
2. How and why evolution is not a religion.
3. The difference between "teaching religion" and "teaching science."
4. How critical thinking threatens many traditional beliefs.

ISSUE SUMMARY

YES: Professor J. Scott Turner argues that the real issue is whether the world is purposeful. Intelligent design can in fact be usefully taught, and doing so avoids intrusions on academic freedom.

NO: The National Academy of Sciences and Institute of Medicine of the National Academies argue that evolution is so firmly ensconced in the foundations of modern science that nonscientific alternatives to evolution such as creationism (including intelligent design) have no place in the public school science curriculum.

It has long been an article of faith for scientists that teleological questions ("why" questions that presume there is an intent behind the phenomena they study) should not be asked, largely because "intent" implies an intender, which is generally taken to mean a divinity of some sort. As a result, there is

a continuing conflict between the forces of faith—which are predicated on the existence of an intender—and the forces of reason. Conservative Christians in many states—California, Texas, Louisiana, and Pennsylvania, among others—have mounted vigorous campaigns to require public school biology classes to give equal time to both biblical creationism and Darwinian evolution. For many years, this meant that evolution was barely mentioned in high school biology textbooks. In Christian schools it still is not mentioned; see Liza Lentini, "One Universe, Under God," *Discover* (October 2007).

For a time, it looked like evolution had scored a decisive victory. In 1982, federal judge William K. Overton struck down an Arkansas law that would have required the teaching of straight biblical creationism, with its explicit talk of God the Creator, as an unconstitutional intrusion of religion into a government activity: education. But the creationists have not given up. They have returned to the fray with something called "scientific creationism" or "intelligent design" (ID), and they have shifted their campaigns from state legislatures and school boards to local school boards, where it is harder for lawyers and biologists to mount effective counterattacks. "Scientific creationism" tries to show that the evolutionary approach is incapable of providing satisfactory explanations. For one thing it says that natural selection relies on random chance to produce structures whose delicate intricacy could only be the product of deliberate design. Therefore, there must have been a designer. There is no mention of God—but, of course, that is the only possible meaning of "designer" (unless one believes in ancient extraterrestrial visitors). For an excellent presentation of the various threads in the debate over ID, see Robert T. Pennock, *Intelligent Design Creationism and Its Critics: Philosophical, Theological, and Scientific Perspectives* (MIT Press, 2001), and Eugenie C. Scott and Glenn Branch, "Antievolutionism: Changes and Continuities," *BioScience* (March 2003).

William Johnson, associate dean of academic affairs at Ambassador University in Big Sandy, Texas, offered another argument for replacing the theory of evolution in a 1994 speech, "Evolution: The Past, Present, and Future Implications," *Vital Speeches of the Day* (February 15, 1995). He argued that the triumph of Darwin's theory "meant the end of the traditional belief in the world as a purposeful created order . . . and the consequent elimination of God from nature has played a decisive role in the secularization of Western society. Darwinian theory broke man's link with God and set him adrift in a cosmos without purpose or end." Johnson suggested that evolution—and perhaps the entire scientific approach to nature—should be abandoned in favor of a return to religion because of the untold damage it has done to the human values that underpin society. See also Evan Ratliff, "The Crusade Against Evolution," *Wired* (October 2004); and Sid Perkins, "Evolution in Action," *Science News* (February 25, 2006).

In 1999, the Kansas Board of Education deleted evolution—as well as much other science that would support the idea of an Earth and universe older than 6000 years—from coverage in state competency tests. Since most teachers could be expected to focus their efforts on material their students would need to score well on the tests, and since the Board had vocal antievolution,

procreation members, the Board's move was widely seen as supporting the antievolution, procreation agenda. See Marjorie George, "And Then God Created Kansas . . . ," *University of Pennsylvania Law Review* (January 2001). Early in 2001, a new Kansas Board of Education took office and promptly put evolution back in the curriculum. See Eugene Russo, "Fighting Darwin's Battles," *The Scientist* (March 19, 2001). Yet, the battle is hardly won. Not even Pope John Paul II's 1996 announcement that "new knowledge leads us to recognize that the theory of evolution is more than a hypothesis" had much impact. Indeed, in November 2004, the balance of power on the Kansas Board of Education had changed again and an effort to move "intelligent design" into the curriculum was growing; see Yudhijit Bhattacharjee, "Kansas Gears Up for Another Battle Over Teaching Evolution," *Science* (April 29, 2005). A similar battle was raging in Dover, Pennsylvania; it was settled in the end by federal district court judge John Jones III, who emphatically declared that ID is not science and thus has no place in a science curriculum. He wrote in his decision that urging the teaching of the controversy, if not of ID itself, "is at best disingenuous and, at worst, a canard. The goal of the ID movement is not to encourage critical thought, but to foment a revolution that would supplant evolutionary theory with ID." See Jeffrey Mervis, "Judge Jones Defines Science—And Why Intelligent Design Isn't," *Science* (January 6, 2006). Harold Morowitz, Robert Hazen, and James Trefil, "Intelligent Design Has No Place in the Science Curriculum," *Chronicle of Higher Education* (September 2, 2005), makes similar points.

Yet, proponents of ID—and/or opponents of Darwinism—never give up; see Glenn Branch and Eugenie C. Scott, "The Latest Face of Creationism," *Scientific American* (January 2009). ID was itself an attempt to bypass opposition to creationism. Now the watchword appears to have changed again. In June 2008, the Louisiana House of Representatives approved a bill to promote "critical thinking" on controversial topics such as evolution, the origins of life, global warming, and human cloning. The bill is widely seen as an attempt to slip ID into the curriculum as an alternative to evolution, which it plainly is not according to "Louisiana's Latest Assault on Darwin," an editorial in *The New York Times* (June 21, 2008). Procreationists such as the Discovery Institute are elated, according to senior fellow John G. West's "Louisiana Confounds the Science Thought Police," *National Review Online* (July 8, 2008) (http://article.nationalreview.com/?q=NjNjYTNjMTVkNmVhMmYxN2JkMWZhMzYzMGNjNzY 4ZDE=).

Among recent books on this issue, Thomas Woodward's *Doubts About Darwin: A History of Intelligent Design* (Baker Books, 2003) argues the case in favor of ID, as does H. Wayne House, ed., *Intelligent Design 101: Leading Experts Explain the Key Issues* (Kregel Publications, 2008). Michael Ruse's *Darwin and Design: Does Evolution Have a Purpose?* (Harvard University Press, 2003) also covers the history but concludes that those who study evolution have an almost religious response to the marvels they find. More critical efforts include Niall Shanks, *God, the Devil, and Darwin: A Critique of Intelligent Design Theory* (Oxford University Press, 2004); Barbara Forrest and Paul R. Gross, *Creationism's Trojan Horse: The Wedge of Intelligent Design* (Oxford University Press, 2004); and Matt Young and Taner Edis, eds., *Why Intelligent Design Fails:*

A Scientific Critique of the New Creationism (Rutgers University Press, 1984). John Brockman, ed., *Intelligent Thought: Science Versus the Intelligent Design Movement* (Vintage, 2006), gathers a number of often quite pungent essays by scientists on ID. In Jill S. Schneiderman and Warren S. Allmon, eds., *For the Rock Record: Geologists on Intelligent Design* (University of California Press, 2009), geologists and paleontologists "systematically demonstrate precisely why geology [the fossil record] destroys all design arguments." For a closely related commentary that is not a book, see John Avise, "Footprints of Nonsentient Design Inside the Human Genome," *Proceedings of the National Academy of Sciences of the United States of America* (supplement, May 11, 2010); Avise finds that the structure of the human genome is not consistent with the idea of an "intelligent" designer.

Criticism of ID also comes from the religious side. The 2008 movie *Expelled: No Intelligence Allowed* charges that Darwinians are guilty of suppressing valid alternatives to the theory of evolution, but Peter Manseau, "Is I.D. Ready for Its Close-Up?" *Science & Spirit* (May–June, 2008), says that "the greatest flaw in this deeply flawed film [is that] not only does *Expelled* treat evolution dishonestly, it does the same with design. Playing fast and loose with the question of whether ID is religion or science (swearing it is the latter but reaching for 'a loving God' when it wants to drive its message home), *Expelled* manages to miss the most intriguing facet of the discussion." Chris Doran, "Intelligent Design: It's Just Too Good to Be True," *Theology & Science* (May 2010), finds "considerable theological problems [in] associating the designer with the God of Jesus Christ."

In the YES selection, Professor J. Scott Turner argues that the real issue is whether the world is purposeful. ID can in fact be usefully taught, and doing so avoids intrusions on academic freedom. In the NO selection, the National Academy of Sciences and Institute of Medicine of the National Academies argue that evolution is so firmly ensconced in the foundations of modern science that nonscientific alternatives to evolution such as creationism (including ID) have no place in the public school science curriculum.

YES

J. Scott Turner

Signs of Design

Because I am a biologist, evolution is at the core of virtually everything I think about. Like most of my colleagues, I've kept an eye on the emerging "intelligent design" movement. Unlike most of my colleagues, however, I don't see ID as a threat to biology, public education or the ideals of the republic. To the contrary, what worries me more is the way that many of my colleagues have responded to the challenge.

ID proponents claim that Darwinism is insufficient to explain the origin and evolution of life on Earth. All is better explained, they say, if there is some kind of designing intelligence guiding things. These assertions are based on two core ideas. The first is essentially a scientific theory of miracles that is the brainchild of philosopher and mathematician William Dembski, one of ID's leading intellectual lights. According to Dembski, one can use rules of probability and information theory to construct "explanatory filters" that can objectively distinguish between purely natural phenomena that come about on their own and phenomena that require some kind of intelligent guidance—a miracle, in a word. Applying an explanatory filter to, say, the origin of life reveals that the probability that life arose by chance is infinitesimal. This in itself is not a particularly novel or controversial idea—no biologist I know would disagree. But Dembski parts company with the rest of us when he insists that a designing intelligence is the only agency that could bring such an improbable event to pass. What heats people up, of course, is that Dembski's "designing intelligence" strikes many as code for "God."

The second core idea comes from microbiologist Michael Behe, who is another of ID's leading lights. He asserts that living systems exhibit a sort of "irreducible complexity" that cannot be derived from the piecemeal evolution that Darwinism demands. The poster child for this argument is the bacterial flagellum, a whiplike device that bacteria use to propel themselves around their environment. This remarkable contrivance, which resembles an electric motor, is built from protein parts and will work only when all the parts are assembled into the complex whole—and this is why Behe calls its complexity irreducible. Whether the flagellum actually is irreducibly complex is questionable: scientists have proposed reasonable models for how its design could have emerged via piecemeal evolution.

Nevertheless, Behe considers irreducible complexity to be proof positive of a designing intelligence at work: how could the flagellum have developed by natural selection if none of its elements by themselves would have made the organism's predecessor more fit to survive? Behe claims that many other attributes of living systems, including the complicated structure of genomes, mechanisms for gene replication, and complex metabolic pathways in cells, are likewise irreducibly complex. What stirs the pot is ID's claim that all this irreducible complexity constitutes a rhetorical dagger pointed at the heart of Darwinism.

If all this sounds familiar, it should: it is essentially natural theology and the argument from design dressed up in modern clothes—William Paley equipped with a computer and electron microscope. Looked at in this way, ID seems not so much like the radical alternative to Darwinism that it claims to be, and more like nostalgia for the Platonic tradition in natural history that prevailed prior to Darwin.

The nostalgia is puzzling: for centuries, the Platonic tradition tied natural history into knots, with some of the most intractable tangles woven around the nature of species and the meaning of the apparent design that abounds in the living world. In a single decisive stroke, Darwin cut a wide path through this Platonic morass with a simple and, most important, reasonable natural explanation for why species exist and why they exist in such marvelous diversity and complexity. To extend Richard Dawkins's famous quip that Darwin made it possible to be an intellectually fulfilled atheist, so too did Darwin make it difficult to be an intellectually credible Platonist.

Nevertheless, ID is as popular as it is controversial, and Platonic nostalgia is not enough to explain why. Something deeper is obviously at play.

To most people who contemplate the natural world, it seems self-evident that the world is a designed place. Despite its many difficulties, the Platonic tradition endured because it offered a satisfying explanation for why: the world reflects God's purposeful design for creation. In dethroning the Platonic tradition, Darwin seemed to take that purpose away, and this has obviously been a difficult pill for many to swallow. It's not so clear, however, that Darwin did divorce design and purpose so decisively from the living world. Indeed, to claim that he did is to misread the history of Darwinism.

Consider, for example, the bedrock concept of Darwinian fitness. Natural selection operates because "fit" individuals are more fecund than "unfit" individuals. This should, over time, produce populations of fitter creatures, even though there is no purpose at work here, no striving for perfection. However, a problem lurks in this seemingly simple explanation. For a scientific idea to be credible, there must at least be the possibility that one can show it to be incorrect. Darwin ran into early difficulty on this score because the conventional depiction of fitness cannot be false—fecundity is fitness, and fitness is fecundity. To Darwin's early critics, a veritable fountain of doubt gushed from this tautology at the heart of his theory.

Edward Drinker Cope, a 19th-century American paleontologist, probably expressed the issue best. The problem is not so much the origin of species as it is the origin of fitness: how, precisely, do organisms become well-crafted—*fit*—things? To Cope, and to many of Darwin's contemporary critics, the way out of the tautology was the very purposefulness that Darwin so adamantly insisted we reject.

Interestingly, Darwin himself was a little muddy on the issue. Asa Gray, the Harvard botanist who was Darwin's most energetic advocate in the 19th-century U.S., actually saw in Darwinian adaptation the vindication of purposefulness in biology—to Darwin's chagrin. Darwin's most enthusiastic German convert, Ernst Haeckel, did Gray one better, crafting his own theory of evolution by melding Darwinian natural selection with the purposeful *Naturphilosophie* of romantics like Goethe—and leaving Darwin not just exasperated but aghast.

One could argue that Gray and Haeckel simply failed to understand Darwin's elegantly simple idea, but that argument doesn't hold water. Alfred Russell Wallace, who independently conceived the idea of natural selection and whose thinking surely would be most closely aligned to Darwin's own, thought that purpose in some form had to have guided the origin of life and the origin of consciousness in the higher animals, particularly humans. One finds similar doubts cropping up among thinkers throughout the late 19th and early 20th centuries—Freud, Louis Agassiz, Carl Jung and Henri Bergson, to name a few—and all were concerned about Darwin's insistence that a purposeless materialism is all there is.

To be fair, much of the ambiguity and unease swirling around during Darwinism's early years was fueled by a lack of knowledge about how another core Darwinian concept—heredity—works. For a time, it was thought that we could resolve Cope's question about how organisms came to be fit by clarifying the material nature of the gene, Mendel's "atom of heredity." That quest succeeded spectacularly, culminating in today's remarkable revolution in molecular biology, and engendering along the way our modern answer to Cope's question: the gene-centered conception of Darwinism—neo-Darwinism, as it is called—in which fitness arises by way of the selection of "good-function genes" at the expense of "poor-function genes."

For a time, neo-Darwinism triumphantly swept away quaint notions of purposeful evolution, to the point where Will Provine, the eminent Darwin historian, could confidently say that there are "no designing agents in evolution." That confident pronouncement may have been premature, however. As we discover more about how genes work, the stranger they become; they are far from the simple specifiers of good and poor function that they were classically thought to be. Paradoxically, this has breathed new life into Cope's question making it more acute, not less so. Indeed, my own scientific work has led me to a conclusion that is precisely the opposite of Provine's: designing agents are in fact everywhere, if only you know how to spot them. The ubiquity of these designing agents may make evolution a far more purposeful phenomenon than neo-Darwinists have been willing to allow.

This puts intelligent design into what I believe is its proper perspective: it is one of multiple emerging critiques of materialism in science and

evolution. Unfortunately, many scientists fail to see this, preferring the gross caricature that ID is simply "stealth creationism." But this strategy fails to meet the challenge. Rather than simply lament that so many people take ID seriously. Scientists would do better to ask *why* so many take it seriously. The answer would be hard for us to bear: ID is popular not because the stupid or ignorant like it, but because neo-Darwinism's principled banishment of purpose seems less defensible with each passing day.

ぐろ

A more constructive response to the ID challenge would ask whether ID is a credible critique of Darwinian materialism. In my opinion, that judgment should turn on one simple criterion: Will ID pose testable answers to Cope's question? By this measure, a fair reading of ID's prospects shows that it is in the game, though it has stepped up to the plate with two self-inflicted strikes against it. The first strike is its philosophical commitment to the argument from design and to the Platonic intelligent designer it implies. The second strike is that the testable ideas it has produced, like Behe's irreducible complexity, have not so far measured up. Whether ID gets a third strike will depend on whether it can come up with a credible and scientific theory of purposeful evolution. Most scientists, including me, doubt that it will be able to, but of all people scientists should know that the world is full of surprising things. ID might surprise us still.

It seems less than sporting, then, to call the pitch while it's still in the air, which is precisely what many of my colleagues insists on doing, sometimes quite vehemently. This, to me, is the most problematic thing about the controversy: it's not ID that keeps me awake at nights, but the tactics and attitudes of certain colleagues who really should know better. In Pogo's immortal words, "We have met the enemy and he is us."

One doesn't have to look far to find examples of conduct unbecoming. There is the recent case of Richard Sternberg, an unpaid staffer at the National Museum of Natural History (part of the Smithsonian), who became the object of a malicious campaign to oust him from the museum. Sternberg's crime? As managing editor of a Smithsonian-affiliated journal, he decided to publish an article that was sympathetic to ID on the seemingly reasonable grounds that a scientific journal is the appropriate venue for an advocate of a controversial theory to state his case. The Justice Department rapped the museum's knuckles for its treatment of Sternberg.

It would be comforting if one could dismiss such incidents as the actions of a misguided few. But the intolerance that gave rise to the Sternberg debacle is all too common: you can see it in its unfiltered glory by taking a look at Web sites . . . and following a few of the threads on ID. The attitudes on display there, which at the extreme verge on antireligious hysteria, can hardly be squared with the relatively innocuous (even if wrong-headed) ideas that sit at ID's core. Why, then, are such attitudes commonplace? The only explanation I can come up with is that many biologists regard ID as a dire existential threat. And that is what really troubles me about the ID controversy: the

animal that feels threatened is the one most likely to do something irrational and destructive.

Consider, for example, the most emotionally charged issue related to ID—whether it has any place in our classrooms. One can render plausible arguments that it does: even if ID is wrong, students are interested in the issue, and it offers a wealth of teachable moments to explore deeper issues of the philosophical roots of biology and the nature of science. What, then, is the harm in allowing teachers to deal with the subject as each sees fit? Advance this seemingly reasonable proposition, and you are likely to see scientists rolling their eyes; some may even become apoplectic.

When pressed to explain why normal standards of tolerance and academic freedom should not apply in the case of ID, scientists typically reply with all manner of evasions and prevarications that are quite out of character for otherwise balanced, intelligent and reasonable people. To give just one argument that has turned up frequently in my correspondence with colleagues: because ID has its roots in fundamentalist Christianity (a dubious proposition in itself), admitting it into our classrooms will foster an exclusionary and hurtful climate, as would admitting other exclusionary sins such as racism or sexism.

Even setting aside the numerous head-turning non sequiturs that weave through this argument, a stroll through most modern universities will quickly reveal how hollow the argument is. Each day as I make my way to my office, for example, I pass the usual gauntlet of Bushitler cartoons and "Duck, it's Dick" posters, and doors plastered with lame jokes and cartoons about Republicans, Christians and conservatives. "Abortion Stops a Beating Heart" posters, on the other hand, are as rare as four-leaf clovers. The display is a stark panorama of what the modern academy is evolving into: a tedious intellectual monoculture where conformity and not contention is the norm. Reflexive hostility to ID is largely cut from that cloth: some ID critics are worried not so much about a hurtful climate as they are about a climate in which people are free to disagree with them.

⁌◎⁍

Such things are easily laughed off as the foibles of the modern academy. My blood chills, however, when these essentially harmless hypocrisies are joined with the all-American tradition of litigiousness, for it is in the hands of courts and lawyers that real damage to cherished academic ideals is likely to be done. This is not mere lawyer-bashing: as universities become more corporatized and politicized, academic freedom and open inquiry are coming under an ever more grave threat. A case in point is the recent federal court decision in *Mayer v. Monroe County Community School Corporation,* which essentially dismisses the notion of academic freedom in high schools. The court found that teachers have no academic autonomy but are only instruments for advancing the interests of school boards.

My university colleagues should not take much comfort in the fact that this decision involved a high school, because it would require only a short step

to apply the same logic to them—a step that some administrators are eager to take. A high-level administrator at the prestigious university near my own has gone on record saving that First Amendment rights of free speech do not apply at an "educational corporation" like a private university. We should take heed: courts, ambitious attorneys and lawsuit-averse administrators are manifestly not academics' friends when it comes to unfettered free speech. Yet the courts are where many of my colleagues seem determined to go with the ID issue. I believe we will ultimately come to regret this.

Take, for example, the recent case in Dover, Pennsylvania, where a group of parents sued the local school board over its requirement that a statement be read to biology students encouraging them to keep an open mind about alternatives to Darwinism. The plaintiffs regarded this requirement as "stealth creationism"—an unanswerable criticism if you think about it—and, backed by the ACLU, they sought relief in the federal courts. There were few heroes to be found in the spectacle that followed. The only bright spot was when a larger group of grown-ups, the Dover electorate, put a stop to the circus by voting out the school board that had put the offending policy in place. Unfortunately, this happy outcome did not keep the judge from ruling for the plaintiffs, decreeing that teaching about ID is constitutionally proscribed.

Many of my scientific colleagues were involved in this case. One would hope that they would have taken a stance of principled neutrality, offering a robust defense of academic freedom tempered with the sober recognition that freedom means that sometimes people will think, speak and even teach things one disagrees with. Instead, my colleagues took sides; many were actively involved as advocates for the plaintiffs, and they were cheered on by many more from the sidelines. Although there was general jubilation at the ruling, I think the joy will be short-lived, for we have affirmed the principle that a federal judge, not scientists or teachers, can dictate what is and what is not science, and what may or may not be taught in a classroom. Forgive me if I do not feel more free.

**National Academy of Sciences
and Institute of Medicine
of the National Academies**

 **NO**

Science, Evolution,
and Creationism

Scientific and technological advances have had profound effects on human life. In the 19th century, most families could expect to lose one or more children to disease. Today, in the United States and other developed countries, the death of a child from disease is uncommon. Every day we rely on technologies made possible through the application of scientific knowledge and processes. The computers and cell phones which we use, the cars and airplanes in which we travel, the medicines that we take, and many of the foods that we eat were developed in part through insights obtained from scientific research. Science has boosted living standards, has enabled humans to travel into Earth's orbit and to the Moon, and has given us new ways of thinking about ourselves and the universe.

Evolutionary biology has been and continues to be a cornerstone of modern science. This booklet documents some of the major contributions that an understanding of evolution has made to human well-being, including its contributions to preventing and treating human disease, developing new agricultural products, and creating industrial innovations. More broadly, evolution is a core concept in biology that is based both in the study of past life forms and in the study of the relatedness and diversity of present-day organisms. The rapid advances now being made in the life sciences and in medicine rest on principles derived from an understanding of evolution. That understanding has arisen both through the study of an ever-expanding fossil record and, equally importantly, through the application of modern biological and molecular sciences and technologies to the study of evolution. Of course, as with any active area of science, many fascinating questions remain, and this booklet highlights some of the active research that is currently under way that addresses questions about evolution.

However, polls show that many people continue to have questions about our knowledge of biological evolution. They may have been told that scientific understanding of evolution is incomplete, incorrect, or in doubt. They may be skeptical that the natural process of biological evolution could have produced such an incredible array of living things, from microscopic bacteria to whales and redwood trees, from simple sponges on coral reefs to humans capable of

contemplating life's history on this planet. They may wonder if it is possible to accept evolution and still adhere to religious beliefs.

This publication speaks to those questions. It is written to serve as a resource for people who find themselves embroiled in debates about evolution. It provides information about the role that evolution plays in modern biology and the reasons why only scientifically based explanations should be included in public school science courses. Interested readers may include school board members, science teachers and other education leaders, policy makers, legal scholars, and others in the community who are committed to providing students with quality science education. This booklet is also directed to the broader audience of high-quality school and college students as well as adults who wish to become more familiar with the many strands of evidence supporting evolution and to understand why evolution is both a fact and a process that accounts for the diversity of life on Earth.

This booklet also places the study of evolution in a broader context. It defines what "theory" means in the scientific community. It shows how evolutionary theory reflects the nature of science and how it differs from religion. It explains why the overwhelming majority of the scientific community accepts evolution as the basis for modern biology. It shows that some individual scientists and religious organizations have described how, for them, evolution and their faith are not in opposition to each other. And it explains why nonscientific alternatives to evolution such as creationism (including intelligent design creationism) should not be part of the science curriculum in the nation's public schools. . . .

Much has happened in evolutionary biology since the release of the first two editions of this booklet, and this new edition provides important updates about these developments. Fossil discoveries have continued to produce new and compelling evidence about evolutionary history. New information and understanding about the molecules that make up organisms has emerged, including the complete DNA sequences of humans. DNA sequencing has become a powerful tool for establishing genetic relationships among species. DNA evidence has both confirmed fossil evidence and allowed studies of evolution where the fossil record is still incomplete. An entirely new field, evolutionary developmental biology, enables scientists to study how the genetic changes that have occurred throughout history have shaped the forms and functions of organisms. The study of biological evolution constitutes one of the most active and far-reaching endeavors in all of modern science.

The public controversies that swirl around evolution also have changed. In the 1980s many people opposed to the teaching of evolution in public schools supported legislation that would have required biology teachers to discuss "scientific creationism"—the assertion that the fossil record and the planet's geological features are consistent with Earth and its living things being created just a few thousand years ago. Major court cases—including a Supreme Court case in 1987—ruled that "creation science" is the product of religious convictions, not scientific research, and that it cannot be taught in public schools because to do so would impose a particular religious perspective on all students.

Since then, the opponents of evolution have taken other approaches. Some have backed the view known as "intelligent design," a new form of creationism based on the contention that living things are too complex to have evolved through natural mechanisms. In 2005 a landmark court case in Dover, Pennsylvania, deemed the teaching of intelligent design unconstitutional, again because it is based on religious conviction and not science.

Others have argued that science teachers should teach the "controversies" surrounding evolution. But there is no controversy in the scientific community about whether evolution has occurred. On the contrary, the evidence supporting descent with modification, as Charles Darwin termed it, is both overwhelming and compelling. In the century and a half since Darwin, scientists have uncovered exquisite details about many of the mechanisms that underlie biological variation, inheritance, and natural selection, and they have shown how these mechanisms lead to biological change over time. Because of this immense body of evidence, scientists treat the occurrence of evolution as one of the most securely established of scientific facts. Biologists also are confident in their understanding of how evolution occurs. . . .

As . . . [this publication] makes clear, the evidence for evolution can be fully compatible with religious faith. Science and religion are different ways of understanding the world. Needlessly placing them in opposition reduces the potential of each to contribute to a better future.

Frequently Asked Questions

Aren't evolution and religion opposing ideas?

Newspaper and television stories sometimes make it seem as though evolution and religion are incompatible, but that is not true. Many scientists and theologians have written about how one can accept both faith and the validity of biological evolution. Many past and current scientists who have made major contributions to our understanding of the world have been devoutly religious. At the same time, many religious people accept the reality of evolution, and many religious denominations have issued emphatic statements reflecting this acceptance. . . .

To be sure, disagreements do exist. Some people reject any science that contains the word "evolution"; others reject all forms of religion. The range of beliefs about science and about religion is very broad. Regrettably, those who occupy the extremes of this range often have set the tone of public discussions. Evolution is science, however, and only science should be taught and learned in science classes. . . .

Isn't belief in evolution also a matter of faith?

Acceptance of evolution is not the same as a religious belief. Scientists' confidence about the occurrence of evolution is based on an overwhelming amount of supporting evidence gathered from many aspects of the natural world. To be accepted, scientific knowledge has to withstand the scrutiny of testing, retesting, and experimentation. Evolution is accepted within the

scientific community because the concept has withstood extensive testing by many thousands of scientists for more than a century. As a 2006 "Statement on the Teaching of Evolution" from the Interacademy Panel on International Issues, a global network of national science academies, said, "Evidence-based facts about the origins and evolution of the Earth and of life on this planet have been established by numerous observations and independently derived experimental results from a multitude of scientific disciplines" (emphasis in original). . . .

Many religious beliefs do not rely on evidence gathered from the natural world. On the contrary, an important component of religious belief is faith, which implies acceptance of a truth regardless of the presence of empirical evidence for or against that truth. Scientists cannot accept scientific conclusions on faith alone because all such conclusions must be subject to testing against observations. Thus, scientists do not "believe" in evolution in the same way that someone believes in God.

How can random biological changes lead to more adapted organisms?

Contrary to a widespread public impression, biological evolution is not random, even though the biological changes that provide the raw material for evolution are not directed toward predetermined, specific goals. When DNA is being copied, mistakes in the copying process generate novel DNA sequences. These new sequences act as evolutionary "experiments." Most mutations do not change traits or fitness. But some mutations give organisms traits that enhance their ability to survive and reproduce, while other mutations reduce the reproductive fitness of an organism.

The process by which organisms with advantageous variations have greater reproductive success than other organisms within a population is known as "natural selection." Over multiple generations, some populations of organisms subjected to natural selection may change in ways that make them better able to survive and reproduce in a given environment. Others may be unable to adapt to a changing environment and will become extinct.

Aren't there many questions that still surround evolution? Don't many famous scientists reject evolution?

As with all active areas of science, there remain questions about evolution. There are always new questions to ask, new situations to consider, and new ways to study known phenomena. But evolution itself has been so thoroughly tested that biologists are no longer examining whether evolution has occurred and is continuing to occur. Similarly, biologists no longer debate many of the mechanisms responsible for evolution. As with any other field of science, scientists continue to study the mechanisms of how the process of evolution operates. As new technologies make possible previously unimaginable observations and allow for new kinds of experiments, scientists continue to propose and examine the strength of evidence regarding the mechanisms for evolutionary change. But the existence of such questions neither reduces nor undermines the fact that evolution has occurred and continues to occur.

Nor do such questions diminish the strength of evolutionary science. Indeed, the strength of a theory rests in part on providing scientists with the basis to explain observed phenomena and to predict what they are likely to find when exploring new phenomena and observations. In this regard, evolution has been and continues to be one of the most productive theories known to modern science.

Even scientific theories that are firmly established continue to be tested and modified by scientists as new information and new technologies become available. For example, the theory of gravity has been substantiated by many observations on Earth. But theoretical scientists, using their understanding of the physical universe, continue to test the limits of the theory of gravity in more extreme situations, such as close to a neutron star or black hole. Someday, new phenomena may be discovered that will require that the theory be expanded or revised, just as the development of the theory of general relativity in the first part of the 20th century expanded knowledge about gravity.

With evolutionary theory, many new insights will emerge as research proceeds. For example, the links between genetic changes and alterations in an organism's form and function are being intensively investigated now that the tools and technologies to do so are available.

Some who oppose the teaching of evolution sometimes use quotations from prominent scientists out of context to claim that scientists do not support evolution. However, examination of the quotations reveals that the scientists are actually disputing some aspect of how evolution occurs, not whether evolution occurred.

What evidence is there that the universe is billions of years old?

This is an important question because evolution of the wide variety of organisms currently existing on Earth required a very long period of time. Several independent dating techniques indicate that the Earth is billions of years old. Measurements of the radioactive elements in materials from the Earth, the Moon, and meteorites provide ages for the Earth and the solar system. These measurements are consistent with each other and with the physical processes of radioactivity. Additional evidence for the ages of the solar system and the galaxy includes the record of crater formation on the planets and their moons, the ages of the oldest stars in the Milky Way, and the rate of expansion of the universe. Measurements of the radiation left over from the Big Bang also support the universe's great age.

What's wrong with teaching critical thinking or "controversies" with regard to evolution?

Nothing is wrong with teaching critical thinking. Students need to learn how to reexamine their ideas in light of observations and accepted scientific concepts. Scientific knowledge itself is the result of the critical thinking applied by generations of scientists to questions about the natural world. Scientific knowledge must be subjected to continued reexamination and skepticism for human knowledge to continue to advance.

But critical thinking does not mean that all criticisms are equally valid.

Critical thinking has to be based on rules of reason and evidence. Discussion of critical thinking or controversies does not mean giving equal weight to ideas that lack essential supporting evidence. The ideas offered by intelligent design creationists are not the products of scientific reasoning. Discussing these ideas in science classes would not be appropriate given their lack of scientific support.

Recent calls to introduce "critical analysis" into science classes disguise a broader agenda. Other attempts to introduce creationist ideas into science employ such phrases as "teach the controversy" or "present arguments for and against evolution." Many such calls are directed specifically at attacking the teaching of evolution or other topics that some people consider as controversial. In this way, they are intended to introduce creationist ideas into science classes, even though scientists have thoroughly refuted these ideas. Indeed, the application of critical thinking to the science curriculum would argue against including these ideas in science classes because they do not meet scientific standards.

There is no scientific controversy about the basic facts of evolution. In this sense the intelligent design movement's call to "teach the controversy" is unwarranted. Of course, there remain many interesting questions about evolution, such as the evolutionary origin of sex or different mechanisms of speciation, and discussion of these questions is fully warranted in science classes. However, arguments that attempt to confuse students by suggesting that there are fundamental weaknesses in the science of evolution are unwarranted based on the overwhelming evidence that supports the theory. Creationist ideas lie outside of the realm of science, and introducing them in science courses has been ruled unconstitutional by the U.S. Supreme Court and other federal courts.

What are common ideas regarding creationism?

"Creationism" is a very broad term. In the most general sense, it refers to views that reject scientific explanations of certain features of the natural world (whether in biology, geology, or other sciences) and instead posit direct intervention (sometimes called "special creation") in these features by some transcendent being or power. Some creationists believe that the universe and Earth are only several thousand years old, a position referred to as "young Earth" creationism. Creationism also includes the view that the complex features of organisms cannot be explained by natural processes but require the intervention of a nonnatural "intelligent designer.". . .

Wouldn't it be "fair" to teach creationism along with evolution?

The goal of science education is to expose students to the best possible scholarship in each field of science. The science curriculum is thus the product of centuries of scientific investigation. Ideas need to become part of the base of accepted scientific knowledge before they are appropriately taught in schools. For example, the idea of continental drift to explain the movements

and shapes of the continents was studied and debated for many years without becoming part of the basic science curriculum. As data accumulated, it became clearer that the surface of the Earth is composed of a series of massive plates, which are not bounded by the continents, that continually move in relation to each other. The theory of plate tectonics (which was proposed in the mid-1960s) grew from these data and offered a more complete explanation for the movement of continents. The new theory also predicted important phenomena, such as where earthquakes and volcanoes are likely to occur. When enough evidence had accumulated for the concept of plate tectonics to be accepted by the scientific community as fact, it became part of the earth sciences curriculum.

Scientists and science educators have concluded that evolution should be taught in science classes because it is the only tested, comprehensive scientific explanation for the nature of the biological world today that is supported by overwhelming evidence and widely accepted by the scientific community. The ideas supported by creationists, in contrast, are not supported by evidence and are not accepted by the scientific community.

Different religions hold very different views and teachings about the origins and diversity of life on Earth. Because creationism is based on specific sets of religious convictions, teaching it in science classes would mean imposing a particular religious view on students and thus is unconstitutional, according to several major rulings in federal district courts and the Supreme Court of the United States.

Does science disprove religion?

Science can neither prove nor disprove religion. Scientific advances have called some religious beliefs into question, such as the ideas that the Earth was created very recently, that the Sun goes around the Earth, and that mental illness is due to possession by spirits or demons. But many religious beliefs involve entities or ideas that currently are not within the domain of science. Thus, it would be false to assume that all religious beliefs can be challenged by scientific findings.

As science continues to advance, it will produce more complete and more accurate explanations for natural phenomena, including a deeper understanding of biological evolution. Both science and religion are weakened by claims that something not yet explained scientifically must be attributed to a supernatural deity. Theologians have pointed out that as scientific knowledge about phenomena that had been previously attributed to supernatural causes increases, a "god of the gaps" approach can undermine faith. Furthermore, it confuses the roles of science and religion by attributing explanations to one that belong in the domain of the other.

Many scientists have written eloquently about how their scientific studies have increased their awe and understanding of a creator. . . . The study of science need not lessen or compromise faith.

EXPLORING THE ISSUE

Should "Intelligent Design" Be Taught in Public Schools?

Critical Thinking and Reflection

1. If creationism is to be taught in the public schools, which one of the various available creation myths should be taught?
2. Is evolution just another religion or tradition?
3. Should morality—standards of right and wrong—be taught in the public schools?
4. Will teaching students the skills of critical analysis wind up favoring acceptance of the theory of evolution by means of natural selection or intelligent design?

Is There Common Ground?

No one in this debate argues that public school students should not be taught how the world and humans came to be. The argument centers on the nature of acceptable evidence—science versus Scripture—and the hazards to society of failing to teach students the difference between right and wrong, or morality. On this last point, there is common ground, for even ardent Darwinians agree that teaching standards of right and wrong is a good idea. They differ from religionists on whether that can be done without also teaching religion.

1. To what extent do standards of right and wrong depend on religion?
2. Can you justify all (or most) of the Ten Commandments using an evolutionary (natural selection) perspective?
3. Look up "Darwinian morality" on the Internet or in the library, and you will find an overwhelming mass of material! Is there a consensus?

ISSUE 3

Should the Internet Be Neutral?

YES: Julius Genachowski, from "Preserving a Free and Open Internet: A Platform for Innovation, Opportunity, and Prosperity," speech at The Brookings Institution (September 21, 2009)

NO: Kyle McSlarrow, from "The Future of the Internet," Testimony before the Senate Committee on Commerce, Science, and Transportation Hearing (April 22, 2008)

Learning Outcomes

After studying this issue, students will be able to explain:

1. The value of network neutrality.
2. Why large content providers are opposed to network neutrality.
3. The difficulty of maintaining network neutrality.
4. The need for government regulation to protect network neutrality.

ISSUE SUMMARY

YES: FCC Chairman Julius Genachowski argues that we must preserve the openness and freedom of the Internet to ensure that the Internet continues to support innovation, opportunity, economic growth, and democracy in the twenty-first century.

NO: Kyle McSlarrow, president and chief executive officer of the National Cable & Telecommunications Association, argues that "net neutrality" mandates would interfere with the ability of broadband providers to improve Internet access and thus would ultimately undermine consumer choice and welfare.

When the Internet was young—not quite two decades ago—any content provider could send any kind of data they wished to any and all users. It was all bits—ones and zeroes—and from the standpoint of the computers or servers that accepted, transferred, and delivered the data, there was no difference between

one stream of bits and another. The Communications Act of 1934, which regulated the phone companies that owned the wires over which almost all network traffic then ran, outlawed treating one kind of traffic or one source's traffic differently from any other. The result was that if one could figure out a way to turn a new kind of data into bits, or a new way to package the bits, or a new way to coordinate different bit streams, one could create a new business. It didn't matter whether one was a teenager in a bedroom in Indiana or a big business in New York. It also didn't matter whether the bits—or "content"—meant stock tips or porn. Everyone had a chance to innovate and make money.

The result was a virtual explosion of innovation. Today it is hard to imagine a world without e-mail, instant messaging, file sharing, Web pages, eBay, PayPal, Google, blogging, social networking, Monster, wireless connectivity, Web cameras, PDAs, Blackberries, Internet (VOIP) phones, and Web-enabled cell phones, among many other things. We have also gone from an Internet that ran on slow dial-up connections to one dominated by much faster broadband—DSL and cable—connections, which make it possible to deliver television and film over the Internet. Media and phone companies now deliver content, and at least some of them would like to facilitate the flow of their own content to their own customers and to interfere with the flow of content from other sources, unless those other sources pay a fee. Such a change has been likened to turning the open highway of the present Internet into a toll road. See Wendy M. Grossman, "Who Pays?" *Scientific American* (July 2006). At the same time, traffic on the Internet has increased tremendously, to the point where the flow of content is sometimes greatly slowed. Tom Giovanetti, "Network Neutrality? Welcome to the Stupid Internet," *Mercury News* (June 9, 2006), argues that a nonneutral Internet that gave priority to such things as VOIP (Internet phone) traffic from police and fire departments, 911 calls, and so on would be vastly preferable to a neutral Internet that did not. The debate has been and continues to be vigorous. Opposition from broadband providers remains strong, however.

In June 2006, the U.S. House of Representatives passed the Communications Opportunity, Promotion and Enhancement Act after deleting a provision that would have mandated network neutrality. As passed, the Act "would let the [Federal Communications Commission] investigate complaints about broadband providers blocking Internet content only after the fact." See Grant Gross, "House Rejects 'Net Neutrality, Passes Telecom Reform Bill'," *Network World* (June 12, 2006). In the Senate, attempts to amend a similar bill to mandate network neutrality failed. See Tom Abate, "Net Neutrality Amendment Dies: Telecommunications Bill Goes to Senate Without Provision Sought By Web Firms," *San Francisco Chronicle* (June 29, 2006). Some have credited the telecommunications industry's heavy investment in lobbyists and campaign contributions with the result to that point. Lauren Weinstein, "Ma Bell's Revenge: The Battle for Network Neutrality," *Communications of the ACM* (January 2007), says that "much of the anti-neutrality argument is simple greed in action" and warns that "most Internet users simply don't realize how drastically and negatively they could be affected if anti-neutrality arguments hold sway. Getting true network neutrality back after it's been lost is likely to

be effectively impossible. Except for the anti-neutrality camp itself, we'd all be worse off with a non-neutral Internet, and that's a risk we simply must not accept."

The overall significance of the issue is discussed by Daniel Krauss, "Net Neutrality and How It Just Might Change Everything," *American Libraries* (September 2006), and Michael Baumann, "Net Neutrality: The Internet's World War," *Information Today* (September 2006). Since then, the debate has gained new impetus with the proposal of new legislation and charges that Comcast and other broadband providers are surreptitiously causing large file downloads to fail (see "Comcast, Cox slowing P2P traffic 24 × 7," *Network World* (May 19, 2008) and "Elude Your ISP's BitTorrent Blockade," *PC World* (July 2008)). In August 2008, the Federal Communications Commission declared network blocking illegal and told Comcast to stop interfering with its customers' use of the Internet (John Eggerton, "FCC: Comcast Violated Internet Open-Access Guidelines," *Broadcasting & Cable* (August 1, 2008), http://www.broadcastingcable.com/article/CA6583586.html). Comcast immediately took the issue to the U.S. Court of Appeals, which ruled in April 2010 that the FCC did not have the authority to enforce network neutrality; see Cecilia Kang, "Court Rules for Comcast Over FCC in 'Net Neutrality' Case," *The Washington Post* (April 7, 2010). In response, the FCC has proposed reversing a past rule, which defined Internet service providers (ISPs) as "information-provider" companies instead of "telecommunications" companies and returning to the old rules, which required network neutrality; see George H. Pike, "What the Future Holds for Net Neutrality," *Information Today* (June 2010).

In testimony before the Senate Committee on Commerce, Science and Transportation Hearing on "The Future of the Internet" (April 22, 2008), professor of law Lawrence Lessig argues that to protect the growth and economic vitality of the Internet, Congress should enact "network neutrality" legislation to prevent broadband providers from interfering with free competition among application and content providers. But net neutrality is not just a matter of promoting innovation, growth, and economic vitality. Devon Greyson, "Net Neutrality: A Library Issue," *Feliciter* (vol. 56, no. 2, 2010), notes that Canadian libraries are defending net neutrality as a matter of intellectual freedom. Joe Dysart, "The Quest for Net Neutrality," *American School Board Journal* (May 2008), says that broadband providers such as AT&T and Comcast are pushing for a two-tiered Internet, with one tier free but slow and a second tier that provides more speed at a premium price. Dysart notes that this would adversely impact institutions such as public schools, whose limited budgets would confine them to the inferior tier. Religious groups have similar concerns. Testifying at the same "The Future of the Internet" hearing that provided the NO selection for this issue, Michele Combs, vice president of Communications for the Christian Coalition of America, argued that net neutrality has been abused by many ISPs: "Verizon Wireless censored text messages sent by the pro-choice advocacy group, NARAL, to its own members who had voluntarily signed up to receive them. . . . AT&T [has] cut off political speech during live concerts . . . [and] Comcast was blocking consumers' ability to download the King James Bible." Combs says, "Increasingly, faith-based groups are turning to the Internet to promote their political rights, to engage in what Ronald Reagan called

'the hard work of freedom.' We should not let the phone and cable companies interfere with that work." Unfortunately, the 2010 election put many anti-net neutrality senators and representatives in office. The conclusion of this debate is by no means clear, but Internet founder Tim Berners-Lee, "Long Live the Web," *Scientific American* (December 2010), considers the Web of interconnected information sources essential to both prosperity and liberty; therefore, he says, it needs defending.

In December 2010, the FCC announced rules intended to protect neutrality; see the FCC press release "FCC Acts to Preserve Internet Freedom and Openness: Action Helps Ensure Robust Internet for Consumers, Innovation, Investment, Economic Prosperity" at http://www.fcc.gov/Daily_Releases/Daily_Business/2010/db1221/DOC-303745A1.pdf. Perhaps unfortunately, they were designed as a compromise and many say they are satisfied. Are better rules needed to keep the Internet neutral? In the following selections, FCC Chairman Julius Genachowski argues that we must preserve the openness and freedom of the Internet to ensure that the Internet continues to support innovation, opportunity, economic growth, and democracy in the twenty-first century. Kyle McSlarrow, president and chief executive officer of the National Cable & Telecommunications Association, argues that "net neutrality" mandates would interfere with the ability of broadband providers to improve Internet access and thus would ultimately undermine consumer choice and welfare.

YES

Julius Genachowski

Preserving a Free and Open Internet: A Platform for Innovation, Opportunity, and Prosperity

. . . **J**ust over forty years ago, a handful of engineers in a UCLA lab connected two computers with a 15-foot gray cable and transferred little pieces of data back and forth. It was the first successful test of the ARPANET, the U.S.-government-funded project that became the Internet—the most transformational communications breakthrough since the printing press.

Today, we can't imagine what our lives would be like without the Internet—any more than we can imagine life without running water or the light bulb. Millions of us depend upon it every day: at home, at work, in school—and everywhere in between. The Internet has unleashed the creative genius of countless entrepreneurs and has enabled the creation of jobs—and the launch of small businesses and the expansion of large ones—all across America.

That's why Congress and the President have charged the FCC with developing a National Broadband Plan to ensure that every American has access to open and robust broadband.

The fact is that we face great challenges as a nation right now, including health care, education, energy, and public safety. While the Internet alone will not provide a complete solution to any of them, it can and must play a critical role in solving each one.

Openness Is the Key

Why has the Internet proved to be such a powerful engine for creativity, innovation, and economic growth? A big part of the answer traces back to one key decision by the Internet's original architects: to make the Internet an open system.

Historian John Naughton describes the Internet as an attempt to answer the following question: How do you design a network that is "future proof"—that can support the applications that today's inventors have not yet dreamed of? The solution was to devise a network of networks that would not be biased in favor of any particular application. The Internet's creators didn't want the network architecture—or any single entity—to pick winners and losers.

Because it might pick the wrong ones. Instead, the Internet's open architecture pushes decision-making and intelligence to the edge of the network—to end users, to the cloud, to businesses of every size and in every sector of the economy, to creators and speakers across the country and around the globe. In the words of Tim Berners-Lee, the Internet is a "blank canvas"—allowing anyone to contribute and to innovate without permission.

It is easy to look at today's Internet giants—and the tremendous benefits they have supplied to our economy and our culture—and forget that many were small businesses just a few years ago, founded on little more than a good idea and a no-frills connection to the Internet. Marc Andreessen was a graduate student when he created Mosaic, which led to Netscape, the first commercially successful Web browser. Mark Zuckerberg was a college student in 2004 when he started Facebook, which just announced that it added its 300 millionth member. Pierre Omidyar originally launched eBay on his own personal website. Today more than 600,000 Americans earn part of their living by operating small businesses on eBay's auction platform, bringing jobs and opportunity to Danvers, Massachusetts, Durham, North Carolina and Lincoln, Nebraska, and many other communities in both rural and urban America. This is the power of the Internet: distributed innovation and ubiquitous entrepreneurship, the potential for jobs and opportunity everywhere there is broadband.

And let us not forget that the open Internet enables much more than commerce. It is also an unprecedented platform for speech, democratic engagement, and a culture that prizes creative new ways of approaching old problems.

In 2000, Jimmy Wales started a project to create a free online encyclopedia. He originally commissioned experts to write the entries, but the project only succeeded after moving to volunteers to write them collaboratively. The result is Wikipedia, one of the top 10 most visited websites in the world and one of the most comprehensive aggregations of human knowledge in our history. The potential of collaboration and social media continues to grow. It is changing and accelerating innovation. And we've seen new media tools like Twitter and YouTube used by democratic movements around the globe.

Even now, the Internet is beginning to transform health care, education, and energy usage for the better. Health-related applications, distributed over a widely connected Internet, can help bring down health care costs and improve medical service. Four out of five Americans who are online have accessed medical information over the Internet, and most say this information affected their decision-making. Nearly four million college students took at least one online course in 2007, and the Internet can potentially connect kids anywhere to the best information and teachers everywhere. And the Internet is helping enable smart grid technologies, which promise to reduce carbon dioxide emissions by hundreds of millions of metric tons.

At the same time, we have also seen great strides in the center of the network. Most Americans' early exposure to the Internet was through analog modems, which allowed a trickle of data through the phone lines to support early electronic bulletin boards and basic email. Over the last two decades, thanks to substantial investment and technological ingenuity, companies devised ways to retrofit networks initially designed for phones and one-way

video to support two-way broadband data streams connecting homes and businesses across the country. And a revolution in wireless technologies— using licensed and unlicensed spectrum—and the creation of path-breaking devices like the Blackberry and iPhone have enabled millions of us to carry the Internet in our pockets and purses.

The lesson of each of these stories, and innumerable others like them, is that we cannot know what tomorrow holds on the Internet, except that it will be unexpected; that the genius of American innovators is unlimited; and that the fewer obstacles these innovators face in bringing their work to the world, the greater our opportunity as citizens and as a nation.

At a Crossroads

Notwithstanding its unparalleled record of success, today the free and open Internet faces emerging and substantial challenges. We've already seen some clear examples of deviations from the Internet's historic openness. We have witnessed certain broadband providers unilaterally block access to VoIP applications (phone calls delivered over data networks) and implement technical measures that degrade the performance of peer-to-peer software distributing lawful content. We have even seen at least one service provider deny users access to political content. And as many members of the Internet community and key Congressional leaders have noted, there are compelling reasons to be concerned about the future of openness.

One reason has to do with limited competition among service providers. As American consumers make the shift from dial-up to broadband, their choice of providers has narrowed substantially. I don't intend that remark as a policy conclusion or criticism—it is simply a fact about today's marketplace that we must acknowledge and incorporate into our policymaking.

A second reason involves the economic incentives of broadband providers. The great majority of companies that operate our nation's broadband pipes rely upon revenue from selling phone service, cable TV subscriptions, or both. These services increasingly compete with voice and video products provided over the Internet. The net result is that broadband providers' rational bottom-line interests may diverge from the broad interests of consumers in competition and choice.

The third reason involves the explosion of traffic on the Internet. With the growing popularity of high-bandwidth applications, Internet traffic is roughly doubling every two years. Technologies for managing broadband networks have become more sophisticated and widely deployed. But these technologies are just tools. They cannot by themselves determine the right answers to difficult policy questions—and they raise their own set of new questions.

In acknowledging the existence of challenging competitive, economic, and technological realities for today's Internet, I want to underscore that this debate, as I see it, isn't about white hats or black hats among companies in and around the network. Rather, there are inevitable tensions built into our system; important and difficult questions that we have an obligation to ask and to answer correctly for our country.

When I worked in the private sector I was fortunate to work with some of the greatest innovators of our time. That taught me some lessons about the importance of innovation and investment. It also taught me the importance of developing clear goals and then being focused and practical in achieving them, making sure to have the best input and ideas from the broadest group possible.

I am convinced that there are few goals more essential in the communications landscape than preserving and maintaining an open and robust Internet. I also know that achieving this goal will take an approach that is smart about technology, smart about markets, smart about law and policy, and smart about the lessons of history.

We Must Choose to Preserve the Open Internet

The rise of serious challenges to the free and open Internet puts us at a crossroads. We could see the Internet's doors shut to entrepreneurs, the spirit of innovation stifled, a full and free flow of information compromised. Or we could take steps to preserve Internet openness, helping ensure a future of opportunity, innovation, and a vibrant marketplace of ideas.

I understand the Internet is a dynamic network and that technology continues to grow and evolve. I recognize that if we were to create unduly detailed rules that attempted to address every possible assault on openness, such rules would become outdated quickly. But the fact that the Internet is evolving rapidly does not mean we can, or should, abandon the underlying values fostered by an open network, or the important goal of setting rules of the road to protect the free and open Internet.

Saying nothing—and doing nothing—would impose its own form of unacceptable cost. It would deprive innovators and investors of confidence that the free and open Internet we depend upon today will still be here tomorrow. It would deny the benefits of predictable rules of the road to all players in the Internet ecosystem. And it would be a dangerous retreat from the core principle of openness—the freedom to innovate without permission—that has been a hallmark of the Internet since its inception, and has made it so stunningly successful as a platform for innovation, opportunity, and prosperity.

In view of these challenges and opportunities, and because it is vital that the Internet continue to be an engine of innovation, economic growth, competition and democratic engagement, I believe the FCC must be a smart cop on the beat preserving a free and open Internet.

What We Can Do

This is how I propose we move forward: To date, the Federal Communications Commission has addressed these issues by announcing four Internet principles that guide our case-by-case enforcement of the communications laws. These principles can be summarized as: Network operators cannot prevent users from accessing the lawful Internet content, applications, and services of their choice, nor can they prohibit users from attaching non-harmful devices to the network.

The principles were initially articulated by Chairman Michael Powell in 2004 as the "Four Freedoms," and later endorsed in a unanimous 2005 policy statement issued by the Commission under Chairman Kevin Martin and with the forceful support of Commissioner Michael Copps, who of course remains on the Commission today. In the years since 2005, the Internet has continued to evolve and the FCC has issued a number of important bipartisan decisions involving openness. Today, I propose that the FCC adopt the existing principles as Commission rules, along with two additional principles that reflect the evolution of the Internet and that are essential to ensuring its continued openness.

Fifth Principle of Non-Discrimination

The fifth principle is one of non-discrimination—stating that broadband providers cannot discriminate against particular Internet content or applications.

This means they cannot block or degrade lawful traffic over their networks, or pick winners by favoring some content or applications over others in the connection to subscribers' homes. Nor can they disfavor an Internet service just because it competes with a similar service offered by that broadband provider. The Internet must continue to allow users to decide what content and applications succeed.

This principle will not prevent broadband providers from reasonably managing their networks. During periods of network congestion, for example, it may be appropriate for providers to ensure that very heavy users do not crowd out everyone else. And this principle will not constrain efforts to ensure a safe, secure, and spam-free Internet experience, or to enforce the law. It is vital that illegal conduct be curtailed on the Internet. As I said in my Senate confirmation hearing, open Internet principles apply only to lawful content, services and applications—not to activities like unlawful distribution of copyrighted works, which has serious economic consequences. The enforcement of copyright and other laws and the obligations of network openness can and must co-exist.

I also recognize that there may be benefits to innovation and investment of broadband providers offering managed services in limited circumstances. These services are different than traditional broadband Internet access, and some have argued they should be analyzed under a different framework. I believe such services can supplement—but must not supplant—free and open Internet access, and that we must ensure that ample bandwidth exists for all Internet users and innovators. In the rulemaking process I will discuss in a moment, we will carefully consider how to approach the question of managed services in a way that maximizes the innovation and investment necessary for a robust and thriving Internet.

I will propose that the FCC evaluate alleged violations of the non-discrimination principle as they arise, on a case-by-case basis, recognizing that the Internet is an extraordinarily complex and dynamic system. This approach, within the framework I am proposing today, will allow the Commission to make reasoned, fact-based determinations based on the Internet

before it—not based on the Internet of years past or guesses about how the Internet will evolve.

Sixth Principle of Transparency

The sixth principle is a transparency principle—stating that providers of broadband Internet access must be transparent about their network management practices.

Why does the FCC need to adopt this principle? The Internet evolved through open standards. It was conceived as a tool whose user manual would be free and available to all. But new network management practices and technologies challenge this original understanding. Today, broadband providers have the technical ability to change how the Internet works for millions of users—with profound consequences for those users and content, application, and service providers around the world.

To take one example, last year the FCC ruled on the blocking of peer-to-peer transmissions by a cable broadband provider. The blocking was initially implemented with no notice to subscribers or the public. It was discovered only after an engineer and hobbyist living in Oregon realized that his attempts to share public domain recordings of old barbershop quartet songs over a home Internet connection were being frustrated. It was not until he brought the problem to the attention of the media and Internet community, which then brought it to the attention of the FCC, that the improper network management practice became known and was stopped.

We cannot afford to rely on happenstance for consumers, businesses, and policymakers to learn about changes to the basic functioning of the Internet. Greater transparency will give consumers the confidence of knowing that they're getting the service they've paid for, enable innovators to make their offerings work effectively over the Internet, and allow policymakers to ensure that broadband providers are preserving the Internet as a level playing field. It will also help facilitate discussion among all the participants in the Internet ecosystem, which can reduce the need for government involvement in network management disagreements.

To be clear, the transparency principle will not require broadband providers to disclose personal information about subscribers or information that might compromise the security of the network, and there will be a mechanism to protect competitively sensitive data.

Application to the Internet, However Accessed

In considering the openness of the Internet, it is also important to recognize that our choice of technologies and devices for accessing the Internet continues to expand at a dizzying pace. New mobile and satellite broadband networks are getting faster every day, and extraordinary devices like smartphones and wireless data cards are making it easier to stay connected while on the go. And I note the beginnings of a trend towards openness among several participants in the mobile marketplace.

Even though each form of Internet access has unique technical characteristics, they are all are different roads to the same place. It is essential that the Internet itself remain open, however users reach it. The principles I've been speaking about apply to the Internet however accessed, and I will ask my fellow Commissioners to join me in confirming this.

Of course, how the principles apply may differ depending on the access platform or technology. The rulemaking process will enable the Commission to analyze fully the implications of the principles for mobile network architectures and practices—and how, as a practical matter, they can be fairly and appropriately implemented. As we tackle these complex questions involving different technologies used for Internet access, let me be clear that we will be focused on formulating policies that will maximize innovation and investment, consumer choice, and greater competition.

Rulemaking Process

I've talked about what we need to do; now I'd like to talk about how we should do it. I will soon circulate to my fellow Commissioners proposed rules prepared by Commission staff embodying the principles I've discussed, and I will ask for their support in issuing a notice of proposed rulemaking. This notice will provide the public with a detailed explanation of what we propose to do and why.

Equally importantly, the notice will ask for input and feedback on the proposed rules and their application, such as how to determine whether network management practices are reasonable, and what information broadband providers should disclose about their network management practices and in what form. And—as I indicated earlier—it will pose a series of detailed questions on how the Internet openness principles should apply to mobile broadband.

While my goals are clear—to ensure the Internet remains a free and open platform that promotes innovation, investment, competition, and users' interests—our path to implementing them is not pre-determined. I will ensure that the rulemaking process will be fair, transparent, fact-based, and data-driven. Anyone will be able to participate in this process, and I hope everyone will. We will hold a number of public workshops and, of course, use the Internet and other new media tools to facilitate participation. Today we've launched a new website, www.openinternet.gov, to kick off discussion of the issues I've been talking about. We encourage everyone to visit the site and contribute to the process.

Moving Forward

Some have argued that the FCC should not take affirmative steps to protect the Internet's openness. Let me be clear about what this is about, and what it isn't.

The fundamental goal of what I've outlined today is preserving the openness and freedom of the Internet.

We have an obligation to ensure that the Internet is an enduring engine for U.S. economic growth, and a foundation for democracy in the 21st century.

We have an obligation to ensure that the Internet remains a vast landscape of innovation and opportunity.

This is not about government regulation of the Internet. It's about fair rules of the road for companies that control access to the Internet. We will do as much as we need to do, and no more, to ensure that the Internet remains an unfettered platform for competition, creativity, and entrepreneurial activity.

This is not about protecting the Internet against imaginary dangers. We're seeing the breaks and cracks emerge, and they threaten to change the Internet's fundamental architecture of openness. This would shrink opportunities for innovators, content creators, and small businesses around the country, and limit the full and free expression the Internet promises. This is about preserving and maintaining something profoundly successful and ensuring that it's not distorted or undermined. If we wait too long to preserve a free and open Internet, it will be too late.

Some will seek to invoke innovation and investment as reasons not to adopt open Internet rules. But history's lesson is clear: Ensuring a robust and open Internet is the best thing we can do to promote investment and innovation. And while there are some who see every policy decision as either pro-business or pro-consumer, I reject that approach; it's not the right way to see technology's role in America.

An open Internet will benefit both consumers and businesses. The principles that will protect the open Internet are an essential step to maximize investment and innovation in the network and on the edge of it—by establishing rules of the road that incentivize competition, empower entrepreneurs, and grow the economic pie to the benefit of all.

I believe we share a common purpose—we want the Internet to continue flourishing as a platform for innovation and communication, with continued investment and increasing deployment of broadband to all Americans. I believe my fellow Commissioners share this purpose, and I look forward to working collaboratively with them in this endeavor.

In closing, we are here because 40 years ago, a bunch of researchers in a lab changed the way computers interact and, as a result, changed the world. We are here because those Internet pioneers had unique insights about the power of open networks to transform lives for the better, and they did something about it. Our work now is to preserve the brilliance of what they contributed to our country and the world. It's to make sure that, in the 21st century, the garage, the basement, and the dorm room remain places where innovators can not only dream but bring their dreams to life. And no one should be neutral about that.

Kyle McSlarrow  **NO**

The Future of the Internet

. . . **T**he cable industry is the nation's largest provider of high-speed Internet access, making cable broadband service available to 92 percent of Americans, and has invested $130 billion to build a two-way interactive network with fiber-optic technology. Cable companies also provide state-of-the-art digital telephone service to more than 15 million American consumers. Cable operators are committed to delivering an open and satisfying Internet experience to their customers, and the dramatic growth in cable broadband subscribers is evidence of their success in doing so.

The cable industry has consistently demonstrated its commitment to policies that ensure all Americans have access to affordable broadband. We supported, for example, proposals advanced by Senator Dorgan and Senator Stevens to create a fund tailored to expanding broadband into unserved areas. We support Senator Inouye's Broadband Data Improvement Act, because we believe that improving federal data collection and dissemination regarding where broadband services have been deployed in the United States is necessary in order to achieve the goal of ubiquitous broadband availability for all Americans. And we continue to support:

- Tax credits or other tax incentives to providers that build out in rural areas that are unserved by an existing broadband provider.
- Reform of the RUS broadband loan program so that funding is targeted specifically to unserved areas.
- Expansion of the FCC's Lifeline and Link-Up Programs to help ensure that broadband access is extended to low-income households.
- Public–private partnerships to provide broadband in unserved areas.

We support these initiatives because we recognize that the government can play an important role in making certain that the economic and social benefits of broadband connectivity are extended to all areas of this country, and we look forward to working with you further to achieve these goals. But while broadband deployment to every community in America merits the full attention of policymakers, legislation calling for "network neutrality" or government intervention into the operation of networks would undermine the goals of broadband deployment and adoption. The development of the Internet, expansion of broadband networks, and creation of innovative Internet applications we have seen would not have occurred at such a rapid pace if providers were restricted in how they could engineer their networks to accommodate

U.S. Senate, April 22, 2008.

these dynamic developments. The government's consistent light regulatory touch since the introduction of broadband has worked. And only that continued regulatory freedom is likely to spur the investment and innovation that consumers have come to expect.

Today, I would like to focus on three points that illustrate why the Internet and broadband services should not be subject to greater and more intrusive government regulation. First, cable broadband providers have demonstrated and remain committed to providing Americans the very best broadband service available. Second, every cable modem subscriber today can access the content he or she seeks over the Internet. Broadband providers do not block access to content. Reasonable network optimization techniques not only enable the growth and development of the Internet, they protect consumers and their legitimate expectations.

Finally, the national policy of leaving the Internet unregulated has been a resounding success. Government intervention in broadband network management would only slow the pace of innovation and prevent the natural development of traffic solutions that is already occurring today.

I. Cable Brought Broadband to America

The industry's commitment to the deployment of broadband is reflected in the plain statistics. By any benchmark, the cable industry is leading efforts to spur broadband use and deployment.

Investment. The cable industry has done more to stimulate broadband growth and innovation than any other industry. Cable operators have invested $130 billion in private capital since the passage of the Telecommunications Act of 1996 to build broadband networks across the United States. Today 92% of American households, or about 117 million homes, have access to cable broadband service, including 96% of American homes to which cable television service is available. This investment and expansion took place without any government subsidies.

Competition. The cable industry's efforts to deploy broadband have stimulated tremendous investment in the provision of Internet access by competing providers, first by telephone companies and now wireless and satellite companies. This competition has spurred cable broadband providers and their competitors to develop better and better networks and applications to meet consumer demand and compete for their business. As former FTC Chairman Timothy Muris has explained, "competition [among providers] spurs producers to meet consumer expectations because the market generally imposes strict discipline on sellers who disappoint consumers and thus lose sales to producers who better meet consumer needs. These same competitive pressures also encourage producers to provide truthful information about their offerings."

Most notably, as the availability of broadband service has grown, the price-per-megabit has fallen significantly, and the speeds cable broadband offers have shot up dramatically. When cable first offered high-speed

broadband service as an alternative to dial-up access in the mid-90s, the speeds were approximately 1–1.5 Mbps. Today, most cable operators offer broadband speeds topping 5 Mbps and some operators, such as Cablevision and Comcast, offer speeds up to 50 Mbps. Comcast and Cox Communications also offer a service that provides for "boosts" of higher speeds that double the throughput on an on-demand, capacity-available basis.

Now the cable industry is on the verge of making the next leap—from "broadband" to "wideband"—with a technology which can enable dramatically higher download and upload speeds well above 100 Megabits per second. Several weeks ago, for example, Comcast launched a "wideband" service in Minneapolis–St. Paul that offers speeds of 50 Megabits per second. Comcast expects to have wideband available to 20% of its systems by year-end 2008 and to all homes passed by mid-2010.

Increased Use and Demand. The high quality and easy availability of cable broadband has led to the widespread adoption of broadband use. Today, the cable industry has more than 35 million broadband customers. Overall, approximately 64 million broadband households nationwide have broadband service, and that number continues to grow.

New Content, Web Services, and Applications. The efforts of broadband network providers to build larger and faster networks have helped ensure the success of countless numbers of new Internet businesses and applications—online video services, social networking websites, data-sharing services, and online interactive game services, to name a few. Despite concerns about alleged limited access to broadband, use of Internet video on demand has grown at the most dramatic rate. In July 2006, 107 million Americans watched video online and about 60% of Internet users downloaded more than 7 billion videos off the Internet. In February 2008, nearly 135 million U.S. Internet users spent an average of 204 minutes viewing 10.1 billion online videos. YouTube represented 34% of those online videos, or nearly 3.5 billion in total. To put it into context, in 2006, YouTube consumed as much bandwidth as the entire Internet consumed in the year 2000.

Television networks are now offering cable modem and other broadband customers video online, such as NBC Universal and News Corp.'s new Hulu service. Book retailers are now offering online digital novels; and music sales websites, such as iTunes, continue to grow. Social networking websites, where users share home videos, pictures, and music content, are also on the rise—in 2007, an estimated 126.5 million people in North America participated in an online social networking website. Internet commerce also continues to grow. Last year, over $135 billion was spent purchasing goods and services over the Internet.

For years, net neutrality proponents have argued that without government intervention, broadband providers would stifle competing services and content providers; Internet development and usage would stagnate; and consumers would be unable to use their broadband connections to download video or access other emerging applications. In fact, cable's investment in broadband has driven innovation and investment in new content and

applications at the edge—the exact opposite of what was predicted by advocates of net regulation.

There is no better proof that there presently exists no "problem" needing a "solution" than YouTube. YouTube would have been a pipe dream in 2002. Six years later, however, YouTube—the proverbial "two guys in a garage" who allegedly could not survive, let alone thrive, unless the Internet were regulated—has become a multibillion dollar enterprise. And YouTube is now owned by Google, which itself has grown to become one of the largest companies in the world with a market capitalization of $169 billion.

Here's an incontrovertible truth: the staggering growth of these companies would not have occurred without cable's investment in and deployment of the reliable high-speed broadband service that provides the ecosystem in which Google, YouTube, Yahoo! and other Internet services can flourish.

II. Network Optimization Enhances and Enables the Internet Experience

In 2006, I testified before this Committee and stated that cable operators do not and would not block subscribers' access to any lawful content, applications or services. That statement remains true today. Cable modem subscribers have the ability to do anything they want to on the Internet. They can download or stream videos, upload and send pictures to friends, or call family across the world. They can also attach gaming devices, or any other computing device they want to use to the network. They can use file-sharing software from peer-to-peer networks. If they couldn't do what they wanted, they would soon not be cable modem subscribers. They would go to our competitors.

Cable subscribers can enjoy the most advanced and cutting-edge Internet sites and applications because of the extensive efforts cable operators constantly undertake to make all content and applications flow smoothly and work seamlessly together over the network. In 1999, there were only 2 million households with broadband service in the United States; today there are approximately 64 million. This is a great success story—but with this success comes the need to manage the network so that every household has good user experience.

Cable providers built a smart infrastructure that has the capability to evolve and meet the challenges of multimedia, file sharing, and other bandwidth-intensive applications. But cable broadband subscribers currently enjoy the full benefits of broadband only because cable operators manage their networks on a content-agnostic basis to provide seamless connectivity, deter spam and viruses, and make sure that a tiny minority of users don't slow down the Internet for everyone else. Various estimates are that as few as 5% of customers use from 50 to 90% of the total capacity of the network. In Japan, it is estimated that 1% of Internet users consume 47% of the total Internet traffic. Faced with these voracious bandwidth consumers, cable operators may engage in reasonable, content-agnostic network management practices—triggered by objective criteria based upon network traffic levels—to ensure that the relatively few customers who utilize bandwidth-heavy applications do not

degrade or otherwise adversely affect broadband Internet access for the vast majority of customers.

There have been some recent concerns that network management practices affecting certain high-bandwidth-consuming peer-to-peer (P2P) applications are "discriminatory." P2P traffic can consume a disproportionately large amount of network resources—far, far more than any other Internet use. If even a small fraction of customers are using these bandwidth-intensive applications at the same time, it can interfere with the ability of the vast majority of all other customers in that area to surf the web, watch streaming video, make voice-over-IP calls, or engage in other routine uses of the Internet.

Providers can't build their way out of this problem—in spite of increasing capacity, many P2P protocols are written specifically to commandeer as much bandwidth as is available. Instead, providers optimize their networks in order to balance the needs of all of their customers.

Far from inhibiting access, smart network techniques protect the ability of our customers to make the greatest and most flexible use of the Internet. They are a reasonable response to an identified congestion problem that has the benefit of allowing all other applications—particularly latency-sensitive applications like VoIP and streaming video—to work better. As the Institute for Policy Innovation recently stated, "[i]n almost all cases, network management today is unnoticed by consumers. The opposite, a total lack of management, would not be true. If network operators were precluded from managing their networks, consumers would be negatively affected." Sound network management is essential to ensuring a stable broadband platform. Google, Yahoo!, Amazon, and service providers like Vonage could not carry on their businesses if bandwidth-consuming applications were allowed to block customers from accessing their Web sites or completing their transactions. Because of network management, such businesses can develop business models that hinge on the expectation that their service will not be crowded out by congestion caused by heavy bandwidth-using software. Far from being "neutral," a network that is not managed simply allows those who want to demand all the bandwidth for themselves to do so unchecked.

Reasonable network management practices are also vital to combating the well-documented, illegal distribution of copyrighted material on the Internet. We cannot ignore the problem of piracy. It is a problem that affects not just broadband service providers, legitimate broadband application providers and content providers, but also law-abiding consumers. Ultimately they are the ones that bear the burden of congestion caused by those who abuse their network access to engage in the widespread distribution of infringing works. Technology is agnostic, but, according to one source, 90 percent of P2P downloads are pirated material. Broadband providers, content owners and others all have a stake in exploring technology solutions that address piracy in ways that respect our customers' expectations and respect the copyright owner's rights, not simply to curtail congestion but for reasons of fairness to those who invest in content and make an important contribution to our economy. Government action that would inhibit development of innovative approaches to thwarting piracy and enhancing the online experience for the vast majority of Internet users would harm content creation and ultimately consumers.

So, is there evidence that these challenges are insurmountable and require more government regulation? Quite the contrary. The same technological innovation that gives rise to some of these challenges has produced creative ways to fight spam and viruses. The same private sector collaboration that allowed the countless number of networks that make up the Internet to exchange traffic and engage in peering has and continues to focus on new challenges.

Some P2P developers are creating new ways to make that technology more bandwidth-efficient and network-friendly, so that it may continue to emerge as a useful way to distribute legal content. Cable companies and other broadband providers are working hard to find ways to address concerns about network congestion and create consumer-friendly options that allow the majority of users to access content at the speeds needed. The "P4P Working Group"—a collaborative industry effort to develop network management solutions that benefit cable and other broadband operators, P2P software firms, and consumers—is one such effort.

Broadband providers have also begun testing and dialogue with P2P applications providers to make networks and P2P applications friendlier to one another. For example, Verizon has been working with Pando Networks, a P2P software developer, and the P4P Working Group to develop a more bandwidth efficient file-sharing protocol. Just last week, Comcast and Pando announced their intention to lead an industry-wide effort to create a "P2P Bill of Rights and Responsibilities." And Comcast and BitTorrent recently reached an agreement in which Comcast pledged to adopt a capacity management technique based on individual users' consumption during peak periods rather than based on a particular protocol.

Broadband providers and Internet content and service providers have mutual incentives to develop workable solutions that enhance customers' Internet experiences. Cable operators' tremendous investments have laid the foundation for robust broadband networks that have spurred the remarkable explosion of new services and innovations on the Internet. In turn, the vast array of applications and services now available on the Internet drive more and more people to become broadband users.

III. The Government Should Continue to Refrain from Regulation

Congress should resist calls to interfere with broadband providers' freedom to manage their respective networks in order to satisfy the evolving needs of American consumers. Cable modem service has never been subject to regulation. Six years after the FCC classified cable's broadband offering as an unregulated information service and nearly three years after the FCC determined that no regulation was needed to encourage broadband deployment and preserve and promote Internet usage and demand, there has been no evidence of any practices that would change those conclusions or warrant government intervention generally or specifically with respect to permissible network

management activities. The disaster scenarios voiced by network neutrality proponents for many years have never happened. In fact, the opposite has happened—the Internet is booming without regulation. There is quite simply no problem requiring a government solution.

Under the guise of preventing discrimination, "net neutrality" proponents would have the government determine which network management techniques are permissible. But putting every network management strategy up for debate before regulators would severely hamper the ability of network providers to ensure high-quality and reliable Internet access for their subscribers. Depriving network operators of certain bandwidth management tools only makes the network less efficient for everyone. Ultimately, interfering with an operator's ability to manage its network would harm consumers and prevent them from accessing the content they desire. Adept network optimization techniques are fundamental to creating and preserving the stable "ecosystem" for online service providers that ensures an optimal customer experience.

Government intervention in a fast-changing technological world could result in very real problems developing very quickly. Network management practices are constantly changing and evolving—as networks grow, consumer usage patterns change, and new technologies emerge. It would be impossible for any regulation to keep up with these changes. Nor does the government have the expertise or resources to second-guess the thousands of network management decisions broadband network engineers must make every day. It is far more likely that government interference in the development of the market could foreclose or prevent the emergence of cross-industry efforts that are more likely to get the solutions right.

Conclusion

Misplaced concerns over legitimate and reasonable network management practices do not justify the enactment of open-ended regulation of the Internet, particularly where the costs of such regulation are foreseeable and substantial. Given the growth of broadband competition and the breathtaking pace of technological change, government intervention is unwarranted. As the Federal Trade Commission has warned, regulation of Internet access at this stage of market development could have "potentially adverse and unintended effects," including reduced product and service innovation. And net neutrality requirements would frustrate the Federal policy of "preserv[ing] the vibrant and competitive free market that presently exists for the Internet . . . , unfettered by Federal or State regulation." Today's hands-off policy has given us the flexibility to innovate and respond to consumer demand. By contrast, proposals for "net neutrality" amount to regulation of the Internet that would undermine—not promote—consumer choice and welfare.

EXPLORING THE ISSUE

Should the Internet Be Neutral?

Critical Thinking and Reflection

1. In what ways does increased traffic on the Internet make it difficult to maintain perfect network neutrality?
2. Society depends on many "networks" (interconnected channels through which something moves) such as the highway system, the electrical grid, and even municipal water distribution systems. In what ways does the concept of "network neutrality" apply to these networks (if it does)?
3. How do users pay for use of these other networks?
4. What are the risks involved in letting broadband providers control what kinds of information can be sent over the Internet?

Is There Common Ground?

Everyone involved in this debate agrees that the Internet is valuable to society. They differ in the nature of that value and to whom that value should accrue. Everyone also agrees that government regulation is a bad idea, but they differ on the reasons why.

1. To those who favor net neutrality, in what ways is the Internet valuable to society?
2. To those who oppose net neutrality, in what ways is the Internet valuable to society?
3. To those who favor net neutrality, what does "government regulation" mean?
4. To those who oppose net neutrality, what does "government regulation" mean?

Internet References . . .

University Corporation for Atmospheric Research

The University Corporation for Atmospheric Research and the National Center for Atmospheric Research are part of a collaborative community dedicated to understanding the atmosphere—the air around us—and the interconnected processes that make up the Earth system, from the ocean floor to the Sun's core. The *UCAR Quarterly* is a journal that presents reports on many issues, including geoengineering (e.g., http://www.ucar.edu/communications/quarterly/fall06/bigfix.jsp).

http://www.ucar.edu/

Department of Energy

The U.S. Department of Energy provides information on nuclear power, hydrogen, and other energy sources, as well as such energy-related issues as global warming.

http://www.energy.gov

Global Warming

The Environmental Protection Agency maintains this site to summarize the current state of knowledge about global warming.

http://www.epa.gov/climatechange/index.html

Intergovernmental Panel on Climate Change

The Intergovernmental Panel on Climate Change (IPCC) was formed by the World Meteorological Organization (WMO) and the United Nations Environment Programme (UNEP) to assess any scientific, technical, and socioeconomic information that is relevant to the understanding of the risk of human-induced climate change.

http://www.ipcc.ch

National Renewable Energy Laboratory

The National Renewable Energy Laboratory (NREL) is the leading center for renewable energy research in the United States.

http://www.nrel.gov

Heritage Foundation

The Heritage Foundation is a think tank whose mission is to formulate and promote conservative public policies based on the principles of free enterprise, limited government, individual freedom, traditional American values, and a strong national defense.

http://www.heritage.org

Energy and the Environment

As the damage that human beings do to their environment in the course of obtaining food, water, wood, ore, energy, and other resources has become clear, many people have grown concerned. Some of that concern is for the environment—the landscapes and living things with which humanity shares its world. Some of that concern is more for human welfare; it focuses on the ways in which environmental damage threatens human health, prosperity, or even survival.

Among the major environmental issues are those related to energy. By releasing vast amounts of carbon dioxide, fossil fuels threaten to change the world's climate. Potential solutions include warding off excess solar heating, greatly expanding the use of nuclear power, and changing our automobile fuel from gasoline to electricity.

- Is It Time to Think Seriously About "Climate Engineering"?

- Is It Time to Revive Nuclear Power?

- Is America Ready for the Electric Car?

ISSUE 4

Is It Time to Think Seriously About "Climate Engineering"?

YES: **Kevin Bullis,** from "The Geoengineering Gambit," *Technology Review* (January/February 2010)

NO: **James R. Fleming,** from "The Climate Engineers," *The Wilson Quarterly* (Spring 2007)

Learning Outcomes

After studying this issue, students will be able to:

1. Compare the benefits of addressing global warming by reducing greenhouse gas emissions with the benefits of addressing global warming by blocking incoming solar radiation.
2. Explain the drawbacks of addressing global warming by blocking incoming solar radiation.
3. Explain why even if the better approach to controlling global warming involves reducing emissions of greenhouse gases, studying geoengineering remains a good idea.
4. Explain the political hazards of geoengineering.

ISSUE SUMMARY

YES: Kevin Bullis, energy editor of *Technology Review*, reviews the latest thinking about "geoengineering" as a solution to the global warming problem, and concludes that despite potential side effects and the risk of unknown impacts on the environment, it may be time to consider technologies that can offset global warming.

NO: James R. Fleming, professor of science, technology, and society, argues that climate engineers fail to consider both the risks of unintended consequences to human life and political relationships and the ethics of the human relationship with nature.

It has been known for a very long time that natural events such as volcanic eruptions can cool climate, sometimes dramatically, by injecting large quantities of dust and sulfates into the stratosphere, where they serve as a "sunshade" that reflects a portion of solar heat back into space before it can warm the Earth. In 1815, the Tambora volcano on Sumbawa island, Indonesia, put so much material (especially sulfates) into the atmosphere that 1816 was known in the United States, Canada, and Europe as the "year without a summer." There was crop-killing frost, snow, and ice all summer long, which gave the year its other name of "eighteen-hundred-and-froze-to-death." See Clive Oppenheimer, "Climatic, Environmental and Human Consequences of the Largest Known Historic Eruption: Tambora Volcano (Indonesia) 1815," *Progress in Physical Geography* (June 2003). In 1992, Mount Pinatubo, in the Philippines, had a similar, if smaller, effect and hid for a time the climate warming otherwise produced by increasing amounts of greenhouse gases. See Alan Robock, "The Climatic Aftermath," *Science* (February 15, 2002). Changes in solar activity can also have effects. Periods of climate chilling and climate warming have been linked to decreases and increases in the amount of energy released by the sun and reaching the Earth; see Caspar M. Ammann et al., "Solar Influence on Climate During the Past Millennium: Results from Transient Simulations with the NCAR Climate System Model," *Proceedings of the National Academy of Sciences of the United States of America* (March 6, 2007).

Such effects have prompted many researchers to think that global warming is not just a matter of increased atmospheric content of greenhouse gases such as carbon dioxide (which slow the loss of heat to space and thus warm the planet) but also of the amount of sunlight that reaches Earth from the sun. So far, most attempts to find a solution to global warming have focused on reducing human emissions of greenhouse gases. But it does not seem unreasonable to consider the other side of the problem, the energy that reaches Earth from the sun. After all, if you are too warm in bed at night, you can remove the blanket or turn down the furnace. Suggestions that something similar might be done on a global scale go back more than 40 years; see Robert Kunzig, "A Sunshade for Planet Earth," *Scientific American* (November 2008).

Paul Crutzen suggested in "Albedo Enhancement by Stratospheric Sulfur Injections: A Contribution to Resolve a Policy Dilemma?" *Climate Change* (August 2006) that adding sulfur compounds to the stratosphere (as volcanoes have done) could reflect some solar energy and help relieve the problem. According to Bob Henson, "Big Fixes for Climate?" *UCAR Quarterly* (Fall 2006) (http://www.ucar.edu/communications/quarterly/fall06/bigfix.jsp), the National Center for Atmospheric Research is currently testing the idea with computer simulations; one conclusion is that a single Pinatubo-sized stratospheric injection could buy 20 years of time before we would have to cut back carbon dioxide emissions in a big way. Such measures would not be cheap, and at present there is no way to tell whether they would have undesirable side effects, although G. Bala, P. B. Duffy, and K. E. Taylor, "Impact of Geoengineering Schemes on the Global Hydrological Cycle," *Proceedings of the National Academy of Sciences of the United States of America* (June 3, 2008), suggest it is likely that precipitation would be significantly reduced.

Roger Angel, "Feasibility of Cooling the Earth with a Cloud of Small Space-craft near the Inner Lagrange Point (L1)," *Proceedings of the National Academy of Sciences of the United States of America* (November 14, 2006), argues that if danger-ous changes in global climate become inevitable, despite greenhouse gas con-trols, it may be possible to solve the problem by reducing the amount of solar energy that hits the Earth by using reflective spacecraft. He does not suggest that climate engineering solutions such as this or injecting sulfur compounds into the stratosphere should be tried *instead of* reducing greenhouse gas emissions. Rather, he suggests that such solutions should be evaluated for use in extremis, if greenhouse gas reductions are not sufficient or if global warming runs out of control. In January 2009, a survey of climate scientists found broad support for exploring the geoengineering approach and even developing techniques; see "What Can We Do to Save Our Planet?" *The Independent* (January 2, 2009) (http://www.independent.co.uk/environment/climate-change/what-can-we-do-to-save-our-planet-1221097.html). However, any such program will require much more international cooperation than is usually available; see Jason J. Blackstock and Jane C. S. Long, "The Politics of Geoengineering," *Science* (January 29, 2010). Jamais Cascio, "The Potential and Risks of Geoengineering," *Futurist* (May/June 2010), argues that there will be a place in international diplomacy for efforts "to control climate engineering technologies and deal with their consequences." Among those consequences may be major changes in the amount and distri-bution of rain and snow; see Gabriele C. Hegerl and Susan Solomon, "Risks of Climate Engineering," *Science* (August 21, 2009).

Chris Mooney, "Climate Repair Made Simple," *Wired* (July 2008), notes that geoengineering proposals might actually work for climate control, but increasing carbon dioxide levels have other consequences too, such as increasing acidity of the oceans. Alternative methods such as ocean fertilization to stimu-late algae to remove carbon dioxide from the atmosphere do not seem likely to be successful; see Noreen Parks, "Fertilizing the Seas for Climate Mitigation—Promising Strategy or Sheer Folly?" *Bioscience* (February 2008). Among other approaches are spraying seawater into the stratosphere and removing carbon dioxide from the atmosphere; see Erik Sofge, "A Geo-Engineered World," *Popular Mechanics* (February 2010), and Erica Engelhaupt, "Engineering a Cooler Earth," *Science News* (June 5, 2010). Robert B. Jackson and James Salzman, "Pursuing Geoengineering for Atmospheric Restoration," *Issues in Science and Technology* (Summer 2010), favors approaches that remove carbon dioxide from the atmos-phere. Awareness of potential problems has already lead to one major meeting that concluded that geoengineering research was essential but should be con-ducted with "humility"; see Eli Kintisch, "'Asilomar 2' Takes Small Steps Toward Rules for Geoengineering," *Science* (April 2, 2010).

James R. Fleming, "The Pathological History of Weather and Climate Modification: Three Cycles of Promise and Hype," *Historical Studies in the Physical and Biological Sciences* (vol. 37, no. 1, 2006), finds the history of attempts to modify weather and climate so marred by excessive optimism that we should doubt the rationality of present climate engineering proposals. Thomas Sterner, et al., "Quick Fixes for the Environment: Part of the Solution or Part of the Problem?" *Environment* (December 2006), say that "Quick fixes

are sometimes appropriate because they work sufficiently well and/or buy time to design longer term solutions . . . [but] when quick fixes are deployed, it is useful to tie them to long-run abatement measures." Fundamental solutions (such as reducing emissions of greenhouse gases to solve the global warming problem) are to be preferred, but they may be opposed because of "lack of understanding of ecological mechanisms, failure to recognize the gravity of the problem, vested interests, and absence of institutions to address public goods and intergenerational choices effectively."

There are two basic problems with "sunshades" solutions such as stratospheric sulfate injections or seawater sprays or reflective spacecraft. One is that they are difficult to test short of full-scale implementation; see Alan Robock et al., "A Test for Geoengineering?" *Science* (January 29, 2010). The second is that even if they work as intended, with few or no undesirable side effects, they must be maintained indefinitely, while the underlying problem continues. If the maintenance falters, as seems reasonable to expect it will given the nature of human politics, the underlying problem will still be there. In fact, atmospheric levels of greenhouse gases will be higher than before because emissions will have continued to rise. The climate will then warm relatively suddenly.

Such solutions also fail to recognize that we face more than one problem. Fossil fuels are finite in supply. We will eventually run out of them. At that time, if we have failed to develop alternative energy sources, we will face a tremendous crisis. But if we reduce greenhouse gas emissions in part by developing alternative energy sources, that crisis will never arrive or will not be as severe when it does. One question with which human society is presently struggling is whether we can shift away from fossil fuels despite the vested interests mentioned by Sterner et al.

It is worth noting that much of the discussion of climate engineering presumes that we will try as a global society to reduce carbon emissions but that our efforts will be insufficient. However, the United Nations Global Climate Change Conference, held in Copenhagen in December 2009, failed to produce a binding agreement to start reducing emissions. Instead, it achieved only an agreement to meet again in 2010 and "start tackling climate change and step up work toward a legally binding treaty." Many people feel that if we do not move faster, geoengineering may be our only option. Robert B. Jackson and James Salzman, "Pursuing Geoengineering for Atmospheric Restoration," *Issues in Science and Technology* (Summer 2010), argue that we need to move toward increased energy efficiency and greater use of renewable energy and explore ways to remove carbon from the atmosphere. If we are successful, we will be less likely to need "sunshades" approaches to geoengineering; however, research into such approaches is essential.

In the YES selection, Kevin Bullis discusses "geoengineering" as a solution to the global warming problem, and concludes that despite potential side effects and the risk of unknown impacts on the environment, it may be time to consider these technologies. In the NO selection, James R. Fleming argues that climate engineers fail to consider risks of unintended consequences to human life and political relationships, and the ethics of the human relationship to nature.

YES

Kevin Bullis

The Geoengineering Gambit

Rivers fed by melting snow and glaciers supply water to over one-sixth of the world's population—well over a billion people. But these sources of water are quickly disappearing: the Himalayan glaciers that feed rivers in India, China, and other Asian countries could be gone in 25 years. Such effects of climate change no longer surprise scientists. But the speed at which they're happening does. "The earth appears to be changing faster than the climate models predicted," says Daniel Schrag, a professor of earth and planetary sciences at Harvard University, who advises President Obama on climate issues.

Atmospheric levels of carbon dioxide have already climbed to 385 parts per million, well over the 350 parts per million that many scientists say is the upper limit for a relatively stable climate. And despite government-led efforts to limit carbon emissions in many countries, annual emissions from fossil-fuel combustion are going up, not down: over the last two decades, they have increased 41 percent. In the last 10 years, the concentration of carbon dioxide in the atmosphere has increased by nearly two parts per million every year. At this rate, they'll be twice preindustrial levels by the end of the century. Meanwhile, researchers are growing convinced that the climate might be more sensitive to greenhouse gases at this level than once thought. "The likelihood that we're going to avoid serious damage seems quite low," says Schrag. "The best we're going to do is probably not going to be good enough."

This shocking realization has caused many influential scientists, including Obama advisors like Schrag, to fundamentally change their thinking about how to respond to climate change. They have begun calling for the government to start funding research into geoengineering—large-scale schemes for rapidly cooling the earth.

Strategies for geoengineering vary widely, from launching trillions of sun shields into space to triggering vast algae blooms in oceans. The one that has gained the most attention in recent years involves injecting millions of tons of sulfur dioxide high into the atmosphere to form microscopic particles that would shade the planet. Many geoengineering proposals date back decades, but until just a few years ago, most climate scientists considered them something between high-tech hubris and science fiction. Indeed, the subject was "forbidden territory," says Ronald Prinn, a professor of atmospheric sciences at MIT. Not only is it unclear how such engineering feats would be accomplished and whether they would, in fact, moderate the climate, but most scientists worry

that they could have disastrous unintended consequences. What's more, relying on geoengineering to cool the earth, rather than cutting greenhouse-gas emissions, would commit future generations to maintaining these schemes indefinitely. For these reasons, mere discussion of geoengineering was considered a dangerous distraction for policy makers considering how to deal with global warming. Prinn says that until a few years ago, he thought its advocates were "off the deep end."

It's not just a fringe idea anymore. The United Kingdom's Royal Society issued a report on geoengineering in September that outlined the research and policy challenges ahead. The National Academies in the United States are working on a similar study. And John Holdren, the director of the White House Office of Science and Technology Policy, broached the idea soon after he was appointed. "Climate change is happening faster than anyone previously predicted," he said during one talk. "If we get sufficiently desperate, we may try to engage in geoengineering to try to create cooling effects." To prepare ourselves, he said, we need to understand the possibilities and the possible side effects. Even the U.S. Congress has now taken an interest, holding its first hearings on geoengineering in November.

Geoengineering might be "a terrible idea," but it might be better than doing nothing, says Schrag. Unlike many past advocates, he doesn't think it's an alternative to reducing greenhouse-gas emissions. "It's not a techno-fix. It's not a Band-Aid. It's a tourniquet," he says. "There are potential side effects, yes. But it may be better than the alternative, which is bleeding to death."

Sunday Storms

The idea of geoengineering has a long history. In the 1830s, James Espy, the first federally funded meteorologist in the United States, wanted to burn large swaths of Appalachian forest every Sunday afternoon, supposing that heat from the fires would induce regular rainstorms. More than a century later, meteorologists and physicists in the United States and the Soviet Union separately considered a range of schemes for changing the climate, often with the goal of warming up northern latitudes to extend growing seasons and clear shipping lanes through the Arctic.

In 1974 a Soviet scientist, Mikhail Budyko, first suggested what is today probably the leading plan for cooling down the earth: injecting gases into the upper reaches of the atmosphere, where they would form microscopic particles to block sunlight. The idea is based on a natural phenomenon. Every few decades a volcano erupts so violently that it sends several millions of tons of sulfur—in the form of sulfur dioxide—more than 10 kilometers into the upper reaches of the atmosphere, a region called the stratosphere. The resulting sulfate particles spread out quickly and stay suspended for years. They reflect and diffuse sunlight, creating a haze that whitens blue skies and causes dramatic sunsets. By decreasing the amount of sunlight that reaches the surface, the haze also lowers its temperature. This is what happened after the 1991 eruption of Mount Pinatubo in the Philippines, which released about 15 million tons of sulfur dioxide into the stratosphere. Over the next 15 months, average

temperatures dropped by half a degree Celsius. (Within a few years, the sulfates settled out of the stratosphere, and the cooling effect was gone.)

Scientists estimate that compensating for the increase in carbon dioxide levels expected over this century would require pumping between one million and five million tons of sulfur into the stratosphere every year. Diverse strategies for getting all that sulfur up there have been proposed. Billionaire investor Nathan Myhrvold, the former chief technology officer at Microsoft and the founder and CEO of Intellectual Ventures, based in Bellevue, WA, has thought of several, one of which takes advantage of the fact that coal-fired power plants already emit vast amounts of sulfur dioxide. These emissions stay close to the ground, and rain washes them out of the atmosphere within a couple of weeks. But if the pollution could reach the stratosphere, it would circulate for years, vastly multiplying its impact in reflecting sunlight. To get the sulfur into the stratosphere, Myhrvold suggests, why not use a "flexible, inflatable hot-air-balloon smokestack" 25 kilometers tall? The emissions from just two coal-fired plants might solve the problem, he says. He estimates that his solution would cost less than $100 million a year, including the cost of replacing balloons damaged by storms.

Not surprisingly, climate scientists are not ready to sign off on such a scheme. Some problems are obvious. No one has ever tried to build a 25-kilometer smokestack, for one thing. Moreover, scientists don't understand atmospheric chemistry well enough to be sure what would happen; far from alleviating climate change, shooting tons of sulfates into the stratosphere could have disastrous consequences. The chemistry is too complex for us to be certain, and climate models aren't powerful enough to tell the whole story.

"We know Pinatubo cooled the earth, but that's not the question," Schrag says. "Average temperature is not the only issue." You've also got to account for regional variations in temperature and effects on precipitation, he explains—the very things that climate models are notoriously bad at accounting for. Prinn concurs: "If we lower levels of sunlight, we are unsure of the exact response of the climate system to doing that, for the same reason that we don't know exactly how the climate will respond to a particular level of greenhouse gases." He adds, "That's the big issue. How can you engineer a system you don't fully understand?"

The actual effects of Mount Pinatubo were, in fact, complex. Climate models at the time predicted that by decreasing the amount of sunlight hitting the surface of the earth, the haze of sulfates produced in such an eruption would reduce evaporation, which in turn would lower the amount of precipitation worldwide. Rainfall did decrease—but by much more than scientists had expected. "The year following Mount Pinatubo had by far the lowest amount of rainfall on record," says Kevin Trenberth, a senior scientist at the National Center for Atmospheric Research in Boulder, CO. "In fact, it was 50 percent lower than the previous low of any year." The effects, however, weren't uniform; in some places, precipitation actually increased. A human-engineered sulfate haze could have similarly unpredictable results, scientists warn.

Even in a best-case scenario, where side effects are small and manageable, cooling the planet by deflecting sunlight would not reduce the carbon dioxide

in the atmosphere, and elevated levels of that gas have consequences beyond raising the temperature. One is that the ocean absorbs more carbon dioxide and becomes more acidic as a result. That harms shellfish and some forms of plankton, a key source of food for fish and whales. The fishing industry could be devastated. What's more, carbon dioxide levels will continue to rise if we don't address them directly, so any sunlight-reducing technology would have to be continually ratcheted up to compensate for their warming effects.

And if the geoengineering had to stop—say, for environmental or economic reasons—the higher levels of greenhouse gases would cause an abrupt warm-up. "Even if the geoengineering worked perfectly," says Raymond Pierrehumbert, a professor of geophysical sciences at the University of Chicago, "you're still in the situation where the whole planet is just one global war or depression away from being hit with maybe a hundred years' worth of global warming in under a decade, which is certainly catastrophic. Geoengineering, if it were carried out, would put the earth in an extremely precarious state."

Smarter Sulfates

Figuring out the consequences of various geoengineering plans and developing strategies to make them safer and more effective will take years, or even decades, of research. "For every dollar we spend figuring out how to actually do geoengineering," says Schrag, "we need to be spending 10 dollars learning what the impacts will be."

To begin with, scientists aren't even sure that sulfates delivered over the course of decades, rather than in one short volcanic blast, will work to cool the planet down. One key question is how microscopic particles interact in the stratosphere. It's possible that sulfate particles added repeatedly to the same area over time would clump together. If that happened, the particles could start to interact with longer-wave radiation than just the wavelengths of electromagnetic energy in visible light. This would trap some of the heat that naturally escapes into space, causing a net heating effect rather than a cooling effect. Or the larger particles could fall out of the sky before they had a chance to deflect the sun's heat. To study such phenomena, David Keith, the director of the Energy and Environmental Systems Group at the University of Calgary, envisions experiments in which a plane would spray a gas at low vapor pressure over an area of 100 square kilometers. The gas would condense into particles in the stratosphere, and the plane would fly back through the particle cloud to take measurements. Systematically altering the size of the particles, the quantity of particles in a given area, the timing of their release, and other variables could reveal key details about their microscale interactions.

Yet even if the behavior of sulfate particles can be understood and managed, it's far from clear how injecting them into the stratosphere would affect vast, complex climate systems. So far, most models have been crude; only recently, for example, did they start taking into account the movement of ice and ocean currents. Sulfates would cool the planet during the day, but they'd make no difference when the sun isn't shining. As a result, nights would probably be warmer relative to days, but scientists have done little to model this

effect and study how it could affect ecosystems. "Similarly, you could affect the seasons," Schrag says: the sulfates would lower temperatures less during the winter (when there's less daylight) and more during the summer. And scientists have done little to understand how stratospheric circulation patterns would change with the addition of sulfates, or precisely how any of these things could affect where and when we might experience droughts, floods, and other disasters.

If scientists could learn more about the effects of sulfates in the stratosphere, it could raise the intriguing possibility of "smart" geoengineering, Schrag says. Volcanic eruptions are crude tools, releasing a lot of sulfur in the course of a few days, and all from one location. But geoengineers could choose exactly where to send sulfates into the stratosphere, as well as when and how fast.

"So far we're thinking about a very simplistic thing," Schrag says. "We're talking about injecting stuff in the stratosphere in a uniform way." The effects that have been predicted so far, however, aren't evenly distributed. Changes in evaporation, for example, could be devastating if they caused droughts on land, but if less rain falls over the ocean, it's not such a big deal. By taking advantage of stratospheric circulation patterns and seasonal variations in weather, it might be possible to limit the most damaging consequences. "You can pulse injections," he says. "You could build smart systems that might cancel out some of those negative effects."

Rather than intentionally polluting the stratosphere, a different and potentially less risky approach to geoengineering is to pull carbon dioxide out of the air. But the necessary technology would be challenging to develop and put in place on large scale.

In his 10th-floor lab in the Manhattan neighborhood of Morningside Heights, Klaus Lackner, a professor of geophysics in the Department of Earth and Environmental Engineering at Columbia University, is experimenting with a material that chemically binds to carbon dioxide in the air and then, when doused in water, releases the gas in a concentrated form that can easily be captured. The work is at an early stage. Lackner's carbon-capture devices look like misshapen test-tube brushes; they have to be hand dipped in water, and it's hard to quickly seal them into the improvised chamber used to measure the carbon dioxide they release. But he envisions automated systems—millions of them, each the size of a small cabin—scattered over the countryside near geologic reservoirs that could store the gases they capture. A system based on this material, he calculates, could remove carbon dioxide from the air a thousand times as fast as trees do now. Others at Columbia are working on ways to exploit the fact that peridotite rock reacts with carbon dioxide to form magnesium carbonate and other minerals, removing the greenhouse gas from the atmosphere. The researchers hope to speed up these natural reactions.

It's far from clear that these ideas for capturing carbon will be practical. Some may even require so much energy that they create a net increase in carbon dioxide. "But even if it takes us a hundred years to learn how to do it," Pierrehumbert says, "it's still useful, because CO_2 naturally takes a thousand years to get out of the atmosphere."

The Seeds of War

Several existing geoengineering schemes, though, could be attempted relatively cheaply and easily. And even if no one knows whether they would be safe or effective, that doesn't mean they won't be tried.

David Victor, the director of the Laboratory on International Law and Regulation at the University of California, San Diego, sees two scenarios in which it might happen. First, "the desperate Hail Mary pass": "A country quite vulnerable to changing climate is desperate to alter outcomes and sees that efforts to cut emissions are not bearing fruit. Crude geoengineering schemes could be very inexpensive, and thus this option might even be available to a Trinidad or Bangladesh—the former rich in gas exports and quite vulnerable, and the latter poor but large enough that it might do something seen as essential for survival." And second, "the Soviet-style arrogant engineering scenario": "A country run by engineers and not overly exposed to public opinion or to dissenting voices undertakes geoengineering as a national mission—much like massive building of poorly designed nuclear reactors, river diversion projects, resettlement of populations, and other national missions that are hard to pursue when the public is informed, responsive, and in power." In either case, a single country acting alone could influence the climate of the entire world.

How would the world react? In extreme cases, Victor says, it could lead to war. Some countries might object to cooling the earth, especially if higher temperatures have brought them advantages such as longer growing seasons and milder winters. And if geoengineering decreases rainfall, countries that have experienced droughts due to global warming could suffer even more.

No current international laws or agreements would clearly prevent a country from unilaterally starting a geoengineering project. And too little is known now for a governing body such as the United Nations to establish sound regulations—regulations that might in any case be ignored by a country set on trying to save itself from a climate disaster. Victor says the best hope is for leading scientists around the world to collaborate on establishing as clearly as possible what dangers could be involved in geoengineering and how, if at all, it might be used. Through open international research, he says, we can "increase the odds—not to 100 percent—that responsible norms would emerge."

Ready or Not

In 2006, Paul Crutzen, the Dutch scientist who won the Nobel Prize in chemistry for his discoveries about the depletion of the stratospheric ozone layer, wrote an essay in the journal *Climatic Change* in which he declared that efforts to reduce greenhouse-gas emissions "have been grossly unsuccessful." He called for increased research into the "feasibility and environmental consequences of climate engineering," even though he acknowledged that injecting sulfates into the stratosphere could damage the ozone layer and cause large, unpredictable side effects. Despite these dangers, he said, climatic engineering

could ultimately be "the only option available to rapidly reduce temperature rises."

At the time, Crutzen's essay was controversial, and many scientists called it irresponsible. But since then it has served to bring geoengineering into the open, says David Keith, who started studying the subject in 1989. After a scientist of Crutzen's credentials, who understood the stratosphere as well as anyone, came out in favor of studying sulfate injection as a way to cool the earth, many other scientists were willing to start talking about it.

Among the most recent converts is David Battisti, a professor of atmospheric sciences at the University of Washington. One problem in particular worries him. Studies of heat waves show that crop yields drop off sharply when temperatures rise 3 °C to 4 °C above normal—the temperatures that MIT's Prinn predicts we might reach even with strict emissions controls. Speaking at a geoengineering symposium at MIT this fall, Battisti said, "By the end of the century, just due to temperature alone, we're looking at a 30 to 40 percent reduction in [crop] yields, while in the next 50 years demand for food is expected to more than double."

Battisti is well aware of the uncertainties that surround geoengineering. According to research he's conducted recently, the first computer models that tried to show how shading the earth would affect climate were off by 2 °C to 3°C in predictions of regional temperature change and by as much as 40 percent in predictions of regional rainfall. But with a billion people already malnourished, and billions more who could go hungry if global warming disrupts agriculture, Battisti has reluctantly conceded that we may need to consider "a climate-engineering patch." Better data and better models will help clarify the effects of geoengineering. "Give us 30 or 40 years and we'll be there," he said at the MIT symposium. "But in 30 to 40 years, at the level we're increasing CO_2, we're going to need this, whether we're ready or not."

James R. Fleming

The Climate Engineers

Beyond the security checkpoint at the National Aeronautics and Space Administration's Ames Research Center at the southern end of San Francisco Bay, a small group gathered in November for a conference on the innocuous topic of "managing solar radiation." The real subject was much bigger: how to save the planet from the effects of global warming. There was little talk among the two dozen scientists and other specialists about carbon taxes, alternative energy sources, or the other usual remedies. Many of the scientists were impatient with such schemes. Some were simply contemptuous of calls for international cooperation and the policies and lifestyle changes needed to curb greenhouse-gas emissions; others had concluded that the world's politicians and bureaucrats are not up to the job of agreeing on such reforms or that global warming will come more rapidly, and with more catastrophic consequences, than many models predict. Now, they believe, it is time to consider radical measures: a technological quick fix for global warming.

"Mitigation is not happening and is not going to happen," physicist Lowell Wood declared at the NASA conference. Wood, the star of the gathering, spent four decades at the University of California's Lawrence Livermore National Laboratory, where he served as one of the Pentagon's chief weapon designers and threat analysts. (He reportedly enjoys the "Dr. Evil" nickname bestowed by his critics.) The time has come, he said, for "an intelligent elimination of undesired heat from the biosphere by technical ways and means," which, he asserted, could be achieved for a tiny fraction of the cost of "the bureaucratic suppression of CO_2." His engineering approach, he boasted, would provide "instant climatic gratification."

Wood advanced several ideas to "fix" the earth's climate, including building up Arctic sea ice to make it function like a planetary air conditioner to "suck heat in from the mid-latitude heat bath." A "surprisingly practical" way of achieving this, he said, would be to use large artillery pieces to shoot as much as a million tons of highly reflective sulfate aerosols or specially engineered nanoparticles into the Arctic stratosphere to deflect the sun's rays. Delivering up to a million tons of material via artillery would require a constant bombardment—basically declaring war on the stratosphere. Alternatively, a fleet of B-747 "crop dusters" could deliver the particles by flying continuously around the Arctic Circle. Or a 25-kilometer-long sky hose could be tethered to a military superblimp high above the planet's surface to pump reflective particles into the atmosphere.

From *The Wilson Quarterly*, Spring 2007, pp. 46, 48–51, 55–58, 59, 60. Copyright © 2007 by James R. Fleming. Reprinted by permission of the author.

Far-fetched as Wood's ideas may sound, his weren't the only Rube Goldberg proposals aired at the meeting. Even as they joked about a NASA staffer's apology for her inability to control the temperature in the meeting room, others detailed their own schemes for manipulating earth's climate. Astronomer J. Roger Angel suggested placing a huge fleet of mirrors in orbit to divert incoming solar radiation, at a cost of "only" several trillion dollars. Atmospheric scientist John Latham and engineer Stephen Salter hawked their idea of making marine clouds thicker and more reflective by whipping ocean water into a froth with giant pumps and eggbeaters. Most frightening was the science-fiction writer and astrophysicist Gregory Benford's announcement that he wanted to "cut through red tape and demonstrate what could be done" by finding private sponsors for his plan to inject diatomaceous earth—the chalk-like substance used in filtration systems and cat litter—into the Arctic stratosphere. He, like his fellow geoengineers, was largely silent on the possible unintended consequences of his plan.

⋯⊚⋯

The inherent unknowability of what would happen if we tried to tinker with the immensely complex planetary climate system is one reason why climate engineering has until recently been spoken of only sotto voce in the scientific community. Many researchers recognize that even the most brilliant scientists have a history of blindness to the wider ramifications of their work. Imagine, for example, that Wood's scheme to thicken the Arctic icecap did somehow become possible. While most of the world may want to maintain or increase polar sea ice, Russia and some other nations have historically desired an ice-free Arctic ocean, which would liberate shipping and open potentially vast oil and mineral deposits for exploitation. And an engineered Arctic ice sheet would likely produce shorter growing seasons and harsher winters in Alaska, Siberia, Greenland, and elsewhere, and could generate super winter storms in the midlatitudes. Yet Wood calls his brainstorm a plan for "global climate stabilization," and hopes to create a sort of "planetary thermostat" to regulate the global climate.

Who would control such a "thermostat," making life-altering decisions for the planet's billions? What is to prevent other nations from undertaking unilateral climate modification? The United States has no monopoly on such dreams. In November 2005, for example, Yuri Izrael, head of the Moscow-based Institute of Global Climate and Ecology Studies, wrote to Russian president Vladimir Putin to make the case for immediately burning massive amounts of sulfur in the stratosphere to lower the earth's temperature "a degree or two"—a correction greater than the total warming since pre-industrial times.

There is, moreover, a troubling motif of militarization in the history of weather and climate control. Military leaders in the United States and other countries have pondered the possibilities of weaponized weather manipulation for decades. Lowell Wood himself embodies the overlap of civilian and military interests. Now affiliated with the Hoover Institution, a think tank at Stanford University, Wood was a protégé of the late Edward Teller, the weapons scientist who was credited with developing the hydrogen bomb and was the

architect of the Reagan-era Star Wars missile defense system (which Wood worked on, too). Like Wood, Teller was known for his advocacy of controversial military and technological solutions to complex problems, including the chimerical "peaceful uses of nuclear weapons." Teller's plan to excavate an artificial harbor in Alaska using thermonuclear explosives actually came close to receiving government approval. Before his death in 2003, Teller was advocating a climate control scheme similar to what Wood proposed.

Despite the large, unanswered questions about the implications of playing God with the elements, climate engineering is now being widely discussed in the scientific community and is taken seriously within the U.S. government. The Bush administration has recommended the addition of this "important strategy" to an upcoming report of the Intergovernmental Panel on Climate Change, the UN-sponsored organization whose February study seemed to persuade even the Bush White House to take global warming more seriously. And climate engineering's advocates are not confined to the small group that met in California. Last year, for example, Paul J. Crutzen, an atmospheric chemist and Nobel laureate, proposed a scheme similar to Wood's, and there is a long paper trail of climate and weather modification studies by the Pentagon and other government agencies.

As the sole historian at the NASA conference, I may have been alone in my appreciation of the irony that we were meeting on the site of an old U.S. Navy airfield literally in the shadow of the huge hangar that once housed the ill-starred Navy dirigible U.S.S. *Macon*. The 785-foot-long *Macon,* a technological wonder of its time, capable of cruising at 87 miles per hour and launching five Navy biplanes, lies at the bottom of the Pacific Ocean, brought down in 1935 by strong winds. The Navy's entire rigid-airship program went down with it. Coming on the heels of the crash of its sister ship, the *Akron,* the *Macon's* destruction showed that the design of these technological marvels was fundamentally flawed. The hangar, built by the Navy in 1932, is now both a historic site and a Superfund site, since it has been discovered that its "galbestos" siding is leaching PCBs into the drains. As I reflected on the fate of the Navy dirigible program, the geoengineers around the table were confidently and enthusiastically promoting techniques of climate intervention that were more than several steps beyond what might be called state of the art, with implications not simply for a handful of airship crewmen but for every one of the 6.5 billion inhabitants of the planet.

Ultimate control of the weather and climate excites some of our wildest fantasies and our greatest fears. It is the stuff of age-old myths. Throughout history, we mortals have tried to protect ourselves against harsh weather. But weather *control* was reserved for the ancient sky gods. Now the power has seemingly devolved to modern Titans. We are undoubtedly facing an uncertain future. With rising temperatures, increasing emissions of greenhouse gases, and a growing world population, we may be on the verge of a worldwide climate crisis. What shall we do? Doing nothing or too little is clearly wrong, but so is doing too much.

Largely unaware of the long and checkered history of weather and climate control and the political and ethical challenges it poses, or somehow considering themselves exempt, the new Titans see themselves as heroic pioneers, the first generation capable of alleviating or averting natural disasters. They are largely

oblivious to the history of the charlatans and sincere but deluded scientists and engineers who preceded them. If we fail to heed the lessons of that history, and fail to bring its perspectives to bear in thinking about public policy, we risk repeating the mistakes of the past, in a game with much higher stakes.

Three stories (there are many more) capture the recurring pathologies of weather and climate control schemes. The first involves 19th-century proposals by the U.S. government's first meteorologist and other "pluviculturalists" to make artificial rain and relieve drought conditions in the American West. The second begins in 1946 with promising discoveries in cloud seeding that rapidly devolved into exaggerated claims and attempts by cold warriors to weaponize the technique in the jungles of Vietnam. And then there is the tale of how computer modeling raised hopes for perfect forecasting and ultimate control of weather and climate—hopes that continue to inform and encourage present-day planetary engineers. . . .

⋅◈⋅

Weather warfare took a macro-pathological turn between 1967 and '72 in the jungles over North and South Vietnam, Laos, and Cambodia. Using technology developed at the naval weapons testing center at China Lake, California, to seed clouds by means of silver iodide flares, the military conducted secret operations intended, among other goals, to "reduce trafficability" along portions of the Ho Chi Minh Trail, which Hanoi used to move men and materiel to South Vietnam. Operating out of Udorn Air Base, Thailand, without the knowledge of the Thai government or almost anyone else, but with the full and enthusiastic support of presidents Lyndon B. Johnson and Richard M. Nixon, the Air Weather Service flew more than 2,600 cloud seeding sorties and expended 47,000 silver iodide flares over a period of approximately five years at an annual cost of some $3.6 million. The covert operation had several names, including "POPEYE" and "Intermediary-Compatriot."

In March 1971, nationally syndicated columnist Jack Anderson broke the story about Air Force rainmakers in Southeast Asia in *The Washington Post*, a story confirmed several months later with the leaking of the Pentagon Papers and splashed on the front page of *The New York Times* in 1972 by Seymour Hersh. By 1973, despite stonewalling by Nixon administration officials, the U.S. Senate had adopted a resolution calling for an international treaty "prohibiting the use of any environmental or geophysical modification activity as a weapon of war." The following year, Senator Claiborne Pell (D.-R.I.), referring to the field as a "Pandora's box," published the transcript of a formerly top-secret briefing by the Defense Department on the topic of weather warfare. Eventually, it was revealed that the CIA had tried rainmaking in South Vietnam as early as 1963 in an attempt to break up the protests of Buddhist monks, and that cloud seeding was probably used in Cuba to disrupt the sugarcane harvest. Similar technology had been employed, yet proved ineffective, in drought relief efforts in India and Pakistan, the Philippines, Panama, Portugal, and Okinawa. All of the programs were conducted under military sponsorship and had the direct involvement of the White House.

Operation POPEYE, made public as it was at the end of the Nixon era, was dubbed the "Watergate of weather warfare." Some defended the use of environmental weapons, arguing that they were more "humane" than nuclear weapons. Others suggested that inducing rainfall to reduce trafficability was preferable to dropping napalm. As one wag put it, "Make mud, not war." At a congressional briefing in 1974, military officials downplayed the impact of Operation POPEYE, since the most that could be claimed were 10 percent increases in local rainfall, and even that result was "unverifiable." Philip Handler, president of the National Academy of Sciences, represented the mainstream of scientific opinion when he observed, "It is grotesquely immoral that scientific understanding and technological capabilities developed for human welfare to protect the public health, enhance agricultural productivity, and minimize the natural violence of large storms should be so distorted as to become weapons of war."

At a time when the United States was already weakened by the Watergate crisis, the Soviet Union caused considerable embarrassment to the Ford administration by bringing the issue of weather modification as a weapon of war to the attention of the United Nations. The UN Convention on the Prohibition of Military or Any Other Hostile Use of Environmental Modification Techniques (ENMOD) was eventually ratified by nearly 70 nations, including the United States. Ironically, it entered into force in 1978, when the Lao People's Democratic Republic, where the American military had used weather modification technology in war only six years earlier, became the 20th signatory.

The language of the ENMOD Convention may become relevant to future weather and climate engineering, especially if such efforts are conducted unilaterally or if harm befalls a nation or region. The convention targets those techniques having "widespread, longlasting or severe effects as the means of destruction, damage, or injury to any other State Party." It uses the term "environmental modification" to mean "any technique for changing—through the deliberate manipulation of natural processes—the dynamics, composition, or structure of the Earth, including its biota, lithosphere, hydrosphere, and atmosphere, or of outer space."

A vision of perfect forecasting ultimately leading to weather and climate control was present at the birth of modern computing, well before the GE cloud seeding experiments. In 1945 Vladimir Zworykin, an RCA engineer noted for his early work in television technology, promoted the idea that electronic computers could be used to process and analyze vast amounts of meteorological data, issue timely and highly accurate forecasts, study the sensitivity of weather systems to alterations of surface conditions and energy inputs, and eventually intervene in and control the weather and climate. He wrote:

> The eventual goal to be attained is the international organization
> of means to study weather phenomena as global phenomena and

to channel the world's weather, as far as possible, in such a way as to minimize the damage from catastrophic disturbances, and otherwise to benefit the world to the greatest extent by improved climatic conditions where possible.

Zworykin imagined that a perfectly accurate machine forecast combined with a paramilitary rapid deployment force able literally to pour oil on troubled ocean waters or even set fires or detonate bombs might someday provide the capacity to disrupt storms before they formed, deflect them from populated areas, and otherwise control the weather.

John von Neumann, the multi-talented mathematician extraordinaire at the Institute for Advanced Study in Princeton, New Jersey, endorsed Zworykin's view, writing to him, "I agree with you completely. . . . This would provide a basis for scientific approach[es] to influencing the weather." Using computer-generated predictions, von Neumann wrote, weather and climate systems "could be controlled, or at least directed, by the release of perfectly practical amounts of energy" or by "altering the absorption and reflection properties of the ground or the sea or the atmosphere." It was a project that neatly fit von Neumann's overall philosophy: "All stable processes we shall predict. All unstable processes we shall control." Zworykin's proposal was also endorsed by the noted oceanographer Athelstan Spilhaus, then a U.S. Army major, who ended his letter of November 6, 1945, with these words: "In weather control meteorology has a new goal worthy of its greatest efforts."

In a 1962 speech to meteorologists, "On the Possibilities of Weather Control," Harry Wexler, the MIT-trained head of meteorological research at the U.S. Weather Bureau, reported on his analysis of early computer climate models and additional possibilities opened up by the space age. Reminding his audience that humankind was modifying the weather and climate "whether we know it or not" by changing the composition of the earth's atmosphere, Wexler demonstrated how the United States or the Soviet Union, perhaps with hostile intent, could alter the earth's climate in a number of ways. Either nation could cool it by several degrees using a dust ring launched into orbit, for example, or warm it using ice crystals lofted into the polar atmosphere by the explosion of hydrogen bombs. And while most practicing atmospheric chemists today believe that the discovery of ozone-destroying reactions dates to the early 1970s, Wexler sketched out a scenario for destroying the ozone layer using chlorine or bromine in his 1962 speech.

"The subject of weather and climate control is now becoming respectable to talk about," Wexler claimed, apparently hoping to reduce the prospects of a geophysical arms race. He cited Soviet premier Nikita Khrushchev's mention of weather control in an address to the Supreme Soviet and a 1961 speech to the United Nations by John F. Kennedy in which the president proposed "cooperative efforts between all nations in weather prediction and eventually in weather control." Wexler was actually the source of Kennedy's suggestions, and had worked on them behind the scenes with the President's

Science Advisory Committee and the State Department. But if weather control's "respectability" was not in question, its attainability—even using computers, satellites, and 100-megaton bombs—certainly was.

·«◉»·

In 1965, the President's Science Advisory Committee warned in a report called *Restoring the Quality of Our Environment* that increases in atmospheric carbon dioxide due to the burning of fossil fuels would modify the earth's heat balance to such an extent that harmful changes in climate could occur. This report is now widely cited as the first official statement on "global warming." But the committee also recommended geoengineering options. "The possibilities of deliberately bringing about countervailing climatic changes . . . need to be thoroughly explored," it said. As an illustration, it pointed out that, in a warming world, the earth's solar reflectivity could be increased by dispersing buoyant reflective particles over large areas of the tropical sea at an annual cost, not considered excessive, of about $500 million. This technology might also inhibit hurricane formation. No one thought to consider the side effects of particles washing up on tropical beaches or choking marine life, or the negative consequences of redirecting hurricanes, much less other effects beyond our imagination. And no one thought to ask if the local inhabitants would be in favor of such schemes. The committee also speculated about modifying high-altitude cirrus clouds to counteract the effects of increasing atmospheric carbon dioxide. It failed to mention the most obvious option: reducing fossil fuel use.

After the embarrassment of the 1978 ENMOD Convention, federal funding for weather modification research and development dried up, although freelance rainmakers continued to ply their trade in the American West with state and local funding. Until recently, a 1991 National Academy of Sciences report, *Policy Implications of Greenhouse Warming,* was the only serious document in decades to advocate climate control. But the level of urgency and the number of proposals have increased dramatically since the turn of the new century.

In September 2001, the U.S. Climate Change Technology Program quietly held an invitational conference, "Response Options to Rapid or Severe Climate Change." Sponsored by a White House that was officially skeptical about global warming, the meeting gave new status to the control fantasies of the climate engineers. According to one participant, "If they had broadcast that meeting live to people in Europe, there would have been riots." . . .

[The] National Research Council issued a study, *Critical Issues in Weather Modification Research,* in 2003. It cited looming social and environmental challenges such as water shortages and drought, property damage and loss of life from severe storms, and the threat of "inadvertent" climate change as justifications for investing in major new national and international programs in weather modification research. Although the NRC study included an acknowledgment that there is "no convincing scientific proof of the efficacy of intentional weather modification efforts," its authors nonetheless argued that there

should be "a renewed commitment" to research in the field of intentional and unintentional weather modification.

⋘◉⋙

The absence of such proof after decades of efforts has not deterred governments here and abroad from a variety of ill-advised or simply fanciful undertakings. . . .

With great fanfare, atmospheric chemist Paul J. Crutzen, winner of a 1995 Nobel Prize for his work on the chemistry of ozone depletion, recently proposed to cool the earth by injecting reflective aerosols or other substances into the tropical stratosphere using balloons or artillery. He estimated that more than five million metric tons of sulfur per year would be needed to do the job, at an annual cost of more than $125 billion. The effect would emulate the 1991 eruption of Mount Pinatubo in the Philippines, which covered the earth with a cloud of sulfuric acid and other sulfates and caused a drop in the planet's average temperature of about 0.5°C for roughly two years. Unfortunately, Mount Pinatubo may also have contributed to the largest ozone hole ever measured. The volcanic eruption was also blamed for causing cool, wet summers, shortening the growing season, and exacerbating Mississippi River flooding and the ongoing drought in the Sahel region of Africa.

Overall, the cooling caused by Mount Pinatubo's eruption temporarily suppressed the greenhouse warming effect and was stronger than the influence of the El Niño event that occurred at the same time. Crutzen merely noted that if a Mount Pinatubo-scale eruption were emulated every year or two, undesired side effects and ozone losses should not be "as large," but some whitening of the sky and colorful sunsets and sunrises would occur. His "interesting alternative" method would be to release soot particles to create minor "nuclear winter" conditions.

Crutzen later said that he had only reluctantly proposed his planetary "shade," mostly to "startle" political leaders enough to spur them to more serious efforts to curb greenhouse-gas emissions. But he may well have produced the opposite effect. The appeal of a quick and seemingly painless technological "fix" for the global climate dilemma should not be underestimated. The more practical such dreams appear, the less likely the world's citizens and political leaders are to take on the difficult and painful task of changing the destiny that global climate models foretell.

⋘◉⋙

These issues are not new. In 1956, F. W. Reichelderfer, then chief of the U.S. Weather Bureau, delivered an address to the National Academy of Sciences, "Importance of New Concepts in Meteorology." Reacting to the widespread theorizing and speculation on the possibilities of weather and climate control at the time, he pointed out that the crucial issue was "practicability" rather than "possibility." In 1956 it was possible to modify a cloud with dry ice or silver iodide, yet it was impossible to predict what the cloud might do after

seeding and impracticable to claim any sense of control over the weather. This is still true today. Yet thanks to remarkable advances in science and technology, from satellite sensors to enormously sophisticated global climate models, the fantasies of the weather and climate engineers have only grown. Now it is possible to tinker with scenarios in computer climate models—manipulating the solar inputs, for example, to demonstrate that artificially increased solar reflectivity will generate a cooling trend in the model.

But this is a far cry from conducting a practical global field experiment or operational program with proper data collection and analysis; full accounting for possible liabilities, unintended consequences, and litigation; and the necessary international support and approval. Lowell Wood blithely declares that if his proposal to turn the polar icecap into a planetary air conditioner were implemented and didn't work, the process could be halted after a few years. He doesn't mention what harm such a failure could cause in the meantime.

There are signs among the geoengineers of an overconfidence in technology as a solution of first resort. Many appear to possess a too-literal belief in progress that produces an anything-is-possible mentality, abetted by a basic misunderstanding of the nature of today's climate models. The global climate system is a "massive, staggering beast," as oceanographer Wallace Broecker describes it, with no simple set of controlling parameters. We are more than a long way from understanding how it works, much less the precise prediction and practical "control" of global climate.

Assume, for just a moment, that climate control were technically possible. Who would be given the authority to manage it? Who would have the wisdom to dispense drought, severe winters, or the effects of storms to some so that the rest of the planet could prosper? At what cost, economically, aesthetically, and in our moral relationship to nature, would we manipulate the climate?

These questions are never seriously contemplated by the climate wizards who dream of mastery over nature. If, as history shows, fantasies of weather and climate control have chiefly served commercial and military interests, why should we expect the future to be different? . . .

When Roger Angel was asked at the NASA meeting last November how he intended to get the massive amount of material required for his space mirrors into orbit, he dryly suggested a modern cannon of the kind originally proposed for the Strategic Defense Initiative: a giant electric rail gun firing a ton or so of material into space roughly every five minutes. Asked where such a device might be located, he suggested a high mountaintop on the Equator.

I was immediately reminded of Jules Verne's 1889 novel *The Purchase of the North Pole*. For two cents per acre, a group of American investors gains rights to the vast and incredibly lucrative coal and mineral deposits under the North Pole. To mine the region, they propose to melt the polar ice. Initially the project captures the public imagination, as the backers promise that their

scheme will improve the climate everywhere by reducing extremes of cold and heat, making the earth a terrestrial heaven. But when it is revealed that the investors are retired Civil War artillerymen who intend to change the inclination of the earth's axis by building and firing the world's largest cannon, public enthusiasm gives way to fears that tidal waves generated by the explosion will kill millions. In secrecy and haste, the protagonists proceed with their plan, building the cannon on Mount Kilimanjaro. The plot fails only when an error in calculation renders the massive shot ineffective. Verne concludes, "The world's inhabitants could thus sleep in peace." Perhaps he spoke too soon.

EXPLORING THE ISSUE

Is It Time to Think Seriously About "Climate Engineering"?

Critical Thinking and Reflection

1. Are we likely to solve the global warming problem without geoengineering?
2. If we cannot, is it ethical to modify global climate deliberately, and thereby affect the world's ecosystems?
3. How could climate engineering lead to war?
4. How does belief in progress lead people to think that anything is possible?

Is There Common Ground?

There is a consensus that the hazards of global warming are so great that humanity must do something to ward them off. When geoengineering was first proposed, the general reaction was, "These guys are out of their minds." In the years since, that reaction has shifted to, "Well, maybe, if everything else fails."

1. Does it seem likely that the world will succeed in reducing greenhouse gas emissions enough to prevent global warming? (To start your research, Google on "congress climate change.")
2. What are the benefits of combining geoengineering with efforts to cut back emissions of greenhouse gases?
3. What kind of geoengineering seems likely to work best in the long term?

ISSUE 5

Is It Time to Revive Nuclear Power?

YES: **Allison MacFarlane**, from "Nuclear Power: A Panacea for Future Energy Needs?" *Environment* (March/April 2010)

NO: **Kristin Shrader-Frechette**, from "Five Myths About Nuclear Energy," *America* (June 23–30, 2008)

Learning Outcomes

After studying this issue, students will be able to:

1. Compare the hazards of nuclear power and global warming.
2. Explain how nuclear power avoids the release of greenhouse gases.
3. Explain why it will be difficult to shift from fossil fuels to nuclear power rapidly.
4. Describe the obstacles that must be overcome before nuclear power can be more widely used.

ISSUE SUMMARY

YES: Allison MacFarlane argues that although nuclear power poses serious problems to be overcome, it "offers a potential avenue to significantly mitigate carbon dioxide emissions while still providing baseload power required in today's world." However, it will take many years to build the necessary number of new nuclear power plants.

NO: Professor Kristin Shrader-Frechette argues that nuclear power is one of the most impractical and risky of energy sources. Renewable energy sources such as wind and solar are a sounder choice.

The technology of releasing for human use the energy that holds the atom together did not get off to an auspicious start. Its first significant application was military, and the deaths associated with the Hiroshima and Nagasaki explosions

have ever since tainted the technology with negative associations. It did not help that for the ensuing half-century, millions of people grew up under the threat of nuclear Armageddon. But almost from the beginning, nuclear physicists and engineers wanted to put nuclear energy to more peaceful uses, largely in the form of power plants. Touted in the 1950s as an astoundingly cheap source of electricity, nuclear power soon proved to be more expensive than conventional sources, largely because safety concerns caused delays in the approval process and prompted elaborate built-in precautions. Safety measures have worked well when needed—Three Mile Island, often cited as a horrific example of what can go wrong, released very little radioactive material to the environment. The Chernobyl disaster occurred when safety measures were ignored. In both cases, human error was more to blame than the technology itself. The related issue of nuclear waste has also raised fears and proved to add expense to the technology.

It is clear that two factors—fear and expense—impede the wide adoption of nuclear power. If both could somehow be alleviated, it might become possible to gain the benefits of the technology. Among those benefits are that nuclear power does not burn oil, coal, or any other fuel, does not emit air pollution and thus contribute to smog and haze, does not depend on foreign sources of fuel and thus weaken national independence, and does not emit carbon. Avoiding the use of fossil fuels is an important benefit; see Robert L. Hirsch, Roger H. Bezdek, and Robert M. Wendling, "Peaking Oil Production: Sooner Rather than Later?" *Issues in Science and Technology* (Spring 2005). But avoiding carbon dioxide emissions may be more important at a time when society is concerned about global warming, and this is the benefit that prompted James Lovelock, creator of the Gaia Hypothesis and hero to environmentalists everywhere, to say, "If we had nuclear power we wouldn't be in this mess now, and whose fault was it? It was [the anti-nuclear environmentalists']." See his autobiography, *Homage to Gaia: The Life of an Independent Scientist* (Oxford University Press, 2001).

Others have also seen this point. The OECD's Nuclear Energy Agency ("Nuclear Power and Climate Change" (Paris, France, 1998); www.nea.fr/html/ndd/climate/climate.pdf) found that a greatly expanded deployment of nuclear power to combat global warming was both technically and economically feasible. Robert C. Morris published *The Environmental Case for Nuclear Power: Economic, Medical, and Political Considerations* (Paragon House) in 2000. "The time seems right to reconsider the future of nuclear power," say James A. Lake, Ralph G. Bennett, and John F. Kotek in "Next-Generation Nuclear Power," *Scientific American* (January 2002). Stewart Brand, for long a leading environmentalist, predicts in "Environmental Heresies," *Technology Review* (May 2005), that nuclear power will soon be seen as the "green" energy technology. David Talbot, "Nuclear Powers Up," *Technology Review* (September 2005), notes, "While the waste problem remains unsolved, current trends favor a nuclear renaissance. Energy needs are growing. Conventional energy sources will eventually dry up. The atmosphere is getting dirtier." Peter Schwartz and Spencer Reiss, "Nuclear Now!" *Wired* (February 2005), argue that nuclear power is the one practical answer to global warming and coming shortages of fossil fuels. Iain Murray, "Nuclear Power? Yes, Please," *National Review* (June 16, 2008),

argues that the world's experience with nuclear power has shown it to be both safe and reliable. Costs can be contained, and if one is concerned about global warming, the case for nuclear power is unassailable.

Robert Evans, "Nuclear Power: Back in the Game," *Power Engineering* (October 2005), reports that a number of power companies are considering new nuclear power plants. See also Eliot Marshall, "Is the Friendly Atom Poised for a Comeback?" and Daniel Clery, "Nuclear Industry Dares to Dream of a New Dawn," *Science* (August 19, 2005). Nuclear momentum is growing, says Charles Petit, "Nuclear Power: Risking a Comeback," *National Geographic* (April 2006), thanks in part to new technologies. Karen Charman, "Brave Nuclear World? (Part I)" *World Watch* (May/June 2006), objects that producing nuclear fuel uses huge amounts of electricity derived from fossil fuels, so going nuclear can hardly prevent all releases of carbon dioxide (although using electricity derived from nuclear power would reduce the problem). She also notes that "Although no comprehensive and integrated study comparing the collateral and external costs of energy sources globally has been done, all currently available energy sources have them. . . . Burning coal—the single largest source of air pollution in the United States—causes global warming, acid rain, soot, smog, and other toxic air emissions and generates waste ash, sludge, and toxic chemicals. Landscapes and ecosystems are completely destroyed by mountain-top removal mining, while underground mining imposes high fatality, injury, and sickness rates. Even wind energy kills birds, can be noisy, and, some people complain, blights landscapes."

Stephen Ansolabehere et al., "The Future of Nuclear Power," *An Interdisciplinary MIT Study* (MIT, 2003), note that in 2000 there were 352 nuclear power plants in the developed world as a whole, and a mere 15 in developing nations, and that even a very large increase in the number of nuclear power plants—from 1000 to 1500—will not stop all releases of carbon dioxide. In fact, if carbon emissions double by 2050 as expected, from 6500 to 13,000 million metric tons per year, the 1800 million metric tons not emitted because of nuclear power will seem relatively insignificant. Nevertheless, say John M. Deutch and Ernest J. Moniz, "The Nuclear Option," *Scientific American* (September 2006), such a cut in carbon emissions would be "significant." Christine Laurent, in "Beating Global Warming with Nuclear Power?" *UNESCO Courier* (February 2001), notes, "For several years, the nuclear energy industry has attempted to cloak itself in different ecological robes. Its credo: nuclear energy is a formidable asset in the battle against global warming because it emits very small amounts of greenhouse gases. This stance, first presented in the late 1980s when the extent of the phenomenon was still the subject of controversy, is now at the heart of policy debates over how to avoid droughts, downpours and floods." Laurent adds that it makes more sense to focus on reducing carbon emissions by reducing energy consumption.

Even though President Obama declared support for "a new generation of safe, clean nuclear power plants" in his January 27, 2010, State of the Union speech and the Department of Energy soon proposed massive loan guarantees for the industry (see Pam Russell and Pam Hunter, "Nuclear Resurgence Poised for Liftoff," *ENR: Engineering News-Record* (March 1, 2010), the debate over the future of nuclear power is likely to remain vigorous for some time to come. But

as Richard A. Meserve says in a *Science* editorial ("Global Warming and Nuclear Power," *Science* (January 23, 2004)), "For those who are serious about confronting global warming, nuclear power should be seen as part of the solution. Although it is unlikely that many environmental groups will become enthusiastic proponents of nuclear power, the harsh reality is that any serious program to address global warming cannot afford to jettison any technology prematurely. . . . The stakes are large, and the scientific and educational community should seek to ensure that the public understands the critical link between nuclear power and climate change." Paul Lorenzini, "A Second Look at Nuclear Power," *Issues in Science and Technology* (Spring 2005), argues that the goal must be energy "sufficiency for the foreseeable future with minimal environmental impact." Nuclear power can be part of the answer, but making it happen requires that we shed ideological biases. "It means ceasing to deceive ourselves about what might be possible." Charles Forsberg, "The Real Path to Green Energy: Hybrid Nuclear-Renewable Power," *Bulletin of the Atomic Scientists* (November/December 2009), suggests that the best use of nuclear power will be to provide energy for biofuel refineries and as backup for solar and wind power.

Alvin M. Weinberg, former director of the Oak Ridge National Laboratory, notes in "New Life for Nuclear Power," *Issues in Science and Technology* (Summer 2003), that to make a serious dent in carbon emissions would require perhaps four times as many reactors as suggested in the MIT study. The accompanying safety and security problems would be challenging. If the challenges can be met, says John J. Taylor, retired vice president for nuclear power at the Electric Power Research Institute, in "The Nuclear Power Bargain," *Issues in Science and Technology* (Spring 2004), there are a great many potential benefits. Are new reactor technologies needed? Richard K. Lester, "New Nukes," *Issues in Science and Technology* (Summer 2006), says that better centralized waste storage is what is needed, at least in the short term, despite the Obama Administration's declaration that Yucca Mountain, the only U.S. storage site under development, will no longer be supported. On the other hand, some new technologies are available already; see Carol Matlack, "A High-End Bet on Nuclear Power," *BusinessWeek* (March 15, 2010).

Environmental groups such as Friends of the Earth are adamantly opposed, but there are signs that some environmentalists do not agree; see William M. Welch, "Some Rethinking Nuke Opposition," *USA Today* (March 23, 2007). Judith Lewis, "The Nuclear Option," *Mother Jones* (May/June 2008), concludes that "When rising seas flood our coasts, the idea of producing electricity from the most terrifying force ever harnessed may not seem so frightening—or expensive—at all."

In the YES selection, Allison MacFarlane argues that although nuclear power poses serious problems to be overcome, it "offers a potential avenue to significantly mitigate carbon dioxide emissions while still providing baseload power required in today's world." However, it will take many years to build the necessary number of new nuclear power plants. Professor Kristin Shrader-Frechette argues that nuclear power is one of the most impractical and risky of energy sources. Renewable energy sources such as wind and solar are a sounder choice.

YES

Allison MacFarlane

Nuclear Power: A Panacea for Future Energy Needs

Each week seems to bring further evidence that the Earth is warming at a faster rate than previously estimated. Pressure is building to replace power sources that emit carbon dioxide with those that do not. It is in this "climate" that nuclear energy is getting a second look. Once relegated to the junk heap after the Three Mile Island and Chernobyl disasters brought the dangers associated with nuclear power to everyone's attention, nuclear power may now be undergoing a "renaissance," as the nuclear industry likes to say. Environmentalists such as Stewart Brand, originator of the Whole Earth Catalog, and Patrick Moore of Greenpeace have started pushing nuclear power as a ready solution to the problem of electricity production without carbon emissions.

Over the past few years, more than 40 countries that currently do not have nuclear power have expressed interest in acquiring it to address their future energy needs, and a few are making significant progress. "Every country has the right to make use of nuclear power, as well as the responsibility to do it in accordance with the highest standards of safety, security, and non-proliferation," stated Mohamed ElBaradei, then–Director General of the International Atomic Energy Agency (IAEA).

All this enthusiasm for nuclear power must be tempered by plain reality. Construction of new nuclear power reactors is still one of the most capital-intensive ventures compared with other energy sources such as coal and natural gas. High-level nuclear waste from the nuclear industry waits in above-ground temporary storage until a final solution is implemented. And the connection between nuclear power and nuclear weapons continues to be perceived as a threat by the international community. Given the pushes and pulls for nuclear power, what is the likelihood that the future will entail a vast expansion of nuclear power on a global scale, and if so, what are its implications, and can this expansion be considered "sustainable" in a development sense?

How Does Nuclear Perform Now?

Globally, there are 436 reactors with a generating capacity of 372 GWe (gigawatts electric) located in 31 countries. [In] 2006, nuclear power generated 15 percent of the world's electricity. Currently, the IAEA estimates that

52 reactors are under construction, whereas the World Nuclear Association lists 71 reactors that will come online between 2009 and 2015. Of the 52 listed by the IAEA, . . . over 85 percent of them are located in Asia and Eastern Europe, and they would add 46 GWe to the existing generating capacity. Of the 52 under construction, 12 of them began construction before 1990, and it is not clear that these projects will ever be completed. At the same time, existing reactors are aging. The average age of the operating fleet in 2007 was 23 years. Most reactors were originally designed for a 40-year life span, but some countries, such as the United States, have recently been granting 20-year life extensions to their fleet.

Carbon Dioxide Emissions Reductions

Nuclear reactors do not emit carbon dioxide to produce electricity because their fuel is uranium-based. This is not to say that nuclear power is emission free—it is not. Carbon dioxide is emitted during the lifecycle of nuclear power production, particularly during the uranium mining, milling, and fuel fabrication processes, and during the construction of new nuclear plants. Nonetheless, nuclear power displaces large volumes of carbon dioxide in comparison with fossil fuel plants.

For instance, in 2006, global nuclear power provided 2594 TWh of electricity. If that electricity was produced by coal and natural gas plants combined, it would have added 3904 million tons of carbon-dioxide equivalent to the atmosphere. Compared to annual emissions of 29,195 million tons of CO_2 equivalent from fossil fuel burning, nuclear power saved about 13 percent.

Certainly if nuclear power grew its capacity, it could contribute significantly to carbon dioxide emissions reductions. Scholars have suggested that 1000 GWe nuclear capacity (in addition to the existing capacity) could reduce potential carbon dioxide emissions growth by 15–25 percent by 2050. Of course, adding 1000 GWe is equivalent to building 1000 new large-scale 1000-MWe plants over the next 40 years, which requires that 25 plants be built per year, an ambitious schedule, but doable. Such plans are not on anyone's drawing board at the moment, though.

Past and Present Safety Issues

Since the Chernobyl accident in 1986, there have been no catastrophic failures at nuclear power plants. That's not to say that there have not been problems, but the overall global safety record since 1986 has been good. This is, in large part, due to vigilant oversight of the nuclear industry and redundant design in safety features.

Issues may arise from aging plants as equipment fails. A case in point is the Davis-Besse reactor in Ohio, which developed an undetected hole in the reactor pressure vessel head, leaving only 0.95 cm of stainless steel to protect against a loss of coolant accident. The hole, which was almost 13 cm in diameter and 17 cm deep, was caused by boric acid corrosion from the borated cooling water in the reactor. The U.S. Nuclear Regulatory Commission's (NRC) Inspector General found that the NRC itself did not demand more rapid action

to address the potentially dangerous issue because it wanted to "lessen the financial impact" on the utility plant operator.

The best way to continue to ensure reactor safety is to follow the advice of the Kemeney Commission, which investigated the 1979 Three Mile Island accident in the United States. They recommended that constant vigilance was required to ensure reactor safety; complacency about the safety of nuclear power would lead to accidents.

Current Waste Management Strategies

With over 50 years of power reactor operation, by 2007 the world had accumulated almost 365,000 m^3 of high-level nuclear waste, including spent nuclear fuel and reprocessing wastes; over 3 million m^3 of long-lived low- and intermediate-level waste; and over 2 million m^3 of short-lived low- and intermediate-level waste. Though many countries have low-level waste disposal facilities and a few have intermediate-level facilities, none have opened a high-level nuclear waste disposal facility. Most spent nuclear fuel remains in cooling pools and dry storage casks at power reactors; some has been reprocessed, and the resulting high-level waste has been vitrified and sits in storage facilities.

Most countries with significant nuclear power generation have decided that high-level nuclear waste should be disposed of in mined geologic repositories. Four countries have been focusing on a single site within their borders. In the United States, the Yucca Mountain, Nevada, site is currently undergoing licensing review for repository construction by the Nuclear Regulatory Commission, although the current Obama Administration has said it will not support the Yucca Mountain site. . . .

Currently there are two management pathways for handling the spent nuclear fuel generated by power reactors. One is the "open cycle," in which spent fuel is considered high-level waste and will be directly disposed of in a repository. The United States, Sweden, Finland, Canada, and others follow this pathway. The second is the "closed cycle," as practiced by France, the United Kingdom, Japan, Russia, and India, in which spent nuclear fuel is reprocessed, the plutonium and uranium extracted, and the remaining waste turned into glass logs destined for a repository. The separated plutonium is then made into new nuclear fuel known as MOX (mixed oxide), but as of yet, it is not reprocessed a second time. The extracted uranium tends to be considered a waste product, as it is too expensive to clean up for reuse.

Reprocessing does reduce the volume of high-level waste by a factor of 4 to 10 times. But this volume reduction does not imply a corresponding capacity reduction in a geologic repository, because volume is not the relevant unit of measure for capacity; heat production and radionuclide composition of the waste are. In addition, reprocessing generates large volumes of low- and intermediate-level wastes, some of which require their own repository. As a result, reprocessing as it is currently practiced has a limited impact on repository size. And no matter which cycle is used, open or closed, a repository will be required in the end.

Issues for the Future

For developed countries, nuclear power can significantly offset carbon dioxide emissions, whereas for developing countries, nuclear power has the potential to electrify the country as well as provide desalination services to address dwindling water supplies. An expansion of nuclear power will not occur without overcoming significant hurdles, though. Whether nuclear power will be sustainable is another issue. The UK Sustainable Development Commission recently concluded that nuclear power was not necessary to achieve a low-carbon future. Some issues associated with nuclear power are unique when compared with other electricity sources, especially in terms of safety and security.

Safety

To operate safely, nuclear power requires a large, active, and well-established infrastructure. The industry needs a trained workforce for plant construction and operation, and also for the regulatory system. In places like the United States, the existing nuclear engineering workforce is aging, and questions remain as to how rapidly it could be replaced. The construction workforce for nuclear power plants requires specialized skills, and the current number of these workers is small. Moreover, there are supply chain issues globally for the nuclear industry. Most significant is the limited capacity for heavy forgings for the reactor pressure vessels. At the moment, a single Japanese plant is capable of making these, and its availability is limited because of commitments to other industries.

For countries with no nuclear plants, an indigenous workforce would have to obtain training abroad, they would need to hire foreign workers, or they would have to rely on the reactor suppliers for a workforce. The same will be true for a regulatory infrastructure. Countries with no existing reactors will need to establish a nuclear infrastructure, again by developing it from the bottom up or by hiring/adapting one from abroad. For example, the United Arab Emirates has hired a former U.S. Nuclear Regulatory Commission official to be the Director-General of its Federal Authority for Nuclear Regulation.

Another key issue for emerging nuclear energy countries is that of liability in the case of nuclear accident for adequate protection of the victims and predictability for nuclear suppliers and insurers. A catastrophic nuclear accident could result in compensation costs that would run into the hundreds of billions of dollars. There is no single global liability regime, and currently 236 of the 436 operating reactors are not covered by liability conventions. Those countries that are party to liability conventions must assure that the legal liability is the responsibility of the reactor operator, and that there are monetary and temporal limits on liability claims.

Cost

Costs associated with the construction of new nuclear reactors may pose the greatest roadblock to the global expansion of nuclear power. . . .

Historically, reactor construction experiences delays and cost escalation. Costs of constructing U.S. nuclear power plants exceed original estimates by 200 percent to 400 percent on average. Experience in the U.S. also shows that increased construction times lead to greatly increased costs from accumulating interest costs. And construction time has not improved that much. Average construction time globally, in most recent experience between 2001–2005, was 6.8 years; at best it was five years, on average.

In the United States, nuclear reactors may cost even more per unit. Florida Power and Light, the utility poised to build two new reactors at its Turkey Point site, recently released figures of $5,780/kW to $8,071/kW, for a total of $12.1 billion to $24.3 billion, depending on the type of plants built. Costs such as these will be prohibitive for many developing countries and even for most utility companies in developed countries. Indeed, the U.S. nuclear industry is seeking further loan guarantees from the federal government over the original $18 billion laid out in the Energy Policy Act of 2005.

All of the reactor designs currently available for construction ("generation III") are large reactors, ranging in size between 600 MWe and 1700 MWe, with most averaging around 1000 MWe. The reason for this is the economies of scale associated with large reactors. Costs associated with reactor design, licensing, regulation, and operation are independent of reactor size, so larger reactors tend to cost less per kilowatt than smaller reactors. These large reactors require large, sophisticated electrical grid networks, something that many developing countries lack. Developing countries seeking nuclear power for electricity production or desalination would be better served by smaller reactors, but none is currently available, though new designs are being put forth.

Capital costs can be decreased by shortening construction time, building standardized designs (in the United States, all existing plants have unique designs), using factory construction of plant components, relying on local resources for labor and construction materials, and building more than one reactor at a site, which allows for costsharing in licensing. For example, Westinghouse's new AP-1000, under construction in Sanmen, China, uses a modular design in which factory prefabricated components can be assembled at the reactor site and put in place using a large crane. Smaller reactors might be helpful in reducing capital costs, because the industry might be able get the economic advantages of producing many units, thus overcoming the problems associated with site-built reactors. Moreover, for small, modular reactors, it may be possible to do the licensing at the manufacturing plant instead of the individual site, greatly reducing costs.

Security

One of the main security concerns about nuclear power programs is their connection to nuclear weapons development. This concern is the reason for international agreements, such as the Nuclear Nonproliferation Treaty (NPT), which guarantees that countries that do not have nuclear weapons are allowed nuclear energy technology, and for institutions such as the IAEA, whose main charge is to monitor nuclear energy programs. The general problem is that the

fuel for nuclear power plants is also the same fuel for nuclear weapons: highly enriched uranium or plutonium.

Running a nuclear power reactor poses little proliferation threat. The problem comes either at the "front-end" of the nuclear fuel cycle, associated with fuel production, or the "back-end," associated with the reprocessing of spent nuclear fuel. . . .

One additional security issue requires comment. Nuclear power plants could become terrorist targets in the future. Terrorists might desire to cause a loss of coolant accident of some sort. Particularly vulnerable in this situation are older plants with near-full or full cooling pools in which the fuel is placed in high density arrangements. These pools are located in different areas depending on the reactor design, though some are located several stories above ground. Were the pool to lose coolant, a fire could ensue, causing the release of huge amounts of radioactivity (more than Chernobyl). Fortunately, unlike dealing with proliferation issues associated with the fuel cycle, there is a relatively straightforward solution to this problem. Older fuel can be moved from the cooling pools into dry cask storage on site. Dry casks are passively cooled and therefore much safer if attacked. One of the only reasons reactors have not gone to low-density fuel arrangement in pools is cost.

Environmental/Health Impacts

Life cycle wastes from nuclear power are relatively small in volume in comparison to other energy sources such as fossil fuels. Nuclear power has low emissions from reactor operation, and overall waste production is low, especially in the open fuel cycle. More wastes are generated by reprocessing spent nuclear fuel, though again, in comparison with fossil fuels, they are small. . . .

The bulk of the volume of wastes associated with nuclear power originates from mining and processing the uranium ore for fabrication into fuel. The largest and most problematic wastes associated with mining are uranium mill tailings, which are the rock residue from the extraction of uranium from the ore. The problem is that all the uranium daughter products, in particular radium (Ra-226) and its daughter radon (Rn-222), from millions to billions of years of decay, remain with the residual rock. These pose risks from windblown dust exposure, radon emissions, and leaching into groundwater. . . .

High-level nuclear wastes will increase if nuclear power expands. At current rates of production, an additional 1000 GWe will produce an extra 20,000–30,000 metric tons of spent fuel annually. This amount is approximately one-third to one-half the currently statutory capacity for the proposed Yucca Mountain repository in the United States. Thus, an expanded nuclear world would require more or larger repositories than are envisaged today.

Prospects for the Future

Nuclear power offers a potential avenue to significantly mitigate carbon dioxide emissions while still providing baseload power required in today's world. But nuclear power cannot provide significant baseload power over the next 15 years or so, because it will take many years before a considerable number of

new plants are licensed and built. The high capital costs of the plants and the risks of investing in this technology will likely enforce a slow start to large-scale nuclear build. New policies that institute a price on carbon dioxide emissions will certainly improve nuclear power's prospects. In some ways, though, nuclear power suffers from a chicken-and-egg situation: more manufacturing experience may reduce prices, but to achieve the necessary experience, many new plants must first be paid for and built.

New reactors in emerging nuclear energy countries will take even longer because of the large infrastructure required and the need for the international community to respond in an organized fashion to the potential proliferation threats posed by nuclear energy. As a result, nuclear power may begin to provide significant carbon emissions relief in the longer term, starting 20 or 30 years from now.

Unlike most other energy sources, nuclear power does have "doomsday" scenarios. History may repeat itself. Both the accidents at Three Mile Island and Chernobyl had a chilling effect on the global nuclear industry. In the United States, no new nuclear plants have been ordered since the Three Mile Island accident. In Sweden in the 1980s, the country voted to end its use of nuclear power (though they have more recently reversed this decision). If a similar accident occurs, nuclear power's future will grow dim. Similarly, if a country breaks out and develops nuclear weapons using its nuclear energy technology, expansion of nuclear power to non-nuclear energy countries will stop. Countries with nuclear energy technology will be loathe to provide it to emerging nuclear energy nations. Unlike fossil fuels and renewable resources, nuclear energy's success rests on the performance and behavior of all of those involved in producing nuclear power, wherever they are. And this is a somewhat tenuous situation on which to base an industry.

 **NO**

Five Myths About Nuclear Energy

Atomic energy is among the most impractical and risky of available fuel sources. Private financiers are reluctant to invest in it, and both experts and the public have questions about the likelihood of safely storing lethal radioactive wastes for the required million years. Reactors also provide irresistible targets for terrorists seeking to inflict deep and lasting damage on the United States. The government's own data show that U.S. nuclear reactors have more than a one-in-five lifetime probability of core melt, and a nuclear accident could kill 140,000 people, contaminate an area the size of Pennsylvania, and destroy our homes and health.

In addition to being risky, nuclear power is unable to meet our current or future energy needs. Because of safety requirements and the length of time it takes to construct a nuclear-power facility, the government says that by the year 2050 atomic energy could supply, at best, 20 percent of U.S. electricity needs; yet by 2020, wind and solar panels could supply at least 32 percent of U.S. electricity, at about half the cost of nuclear power. Nevertheless, in the last two years, the current U.S. administration has given the bulk of taxpayer energy subsidies—a total of $20 billion—to atomic power. Why? Some officials say nuclear energy is clean, inexpensive, needed to address global climate change, unlikely to increase the risk of nuclear proliferation and safe.

On all five counts they are wrong. Renewable energy sources are cleaner, cheaper, better able to address climate change and proliferation risks, and safer. The government's own data show that wind energy now costs less than half of nuclear power; that wind can supply far more energy, more quickly, than nuclear power; and that by 2015, solar panels will be economically competitive with all other conventional energy technologies. The administration's case for nuclear power rests on at least five myths. Debunking these myths is necessary if the United States is to abandon its current dangerous energy course.

Myth 1. Nuclear Energy Is Clean

The myth of clean atomic power arises partly because some sources, like a pro-nuclear energy analysis published in 2003 by several professors at the Massachusetts Institute of Technology, call atomic power a "carbon-free source" of energy. On its Web site, the U.S. Department of Energy, which is

also a proponent of nuclear energy, calls atomic power "emissions free." At best, these claims are half-truths because they "trim the data" on emissions.

While nuclear reactors themselves do not release greenhouse gases, reactors are only part of the nine-stage nuclear fuel cycle. This cycle includes mining uranium ore, milling it to extract uranium, converting the uranium to gas, enriching it, fabricating fuel pellets, generating power, reprocessing spent fuel, storing spent fuel at the reactor and transporting the waste to a permanent storage facility. Because most of these nine stages are heavily dependent on fossil fuels, nuclear power thus generates at least 33 grams of carbon-equivalent emissions for each kilowatt-hour of electricity that is produced. (To provide uniform calculations of greenhouse emissions, the various effects of the different greenhouse gases typically are converted to carbon-equivalent emissions.) Per kilowatt-hour, atomic energy produces only one-seventh the greenhouse emissions of coal, but twice as much as wind and slightly more than solar panels.

Nuclear power is even less clean when compared with energy-efficiency measures, such as using compact-fluorescent bulbs and increasing home insulation. Whether in medicine or energy policy, preventing a problem is usually cheaper than curing or solving it, and energy efficiency is the most cost-effective way to solve the problem of reducing greenhouse gases. Department of Energy data show that one dollar invested in energy-efficiency programs displaces about six times more carbon emissions than the same amount invested in nuclear power. Government figures also show that energy-efficiency programs save $40 for every dollar invested in them. This is why the government says it could immediately and cost-effectively cut U.S. electricity consumption by 20 percent to 45 percent, using only existing strategies, like time-of-use electricity pricing. (Higher prices for electricity used during daily peak-consumption times—roughly between 8 a.m. and 8 p.m.—encourage consumers to shift their time of energy use. New power plants are typically needed to handle only peak electricity demand.)

Myth 2. Nuclear Energy Is Inexpensive

Achieving greater energy efficiency, however, also requires ending the lopsided system of taxpayer nuclear subsidies that encourage the myth of inexpensive electricity from atomic power. Since 1949, the U.S. government has provided about $165 billion in subsidies to nuclear energy, about $5 billion to solar and wind together, and even less to energy-efficiency programs. All government efficiency programs—to encourage use of fuel-efficient cars, for example, or to provide financial assistance so that low-income citizens can insulate their homes—currently receive only a small percentage of federal energy monies.

After energy-efficiency programs, wind is the most cost-effective way both to generate electricity and to reduce greenhouse emissions. It costs about half as much as atomic power. The only nearly finished nuclear plant in the West, now being built in Finland by the French company Areva, will generate electricity costing 11 cents per kilowatt-hour. Yet the U.S. government's Lawrence Berkeley National Laboratory calculated actual costs of new wind

WHAT DOES THE CHURCH SAY?

Though neither the Vatican nor the U.S. bishops have made a statement on nuclear power, the church has outlined the ethical case for renewable energy. In *Centesimus Annus* Pope John Paul II wrote that just as Pope Leo XIII in 1891 had to confront "primitive capitalism" in order to defend workers' rights, he himself had to confront the "new capitalism" in order to defend collective goods like the environment. Pope Benedict XVI warned that pollutants "make the lives of the poor especially unbearable." In their 2001 statement *Global Climate Change*, the U.S. Catholic bishops repeated his point: climate change will "disproportionately affect the poor, the vulnerable, and generations yet unborn."

The bishops also warn that "misguided responses to climate change will likely place even greater burdens on already desperately poor peoples." Instead they urge "energy conservation and the development of alternate renewable and clean-energy resources." They argue that renewable energy promotes care for creation and the common good, lessens pollution that disproportionately harms the poor and vulnerable, avoids threats to future generations and reduces nuclear-proliferation risks.

---

plants, over the last seven years, at 3.4 cents per kilowatt-hour. Although some groups say nuclear energy is inexpensive, their misleading claims rely on trimming the data on cost. The 2003 M.I.T. study, for instance, included neither the costs of reprocessing nuclear material, nor the full interest costs on nuclear-facility construction capital, nor the total costs of waste storage. Once these omissions—from the entire nine-stage nuclear fuel cycle—are included, nuclear costs are about 11 cents per kilowatt-hour.

The cost-effectiveness of wind power explains why in 2006 utility companies worldwide added 10 times more wind-generated, than nuclear, electricity capacity. It also explains why small-scale sources of renewable energy, like wind and solar, received $56 billion in global private investments in 2006, while nuclear energy received nothing. It explains why wind supplies 20 percent of Denmark's electricity. It explains why, each year for the last several years, Germany, Spain and India have each, alone, added more wind capacity than all countries in the world, taken together, have added in nuclear capacity.

In the United States, wind supplies up to 8 percent of electricity in some Midwestern states. The case of Louis Brooks is instructive. Utilities pay him $500 a month for allowing 78 wind turbines on his Texas ranch, and he can still use virtually all the land for farming and grazing. Wind's cost-effectiveness also explains why in 2007 wind received $9 billion in U.S. private investments, while nuclear energy received zero. U.S. wind energy has been growing by nearly 3,000 megawatts each year, annually producing new electricity

equivalent to what three new nuclear reactors could generate. Meanwhile, no new U.S. atomic-power reactors have been ordered since 1974.

Should the United States continue to heavily subsidize nuclear technology? Or, as the distinguished physicist Amory Lovins put it, is the nuclear industry dying of an "incurable attack of market forces"? Standard and Poor's, the credit- and investment-rating company, downgrades the rating of any utility that wants a nuclear plant. It claims that even subsidies are unlikely to make nuclear investment wise. *Forbes* magazine recently called nuclear investment "the largest managerial disaster in business history," something pursued only by the "blind" or the "biased."

Myth 3. Nuclear Energy Is Necessary to Address Climate Change

Government, industry and university studies, like those recently from Princeton, agree that wind turbines and solar panels already exist at an industrial scale and could supply one-third of U.S. electricity needs by 2020, and the vast majority of U.S. electricity by 2050—not just the 20 percent of electricity possible from nuclear energy by 2050. The D.O.E. says wind from only three states (Kansas, North Dakota and Texas) could supply all U.S. electricity needs, and 20 states could supply nearly triple those needs. By 2015, according to the D.O.E., solar panels will be competitive with all conventional energy technologies and will cost 5 to 10 cents per kilowatt hour. Shell Oil and other fossil-fuel companies agree. They are investing heavily in wind and solar.

From an economic perspective, atomic power is inefficient at addressing climate change because dollars used for more expensive, higher-emissions nuclear energy cannot be used for cheaper, lower-emissions renewable energy. Atomic power is also not sustainable. Because of dwindling uranium supplies, by the year 2050 reactors would be forced to use low-grade uranium ore whose greenhouse emissions would roughly equal those of natural gas. Besides, because the United States imports nearly all its uranium, pursuing nuclear power continues the dangerous pattern of dependency on foreign sources to meet domestic energy needs.

Myth 4. Nuclear Energy Will Not Increase Weapons Proliferation

Pursuing nuclear power also perpetuates the myth that increasing atomic energy, and thus increasing uranium enrichment and spent-fuel reprocessing, will increase neither terrorism nor proliferation of nuclear weapons. This myth has been rejected by both the International Atomic Energy Agency and the U.S. Office of Technology Assessment. More nuclear plants means more weapons materials, which means more targets, which means a higher risk of terrorism and proliferation. The government admits that Al Qaeda already has targeted U.S. reactors, none of which can withstand attack by a large airplane. Such an attack, warns the U.S. National Academy of Sciences, could cause fatalities as

far away as 500 miles and destruction 10 times worse than that caused by the nuclear accident at Chernobyl in 1986.

Nuclear energy actually increases the risks of weapons proliferation because the same technology used for civilian atomic power can be used for weapons, as the cases of India, Iran, Iraq, North Korea and Pakistan illustrate. As the Swedish Nobel Prize winner Hannes Alven put it, "The military atom and the civilian atom are Siamese twins." Yet if the world stopped building nuclear-power plants, bomb ingredients would be harder to acquire, more conspicuous and more costly politically, if nations were caught trying to obtain them. Their motives for seeking nuclear materials would be unmasked as military, not civilian.

Myth 5. Nuclear Energy Is Safe

Proponents of nuclear energy, like Patrick Moore, cofounder of Greenpeace, and the former Argonne National Laboratory adviser Steve Berry, say that new reactors will be safer than current ones—"meltdown proof." Such safety claims also are myths. Even the 2003 M.I.T. energy study predicted that tripling civilian nuclear reactors would lead to about four core-melt accidents. The government's Sandia National Laboratory calculates that a nuclear accident could cause casualties similar to those at Hiroshima or Nagasaki: 140,000 deaths. If nuclear plants are as safe as their proponents claim, why do utilities need the U.S. Price-Anderson Act, which guarantees utilities protection against 98 percent of nuclear-accident liability and transfers these risks to the public? All U.S. utilities refused to generate atomic power until the government established this liability limit. Why do utilities, but not taxpayers, need this nuclear-liability protection?

Another problem is that high-level radioactive waste must be secured "in perpetuity," as the U.S. National Academy of Sciences puts it. Yet the D.O.E. has already admitted that if nuclear waste is stored at Nevada's Yucca Mountain, as has been proposed, future generations could not meet existing radiation standards. As a result, the current U.S. administration's proposal is to allow future releases of radioactive wastes, stored at Yucca Mountain, provided they annually cause no more than one person—out of every 70 persons exposed to them—to contract fatal cancer. These cancer risks are high partly because Yucca Mountain is so geologically unstable. Nuclear waste facilities could be breached by volcanic or seismic activity. Within 50 miles of Yucca Mountain, more than 600 seismic events, of magnitude greater than two on the Richter scale, have occurred since 1976. In 1992, only 12 miles from the site, an earthquake (5.6 on the Richter scale) damaged D.O.E. buildings. Within 31 miles of the site, eight volcanic eruptions have occurred in the last million years. These facts suggest that Alvin Weinberg was right. Four decades ago, the then-director of the government's Oak Ridge National Laboratory warned that nuclear waste required society to make a Faustian bargain with the devil. In exchange for current military and energy benefits from atomic power, this generation must sell the safety of future generations.

Yet the D.O.E. predicts harm even in this generation. The department says that if 70,000 tons of the existing U.S. waste were shipped to Yucca

Mountain, the transfer would require 24 years of dozens of daily rail or truck shipments. Assuming low accident rates and discounting the possibility of terrorist attacks on these lethal shipments, the D.O.E. says this radioactive-waste transport likely would lead to 50 to 310 shipment accidents. According to the D.O.E., each of these accidents could contaminate 42 square miles, and each could require a 462-day cleanup that would cost $620 million, not counting medical expenses. Can hundreds of thousands of mostly unguarded shipments of lethal materials be kept safe? The states do not think so, and they have banned Yucca Mountain transport within their borders. A better alternative is onsite storage at reactors, where the material can be secured from terrorist attack in "hardened" bunkers.

Where Do We Go From Here?

If atomic energy is really so risky and expensive, why did the United States begin it and heavily subsidize it? As U.S. Atomic Energy Agency documents reveal, the United States began to develop nuclear power for the same reason many other nations have done so. It wanted weapons-grade nuclear materials for its military program. But the United States now has more than enough weapons materials. What explains the continuing subsidies? Certainly not the market. *The Economist* (7/7/05) recently noted that for decades, bankers in New York and London have refused loans to nuclear industries. Warning that nuclear costs, dangers and waste storage make atomic power "extremely risky," *The Economist* claimed that the industry is now asking taxpayers to do what the market will not do: invest in nuclear energy. How did *The Economist* explain the uneconomical $20 billion U.S. nuclear subsidies for 2005–7? It pointed to campaign contributions from the nuclear industry.

Despite the problems with atomic power, society needs around-the-clock electricity. Can we rely on intermittent wind until solar power is cost-effective in 2015? Even the Department of Energy says yes. Wind now can supply up to 20 percent of electricity, using the current electricity grid as backup, just as nuclear plants do when they are shut down for refueling, maintenance and leaks. Wind can supply up to 100 percent of electricity needs by using "distributed" turbines spread over a wide geographic region—because the wind always blows somewhere, especially offshore.

Many renewable energy sources are safe and inexpensive, and they inflict almost no damage on people or the environment. Why is the current U.S. administration instead giving virtually all of its support to a riskier, more costly nuclear alternative?

EXPLORING THE ISSUE

Is It Time to Revive Nuclear Power?

Critical Thinking and Reflection

1. Which is more dangerous? Nuclear power or global warming? (See *The Anatomy of a Silent Crisis*, Global Humanitarian Forum Geneva (2009), www.ghfgeneva.org/LinkClick.aspx?fileticket=pg6PNloVEoA%3d.)
2. How are nuclear wastes handled today?
3. Pretend that your campus is a nuclear power plant. Now devise an evacuation plan to protect the residents of neighboring communities in case of a serious accident.
4. What are the advantages of a "closed cycle" approach to handling spent nuclear fuel?

Is There Common Ground?

There is no argument that today's society needs vast amounts of energy to function. The debate largely centers on how to meet the need (which is projected to grow greatly in the future). The greatest agreement may well be in the solutions people refuse to consider. As an exercise, consider the following major uses of energy:

Global trade

Commuting

Air-conditioning

Central heating

1. In what ways could we change our lifestyles to reduce energy use in each of these areas?
2. Would reducing population help?

ISSUE 6

Is America Ready for the Electric Car?

YES: Michael Horn, from "Roadmap to the Electric Car Economy," *The Futurist* (April 2010)

NO: Rick Newman, from "A Stuttering Start for Electric Cars," *U.S. News & World Report* (April 2010)

Learning Outcomes

After studying this issue, students will be able to explain:

1. The advantages of electric vehicles over fossil fuel–powered vehicles.
2. The shortcomings of electric vehicles.
3. Why even perfect electric vehicles will not replace fossil fuel–powered vehicles quickly.
4. Why electric-vehicle charging systems should be standardized.

ISSUE SUMMARY

YES: Michael Horn argues that the technology already exists to replace gasoline-burning cars with electric cars and thereby save money, reduce dependence on foreign oil sources, and reduce pollution. All we need is organization and determination.

NO: Rick Newman argues that because electric car technology is still new, expensive, and unreliable, it will be at least a decade before consumers are willing to shift from gas burners to electric cars.

$\mathbf{T}$he 1973 "oil crisis" heightened awareness that the world—even if it was not yet running out of oil—was extraordinarily dependent on that fossil fuel (and therefore on supplier nations) for transportation, home heating, and electricity generation. Since the supply of oil and other fossil fuels is clearly finite, some people have worried that there would come a time when demand could not be satisfied, and our dependence would leave us helpless. At the

same time, we have become acutely aware of the many unfortunate side-effects of fossil fuels, including air pollution, strip mines, oil spills, global warming, and more.

The 1970s saw the modern environmental movement gain momentum. The first Earth Day was in 1970. Numerous steps were taken by governments to deal with air pollution, water pollution, and other environmental problems. In response to the oil crisis, a great deal of public money went into developing alternative energy supplies. The emphasis was on "renewable" energy, meaning conservation, wind, solar, geothermal, and tidal energy. However, when the crisis passed and oil supplies were once more ample (albeit it did cost more to fill a gasoline tank), most public funding for alternative-energy research and demonstration projects vanished. What work continued was at the hands of a few enthusiasts and those corporations that saw future opportunities.

The electric car is not a new idea. Such cars existed in the early years of the twentieth century, although they soon gave way to gasoline-burning cars, which could run longer on a charge (or fill-up). The idea has been revived in recent decades, however. Its most common form is the gas-electric hybrid (e.g., the Toyota Prius), but all-electric cars have been built. GM's EV never hit the market (see the documentary *Who Killed the Electric Car?* available on DVD), but the Chevy Volt (www.chevrolet.com/pages/open/default/fuel/electric.do) is already rolling off assembly lines. Unfortunately, perhaps, the Chevy Volt is not a pure electric car; it is a "plug-in hybrid," meaning that its battery can be charged from a wall socket, but it also uses a gas-powered engine to charge its battery while on the road. Several all-electric cars will be at dealers soon, but they will not be cheap. Improvements in price and performance are frequently promised, but they depend mostly on finding a way to store an amount of electrical energy equivalent to the energy content of a tankful of gasoline in a compact package that does not cost a huge amount to replace. A great deal of research effort is currently devoted to improving batteries and developing alternative electricity-storage devices such as supercapacitors. Entrepreneurs are also working on battery-leasing plans and other methods of making electric cars more affordable.

The prospective benefits of electric cars are well established. In August 2009, the Center for Entrepreneurship & Technology at the University of California, Berkeley, published Thomas A. Becker, Ikhlaq Sidhu, and Burghardt Tenderich, "Electric Vehicles in the United States: A New Model with Forecasts to 2030" (http://cet.berkeley.edu/dl/CET_Technical%20Brief_EconomicModel2030_f .pdf). Among their premises were that electric cars will have batteries that are not charged in situ but are swapped for charged batteries (Shai Agassi is working to establish such a system in Israel at the moment; see Steve Hamm, "The Electric Car Acid Test," *Businessweek* [February 4, 2008]) and that charging networks will be financed by pay-per-mile contracts. In their baseline forecast, by 2030 electric cars will account for 64 percent of U.S. light vehicle sales. Of light vehicles on the road, electrics will be 24 percent. Oil imports will be almost 40 percent lower than if all we do is improve the efficiency of internal combustion engines. The annual trade deficit will be down by as much as a quarter trillion dollars. Employment will be boosted by as much as 350,000 jobs. If

the electric cars are charged using nonpolluting sources of electricity (wind, solar, etc.), there will be $100–200 billion in savings in health care costs due to reduced pollution. And carbon dioxide emissions will be greatly reduced. Unfortunately, the extent of those emissions reductions depends on where you live and how your electricity is generated; see Michael Moyer, "The Dirty Truth about Plug-In Hybrids," *Scientific American* (July 2010). For an overview of what is now available, see "Should You Plug In?" *Consumer Reports* (October 2010).

In 2010, the National Research Council's Committee on Assessment of Resource Needs for Fuel Cell and Hydrogen Technologies published "Transitions to Alternative Transportation Technologies—Plug-in Hybrid Electric Vehicles" (www.nap.edu/catalog.php?record_id=12826). The more cautious focus—on plug-in hybrids instead of all-electric cars—makes the results not quite comparable to the earlier report. In addition their conclusions are less optimistic. For instance, they forecast that the maximum practical market penetration would result in 2030 in an on-the-road fleet that is no more than 15 percent plug-in hybrids. There will still be marked reductions in gasoline use, pollution, and carbon emissions.

According to Julian Edgar, "Electric Cars Now!" *Autospeed* (http://autospeed .com/cms/A_111205/printArticle.html), recent improvements in battery and charging technology mean that "The arguments against electric cars are now so weak they're effectively gone." Indeed, it is hard to find anyone who seriously argues that electric cars are a bad idea. The real question is whether people will buy them, and costs of vehicles and batteries will play a large part in shaping the answer to this question. Reliability of the technology may be demonstrated very soon. The Chevy Volt—a plug-in hybrid—will be on the market in 2011. Also in 2011, Nissan's all-electric Leaf is scheduled to hit the U.S. market; see http://nissanusa.com/leaf-electric-car. More electric cars are due soon from Ford, Hyundai, Volvo, Toyota, and Audi. The next few years will tell the tale.

In the YES selection, retired aerospace scientist Michael Horn argues that the technology already exists to replace gasoline-burning cars with electric cars and thereby save money, reduce dependence on foreign oil sources, and reduce pollution. All we need is organization and determination. In the NO selection, Journalist Rick Newman argues that because electric car technology is still new, expensive, and unreliable, it will be at least a decade before consumers are willing to shift from gas burners to electric cars. It will be longer than that before they replace more than a small fraction of the gas burner fleet.

YES

Michael Horn

Roadmap to the Electric Car Economy

By the middle of this century, the United States may have completely transitioned from gasoline to electric vehicles, or EVs. Its economy will then enjoy an EV-energy bonus, somewhat like the peace bonus at the end of the Cold War, but this one will result from saving half of the money that U.S. consumers previously spent on oil imports to make gasoline for all their cars.

By then, the bankruptcies of GM and Chrysler will be a long-forgotten anomaly in the history of the auto industry, because once the auto companies replace the 254.4 million gasoline-powered cars in the United States with electric ones by mid-century, they will create a manufacturing boom that completely wipes out the losses that they sustained during the 2008 recession.

These electric cars will have come a long way from the twentieth-century electric prototypes that required drivers to stop frequently to recharge the batteries, making highway driving nearly impossible. In the coming decades, highways might be outfitted with guardrails that emit harmless radio-frequency charging waves. Special coils inside each car will receive the waves and harness them to recharge the battery continuously while the car is driving. The human passengers will have the luxury of never having to stop for a refueling.

The chore of pumping gas will seem akin to shoveling coal, and the ignominy of driving out of a gas station with the smell of gasoline on your hands from the pump handle will be memories only older folks might recall. The electric car, emitting no fumes and being virtually silent in operation, will make the gasoline-powered cars of the past seem utterly primordial by comparison.

Late in the century, historians may even debate why it took so long to make the transition from oil to electricity, when oil was so inefficient, involved so much peril, and all the elements necessary for transition to electric were well in hand by the end of the twentieth century.

Gasoline's Problems

But back to the present, where for the last 100 years, the U.S. economy has continued to depend on the gasoline-fueled, internal-combustion engine for powering cars and trucks. This engine is only a small technological step above the steam engine. The fact that it's primitive is not the problem; it's that it is so inefficient. For every $1 that we spend on gas, 85¢ is wasted in heating

the engine block and the surrounding air (the reason it needs both an oil and water pump to cool it); only 15¢ goes into moving the car down the road.

Obtaining the gasoline is fraught with serious environmental and political perils. We are facing many questions concerning global warming, not the least of which is how much automobile exhaust contributes. Then there's the question of what happens to our frail economy if our oil supplies are disrupted. But our societal attitude is curiously sanguine concerning how imperiled we make ourselves when we rely so heavily upon the gasoline-powered engine. We seriously need to reconsider our options.

Continued Dependence On Oil

Over the last 30 years, each American president has vowed to reduce the nation's consumption and dependence on oil (i.e., gasoline) by increasing gas mileage of all cars and light trucks through a program called CAFE (Corporate Average Fuel Economy). After 30 years, however, the United States is still locked into an oil economy, and CAFE, which has done little to alleviate the situation, continues to be its only option for reducing oil imports.

President Obama has continued to follow the course of previous presidents and recently raised the CAFE standards from 27 mpg to 35 mpg. He also enacted a $3 billion cash-forclunkers program in an effort to get gas-guzzlers off the road. At the same time, billions are being spent on alternative-fuel cars, with research money still being spent on getting fuel out of corn. America is desperately trying to wean itself off oil imports from unstable sources around the world, but has yet to come up with a winning formula for doing so. When the CAFE was introduced in the 1970s, the average fuel economy mandated was 18 mpg. Now more than three decades later the fuel standards have gotten to 35 miles per gallon.

At that rate of development, it would take about 350 years for the internal-combustion engine cars to reach the more than 200 mpg efficiency already realized by battery-powered cars today! So why not put all available resources into making the electric car the successful replacement to the gasoline-powered car? It's been tried before, and we see the result all around us: Electric cars are far from becoming mainstream.

The problems were not so much with the cars, but with the environment into which the cars were cast. Back in 1990, the California Air Resources Board (CARB) introduced new regulations mandating that progressively larger shares of auto manufacturers' fleets of cars must produce zero emissions: By 1998, according to the CARB mandate, 2% of all the vehicles on California's roadways would have to be zero-emissions vehicles (ZEVs); by 2003, 10%. The only ZEVs circa 1990 were battery-powered cars. So, somewhat reluctantly, the auto industry began projects to develop battery-powered cars. GM and Toyota produced very impressive electric cars (based on relatively primitive battery technology compared to today) that eventually attained ranges of over 100 miles.

After huge investments and low sales, however, General Motors and Chrysler filed a lawsuit against CARB in 2002 to reverse the ZEV regulations. The auto companies got their way, and CARB was forced to repeal its mandates

for 2003 and 2004. The program resumed in 2005, but with vastly lowered expectations. Today, of the more than 28 million cars registered in California, only 30,400 of them—less than a tenth of one percent—run on batteries.

Regardless of the reasons, the electric cars were doomed from the start because there were few places to recharge them, recharging them was time consuming, and the vehicles have limited range.

The electric car still faces the obstacle of having places to recharge, and now the Obama administration is putting money into electric car technology research without, once again, providing for an infrastructure to support it. It's like planning an aquarium and buying the fish before you build the tanks for the fish to swim in. Right now the electric car is like a fish out of water.

The other side of this issue is the auto industry, which has been burned by the hundreds of millions of dollars lost in the last round of electrics that failed to capture the imagination of all but a small sector of the car-buying public. Auto manufacturers realize the issues and limitations of the electric car and don't want to invest millions or maybe billions more in a car that might not sell. So the bottom line becomes this: Above and beyond getting society away from dependence on oil, what makes the electric car worth all the trouble?

Benefits of the Electric Car

The thing that makes the electric car worth all the trouble is its efficiency. Money and energy are interchangeable. When we waste energy, we waste money, and we waste a tremendous amount of money on oil. Half of all the oil that the United States imports goes into making gasoline. Switching to electric cars would eliminate about half of U.S. oil consumption and dependency.

According to the Energy Information Administration, America used about 137.8 billion gallons of gasoline in 2008. With an average price of $3.55 per gallon that year, the nation spent nearly half a trillion dollars on gasoline! But the worst part is that, since the gasoline engine is only 15% efficient, 85% of the money spent went up in smoke. That's $400 billion that was simply wasted. Any economy that has to contend with that degree of wasted resources is going to be in trouble, sooner or later.

In EVs' favor, most of the extra electricity needed to charge up the new swarm of electric cars wouldn't be coming from burning oil, because it's not the fuel of choice for the electric power industry. Moreover, most of the cost to charge up a battery-powered electric car actually goes into moving the car and is not wasted. That's what I mean by efficiency. Even the charging process is pretty efficient, at better than 85%, according to a study by Sandia Labs.

Along with all the efficiency there's also the immediate and complete cessation of direct air pollution. Despite what detractors of the electric car say, there is no pollution coming out of an electric car itself. There may be pollution created at the point where fossil fuels are burned to make electricity, but at least there are not engines pumping out fumes on every street corner of your city. And besides, there are ways to cap pollution from power plants and keep it from escaping into the atmosphere.

Making the EV Future Viable

Despite public perception of electric vehicles as slow, ugly "golf carts," they can be made to accelerate as fast as any gasoline-powered cars. In fact, an electric motor can accelerate a car faster than any gas engine, and it has done so many times—just check out the YouTube video, "unveiling of the Tesla." The electric car is also virtually silent and very clean, with no oil drips on the driveway or fumes filling up the garage while you warm up the engine in the winter—their motors don't even need to be warmed up!

Electric cars only expend energy when they're moving, so if you're stuck in a traffic jam, at least you can take comfort in knowing that your electric isn't using any energy at all. Also, it's nearly as efficient going 50 mph as it is going 5 mph. Electric cars can be made large or small, and can carry as many people and look as cool or sophisticated as any gas-powered car. They can be made in two-wheel or four-wheel drive. Electric motors are small enough to be the basis of more-flexible interior cabin designs.

The electric motor will also last much longer than its gasoline-powered counterpart because it contains only one moving part. The electric car will be another electrical appliance that runs for years with virtually no maintenance. Just think, when was the last time you needed to have your clothes dryer taken in for an oil change or new spark plugs? They both have similar electric motors. A gasoline car needs something done to it starting around the first three months and then every 3,000 miles—from oil changes to timing-belt replacements, ad nauseam. That in itself is part of the problem in breaking the auto industry away from the gas-engine cars: The industry's business model is based as much on service and parts as it is on sales. Look how much more space at the dealership is devoted to the service and parts department compared to the sales showroom. Clearly, the auto industry will need a better business model than the planned obsolescence that got it so much mileage in the 1950s, '60s, and '70s.

Being so reliable, the electric car may spawn some other novel approaches that would change the way we look at cars. For example, as styling fads change over a few years, instead of buying whole new cars, vehicle owners might just have the recyclable, outer body panels swapped to keep up with the latest trends or just for the sake of change. The auto industry would realize a way to augment money lost on service and parts by marketing newly styled outer panels over the durable electric-drive machinery. GM proposed such a swappable body in its "Skateboard" design, built around a fuel-cell electric vehicle.

Prospects for an "Electric Car Economy"

The electric car economy is one that has eliminated its dependence on oil and transitioned to a vastly more efficient means of powering its cars and trucks. It has removed the addiction to oil that binds consumers to perilous sources of energy. It has removed the issues that distract researchers from developing alternative sources of energy. And it's an economy that provides everyone,

businesses and individuals alike, with hundreds of billions of dollars to spend on other things besides the oil they formerly imported to make gasoline. It's an economy that's pumped up by its newly found efficiency. But to create the electric car economy, we first have to make the electric car a real and complete replacement for the gas-powered car.

The first thing required to make the electric car a viable replacement for the gasoline-powered car is to create the infrastructure that supports the electric car. This infrastructure will be, by its very far-flung, distributed nature, enormous. According to the U.S. Census Bureau, there are 117,000 gas stations in the United States—or as they prefer to put it, one gas station for every 2,500 people. That's the reason that the gasoline-powered car is so successful—it has a vast gasoline distribution infrastructure.

To be as successful, the electric car needs a comparable infrastructure, but we won't need to start from scratch. Electricity is much simpler than liquid or gaseous fuels, which need to be piped or trucked and then stored in huge tanks at the point of sales. Electricity is available everywhere through power lines. Gas stations already have plenty of electric power to run anywhere from four to 12 big pumps and dozens of high-wattage light fixtures. Every gas station will need to conform to a government regulation to have at least one electric car-battery charger to begin with, by a reasonable deadline. Eventually, they'll need more than one charger per station, as people catch on that the electric car can now go further than the city limits. The planned Smart Grid will help accommodate the gradually rising load.

In order for the plan to work, these battery chargers will have to charge a car battery quickly, unlike the home plug-in power sources that take all night. Fortunately, the rapid-charge technology is a reality right now. In fact, one such system, called PosiCharge, was able to charge an electric car battery made by Altairnano in less than 10 minutes.

Standardization is another issue that must be addressed. The batteries and charging-control modules on electric cars have to be standardized so that any vehicle can be recharged anywhere. The plan won't work if you need to go to special recharging stations for a charger that works for your car. At present, different automakers are planning to use different chemistries and internal structures in their batteries. Consequently, not every battery would fit a given service station's charging system. This would put an electric car in the same position a gas-powered car would be in if there was no gas station in the community. How far would a gas-powered car go if there were no gas stations? The government and the auto industry will need to implement standards so that there is a uniform infrastructure of chargers and a uniform code, and that cars everywhere comply with the uniform code. That way, drivers everywhere will be able to quickly charge up their cars without damaging them.

My idea is really quite simple, but it will require some government regulations: Put rapid electric chargers in every gas station, because that's where people already go for gas. Drivers can pull into their local gas station, just as they always had in the past, and quickly charge up their shiny new electrics. Nothing much changes for the driving public except that everyone will be saving that huge amount that was once wasted on gasoline.

   The advantages of promoting an all-electric-car economy are manifold, including the enormous savings in money and the substantial reduction in need for foreign oil supplies, which threaten further economic distress. Air quality would improve significantly. The electric-car economy represents a monumental plan that doesn't actually cost that much — an estimated $3.5 billion. With the right organization and determination, a future of clean, efficient, oil-free electric cars is attainable.

Rick Newman

A Stuttering Start for Electric Cars

Y OUNG TECHNOLOGY MEANS CONSUMERS MAY SIT ON THE SIDELINES
You might get the impression, over the next year or so, that driving as you know it will never be the same again. The electric vehicle, you see, is about to arrive.

The much-heralded Chevrolet Volt, able to travel up to 40 miles on a battery charged through a household outlet, is set to go on sale late this year. So is the Nissan Leaf, with a range of up to 100 miles. A plug-in version of the Toyota Prius will be right behind them. Once the numbers are official, fuel economy for these newfangled machines, when converted to conventional measures, could easily exceed the mystical mark of 100 miles per gallon.

Such eye-popping mileage, plus a dramatic cutback in tailpipe emissions, represents the kind of automotive breakthrough that clean energy advocates have been seeking for decades. And now, they've got powerful allies in government and industry. The Obama administration has offered generous subsidies to manufacturers that build electric vehicles and consumers who buy them. In response, many automakers are ramping up their EV plans, with venture capitalists starting to gamble on electric cars, too. And a number of cities are developing plans to build charging stations and an EV-friendly infrastructure.

The only question is whether drivers will go along. They may just sit on the sidelines as electric vehicles start to roll off the assembly lines. Despite loads of hype and a government jump-start, price premiums will still be high, even with government subsidies. Practical limitations may force Americans to drive differently. And automakers themselves will develop other innovations that buyers may prefer. "Consumers are happy with hybrids and gas-powered cars that get 30 miles per gallon," says Mike Omotoso, a powertrain analyst with J. D. Power & Associates. "As long as gas stays below $3 per gallon, it will probably stay that way."

On paper, the appeal of EVs is, well, electrifying. Unlike hybrids, which are powered by a gas engine and a battery-powered electric motor working more or less in tandem, electrics will run purely on battery power, at least part of the time. That will allow them to take advantage of electricity rates that, mile for mile, are significantly cheaper than gas. General Motors has designed the Volt to travel up to 40 miles on an electrical charge and be chargeable from

a 120-volt household outlet, the kind you use to plug in your washer or dryer. Once the battery runs low, a gas-powered engine kicks in and powers a generator that can move the car for about 300 miles more.

The Prius Plug-In will go 10 to 15 miles on battery power before reverting to the same hybrid operation as in the conventional Prius. On the Volt and the Prius, the gas-powered engine spares drivers "range anxiety": the worry that your car will run out of juice before you reach your destination. The Leaf, by contrast, would be a "pure electric" vehicle able to travel 100 miles or so on a charge—but without a second power source to prevent drivers from being stranded. "Don't worry, there will be lots of charging reminders," says Mark Perry, a top product planner at Nissan.

Saving Money

The potential savings in fuel costs are dramatic. The government hasn't yet developed official mileage ratings for electric vehicles, but General Motors drew headlines last year when it said that the Volt could get the equivalent of 230 mpg in city driving. Nissan scoffed at GM's methodology, saying that by the same metrics the Leaf would get 300 mpg. Tony Posawatz of GM's Volt program acknowledges that the Volt's official mileage number could be lower than 230 mpg, because it will have to account for time spent tooling around on the less efficient gas engine. But overall mileage, he says, "will be better than any conventional car out there." That means the Volt would handily beat the current Prius, which has a combined 50 mpg and is the reigning gas-mileage champ among ordinary production cars.

Comparing EVs with conventional cars is bound to be confusing, with a learning curve that regulators and consumers will have to scale together. The fuel economy for the $109,000 Tesla Roadster, for example—the only full-speed electric vehicle on U.S. roads today—is 110 watt-hours per kilometer, allowing it to travel 244 miles on a charge that takes about 3½ hours. Enthusiasts estimate that the mpg-equivalent ranges from 135 mpg to 400 mpg, depending on how the equivalency between gas and electricity is computed. (The Roadster also rockets from zero to 60 in 3.9 seconds, highlighting one feature of electric powertrains that drivers will love: instantly available torque, which translates into zesty acceleration.)

Drivers may ultimately compare fuel efficiency through another measure: cost per mile. If gas costs $3 per gallon and typical mileage is 25 mpg, it will take 4 gallons of gas to go 100 miles, at a total cost of $12. The per-mile cost is one hundredth of that, or 12 cents per mile. For the Prius, at 50 mpg, fueling costs are half that: 6 cents per mile.

GM says that 100 miles of battery-powered travel in the Volt will require about $2.75 worth of electricity. That adds up to less than 3 cents per mile based on average electricity rates of about 11 cents per kilowatt-hour. If drivers charge their Volt overnight, when off-peak electricity rates are much lower, the cost could be as little as 1 cent per mile, according to Posawatz. At those rates, the annual cost savings on fuel could easily be more than $1,000 in typical driving.

Potential Problems

That's on paper. In the real world, lots of unanticipated things can go wrong. Toyota's recent recalls of millions of vehicles, for instance, involved gas pedals and brakes, hardly exotic components. Some experts think electronics may have played a role in the "sudden acceleration" reported by some Toyota owners, which highlights the risks that come even with the gradual introduction of new technology.

Electric vehicles represent an entirely new set of hardware and software, and it could take years to work out the bugs. Lithium-ion batteries, for instance, have been used for years in cellphones and laptops, but scaling them up for use in cars is a technological leap that's only in the early stages. Poor driving techniques or other unforeseen factors could produce driving range that's lower than manufacturers expect. And any bad press could dent public confidence in the precocious cars.

Then there's the cost of the vehicles themselves. Consulting firm CSM Worldwide estimates that new EV technology generates a price premium of about $20,000 per vehicle, mostly on account of the costly batteries. With gas at $3, it would take nearly 15 years, longer than the life span of most cars, to earn that back through savings on fuel. That's why manufacturers will eat some of the cost, and a $7,500 federal tax credit will bring prices down further. But EVs will still be expensive compared with regular cars. Manufacturers haven't announced prices yet, but the Volt is likely to cost about $40,000 before the tax credit. The Leaf could be $30,000 or so. Consumer reluctance to pay extra for unproven technology is one reason the take rate for EVs is expected to be very low. J. D. Power estimates that by 2015, plug-ins and pure electrics will account for just 0.3 percent of all car sales, or approximately 50,000 vehicles. The Prius alone tallies about 150,000 in annual sales today.

EVs could still change the automotive landscape, however, and the history of hybrids helps explain how. Toyota and Honda began developing hybrids in the early 1990s, with help from the Japanese government. In the United States, the Honda Insight appeared in 1999, the Prius in 2000. While praised for their fuel-sipping engines, as automobiles, they were widely panned. The Insight two-seater was odd and impractical. The pod-shaped Prius was slow and unsure on the highway. Still, some environmentalists flocked to the hybrids, and the unexpected endorsement of a few celebrities pushed Prius sales above expectations.

A Bigger Impact

Toyota lost money on the Prius for at least a decade, and only now does it say its hybrids are profitable. And the Prius has grown from a niche vehicle into Toyota's No. 4 seller. The Prius also paved the way for hybrid versions of the Camry, Highlander, and several Lexuses. Competitors like GM, which once dismissed hybrids as a glorified science experiment, now embrace them. Overall, hybrids represent nearly 3 percent of the market today, and J. D. Power predicts they'll account for nearly 9 percent of sales in 2015.

EVs could make a bigger impact sooner. GM actually developed an electric vehicle in the 1990s—the EV-1—which it abandoned because of low gas prices, weak consumer interest, and the lack of a backup engine. The technology is back because of tough new fuel efficiency and pollution requirements, adopted in both the Bush and Obama administrations, that will force automakers to find new ways to boost fuel economy 4 percent per year, on average, through 2015—an aggressive target that can't be met simply by tweaking existing engines.

But the American market may be the last to see a widespread rollout of EVs, largely because of low gas prices. In Europe and Japan, high taxes keep gas prices well above $6 per gallon, which cuts in half the "payback period" required to recoup the added cost of new technology. With gas prices at $6, for example, an EV would pay for itself in fuel savings after 6.2 years, according to CSM; with $8 gas, that drops to 4.5 years. And greater sales always bring down the cost per unit. If EVs catch on, the added cost could fall by 15 percent a year or so, which is similar to the cost decrease for hybrids and other new technology.

CSM and other forecasting firms believe electric vehicles will start to penetrate the mainstream market by 2020 or so, as costs come down, the technology becomes more reliable, and consumers make the mental shift into a new driving paradigm. In the meantime, collateral benefits of electrification will filter into the mainstream fleet in smaller ways. More cars, for example, will start to feature "start stop" systems, standard on hybrids, which shut down the engine when the car is idling and can boost fuel economy by 5 percent or more. Virtually every automaker plans to roll out more hybrids. There will also be more "clean diesels" and perhaps ethanol-powered vehicles.

The most striking thing about the auto fleet in 2015 will be the shrinking proportion of conventional gas-powered cars, which J. D. Power expects to be just 73 percent, down from 89 percent today. That in itself could foretell an automotive revolution. But what will fuel it is unknown.

EXPLORING THE ISSUE

Is America Ready for the Electric Car?

Critical Thinking and Reflection

1. What are the advantages of electric cars?
2. What are the disadvantages of electric cars?
3. How will standardization benefit the electric car economy?
4. What can government do to encourage adoption of electric cars?
5. Would electric vehicles be more acceptable in a less spread-out society (such as, for instance, Holland)?

Is There Common Ground?

There is little disagreement on the basic question of whether electric vehicles are a "good idea." However, optimists see the technology as ready to be adopted, with the big question being why society is not rushing to adopt the technology. Pessimists do not think the technology is quite ready yet.

1. When the gasoline-powered car was new, there was very little infrastructure to support it. How much paved road was there? Where were gas pumps located, and how common were they?
2. Electric vehicles will also need infrastructure. Roads exist, but what about charging stations? How many will be needed? Where will they be? And how long will it take to provide enough?
3. Do electric vehicles seem more acceptable if you consider only urban driving? Why?

Internet References . . .

Facing the Future: People and the Planet

Facing the Future strives to educate people about critical global issues, including population growth, poverty, overconsumption, and environmental destruction.

http://www.facingthefuture.org/

Cell Phone Facts

The Food and Drug Administration (FDA) summarizes current knowledge of health risks from cell phone use at its Cell Phone Facts page.

**http://www.fda.gov/radiation-emittingproducts/
radiationemittingproductsandprocedures/
homebusinessandentertainment/cellphones/default.htm**

World Health Organization

The World Health Organization of the United Nations provides links to recent reports and meetings about the safety of GM foods on its Biotechnology page.

http://www.who.int/foodsafety/biotech/en/

Malaria Foundation International

The Malaria Foundation International seeks "to facilitate the development and implementation of solutions to the health, economic and social problems caused by malaria."

http://www.malaria.org/

Plum Island Animal Disease Center

Since 1954, the Plum Island Animal Disease Center has been protecting America's livestock from foreign animal diseases (diseases that are not present in the United States) such as foot-and-mouth disease.

http://www.ars.usda.gov/main/site_main.htm?modecode=19-40-00-00

National Institute of Environmental Health Sciences

The National Institute of Environmental Health Sciences studies the health risks of numerous environmental factors, many of which are associated with the use of technology.

http://www.niehs.nih.gov

Human Health and Welfare

*M*any people are concerned about new technological and scientific discoveries because they fear their potential impacts on human health and welfare. In the past, fears have been expressed concerning nuclear bombs and power plants, irradiated food, the internal combustion engine, medications such as thalidomide and diethylstilbestrol, vaccines, pesticides and other chemicals, and more. Because human birth rates have declined, at least in developed nations, the hazards of excess population have fallen out of the headlines, but a few people do still struggle to remind us that a smaller population makes many problems less worrisome. On the public health front, people worry about the best way to control tropical diseases such as malaria and about whether research into infectious animal diseases such as hoof-and-mouth disease should be kept far away from livestock operations. It is worth stressing that risks may be real (as they are with insecticides such as DDT), but there may be a trade-off for genuine health benefits.

- Do Falling Birth Rates Pose a Threat to Human Welfare?
- Is There Sufficient Scientific Evidence to Conclude That Cell Phones Cause Cancer?
- Should DDT Be Banned Worldwide?
- Can Infectious Animal Diseases Be Studied Safely in Kansas?
- Are Genetically Modified Foods Safe to Eat?

ISSUE 7

Do Falling Birth Rates Pose a Threat to Human Welfare?

YES: **Michael Meyer, et al.,** from "Birth Dearth," *Newsweek* (September 27, 2004)

NO: **Julia Whitty,** from "The Last Taboo," *Mother Jones* (May–June 2010)

Learning Outcomes

After studying this issue, students will be able to explain:

1. The nature of the "population problem."
2. The concept of "carrying capacity."
3. The potential benefits of stabilizing or reducing population.
4. The potential drawbacks of stabilizing or reducing population.

ISSUE SUMMARY

YES: Michael Meyer argues that when world population begins to decline after about 2050, economies will no longer continue to grow, government benefits will decline, young people will have to support an elderly population, and despite some environmental benefits, quality of life will suffer.

NO: Writer Julia Whitty argues that even though the topic of overpopulation has become unpopular, it is clear that we are already using the Earth's resources faster than they can be replenished, and the only answer is to slow and eventually reverse population growth.

In 1798, the British economist Thomas Malthus published his *Essay on the Principle of Population.* In this, he pointed with alarm at the way the human population grew geometrically (a hockey stick–shaped curve of increase) and at how agricultural productivity grew only arithmetically (a straight-line

increase). It was obvious, he said, that the population must inevitably outstrip its food supply and experience famine. Contrary to the conventional wisdom of the time, population growth was not necessarily a good thing. Indeed, it led inexorably to catastrophe. For many years, Malthus was something of a laughing stock. The doom he forecast kept receding into the future as new lands were opened to agriculture, new agricultural technologies appeared, new ways of preserving food limited the waste from spoilage, and the birth rate dropped in the industrialized nations (the "demographic transition"). The food supply kept ahead of population growth and seemed likely—to most observers—to continue to do so. Malthus's ideas were dismissed as irrelevant fantasies.

Yet, overall population kept growing. In Malthus's time, there were about 1 billion human beings on the Earth. By 1950—when Warren S. Thompson worried that civilization would be endangered by the rapid growth of Asian and Latin American populations during the next five decades (see "Population," *Scientific American* [February 1950])—there were a little more than 2.5 billion people. In 1999, the tally passed 6 billion. By 2025, it will be more than 8 billion. Statistics like these, which are presented in *World Resources 2008: Roots of Resilience—Growing the Wealth of the Poor* (World Resources Institute, 2008) (http://www.wri.org/publication/world-resources-2008-roots-of-resilience), published in collaboration with the United Nations Development Programme, the United Nations Environment Programme, and the World Bank, are positively frightening. The Worldwatch Institute's yearly *State of the World* reports (W.W. Norton) are no less so. By 2050, the UN expects the world population to be about 9 billion (see *World Population Prospects: The 2008 Revision Population Database;* http://esa.un.org/wup2009/unup/index.asp; United Nations, 2009). Although global agricultural production has also increased, it has not kept up with rising demand, and—because of the loss of topsoil to erosion, the exhaustion of aquifers for irrigation water, and the high price of energy for making fertilizer (among other things)—the prospect of improvement seems exceedingly slim to many observers.

Two centuries never saw Malthus's forecasts of doom come to pass. Population continued to grow, and environmentalists pointed with alarm at a great many problems that resulted from human use of the world's resources (air and water pollution, erosion, loss of soil fertility and groundwater, loss of species, and a great deal more). "Cornucopian" economists such as the late Julian Simon insisted that the more people there are on the Earth, the more people there are to solve problems and that humans can find ways around all possible resource shortages. See Simon's essay, "Life on Earth Is Getting Better, Not Worse," *The Futurist* (August 1983).

Was Malthus wrong? Both environmental scientists and many economists now say that if population continues to grow, problems are inevitable. But earlier predictions of a world population of 10 or 12 billion by 2050 are no longer looking very likely. The UN's population statistics show a slowing of growth, to be followed by an actual decline in population size.

Fred Pearce, *The Coming Population Crash: and Our Planet's Surprising Future* (Beacon, 2010), is optimistic about the effects on human well-being of the coming decline in population. Do we still need to work on controlling

population? Historian Matthew Connolly, *Fatal Misconception: The Struggle to Control World Population* (Belknap Press, 2010), argues that the twentieth-century movement to control population was an oppressive movement that failed to deliver on its promises. Now that population growth is slowing, the age of population control is over. Yet there remains the issue of "carrying capacity," defined very simply as the size of the population that the environment can support, or "carry," indefinitely, through both good and bad years. It is not the size of the population that can prosper in good times alone, for such a large population must suffer catastrophically when droughts, floods, or blights arrive or the climate warms or cools. It is a long-term concept, where "long term" means not decades or generations, nor even centuries, but millennia or more. See Mark Nathan Cohen, "Carrying Capacity," *Free Inquiry* (August/September 2004) and T.C.R. White, "The Role of Food, Weather, and Climate in Limiting the Abundance of Animals," *Biological Reviews* (August 2008).

What is the Earth's carrying capacity for human beings? It is surely impossible to set a precise figure on the number of human beings the world can support for the long run. As Joel E. Cohen discusses in *How Many People Can the Earth Support?* (W.W. Norton, 1996), estimates of the Earth's carrying capacity range from less than a billion to more than a trillion. The precise number depends on our choices of diet, standard of living, level of technology, willingness to share with others at home and abroad, and desire for an intact physical, chemical, and biological environment (including wildlife and natural environments), as well as on whether or not our morality permits restraint in reproduction and our political or religious ideology permits educating and empowering women. The key, Cohen stresses, is human choice, and the choices are ones we must make within the next 50 years. Phoebe Hall, "Carrying Capacity," *E—The Environmental Magazine* (March/April 2003), notes that even countries with large land areas and small populations, such as Australia and Canada, can be overpopulated in terms of resource availability. The critical resource appears to be food supply; see Russell Hopfenberg, "Human Carrying Capacity Is Determined by Food Availability," *Population & Environment* (November 2003).

Andrew R.B. Ferguson, in "Perceiving the Population Bomb," *World Watch* (July/August 2001), sets the maximum sustainable human population at about 2 billion. Sandra Postel, in the Worldwatch Institute's *State of the World 1994* (W.W. Norton, 1994), says, "As a result of our population size, consumption patterns, and technology choices, we have surpassed the planet's carrying capacity. This is plainly evident by the extent to which we are damaging and depleting natural capital" (including land and water).

If population growth is now declining and world population will actually begin to decline during this century, there is clearly a hope. But the question of carrying capacity remains. Most estimates of carrying capacity put it at well below the current world population size, and it will take a long time for global population to fall far enough to reach such levels. We seem to be moving in the right direction, but it remains an open question whether our numbers will decline far enough soon enough (i.e., before environmental problems become critical). On the other hand, Jeroen Van den Bergh and Piet

Rietveld, "Reconsidering the Limits to World Population: Meta-Analysis and Meta-Prediction," *Bioscience* (March 2004), set their best estimate of human global carrying capacity at 7.7 billion, which is distinctly reassuring. However, there is still a concern that global population will not stop at that point; see David R. Francis, "'Birth Dearth' Worries Pale in Comparison to Overpopulation," *Christian Science Monitor* (July 14, 2008).

How high a level will population actually reach? Fertility levels are definitely declining in many developed nations; see Alan Booth and Ann C. Crouter (eds.), *The New Population Problem: Why Families in Developed Countries Are Shrinking and What It Means* (Lawrence Erlbaum Associates, 2005). The visibility of this fertility decline is among the reasons mentioned by Martha Campbell, "Why the Silence on Population?" *Population and Environment* (May 2007). Is there an actual "birth dearth?" Not according to Doug Moss, "What Birth Dearth?" *E—The Environmental Magazine* (November–December 2006), who reminds us that there is still a large surplus of births—and therefore a growing population—in the less developed world. If we think globally, there is no shortage of people. However, many countries are so concerned about changing age distributions that they are trying to encourage larger—not smaller—families. See Robert Engelman, "Unnatural Increase? A Short History of Population Trends and Influences," *World Watch* (September/October 2008—a special issue on population issues) and his book *More: Population, Nature, and What Women Want* (Island Press, 2008).

Some people worry that a decline in population will not be good for human welfare. In the YES selection, Michael Meyer argues that a shrinking population will mean that the economic growth that has meant constantly increasing standards of living must come to an end, government programs (from war to benefits for the poor and elderly) will no longer be affordable, a shrinking number of young people will have to support a growing elderly population, and despite some environmental benefits, quality of life will suffer. In the NO selection, writer Julia Whitty argues that even though the topic of overpopulation has become unpopular, it is clear that we are already using the Earth's resources faster than they can be replenished and the only answer is to slow and eventually reverse population growth.

YES

Michael Meyer

Birth Dearth

Everyone knows there are too many people in the world. Whether we live in Lahore or Los Angeles, Shanghai or Sao Paulo, our lives are daily proof. We endure traffic gridlock, urban sprawl and environmental depredation. The evening news brings variations on Ramallah or Darfur—images of Third World famine, poverty, pestilence, war, global competition for jobs and increasingly scarce natural resources.

Just last week the United Nations warned that many of the world's cities are becoming hopelessly overcrowded. Lagos alone will grow from 6.5 million people in 1995 to 16 million by 2015, a miasma of slums and decay where a fifth of all children will die before they are 5. At a conference in London, the U.N. Population Fund weighed in with a similarly bleak report: unless something dramatically changes, the world's 50 poorest countries will triple in size by 2050, to 1.7 billion people.

Yet this is not the full story. To the contrary, in fact. Across the globe, people are having fewer and fewer children. Fertility rates have dropped by half since 1972, from six children per woman to 2.9. And demographers say they're still falling, faster than ever. The world's population will continue to grow—from today's 6.4 billion to around 9 billion in 2050. But after that, it will go sharply into decline. Indeed, a phenomenon that we're destined to learn much more about—depopulation—has already begun in a number of countries. Welcome to the New Demography. It will change everything about our world, from the absolute size and power of nations to global economic growth to the quality of our lives.

This revolutionary transformation will be led not so much by developed nations as by the developing ones. Most of us are familiar with demographic trends in Europe, where birthrates have been declining for years. To reproduce itself, a society's women must each bear 2.1 children. Europe's fertility rates fall far short of that, according to the 2002 U.N. population report. France and Ireland, at 1.8, top Europe's childbearing charts. Italy and Spain, at 1.2, bring up the rear. In between are countries such as Germany, whose fertility rate of 1.4 is exactly Europe's average. What does that mean? If the U.N. figures are right, Germany could shed nearly a fifth of its 82.5 million people over the next 40 years—roughly the equivalent of all of east Germany, a loss of population not seen in Europe since the Thirty Years' War.

And so it is across the Continent. Bulgaria will shrink by 38 percent, Romania by 27 percent, Estonia by 25 percent. "Parts of Eastern Europe, already sparsely populated, will just empty out," predicts Reiner Klingholz, director of the Berlin Institute for Population and Development. Russia is already losing close to 750,000 people yearly. (President Vladimir Putin calls it a "national crisis.") So is Western Europe, and that figure could grow to as much as 3 million a year by midcentury, if not more.

The surprise is how closely the less-developed world is following the same trajectory. In Asia it's well known that Japan will soon tip into population loss, if it hasn't already. With a fertility rate of 1.3 children per woman, the country stands to shed a quarter of its 127 million people over the next four decades, according to U.N. projections. But while the graying of Japan (average age: 42.3 years) has long been a staple of news headlines, what to make of China, whose fertility rate has declined from 5.8 in 1970 to 1.8 today, according to the U.N.? Chinese census data put the figure even lower, at 1.3. Coupled with increasing life spans, that means China's population will age as quickly in one generation as Europe's has over the past 100 years, reports the Center for Strategic and International Studies in Washington. With an expected median age of 44 in 2015, China will be older on average than the United States. By 2019 or soon after, its population will peak at 1.5 billion, then enter a steep decline. By midcentury, China could well lose 20 to 30 percent of its population every generation.

The picture is similar elsewhere in Asia, where birthrates are declining even in the absence of such stringent birth-control programs as China's. Indeed, it's happening despite often generous official incentives to procreate. The industrialized nations of Singapore, Hong Kong, Taiwan and South Korea all report subreplacement fertility, says Nicholas Eberstadt, a demographer at the American Enterprise Institute in Washington. To this list can be added Thailand, Burma, Australia and Sri Lanka, along with Cuba and many Caribbean nations, as well as Uruguay and Brazil. Mexico is aging so rapidly that within several decades it will not only stop growing but will have an older population than that of the United States. So much for the cliche of those Mexican youths swarming across the Rio Grande. "If these figures are accurate," says Eberstadt, "just about half of the world's population lives in subreplacement countries."

There are notable exceptions. In Europe, Albania and the outlier province of Kosovo are reproducing energetically. So are pockets of Asia: Mongolia, Pakistan and the Philippines. The United Nations projects that the Middle East will double in population over the next 20 years, growing from 326 million today to 649 million by 2050. Saudi Arabia has one of the highest fertility rates in the world, 5.7, after Palestinian territories at 5.9 and Yemen at 7.2. Yet there are surprises here, too. Tunisia has tipped below replacement. Lebanon and Iran are at the threshold. And though overall the region's population continues to grow, the increase is due mainly to lower infant mortality; fertility rates themselves are falling faster than in developed countries, indicating that over the coming decades the Middle East will age far more rapidly than other regions of the world. Birthrates in Africa remain high, and despite the AIDS

epidemic its population is projected to keep growing. So is that of the United States.

We'll return to American exceptionalism, and what that might portend. But first, let's explore the causes of the birth dearth, as outlined in a pair of new books on the subject. "Never in the last 650 years, since the time of the Black Plague, have birth and fertility rates fallen so far, so fast, so low, for so long, in so many places," writes the sociologist Ben Wattenberg in "Fewer: How the New Demography of Depopulation Will Shape Our Future." Why? Wattenberg suggests that a variety of once independent trends have conjoined to produce a demographic tsunami. As the United Nations reported last week, people everywhere are leaving the countryside and moving to cities, which will be home to more than half the world's people by 2007. Once there, having a child becomes a cost rather than an asset. From 1970 to 2000, Nigeria's urban population climbed from 14 to 44 percent. South Korea went from 28 to 84 percent. So-called megacities, from Lagos to Mexico City, have exploded seemingly overnight. Birthrates have fallen in inverse correlation.

Other factors are at work. Increasing female literacy and enrollment in schools have tended to decrease fertility, as have divorce, abortion and the worldwide trend toward later marriage. Contraceptive use has risen dramatically over the past decade; according to U.N. data, 62 percent of married or "in union" women of reproductive age are now using some form of nonnatural birth control. In countries such as India, now the capital of global HIV, disease has become a factor. In Russia, the culprits include alcoholism, poor public health and industrial pollution that has whacked male sperm counts. Wealth discourages childbearing, as seen long ago in Europe and now in Asia. As Wattenberg puts it, "Capitalism is the best contraception."

The potential consequences of the population implosion are enormous. Consider the global economy, as Phillip Longman describes it in another recent book, "The Empty Cradle: How Falling Birthrates Threaten World Prosperity and What to Do About It." A population expert at the New America Foundation in Washington, he sees danger for global prosperity. Whether it's real estate or consumer spending, economic growth and population have always been closely linked. "There are people who cling to the hope that you can have a vibrant economy without a growing population, but mainstream economists are pessimistic," says Longman. You have only to look at Japan or Europe for a whiff of what the future might bring, he adds. In Italy, demographers forecast a 40 percent decline in the working-age population over the next four decades—accompanied by a commensurate drop in growth across the Continent, according to the European Commission. What happens when Europe's cohort of baby boomers begins to retire around 2020? Recent strikes and demonstrations in Germany, Italy, France and Austria over the most modest pension reforms are only the beginning of what promises to become a major sociological battle between Europe's older and younger generations.

That will be only a skirmish compared with the conflict brewing in China. There market reforms have removed the cradle-to-grave benefits of the planned economy, while the Communist Party hasn't constructed an adequate social safety net to take their place. Less than one quarter of the population is covered

by retirement pensions, according to CSIS. That puts the burden of elder care almost entirely on what is now a generation of only children. The one-child policy has led to the so-called 4-2-1 problem, in which each child will be potentially responsible for caring for two parents and four grandparents.

Incomes in China aren't rising fast enough to offset this burden. In some rural villages, so many young people have fled to the cities that there may be nobody left to look after the elders. And the aging population could soon start to dull China's competitive edge, which depends on a seemingly endless supply of cheap labor. After 2015, this labor pool will begin to dry up, says economist Hu Angang. China will have little choice but to adopt a very Western-sounding solution, he says: it will have to raise the education level of its work force and make it more productive. Whether it can is an open question. Either way, this much is certain: among Asia's emerging economic powers, China will be the first to grow old before it gets rich.

Equally deep dislocations are becoming apparent in Japan. Akihiko Matsutani, an economist and author of a recent best seller, "The Economy of a Shrinking Population," predicts that by 2009 Japan's economy will enter an era of "negative growth." By 2030, national income will have shrunk by 15 percent. Speculating about the future is always dicey, but economists pose troubling questions. Take the legendarily high savings that have long buoyed the Japanese economy and financed borrowing worldwide, especially by the United States. As an aging Japan draws down those assets in retirement, will U.S. and global interest rates rise? At home, will Japanese businesses find themselves competing for increasingly scarce investment capital? And just what will they be investing in, as the country's consumers grow older, and demand for the latest in hot new products cools off? What of the effect on national infrastructure? With less tax revenue in state coffers, Matsutani predicts, governments will increasingly be forced to skimp on or delay repairs to the nation's roads, bridges, rail lines and the like. "Life will become less convenient," he says. Spanking-clean Tokyo might come to look more like New York City in the 1970s, when many urban dwellers decamped for the suburbs (taking their taxes with them) and city fathers could no longer afford the municipal upkeep. Can Japanese cope? "They will have to," says Matsutani. "There's no alternative."

Demographic change magnifies all of a country's problems, social as well as economic. An overburdened welfare state? Aging makes it collapse. Tensions over immigration? Differing birthrates intensify anxieties, just as the need for imported labor rises—perhaps the critical issue for the Europe of tomorrow. A poor education system, with too many kids left behind? Better fix it, because a shrinking work force requires higher productivity and greater flexibility, reflected in a new need for continuing job training, career switches and the health care needed to keep workers working into old age.

In an ideal world, perhaps, the growing gulf between the world's wealthy but shrinking countries and its poor, growing ones would create an opportunity. Labor would flow from the overpopulated, resource-poor south to the depopulating north, where jobs would continue to be plentiful. Capital and remittance income from the rich nations would flow along the reverse path, benefiting all. Will it happen? Perhaps, but that presupposes considerable labor mobility.

Considering the resistance Europeans display toward large-scale immigration from North Africa, or Japan's almost zero-immigration policy, it's hard to be optimistic. Yes, attitudes are changing. Only a decade ago, for instance, Europeans also spoke of zero immigration. Today they recognize the need and, in bits and pieces, are beginning to plan for it. But will it happen on the scale required?

A more probable scenario may be an intensification of existing tensions between peoples determined to preserve their beleaguered national identities on the one hand, and immigrant groups on the other seeking to escape overcrowding and lack of opportunity at home. For countries such as the Philippines—still growing, and whose educated work force looks likely to break out of low-status jobs as nannies and gardeners and move up the global professional ladder—this may be less of a problem. It will be vastly more serious for the tens of millions of Arab youths who make up a majority of the population in the Middle East and North Africa, at least half of whom are unemployed.

America is the wild card in this global equation. While Europe and much of Asia shrinks, the United States' indigenous population looks likely to stay relatively constant, with fertility rates hovering almost precisely at replacement levels. Add in heavy immigration, and you quickly see that America is the only modern nation that will continue to grow. Over the next 45 years the United States will gain 100 million people, Wattenberg estimates, while Europe loses roughly as many.

This does not mean that Americans will escape the coming demographic whammy. They, too, face the problems of an aging work force and its burdens. (The cost of Medicare and Social Security will rise from 4.3 percent of GDP in 2000 to 11.5 percent in 2030 and 21 percent in 2050, according to the Congressional Budget Office.) They, too, face the prospect of increasing ethnic tensions, as a flat white population and a dwindling black one become gradually smaller minorities in a growing multicultural sea. And in our interdependent era, the troubles of America's major trading partners—Europe and Japan—will quickly become its own. To cite one example, what becomes of the vaunted "China market," invested in so heavily by U.S. companies, if by 2050 China loses an estimated 35 percent of its workers and the aged consume an ever-greater share of income?

America's demographic "unipolarity" has profound security implications as well. Washington worries about terrorism and failing states. Yet the chaos of today's fragmented world is likely to prove small in comparison to what could come. For U.S. leaders, Longman in "The Empty Cradle" sketches an unsettling prospect. Though the United States may have few military competitors, the technologies by which it projects geopolitical power—from laser-guided missiles and stealth bombers to a huge military infrastructure—may gradually become too expensive for a country facing massively rising social entitlements in an era of slowing global economic growth. If the war on terrorism turns out to be the "generational struggle" that national-security adviser Condoleezza Rice says it is, Longman concludes, then the United States might have difficulty paying for it.

None of this is writ, of course. Enlightened governments could help hold the line. France and the Netherlands have instituted family-friendly policies

that help women combine work and motherhood, ranging from tax credits for kids to subsidized day care. Scandinavian countries have kept birthrates up with generous provisions for parental leave, health care and part-time employment. Still, similar programs offered by the shrinking city-state of Singapore—including a state-run dating service—have done little to reverse the birth dearth. Remember, too, that such prognoses have been wrong in the past. At the cusp of the postwar baby boom, demographers predicted a sharp fall in fertility and a global birth dearth. Yet even if this generation of seers turns out to be right, as seems likely, not all is bad. Environmentally, a smaller world is almost certainly a better world, whether in terms of cleaner air or, say, the return of wolves and rare flora to abandoned stretches of the East German countryside. And while people are living longer, they are also living healthier—at least in the developed world. That means they can (and probably should) work more years before retirement.

Yes, a younger generation will have to shoulder the burden of paying for their elders. But there will be compensations. As populations shrink, says economist Matsutani, national incomes may drop—but not necessarily per capita incomes. And in this realm of uncertainty, one mundane thing is probably sure: real-estate prices will fall. That will hurt seniors whose nest eggs are tied up in their homes, but it will be a boon to youngsters of the future. Who knows? Maybe the added space and cheap living will inspire them to, well, do whatever it takes to make more babies. Thus the cycle of life will restore its balance. . . .

Julia Whitty  **NO**

The Last Taboo

What unites the Vatican, lefties, conservatives, environmentalists, and scientists in a conspiracy of silence?

It's midnight on the streets of Calcutta. Old women cook over open fires on the sidewalks. Men wait in line at municipal hand pumps to lather skin, hair, and lungis (skirts), bathing without undressing. Girls sit in the open beds of bicycle-powered trucks, braiding their hair. The monsoon's not yet over, and grandfathers under umbrellas squat on their heels, arguing over card games, while mothers hold bare-bottomed toddlers over open latrines. On every other block, shops the size of broom closets are still open, kerosene lights blazing, their proprietors seated cross-legged on tiny shelves built above their wares of plastic buckets or machetes or radios. Many people sleep through the lively darkness, draped over sacks or on work carts full of paper or rags or hay. Groups of men and women, far from their home villages, sprawl haphazardly across the sidewalks, snoring.

I'm crossing the city in one of Calcutta's famously broken-down Ambassador taxis. The seat's been replaced with a box, the windows don't work, there never were seat belts. Sneezes of rain blow through. It's always like this, arriving in the dead of night after incomprehensibly long international flights, exiting the hermetically sealed jet onto humid and smoky streets perfumed with gardenias and shit. The coal haze is thick as magician's smoke. Out of the dark, suddenly, the huge haunches of a working elephant appear, tail switching, big feet plodding carefully over piles of garbage, each footfall spooking a hungry dog. The mahout tucked between her ears nonchalantly chats on a cell phone. . . .

That so many can live among the ruins seems impossible. Yet so many do. The city is home to about 5 million people, at a population density of 70,000 per square mile—2.5 times more crowded than New York City. Another 9 million live in the urban agglomeration, bringing the population of greater Kolkata to 14 million. More are added every day—though not as many as you might expect from births. Kolkata's fertility rate (the average number of children born to a woman) is only 1.35, well below the global replacement average of 2.34 (the number where population stabilizes as births balance with deaths). Instead, the city's growth is fueled largely through migration from a poorer and more fertile countryside.

What supports the crowds of Kolkata are what supports life everywhere: air, water, food, fuel, climate. Three hundred miles north of the city rises the mighty buttress of the Himalayas, home to 18,000 glaciers covering an area of ice larger than Maryland. After the Arctic and Antarctic, this "third pole" holds Earth's greatest freshwater reserve, supplying the outflows of some of the globe's mightiest rivers—Ganges, Yarlung Tsangpo, Brahmaputra—water for one in seven people on Earth. Fifty miles to the south of Kolkata, at the end of those rivers, lies the enormous Bay of Bengal, where 3 million tons of seafood are netted, hooked, and trawled annually. In highlands to the north and south lie the seams of coal that fuel the city.

Seen from above, the circulatory system of roads and railroads of the Indian east—home to 300 million people, roughly the same as the US—funnels into Kolkata, with trucks and freight trains running day and night, laden with fuel, fish, and food. The city itself funnels into a central core, a defensible bend in the Hooghly River and the classic star-shaped, 18th-century Fort William—a stronghold harking back to a time when wealth was measured in tea, silk, jute, ivory, and gemstones, and when survival was assured with cannon fire.

Survival in the 21st century is different. Its real measure lies in the depth of the snowpack in the Himalayas, in the sustainable tonnage of fish caught in the Bay of Bengal, in the inches of topsoil remaining on the Indian plains, and in the parts per million of coal smoke in the air. The root cause of India's dwindling resources and escalating pollution is the same: the continued exponential growth of humankind.

As recently as 1965, when the world population stood at 3.3 billion, we collectively taxed only 70 percent of the Earth's biocapacity each year. That is, we used only 7/10 of the land, water, and air the planet could regenerate or repair yearly to produce what we consumed and to absorb our greenhouse gas emissions. According to the Global Footprint Network, a California think tank, we first overdrew our accounts in 1983, when our population of nearly 4.7 billion began to consume natural resources faster than they could be replenished—a phenomenon called "ecological overshoot." Last year, 6.8 billion of us consumed the renewable resources of 1.4 Earths.

The United Nations projects that world population will stabilize at 9.1 billion in 2050. This prediction assumes a decline from the current average global fertility rate of 2.56 children per woman to 2.02 children per woman in the years between 2045 and 2050. But should mothers average half a child more in 2045, the world population will peak at 10.5 billion five years later. Half a child less, and it stabilizes at 8 billion. The difference in those projections—2.5 billion—is the total number of people alive on Earth in 1950.

The only known solution to ecological overshoot is to decelerate our population growth faster than it's decelerating now and eventually reverse it—at the same time we slow and eventually reverse the rate at which we consume the planet's resources. Success in these twin endeavors will crack our most pressing global issues: climate change, food scarcity, water supplies, immigration, health care, biodiversity loss, even war. On one front, we've already made unprecedented strides, reducing global fertility from an average 4.92 children per woman in 1950 to 2.56 today—an accomplishment of

trial and sometimes brutally coercive error, but also a result of one woman at a time making her individual choices. The speed of this childbearing revolution, swimming hard against biological programming, rates as perhaps our greatest collective feat to date.

But it's not enough. And it's still not fast enough. Faced with a world that can support either a lot of us consuming a lot less or far fewer of us consuming more, we're deadlocked: individuals, governments, the media, scientists, environmentalists, economists, human rights workers, liberals, conservatives, business and religious leaders. On the supremely divisive question of the ideal size of the human family, we're amazingly united in a pact of silence.

"Overpopulation, combined with overconsumption, is the elephant in the room," says Paul Ehrlich, 42 years after he wrote his controversial book, *The Population Bomb.* "We don't talk about overpopulation because of real fears from the past—of racism, eugenics, colonialism, forced sterilization, forced family planning, plus the fears from some of contraception, abortion, and sex. We don't really talk about overconsumption because of ignorance about the economics of overpopulation and the true ecological limits of Earth."

Core differences about how the population issue is viewed have reinforced the paralysis. Conservationists tended to frame the issue as people vs. nature, while human rights activists found this analysis simplistic and even racist, failing to address what they saw as the core problems of poverty and environmental injustice. Yet they in turn have tended to deny the limits of growth. Add the tension between rich and poor nations, and the issue quickly becomes radioactive. "In the developing world," says Kavita Ramdas, the president and CEO of the San Francisco-based Global Fund for Women, "the problem of population is seen less as a matter of human numbers than of Western overconsumption. Yet within the development community, the only solution to the problems of the developing world is to export the same unsustainable economic model fueling the overconsumption of the West."

I'm returning to India, where the dynamics of overpopulation and overconsumption are most acute, where the lifelines between water, food, fuel, and 1.17 billion people—17 percent of humanity subsisting on less than 2.5 percent of the globe's land—are already stretched dangerously thin. India's population is projected to surpass China's by 2030 in a country only a third China's size—adding 400 million citizens between now and 2050. But that's the mid-level projection. A slight up-tick in global fertility, and it may be home to a staggering 2 billion people by 2050. Here, before anywhere else on Earth, the challenges of 20th-century family planning will become a 21st-century fight for survival.

Eden Hospital is a 19th-century marble marvel hidden behind spindly bamboo scaffolding at Kolkata's Medical College. Its threshold is swamped by an outpouring of families, each shielding a mother and a swaddled newborn. It takes me a while to ford the flood. Inside, up an ancient, dark, and gritty central stairway, down a veranda lined with multi-bed wards and separated by jalousie doors hanging from rusted hinges, my mother was born 80 years ago, as were many of my relatives before and after her.

Eden maternity hospital was a wonder in its day, opened optimistically in 1881 to accommodate some 80 women, primarily Europeans and Anglo-Indians: the biracial Eurasian community sired by the Raj. In 1881, there was an understanding that human population was growing, thanks to the Reverend Thomas Robert Malthus' 1798 *An Essay on the Principle of Population*. Malthus, a political economist, argued that humans were destined to grow geometrically, while food production could increase only arithmetically, guaranteeing that famine would cinch the growth of humankind within the scarce purse of resources.

And so it did. For 150 years after Malthus, hunger killed millions: perhaps 50 million Chinese in multiple famines of the 19th century; upwards of 20 million Indians during a dozen major famines in the latter half of the 19th century; a million in the Great Famine of Ireland between 1845 and 1852; one-third of the local population in the Ethiopian Great Famine of 1888 to 1892; 3 million in Bengal in 1943.

Malthus' mathematical concerns about population growth developed inside an 18th-century moral framework we still wrestle with today. According to him, poor people grew their numbers irresponsibly and were kept in check by their own bad habits and addictions: "The vices of mankind are active and able ministers of depopulation." He opposed government assistance to the poor on the grounds that it enabled more people to reproduce without the means to support themselves. He advocated that the surplus population be allowed to decrease of its own accord—a suggestion that reportedly inspired Charles Dickens to pen the tale of misanthrope Ebenezer Scrooge.

In later editions of his essay, Malthus suggested a solution to the growing numbers of impoverished people he considered poor specimens, a eugenics-like answer popular in his time, based on animal husbandry and designed to "upgrade" the human race: "[B]y an attention to breed, a certain degree of improvement similar to that among animals might take place among men," he wrote. "Whether intellect could be communicated may be a matter of doubt; but size, strength, beauty, complexion, and, perhaps, even longevity, are in a degree transmissible." . . .

India today prides itself on being the world's largest democracy. But it's also the hungriest, only recently and barely liberated from "the most dreadful famines" Malthus wrote of. One of every two underfed people on Earth lives here. Forty percent of Indian children under the age of five are underweight and stunted. More than 4 percent of the 26 million babies born here every year die within their first month of life, a neonatal mortality rate surpassing even India's war-torn neighbor, Sri Lanka. Worse, India's underfed are not decreasing, as one might expect from one of the world's fastest growing economies, but increasing. India's economic boom has surged past most Indians, leaving 53 percent in poverty, according to the calculations of one Indian government commission. In the state of Bihar, next door to West Bengal, 9 of 10 rural children are anemic, a telltale marker of hunger and malnutrition.

In *The Population Bomb,* Ehrlich predicted inevitable mass starvation as early as the 1970s and 1980s—notably in India, which he claimed could not possibly attain food self-sufficiency. Instead, American agronomist Norman Borlaug's "Green Revolution" brought dwarf wheat strains and chemical fertilizers to increase India's crop yields 168 percent within a decade. This monumental achievement defused the bomb and earned Ehrlich the dismissive title of Malthusian: just one more in a line of pessimists forecasting phantom famines. Ever since, the subject has been largely taboo. Scientists from a variety of fields privately tell me the issue of overpopulation is simply too controversial—too inflamed with passions to get funded, too strong a magnet for ideologues. Those who've tackled it tell me of harassment, even physical threats, from a frightening fringe.

Take the near-civil war within the Sierra Club—whose former executive director, David Brower, originally suggested Ehrlich write *The Population Bomb.* The Sierra Club had long supported population stabilization. But started in the early 1990s, anti-immigration activists spurred by John Tanton—who controls an array of English-only, zero-immigration, and nativist groups—stealthily twice attempted to take over the board. Perhaps naively, some Sierra Club stalwarts concerned with population joined their cause. The battle lasted for a decade, culminating when Morris Dees of the Southern Poverty Law Center ran for Sierra's board in an effort to expose Tanton's true agenda—and the fact that one of his groups had accepted money from white supremacists. Ehrlich's NGO Zero Population Growth then parted ways with Tanton (a past president), renamed itself the Population Connection, and embraced an end-poverty-to-curb-population approach. Ehrlich and his wife Anne, a conservation biologist, also left the board of Tanton's Federation for American Immigration Reform. Yet the scars between environmentalists and the development community are only beginning to heal. "When you talk about population," says Larry Fahn, Sierra Club president during some of the bitterest infighting, "the immigration people come out of the woodwork with their hate mongering. It's unfortunate that the subject brings out a racist agenda."

Abortion is even more toxically associated with population debates. "Many conservation and nongovernmental organizations that run on member support, even the big ones, shy away from the population issue," says Ed Barry of the Population Institute in Washington, DC, a nonprofit founded in 1969 by a United Methodist Church minister. "That's because it puts their funding at risk. Even if you're talking about population as a sustainability issue, there's often an automatic assumption you'll be talking about abortion."

Voiced or not, addressed or not; the problem of overpopulation has not gone away. The miracle of the Green Revolution, which fed billions and provided the world a sense of limitless hope, also disguised four ominous truths about Earth's limits. First, the revolution's most effective agents, chemical fertilizers of nitrogen and phosphorus, are destined to run out, along with the natural resources used to produce them. Second, the fertilizers, pesticides, and herbicides that grew the food that enabled our enormous population growth in the 20th century bore expensive downstream costs in the form of polluted land, water, and air that now threaten life. Third, crop yields today are holding

stubbornly stable and even beginning to fall in some places, despite increasing fertilizer use, in soils oversaturated with nitrogen.

The Green Revolution's duplicitous harvest—giving life with one hand, robbing life-support with the other—also masked a fourth ominous truth. We're running out of topsoil, tossing it to the wind via mechanized agriculture and losing it to runoff and erosion. Geomorphologist David Montgomery, author of *Dirt: The Erosion of Civilizations* and 2008 recipient of a MacArthur "genius" fellowship, calculates that human activities are eroding topsoil 10 times faster than it can be replenished. "Just when we need more soil to feed the 10 billion people of the future," he says, "we'll actually have less—only a quarter of an acre of cropland per person in 2050, versus the half-acre we use today on the most efficient farms." Plus there's little new land to bring into production: "We could, with crippling environmental costs, raze the Amazonian rainforests and reap 5 to 10 years of crops before the tropical soils failed. But the fertile prairies of the Midwest, northern China, and northern Europe are already plowed to capacity and shrinking."

In India, the problem of peak soil is already acute. Nearly a quarter of its lands, more than 314,000 square miles, are desert or in the process of becoming desert, according to a recent Indian government report. Desertification will double India's current water usage by 2030, as more water is rerouted to irrigate an increasingly drier landscape to grow rice, wheat, and sugar for an increasing population, including the growing demands of a growing middle class. McKinsey & Co., the global management consulting firm, forecasts severe deficits in water—and, by default, food—in India by 2030.

Combine peak oil and peak topsoil with global warming, and a study in the peer-reviewed journal *Science* predicts a 20 to 30 percent decline in crop yields in the next 80 years. Alarmingly, the process of photosynthesis itself declines precipitously as temperatures rise above 86 degrees Fahrenheit, making it increasingly difficult to maintain—let alone increase—crop yields. (The European heat wave of 2003 that killed up to 50,000 people also slashed crop harvests by as much as 36 percent.) Rising temperatures and the resulting drier landscapes will put our major food crops in the lower latitudes (including all of India) at risk in the near future. "I grow increasingly concerned that we have not yet understood what it will take to feed a growing population on a warming planet," says Penn State biologist and lead author Nina Fedoroff. Furthermore, India's "atmospheric brown cloud"—the smog that fouls the subcontinent between monsoons—could undermine crop yields by up to 40 percent. Not only is there more smog in Asia, but Asian crops appear more sensitive to smog than crops in North America or Europe, even crops of the same variety. No one knows why.

The UN calculates that 36 million die of hunger and malnutrition every year—a person every second, mostly women and children. Famine is no phantom, and history may yet remember Paul Ehrlich as the premature prophet, not the false one, his predictions off by decades rather than degree. . . .

The problem is long in the making. Ever since Homo sapiens invented agriculture, we've sported super-prolific birth rates, counterbalanced by brutishly short life expectancies averaging a mere 10 years. We bred and died in

boom cycles busted by famines, natural disasters, diseases, and violence. Beginning around 500 AD, we suffered centuries of bust, ravaged by the Black Death and its piggybacking disasters sweeping west from Asia—the last check on our growth. Nothing since then, not the lethal 20th century, with two world wars, an influenza pandemic, and the emergence of HIV/AIDS, has reversed our growth.

Driven by inescapable biology that seduces us with the joys of sex, we populate, and then some. We plan our families. Or we don't. Two hundred million women have no access whatsoever to contraception, contributing to the one in four unplanned births worldwide and the 50 million pregnancies aborted each year, half of them performed clandestinely, killing 68,000 women in the process. As for the conventional wisdom that poor rural couples actively plan to have large families because of high child mortality or to provide for their care in old age, not true, says John Guillebaud, emeritus professor of family planning and reproductive health at University College, London. Instead, poor people have large families simply because they, like most of us, have sex many, many times in their lifetimes and some of those times, or even all of those times, they do not have, or do not use, contraceptives, or their contraceptives fail. "For a fertile couple, nothing is easier," says Guillebaud. Planned or not, wanted or not, 139 million new people are added every year: more than an entire Japan, nearly an entire Russia, minus the homelands and the resources to go along with them. Countered against the 56 million deaths annually, our world gains 83 million extra people every year, the equivalent of another Iran. That's 1.6 million more humans alive this week than last week and 227,000 more people today than yesterday—all needing food, water, homes, and medicine for an average lifespan of 69 years. We are asking our world to supply an additional 2.1 trillion human-days of life support every single year. Eventually, most of these 83 million new people added every year will have kids, too.

Understood or not, the exponential growth model—also known as the Malthusian growth model—runs in the background, amplifying our child-bearing choices. In a new twist on the downstream effects, statistician Paul Murtaugh of Oregon State University decided to investigate the environmental price tag of a baby. "Suddenly we can gauge our carbon emissions from all kinds of lifestyle choices, like cars, appliances, and airplane flights," he says. "But there's no calculator computing the carbon emissions of a child—and her children, and her children." (Murtaugh ran the statistical analysis on mothers, because following lineages of both parents was computationally prohibitive.)

"The results surprised me," he says. "Using United Nations projections of fertility, and projecting statistically through the lifespan of the mother's line—some lineages being short-lived, others indefinitely long—an American child born today adds an average 10,407 tons of carbon dioxide to the carbon legacy of her mother. That's almost six times more CO_2 than the mother's own lifetime emissions. Furthermore, the ecological costs of that child and her children far outweigh even the combined energy-saving choices from all a mother's other good decisions, like buying a fuel-efficient car, recycling, using energy-saving appliances and lightbulbs. The carbon legacy of one American

child and her offspring is 20 times greater than all those other sustainable maternal choices combined."

Murtaugh's research shows that even though India has a much larger population and a higher rate of population growth than the US, its overall carbon legacy is vastly reduced, due to its population's drastically lower levels of consumption combined with shorter lifespans (63.8 years on average for India, versus 80.2 years for the US): At current rates, an American child has 55 times the carbon legacy of a child born to a family in India. While India is conservatively predicted to grow by 400 million people by 2050, the US is projected to grow by 86 million. But take those additional Americans and factor in their 55-times-higher carbon legacy (at current national consumption rates), and they will equal the legacy of 4.7 billion Indians.

"The irony," says Ramdas of the Global Fund for Women, "is that just as some Americans are starting to learn to live more like traditional Indians— becoming vegetarian, buying locally, eating organic—aspiring middle-class Indians are trying to live more like overconsuming Americans. The question really is, which kind of people do we want less of?" . . .

Looking back now, we can see that India's population course in the 20th century took a surprisingly predictable path—because we know what Thomas Robert Malthus could not know: that nations wend through multiple stages of a demographic transition on their way to and through industrialization.

Until the late 18th century, everyone everywhere subsisted in the nasty, brutish, and short conditions of stage one: extremely high birth rates coupled with extremely high death rates, resulting in slow population growth. Malthus himself lived through Britain's stage two: the onset of urbanization and industrialization and a true population explosion, as birth rates leveled but death rates plunged dramatically. Stage two first occurred in northern Europe and was spawned (ironically, despite Malthus' fears) by more and better food: the superior nutrition of corn and potatoes imported from the Americas, and an agricultural revolution brought on by scientific advances in farming. Stage two was also triggered by a revolution in our understanding of disease, which led to better handling of water, sewage, food, and ourselves. The primary driver behind this new science of hygiene was increased literacy among women, who wrote and read health-education pamphlets, and who managed the daily cleanliness of families and hospitals.

India today is navigating stage three, as fertility rates drop closer to death rates. Stage three includes a contraceptive revolution, different in every time and place: in Europe 200 years ago, a revolution of coitus interruptus and condoms; in India today, birth control pills and, often, sterilization after the first son is born. This pivotal phase coincides with profound cultural changes, as women end their isolation in the home to enter the workplace and network with other women. Wage-earning women claim more responsibility for childbearing and child-rearing decisions, leading to a revolution in children's lives, as the decision is made to pay for schooling—a costly choice necessitating smaller families. This choice is strongly influenced by female literacy, since women who can read even slightly are more likely to send their daughters to school.

In India today, 75 percent of men are literate, compared to only 54 percent of women—one of the most lopsided ratios among newly industrialized nations. The statistic corresponds directly to fertility. In the state of Bihar, next door to West Bengal, where literacy falls below the national average—to 60 percent for males and 33 percent for females—the total fertility rate swings up to four children per woman. Conversely, the southern Indian state of Kerala, which boasts 94 percent male literacy and 88 percent female literacy, has reached a below-replacement-rate fertility that resembles the industrialized world's, at only 1.9 children per woman.

Whether we are a world of 8, 9.1, or 10.5 billion people in 2050 will be decided in no small part by the number of illiterate women on Earth. Of the more than 1 in 10 people who can't read or write today, two-thirds are female. Locate them, and you'll find an uncannily accurate roadmap of societal strife—of civil wars, foreign wars, the wars against reason embedded in religiosity, the wars against equality ingrained in patriarchal and caste systems.

Sheryl WuDunn, the Pulitzer Prize-winning coauthor (along with her husband, *New York Times* columnist Nicholas Kristof) of *Half the Sky: Turning Oppression into Opportunity for Women Worldwide,* explains: "When women are educated, they tend to marry later in life, to have children later in life, and to have fewer children. In effect, you have a form of population control that's peaceful, voluntary, and efficient. Plus, educated women do better in business, raising economic growth rates, and lowering societal conflict. If we could achieve universal literacy for women, we'd have a much better shot at peace around the world." . . .

⋘◈⋙

The best family plans, the best intentions of any woman, can be waylaid by her government, since politics control fertility with godlike powers. In 2003, the predominantly Catholic Philippines bowed to church demands to support only "natural family planning"—otherwise known as the rhythm method, and grimly referred to as Vatican roulette. The Filipino government no longer provides contraceptives for poor Filipinas, and government clinics no longer distribute donated contraceptives, including the wealth of modern birth control once provided by the US Agency for International Development. (Filipina Health Secretary Esperanza Cabral, however, continues defiantly to distribute free condoms to combat rising HIV infection rates.)

Today more than half of all pregnancies in the Philippines are unplanned—10 percent more than a decade ago. In a first-of-its-kind study in the Philippines, the Guttmacher Institute calculates that easy access to contraception would reduce those births by 800,000 and abortions by half a million a year. Furthermore, it would deliver a net savings to the government on the order of $16.5 million a year in reduced health costs from unwanted pregnancies, including the brutal medical consequences of illegal back-alley abortions.

In Iran, the fertility pendulum has gone the other way in recent years. From a high of 7.7 in 1966, total fertility fell to 6 during the Shah's reign; spiked to 7 during the Islamic Revolution (when marriage became legal for 12-year-old

boys and 9-year-old girls), then plummeted 50 percent between 1988 and 1996, continuing down to 1.7 today. That plunge, known as the "Iranian miracle," was one of the most rapid fertility declines ever recorded.

Iran's demographic reversal was swift, uniform, and voluntary. Women of all childbearing ages in urban and rural parts of the country simply began to have smaller families practically overnight. Demographer Mohammad Jalal Abbasi-Shavazi of the University of Tehran writes that the feat was engineered through a mobilization between government and media: Information was broadcast nationwide about the value of small families, followed up with education about birth control, implemented with free contraceptives. Progressive social measures further primed Iran: increasing public education for girls (today more than 60 percent of Iranian university students are women); a new health care system; access to electricity, safe water, transportation, and communication. Similar fertility reversals have occurred in Costa Rica, Cuba, South Korea, Taiwan, Thailand, Tunisia, and Morocco—as quickly as in China but minus the brutal one-child policy.

The United States, plagued by its own ping-pong policy, has been little help. Beginning with Ronald Reagan in 1984, the "global gag rule," also known as the Mexico City Policy, prohibited US funding of any foreign family planning organizations providing abortions. The gag rule barred the discussion of abortion or any critique of unsafe abortions, even if these medical services were implemented with the group's own money (a ruling that would have been unconstitutional in the US). Bill Clinton rescinded the policy in 1993, but George W. Bush reinstated it in 2001, and before Barack Obama could rescind it again, the flow of aid to developing countries slowed or even stopped, eviscerating health care and severely undermining family planning efforts in at least 26 developing nations, primarily in Africa. (See "Sex, American Style," page 45.)

Joanna Nerquaye-Tetteh, former executive director of the Planned Parenthood Association of Ghana, testified before Congress in 2004 on the policy's effects in her country. "The gag rule completely disrupted decades of investment in building up health care services," she said. "We couldn't provide contraceptives and services to nearly 40,000 women who had formerly used our services. We saw within a year a rise in sexually transmitted infections and more women coming to our clinics for post-abortion care as a result of unsafe abortions."

Although it's unclear how many babies were added to the human family as a result of the global gag rule, the UN estimates that at its height in 2005, the unmet demand for contraceptives and family planning drove up fertility rates between 15 and 35 percent in Latin America, the Caribbean, the Arab states, Asia, and Africa—a whole generation of unplanned Bush babies. . . .

Rajendra Pachauri, cowinner of a Nobel Prize for his chairmanship of the Intergovernmental Panel on Climate Change, warns that India's growing population can't afford increased consumption levels. "We can't support lifestyles

even remotely like those in Europe and North America," he says. "We need policy initiatives to assure this doesn't happen. But the movement has to take place in both hemispheres. Awareness has to be raised in both the East and the West to deglamorize unsurvivable consumerism."

On the top floor of the Tiger Hill Pavilion, the people in the super deluxe lounge are sipping their complimentary tea. Among them are Indians who have returned from abroad, a few Europeans, Australians, and North Americans—the representatives of the fourth stage of the model of demographic transition, where population is stable and aging. In most industrialized countries, fertility has fallen below replacement level, and population is declining. Many aging nations introduce pro-natalist policies, so-called, baby bonuses designed to keep their retired populace comfortably retired, supported by younger, working people. It's an effective strategy. "But it's nutty," says Paul Ehrlich. "These highest-consuming populations are exactly the ones we need to allow to naturally shrink."

Meanwhile, somewhere in the super deluxe lounge may be a person or two representing a trend that's taken demographers by surprise. It's the unexpected emergence of what appears to be a fifth stage in the demographic transition, a development important enough to warrant another paper in the preeminent scientific journal, *Nature*. This fifth stage is upending a key tenet of social science: that increasing wealth, education, and gender equality invariably and irreversibly trigger a decline in fertility and a smaller population. Instead, demographers have discovered that in 18 of the 24 most highly developed countries—the US, Denmark, Germany, Spain, Norway, the Netherlands, Belgium, Luxembourg, Finland, Israel, Italy, Sweden, France, Iceland, the UK, New Zealand, Greece, and Ireland (the exceptions: Japan, Canada, Australia, Austria, Switzerland, and South Korea)—fertility has flipped. As of 2005, women in these countries were having more children than in previous years—stalling out their nation's straightforward decline in fertility (though birth rates still remain below replacement rates). This small but important fertility increase is good news for those who worry about Social Security deficits, but bad news for those who worry about societal security on a planet with finite resources.

The study leaves the causes unaddressed, leaving us to wonder: What portion is due to the cultural norms of new immigrants? Or to abstinence education? The only known correlates are the highest levels of economic and social development. Perhaps the core question is, how much has our silence around population growth contributed to the emergence of this fifth demographic stage? Even in rich nations, most families calculate the costs of each child in their household budget—in the size of their house, the need for quality child care, and college costs. So would these same families make different decisions if they were calculating the costs of each child in their (equally limited) planetary budget—in the costs of clean air, water, and adequate food for all?

Four decades ago, Norman Borlaug warned in his Nobel acceptance speech that his Green Revolution would grant only a temporary respite from the issue of our own population: "There can be no permanent progress in the battle against hunger until the agencies that fight for increased food production and

those that fight for population control unite in a common effort." In the next 40 years, as we add somewhere between 1 and nearly 4 billion more people, as at least some of these newcomers achieve a deservedly better standard of living, the challenges to survival will become daunting—not just for the people of India but for people everywhere.

The paradox embedded in our future is that the fastest way to slow our population growth is to reduce poverty, yet the fastest way to run out of resources is to increase wealth. The trial ahead is to strike the delicate compromise: between fewer people, and more people with fewer needs . . . all within a new economy geared toward sustainability. Perhaps this is the sixth stage in our demographic maturity: the transition from 20th-century family planning to 21st-century civilizational planning. The shift may seem daunting, but some of it's already happening. Birth rates continue to fall. And slowly but surely our focus converges as we realize that our common future is entwined with the fate of this small world. . . .

EXPLORING THE ISSUE

Do Falling Birth Rates Pose a Threat to Human Welfare?

Critical Thinking and Reflection

1. Is it possible to have too many people on the Earth?
2. What is wrong with the statement that there is no population problem because all of Earth's human population could fit inside the state of Texas?
3. What does population have to do with sustainability?
4. Why is talking about the population problem taboo?

Is There Common Ground?

The essayists for this issue agree that human welfare is the paramount goal. They disagree on the best way to maintain and improve it.

1. Does quality of life seem likely to suffer more with a declining population or a growing population?
2. What are the key features of "quality of life?" (One good place to start your research is http://www.foe.co.uk/community/tools/isew/.)
3. How might we determine what the Earth's carrying capacity for human beings really is?

ISSUE 8

Is There Sufficient Scientific Evidence to Conclude That Cell Phones Cause Cancer?

YES: Olga V. Naidenko, from testimony before Senate Committee on Appropriations, Subcommittee on Labor, Health and Human Services, and Education, and Related Agencies, hearing on "The Health Effects of Cell Phone Use" (September 14, 2009)

NO: Linda S. Erdreich, from testimony before Senate Committee on Appropriations, Subcommittee on Labor, Health and Human Services, and Education, and Related Agencies, hearing on "The Health Effects of Cell Phone Use" (September 14, 2009)

Learning Outcomes

After studying this issue, students will be able to explain:

1. What the evidence says about the link between cell phone use and brain cancer.
2. Why the scientific method does not require a mechanism that produces an effect to be confident the effect exists.
3. What the greatest risks associated with cell phone use are.
4. How one may reduce possible cell phone cancer risks without giving up the technology.

ISSUE SUMMARY

YES: Olga V. Naidenko argues that even though past research into the link between cell phones and cancer has produced ambiguous results, more recent research on people who have used cell phones for many years has produced more worrisome results. More research is needed, but concern is already amply justified, especially in connection with children's exposure to cell phone emissions of radio waves.

NO: Linda S. Erdreich argues that independent scientific organizations have reviewed the research to date on the supposed link

between cell phones and cancer and concluded that current evidence does not demonstrate that wireless phones cause cancer or have other adverse health effects.

It seems inevitable that new technologies will alarm people. For example, in the late 1800s, when electricity was new, people feared the new wires that were strung overhead. See Joseph P. Sullivan, "Fearing Electricity: Overhead Wire Panic in New York City," *IEEE Technology and Society Magazine* (Fall 1995). More recently, electromagnetic fields (EMFs) have drawn attention. Now cell phones and other forms of wireless communications technology, including wireless networks (wi-fi), are the focus of controversy.

EMFs are emitted by any device that uses electricity. They weaken rapidly as one gets farther from the source, but they can be remarkably strong close to the source. Users of electric blankets (before the blankets were redesigned to minimize EMFs) and personal computers are thus subject to high exposures. Since EMF strength also depends on how much electricity is flowing through the source, people who live near power lines, especially high-tension, long-distance transmission lines, are also open to high EMF exposure.

Are EMFs dangerous? There have been numerous reports suggesting a link between EMF exposure and cancer, but inconsistency has been the curse of research in this area. In 1992 the Committee on Interagency Radiation Research and Policy Coordination, an arm of the White House's Office of Science and Technology Policy, released *Health Effects of Low Frequency Electric and Magnetic Fields,* a report that concluded, "There is no convincing [published] evidence . . . to support the contention that exposures to extremely low frequency electric and magnetic fields generated by sources such as household appliances, video terminals, and local powerlines are demonstrable health hazards." Jon Palfreman, in "Apocalypse Not," *Technology Review* (April 1996), summarized the controversy and the evidence against any connection between cancer and EMFs. And in "Residential Exposure to Magnetic Fields and Acute Lymphoblastic Leukemia in Children," *The New England Journal of Medicine* (July 3, 1997), Martha S. Linet, et al. report that they failed to find any support for such a connection.

Since cell phones are electrical devices, they emit EMFs. But they—or their antennae—also emit electromagnetic radiation in the form of radio signals. And after a few cell phone users developed brain cancer and sued the phone makers, people began to worry. See Gordon Bass, "Is Your Cell Phone Killing You?" *PC Computing* (December 1999). George Carlo and Martin Schram, *Cell Phones: Invisible Hazards in the Wireless Age: An Insider's Alarming Discoveries about Cancer and Genetic Damage* (Basic Books, 2002), contend that there is a genuine risk that cell phone EMFs may cause cancer and other health problems. Tamar Nordenberg, "Cell Phones and Brain Cancer: No Clear Connection," *FDA Consumer* (November–December 2000), reported no real signs that cell phones caused cancer but noted that the evidence was sufficient to justify continuing research.

Do cell phones pose a genuine hazard? L. Hardell, et al. reported, in "Cellular and Cordless Telephones and the Risk for Brain Tumours," *European Journal of Cancer Prevention* (August 2002), that long-term users of older, analog phones were more likely to suffer brain tumors. U.S. District Judge Catherine Blake, presiding over the most famous phone cancer lawsuit, was not swayed. She declared that the claimant had provided "no sufficiently reliable and relevant scientific evidence" and said she intended to dismiss the case (Mark Parascandola, "Judge Rejects Cancer Data in Maryland Cell Phone Suit," *Science*, October 11, 2002). Robert Clark, "Clean Bill of Health for Cell Phones," *America's Network* (April 1, 2004), reports that "A survey by the Danish Institute of Cancer Epidemiology . . . says there is no short-term danger of developing brain tumors." Studies mentioned by Olga Naidenko in her essay as supporting worries about the link between cell phones and cancer have not been supported by other studies. There are even apparent reasons to doubt reports of DNA damage from cell phone radiation; see Gretchen Vogel, "Fraud Charges Cast Doubt on Claims of DNA Damage from Cell Phone Fields," *Science* (August 29, 2008). In addition, warns Michael Repacholi, "The Reality of Mobile Phones and Cancer," *New Scientist* (December 12, 2009), there are serious weaknesses in many studies of the association between cell phones and cancer. E. Cardis, et al. (The Interphone Study Group), "Brain Tumour Risk in Relation to Mobile Telephone Use: Results of the Interphone International Case-Control Study," *International Journal of Epidemiology* (vol. 39, no. 3, 2010), conclude, "Overall, no increase in risk of glioma or meningioma was observed with use of mobile phones. There were suggestions of an increased risk of glioma at the highest exposure levels, but biases and error prevent a causal interpretation. The possible effects of long-term heavy use of mobile phones require further investigation." Janet Raloff, "Cell Phone-Cancer Study an Enigma," *Science News* (June 19, 2010), notes that the same study actually suggests that moderate cell phone users experience *less* risk of brain cancer than users of landlines.

Skeptics insist that the threat is real. However, if it is real, it is not yet clear beyond a doubt. Unfortunately, society cannot always wait for certainty. In connection with EMFs, Gordon L. Hester, in "Electric and Magnetic Fields: Managing an Uncertain Risk," *Environment* (January/February 1992), asserts that just the possibility of a health hazard is sufficient to justify more research into the problem. The guiding principle, says Hester, is "'prudent avoidance,' which was originally intended to mean that people should avoid fields 'when this can be done with modest amounts of money and trouble.'" The same guideline surely applies to cell phone radiation. Sari N. Harar, "Do Cell Phones Cause Cancer?" *Prevention* (August 2006), notes that the consensus answer is that the risks are low and adds that risk can easily be reduced even further by using hands-free headsets and keeping calls short. In July 2008, Ronald B. Herberman, director of the University of Pittsburgh Cancer Institute, warned staff and faculty to limit cell phone use because of the possible health risks, basing his warning on early unpublished data.

Is it possible to prove that cell phones do *not* cause cancer? Unfortunately, no, because small, sporadic effects might not be detected even in massive

studies. Thus, for some people, the jury will forever be out. Meanwhile, the jury is getting new charges to consider: George Carlo is now contending that wireless computer networks (Wi-Fi) also involve radiation that can cause tumors (see "Wi-Fi Fear," *The Ecologist*, April 2007). As with cell phones, there is a lack of evidence to support the charges. What should society do in the face of weak, uncertain, and even contradictory data? Can we afford to conclude that there is no hazard? Or must we ban or redesign a useful technology with no justification other than our fear that there might be a real hazard? Many scientists and politicians argue that even if there is no genuine medical risk, there is a genuine impact in terms of public anxiety. See Gary Stix, "Closing the Book," *Scientific American* (March 1998). It is therefore appropriate, they say, to fund further research and to take whatever relatively inexpensive steps to minimize exposure are possible. Failure to do so increases public anxiety and distrust of government and science. Some of those "relatively inexpensive steps are pretty simple"; as Olga Naidenko notes, they include using headsets and even texting instead of talking. But as Tamar Nordenberg, "Cell Phones and Brain Cancer: No Clear Connection," *FDA Consumer* (November–December 2000), says, quoting Professor John Moulder, using a cell phone while driving is much more hazardous even than using a conventional high-radiation cell phone. By 2003, cell phones were being broadly indicted as hazards on the highway. The basic problem is that using a cell phone increases the mental workload on the driver, according to Roland Matthews, Stephen Legg, and Samuel Charlton, "The Effect of Cell Phone Type on Drivers' Subjective Workload During Concurrent Driving and Conversing," *Accident Analysis & Prevention* (July, 2003); they too recommend using a hands-free phone. As a result of such studies, many states have already banned the use of handheld phones while driving, with initial good effect; see Anne T. McCartt, Elisa R. Braver, and Lori L. Geary, "Drivers' Use of Handheld Cell Phones Before and After New York State's Cell Phone Law," *Preventive Medicine* (May 2003). Unfortunately, the initial good results have not lasted. See "Motorists' Cell Phone Use Rising: NHTSA," *Safety & Health* (May 2005).

For a time, it seemed that the lack of evidence for a connection between cell phones and cancer had quieted the debate. However, in September 2009, Environmental Working Group (EWG), a nonprofit advocacy group, released a report claiming that new evidence justified concern. In the YES selection, EWG's Olga V. Naidenko argues that even though past research into the link between cell phones and cancer has produced ambiguous results, more recent research on people who have used cell phones for many years has produced more worrisome results. More research is needed, but concern is already amply justified, especially in connection with children's exposure to cell phone emissions of radio waves. In the NO selection, Linda S. Erdreich argues that independent scientific organizations have reviewed the research to date on the supposed link between cell phones and cancer and concluded that current evidence does not demonstrate that wireless phones cause cancer or have other adverse health effects.

YES

Olga V. Naidenko

The Health Effects of Cell Phone Use

Mr. Chairman and distinguished Members of the Subcommittee . . . I thank [you] for holding this important hearing and for the opportunity to testify.

Last week, EWG released the results of a 10-month investigation of more than 200 peer-reviewed studies, government advisories, and industry documents on the safety of cell phone radiation. We found that the studies amassed during the first two decades of cell phone use produced conflicting results and few definitive conclusions on cell phone safety. But the latest research, in which scientists are for the first time able to study people who have used cell phones for many years, suggests the potential for serious safety issues.

Studies published over the past several years find significantly higher risks for brain and salivary gland tumors among people using cell phones for 10 years or longer. The state of the science is provocative and troubling, and more research is essential. We at Environmental Working Group are still using our cell phones, but we also believe that until scientists know much more about cell phone radiation, it's smart for consumers to buy phones with the lowest emissions.

As of December 2008, U.S. wireless subscribers numbered 270.3 million— 87 percent of Americans—a 30 percent jump in three years. Some 60 percent of the global population—four billion people—subscribe to wireless service. As the market for new devices has grown, so has the urgency that cell phone safety be well understood, and that cell phone radiation standards be sufficient to protect public health.

In this testimony we highlight five key areas of concern:

- Consumers have a right to know the level of radiation their phones emit;
- Latest science points to potential risks to children's health;
- Federal standards for cell phone radiation need to be modernized;
- What consumers can do to reduce exposures to cell phone radiation;
- EWG's recommendations to the government, industry, and the public.

U.S. Senate, September 14, 2009.

1. Consumers Have a Right to Know the Level of Radiation Their Phones Emit

EWG advocates that cell phone companies label their products' radiation output so that consumers can make informed choices at the point of sale, and that the government require this disclosure. Currently, most people are given no information at all about radiation emissions when they purchase a phone.

To fill this information void, EWG's research team created a user-friendly, interactive online guide to cell phone emissions, covering over 1,200 phones currently on the market. Consumers can use this free online database to make informed decisions about which cell phones to buy. The EWG guide uses easy-to-read graphics to illustrate each phone's radiofrequency emissions, enabling consumers to make quick comparisons of radiation output of various wireless devices.

In the 64 hours following the publication of our science review and cell phone radiation database, 442,000 people accessed these materials on our website, collectively viewing 1.4 million online pages. During those same 3 days our findings were reported in 100 news articles and in national and local broadcast news, including *The New York Times*, *NBC Nightly News*, *WebMD*, and *USA Today*. This powerful response from the public and from news media outlets reflects consumers' keen interest in the issue of cell phone safety. Clearly, people are eager to know if cell phones are safe and how they can protect themselves and their families from potential adverse effects of excessive exposure to cell phone radiation.

2. The Latest Science Point to Potential Risks to Children's Health

Prior to 2003, studies of cancer risk and cell phone use produced conflicting results. The Food and Drug Administration (FDA) told consumers that scientists had found no harmful health effects from exposure to cell phone emissions. But FDA's assurances were based on studies of people who had used cell phones for just 3 years, on average, not long enough to develop cancer. At that time, studies had not addressed the risks of longer-term cell phone radiation exposures. The research gap is closing. Recent studies find significantly higher risks for brain and salivary gland tumors among people using cell phones for 10 years or longer. The state of the science is provocative and troubling, especially for the health of children. Among recent findings are the following:

- A joint study by researchers in Denmark, Finland, Norway, Sweden and the United Kingdom found that people who had used cell phones for more than 10 years had a significantly increased risk of developing glioma, a usually malignant brain tumor, on the side of the head they had favored for cell phone conversations.
- French and German scientists reported an increased risk of glioma for long-term cell phone users. Analysis of all published cell phone-brain tumor studies found that people who had used a cell phone for 10 or

more years, the overall risk for developing a glioma on the cell phone side of the head increased by 90 percent.

- Cell phone use for 10 years and longer has been also associated with significantly increased risk of acoustic neuroma, a type of benign brain tumor, on the primary side of cell phone use. An extensive review of published studies of acoustic neuroma found that long-term cell phone users had a 60 percent greater risk of being diagnosed with the disease.
- A study from Israel reported an association between frequent and prolonged mobile phone use and parotid (salivary) gland tumors. Scientists analyzing data from Sweden and Denmark combined found that people who had used cell phones for at least 10 years ran an increased risk of benign parotid gland tumors.

The National Research Council (NRC) has observed that "with the rapid advances in technologies and communications utilizing [radiation in the range of cell phone frequencies], children are increasingly exposed . . . at earlier ages (starting at age 6 or before)." Research by France Telecom scientists showed that under standard conditions of use, twice as much cell phone radiation would penetrate a child's thinner, softer skull than an adult's. Children will be exposed to cell phone radiation for more years and therefore in greater total amounts than the current generation of adults.

Children are likely to be more susceptible than adults to effects from cell phone radiation, since the brain of a child is still developing and its nervous tissues absorb a greater portion of incoming radiation compared to that of an adult. Much more research is essential. However, in response to the information already available over the potential health risks of cell phone emissions, government agencies in Germany, Switzerland, Israel, United Kingdom, France, and Finland and the European Parliament have recommended actions to help consumers reduce exposures to cell phone radiation, especially for young children. Among warnings issued by government agencies are the following:

- **United Kingdom Department of Health.** "UK Chief Medical Officers strongly advise that where children and young people do use mobile phones, they should be encouraged to: use mobile phones for essential purposes only; keep all calls short—talking for long periods prolongs exposure and should be discouraged."
- **Canada—City of Toronto Department of Public Health.** "Today's children have started to use cell phones at a younger age, therefore their lifetime exposure to cell phone RFs will likely be greater. As a result, the chances that a child could develop harmful health effects from using a cell phone for a long time may be greater . . . Toronto Public Health is recommending that children, especially pre-adolescent children, use landlines whenever possible, keeping the use of cell phones for essential purposes only, limiting the length of cell phone calls and using headsets or hands-free options, whenever possible."
- **Finland—Finnish Radiation and Nuclear Safety Authority.** "It would be good to restrict children's use of mobile phones." "Precaution is recommended for children as all of the effects are not known. . . . Parents are

recommended to guide their children to use a handsfree that minimises the exposure of head significantly. When using a hands-free it is recommended to keep the mobile phone at least a few centimetres away from the body."

In contrast, the two U.S. federal agencies that regulate cell phones, the FDA and the Federal Communications Commission (FCC), have all but ignored evidence that long-term cell phone use may be risky.

3. Federal Standards for Cell Phone Radiation Need to Be Modernized

The FCC set cell phone radiation standards 17 years ago, when few people used cell phones. These standards fail to provide an adequate margin of safety for cell phone radiation exposure and do not account for risks to children. The FCC standards closely follow the 1992 recommendations of the Institute of Electrical and Electronics Engineers (IEEE). The FCC adopted IEEE's proposal to allow 20 times more radiation to the head than the average amount allowed for the whole body, even though the brain may well be one of the most sensitive parts of human body with respect to radiofrequency radiation and should have more protection. EWG's conclusion: current U.S. cell phone radiation standards are outdated and may not be sufficiently protective. EWG urges the FDA and the FCC to upgrade its standards to take account of the newest scientific evidence and also increasing cell phone use by children.

4. What Consumers Can Do to Reduce Exposures to Cell Phone Radiation

EWG recommends a number of simple actions consumers can take to reduce exposures to cell phone radiation. We recommend these simple precautionary measures until the science on cell phone risks is settled, and until the federal government modernizes current radiation limits to reflect the latest research.

- **Use a low-radiation phone.** Consumers can find radiation emissions for their current phone on EWG's database (www.ewg.org/cellphone-radiation), in their user's manual, or by contacting the manufacturer. EWG's database lists alternate, low-radiation phones, allowing people to consider purchasing a phone that emits the lowest radiation possible and still meets their needs.
- **Use a headset or speakers.** Headsets emit much less radiation than phones. Experts are split on whether wireless or wired is safer. Some wireless headsets emit continuous, low-level radiation, so EWG advises removing the headset from the ear between calls. Using a phone in speaker mode also reduces radiation to the head.
- **Listen more, talk less.** Cell phones emit radiation to transmit voice or text messages, but not to receive messages. Listening more and talking less reduces exposures.

- **Hold phone away from the body.** Holding the phone away from the torso when talking (while using the headset or speaker) reduces radiation exposures. EWG advises against holding the phone against the ear, in a pocket, or on the belt where soft body tissues absorb radiation.
- **Choose texting over talking.** Phones use less power (less radiation) to send text than voice. And unlike speaking with the phone at the ear, texting keeps radiation away from the head.
- **Stay off the phone if the signal is poor.** Fewer signal bars on the phone means that it emits more radiation to get the signal to the tower. EWG recommends that people make and take calls when the phone has a strong signal.
- **Limit children's phone use.** Young children's brains absorb twice the cell phone radiation as an adult's. EWG joins health agencies in at least six countries in recommending limits for children's phone use, such as for emergency situations only.
- **Skip the "radiation shield."** Radiation shields such as antenna caps or keypad covers reduce the connection quality and force the phone to transmit at a higher power with higher radiation.

5. Recommendations

The government should invest in additional research on the health effects of cell phone radiation, with special emphasis on children and teens.

The government should require industry to make cell phone radiation level information available at the point of sale, so consumers can make informed decisions about the phones they buy.

Given the troubling questions raised by the research thus far, the cell phone industry should not wait for government action, but instead, offer consumers phones that operate with the least possible radiation, and should offer radiation information at the point of sale.

In the meanwhile, cell phone users can protect themselves and their families by buying low-radiation phones. Cell phone users can also reduce radiation exposures by using their phone in speaker mode or with a headset.

In conclusion, EWG strongly believes that the government should support additional research into this important health question, and that the public has the right to know what levels of radiation they may be exposed to, what may be the potential risks, and what precautionary measures they can take to protect themselves and their families from any adverse health effects of cell phone radiation. . . .

Linda S. Erdreich

 **NO**

The Health Effects of Cell Phone Use

. . . **M**obile phones operate using radio waves. Radio waves, or radiofrequency (RF) energy, is a range of the electromagnetic spectrum that includes AM and FM broadcast radio, television, and many other devices and technologies including cordless phones, baby monitors, radar, and microwave ovens. Visible light is also part of the electromagnetic spectrum, but is at a higher frequency and shorter wavelength than RF. RF energy is not "radiation" in the same sense as used for high frequency X rays, because the energy of RF is so much lower and is unable to change the DNA of cells. Although RF energy is sometimes referred to as "EMF" the contemporary usage of EMF refers primarily to the electric and magnetic fields associated with electricity from power lines and all electric devices. Electricity operates in the extremely low frequency (ELF) range, 60 cycles per second (60 Hz), in the United States. To avoid confusion, I will use RF in my discussion of mobile phones.

Standard Scientific Methods Are Used to Access Possible Risks to Human Health

The standard scientific approach used to determine whether an exposure source, such as to RF energy, poses a health risk, is to look at all of the available research, including both studies that have reported effects, and those that did not. The goal is an objective, comprehensive review, in which the strengths and weaknesses of each study are evaluated, and more weight is given to studies of better quality. This approach is designed to ensure that reviewers do not single out studies, consciously or inadvertently, to support a preconceived opinion. Then, all of the studies are evaluated together to arrive at a conclusion. This is the method that I have used for evaluating the RF research and for other assessments throughout my career.

The relevant research to be considered includes a broad spectrum of scientific research that uses different approaches to study potential effects of RF energy on humans. These different approaches have different strengths and limitations and provide complementary information: laboratory studies in cells and in animals, experimental studies of human volunteers,

U.S. Senate, September 14, 2009.

and epidemiologic studies of human populations. For this reason, scientific organizations convene panels of independent experts from the various areas of expertise (e.g. health physics, engineering, toxicology, clinical medicine, and epidemiology) relevant to the topic. Many scientific organizations consider pertinent studies to be those reports of scientific research or reviews that have been published or accepted for publication in the peer-reviewed scientific literature.

Independent Scientific Organizations Worldwide Have Reviewed the Research

Independent scientific organizations worldwide have reviewed the research and proposed exposure limits. Many studies have been conducted over the past 50 years to examine whether exposure to RF energy has adverse effects on health, and to determine allowable levels of exposure. Several scientific organizations have reviewed the laboratory and epidemiologic research to assess the potential for health effects from RF exposure, and to set exposure limits to ensure occupational and public safety. These expert groups have included scientists with diverse skills to reflect the different research expertise required to answer questions about RF energy and health. Numerous government agencies and professional organizations have reviewed the science related to potential health effects from using wireless phones. While the specific conclusions vary, all of the reports that assess the evidence using multidisciplinary panels and a comprehensive approach reach similar conclusions; the current scientific evidence does not demonstrate that wireless phones cause cancer or other adverse health effects.

The Federal Communications Commission (FCC) and the Food and Drug Administration (FDA), the agencies with regulatory authority over radiofrequency emissions in the U.S., have both concluded that the current scientific evidence does not indicate that there are health hazards from using a wireless phone. The FCC's website states that "[t]here is no scientific evidence that proves that wireless phone usage can lead to cancer or a variety of other problems, including headaches, dizziness or memory loss."(www.fcc.gov/cgb/cellular .html#evidence) The FDA's website similarly states that "[t]he weight of scientific evidence has not linked cell phones with any health problems."(http:// www.fda.gov/Radiation-EmittingProducts/RadiationEmittingProductsandProcedures/ HomeBusinessandEntertainment/CellPhones/ucm116282.htm)

In September 2008, the National Cancer Institute (NCI), the U.S. government's principal agency for cancer research, published a Fact Sheet on Cellular Telephone Use and Cancer Risk that concluded that there is no consistent link between cellular telephone use and cancer.[1] The NCI also stated that "incidence data from the Surveillance, Epidemiology, and End Results (SEER) program of the National Cancer Institute have shown no increase between 1987 and 2005 in the age-adjusted incidence of brain or other nervous system cancers despite the dramatic increase in use of cellular telephones."[2] http://www .cancer.gov/cancertopics/factsheet/Risk/cellphones.

The conclusions of these U.S. agencies are similar to the conclusions reached in reports prepared by various commissions and agencies around the world, including for example:

- **The Australian Radiation Protection and Nuclear Safety Agency**

"There is essentially no evidence that microwave exposure from mobile telephones causes cancer, and no clear evidence that such exposure accelerates the growth of an already-existing cancer." http://www.arpansa.gov.au/mobilephones/index.cfm

- **Health Canada**

"There is no convincing scientific evidence that RF exposures have any link to cancer initiation or promotion. The body of peer-reviewed literature in this area overwhelmingly demonstrates a lack of linkage, and where the few reports of linkage effects were found, some may be attributed to factors other than RF energy."

- **The Health Council of the Netherlands**

"The Committee maintained its conclusion that no causal link has thus far been demonstrated between health problems and exposure to electromagnetic fields generated by mobile phones or base stations for mobile telephony." http://www.gezondheidsraad.nl/sites/default/files/200902.pdf.

- **The Scientific Committee on Emerging and Newly Identified Health Risks of the European Commission**

"Overall, research indicates that mobile phone use does not increase the risk of cancer, especially when used for less than ten years." http://ec.europa.eu/health/opinions2/en/electromagnetic-fields/index.htm#3

- **The World Health Organization**

"Considering the very low exposure levels and research results collected to date, there is no convincing scientific evidence that the weak RF signals from base stations and wireless networks cause adverse health effects." http://www.who.int/mediacentre/factsheets/fs304/en/index.html

The United Kingdom's Health Protection Agency and New Zealand Ministry of Health's National Radiation Laboratory also have reached similar conclusions after reviewing the available science.

In September 2009, the International Commission on Non-Ionizing Radiation Protection's (ICNRP) Standing Committee on Epidemiology published a scientific review of all of the available epidemiologic evidence on wireless phones and brain tumors. That review concludes:

"In the last few years, the epidemiologic evidence on mobile phone use and risk of brain and other tumors of the head has grown considerably.

In our opinion, overall the studies published to date do not demonstrate a raised risk within approximately 10 years of use for any tumor of the brain or any other head tumor."

Conclusion

Based on my review of the epidemiologic studies and consideration of experimental data in animals, I agree with the conclusions of the scientific organizations: The current scientific evidence does not demonstrate that wireless phones cause cancer or other adverse health effects.

Notes

1. *See* http://www.cancer.gov/cancertopics/factsheet/Risk/cellphones.
2. *Id.*

EXPLORING THE ISSUE

Is There Sufficient Scientific Evidence to Conclude That Cell Phones Cause Cancer?

Critical Thinking and Reflection

1. How could one tell whether there is really a causative link between cell phones and brain cancer? How could one rule out coincidence?
2. Some people think there is also a problem with Wi-Fi radiation. Should we also worry about Bluetooth headsets?
3. How certain do we have to be before we can justify spending large sums of money on possible problems?
4. Should we accept as real a proposed association between an environmental agent and a disease if there is no biologically plausible mechanism for the effect?

Is There Common Ground?

The "common ground" with this issue lies in the repeated use of the phrase "no convincing evidence," with stress on the word "convincing." Many studies have found weak hints of an association between cell phone use and brain cancer, but when the results of the studies are analyzed statistically, those hints are not strong enough to rule out coincidence.

1. Go back to the introduction to this book and re-read the material on the use of controls in research. What is the purpose of using controls?
2. How does the use of controls help to rule out coincidence?
3. Can one ever totally rule out the role of coincidence? Look up "confidence intervals" in a statistics text.

ISSUE 9

Should DDT Be Banned Worldwide?

YES: Anne Platt McGinn, from "Malaria, Mosquitoes, and DDT," *World Watch* (May/June 2002)

NO: Donald R. Roberts, from "The Role of Science in Environmental Policy-Making," Statement before U.S. Senate Committee on Environment & Public Works (September 28, 2005)

Learning Outcomes
After studying this issue, students will be able to explain:
1. How mosquitoes spread malaria.
2. Why there are few or no reliable methods for preventing infection with malaria.
3. Why natural selection makes the use of pesticides a short-term solution at best.
4. The difficulty of choosing among competing priorities, in this case the lives of children versus the lives of wildlife.

ISSUE SUMMARY

YES: Anne Platt McGinn, a senior researcher at the Worldwatch Institute, argues that although DDT is still used to fight malaria, there are other more effective and less environmentally harmful methods. She maintains that DDT should be banned or reserved for emergency use.

NO: Donald R. Roberts argues that the scientific evidence regarding the environmental hazards of DDT has been seriously misrepresented by antipesticide activists. The hazards of malaria are much greater and, properly used, DDT can prevent them and save lives.

The story of DDT is a crucial element in the story of how science and technology interact with society. The chemical was first synthesized in 1874.

Its insecticidal properties were first noticed by Paul Mueller, and it was very quickly realized that this implied the chemical could save human lives. It had long been known that in wars, more soldiers died because of disease than because of enemy fire. During World War I, some 5 million lives were lost to typhus, a disease carried by body lice. DDT was first deployed during World War II to halt a typhus epidemic in Naples, Italy. Dramatic success soon meant that DDT was used routinely as a dust for soldiers and civilians. During and after the war, it was also successfully deployed against the mosquitoes that carry malaria and other diseases. In the United States, cases of malaria fell from 120,000 in 1934 to 72 in 1960. Yellow fever cases dropped from 100,000 in 1878 to none. In 1948, Mueller received the Nobel Prize for Medicine and Physiology because DDT had saved so many civilian lives. Roger Bate, director of Africa Fighting Malaria, argues, in "A Case of the DDTs," *National Review* (May 14, 2001), that DDT remains the cheapest and most effective way to combat malaria and that it should remain available for use.

DDT was by no means the first pesticide. But its predecessors were such things as arsenic, strychnine, cyanide, copper sulfate, and nicotine, all of which had such marked toxicity to humans that they gave rise to a host of murder mysteries such as the play "Arsenic and Old Lace." DDT was not only more effective as an insecticide; it was also less hazardous to users (not to mention potential murder victims). It is thus not surprising that DDT was seen as a beneficial substance and was soon applied routinely to agricultural crops and used to control mosquito populations in American suburbs ("Rachel Carson's Silent Spring," a PBS American Experience video, includes footage of children at a picnic being engulfed in a cloud of DDT). However, insects quickly became resistant to the insecticide (in any population of insects, some will be more resistant than others; when the insecticide kills the more vulnerable members of the population, the resistant ones are left to breed and multiply; this is an example of natural selection). In *Silent Spring* (1961), Rachel Carson documented that DDT was concentrated in the food chain and affected the reproduction of predators such as hawks and eagles. In 1972, the U.S. Environmental Protection Agency banned almost all DDT uses (it could still be used to protect public health). Other developed countries soon banned it as well, but developing nations, especially in the tropics, saw it as an essential tool for fighting diseases such as malaria, which infects up to half a billion people per year and kills more than a million, most of them under age five. See Michael Finkel, "Bedlam in the Blood," *National Geographic* (July 2007).

DDT is by no means the only pesticide or organic toxin with environmental effects. On May 24, 2001, the United States joined 90 other nations in signing the Stockholm Convention on Persistent Organic Pollutants (POPs). This treaty aims to eliminate from use the entire class of chemicals to which DDT belongs, beginning with the "dirty dozen" pesticides, DDT, aldrin, dieldrin, endrin, chlordane, heptachlor, mirex, toxaphene, and the industrial chemicals polychlorinated biphenyls (PCBs), hexachlorobenzene (HCB), dioxins, and furans. Since then, 59 countries, not including the United States and the European Union, have formally ratified the treaty, which took effect in

May 2004. Fiona Proffitt, "U.N. Convention Targets Dirty Dozen Chemicals," *Science* (May 21, 2004), notes that "About 25 countries will be allowed to continue using DDT against malaria-spreading mosquitoes until a viable alternative is found."

Angela Logomasini comes close to accusing environmentalists of condemning DDT more on the basis of politics or ideology than of science in "Chemical Warfare: Ideological Environmentalism's Quixotic Campaign Against Synthetic Chemicals," in Ronald Bailey, ed., *Global Warming and Other Eco-Myths: How the Environmental Movement Uses False Science to Scare Us to Death* (Prima Publishing, 2002). Her admission that public health demands have softened some environmentalists' resistance to the use of DDT points to a basic truth about environmental debates. Over and over again, they come down to what we should do first: Should we meet human needs whether or not species die and air and water are contaminated? Or should we protect species, air, water, and other aspects of the environment even if some human needs must go unmet? Even if those human needs are the lives of children? This opposition is very clear in the debate over DDT. The human needs are clear, for insect-borne diseases have killed and continue to kill a great many people. Yet the environmental needs are also clear; the title of Rachel Carson's *Silent Spring* says it all. The question is one of choosing priorities and balancing risks. See John Danley, "Balancing Risks: Mosquitoes, Malaria, Morality, and DDT" (*Business & Society Review [1974]*, Spring 2002). It is worth noting that John Beard, "DDT and Human Health," *Science of the Total Environment* (February 2006), finds the evidence for the ill effects of DDT more convincing and says that it is still too early to say it does not contribute to human disease.

Malaria can be treated with drugs, but the parasite has developed resistance to standard medications such as chloroquine and its successors, the artemisinins; see Martin Enserink, "Malaria's Drug Miracle in Danger," *Science* (May 14, 2010). Mosquitoes can be controlled in various ways: Swamps can be drained (which carry their own environmental price), other breeding opportunities (such as old tires containing pools of water) can be eliminated, and larvae can be destroyed by hand (see Jeffrey Marlow, "Malaria," *World Watch,* May/June 2008). Fish can be introduced to eat mosquito larvae. Bednets can keep the mosquitoes away from people. But these (and other) alternatives do not mean that there does not remain a place for chemical pesticides. In "Pesticides and Public Health: Integrated Methods of Mosquito Management," *Emerging Infectious Diseases* (January–February 2001), Robert I. Rose, an arthropod biotechnologist with the Animal and Plant Health Inspection Service of the U.S. Department of Agriculture, says, "Pesticides have a role in public health as part of sustainable integrated mosquito management. Other components of such management include surveillance, source reduction or prevention, biological control, repellents, traps, and pesticide-resistance management." "The most effective programs today rely on a range of tools," says Anne Platt McGinn in "Combating Malaria," *State of the World 2003* (W.W. Norton, 2003). Indeed, multiple techniques are essential to efforts to eradicate malaria in Africa and elsewhere; see Leslie Roberts, "Elimination Meets Reality in Hispaniola" and "Shrinking the Malaria Map from the Outside in," *Science* (May 14, 2010).

Today some countries see DDT as essential. See Tina Rosenberg, "What the World Needs Now Is DDT," *The New York Times Magazine* (April 11, 2004). However, when the World Health Organization (WHO) endorsed the use of DDT to fight malaria, there was immediate outcry; see Allan Schapira, "DDT: A Polluted Debate in Malaria Control," *Lancet* (December 16, 2006).

It has proven difficult to find effective, affordable drugs against malaria; see Ann M. Thayer, "Fighting Malaria," *Chemical and Engineering News* (October 24, 2005), and Claire Panosian Dunavan, "Tackling Malaria," *Scientific American* (December 2005). A great deal of effort has gone into developing vaccines against malaria; the parasite has demonstrated a persistent talent for evading all attempts to arm the immune system against it, but the work goes on. See Michael Finkel, "Bedlam in the Blood," *National Geographic* (July 2007). Research into vaccines that block transmission of the malaria parasite rather than infection is providing promising results; see Gretchen Vogel, "The 'Do Unto Others' Malaria Vaccine," *Science* (May 14, 2010), and Mary Carmichael, "Halting the World's Most Lethal Parasite," *Scientific American* (November 2010). On the other hand, Nicholas J. White, "Malaria—Time to Act," *The New England Journal of Medicine* (November 9, 2006), argues that rather than wait for a perfect solution, we should recognize that present tools—including DDT—are effective enough now that there is no excuse to avoid using them.

It is worth stressing that malaria is only one of several mosquito-borne diseases that pose threats to public health (even in the United States). Three others are yellow fever, dengue, and West Nile virus. It is also worth stressing that global warming means climate changes that may increase the geographic range of disease-carrying mosquitoes. Many climate researchers are concerned that malaria, yellow fever, and other now mostly tropical and subtropical diseases may return to temperate-zone nations and even spread into areas where they have never been known. See Atul A. Khasnis and Mary D. Nettleman, "Global Warming and Infectious Disease," *Archives of Medical Research* (November 2005). However, Peter W. Gething, *et al.*, "Climate Change and the Global Malaria Recession," *Nature* (May 20, 2010), find that despite past warming malaria's range has shrunk and is now less correlated with climate.

In the YES selection, Worldwatch researcher Anne Platt McGinn grants that malaria remains a serious problem in the developing nations of the tropics, especially in Africa. DDT is still used to fight malaria in these nations, but because of resistance, it is far less effective than it used to be and environmental effects are serious concerns. She argues that alternative measures such as mosquito nets impregnated with pyrethrin insecticides are more effective and less environmentally harmful. DDT should be banned or reserved for emergency use. In the NO selection, Professor Donald R. Roberts argues that the scientific evidence regarding the environmental hazards of DDT has been seriously misrepresented by antipesticide activists. The hazards of malaria are much greater and, properly used, DDT can prevent them and save lives. Efforts to prevent the use of DDT have produced a "global humanitarian disaster."

YES

Anne Platt McGinn

Malaria, Mosquitoes, and DDT

This year, like every other year within the past couple of decades, uncountable trillions of mosquitoes will inject malaria parasites into human blood streams billions of times. Some 300 to 500 million full-blown cases of malaria will result, and between 1 and 3 million people will die, most of them pregnant women and children. That's the official figure, anyway, but it's likely to be a substantial underestimate, since most malaria deaths are not formally registered, and many are likely to have escaped the estimators. Very roughly, the malaria death toll rivals that of AIDS, which now kills about 3 million people annually.

But unlike AIDS, malaria is a low-priority killer. Despite the deaths, and the fact that roughly 2.5 billion people (40 percent of the world's population) are at risk of contracting the disease, malaria is a relatively low public health priority on the international scene. Malaria rarely makes the news. And international funding for malaria research currently comes to a mere $150 million annually. Just by way of comparison, that's only about 5 percent of the $2.8 billion that the U.S. government alone is considering for AIDS research in fiscal year 2003.

The low priority assigned to malaria would be at least easier to understand, though no less mistaken, if the threat were static. Unfortunately it is not. It is true that the geographic range of the disease has contracted substantially since the mid-20th century, but over the past couple of decades, malaria has been gathering strength. Virtually all areas where the disease is endemic have seen drug-resistant strains of the parasites emerge—a development that is almost certainly boosting death rates. In countries as various as Armenia, Afghanistan, and Sierra Leone, the lack or deterioration of basic infrastructure has created a wealth of new breeding sites for the mosquitoes that spread the disease. The rapidly expanding slums of many tropical cities also lack such infrastructure; poor sanitation and crowding have primed these places as well for outbreaks—even though malaria has up to now been regarded as predominantly a rural disease.

What has current policy to offer in the face of these threats? The medical arsenal is limited; there are only about a dozen antimalarial drugs commonly in use, and there is significant malaria resistance to most of them. In the absence of a reliable way to kill the parasites, policy has tended to focus on killing the mosquitoes that bear them. And that has led to an abundant use of synthetic pesticides, including one of the oldest and most dangerous: dichlorodiphenyl trichloroethane, or DDT.

From *World Watch* magazine, vol. 15, no. 3, May/June 2002. Copyright © 2002 by Worldwatch Institute. Reprinted by permission. http://www.worldwatch.org.

DDT is no longer used or manufactured in most of the world, but because it does not break down readily, it is still one of the most commonly detected pesticides in the milk of nursing mothers. DDT is also one of the "dirty dozen" chemicals included in the 2001 Stockholm Convention on Persistent Organic Pollutants [POPs]. The signatories to the "POPs Treaty" essentially agreed to ban all uses of DDT except as a last resort against disease-bearing mosquitoes. Unfortunately, however, DDT is still a routine option in 19 countries, most of them in Africa. (Only 11 of these countries have thus far signed the treaty.) Among the signatory countries, 31—slightly fewer than one-third—have given notice that they are reserving the right to use DDT against malaria. On the face of it, such use may seem unavoidable, but there are good reasons for thinking that progress against the disease is compatible with *reductions* in DDT use.

꒰◯꒱

Malaria is caused by four protozoan parasite species in the genus *Plasmodium.* These parasites are spread exclusively by certain mosquitoes in the genus *Anopheles.* An infection begins when a parasite-laden female mosquito settles onto someone's skin and pierces a capillary to take her blood meal. The parasite, in a form called the *sporozoite,* moves with the mosquito's saliva into the human bloodstream. About 10 percent of the mosquito's lode of sporozoites is likely to be injected during a meal, leaving plenty for the next bite. Unless the victim has some immunity to malaria—normally as a result of previous exposure—most sporozoites are likely to evade the body's immune system and make their way to the liver, a process that takes less than an hour. There they invade the liver cells and multiply asexually for about two weeks. By this time, the original several dozen sporozoites have become millions of *merozoites*—the form the parasite takes when it emerges from the liver and moves back into the blood to invade the body's red blood cells. Within the red blood cells, the merozoites go through another cycle of asexual reproduction, after which the cells burst and release millions of additional merozoites, which invade yet more red blood cells. The high fever and chills associated with malaria are the result of this stage, which tends to occur in pulses. If enough red blood cells are destroyed in one of these pulses, the result is convulsions, difficulty in breathing, coma, and death.

As the parasite multiplies inside the red blood cells, it produces not just more merozoites, but also *gametocytes,* which are capable of sexual reproduction. This occurs when the parasite moves back into the mosquitoes; even as they inject sporozoites, biting mosquitoes may ingest gametocytes if they are feeding on a person who is already infected. The gametocytes reproduce in the insect's gut and the resulting eggs move into the gut cells. Eventually, more sporozoites emerge from the gut and penetrate the mosquito's salivary glands, where they await a chance to enter another human bloodstream, to begin the cycle again.

Of the roughly 380 mosquito species in the genus *Anopheles,* about 60 are able to transmit malaria to people. These malaria vectors are widespread throughout the tropics and warm temperate zones, and they are very efficient

at spreading the disease. Malaria is highly contagious, as is apparent from a measurement that epidemiologists call the "basic reproduction number," or BRN. The BRN indicates, on average, how many new cases a single infected person is likely to cause. For example, among the nonvectored diseases (those in which the pathogen travels directly from person to person without an intermediary like a mosquito), measles is one of the most contagious. The BRN for measles is 12 to 14, meaning that someone with measles is likely to infect 12 to 14 other people. (Luckily, there's an inherent limit in this process: as a pathogen spreads through any particular area, it will encounter fewer and fewer susceptible people who aren't already sick, and the outbreak will eventually subside.) HIV/AIDS is on the other end of the scale: it's deadly, but it burns through a population slowly. Its BRN is just above 1, the minimum necessary for the pathogen's survival. With malaria, the BRN varies considerably, depending on such factors as which mosquito species are present in an area and what the temperatures are. (Warmer is worse, since the parasites mature more quickly.) But malaria can have a BRN in excess of 100: over an adult life that may last about a week, a single, malaria-laden mosquito could conceivably infect more than 100 people.

Seven Years, Seven Months

"Malaria" comes from the Italian "mal'aria." For centuries, European physicians had attributed the disease to "bad air." Apart from a tradition of associating bad air with swamps—a useful prejudice, given the amount of mosquito habitat in swamps—early medicine was largely ineffective against the disease. It wasn't until 1897 that the British physician Ronald Ross proved that mosquitoes carry malaria.

The practical implications of Ross's discovery did not go unnoticed. For example, the U.S. administration of Theodore Roosevelt recognized malaria and yellow fever (another mosquito-vectored disease) as perhaps the most serious obstacles to the construction of the Panama Canal. This was hardly a surprising conclusion, since the earlier and unsuccessful French attempt to build the canal—an effort that predated Ross's discovery—is thought to have lost between 10,000 and 20,000 workers to disease. So the American workers draped their water supplies and living quarters with mosquito netting, attempted to fill in or drain swamps, installed sewers, poured oil into standing water, and conducted mosquito-swatting campaigns. And it worked: the incidence of malaria declined. In 1906, 80 percent of the workers had the disease; by 1913, a year before the Canal was completed, only 7 percent did. Malaria could be suppressed, it seemed, with a great deal of mosquito netting, and by eliminating as much mosquito habitat as possible. But the labor involved in that effort could be enormous.

That is why DDT proved so appealing. In 1939, the Swiss chemist Paul Müller discovered that this chemical was a potent pesticide. DDT was first used during World War II, as a delousing agent. Later on, areas in southern Europe, North Africa, and Asia were fogged with DDT, to clear malaria-laden mosquitoes from the paths of invading Allied troops. DDT was cheap and it seemed to

be harmless to anything other than insects. It was also long-lasting: most other insecticides lost their potency in a few days, but in the early years of its use, the effects of a single dose of DDT could last for up to six months. In 1948, Müller won a Nobel Prize for his work and DDT was hailed as a chemical miracle.

A decade later, DDT had inspired another kind of war—a general assault on malaria. The "Global Malaria Eradication Program," launched in 1955, became one of the first major undertakings of the newly created World Health Organization [WHO]. Some 65 nations enlisted in the cause. Funding for DDT factories was donated to poor countries and production of the insecticide climbed.

The malaria eradication strategy was not to kill every single mosquito, but to suppress their populations and shorten the lifespans of any survivors, so that the parasite would not have time to develop within them. If the mosquitoes could be kept down long enough, the parasites would eventually disappear from the human population. In any particular area, the process was expected to take three years—time enough for all infected people either to recover or die. After that, a resurgence of mosquitoes would be merely an annoyance, rather than a threat. And initially, the strategy seemed to be working. It proved especially effective on islands—relatively small areas insulated from reinfestation. Taiwan, Jamaica, and Sardinia were soon declared malaria-free and have remained so to this day. By 1961, arguably the year at which the program had peak momentum, malaria had been eliminated or dramatically reduced in 37 countries.

One year later, Rachel Carson published *Silent Spring,* her landmark study of the ecological damage caused by the widespread use of DDT and other pesticides. Like other organochlorine pesticides, DDT bioaccumulates. It's fat soluble, so when an animal ingests it—by browsing contaminated vegetation, for example—the chemical tends to concentrate in its fat, instead of being excreted. When another animal eats that animal, it is likely to absorb the prey's burden of DDT. This process leads to an increasing concentration of DDT in the higher links of the food chain. And since DDT has a high chronic toxicity—that is, long-term exposure is likely to cause various physiological abnormalities—this bioaccumulation has profound implications for both ecological and human health.

With the miseries of malaria in full view, the managers of the eradication campaign didn't worry much about the toxicity of DDT, but they were greatly concerned about another aspect of the pesticide's effects: resistance. Continual exposure to an insecticide tends to "breed" insect populations that are at least partially immune to the poison. Resistance to DDT had been reported as early as 1946. The campaign managers knew that in mosquitoes, regular exposure to DDT tended to produce widespread resistance in four to seven years. Since it took three years to clear malaria from a human population, that didn't leave a lot of leeway for the eradication effort. As it turned out, the logistics simply couldn't be made to work in large, heavily infested areas with high human populations, poor housing and roads, and generally minimal infrastructure. In 1969, the campaign was abandoned. Today, DDT resistance is widespread in *Anopheles,* as is resistance to many more recent pesticides.

Undoubtedly, the campaign saved millions of lives, and it did clear malaria from some areas. But its broadest legacy has been of much more dubious value. It engendered the idea of DDT as a first resort against mosquitoes and it established the unstable dynamic of DDT resistance in *Anopheles* populations. In mosquitoes, the genetic mechanism that confers resistance to DDT does not usually come at any great competitive "cost"—that is, when no DDT is being sprayed, the resistant mosquitoes may do just about as well as nonresistant mosquitoes. So once a population acquires resistance, the trait is not likely to disappear even if DDT isn't used for years. If DDT is reapplied to such a population, widespread resistance will reappear very rapidly. The rule of thumb among entomologists is that you may get seven years of resistance-free use the first time around, but you only get about seven months the second time. Even that limited respite, however, is enough to make the chemical an attractive option as an emergency measure—or to keep it in the arsenals of bureaucracies committed to its use.

Malaria Taxes

In December 2000, the POPs Treaty negotiators convened in Johannesburg, South Africa, even though, by an unfortunate coincidence, South Africa had suffered a potentially embarrassing setback earlier that year in its own POPs policies. In 1996, South Africa had switched its mosquito control programs from DDT to a less persistent group of pesticides known as pyrethroids. The move seemed solid and supportable at the time, since years of DDT use had greatly reduced *Anopheles* populations and largely eliminated one of the most troublesome local vectors, the appropriately named *A. funestus* ("funestus" means deadly). South Africa seemed to have beaten the DDT habit: the chemical had been used to achieve a worthwhile objective; it had then been discarded. And the plan worked—until a year before the POPs summit, when malaria infections rose to 61,000 cases, a level not seen in decades. *A. funestus* reappeared as well, in KwaZulu-Natal, and in a form resistant to pyrethroids. In early 2000, DDT was reintroduced, in an indoor spraying program. (This is now a standard way of using DDT for mosquito control; the pesticide is usually applied only to walls, where mosquitoes alight to rest.) By the middle of the year, the number of infections had dropped by half.

Initially, the spraying program was criticized, but what reasonable alternative was there? This is said to be the African predicament, and yet the South African situation is hardly representative of sub-Saharan Africa as a whole.

Malaria is considered endemic in 105 countries throughout the tropics and warm temperate zones, but by far the worst region for the disease is sub-Saharan Africa. The deadliest of the four parasite species, *Plasmodium falciparum,* is widespread throughout this region, as is one of the world's most effective malaria vectors, *Anopheles gambiae.* Nearly half the population of sub-Saharan Africa is at risk of infection, and in much of eastern and central Africa, and pockets of west Africa, it would be difficult to find anyone who has not been exposed to the parasites. Some 90 percent of the world's malaria infections and deaths occur in sub-Saharan Africa, and the disease now accounts

for 30 percent of African childhood mortality. It is true that malaria is a grave problem in many parts of the world, but the African experience is misery on a very different order of magnitude. The average Tanzanian suffers more infective bites each *night* than the average Thai or Vietnamese does in a year.

As a broad social burden, malaria is thought to cost Africa between $3 billion and $12 billion annually. According to one economic analysis, if the disease had been eradicated in 1965, Africa's GDP would now be 35 percent higher than it currently is. Africa was also the gaping hole in the global eradication program: the WHO planners thought there was little they could do on the continent and limited efforts to Ethiopia, Zimbabwe, and South Africa, where eradication was thought to be feasible.

But even though the campaign largely passed Africa by, DDT has not. Many African countries have used DDT for mosquito control in indoor spraying programs, but the primary use of DDT on the continent has been as an agricultural insecticide. Consequently, in parts of west Africa especially, DDT resistance is now widespread in *A. gambiae*. But even if *A. gambiae* were not resistant, a full-bore campaign to suppress it would probably accomplish little, because this mosquito is so efficient at transmitting malaria. Unlike most *Anopheles* species, *A. gambiae* specializes in human blood, so even a small population would keep the disease in circulation. One way to get a sense for this problem is to consider the "transmission index"—the threshold number of mosquito bites necessary to perpetuate the disease. In Africa, the index overall is 1 bite per person per month. That's all that's necessary to keep malaria in circulation. In India, by comparison, the TI is 10 bites per person per month.

And yet Africa is not a lost cause—it's simply that the key to progress does not lie in the general suppression of mosquito populations. Instead of spraying, the most promising African programs rely primarily on "bednets"—mosquito netting that is treated with an insecticide, usually a pyrethroid, and that is suspended over a person's bed. Bednets can't eliminate malaria, but they can "deflect" much of the burden. Because *Anopheles* species generally feed in the evening and at night, a bednet can radically reduce the number of infective bites a person receives. Such a person would probably still be infected from time to time, but would usually be able to lead a normal life.

In effect, therefore, bednets can substantially reduce the disease. Trials in the use of bednets for children have shown a decline in malaria-induced mortality by 25 to 40 percent. Infection levels and the incidence of severe anemia also declined. In Kenya, a recent study has shown that pregnant women who use bednets tend to give birth to healthier babies. In parts of Chad, Mali, Burkina Faso, and Senegal, bednets are becoming standard household items. In the tiny west African nation of The Gambia, somewhere between 50 and 80 percent of the population has bednets.

Bednets are hardly a panacea. They have to be used properly and retreated with insecticide occasionally. And there is still the problem of insecticide resistance, although the nets themselves are hardly likely to be the main cause of it. (Pyrethroids are used extensively in agriculture as well.) Nevertheless, bednets can help transform malaria from a chronic disaster to a manageable public health problem—something a healthcare system can cope with.

So it's unfortunate that in much of central and southern Africa, the nets are a rarity. It's even more unfortunate that, in 28 African countries, they're taxed or subject to import tariffs. Most of the people in these countries would have trouble paying for a net even without the tax. This problem was addressed in the May 2000 "Abuja Declaration," a summit agreement on infectious diseases signed by 44 African countries. The Declaration included a pledge to do away with "malaria taxes." At last count, 13 countries have actually acted on the pledge, although in some cases only by reducing rather than eliminating the taxes. Since the Declaration was signed, an estimated 2 to 5 million Africans have died from malaria.

This failure to follow through with the Abuja Declaration casts the interest in DDT in a rather poor light. Of the 31 POPs treaty signatories that have reserved the right to use DDT, 21 are in Africa. Of those 21, 10 are apparently still taxing or imposing tariffs on bednets. (Among the African countries that have *not* signed the POPs treaty, some are almost certainly both using DDT and taxing bednets, but the exact number is difficult to ascertain because the status of DDT use is not always clear.) It is true that a case can be made for the use of DDT in situations like the one in South Africa in 1999—an infrequent flare-up in a context that lends itself to control. But the routine use of DDT against malaria is an exercise in toxic futility, especially when it's pursued at the expense of a superior and far more benign technology.

Learning to Live with the Mosquitoes

A group of French researchers recently announced some very encouraging results for a new anti-malarial drug known as G25. The drug was given to infected aotus monkeys, and it appears to have cleared the parasites from their systems. Although extensive testing will be necessary before it is known whether the drug can be safely given to people, these results have raised the hope of a cure for the disease.

Of course, it would be wonderful if G25, or some other new drug, lives up to that promise. But even in the absence of a cure, there are opportunities for progress that may one day make the current incidence of malaria look like some dark age horror. Many of these opportunities have been incorporated into an initiative that began in 1998, called the Roll Back Malaria (RBM) campaign, a collaborative effort between WHO, the World Bank, UNICEF, and the UNDP [United Nations Development Programme]. In contrast to the earlier WHO eradication program, RBM grew out of joint efforts between WHO and various African governments specifically to address African malaria. RBM focuses on household- and community-level intervention and it emphasizes apparently modest changes that could yield major progress. Below are four "operating principles" that are, in one way or another, implicit in RBM or likely to reinforce its progress.

1. Do away with all taxes and tariffs on bednets, on pesticides intended for treating bednets, and on antimalarial drugs. Failure to act on this front certainly undercuts claims for the necessity of DDT; it may also undercut claims for antimalaria foreign aid.

2. Emphasize appropriate technologies. Where, for example, the need for mud to replaster walls is creating lots of pothole sized cavities near houses—cavities that fill with water and then with mosquito larvae—it makes more sense to help people improve their housing maintenance than it does to set up a program for squirting pesticide into every pothole. To be "appropriate," a technology has to be both affordable and culturally acceptable. Improving home maintenance should pass this test; so should bednets. And of course there are many other possibilities. In Kenya, for example, a research institution called the International Center for Insect Physiology and Ecology has identified at least a dozen native east African plants that repel *Anopheles gambiae* in lab tests. Some of these plants could be important additions to household gardens.

3. Use existing networks whenever possible, instead of building new ones. In Tanzania, for example, an established healthcare program (UNICEF's Integrated Management of Childhood Illness Program) now dispenses antimalarial drugs—and instruction on how to use them. The UNICEF program was already operating, so it was simple and cheap to add the malaria component. Reported instances of severe malaria and anemia in infants have declined, apparently as a result. In Zambia, the government is planning to use health and prenatal clinics as the network for a coupon system that subsidizes bednets for the poor. Qualifying patients would pick up coupons at the clinics and redeem them at stores for the nets.

4. Assume that sound policy will involve action on many fronts. Malaria is not just a health problem—it's a social problem, an economic problem, an environmental problem, an agricultural problem, an urban planning problem. Health officials alone cannot possibly just make it go away. When the disease flares up, there is a strong and understandable temptation to strap on the spray equipment and douse the mosquitoes. But if this approach actually worked, we wouldn't be in this situation today. Arguably the biggest opportunity for progress against the disease lies, not in our capacity for chemical innovation, but in our capacity for *organizational innovation*—in our ability to build an awareness of the threat across a broad range of policy activities. For example, when government officials are considering loans to irrigation projects, they should be asking: has the potential for malaria been addressed? When foreign donors are designing antipoverty programs, they should be asking: do people need bednets? Routine inquiries of this sort could go a vast distance to reducing the disease.

Where is the DDT in all of this? There isn't any, and that's the point. We now have half a century of evidence that routine use of DDT simply will not prevail against the mosquitoes. Most countries have already absorbed this lesson, and banned the chemical or relegated it to emergency only status. Now the RBM campaign and associated efforts are showing that the frequency and intensity of those emergencies can be reduced through systematic attention to the chronic aspects of the disease. There is less and less justification for DDT, and the futility of using it as a matter of routine is becoming increasingly apparent: in order to control a disease, why should we poison our soils, our waters, and ourselves?

Donald R. Roberts

The Role of Science in Environmental Policy-Making

Thank you, Chairman Inhofe, and distinguished members of the Committee on Environment and Public Works, for the opportunity to present my views on the misuse of science in public policy. My testimony focuses on misrepresentations of science during decades of environmental campaigning against DDT.

Before discussing how and why DDT science has been misrepresented, you first must understand why this misrepresentation has not helped, but rather harmed, millions of people every year all over the world. Specifically you need to understand why the misrepresentation of DDT science has been and continues to be deadly. By way of explanation, I will tell you something of my experience.

I conducted malaria research in the Amazon Basin in the 1970s. My Brazilian colleague—who is now the Secretary of Health for Amazonas State—and I worked out of Manaus, the capitol of Amazonas State. From Manaus we traveled two days to a study site where we had sufficient numbers of cases for epidemiological studies. There were no cases in Manaus, or anywhere near Manaus. For years before my time there and for years thereafter, there were essentially no cases of malaria in Manaus. However, in the late 1980s, environmentalists and international guidelines forced Brazilians to reduce and then stop spraying small amounts of DDT inside houses for malaria control. As a result, in 2002 and 2003 there were over 100,000 malaria cases in Manaus alone.

Brazil does not stand as the single example of this phenomenon. A similar pattern of declining use of DDT and reemerging malaria occurs in other countries as well, Peru for example. Similar resurgences of malaria have occurred in rural communities, villages, towns, cities, and countries around the world. As illustrated by the return of malaria in Russia, South Korea, urban areas of the Amazon Basin, and increasing frequencies of outbreaks in the United States, our malaria problems are growing worse. Today there are 1 to 2 million malaria deaths each year and hundreds of millions of cases. The poorest of the world's people are at greatest risk. Of these, children and pregnant women are the ones most likely to die.

We have long known about DDT's effectiveness in curbing insect-borne disease. Othmar Zeidler, a German chemistry student, first synthesized DDT in 1874. Over sixty years later in Switzerland, Paul Müller discovered the

U.S. Senate Committee on Environment and Public Works, September 28, 2005.

insecticidal property of DDT. Allied forces used DDT during WWII, and the new insecticide gained fame in 1943 by successfully stopping an epidemic of typhus in Naples, an unprecedented achievement. By the end of the war, British, Italian, and American scientists had also demonstrated the effectiveness of DDT in controlling malaria-carrying mosquitoes. DDT's proven efficacy against insect-borne diseases, diseases that had long reigned unchecked throughout the world, won Müller the Nobel Prize for Medicine in 1948. After WWII, the United States conducted a National Malaria Eradication Program, commencing operations on July 1, 1947. The spraying of DDT on internal walls of rural homes in malaria endemic counties was a key component of the program. By the end of 1949, the program had sprayed over 4,650,000 houses. This spraying broke the cycle of malaria transmission, and in 1949 the United States was declared free of malaria as a significant public health problem. Other countries had already adopted DDT to eradicate or control malaria, because wherever malaria control programs sprayed DDT on house walls, the malaria rates dropped precipitously. The effectiveness of DDT stimulated some countries to create, for the first time, a national malaria control program. Countries with pre-existing programs expanded them to accommodate the spraying of houses in rural areas with DDT. Those program expansions highlight what DDT offered then, and still offers now, to the malaria endemic countries. As a 1945 U.S. Public Health Service manual explained about the control of malaria: "Drainage and larviciding are the methods of choice in towns of 2,500 or more people. But malaria is a rural disease. Heretofore there has been no economically feasible method of carrying malaria control to the individual tenant farmer or sharecropper. Now, for the first time, a method is available—the application of DDT residual spray to walls and ceilings of homes." Health workers in the United States were not the only ones to recognize the particular value of DDT. The head of malaria control in Brazil characterized the changes that DDT offered in the following statement: "Until 1945–1946, preventive methods employed against malaria in Brazil, as in the rest of the world, were generally directed against the aquatic phases of the vectors (draining, larvicides, destruction of bromeliads, etc. . . .). These methods, however, were only applied in the principal cities of each state and the only measure available for rural populations exposed to malaria was free distribution of specific drugs."

DDT was a new, effective, and exciting weapon in the battle against malaria. It was cheap, easy to apply, long-lasting once sprayed on house walls, and safe for humans. Wherever and whenever malaria control programs sprayed it on house walls, they achieved rapid and large reductions in malaria rates. Just as there was a rush to quickly make use of DDT to control disease, there was also a rush to judge how DDT actually functioned to control malaria. That rush to judgment turned out to be a disaster. At the heart of the debate—to the extent there was a debate—was a broadly accepted model that established a mathematical framework for using DDT to kill mosquitoes and eradicate malaria. Instead of studying real data to see how DDT actually worked in controlling malaria, some scientists settled upon what

they thought was a logical conclusion: DDT worked solely by killing mosquitoes. This conclusion was based on their belief in the model. Scientists who showed that DDT did not function by killing mosquitoes were ignored. Broad acceptance of the mathematical model led to strong convictions about DDT's toxic actions. Since they were convinced that DDT worked only by killing mosquitoes, malaria control specialists became very alarmed when a mosquito was reported to be resistant to DDT's toxic actions. As a result of concern about DDT resistance, officials decided to make rapid use of DDT before problems of resistance could eliminate their option to use DDT to eradicate malaria. This decision led to creation of the global malaria eradication program. The active years of the global malaria eradication program were from 1959 to 1969. Before, during, and after the many years of this program, malaria workers and researchers carried out their responsibilities to conduct studies and report their research. Through those studies, they commonly found that DDT was functioning in ways other than by killing mosquitoes. In essence, they found that DDT was functioning through mechanisms of repellency and irritancy. Eventually, as people forgot early observations of DDT's repellent actions, some erroneously interpreted new findings of repellent actions as the mosquitoes' adaptation to avoid DDT toxicity, even coining a term, "behavioral resistance," to explain what they saw. This new term accommodated their view that toxicity was DDT's primary mode of action and categorized behavioral responses of mosquitoes as mere adaptations to toxic affects. However this interpretation depended upon a highly selective use of scientific data. The truth is that toxicity is not DDT's primary mode of action when sprayed on house walls. Throughout the history of DDT use in malaria control programs there has always been clear and persuasive data that DDT functioned primarily as a spatial repellent. Today we know that there is no insecticide recommended for malaria control that rivals, much less equals, DDT's spatial repellent actions, or that is as long-acting, as cheap, as easy to apply, as safe for human exposure, or as efficacious in the control of malaria as DDT. . . . The 30 years of data from control programs of the Americas plotted . . . illustrate just how effective DDT is in malaria control. The period 1960s through 1979 displays a pattern of malaria controlled through house spraying. In 1979 the World Health Organization (WHO) changed its strategy for malaria control, switching emphasis from spraying houses to case detection and treatment. In other words, the WHO changed emphasis from malaria prevention to malaria treatment. Countries complied with WHO guidelines and started to dismantle their spray programs over the next several years. . . .

I find it amazing that many who oppose the use of DDT describe its earlier use as a failure. Our own citizens who suffered under the burden of malaria, especially in the rural south, would hardly describe it thus.

Malaria was a serious problem in the United States and for some localities, such as Dunklin County, Missouri, it was a very serious problem indeed. For four counties in Missouri, the average malaria mortality from 1910 to 1914 was 168.8 per 100,000 population. For Dunklin County, it was 296.7 per 100,000, a rate almost equal to malaria deaths in Venezuela and actually

greater than the mortality rate for Freetown, Sierra Leone. Other localities in other states were equally as malarious. Growing wealth and improved living conditions were gradually reducing malaria rates, but cases resurged during WWII. The advent of DDT, however, quickly eradicated malaria from the United States.

DDT routed malaria from many other countries as well. The Europeans who were freed of malaria would hardly describe its use as a failure. After DDT was introduced to malaria control in Sri Lanka (then Ceylon), the number of malaria cases fell from 2.8 million in 1946 to just 110 in 1961. Similar spectacular decreases in malaria cases and deaths were seen in all the regions that began to use DDT. The newly formed Republic of China (Taiwan) adopted DDT use in malaria control shortly after World War II. In 1945 there were over 1 million cases of malaria on the island. By 1969 there were only 9 cases and shortly thereafter the disease was eradicated from the island and remains so to this day. Some countries were less fortunate. South Korea used DDT to eradicate malaria, but without house spray programs, malaria has returned across the demilitarized zone with North Korea. As DDT was eliminated and control programs reduced, malaria has returned to other countries such as Russia and Argentina. Small outbreaks of malaria are even beginning to appear more frequently in the United States.

These observations have been offered in testimony to document first that there were fundamental misunderstandings about how DDT functioned to exert control over malaria. Second, that regardless of systematic misunderstandings on the part of those who had influence over malaria control strategies and policies, there was an enduring understanding that DDT was the most cost-effective compound yet discovered for protecting poor rural populations from insect-borne diseases like malaria, dengue, yellow fever, and leishmaniasis. I want to emphasize that misunderstanding the mode of DDT action did not lead to the wholesale abandonment of DDT. It took an entirely new dimension in the misuse of science to bring us to the current humanitarian disaster represented by DDT elimination.

The misuse of science to which I refer has found fullest expression in the collection of movements within the environmental movement that seek to stop production and use of specific man-made chemicals. Operatives within these movements employ particular strategies to achieve their objectives. By characterizing and understanding the strategies these operatives use, we can identify their impact in the scientific literature or in the popular press.

The first strategy is to develop and then distribute as widely as possible a broad list of claims of chemical harm. This is a sound strategy because individual scientists can seldom rebut the scientific foundations of multiple and diverse claims. Scientists generally develop expertise in a single, narrow field and are disinclined to engage issues beyond their area of expertise. Even if an authoritative rebuttal of one claim occurs, the other claims still progress. A broad list of claims also allows operatives to tailor platforms for constituencies, advancing one set of claims with one constituency and a different combination for another. Clever though this technique is, a list of multiple claims of harm is hardly sufficient to achieve the objective of a ban. The second strategy then

is to mount an argument that the chemical is not needed and propose that alternative chemicals or methods can be used instead. The third strategy is to predict that grave harm will occur if the chemical continues to be used.

The success of Rachel Carson's *Silent Spring* serves as a model for this tricky triad. In *Silent Spring*, Rachel Carson used all three strategies on her primary target, DDT. She described a very large list of potential adverse effects of insecticides, DDT in particular. She argued that insecticides were not really needed and that the use of insecticides produces insects that are insecticide resistant, which only exacerbates the insect control problems. She predicted scary scenarios of severe harm with continued use of DDT and other insecticides. Many have written rebuttals to Rachel Carson and others who have, without scientific justification, broadcast long lists of potential harms of insecticides. . . .

[T]ime and science have discredited most of Carson's claims. Rachel Carson's descriptions of inappropriate uses of insecticides that harmed wildlife are more plausible. However, harm from an inappropriate use does not meet the requirements of anti-pesticide activists. They can hardly lobby for eliminating a chemical because someone used it wrongly. No, success requires that even the proper use of an insecticide will cause a large and systematic adverse effect. However, the proper uses of DDT yield no large and systematic adverse effects. Absent such adverse actions, the activists must then rely on claims about insidious effects, particularly insidious effects that scientists will find difficult to prove one way or the other and that activists can use to predict a future catastrophe.

Rachel Carson relied heavily on possible insidious chemical actions to alarm and frighten the public. Many of those who joined her campaign to ban DDT and other insecticides made extensive use of claims of insidious effects. These claims were amplified by the popular press and became part of the public perception about modern uses of chemicals. For example, four well-publicized claims about DDT were:

1. DDT will cause the obliteration of higher trophic levels. If not obliterated, populations will undergo reproductive failure. Authors of this claim speculated that, even if the use of DDT were stopped, systematic and ongoing obliterations would still occur.
2. DDT causes the death of algae. This report led to speculations that use of DDT could result in global depletion of oxygen.
3. DDT pushed the Bermuda petrel to the verge of extinction and that full extinction might happen by 1978.
4. DDT was a cause of premature births in California sea lions.

Science magazine, the most prestigious science journal in the United States, published these and other phantasmagorical allegations and/or predictions of DDT harm. Nonetheless, history has shown that each and every one of these claims and predictions were false.

1. The obliteration of higher trophic levels did not occur; no species became extinct; and levels of DDT in all living organisms declined

precipitously after DDT was de-listed for use in agriculture. How could the prediction have been so wrong? Perhaps it was so wrong because the paper touting this view used a predictive model based on an assumption of no DDT degradation. This was a startling assertion even at the time as *Science* and other journals had previously published papers that showed DDT was ubiquitously degraded in the environment and in living creatures. It was even more startling that *Science* published a paper that flew so comprehensively in the face of previous data and analysis.

2. DDT's action against algae reportedly occurred at concentrations of 500 parts per billion. But DDT cannot reach concentrations in water higher than about 1.2 parts per billion, the saturation point of DDT in water.

3. Data on the Bermuda petrel did not show a cause-and-effect relationship between low numbers of birds and DDT concentrations. DDT had no effect on population numbers, for populations increased before DDT was de-listed for use in agriculture and after DDT was de-listed as well.

4. Data gathered in subsequent years showed that "despite relatively high concentrations [of DDT], no evidence that population growth or the health of individual California sea lions have been compromised. The population has increased throughout the century, including the period when DDT was being manufactured, used, and its wastes discharged off southern California."

If time and science have refuted all these catastrophic predictions, why do many scientists and the public not know these predictions were false? In part, we do not know the predictions were false because the refutations of such claims rarely appear in the literature.

When scientists hear the kinds of claims described above, they initiate research to confirm or refute the claims. After Charles Wurster published his claim that DDT kills algae and impacts photosynthesis, I initiated research on planktonic algae to quantify DDT's effects. From 1968–1969, I spent a year of honest and demanding research effort to discover that not enough DDT would even go into solution for a measurable adverse effect on planktonic algae. In essence, I conducted a confirmatory study that failed to confirm an expected result. I had negative data, and journals rarely accept negative data for publication. My year was practically wasted. Without a doubt, hundreds of other scientists around the world have conducted similar studies and obtained negative results, and they too were unable to publish their experimental findings. Much in the environmental science literature during the last 20–30 years indicates that an enormous research effort went into proving specific insidious effects of DDT and other insecticides. Sadly, the true magnitude of such efforts will never be known because while the positive results of research find their way into the scientific literature, the negative results rarely do. Research on insidious actions that produce negative results all too often ends up only in laboratory and field notebooks and is forgotten. For this reason, I place considerable weight on a published confirmatory study that fails to confirm an expected result.

The use of the tricky triad continues. A . . . recent paper . . . published in *The Lancet* illustrates the triad's modern application. Two scientists at the National Institute of Environmental Health Sciences, Walter Rogan and Aimin Chen, wrote this paper, entitled "Health risks and benefits of bis(4-chlorophenyl)-1,1,1-trichloroethane (DDT)." It is interesting to see how this single paper spins all three strategies that gained prominence in Rachel Carson's *Silent Spring*.

The journal *Emerging Infectious Diseases* had already published a slim version of this paper, which international colleagues and I promptly rebutted. The authors then filled in some parts, added to the claims of harm, and republished the paper in the British journal, *The Lancet*. To get the paper accepted by editors, the authors described studies that support (positive results) as well as studies that do not support (negative results) each claim. Complying with strategy number 1 of the triad, Rogan and Chen produce a long list of possible harms, including the charge that DDT causes cancer in nonhuman primates. The literature reference for Rogan and Chen's claim that DDT causes cancer in nonhuman primates was a paper by Takayama et al. Takayama and coauthors actually concluded from their research on the carcinogenic effect of DDT in nonhuman primates that "the two cases involving malignant tumors of different types are inconclusive with respect to a carcinogenic effect of DDT in nonhuman primates." Clearly, the people who made the link of DDT with cancer were not the scientists who actually conducted the research.

The authors enacted strategy number two of the triad by conducting a superficial review of the role of DDT in malaria control with the goal of discrediting DDT's value in modern malaria control programs. The authors admitted that DDT had been very effective in the past, but then argued that malaria control programs no longer needed it and should use alternative methods of control. Their use of the second strategy reveals, in my opinion, the greatest danger of granting authority to anti-pesticide activists and their writings. As *The Lancet* paper reveals, the NIEHS scientists assert great authority over the topic of DDT, yet they assume no responsibility for the harm that might result from their erroneous conclusions. After many malaria control specialists have expressed the necessity for DDT in malaria control, it is possible for Rogan and Chen to conclude that DDT is not necessary in malaria control only if they have no sense of responsibility for levels of disease and death that will occur if DDT is not used.

Rogan and Chen also employ the third strategy of environmentalism. Their list of potential harms caused by DDT includes toxic effects, neurobehavior effects, cancers, decrements in various facets of reproductive health, decrements in infant and child development, and immunology and DNA damage. After providing balanced coverage of diverse claims of harm, the authors had no option but to conclude they could not prove that DDT caused harm. However, they then promptly negated this honest conclusion by asserting that if DDT is used for malaria control, then great harm might occur. So, in an amazing turn, they conclude they cannot prove DDT causes harm, but still predict severe harm if it is used.

Rogan and Chen end their paper with a call for more research. One could conclude that the intent of the whole paper is merely to lobby for research to better define DDT harm, and what's the harm in that? Surely increasing knowledge

is a fine goal. However, if you look at the specific issue of the relative need for research, you will see that the harm of this technique is great. Millions of children and pregnant women die from malaria every year, and the disease sickens hundreds of millions more. This is an indisputable fact: impoverished people engage in real life and death struggles every day with malaria. This also is a fact: not one death or illness can be attributed to an environmental exposure to DDT. Yet, a National Library of Medicine literature search on DDT reveals over 1,300 published papers from the year 2000 to the present, almost all in the environmental literature and many on potential adverse effects of DDT. A search on malaria and DDT reveals only 159 papers. DDT is a spatial repellent and hardly an insecticide at all, but a search on DDT and repellents will reveal only 7 papers. Is this not an egregiously disproportionate research emphasis on non-sources of harm compared to the enormous harm of malaria? Does not this inequity contribute to the continued suffering of those who struggle with malaria? Is it possibly even more than an inequity? Is it not an active wrong?

Public health officials and scientists should not be silent about enormous investments into the research of theoretical risks while millions die of preventable diseases. We should seriously consider our motivations in apportioning research money as we do. Consider this: the U.S. used DDT to eradicate malaria. After malaria disappeared as an endemic disease in the United States, we became richer. We built better and more enclosed houses. We screened our windows and doors. We air conditioned our homes. We also developed an immense arsenal of mosquito control tools and chemicals. Today, when we have a risk of mosquito borne disease, we can bring this arsenal to bear and quickly eliminate risks. And, as illustrated by aerial spray missions in the aftermath of hurricane Katrina, we can afford to do so. Yet, our modern and very expensive chemicals are not what protect us from introductions of the old diseases. Our arsenal responds to the threat; it does not prevent the appearance of old diseases in our midst. What protects us is our enclosed, screened, air-conditioned housing, the physical representation of our wealth. Our wealth is the factor that stops dengue at the border with Mexico, not our arsenal of new chemicals. Stopping mosquitoes from entering and biting us inside our homes is critical in the prevention of malaria and many other insect-borne diseases. This is what DDT does for poor people in poor countries. It stops large proportions of mosquitoes from entering houses. It is, in fact, a form of chemical screening, and until these people can afford physical screening or it is provided for them, this is the only kind of screening they have.

DDT is a protective tool that has been taken away from countries around the world, mostly due to governments acceding to the whims of the anti-pesticide wing of environmentalism, but it is not only the anti-pesticide wing that lobbies against DDT. The activists have a sympathetic lobbying ally in the pesticide industry. As evidence of insecticide industry working to stop countries from using DDT, I am attaching an email message dated 23rd September and authored by a Bayer official. . . . The Bayer official states

"[I speak] Not only as the responsible manager for the vector control business in Bayer, being the market leader in vector control and pointing out by that we know what we are talking about and have decades of

experiences in the evolution of this very particular market. [but] Also as one of the private sector representatives in the RBM Partnership Board and being confronted with that discussion about DDT in the various WHO, RBM et al circles. So you can take it as a view from the field, from the operational commercial level—but our companies [sic] point of view. I know that all of my colleagues from other primary manufacturers and internationally operating companies are sharing my view."

The official goes on to say that

"DDT use is for us a commercial threat (which is clear, but it is not that dramatical because of limited use), it is mainly a public image threat."

However the most damning part of this message was the statement that

"we fully support EU to ban imports of agricultural products coming from countries using DDT"

[There is] . . . clear evidence of international and developed country pressures to stop poor countries from using DDT to control malaria. This message also shows the complicity of the insecticide industry in those internationally orchestrated efforts.

Pressures to eliminate spray programs, and DDT in particular, are wrong. I say this not based on some projection of what might theoretically happen in the future according to some model, or some projection of theoretical harms, I say this based firmly on what has already occurred. The track record of the anti-pesticide lobby is well documented, the pressures on developing countries to abandon their spray programs are well documented, and the struggles of developing countries to maintain their programs or restart their uses of DDT for malaria control are well documented. The tragic results of pressures against the use of DDT, in terms of increasing disease and death, are quantified and well documented. How long will scientists, public health officials, the voting public, and the politicians who lead us continue policies, regulations and funding that have led us to the current state of a global humanitarian disaster? How long will support continue for policies and programs that favor phantoms over facts?

EXPLORING THE ISSUE

Should DDT Be Banned Worldwide?

Critical Thinking and Reflection

1. How can DDT be used to control malaria without harming the environment?
2. How do mosquitoes develop resistance to pesticides?
3. Why are bednets *not* a perfect preventative for mosquito-borne malaria?
4. Which is more important, the lives of humans (threatened by malaria) or the lives of birds (threatened by DDT)?

Is There Common Ground?

There is no disagreement that malaria is a major public health problem, especially in tropical countries. Nor is there disagreement that it needs to be controlled. The debate is over methods of control, and it is complicated by the simple fact that many countries with large malaria burdens are poor countries whose people cannot afford some things we take for granted, such as window screens.

1. Why do efforts to supply malaria-afflicted populations require international financial assistance?
2. Why do rich countries not invest more money in antimalaria research?
3. Why do poor, malaria-afflicted countries favor the use of DDT?

ISSUE 10

Can Infectious Animal Diseases Be Studied Safely in Kansas?

YES: Bruce Knight, from "Statement on the National Bio- and Agro-Defense Facility," before the Subcommittee on Oversight and Investigation, House Energy and Commerce Committee (May 22, 2008)

NO: Ray L. Wulf, from "Written Testimony," submitted for the Record to the Subcommittee on Oversight and Investigation, House Energy and Commerce Committee (May 22, 2008)

Learning Outcomes

After studying this issue, students will be able to:

1. Explain the need for reliable isolation or containment measures when doing research on infectious animal and human diseases.
2. Compare the advantages of geographic and technological isolation or containment measures.
3. Discuss the economic impact of an outbreak of foot-and-mouth disease.

ISSUE SUMMARY

YES: Bruce Knight argues that although the U.S. Department of Agriculture's research facility at Plum Island, New York, has served well since it was built over half a century ago, modern technology is capable of ensuring safety at a mainland facility, which would also be cheaper to operate, more easily accessible, and more responsive to potential disease threats.

NO: Ray L. Wulf argues that an island location is much more effective at containing infectious diseases such as foot-and-mouth disease. A mainland research facility would permit unhampered spread of such diseases throughout the continental United States, with devastating consequences for the agricultural economy. Modern technology is not adequate to ensure safety, and federal, state, and local authorities are not prepared to deal with an outbreak.

Plum Island, located off the coast of Long Island in New York State, became a center of research into deadly animal diseases in 1954. At that time, responding to outbreaks of foot-and-mouth disease (FMD) in Mexico and Canada, the U.S. Army gave the island to the U.S. Department of Agriculture (USDA) to establish a research center for studying FMD. The island location was chosen because it was isolated from the mainland and the prevailing winds blow out to sea. FMD can be spread by the wind, and it is highly contagious. The island location was regarded as the safest possible place to work with diseases such as FMD.

Today, the Plum Island Animal Disease Center is responsible for protecting the U.S. livestock industry against catastrophic economic losses caused by foreign animal disease agents accidentally or deliberately introduced into the United States. It does this by performing research into disease detection and diagnosis, vaccines, drugs, and risk assessment. It also trains animal health professionals. It is proud of its safety record; its Web site claims that "Not once in our nearly 50 years of operation has an animal pathogen escaped from the island."

The island was transferred from the USDA to the Department of Homeland Security (DHS) in 2003. The DHS soon began to rethink the facility as the National Bio- and Agro-Defense Facility, upgraded to provide more space for the study of diseases that can infect both animals and humans. Such research would require Biosafety Level 4 laboratories, the highest security level. Plum Island at the time had only Biosafety Level 3 laboratories, and area residents had resisted proposals to upgrade the laboratories to Level 4. DHS also thought it would be advantageous to move the research facility to the mainland and soon narrowed the list of candidate sites to six (including Plum Island). The final choice was Manhattan, Kansas, near to a major university and research community but also very close to large populations of livestock. Critics have objected that the choice of Kansas was unduly influenced by aggressive lobbying by the state's senators and governor; see Yudhijit Bhattacharjee, "How Kansas Nabbed the New Bio- and Agro-Defense Lab," *Science* (December 12, 2008). As of late 2010, the Kansas choice stands, and Plum Island is to be sold.

At the hearing of the Subcommittee on Oversight and Investigation, House Energy and Commerce Committee, for which the testimony presented in the NO selection was prepared, the U.S. Government Accounting Office (GAO) testified that the DHS had not suitably evaluated the risks of moving the Plum Island Animal Disease Center to the mainland. On December 12, 2008, DHS released a final Environmental Impact Statement (EIS), and on January 16, 2009, it announced its choice of Manhattan, Kansas, as the new location, basing the choice on the information and analysis in the final EIS (http://www.dhs.gov) and other factors.

The GAO then undertook to analyze the EIS, noting that DHS was restricted by law from moving the Plum Island facility to the mainland until it had completed a risk assessment on whether FMD research can be done there as safely as on the island. The GAO specifically assessed the evidence DHS said supported its decision. Unfortunately, said the GAO, "DHS's analyses did not

effectively characterize and differentiate the risks associated with the release of FMD virus at the six sites. . . . The economic analyses did not incorporate market response to an FMD outbreak—which would be related to the number of livestock in the site's vicinity. They also did not consider the effect of establishing a containment zone to control the effects of a national export ban on the domestic livestock industry—which could have been used to differentiate across National Bio and Agro-Defense Facility sites. The analyses were constrained by limited scope and detail. They did not incorporate worst-case outbreak scenarios. . . . Given the significant limitations in DHS's analyses that we found, the conclusion that FMD work can be done as safely on the mainland as on Plum Island is not supported." See the GAO report at http://www .gao.gov/products/GAO-09-747. In November 2010, the National Research Council issued a safety report, which concluded that there is a 70 percent chance of pathogen release from the proposed Manhattan, Kansas BioLab-4 over a 50-year period; see "National Research Council Questions Safety of Proposed Biocontainment Lab in Kansas," http://www.thefreelibrary.com/National+research+council+ questions+safety+of+proposed+biocontainment...-a0243277969. New York officials are objecting to the move on the grounds of expense and jobs, among other things.

According to Carol D. Leonnig, "Infectious Diseases Study Site Questioned: Tornado Alley May Not Be Safe, GAO Says," *Washington Post* (July 27, 2009), DHS officials are claiming that the GAO exceeded its authority in reviewing the DHS risk assessment. They are also pushing to delay further hearings of the Subcommittee on Oversight and Investigation, House Energy and Commerce Committee. No such hearings had been held by the end of 2010.

It is worth noting that risk assessment is a complex activity. One recent textbook, Paolo F. Ricci's *Environmental and Health Risk Assessment and Management: Principles and Practices* (Springer Netherlands, 2009), stresses the need for "sound causal arguments," which is where the GAO says the DHS falls short. However, the president of Kansas State University in Manhattan, Kansas, remains delighted that his campus was chosen by DHS to house Plum Island's replacement, according to a press release, "President Kirk Schulz Keeping K-State at the Forefront of National Animal Health."

In the YES selection taken from testimony before the Subcommittee on Oversight and Investigation, House Energy and Commerce Committee, Bruce Knight, then the USDA's Under Secretary for Marketing and Regulatory Programs, argues that although the USDA's research facility at Plum Island, New York, has served well since it was built over half a century ago, modern technology is capable of ensuring safety at a mainland facility, which would also be cheaper to operate, more easily accessible, and more responsive to potential disease threats. In the NO selection, farmer and rancher Ray L. Wulf argues that an island location is much more effective at containing infectious diseases such as FMD. A mainland research facility would permit unhampered spread of such diseases throughout the continental United States, with devastating consequences for the agricultural economy. Modern technology is not adequate to ensure safety, and federal, state, and local authorities are not prepared to deal with an outbreak.

YES

Bruce Knight

Statement on the National Bio- and Agro-Defense Facility

. . . **A**griculture is a vital component of our nation's economy. Of particular importance to homeland security is the significant increase in agricultural trade. This year, we expect agriculture exports to reach approximately $101 billion, making it the highest export sales year ever in our history—and significant to our balance of trade. Agriculture imports are rising as well—increasing from nearly $58 billion in 2005 to an estimated $76.5 billion this year.

We face many challenges in protecting this important infrastructure. As goods move back and forth across the border, we must remain vigilant to safeguard U.S. agriculture from unwelcome pest and disease threats. Our sector is particularly concerned about security because food production is not constrained by political boundaries, and as we all know, diseases and pathogens do not respect state or national borders. The interconnected nature of the global food system is our strength and allows us to feed the world, but it is also a disadvantage in the event of attack or natural disease outbreak. Additionally, one of the agricultural sector's greatest contributions to the quality of life is the fact that products flow quickly through interstate commerce—one of our greatest assets is also one of our greatest concerns because intentionally or unintentionally contaminated products could quickly spread a pest, disease, or other agent.

USDA works diligently to protect U.S. agriculture from the potential introduction of human and animal disease agents, whether unintentionally or through agroterrorism. Many of these pathogens such as the Nipah and Hendra viruses are zoonotic, that is, they cause both human and animal disease, and can pass from animals to humans. If a significant zoonotic or animal disease were to penetrate our borders, it could devastate the agricultural industry, cause numerous casualties, and harm the economy.

We've seen just how disastrous the effects of a foreign animal disease outbreak can be in the 2001 foot-and-mouth disease (FMD) outbreak in the United Kingdom. In that case, over 6 million pigs, sheep, and cattle were destroyed, with the epidemic costing the U.K. economy an estimated $13 billion. This example highlights the need for the best tools and diagnostics to safeguard the U.S. livestock industry from significant foreign animal disease threats such as FMD. At the same time, the 2007 suspected release of live FMD virus from the Pirbright campus in England amplifies the balance needed in

U.S. House of Representatives, May 22, 2008.

undertaking such work. This is why USDA and the Department of Homeland Security (DHS) will use the most modern biosafety practices and procedures, and stringent and rigorous safety measures within NBAF.

Because of the continued emergence of new animal diseases, the leaping of dangerous animal diseases across species, and the possibility of a bioterrorist release, it is even more essential that USDA have a sufficient understanding of these diseases and be well prepared to protect the U.S. livestock industry from their damage. To achieve this, USDA works through its Agricultural Research Service (ARS) and Animal and Plant Health Inspection Service (APHIS) to meet its responsibilities in animal health. ARS is the primary intramural science research agency of USDA, operating a network of over 100 research laboratories across the nation that work on all aspects of agricultural science. APHIS is responsible for safeguarding U.S. agricultural health from foreign pests and diseases of plants and animals.

In order to be able to rapidly identify, respond to, and control outbreaks of foreign animal and zoonotic disease, USDA needs secure, state-of-the-art biocontainment laboratories with adequate space for advanced research, diagnostics, and training. Recognizing this need, the President directed USDA and DHS, via Homeland Security Presidential Directive 9: "Defense of the United States Agriculture and Food," to develop a plan to provide for such facilities. As I will explain further, USDA is working closely with our partners in DHS to fulfill this important need.

Plum Island Animal Disease Center

In 1954, USDA began work at the Plum Island Animal Disease Center (PIADC) in research and diagnostics on foreign animal diseases that, either by accidental or deliberate introduction to the United States, pose significant health and/or economic risks to the U.S. livestock industry. The Plum Island Animal Disease Center has served U.S. agriculture well. It's no accident that this country has the healthiest and most abundant livestock populations in the world. Producers and all of us at USDA work hard every day to keep this up.

An integral part of maintaining animal health is preventing the entry of exotic pest and disease threats. The Plum Island Animal Disease Center, through its diagnostic, research, and reagent production and distribution activities, has stood as American agriculture's bulwark against potentially devastating foreign animal diseases. Each working day since the facility opened over 50 years ago, the dedicated and highly skilled Plum Island Animal Disease Center staff has equipped veterinarians, scientists, professors, and other animal health professionals here and around the world with the tools they need to fight exotic disease incursions that threaten livestock. In addition to FMD and classical swine fever, other livestock diseases that our scientists have studied at the Plum Island Animal Disease Center include African swine fever, rinderpest, Rift Valley fever, West Nile fever, vesicular stomatitis, and Capri pox (sheep pox and lumpy skin disease).

As you know, in June 2003, operational responsibility for the Plum Island Animal Disease Center transferred from USDA to DHS under the Homeland

Security Act of 2002. Since the transfer, we've developed a strong, collaborative partnership with DHS and put in place an interagency agreement to clarify roles and responsibilities. A Board of Directors and Senior Leadership Group were created to facilitate decision-making regarding facility operations and policies, while also allowing the three agencies to focus on accomplishing their specific missions and goals. I believe our relationship with DHS is a very positive one that allows both Departments to achieve our similar goals while making the most of each other's specialized expertise.

After the Plum Island Animal Disease Center transfer, USDA remained responsible for conducting basic and applied research and diagnostic activities at the Plum Island Animal Disease Center to protect U.S. agriculture from foreign animal disease agents. DHS, in turn, assumed responsibility for coordinating the overall national effort to protect key U.S. resources and infrastructure, including agriculture. Science programs at the Plum Island Animal Disease Center now include the APHIS Foreign Animal Disease Diagnostic Laboratory (FADDL), ARS' Foreign Animal Disease Research Unit, and DHS' Targeted Advanced Development Unit. . . .

APHIS scientists perform diagnostic testing of samples collected from U.S. livestock that are showing clinical signs consistent with an exotic disease, as well as testing animal products and live animals being imported into the United States to ensure that unwanted diseases are not accidentally introduced through importation. APHIS scientists at the Plum Island Animal Disease Center have the capability to diagnose more than 30 exotic animal diseases, and perform thousands of diagnostic tests each year. They also prepare diagnostic reagents and distribute them to laboratories throughout the world, and test the safety and efficacy of vaccines for selected foreign animal diseases. Other APHIS activities include improving techniques for the diagnosis or control of foreign animal diseases and validating tests for foreign animal diseases that are deployed to the National Animal Health Laboratory Network (NAHLN). Through the use of these tests in surveillance, the NAHLN provides for early detection and the surge capability needed in the case of an outbreak.

In addition, FADDL staff, in conjunction with APHIS' Professional Development Staff, train veterinarians, scientists, professors, and veterinary students on recognition of clinical signs and pathological changes caused by foreign animal diseases. This training provides the backbone of APHIS' animal disease surveillance and safeguarding programs. These foreign animal disease diagnosticians trained by FADDL are located throughout the country, and can be on-site to conduct an investigation and collect samples within 16 hours of receiving a report of a suspect foreign animal disease. Based on their assessment of the situation and prioritization of the threat, APHIS can then take appropriate steps if necessary to protect the U.S. livestock industry.

Through its involvement in the Plum Island Animal Disease Center, ARS develops new strategies to prevent and control foreign or emerging animal disease epidemics through a better understanding of the nature of infectious organisms, pathogenesis in susceptible animals, host immune responses, and the development of novel vaccines and diagnostic tests. The ARS Foreign Animal Disease Research Unit focuses on developing vaccines that can be

produced safely in the United States and used safely on U.S. farms, diagnostic techniques to differentiate between a vaccinated and an infected animal, and methods for identifying carrier animals. Currently, ARS' work at the Plum Island Animal Disease Center includes active research programs working with FMD, Classical Swine Fever, and vesicular stomatitis viruses.

ARS scientists have recently carried out extensive work on FMD, including early development of a FMD vaccine that is safe to produce on the mainland; discovery of an antiviral treatment that prevents FMD replication and spread within 24 hours; and determination of many key aspects of FMD virus structure, function, and replication at the molecular level, leading to highly specific diagnostic tests.

Meeting the Needs of American Agriculture

The Plum Island Animal Disease Center has played a critical role in developing the tools and expertise needed to protect the country from the deliberate or unintentional introduction of significant foreign animal diseases. However, much has changed since the Plum Island Animal Disease Center was first built, and we are even more cognizant of the threat from foreign animal diseases due to the increasingly interconnected world we live in. This need is echoed by our American livestock industries that could be devastated by the introduction of a significant foreign animal disease. Groups such as the United States Animal Health Association and National Institute for Animal Agriculture have appealed for accelerated research to protect their industries. Also, the National Cattlemen's Beef Association, Animal Agriculture Coalition, and National Milk Producers Federation have written to Congress, to show their support for NBAF.

To continue providing U.S. agriculture with the latest research and technological services, as well as world-class approaches to agricultural health safeguarding and foreign-animal disease diagnostics, USDA needs additional space and upgraded biosecurity measures to work on those animal-borne diseases that pose the greatest risk to U.S. livestock industries, and those that can also be transmitted to humans. The Plum Island Animal Disease Center is aging and nearing the end of its lifecycle, and the state of current facilities has created a backlog of needed space for important experiments, diagnostic development, and training efforts.

In particular, USDA is in need of enhanced research and diagnostic capabilities for animal diseases, particularly zoonotic diseases of large animals that require agriculture BSL-3 and BSL-4 capabilities. However, since we cannot currently carry out BSL-4 activities at the Plum Island Animal Disease Center, the nation is left lacking a large animal facility to address high-consequence animal diseases that can be transmitted to humans, such as Nipah and Hendra, as well as Rift Valley Fever (which requires vaccinated personnel; however vaccine is in short supply).

Specifically, USDA would utilize the BSL-4 space to develop diagnostic assays for Rift Valley Fever and Nipah and Hendra viruses, using specimens collected from animals in the BSL-4 lab. In addition, in the event of an emerging pathogen, it would often be necessary to inoculate animals in a BSL-4 suite

in order to determine the clinical course of the disease, determine appropriate diagnostic specimens, isolate the agent, and develop diagnostic tools.

In order to protect U.S. agriculture and human health, it is critical that USDA have the capability of diagnosing and working with the disease agents I have mentioned, as well as any new highly infectious pathogen that may emerge. In response, our agencies have begun planning for the next generation facility which we call the NBAF, to replace the current structures at the Plum Island Animal Disease Center. NBAF will integrate research, development, and testing in foreign animal diseases and zoonotic diseases, which will support the complimentary missions of USDA and DHS. NBAF will address USDA needs that are currently not being met by the facilities at the Plum Island Animal Disease Center, including inadequate lab space for processing diagnostic samples, limitations in diagnostic capability for BSL-4 agents, and lack of space to expand to include the development, feasibility testing, and validation of new and emerging technologies for detection of exotic and emerging diseases. In addition, it will provide room to grow as we further enhance our abilities to respond to increasing threats to the U.S. livestock industry.

The NBAF will also have a synergistic effect, to the benefit of each of our agencies, by utilizing the expertise of the academic and scientific community in the area. In addition, we expect that by sharing a well-equipped core facility, we will see a more cost effective utilization of funding. This will also continue to provide a number of opportunities for enhanced interaction among the three agencies. For example, research done by ARS and DHS may identify possible new diagnostic tools that APHIS can use; APHIS' repository of foreign animal disease agents obtained from outbreaks around the world will provide a resource for ARS and DHS research and bioforensics; and APHIS' diagnostic investigations and surveillance will help identify emerging or re-emerging diseases in the field, in turn helping set research priorities for ARS and DHS.

Site Selection

At the time Plum Island was built, biosecurity was much different than it is today. Agriculture biosecurity was defined by biological isolation, so that if there was a problem at the laboratory, there was physical separation from susceptible livestock populations and any breaches were localized. Today, with much more advanced technologies, the ability to manage effective biosecurity and biosafety practices is not dictated by location or physical barriers.

We recognize that there is concern about building the NBAF on the mainland. Since the determination was made over 60 years ago to build the Plum Island Animal Disease Center on an island, assessments have shown that technological advances would allow for safe research and diagnostics of foreign animal diseases to take place on the U.S. mainland. A 2002 study completed by the Science Applications International Corporation (SAIC) and commissioned by USDA found that the FMD virus and other exotic foreign animal diseases of concern to the Department could be fully and safely contained within a BSL-3 laboratory, as was being done in other countries at the time including Canada, Germany, and Brazil. A second SAIC study also concluded that there was a

valid USDA need for a BSL-4 facility, and that a BSL-4 facility for large animal work could be safely located on the mainland.

In planning for the NBAF, we recognize the absolutely essential need for state-of-the-art biosafety practices and procedures, including stringent and rigorous safety measures within the laboratories themselves, to prevent disease organisms from escaping into the environment. Situations such as the recent suspected release of live FMD virus from the Pirbright campus in England only serve to highlight this importance. We can use that example as a learning opportunity and make sure that the design and maintenance of the NBAF facility enables us to carry out the essential activities needed to protect the nation from foreign animal diseases while ensuring the highest level of biosafety.

This is why the NBAF will utilize the redundancies built into modern research laboratory designs and the latest biosecurity and containment systems, coupled with continued training and monitoring of employees, to effectively minimize any risks. Personnel controls for the NBAF will include background checks, biometric testing for lab entry, and no solitary access to BSL-4 microorganisms. The NBAF will also feature biological safety cabinets in the wet labs designed to meet the needs of BSL-3 labs, while in BSL-4 labs, these biological safety cabinets will include additional security measures or be used in combination with full-body, air-supplied personal protective suits.

In terms of facility design, the BSL-4 lab at the NBAF will employ a box-in-box principle with a pressure-controlled buffer. All water and air leaving the lab will be purified—that is, no research microorganism will enter the sewage system or outside air. All critical functions will have redundant systems. The design of the BSL-4 laboratories and animal space will comply with the appropriate recommendations and requirements of the Centers for Disease Control and Prevention, National Institutes of Health, Department of Defense, and National Research Council.

I would also like to note some potential advantages to locating the NBAF on the mainland. For example, the lower cost of living, as compared to that in the communities surrounding the Plum Island Animal Disease Center, would likely make recruiting personnel easier for our agencies. This would also eliminate the costs of moving people on and off an island every day, as we currently do. A mainland facility would be more accessible if air traffic is shut down due to weather conditions or an emergency situation, and would not be subject to the occasional wind closures that we experience at the Plum Island Animal Disease Center due to rough waters. And, as I mentioned earlier, locating the facility near an established research community would facilitate innovative collaboration.

A key advantage to locating NBAF on the mainland would be the ability to quickly respond to a potential foreign animal disease threat. Placing the NBAF on the mainland could eliminate the need for additional transport of samples to the island via boat or aircraft, as is currently done at Plum Island. Having a more accessible location, where diagnostic capabilities could be utilized within the first 24 hours of an emergency, is essential. For example, in June 2007, APHIS conducted an investigation into swine showing signs consistent with a significant foreign animal disease. In such a situation, every hour counts when

it comes to being able to quickly rule out major diseases. Incidents such as this can have a significant impact on the economy, stop movement and trade in multiple species of livestock, and spread fear throughout the industry.

Although DHS is ultimately responsible for the selection of a NBAF site, USDA has been closely involved throughout this process. APHIS and ARS have provided detailed program requirements to DHS, and have representatives on the site selection committee and site inspection team. We support the criteria used to select the sites: proximity to research capabilities linked to the NBAF mission requirements, site proximity to a skilled workforce, as well as acquisition/construction/operations, and community acceptance, and look forward to the next steps in the process.

DHS is currently preparing an environmental impact statement (EIS) looking at the six sites, which include Plum Island and five mainland locations. The EIS, on which USDA and DHS are working, will consider the risk and potential consequences of an accidental release of a foreign animal disease, and will be integral to moving forward with a sound NBAF site selection.

It is important that we move forward in a timely manner with planning and construction of NBAF so that we can develop the diagnostics and tools needed to protect U.S. agriculture from the threats of dangerous foreign animal diseases. Just as the science behind bioterrorism has advanced in recent years, and new and changing diseases continue to emerge, so too must we arm ourselves with more sophisticated ways of preventing harm to the U.S. livestock industry. If we don't, then bioterrorists will continue to find innovative ways to attack our livestock, new diseases will continue to emerge, and U.S. agriculture will be left vulnerable to these dangers. This is why USDA is committed to working with DHS to move forward with plans for NBAF, after a thorough analysis of the options and development of plans to ensure the utmost biosafety and biosecurity.

Authority to Conduct FMD Research on the Mainland

Lastly, I would like to briefly mention recent legislative activity related to live FMD virus. Current statute (21 U.S.C. 113a.) restricts research involving live FMD virus and other animal diseases that present a significant risk to domestic U.S. livestock to laboratories on coastal islands separated from the mainland United States by deep water. Research involving live FMD virus is carried out at the Plum Island Animal Disease Center under this statute, which dates back to the 1950s. The statute was amended by the 1990 Farm Bill to authorize the Secretary of Agriculture, when necessary, to allow the movement of live FMD virus, under permit, to research facilities on the U.S. mainland.

USDA recognizes DHS' interest in the Secretary being directed, via statute, to issue a permit for live FMD virus at the NBAF. This direction will provide clarity in this important area as DHS moves forward in selecting a site for the NBAF and then in contracting for the construction of the facility. For these reasons, the Administration included in our Farm Bill Proposal an authorization for USDA to conduct research and diagnostics for highly infectious disease

agents, such as FMD and rinderpest, on the U.S. mainland. Consistent with the Administration's proposal, section 7524 of the Food, Conservation, and Energy Act of 2008 directs the Secretary to issue a permit for live FMD virus at NBAF, while preserving the Secretary's discretion and ensuring that all biosafety and select agent requirements are being met at the facility.

Conclusion

... We believe the planned NBAF is necessary to replace the aging Plum Island Animal Disease Center and provide additional capacity for much needed animal disease research, diagnostics, training, and countermeasures development. The NBAF will play a crucial role in protecting against the future introduction of foreign animal and zoonotic diseases, and ensuring the continued health and vitality of our agricultural industries. We are committed to continuing our work in partnership with DHS in planning the NBAF and making the facility a reality.

Ray L. Wulf  **NO**

Written Testimony

... **O**n behalf of American Farmers & Ranchers [I] thank you for the opportunity to testify on the Department of Homeland Security's recent proposal to close the Plum Island Animal Disease Center and move its biological research laboratory, including, but not limited to, research on foot-and-mouth disease, to a new location on the mainland United States. This is an issue that is of particular interest and concern to our organization and companies.

At the committee's request I will address the following questions:

- Does your organization support moving foot-and-mouth disease from Plum Island to a research facility on the mainland United States?
- What would be the estimated cost to your membership of an outbreak of foot-and-mouth disease in the United States?
- Does your organization believe modern technology is adequate to prevent the accidental release of foot-and-mouth disease—or other contagious diseases affecting livestock—from a research facility located on the mainland United States?
- If an outbreak of foot-and-mouth disease were to occur on the mainland United States, does your organization believe that Federal, State, and local authorities are prepared to identify, isolate, and halt the spread of such an outbreak before it caused significant damage?

Does your organization support moving foot-and-mouth disease from Plum Island to a research facility on the mainland United States?

NO, AFR is *opposed* to the movement of the Plum Island Animal Disease Center to a research facility on the mainland U.S. The Plum Island Animal Disease Center is the only place in the country where certain highly infectious foreign animal diseases are studied, such as foot-and-mouth disease. Foot-and-mouth disease is a highly contagious virus that affects cloven-hoofed animals such as cattle, sheep, pigs, goats and deer.

Foot-and-mouth disease can be carried by the wind, on clothing, footwear, skin, through nasal passages, and on equipment. The current location or one with similar natural barriers should continue to be the site for research and diagnostic activities that protect our nation's food supply. There are simply too many possibilities for error, either by negligence, or accident, that could pose extreme economic impacts on U.S. agriculture producers and consumers.

U.S. House of Representatives, May 22, 2008.

Specifically foot-and-mouth disease creates a serious threat to the U.S. livestock industry, the overall agriculture economy, as well as the U.S. economy. A GAO report released December of 2005 stated that nationally recognized animal disease experts were interviewed and agreed that foot-and-mouth disease constitutes the greatest threat to American livestock. Furthermore GAO provided a letter on December 17, 2007 stating that some of the pathogens maintained at Plum Island, such as foot-and-mouth disease, are highly contagious to livestock and could cause catastrophic economic losses in the agricultural sector if it was released outside of the facility.

Infrastructure

The results of a possible outbreak on the mainland are magnified and accelerated by the efficiencies of the U.S. infrastructure and the transportation industry. The U.S. infrastructure for moving livestock is second to none, allowing livestock to move rapidly across the U.S. [In] five days cattle were trucked from the Oklahoma City National Livestock Market to 39 states. In addition, other animals that carry foot-and-mouth disease, such as swine, sheep, and goats are also rapidly distributed. Within a matter of days livestock can be transported hundreds to thousands of miles away and intermingled with other livestock. Amplifying the situation is the fact that foot-and-mouth disease is expelled over four to five days after an animal has been infected and may occur several days before the onset of clinical signs. In a matter of a couple of weeks the entire country could be infected.

What would be the estimated cost to your membership of an outbreak of foot-and-mouth disease in the United States?

The economic impacts to AFR members would no doubt be severe and devastating and reach far beyond the livestock industry. Quarantines affecting large areas would be established stopping all incoming and outgoing commerce in the quarantined area. Depending on the time of year, a quarantine could halt grain harvest, a major economic impact to many areas. Trucks and equipment would not be allowed in or out for harvesting, milk trucks would not be allowed in or out and, in addition, travel to and from school, for business or leisure would be halted. The impact would not only be felt by the producer, but also the local community, region, nation and could cause irreparable damage to the financial community. In addition the U.S. could expect severe economic consequences in the global market.

Many studies have attempted to assess the economic implications of an outbreak of foot-and-mouth disease in the U.S. Results can vary, but at the same time all point out the significant economic losses as a result of a foot-and-mouth outbreak. Direct economic losses would result from lost production, the cost of destroying disease-ridden livestock, indemnification and the cost of disease containment measures, such as drugs, diagnostics, vaccines, and veterinary services. Indirect costs and multiplier effects from dislocations in agriculture sectors would include the feed and inputs industry, transportation, retail and the loss of export markets.

A foot-and-mouth outbreak would not only be a problem for agriculture. In Britain the outbreak of foot-and-mouth disease resulted in postponing a general election for a month, the cancellation of many sporting events and leisure activities, the cancellation of large events likely to be attended by those from infected areas.

Research at Oklahoma State University

Dr. Clem Ward of Oklahoma State University outlines how estimating the effects is difficult to gauge:

- First, the effects would depend upon how isolated or widespread the incidence was and how quickly it was contained.
- Second, the effects would depend upon the type of livestock operations that were infected and how frequently or recently animals have moved from the sites.
- Third, impacts would depend on how the media handles the news reporting of the outbreak.
- And fourth, markets would likely react immediately to the news, and how long it would take them to rebound to a more normal level would depend on the first three factors mentioned.

Dr. Ward also looked at two studies that estimate the economic impacts of a foot-and-mouth outbreak based on a given set of wide ranging scenarios.

1. A 1979 study with impacts adjusted to 2000; estimated economic impacts from $2.4 billion to $27.6 billion.
2. A 1999 study estimated the impacts for California alone at $8.5 billion to $13.5 billion.

Kansas Research

An article in ScienceDaily (Nov. 29, 2007), "Foot-and-mouth Disease Could Cost Kansas Nearly A Billion Dollars," referenced research by Dustin L. Pendell, John Leatherman, Ted C. Schroeder, and Gregory S. Alward—THE ECONOMIC IMPACTS OF A FOOT-AND-MOUTH DISEASE OUTBREAK: A REGIONAL ANALYSIS. The team of researchers analyzed a 14-county region in southwest Kansas that has a high concentration of large cattle feeding operations, as well as other livestock enterprises and beef processing plants. They considered three scenarios:

- one where the disease was introduced at a single cow-calf operation;
- one where a medium-sized feedlot, 10,000 to 20,000 head of cattle, was initially infected;
- one where five large feedlots, each with more than 40,000 head of cattle, were simultaneously exposed.

Schroeder said the first two scenarios were used to predict what could happen if the disease were introduced accidentally, while the larger scenario shows what could happen were there an intentional release.

Generally, researchers found that the greater the number of animals infected in an operation, the longer an outbreak would last and the more it would likely spread—all directly correlating to the level of economic ruin.

- Under the small cow-calf scenario, researchers predicted that 126,000 head of livestock would have to be destroyed and that a foot-and-mouth disease outbreak would last 29 days.
- In the medium-sized operation, those numbers went up to 407,000 animals and 39 days.
- In the scenario where five large feedlots were exposed at the same time, researchers predicted that 1.7 million head of livestock would have to be destroyed and that an outbreak would last nearly three months.

From smallest to largest operation, that translated into regional economic losses of $23 million, $140 million and $685 million, respectively. For the state of Kansas as a whole, those numbers climb to $36 million, $199 million and $945 million.

"Kansas produces about 1.5 million calves, markets 5.5 million head of fed cattle, and slaughters 7.5 million head of cattle annually. The large commercial cattle feedlot and beef packing industries together bring more than 100,000 head of cattle per week on average into the state for feeding or processing," Schroeder said. "Such large volumes of livestock movement provide avenues for contagious animal disease to spread."

Leatherman estimated the statewide impacts of foot-and-mouth for this study and said the effects of an outbreak would go way beyond producers. "This study tells us what the overall stake of the region and state has in preventing such an occurrence," he said. "It isn't just farmers, ranchers, feed lots and packers who would suffer—it's all of us, in some measure."

Other Research

Another report titled "Potential Revenue Impact of an Outbreak of Foot-and-Mouth Disease in the United Sates" by Paarlbwerg, Lee, and Seitzinger was published in the *Journal of American Veterinary Medical Association* in April of 2002. The report stated an outbreak similar to that which occurred in the U.K. during 2001, would cause an estimated U.S. farm income losses of $14 billion. Losses in gross revenue for each sector were estimated to be the following: live swine, −34%; pork, −24%; live cattle −17%; beef, −20%; milk, −16%; live lambs and sheep, −14%; lamb and sheep meat, −10%; forage, −15%; and soybean meal, −7%.

Other Agriculture Markets Impacted

Livestock markets are not the only markets impacted by an outbreak. Feed grains and protein meal feeds would also be impacted. A CRS Report titled "Agroterrorism: Options in Congress," December 19, 2001 states—According

to industry officials, every other bushel of U.S. grain goes to animal feed. In addition, information from the U.S. Meat Export Federation states that:

- One milk cow will eat 3 tons of hay and 1,460 lbs of distiller's grain over the course of a year
- It takes 150 lbs of soybean meal to feed a pig to its finished weight
- Every pound of U.S. pork exported utilizes 1.5 pounds of U.S. soybeans
- More than 54 million bushels of soybeans were exported through U.S. red meat in 2006
- More than 300 million bushels of corn were exported through U.S. red meat in 2006
- While direct corn exports have increased by 25% since 1990, indirect exports of corn through the value added process of exporting red meat has increased by 196%

Trade Impact

Ninety four to ninety six percent of the world's consumers live outside the U.S. making trade a critical part of U.S. Agriculture. Examples from the pork industry are as follows:

- Source: USDA
  - U.S. has 27% share of the world pork exports
- Source: U.S. Meat Export Federation
  - 2007 Pork Exports add $22.00 per hog
  - The net benefit of U.S. pork exports to the pork industry in 2007 equates to $22 added dollars per market hog
  - Japan, Mexico, Canada and Korea account for 75% of all U.S. pork exports—10% of total production
  - One in every four pounds of pork traded in the world originates from the U.S.
  - The U.S. exports the equivalent of 49,500 market hogs daily

Foot-and-mouth disease is a *"Trade Disease."* To avoid foot-and-mouth disease it is common practice among foot-and-mouth disease-free countries to allow imports only from other foot-and-mouth disease-free countries. This action by countries that are foot-and-mouth disease free is consistent with the provisions of the World Trade Organization's "Agreement on Application of Sanitary and Phytosanitary Measures," which allows countries to adopt and enforce measures necessary to protect human, animal, or plant health. The World Organization of Animal Health (OIE), an independent international organization founded in 1924, monitors and disseminates information about animal diseases throughout the world, and provides a list of countries declared free of foot-and-mouth disease.

Global competition is fierce and in the event a foot-and-mouth outbreak occurred in the U.S., life as we know would no longer exist. Operating as a foot-and-mouth positive country would exclude the U.S. from premium meat markets.

While a foot-and-mouth disease vaccine is available it is used only in emergencies, to create a "disease-free" buffer zone around an infected area.

Because vaccinated animals will test positive, they cannot be shipped internationally and protocols require the animals to be destroyed as soon as the disease is eradicated.

Consumer Issues

Foot-and-mouth is not readily transmissible to humans. Only a few cases of human infections, none requiring hospitalization, occurring as a result of direct contact with infected animals have been documented. Even though foot-and-mouth disease does not pose a health risk to humans, consumer fear would occur. Because the average consumer has a lack of knowledge about the disease, more than likely there would be a drop in meat consumption.

. . .

Does your organization believe modern technology is adequate to prevent the accidental release of foot-and-mouth disease—or other contagious diseases affecting livestock—from a research facility located on the mainland United States?

NO, AFR does not believe that there are adequate technologies and safety precautions that can assure U.S. producers and consumers that there would not be an accidental or intentional release of foot-and mouth disease or for that fact any other contagious disease affecting livestock from a research facility located on the mainland U.S. Regardless of how much technology has improved, it does not safeguard from human error, harmful intentions or lack of preparedness.

Plum Island's research and diagnostic activities work to accomplish an important mission to protect U.S. animal industries and exports from deliberate or accidental introductions of foreign animal diseases. Although steps have been taken to implement better security measures at Plum Island, an outbreak is not out of the question. The U.S. should take note of the most recent U.K. outbreak in August of 2007. Investigations determined that the U.K. outbreak was caused by a strain of virus used for vaccine research at laboratories associated with the institute for Animal Health at Pirbright.

If an outbreak of foot-and-mouth disease were to occur on the mainland United States, does your organization believe that Federal, State, and local authorities are prepared to identify, isolate, and halt the spread of such an outbreak before it caused significant damage?

NO, Although Federal, State and local authorities continue to try to prepare themselves for a foreign animal disease outbreak, AFR believes there are entirely too many unknown variables that would hinder a successful containment of the disease. A U.S. Government simulated outbreak in 2002 called "Crimson Sky" ended with fictional riots in the streets after the simulation's National Guardsmen were ordered to kill tens of millions of farm animals, so many that troops ran out of bullets. In the exercise, the government said it would have been forced to dig a ditch in Kansas 25 miles long to bury carcasses. In the simulation, protests broke out in some cities amid food shortages.

In addition, AFR has concerns about the transportation of infectious disease samples that may need to come into or out of the facility and travel through populated areas. Furthermore AFR has concerns about the number of employees that would be traveling in and out of the facility. The Department of Homeland Security states that a new proposed National Bio and Agro-Defense Facility would generally include between 250 and 350 employees.

Traceability Is Critical

AFR believes that a critical part of being able to control the spread of foot-and-mouth or any animal disease is a national animal identification system. The capacity to trace livestock and product movements is critical for the early control of an outbreak. USDA has been pursuing implementation of an effective animal identification system since the BSE discovery in a U.S. cow in 2003. The U.S. has yet to establish a workable I.D. program. Until traceability is mandatory and in place moving the Plum Island Animal Disease Center to the mainland should *not* be considered and even then it should be reviewed carefully and any consideration should be focused on a remote area with little or no livestock or wild game habitation.

Conclusion

In conclusion, AFR strongly supports full funding for the research performed at Plum Island, including research on foot-and-mouth disease. In addition AFR fully supports funding to update research facilities to the highest standards.

However, AFR believes the U.S. should not risk bringing highly contagious animal disease research to the mainland with so many variables that could wreak havoc on the U.S. livestock industry, communities, the U.S. and global economy.

AFR believes further activities are needed to prepare for an animal disease outbreak. Activities should include:

- An analysis of communication between all stakeholders
- A full economic study that includes control and compensation including businesses reliant on livestock and global trade impacts
- How to adequately establish a quarantine area around an outbreak
- How movement restrictions will be handled
- Procedures in regard to slaughtering all infected herds and other herds that have been in contact with them
- Disposing of animals—Environmental impacts—burial contamination of ground water by leakages from a disposal pit
- Disinfecting properties
- Compensating stock owners for the livestock slaughtered
- Carrying out clinical inspection a surveillance to ensure the disease has not spread

EXPLORING THE ISSUE

Can Infectious Animal Diseases Be Studied Safely in Kansas?

Critical Thinking and Reflection

1. Why was Plum Island initially favored for working with highly infectious animal diseases?
2. Why does the Department of Homeland Security think Plum Island is no longer an appropriate location?
3. Why is foot-and-mouth disease considered a "trade disease?"
4. How would an outbreak of foot-and-mouth disease affect the U.S. economy?

Is There Common Ground?

All involved in this debate agree that infectious diseases—whether of animals or of humans—should not be permitted to escape from research facilities. One significant difference is in the degree of trust people are willing to put in technological means of preventing such escape.

1. Google on "biodefense labs" and summarize the news stories and reports you find.
2. Do people seem willing to trust isolation or containment measures to work? Why not?
3. What could be done to make isolation or containment measures more reliable, or at least more worthy of public trust?

ISSUE 11

Are Genetically Modified Foods Safe to Eat?

YES: Henry I. Miller and Gregory Conko, from "Scary Food," *Policy Review* (June/July 2006)

NO: Jeffrey M. Smith, from "Not in My Fridge!" *Ecologist* (November 2007)

Learning Outcomes

After studying this issue, students will be able to:

1. Describe the potential benefits of applying genetic engineering to food crops.
2. Describe the potential adverse effects of genetically modified foods.
3. Explain why and on what basis new technologies should be regulated.

ISSUE SUMMARY

YES: Henry I. Miller and Gregory Conko of the Hoover Institution argue that genetically modified (GM) crops are safer for the consumer and better for the environment than non-GM crops.

NO: Jeffrey M. Smith, director of the Institute for Responsible Technology and the Campaign for Healthier Eating in America, argues that GM foods are dangerous to health and should be removed from the marketplace.

In the early 1970s scientists first discovered that it was technically possible to move genes—biological material that determines a living organism's physical makeup—from one organism to another and thus (in principle) to give bacteria, plants, and animals new features and to correct genetic defects of the sort that cause many diseases, such as cystic fibrosis. Most researchers in molecular genetics were excited by the potentialities that suddenly seemed within

their grasp. However, a few researchers—as well as many people outside the field—were disturbed by the idea; they thought that genetic mix-and-match games might spawn new diseases, weeds, and pests. Some people even argued that genetic engineering should be banned at the outset, before unforeseeable horrors were unleashed.

Researchers in support of genetic experimentation responded by declaring a moratorium on their own work until suitable safeguards could be devised. Once those safeguards were in place in the form of government regulations, work resumed. James D. Watson and John Tooze document the early years of this research in *The DNA Story: A Documentary History of Gene Cloning* (W.H. Freeman, 1981). For a shorter, more recent review of the story, see Bernard D. Davis, "Genetic Engineering: The Making of Monsters?" *The Public Interest* (Winter 1993).

By 1989 the technology had developed tremendously: researchers could obtain patents for mice with artificially added genes ("transgenic" mice); firefly genes had been added to tobacco plants to make them glow (faintly) in the dark; and growth hormone produced by genetically engineered bacteria was being used to grow low-fat pork and increase milk production by cows. Critics argued that genetic engineering was unnatural and violated the rights of both plants and animals to their "species integrity"; that expensive, high-tech, tinkered animals gave the competitive advantage to big agricultural corporations and drove small farmers out of business; and that putting human genes into animals, plants, or bacteria was downright offensive. See Betsy Hanson and Dorothy Nelkin, "Public Responses to Genetic Engineering," *Society* (November/December 1989). Most of the initial attention aimed at genetic engineering focused first on its use to modify bacteria and other organisms to generate drugs needed to fight human disease and second on its potential to modify human genes and attack hereditary diseases at their roots. See Eric B. Kmiec, "Gene Therapy," *American Scientist* (May–June 1999).

Despite some successes, gene therapy has not yet become a multimillion dollar industry. Nevertheless, thoughts of tinkering with humans themselves have prompted such comments as the following from Richard Hayes, "In the Pipeline: Genetically Modified Humans?" *Multinational Monitor* (January/February 2000): "No one can be sure how the technology will evolve, but a techno-eugenic future appears ever more likely unless an organized citizenry demands such visions be consigned to science fiction dystopias" (see Issue 19 in this book).

Pharmaceutical and agricultural applications of genetic engineering have been much more successful, the latter largely because, as Robert Shapiro, CEO of Monsanto Corporation, said in June 1998, it "represents a potentially sustainable solution to the issue of feeding people." In "Biotech's Plans to Sustain Agriculture," *Scientific American* (October 2009) interviewed several industry representatives, who see biotechnology—including genetic engineering—as essential to meeting future food demand in a sustainable way.

Between 1996 and 2009, the area planted with genetically engineered crops jumped from 1.7 million hectares to 134 million hectares (www.gmo-compass.org/eng/agri_biotechnology/gmo_planting/). Many people are not reassured

by such data. They see potential problems in nutrition, toxicity, allergies, and ecology. Brian Halweil, "The Emperor's New Crops," *World Watch* (July/August 1999), notes that although genetically engineered crops may have potential benefits, they may also have disastrous effects on natural ecosystems and—because high-tech agriculture is controlled by major corporations such as Monsanto—on less developed societies. He argues that "ecological" agriculture (using, e.g., organic fertilizers and natural enemies instead of pesticides) offers much more hope for the future. Similar arguments are made by those who demonstrate against genetically modified (GM) foods—sometimes by destroying research labs and test plots of trees, strawberries, and corn—and lobby for stringent labeling requirements or for outright bans on planting and importing these crops. See Claire Hope Cummings, "Risking Corn, Risking Culture," *World Watch* (November/December 2002). Many protestors argue against GM technology in terms of the precautionary principle; see "GMOs and Precaution in EU Countries," *Outlook on Science Policy* (September 2005). Georgina Gustin, "Seeds of Change?" *Columbia Journalism Review* (January/February 2010), reviews press coverage of GM crops and notes that despite the numerous objections by environmental groups there are no data that indicate problems. She adds that there is a need for more research on safety.

Many researchers see great hope in GM foods. In July 2000, the Royal Society of London, the U.S. National Academy of Sciences, the Brazilian Academy of Sciences, the Chinese Academy of Sciences, the Indian Academy of Sciences, the Mexican Academy of Sciences, and the Third World Academy of Sciences issued a joint report titled "Transgenic Plants and World Agriculture" (available at http://royalsociety.org/Transgenic-plants-and-world-agriculture/). This report stresses that during the twenty-first century, both the population and the need for food are going to increase dramatically, especially in developing nations. According to the report, "Foods can be produced through the use of GM [genetic modification] technology that are more nutritious, stable in storage and in principle, health promoting. . . . New public sector efforts are required for creating transgenic crops that benefit poor farmers in developing nations and improve their access to food. . . . Concerted, organised efforts must be undertaken to investigate the potential environmental effects, both positive and negative, of GM technologies [compared to those] from conventional agricultural technologies. . . . Public health regulatory systems need to be put in place in every country to identify and monitor any potential adverse human health effects." The United States' National Research Council reports that the economic and environmental benefits of GM crops are clear; see Erik Stokstad, "Biotech Crops Good for Farmers and Environment, Academy Finds," *Science* (April 16, 2010), and Committee on the Impact of Biotechnology on Farm-Level Economics and Sustainability, *The Impact of Genetically Engineered Crops on Farm Sustainability in the United States* (National Academies Press, 2010) (www.nap.edu/catalog.php?record_id=12804).

The worries surrounding GM foods and the scientific evidence to support them are summarized by Kathryn Brown, in "Seeds of Concern," and Karen Hopkin, in "The Risks on the Table," both in *Scientific American* (April 2001). In the same issue, Sasha Nemecek poses the question "Does the World Need GM

Foods?" to two prominent figures in the debate: Robert B. Horsch, a Monsanto vice president and recipient of the 1998 National Medal of Technology for his work on modifying plant genes, who says yes, and Margaret Mellon, of the Union of Concerned Scientists, who says no, adding that much more work needs to be done on safety. Jeffrey M. Smith, *Seeds of Deception: Exposing Industry and Government Lies about the Safety of the Genetically Engineered Foods You're Eating* (Chelsea Green, 2003), argues that the dangers of GM foods have been deliberately concealed. Henry I. Miller and Gregory Conko, in *The Frankenfood Myth: How Protest and Politics Threaten the Biotech Revolution* (Praeger, 2004), address at length the fallacy that GM foods are especially risky. Rod Addy and Elaine Watson, "Forget 'Frankenfood,' GM Crops Can Feed the World, Says FDF," *Food Manufacture* (December 2007), note that "EU trade commissioner Peter Mandelson said that the inability of European politicians to engage in a rational debate about GM was a source of constant frustration. They were also creating barriers to trade by banning GM crops that had repeatedly been pronounced safe by the European Food Safety Authority (EFSA)." Early in 2010, the EFSA reinforced the point; see "EFSA Rejects Study Claiming Toxicity of GMOs," *European Environment & Packaging Law Weekly* (February 24, 2010). Mac Margolis, et al., "Beakers to the Rescue," *Newsweek* (May 19, 2008), are also optimistic about the potential of GM foods to help feed the world. Maywa Montenegro, "Green Revolution 2.0," *Seed* (July/August 2008), argues that the world's food shortages of 2008 indicate that the limits of agriculture to meet needs for food and biofuels are being strained and that genetic engineering holds the seeds of a solution (though not in its current corporate form). Richard Stone, "China Plans $3.5 Billion GM Crops Initiative," *Science* (September 5, 2008), notes that "with questions mounting about China's ability to feed itself . . . not pushing ahead with GM varieties could be more detrimental than any theoretical hazard." Andrew Batson and James T. Areddy note that "Beijing Gives Nod to Modified Rice," *Wall Street Journal* (Eastern ed., December 1, 2009).

Harihara M. Mehendale, "Genetically Modified Foods: Why the Public Frenzy? Role of Mainstream News Media," *International Journal of Toxicology* (September 2004), blames "the role of the press in spreading misleading facts related to the technology." Robert Falkner, "The Global Biotech Food Fight: Why the United States Got It So Wrong," *Brown Journal of World Affairs* (Fall/Winter 2007), says that food safety fears are a major driver for the antibiotech movement and the government's insistence that a separate regulatory approach is not needed has strengthened "the perception that biotech food is being forced upon reluctant societies."

Is the issue safety? Human welfare? Or economics? In the YES selection, Henry I. Miller and Gregory Conko of the Hoover Institution argue that GM crops are safer for the consumer and better for the environment than non-GM crops. People have failed to embrace them because news coverage has been dominated by the outlandish claims and speculations of antitechnology activists. In the NO selection, Jeffrey M. Smith, director of the Institute for Responsible Technology and the Campaign for Healthier Eating in America, argues that GM foods are dangerous to health and should be removed from the marketplace.

YES

Henry I. Miller and
Gregory Conko

Scary Food

Like a scene from some Hollywood thriller, a team of U.S. Marshals stormed a warehouse in Irvington, New Jersey, last summer to intercept a shipment of evildoers from Pakistan. The reason you probably haven't heard about the raid is that the objective was not to seize Al Qaeda operatives or white slavers, but $80,000 worth of basmati rice contaminated with weevils, beetles, and insect larvae, making it unfit for human consumption. In regulation-speak, the food was "adulterated," because "it consists in whole or in part of any filthy, putrid, or decomposed substance, or if it is otherwise unfit for food."

Americans take food safety very seriously. Still, many consumers tend to ignore Mother Nature's contaminants while they worry unduly about high technology, such as the advanced technologies that farmers, plant breeders, and food processors use to make our food supply the most affordable, nutritious, varied, and safe in history.

For example, recombinant DNA technology—also known as food biotechnology, gene-splicing, or genetic modification (GM)—is often singled out by critics as posing a risk that new allergens, toxins, or other nasty substances will be introduced into the food supply. And, because of the mainstream media's "if it bleeds, it leads" approach, news coverage of food biotech is dominated by the outlandish claims and speculations of anti-technology activists. This has caused some food companies—including fastfood giant McDonald's and baby-food manufacturers Gerber and Heinz—to forgo superior (and even cost-saving) gene-spliced ingredients in favor of ones the public will find less threatening.

Scientists agree, however, that gene-spliced crops and foods are not only better for the natural environment than conventionally produced food crops, but also safer for consumers. Several varieties now on the market have been modified to resist insect predation and plant diseases, which makes the harvested crop much cleaner and safer. Ironically (and also surprisingly in these litigious times), in their eagerness to avoid biotechnology, some major food companies may knowingly be making their products less safe and wholesome for consumers. This places them in richly deserved legal jeopardy.

Don't Trust Mother Nature

Every year, scores of packaged food products are recalled from the American market due to the presence of all-natural contaminants like insect parts, toxic molds, bacteria, and viruses. Because farming takes place out-of-doors and in dirt, such contamination is a fact of life. Fortunately, modern technology has enabled farmers and food processors to minimize the threat from these contaminants.

The historical record of mass food poisoning in Europe offers a cautionary tale. From the ninth to the nineteenth centuries, Europe suffered a succession of epidemics caused by the contamination of rye with ergot, a poisonous fungus. Ergot contains the potent toxin ergotamine, the consumption of which induces hallucinations, bizarre behavior, and violent muscle twitching. These symptoms gave rise at various times to the belief that victims were possessed by evil spirits. Witch-hunting and persecution were commonplace—and the New World was not immune. One leading explanation for the notorious 1691–92 Salem witch trials also relates to ergot contamination. Three young girls suffered violent convulsions, incomprehensible speech, trance-like states, odd skin sensations, and delirious visions in which they supposedly saw the mark of the devil on certain women in the village. The girls lived in a swampy meadow area around Salem; rye was a major staple of their diet; and records indicate that the rye harvest at the time was complicated by rainy and humid conditions, exactly the situation in which ergot would thrive.

Worried villagers feared the girls were under a spell cast by demons, and the girls eventually named three women as witches. The subsequent panic led to the execution of as many as 20 innocent people. Until a University of California graduate student discovered this link, a reasonable explanation had defied historians. But the girls' symptoms are typical of ergot poisoning, and when the supply of infected grain ran out, the delusions and persecution likewise disappeared.

In the twenty-first century, modern technology, aggressive regulations, and a vigorous legal liability system in industrialized countries such as the United States are able to mitigate much of this sort of contamination. Occasionally, though, Americans will succumb to tainted food picked from the woods or a backyard garden. However, elsewhere in the world, particularly in less-developed countries, people are poisoned every day by fungal toxins that contaminate grain. The result is birth defects, cancer, organ failure, and premature death.

About a decade ago, Hispanic women in the Rio Grande Valley of Texas were found to be giving birth to an unusually large number of babies with crippling and lethal neural tube defects (NTDS) such as spina bifida, hydrocephalus, and anencephaly—at a rate approximately six times higher than the national average for non-Hispanic women. The cause remained a mystery until recent research revealed a link between NTDS and consumption of large amounts of unprocessed corn like that found in tortillas and other staples of the Latino diet.

The connection is obscure but fascinating. The culprit is fumonisin, a deadly mycotoxin, or fungal toxin, produced by the mold *Fusarium* and sometimes found in unprocessed corn. When insects attack corn, they open wounds in the plant that provide a perfect breeding ground for *Fusarium.* Once molds get a foothold, poor storage conditions also promote their postharvest growth on grain.

Fumonisin and some other mycotoxins are highly toxic, causing fatal diseases in livestock that eat infected corn and esophageal cancer in humans. Fumonisin also interferes with the cellular uptake of folic acid, a vitamin that is known to reduce the risk of NTDS in developing fetuses. Because fumonisin prevents the folic acid from being absorbed by cells, the toxin can, in effect, induce functional folic acid deficiency—and thereby cause NTDS—even when the diet contains what otherwise would be sufficient amounts of folic acid.

The epidemiological evidence was compelling. At the time that the babies of Hispanic women in the Rio Grande Valley experienced the high rate of neural tube defects, the fumonisin level in corn in that locale was two to three times higher than normal, and the affected women reported much higher dietary consumption of homemade tortillas than in women who were unaffected.

Acutely aware of the danger of mycotoxins, regulatory agencies such as the U.S. Food and Drug Administration and Britain's Food Safety Agency have established recommended maximum fumonisin levels in food and feed products made from corn. Although highly processed cornstarch and corn oil are unlikely to be contaminated with fumonisin, unprocessed corn or lightly processed corn (e.g., cornmeal) can have fumonisin levels that exceed recommended levels.

In 2003, the Food Safety Agency tested six organic cornmeal products and twenty conventional cornmeal products for fumonisin contamination. All six organic cornmeals had elevated levels—from nine to 40 times greater than the recommended levels for human health—and they were voluntarily withdrawn from grocery stores.

A Technical Fix

The conventional way to combat mycotoxins is simply to test unprocessed and processed grains and throw out those found to be contaminated—an approach that is both wasteful and dubious. But modern technology—specifically in the form of gene-splicing—is already attacking the fungal problem at its source. An excellent example is "Bt corn," crafted by splicing into commercial corn varieties a gene from the bacterium *Bacillus thuringiensis.* The "Bt" gene expresses a protein that is toxic to corn-boring insects but is perfectly harmless to birds, fish, and mammals, including humans.

As the Bt corn fends off insect pests, it also reduces the levels of the mold *Fusarium,* thereby reducing the levels of fumonisin. Thus, switching to the gene-spliced, insect-resistant corn for food processing lowers the levels of fumonisin—as well as the concentration of insect parts—likely to be found in the final product. Researchers at Iowa State University and the U.S. Department

of Agriculture found that Bt corn reduces the level of fumonisin by as much as 80 percent compared to conventional corn.

Thus, on the basis of both theory and empirical knowledge, there should be potent incentives—legal, commercial, and ethical—to use such gene-spliced grains more widely. One would expect public and private sector advocates of public health to demand that such improved varieties be cultivated and used for food—not unlike requirements for drinking water to be chlorinated and fluoridated. Food producers who wish to offer the safest and best products to their customers—to say nothing of being offered the opportunity to advertise "New and Improved!"—should be competing to get gene-spliced products into the marketplace.

Alas, none of this has come to pass. Activists have mounted intractable opposition to food biotechnology in spite of demonstrated, significant benefits, including reduced use of chemical pesticides, less runoff of chemicals into waterways, greater use of farming practices that prevent soil erosion, higher profits for farmers, and less fungal contamination. Inexplicably, government oversight has also been an obstacle, by subjecting the testing and commercialization of gene-spliced crops to unscientific and draconian regulations that have vastly increased testing and development costs and limited the use and diffusion of food biotechnology.

The result is jeopardy for everyone involved in food production and consumption: Consumers are subjected to avoidable and often undetected health risks, and food producers have placed themselves in legal jeopardy. The first point is obvious, the latter less so, but as described first by Drew Kershen, professor of law at the University of Oklahoma, it makes a fascinating story: Agricultural processors and food companies may face at least two kinds of civil liability for their refusal to purchase and use fungus-resistant, gene-spliced plant varieties, as well as other superior products.

Food for Thought

In 1999 the Gerber foods company succumbed to activist pressure, announcing that its baby food products would no longer contain any gene-spliced ingredients. Indeed, Gerber went farther and promised it would attempt to shift to organic ingredients that are grown without synthetic pesticides or fertilizers. Because corn starch and corn sweeteners are often used in a range of foods, this could mean changing Gerber's entire product line.

But in its attempt to head off a potential public relations problem concerning the use of gene-spliced ingredients, Gerber has actually increased the health risk for its baby consumers—and, thereby, its legal liability. As noted above, not only is gene-spliced corn likely to have lower levels of fumonisin than conventional corn; organic corn is likely to have the highest levels, because it suffers greater insect predation due to less effective pest controls.

If a mother some day discovers that her "Gerber baby" has developed liver or esophageal cancer, she might have a legal case against Gerber. On the child's behalf, a plaintiff's lawyer can allege liability based on mycotoxin contamination in the baby food as the causal agent of the cancer. The contamination

would be considered a *manufacturing defect* under product liability law because the baby food did not meet its intended product specifications or level of safety. According to Kershen, Gerber could be found liable "even though all possible care was exercised in the preparation and marketing of the product," simply because the contamination occurred.

The plaintiff's lawyer could also allege a *design defect* in the baby food, because Gerber knew of the existence of a less risky design—namely, the use of gene-spliced varieties that are less prone to *Fusarium* and fumonisin contamination—but deliberately chose not to use it. Instead, Gerber chose to use non-gene-spliced, organic food ingredients, knowing that the foreseeable risks of harm posed by them could have been reduced or avoided by adopting a reasonable alternative design—that is, by using gene-spliced Bt corn, which is known to have a lower risk of mycotoxin contamination.

Gerber might answer this design defect claim by contending that it was only responding to consumer demand, but that alone would not be persuasive. Product liability law subjects defenses in design defect cases to a risk-utility balancing in which consumer expectations are only one of several factors used to determine whether the product design (e.g., the use of only non-gene-spliced ingredients) is reasonably safe. A jury might conclude that whatever consumer demand there may be for non-biotech ingredients does not outweigh Gerber's failure to use a technology that is known to lower the health risks to consumers.

Even if Gerber was able to defend itself from the design defect claim, the company might still be liable because it failed to provide adequate instructions or warnings about the potential risks of non-gene-spliced ingredients. For example, Gerber could label its non-gene-spliced baby food with a statement such as: "This product does not contain gene-spliced ingredients. Consequently, this product has a very slight additional risk of mycotoxin contamination. Mycotoxins can cause serious diseases such as liver and esophageal cancer and birth defects."

Whatever the risk of toxic or carcinogenic fumonisin levels in non-biotech corn may be (probably low in industrialized countries, where food producers generally are cautious about such contamination), a more likely scenario is potential liability for an allergic reaction.

Six percent to 8 percent of children and 1 to 2 percent of adults are allergic to one or another food ingredient, and an estimated 150 Americans die each year from exposure to food allergens. Allergies to peanuts, soybeans, and wheat proteins, for example, are quite common and can be severe. Although only about 1 percent of the population is allergic to peanuts, some individuals are so highly sensitive that exposure causes anaphylactic shock, killing dozens of people every year in North America.

Protecting those with true food allergies is a daunting task. Farmers, food shippers and processors, wholesalers and retailers, and even restaurants must maintain meticulous records and labels and ensure against cross-contamination. Still, in a country where about a billion meals are eaten every day, missteps are inevitable. Dozens of processed food items must be recalled every year due to accidental contamination or inaccurate labeling.

Fortunately, biotechnology researchers are well along in the development of peanuts, soybeans, wheat, and other crops in which the genes coding for allergenic proteins have been silenced or removed. According to University of California, Berkeley, biochemist Bob Buchanan, hypoallergenic varieties of wheat could be ready for commercialization within the decade, and nuts soon thereafter. Once these products are commercially available, agricultural processors and food companies that refuse to use these safer food sources will open themselves to products-liability, design-defect lawsuits.

Property Damage and Personal Injury

Potato farming is a growth industry, primarily due to the vast consumption of french fries at fast-food restaurants. However, growing potatoes is not easy, because they are preyed upon by a wide range of voracious and difficult-to-control pests, such as the Colorado potato beetle, virus-spreading aphids, nematodes, potato blight, and others.

To combat these pests and diseases, potato growers use an assortment of fungicides (to control blight), insecticides (to kill aphids and the Colorado potato beetle), and fumigants (to control soil nematodes). Although some of these chemicals are quite hazardous to farm workers, forgoing them could jeopardize the sustainability and profitability of the entire potato industry. Standard application of synthetic pesticides enhances yields more than 50 percent over organic potato production, which prohibits most synthetic inputs.

Consider a specific example. Many growers use methamidophos, a toxic organophosphate nerve poison, for aphid control. Although methamidophos is an EPA-approved pesticide, the agency is currently reevaluating the use of organophosphates and could ultimately prohibit or greatly restrict the use of this entire class of pesticides. As an alternative to these chemicals, the Monsanto Company developed a potato that contains a gene from the bacterium *Bacillus thuringiensis* (Bt) to control the Colorado potato beetle and another gene to control the potato leaf roll virus spread by the aphids. Monsanto's NewLeaf potato is resistant to these two scourges of potato plants, which allowed growers who adopted it to reduce their use of chemical controls and increase yields.

Farmers who planted NewLeaf became convinced that it was the most environmentally sound and economically efficient way to grow potatoes. But after five years of excellent results it encountered an unexpected snag. Under pressure from anti-biotechnology organizations, McDonald's, Burger King, and other restaurant chains informed their potato suppliers that they would no longer accept gene-spliced potato varieties for their french fries. As a result, potato processors such as J.R. Simplot inserted a nonbiotech-potato clause into their farmer-processor contracts and informed farmers that they would no longer buy gene-spliced potatoes. In spite of its substantial environmental, occupational safety, and economic benefits, NewLeaf became a sort of contractual poison pill and is no longer grown commercially. Talk about market distortions.

Now, let us assume that a farmer who is required by contractual arrangement to plant nonbiotech potatoes sprays his potato crop with methamidophos (the organophosphate nerve poison) and that the pesticide drifts into a nearby stream and onto nearby farm laborers. Thousands of fish die in the stream, and the laborers report to hospital emergency rooms complaining of neurological symptoms.

This hypothetical scenario is, in fact, not at all far-fetched. Fish-kills attributed to pesticide runoff from potato fields are commonplace. In the potato-growing region of Prince Edward Island, Canada, for example, a dozen such incidents occurred in one 13-month period alone, between July 1999 and August 2000. According to the UN's Food and Agriculture Organization, "normal" use of the pesticides parathion and methamidophos is responsible for some 7,500 pesticide poisoning cases in China each year.

In our hypothetical scenario, the state environmental agency might bring an administrative action for civil damages to recover the cost of the fish-kill, and a plaintiff's lawyer could file a class-action suit on behalf of the farm laborers for personal injury damages.

Who's legally responsible? Several possible circumstances could enable the farmer's defense lawyer to shift culpability for the alleged damages to the contracting food processor and to the fast-food restaurants that are the ultimate purchasers of the potatoes. These circumstances include the farmer's having planted Bt potatoes in the recent past; his contractual obligation to the potato processor and its fast-food retail buyers to provide only nonbiotech varieties; and his demonstrated preference for planting gene-spliced, Bt potatoes, were it not for the contractual proscription. If these conditions could be proved, the lawyer defending the farmer could name the contracting processor and the fast-food restaurants as cross-defendants, claiming either contribution in tort law or indemnification in contract law for any damages legally imposed upon the farmer client.

The farmer's defense could be that those companies bear the ultimate responsibility for the damages because they compelled the farmer to engage in higher-risk production practices than he would otherwise have chosen. The companies chose to impose cultivation of a non-gene-spliced variety upon the farmer although they knew that in order to avoid severe losses in yield, he would need to use organophosphate pesticides. Thus, the defense could argue that the farmer should have a legal right to pass any damages (arising from contractually imposed production practices) back to the processor and the fast-food chains.

Why Biotech?

Companies that insist upon farmers' using production techniques that involve foreseeable harms to the environment and humans may be—we would argue, *should* be—legally accountable for that decision. If agricultural processors and food companies manage to avoid legal liability for their insistence on nonbiotech crops, they will be "guilty" at least of externalizing their environmental costs onto the farmers, the environment, and society at large.

Food biotechnology provides an effective—and cost-effective—way to prevent many of these injurious scenarios, but instead of being widely encouraged, it is being resisted by self-styled environmental activists and even government officials.

It should not fall to the courts to resolve and reconcile what are essentially scientific and moral issues. However, other components of society—industry, government, and "consumer advocacy" groups—have failed abjectly to fully exploit a superior, life-enhancing, and life-saving technology. Even the biotechnology trade associations have been unhelpful. All are guilty, in varying measures, of sacrificing the public interest to self-interest and of helping to perpetuate a gross public misconception—that food biotechnology is unproven, untested, and unregulated.

If consumers genuinely want a safer, more nutritious, and more varied food supply at a reasonable cost, they need to know where the real threats lie. They must also become better informed, demand public policy that makes sense, and deny fringe anti-technology activists permission to speak for consumers.

Jeffrey M. Smith  **NO**

Not in My Fridge!

It was a bad year for the biotech barons. At a conference in January 1999, the consulting firm Arthur Andersen revealed Monsanto executives' vision of an ideal future—a world in which natural seeds were virtually all extinct and where commercial seeds were genetically modified (GM) and patented. Andersen Consulting then worked backwards from that goal, developing the strategy and tactics to help Monsanto achieve industry dominance in a GM world. At the same meeting another biotech company, apparently with the same aspiration, showed a graph that projected a 95 per cent replacement of all natural seeds by GM varieties in just five years. Within weeks, their ideal future crashed.

By mid-February, Parliament had invited scientist Árpád Pusztai to tell what he knew. Just a few years earlier, in 1996, Pusztai had been given a grant of £1.6 million by the UK government to design a rigorous safety assessment protocol for testing GM foods. In the course of his studies under the auspices of the Rowett Institute in Aberdeen, Pusztai, a pro-GM scientist with a stellar reputation, discovered that the GM potato he was working on caused massive systemic health problems in rats. Virtually every organ in the animals' bodies was affected by eating the GM potato—their brains, livers and testicles were generally smaller, pathological changes in the thymus and spleen were detected and the animals' immune systems were damaged.

Since most GM foods were created using the same process and genetic material, the results raised serious questions about the safety of all GM foods. Pusztai went public in 1998 and paid dearly for his integrity: he lost his job of 35 years, was silenced with threats of lawsuits, his 20-member team was disbanded and the project terminated.

In the same year, the US Food and Drug Administration (FDA) records—44,000 pages of them, kept secret since 1992—revealed that references made by US government scientists to 'unintended negative effects . . . were progressively deleted from drafts of the policy statements (over the protests of Agency scientists)' and that the FDA was under orders from the White House to promote GM crops.

Concern about the safety of GM food was growing. Pusztai's parliamentary invitation forced the Rowett Institute to lift its long-standing gag order. When the scientist finally spoke out about the GM potatoes that had caused such substantial damage to rats, and how the biotech industry had scrambled

From *The Ecologist*, vol. 37, issue 9, November 2007. Copyright © 2007 by The Ecologist. Reprinted by permission.

to protect its reputation by rubbishing his, the press went wild. By week's end they had spewed out 159 'column feet' of text, which, according to one columnist, 'divided society into two warring blocs.' An editorial stated, 'Within a single week the spectre of a food scare has become a full-scale war.'

The resulting overwhelming consumer resistance was too much for the food industry. GM food became a liability and, in April 1999, Unilever publicly committed to removing GM ingredients from its European brands. Within a week, nearly all major food companies followed suit, leaving Monsanto's ideal future in tatters. That rejection by manufacturers has kept nearly all GM foods (other than milk and meat products from GM-fed animals) out of Europe in spite of official approvals of GM varieties by the EU Commission.

But the biotech industry did not roll over. It has steadily pushed its agenda, but more quietly than before. Nearly every natural food crop now has a genetically engineered version produced in a lab somewhere, with at least 172 species grown outdoors in field trials. With pressure from the industry and the US, and in spite of doubts over their impact in terms of health and the environment, the European Commission last year approved new GM crops for cultivation for the first time since the 1999 consumer revolt, and in a vote in June this year, the European Commission allowed accidental GM contamination of organic products at levels up to 0.9 per cent.

Animals Reject GM

Eyewitness reports from farmers and scientists across North America describe how, when given the choice, several varieties of animals—including cows, pigs, deer, elk, raccoons, geese, squirrels, mice and rats—avoid eating GM plants and feed. It's possible the animals instinctively know or sense what we are only just beginning to see.

Lab animals forced to eat GM food showed damage to virtually every system studied. They had stunted growth, bleeding stomachs, abnormal and potentially pre-cancerous cell growth in the intestines, impaired blood cell development, misshapen cell structures in the liver, pancreas and testicles, altered gene expression and cell metabolism, liver and kidney lesions, partially atrophied livers, inflamed kidneys, less developed brains and testicles, enlarged livers, pancreases and intestines, reduced digestive enzymes, higher blood sugar levels, increased death rates, higher offspring mortality and immune system dysfunction.

Reports from the field are similarly alarming. About two dozen US farmers report that GM corn varieties caused thousands of pigs to become sterile. Some also reported sterility among cows and bulls. German farmers link cow deaths to one variety of GM corn, while Filipinos link another variety to deaths among water buffaloes, chickens and horses. When 71 Indian shepherds let their sheep graze on Bt cotton plants after harvest, within five to seven days 25 per cent had died. The 2006 death rate for the region is estimated at 10,000 sheep. This year, more deaths were identified and toxins were also found in Bt cotton fields. Post mortems showed severe irritation and black patches in the intestines and liver of the sheep, as well as enlarged bile ducts. Investigators

concluded that preliminary evidence 'strongly suggests the sheep mortality was due to a toxin . . . most probably Bt-toxin.'

Should Humans Be Worried?

The biotech industry argument is that millions have eaten GM foods for years without a problem—but how would it know? There is no surveillance system in place that could identify problems if they did arise. The Canadian government announced in 2002 that it would undertake such monitoring, but abandoned its plans within a year on the grounds that it was too difficult. There are not even human clinical trials. Some GM varieties are approved before any human has ever eaten them.

Soon after GM soya was introduced into the UK, researchers at York Nutritional Laboratory, Yorkshire, reported that allergies to soya had skyrocketed by 50 per cent in a single year. Although no follow-up studies were done, there are many ways in which genetic engineering could be the culprit. Allergic reactions occur when the immune system encounters something it interprets as foreign, different and offensive, and reacts accordingly. All GM foods, by definition, have something foreign and different about them. And several studies show that they provoke reactions.

Although biotech advocates describe genes in terms of Lego, snapping cleanly into place, the process of creating a GM crop can produce massive collateral damage in plant DNA. Native genes can be mutated, deleted or permanently turned on or off, and hundreds may change their levels of protein expression. The result may be an increase in an existing allergen or the production of an entirely new one. Both appear to have happened in GM soya.

Levels of one soya allergen, trypsin inhibitor, were as much as seven times higher in cooked GM soya when compared with a non-GM variety. Another study verified that GM soybeans contain a unique, unexpected protein, not found in controls, that reacts with immunoglobulin E (IgE), the principal antibody involved in allergic reactions. This suggests the potential for dangerous allergic reactions. The same study revealed that one human subject showed a skin-prick immune response to GM soya only, not to natural soya.

In addition, a protein in natural soya cross-reacts with peanut allergies. This means soya may trigger reactions in some people who are allergic to peanuts. This cross-reactivity could theoretically increase in GM varieties. Thus, the doubling of US peanut allergies in the five years immediately after the introduction of GM soya might not be a coincidence.

GM soya also produces an unpredicted side effect in the pancreas of mice—a dramatic reduction in the production of digestive enzymes. If fewer enzymes cause food proteins to break down more slowly, there is more time for allergic reactions to develop. Thus, digestive problems from GM soya might promote allergic reactions to a wide range of proteins, not just to soya.

To make matters worse, the only published human feeding study on GM foods verified that portions of the gene inserted into GM soya transfers into the DNA of human gut bacteria. This means that, years after people stop eating

GM soya, they may still be exposed to its potentially allergenic protein, which is continuously produced inside their intestines.

Monsanto's 'Roundup Ready' GM soya is planted in 89 per cent of US soya acres. A foreign gene from bacteria (with parts of virus and petunia DNA) is inserted, which allows the plant to survive applications of the otherwise deadly Roundup herbicide. Because people aren't usually allergic to a food until they have eaten it several times, we don't know in advance if the protein produced by bacteria, which has never been part of the human food supply, will provoke a reaction.

As a precaution, scientists compare the amino acid sequence of the novel protein with a database of known allergens. If there is a match, according to criteria recommended by the World Health Organization (WHO) and others, the GM crop should either not be commercialised or additional testing should be done. Sections of the protein produced in GM soya are identical to known allergens, but the soybean was introduced before WHO criteria were established, and the recommended additional tests not conducted.

GM corn is also problematic. Rats fed Monsanto's GM corn, for example, were found to have a significant increase in blood ceils related to the immune system. GM potatoes caused the rats' immune system to respond more slowly. And, when produced within GM peas, a harmless protein was transformed into a potentially deadly allergen. The peas and potatoes were not commercialised, but they had passed the superficial tests usually carried out in the approval of most GM crops. Crops that did make it to the market, however, may be triggering immune responses in the unsuspecting population.

Cleaning Up the Food Chain

In 2003, I interviewed GMO campaigners worldwide about their methods and successes, in order to develop a plan for the Institute for Responsible Technology (IRT) that would help remove GMOs from the marketplace. Unlike many other organisations, which are focused on containing GMOs—by limiting the territory of cultivation or preventing new varieties, for instance—IRT's goal is to eliminate the current generation of GM crops, which it believes is unsafe. Intelligent activism from individual consumers and groups could easily accomplish this in as little as 24 months.

The undisputed driver of the GMO doctrine is the United States. The first Bush Administration fast-tracked the GM approval process in 1992, hoping this would increase exports and US dominance of food markets. The opposite ensued, and soon the government was shelling out $3 billion to $5 billion a year in subsidies to prop up prices on the GM crops no-one wanted. Rather than giving up on the unpopular technology, the US tried to force other countries to accept GM, resorting to World Trade Organization (WTO) lawsuits against the European Union, GM food aid for famine-stricken nations, even threats to withdraw funds for AIDS relief if GMOs weren't adopted by African nations.

If GMOs are to implode worldwide, the US must be ground zero.

About 9 out of 10 processed foods in the US contain unlabelled GM ingredients, many produced by the same companies that sell only non-GM

products in Europe. Why didn't US consumers react like the Europeans in the wake of the Pusztai scandal? The fact is that the US press did not even mention the story. Project Censored—a group that tracks the news published in independent journals and newsletters and compiles an annual list of stories of social significance that have been overlooked, underreported or self-censored by the major national news media—described it as one of the 10 most underreported events of the year.

Because the US press rarely mentions GM foods at all, if you ask the average American whether he or she has ever eaten a GM food in their life, 60 per cent will so 'no' and 15 per cent will say 'I don't know.' GMOs flourish on the basis of consumer ignorance, but this leaves the biotech industry extremely vulnerable. If some campaign or event were to push this issue above the national radar screen, causing sufficient consumer concern, US manufacturers would respond like their European counterparts and swear off GMOs.

The Power of the Market

The tipping point to trigger a non-GMO food revolution in the US does not require that a majority of shoppers reject GM foods—if even a small percentage started switching brands based on GMO content, major companies would spot the trend, see a loss in market share and respond. This is facilitated by the fact that manufacturers gain no benefits from GM ingredients; requesting their removal is not like asking them to take out sugar or fat. GMOs do not make a product tastier, healthier or more appealing.

Even five per cent of the US population—15 million people or 5.6 million households—making brand choices based on GM content may be more than the critical mass needed to force change. With little exaggeration, Oprah Winfrey could end the genetic engineering of the food supply in 60 minutes. A popular film such as a GMO version of *An Inconvenient Truth* might accomplish it as well.

Even if these things are not forthcoming, however, there are several subgroups within the US that are large enough and receptive enough to drive a transformation. Chief among these are health-conscious shoppers, and they are already being rallied to the cause.

Currently, 28 million Americans buy organic products on a regular basis. Another 54 million are considered 'temperate' organic shoppers. Together they account for approximately 27 per cent of the population. According to a December 2006 poll, 29 per cent of Americans (probably many of the organic buyers) are strongly opposed to GM foods and believe they are unsafe. But most do not conscientiously avoid GM ingredients in their non-organic purchases; they usually don't know how. That's about to change.

In spring 2007, a coalition of food manufacturers, distributors and retailers in the natural products industry, along with the IRT, launched an initiative to remove GM ingredients from the entire natural food sector. This comprehensive initiative—called the Campaign for Healthier Eating in America . . .—will educate consumers about the health risks of GM foods and promote non-GMO brands through in-store non-GMO shopping guides. Within approximately 18–24 months, it is expected that nearly all the food brands sold in natural food

markets will have achieved non-GMO status. At that point the campaign will provide in-store, on-shelf labels for retailers to indicate to consumers any of the few remaining holdout products that still 'May contain GM ingredients.'

Shopper education will be provided through GMO-education centres in natural food stores nationwide, as well as regular features on websites and in magazines and newsletters. By providing health-conscious shoppers with information showing that 'Healthy Eating Means No GMOs,' and by offering clear choices in the store, brands that do not contain GM ingredients will have the clear advantage.

The mechanics of the sector-wide cleanout is being orchestrated by an organisation called The Non-GMO Project . . . , which is establishing a uniform standard for defining non-GMO and a low-cost, online, third-party verification programme to ensure that farming and production methods meet that standard. The membership of their board of directors illustrates the far-reaching support for this unprecedented initiative in self-regulation. It includes executives from the multi-billion-dollar Whole Foods Market and United Natural Foods, as well as industry leaders such as Eden Foods, Lundberg Family Farms, Organic Valley and Nature's Path.

Organic products are included in this programme: they are not allowed to use GMOs and have been an important oasis for non-GMO shoppers—and yet research shows that some batches of organic seed and crops contain tiny amounts of GM contamination. If unchecked, this can grow over time. By including the organic sector in the campaign, organic producers will use GMO testing methods and procedures that will help clean up seeds and crops and ensure that certified organic foods continue to be a trusted source of non-GMO products. Unlike the recently enacted EU threshold for allowable 'adventitious' contamination of organic products by as much as 0.9 per cent, the standard for non-GMO claims will take into consideration current levels of purity and will in all likelihood require progressively cleaner levels in subsequent years, based on successful efforts to remove GMO contamination.

This initiative, which is akin to an immune response to GMOs by the natural food industry, could easily set the stage for the elimination of GM ingredients throughout the conventional foods industry as well.

Mobilising Support

Health-conscious individuals and groups outside the food industry also have a major role to play in cleaning up the food chain. Parents with young children, for example, are the ones most likely to switch to a healthier diet—for the sake of the children. Such care is warranted, as young, fast-growing bodies are more at risk from potential toxins, allergens and nutritional problems—all three of which are associated with GMOs.

With the epidemics of obesity and diabetes, as well as the increased medication of children for ADHD and depression, the focus on their diets, both at home and at school, is now 'on fire' in the US and elsewhere. Adding compelling information about the impact of GM foods on children's health can leverage the media coverage, community organising, and school-meal

reorganisation already taking place. In the US this is the role of the GM-Free Schools campaign . . . , which is active in several states.

On the basis of potential adverse health effects, several healthcare organisations in the US are now providing educational materials to healthcare providers in order to help patients follow the prescription to avoid GM foods. Many religious organisations, too, have denounced GM foods on the basis that such mixing of species is against natural law. They equate the concept of 'GMO' with 'God, Move Over'. Large religious organisations have not yet asked their membership to avoid buying and eating GM foods, however. With the ability to activate millions, religions are the sleeping giants in this debate.

On their own, action by any of these groups is capable of forcing the hand of the US food industry. When company executives learn that a major religion is instructing millions of its followers to avoid their brand, that doctors are prescribing the same, that parents believe the company's foods can hurt children or that millions of trend-setting health-conscious shoppers shun their products, the end is near for GM foods. Over the next two years, through these education-based strategies, the IRT expects the synergy of information and activism to take effect.

A key advantage of addressing the problem of GM food in this way is that it does not rely on governments to step in; it places the mantle of leadership on consumers who are, after all, at the top of our food chain. By making healthier choices for themselves and for their families, they can quite quickly, and quite literally, change the world.

GM-Free Zones?

The advancement of GMOs in Europe and elsewhere has not been without protests. Indeed, the stream of GM crops approved for import have consistently been rejected by the majority of member states. Poland, Greece, northern Austria and, as of June, Ireland are seeking to enforce a ban against planting GM crops, but the European Commission has branded these GM-free zones illegal. Brazil, which grows GM soya, may be introducing corn and cotton starting this year, but approvals are being challenged in the court. Australian states' moratoria on GM crops will expire in 2008 and there is a pitched battle over possible renewals. GM cotton has gained a foothold in India, but thousands of farmer suicides linked to poor crop performance, as well as animal deaths and allergic reactions among cotton workers, are fuelling resistance there. And looming large on the horizon are GM biofuels, the new poster child of the industry, which hopes that biotechnology will be embraced as a solution for global warming.

Decisions being made in Europe and around the world at this time are critical, and will help decide whether the biotech industry can reincarnate its genetically engineered future. The industry paints the picture that agricultural biotechnology is a 'done deal' that must coexist with natural varieties, but this is not the case. GM can be stopped. Given the substantial evidence for adverse health effects and the difficulties of containing GM contamination in the wild, ending the genetic engineering of the food supply appears easier than managing it. . . .

EXPLORING THE ISSUE

Are Genetically Modified Foods Safe to Eat?

Critical Thinking and Reflection

1. What does it mean to say that a particular technology is "unnatural?"
2. What is the greatest threat to human health posed by genetically modified (GM) foods?
3. Should tests of GM foods performed by industry scientists be trusted?
4. Should regulation of a new technology be based on demonstrated risks? On potential risks? On the nature of the press coverage?

Is There Common Ground?

The participants in the debate over GM foods agree that it is important to ensure a healthy, safe, and abundant food supply. They differ on whether genetic engineering helps to achieve this aim.

1. It can be instructive to consider other threats to a healthy, safe, and abundant food supply. Among these threats are plant diseases known as rusts and blights. Read Rachel Ehrenberg, "Rust Never Sleeps," *Science News* (September 25, 2010), and discuss the global effects of a massive rust outbreak.
2. List as many other threats to a healthy, safe, and abundant food supply as you can.
3. How many of these threats might be addressed using genetic engineering? Using other technologies?

Internet References . . .

National Aeronautics and Space Administration

At this site, you can find out the latest information on the International Space Shuttle, space exploration, and other space-related news.

http://www.nasa.gov

SETI Institute

The SETI Institute serves as a home for scientific research in the general field of life in the universe, with an emphasis on the search for extraterrestrial intelligence (SETI).

http://www.seti.org

Close Approaches

NASA's Near Earth Object Program lists past and future close approaches to Earth.

http://neo.jpl.nasa.gov/ca/

Near Earth Objects

The Near Earth Object Dynamic Site (NEODyS) provides information on all near earth asteroids (NEAs). Each NEA has its own dynamically generated home page. Note the Risk Page, which presents information on the likelihood of impacts with Earth.

http://newton.dm.unipi.it/neodys/

Space

*M*any interesting controversies arise in connection with technologies
that are so new that they may sound more like science fiction than fact.
Some examples are technologies that allow the exploration of space, the
detection (and perhaps prevention) of space-based threats, and the search
for extraterrestrial intelligence. We have capabilities undreamed of in earlier ages, and they raise genuine, important questions about what it is to
be a human being, the limits on human freedom in a technological age,
the degree to which humans are helpless victims of fate, and the place of
humanity in the broader universe. They also raise questions of how we
should respond: Should we accept the new devices and abilities offered by
scientists and engineers? Or should we reject them? Should we use them
to make human life safer and more secure? Or should we remain, as in
past ages, at the mercy of the heavens?

- Are We Doing Enough to Protect the Earth from Asteroid and Comet
  Impacts?

- Will the Search for Extraterrestrial Life Ever Succeed?

- Do Humans Belong in Space?

ISSUE 12

Are We Doing Enough to Protect the Earth from Asteroid and Comet Impacts?

YES: J. Anthony Tyson, from "Near-Earth Objects (NEOs)—Status of the Survey Program and Review of NASA's Report to Congress," Testimony before the House Committee on Science and Technology, Subcommittee on Space and Aeronautics (November 8, 2007)

NO: Russell L. Schweickart, from *Asteroid Threats: A Call for Global Response* (Association of Space Explorers International Panel on Asteroid Threat Mitigation, September 25, 2008)

Learning Outcomes

After studying this issue, students will be able to explain:

1. Why asteroid and comet impacts are considered a risk to society.
2. What options are available to prevent asteroid and comet impacts.
3. The importance of advance planning to deal with potential disasters such as asteroid and comet impacts.
4. The factors that go into defining how big a near-Earth object must be before we consider it worrisome.

ISSUE SUMMARY

YES: Physics professor J. Anthony Tyson argues that NASA can fulfill its congressionally mandated mission of surveying near-Earth objects (NEOs) that may pose future hazards to Earth by funding the proposed Large Synoptic Survey Telescope (LSST) project.

NO: Russell L. Schweickart, chair of the Association of Space Explorers International Panel on Asteroid Threat Mitigation, argues that to deal with the potential threat of asteroid and comet impacts, the United Nations must oversee an international effort not only to

catalog potential threats but also to decide when and how to ward off potential impacts.

Thomas Jefferson once said that he would rather think scientists were crazy than believe that rocks could fall from the sky. Since then, we have recognized that rocks do indeed fall from the sky. Most are quite small and do no more than make pretty streaks across the sky as they burn up in the atmosphere; they are known as meteors. Some—known as meteorites—are large enough to reach the ground and even to do damage. Every once in a while, the news reports one that crashed through a car or house roof, as indeed one did in January 2007 in New Jersey. Very rarely, a meteorite is big enough to make a crater in the Earth's surface, much like the ones that mark the face of the Moon. An example is Meteor Crater in Arizona, almost a mile across, created some 50,000 years ago by a meteorite 150 feet in diameter. (The Meteor Crater Web site, http://www.meteorcrater.com/, includes an animation of the impact.) A more impressive impact is the one that occurred 65 million years ago; the scar has been found at Chicxulub, Mexico: The results included the extinction of the dinosaurs (as well as a great many other species). Chicxulub-scale events are very rare; a hundred million years may pass between them. Meteor Crater-scale events may occur every thousand years, releasing as much energy as a 100-megaton nuclear bomb and destroying an area the size of a city. And it has been calculated that a human being is more likely to die as the result of such an event than in an airplane crash.

It is not just Hollywood sci-fi, *Deep Impact* and *Armageddon*. Some people think we really should be worried. We should be doing our best to identify meteoroids (as they are called before they become meteors or meteorites) in space, plot their trajectories, tell when they are coming our way, and even develop ways of deflecting them before they cause enormous loss of life. In 1984, Thomas Gehrels, a University of Arizona astronomer, initiated the Spacewatch project, which aimed to identify space rocks that cross Earth's orbit. In the early 1990s, NASA workshops considered the hazards of these rocks. NASA now funds the international Spaceguard Survey, which finds about 25 new near-Earth asteroids every month, and has identified more than 600 asteroids over 1 kilometer in diameter (1000 meters; 1.6 kilometres equal 1 mile); none seem likely to strike Earth in the next century. See Duncan Steel, *Target Earth: How Rogue Asteroids and Doomsday Comets Threaten Our Planet* (Reader's Digest Association, 2000), David Morrison, "Asteroid and Comet Impacts: The Ultimate Environmental Catastrophe," *Philosophical Transactions: Mathematical, Physical & Engineering Sciences* (August 2006), and Mark Williamson, "The Asteroid Threat: Should We Worry?" *Engineering & Technology* (May 23–June 5, 2009). However, the news periodically issues alarming reports. In 2004, the 130-foot-wide asteroid 99942 Apophis looked for a time as if it would strike Earth in 2029 with the equivalent of a 10,000-megaton nuclear bomb. Improved data pushed the date of impact off to 2036. Still more data reduced the probability of an impact in that year to 1 in 45,000. This might seem reassuring, but there are many other large rocks in space, and eventual large impacts on Earth are very likely. David Noland, "The Threat Is Out There,"

Popular Mechanics (December 2006), reviews the story and covers what we might do if this (or another) asteroid takes a closer swing at us. Greg Easterbrook, "The Sky Is Falling," *Atlantic* (June 2008), argues that human society faces so much risk from asteroid and comet impacts that Congress should place a much higher priority on detecting potential impactors and devising ways to stop them.

In the debate over the risks of near-Earth object (NEO) impacts on Earth, there are a few certainties: They have happened before, they will happen again, and they come in various sizes. As Mike Reynolds says, in "Earth Under Fire," *Astronomy* (August 2006), the question is not whether impacts will happen in the future. "It's just a matter of when and how big the object will be." Many past craters mark the Earth, even though many more have been erased by plate tectonics and erosion. Ivan Semeniuk, "Asteroid Impact," *Mercury* (November/December 2002), says, "If there is one question that best sums up the current state of thinking about the impact hazard, it is this: At what size do we need to act? In the shooting gallery that is our solar system, everyone agrees we are the target of both cannonballs and BBs. The hard part is deciding where to draw the line that separates them. For practical reasons, that line is now set at 1 kilometer. Not only are objects of this diameter a global threat (no matter where they hit, we're all affected to some degree), they are also the easiest to spot. Under a mid-1990s congressional mandate, NASA currently funds search efforts to the tune of about $3.5 million per year. . . . 'The existing commitment to 1 kilometer and larger is to retire the risk,' says Tom Morgan, who heads NASA's NEO group. 'By the end of this decade we'll be able to tell you if any of these objects presents a threat in the foreseeable future.'" However, as Richard A. Kerr notes, "The Small Ones Can Kill You, Too," *Science* (September 19, 2003).

What if a "killer rock" does present a threat? In September 2002, NASA held a "Workshop on Scientific Requirements for Mitigation of Hazardous Comets and Asteroids," which concluded "that the prime impediment to further advances in this field is the lack of any assigned responsibility to any national or international governmental organization to prepare for a disruptive collision and the absence of any authority to act in preparation for some future collision mitigation attempt" and urged that "NASA be assigned the responsibility to advance this field" and "a new and adequately funded program be instituted at NASA to create, through space missions and allied research, the specialized knowledge base needed to respond to a future threat of a collision from an asteroid or comet nucleus." The results of the workshop appeared as *Mitigation of Hazardous Impacts Due to Asteroids and Comets* (Cambridge University Press, 2004).

The Organization for Economic Cooperation and Development (OECD) Global Science Forum held a "Workshop on Near Earth Objects: Risks, Policies and Actions" in January 2003. It too concluded that more work is needed. In May 2005, the House Science Committee approved a bill to establish and fund a NASA program to detect and assess near-Earth asteroids and comets down to 100 meters in diameter. See also David H. Levy, "Asteroid Alerts: A Risky Business," *Sky & Telescope* (April 2006). NASA's March 2007 "Near-Earth Object Survey and Deflection Analysis of Alternatives, Report to Congress" argues that although progress is being made, much more would be possible if Congress increased funding.

Given political will and funding, what could be done if a threat were identified? Richard Stone, "Target Earth," *National Geographic* (August 2008), says that "Two facts are clear: Whether in 10 years or 500, a day of reckoning is inevitable. More heartening, for the first time ever we have the means to prevent a natural disaster of epic proportions." There have been numerous proposals, from launching nuclear missiles to pulverize approaching space rocks to sending astronauts (or robots) to install rocket engines and deflect the rocks onto safe paths (perhaps into the sun to forestall future hazards).

In 2009 the U.S. National Research Council published *Near-Earth Object Surveys and Hazard Mitigation Strategies: Interim Report,* concluding that although the United States leads the effort to evaluate the hazard and develop methods of coping, Congress should be providing funds to let NASA do much more. Possible countermeasures are discussed by W. Huebner et al., "A Comprehensive Program for Countermeasures against Potentially Hazardous Objects," *Solar System Research* (August 2009). See also Brian Fisher Johnson, "How to Deflect an Incoming Asteroid," *Earth* (October 2009). Russell L. Schweickart expands his essay, reprinted in the NO selection, in "Decision Program on Asteroid Threat Mitigation," *Acta Astronautica* (November 2009).

A December 2008 study by the U.S. Air Force found that we are woefully unprepared for a NEO impact; see David Shiga, "Asteroid Attack: Putting Earth's Defences to the Test," *New Scientist* (September 23, 2009). Not much has changed since Bill Cooke, "Killer Impact," *Astronomy* (December 2004), warned that for the foreseeable future, our only real hope will be evacuation of the target zone. All proposed methods of warding off disaster require a stronger space program than any nation now has. Lacking such a program, knowing that a major rock is on the way would surely be little comfort. However, given sufficient notice—on the order of decades—a space program might be mobilized to deal with the threat. Indeed, David Adam, "Russia's Armageddon Plan to Save Earth from Collision with Asteroid," *The Guardian* (December 30, 2009), reports that Russia's space agency is currently considering plans to deflect the Apophis asteroid away from any possible collision with Earth. The probability of such a collision in 2029 or 2036 is low, but it is finite, and Apophis offers a good opportunity to develop necessary technology.

In the YES selection, physics professor J. Anthony Tyson argues that NASA can fulfill its congressionally mandated mission of surveying NEOs that may pose future hazards to Earth by funding the proposed Large Synoptic Survey Telescope (LSST) project (www.lsst.org/lsst). Russell L. Schweickart, chair of the Association of Space Explorers International Panel on Asteroid Threat Mitigation, argues that more is needed. To deal with the potential threat of asteroid and comet impacts, the United Nations must oversee an international effort not only to catalog potential threats but also to decide when and how to ward off potential impacts.

YES

J. Anthony Tyson

Near-Earth Objects (NEOs)—Status of the Survey Program and Review of NASA's Report to Congress

. . . The House Committee on Science has been a leader on a bipartisan basis for over two decades in focusing attention on the need to detect, characterize, and catalog near-Earth asteroids. The passage of the "George E. Brown Jr. Near Earth Object Survey Act" was a landmark piece of legislation that sets a goal of cataloging 90% of NEOs of 140 meters in diameter and larger within 15 years. The Committee is properly looking at the existing and future capabilities for carrying out this goal and expanding the existing Spaceguard program. [The Large Synoptic Survey Telescope] (LSST) adopted the goal of surveying NEOs at the outset as one of its major science capabilities.

Until recently, the discussion of risk associated with an impact of a NEO has been statistical; what is the probability? This is similar to considerations of risk in many other areas such as weather and traffic accidents. What if it were feasible to deploy a system that would alert me of an impending traffic accident well in advance? That would change the very nature of that risk from a probabilistic worry to a deterministic actionable situation. The ability to detect virtually every potentially hazardous near-Earth object and determine its orbit with precision transforms that statistical threat into a deterministic prediction. We face many threats, and virtually all of them are either so complex or unpredictable that they are treated probabilistically even though the social and financial consequences are legion. With a comparatively small investment the NEO risk can be transformed from a probabilistic one to a deterministic one, enabling mitigation.

The First Job: Finding the NEOs

Ground-based optical surveys are the most efficient tool for comprehensive NEO detection, determination of their orbits and subsequent tracking. (Radar also plays an important role once a threatening NEO has been found, in refining its orbit when the NEO is near.) The first job is to find the NEOs which are potentially hazardous (so-called Potentially Hazardous Asteroids) from among the swarm of ten million other asteroids. A survey capable of extending these tasks to NEOs with diameters as small as 140 m, as mandated by Congress, requires a large telescope, a large camera, and a sophisticated data acquisition,

From U.S. House of Representatives, November 8, 2007.

processing and dissemination system. The Congressional mandate drives the requirement for an 8-meter class telescope with a 3000 Megapixel camera and a sophisticated and robust data processing system. These requirements are met by the LSST.

Why is a large telescope required? A typical 140-meter NEO appears very faint (visual magnitude of 25). Multiple NEO detections in a single night are required to estimate its motion, so that its future or past detections can be linked together. This linkage has to be done exceedingly robustly because the near-Earth objects will be outnumbered nearly a thousand to one by main-belt asteroids (between Mars and Jupiter) which present no threat to Earth. By reliably linking detections on multiple nights, the NEO's orbit can be reconstructed and used to compute its impact probability with Earth. Despite their name, NEOs are typically found far from Earth. In principle, very faint objects can be detected using long exposures, but for objects moving as fast as typical NEOs, the so-called trailing losses limit the exposure time to about 30 seconds. In order to detect 140-meter NEOs in 30 seconds, an 8-meter class telescope is required.

Why is a large camera required? The need for a very large field of view comes from the requirement that the whole observable sky should be observed at least every four to five nights. For comparison, we need a field of view thousands of times larger than the Hubble Space Telescope's Advanced Camera for Surveys. With its 10 square degree field of view, LSST will be able to reach the mandated high NEO completeness.

Finding Near-Earth Objects with Ground-based Surveys

Ground-based optical surveys are a very cost-effective tool for comprehensive NEO detection, determination of orbits, and subsequent tracking. A survey capable of extending these tasks to NEOs with diameters as small as 140 m, as mandated by Congress, drives the requirement for a large telescope, a large camera, and a sophisticated data acquisition, processing and dissemination system.

To find a significant fraction of the faint NEOs one must essentially make a movie of the deep sky. Each faint asteroid must be captured in many separate exposures in order for computers to distinguish it from the numerous other asteroids and then piece together its orbit. A large area of the sky (ideally all the sky visible from some location on Earth, at least 20,000 square degrees) must be surveyed rapidly and deeply in order to survey a large volume for these faint asteroids. The ability of a telescope and camera to take rapid deep repeated images of the entire sky is proportional to its "throughput." Throughput (sometimes called etendue) is simply the product of the telescope light collection area (units: square meters) times the camera field of view in a single snapshot (units: square degrees). Thus throughput of a survey facility is measured in units of square meters square degrees. The throughput of LSST is 320 square meters square degrees. High throughput is a necessary condition for such a facility to carry out its mission, but not a sufficient condition: one must also arrange to have high observing efficiency (access to the sky) and

highly efficient optics and imaging detectors in the camera, as well as superb image quality.

For an efficient NEO survey, the whole observable sky should be observed at least every four to five nights, with multiple observations per night. In order to do so with exposure time of about 30 seconds per observation, a 10 square degree large field of view is required. Such a large field of view, with pixel size sufficiently small to fully sample the image at a good observing site, implies a multi-billion pixel camera. Indeed, at the time of its completion, the 3.2 billion pixel LSST camera will be the largest astronomical camera in the world.

With a 3.2 billion pixel camera obtaining images every 15 seconds (individual 30 second exposures are split into two 15 second exposures for technical reasons), the data rate will be about 20 thousand gigabytes per night. Not only is this a huge data rate, but the data have to be processed and disseminated in real time, and with exquisite accuracy. It is estimated that the LSST data system will incorporate several million lines of state-of-the-art custom computer code.

State of the LSST Project

The Large Synoptic Survey Telescope (LSST) is currently by far the most ambitious proposed survey of the sky. With initial funding from the US National Science Foundation (NSF), Department of Energy (DOE) laboratories and private sponsors, the design and development efforts are well underway at many institutions, including top universities and leading national laboratories. The main science themes that drive the LSST system design are Dark Energy and Dark Matter, the Solar System Inventory, Transient Optical Sky and the Milky Way Mapping. It is this diverse array of science goals that has generated the widespread excitement of scientists ranging from high-energy physicists to astronomers and planetary scientists, and earned LSST the endorsement of a number of committees commissioned by the National Academy of Sciences.

Fortunately, the same hardware and software requirements are driven by science unrelated to NEOs: LSST reaches the threshold where different science drivers and different agencies (NSF, DOE and NASA) can work together to efficiently achieve seemingly disjoint, but deeply connected, goals. Because of this synergy the Congressional mandate can be reached at only a fraction of the cost of a mission dedicated exclusively to NEO search.

The scientific priority for constructing a large aperture ground based survey telescope was recommended in the astronomy and astrophysics Decadal Survey 2000 report entitled Astronomy and Astrophysics in the New Millennium. Since then, LSST has reached a high state of design maturity. LSST has recently passed the NSF Conceptual Design Review for construction, which puts it on track for transition to Readiness in spring 2008. LSST is a public–private project. To date $44M in private funding has been raised. Twenty-two institutions have joined the effort and have contributed significant in-kind technical labor. LSST R&D continues for another 3 years under NSF support along with in-kind contributions. The project is on track for first light in 2014. It is proposed that the DOE (because of the importance of LSST for addressing the mystery of dark energy) support the $80M cost of constructing

the camera. Foreign support now appears likely, and this in-kind would offset the camera cost.

Method of Study: The LSST Operations Simulator

The LSST Operations Simulator was developed to be able to do just the sort of assessment described in this document. It contains detailed models of site conditions, hardware and software performance, and an algorithm for scheduling observations which will, eventually, drive the robotic LSST observatory. . . .

For the currently planned LSST baseline cadence, objects counted as cataloged are observed on 20 different nights on average. A more stringent requirement could decrease the completeness by up to 3%. The completeness is also a function of the assumed size distribution: the flatter the distribution, the higher the completeness. If the latest results for the NEO size distribution by A. Harris are taken into account, the completeness increases by 1–2%. Due to these issues, the completeness estimates have a systematic uncertainty of 2%. Our analysis assumes that no NEOs are known prior to LSST. Current surveys make a negligible contribution to the 90% completeness for NEOs of 140 m and up.

The NEO Survey Completeness Achievable with LSST

The LSST system is the only proposed astronomical facility that can detect 140-meter objects in the main asteroid belt in less than a minute. The LSST system will be sited at Cerro Pachon in northern Chile, with first light scheduled for 2014. In a continuous observing campaign, LSST will cover the entire available sky every four nights, with at least two observations of an NEO per night. Over the baseline survey lifetime of 10 years, each sky location would be observed over 800 times. Two NEO detections in a single night are required to estimate its motion, so that its future or past detections can be linked together. This linkage has to be done exceedingly robustly because the near-Earth objects will be outnumbered a hundred to one by main-belt asteroids which present no threat to Earth. By reliably linking detections on multiple nights, the NEO's orbit can be reconstructed and used to compute its impact probability with Earth.

The currently planned LSST baseline observing cadence on the sky, described in the Major Research Equipment and Facilities Construction proposal submitted to NSF, is simultaneously optimized for all four main science drivers: Characterizing Dark Energy and Dark Matter, the Solar System Inventory, Transient Optical Sky, and the Milky Way Mapping. Computer simulations of LSST observing show that the data stream resulting from this baseline cadence on the sky is capable of providing orbits for 82% of Potentially Hazardous Asteroids (PHA) larger than 140 meters after 10 years of

operations. . . . This baseline cadence spends 5% of the total observing time on NEO-optimized observations in the north region of the ecliptic (plane of the solar system).

Various adjustments to this baseline cadence can boost the completeness for 140 m and larger PHAs to 90%. Based on about 100 different simulations, we find that such adjustments to the baseline cadence or filter choices can have unacceptably large impact on other science programs, if the 90% completeness is to be reached within 10 years from the beginning of the survey. However, with a minor adjustment of the baseline cadence and additional specialized observing for NEOs, this completeness level can be reached with a 12-year long survey, and with a negligible effect on the rest of science goals.

These specialized observations would be of limited use to other science programs, and they require 15% of the observing time. . . .

Conclusions

The ability of LSST to reach the mandated 90% completeness for 140 m and larger PHAs in 10 years by the so-called "dedicated" option described in the 2007 NASA NEO report is supported by our detailed and realistic simulations. An important additional insight from these simulations is that we can deliver the performance of a "dedicated" system by spending 85% of the total observing time on a general survey useful for all LSST science programs, and by specializing only about 15% of the total observing time for NEO surveying. If such an NEO-optimized program is executed for 12 years, the 90% completeness for 140 m and larger PHAs can be reached without a significant negative impact on other science programs.

The current cost estimate for LSST in 2006 dollars is $389M for construction and $37M per year for operations. For a 12-year long survey, 15% of the total cost is $125M. Thus, we could deliver the performance of a full NEO-dedicated LSST to NASA at a small fraction of the total cost to build and operate such a system. This cost is equivalent to 30% of operations, which would commence in 2014. To assure LSST keeps on schedule, about $5M should be spent on optimized NEO orbit software pipeline development in the last phase of R&D and the construction phase, 2009–2014.

Executive Summary

In December 2005 Congress directed NASA to implement a near-Earth object (NEO) survey that would catalog 90% of NEOs larger than 140 meters in 15 years. In order to fulfill the Congressional mandate using a ground-based facility, an 8-meter class telescope equipped with a 3200 Megapixel camera, and a sophisticated and robust data processing system are required. These criteria are met by the Large Synoptic Survey Telescope (LSST). We have carried out over 100 simulations of the LSST operations for a variety of NEO-optimized scenarios. The planned LSST baseline survey cadence on the sky, simultaneously optimized for all main science drivers, is capable of providing orbits for 82% of PHAs larger than 140 meters after 10 years of operation, and is 90%

complete for objects larger than 230 meters. This baseline cadence assumes that 5% of the total observing time is spent on NEO-specialized observing. This is what is currently planned. By increasing this fraction to 15% and by running the survey longer, the Congressional mandate of 90% completeness for NEOs of 140 m and greater size can be fulfilled after 12 years of operation, with 60% completeness level reached after only 3 years.

Note that by operating LSST in this special NEO-enhanced mode we would have the performance equivalent of an LSST fully dedicated to NEO surveying. By supporting only 15% of the total cost, NASA would be essentially getting a NEO-dedicated LSST. This is a key new insight relative to the costing model in the 2007 NASA NEO report to Congress.

Russell L. Schweickart

 **NO**

Asteroid Threats: A Call for Global Responses

. . .

1. Introduction

The Association of Space Explorers and its international Panel on Asteroid Threat Mitigation submits this document, *Asteroid Threats: A Call for Global Response*, for consideration and necessary action by the United Nations on behalf of the international community, comprised of all the nations on Earth. The document's purpose is to urge the global community to establish necessary institutional decision-making capacities to prevent an asteroid impact with Earth.

International NEO decision-making should take the following factors into consideration:

- Damage caused by asteroids and other near-Earth objects might affect the entire international community and/or major parts of the world. A truly global response is required.
- Capabilities (unevenly spread among the international community) are available to humankind to undertake responsive action against NEO threats, especially if the appropriate decisions are made sufficiently in advance.
- The discovery rate of NEOs posing a potential threat will increase significantly within the next 10–15 years.
- Because a substantial lead time is usually required to execute an asteroid deflection operation, the international community may have to act before it would be certain an impact would occur.
- Efforts to deflect a NEO could cause a temporary shift in the impact site from one populated region of the planet to another.
- Delays in decisions to undertake responsive actions will limit the relevant options. Such delays will increase the risk that the remaining options may cause undesirable political consequences or even physical impact damage.

For these reasons, the Association of Space Explorers and its international Panel on Asteroid Threat Mitigation consider it necessary that a decision-making

program for global action in response to asteroid threats should be developed at the earliest opportunity. Such a program requires high level acceptance by the international community as a whole. Accordingly, the ASE and its international Panel on Asteroid Threat Mitigation believe that the United Nations is the most appropriate forum to begin addressing and implementing such a decision-making program.

2. Dealing with the Impact Hazard

2.1 The Impact Hazard

Our planet's geological and biological history is punctuated by evidence of repeated, devastating cosmic impacts. Since its formation 4.5 billion years ago, Earth has absorbed repeated impacts from asteroids and comets. These remnants of solar system formation delivered to Earth the water and organic materials which created a favorable environment for life. But as life emerged and developed here, cosmic impacts continued, sometimes with effects devastating enough to shift the course of evolution. Today, our complex and interdependent society is more vulnerable than ever to catastrophic disruption by a major impact.

Our planet orbits the Sun amid a swarm of hundreds of thousands of inner solar system objects capable of causing destruction on Earth. They range in size from 45-meter Tunguska-like objects to the extremely rare 10-kilometer objects which can cause a catastrophic mass extinction.

The Cretaceous-Tertiary (K-T) Extinction, 65 million years ago, was probably triggered by the impact of a 12-kilometer-diameter asteroid in what is now the Yucatan Peninsula of Mexico. The planet-wide effects of Chicxulub eliminated about 70% of all living species, including the dinosaurs.

Tons of cosmic material fall on the Earth every day, but nearly all disintegrates and burns during passage through the atmosphere. However, when objects larger than approximately 45 meters in diameter strike, the atmosphere cannot fully screen us. Even NEOs which do not make it all the way to the ground can cause destruction through the production of a damaging fireball and shock wave. The most famous example occurred in 1908, when 2,000 square kilometers of Siberian forest were destroyed by a multi-megaton impact called the Tunguska Event. When larger objects make it through the atmosphere and strike Earth's surface, they produce an explosion and crater.

The human species has always been vulnerable to this cosmic impact process, which has often altered the course of life on Earth. But the advanced telescopes and technology available today provide us with the necessary early warning and deflection capabilities to prevent these infrequent but terribly devastating natural disasters. We need no longer remain passive victims of the impact process.

2.2 The Coming Wave of NEO Discoveries

As of late 2008, we know of approximately 5,600 near-Earth objects, and some 967 of those are known as Potentially Hazardous Asteroids: objects 150 m or larger which come within 0.05 astronomical units (about 7.5 million km) of

Earth. Current United States law directs the National Aeronautics and Space Administration (NASA) by 2020 to discover, track, catalog and characterize 90% of all near-Earth objects over 140 m in diameter. Advanced telescopes planned for operation within the next 5–7 years will greatly increase our ability to find more and smaller NEOs. Over the next 10–15 years, the NEO discovery rate will increase dramatically.

Based on what we know about the statistics of the NEO population, search programs over the next 15 years will add to the NEO database 200,000 to 400,000 potential impactors large enough to do substantial damage to Earth. Approximately 6,000 of these objects will have a "non-zero" probability of impacting Earth within the next 100 years. Generally these "non-zero" probabilities are very small, typically one in several hundred thousand or less, but it is likely that hundreds will have impact probabilities that are worrisome. Dozens of NEOs will likely be threatening enough that they will require a proactive decision about whether to take action to prevent an impact.

2.3 Impact Warning Scenarios and Reaction Time

. . . In describing these impact scenarios, we emphasize that of all the near-Earth asteroids discovered, only a very small fraction (3% or so) possess even a small possibility of impacting Earth in the next century. Of this small fraction, most will cease to be a threat entirely once we obtain multiple tracking "apparitions" for each NEO and better determine its orbit. Still, we must search for the rare case of an ultimately threatening NEO, for only by discovering it can we prevent or minimize what may be a disaster of unprecedented magnitude.

Near-Term Potential Impacts (Mitigation)
Asteroid impacts occur on both the daylight and night sides of the Earth in roughly equal numbers. While there are exceptions, asteroids impacting on the sunlit hemisphere appear to approach the Earth from the direction of the Sun, while those impacting at night appear to approach from the anti-Sun direction. As a result, while ground-based optical telescopes can observe the approach of night impactors, they cannot (due to solar glare), be used to detect and track those close to impact on the day side.

From the daylight hemisphere, NEO detection and tracking are restricted to radar telescopes, which are insensitive to the bright sky. Furthermore, while optical telescopes can detect and track the smallest NEOs of concern from 1 to 6 months before impact, radar systems with their limited range can only "see" objects this size within 3 to 6 days of impact, provided the operators know precisely where to look.

Thus, for an impactor approaching from the sunlit side, there will be a maximum of 3–6 days of warning time for the evacuation of a potentially large target zone. Even that minimal warning would be available only for those asteroids detected on a previous close pass by the Earth; that earlier tracking would provide us with the predicted impact time and direction of approach necessary for aiming our radar telescopes. Because radar observatories have

small fields of view and cannot view the entire sky, an undetected asteroid approaching Earth from the daylight side will give us little or no warning.

For NEOs approaching from Earth's night side (about 50% of the cases), the situation is slightly better. Optical telescopes should detect both known asteroids and those not in our database a month or more prior to impact. This should be true even for the smallest (and most numerous) asteroids of concern. For those previously discovered NEOs headed for nighttime impact, a fairly precise impact point can be determined when they are first optically recovered a month or more pre-impact.

For "new" asteroids (those on their first apparition), astronomers cannot determine the specific impact point until a few weeks prior to impact, or perhaps until they come within radar range, 3–6 days from Earth. Although we can issue a general alert for the target region (perhaps 1,000 km across), we may not be able to give the precise impact point until a few days prior to the collision.

Long-Term Potential Impacts (Deflection)

To discover and track near-Earth asteroids early enough to obtain accurate orbits and predict any possible impacts far in advance, a dedicated NEO search program is necessary. With good, early orbit knowledge, we can initiate a deflection campaign and avert an impact. This outcome, while entirely feasible, is highly dependent on possessing all three elements of an effective NEO defense, namely:

1. The early warning system must discover and track the entire cohort of sizeable near-Earth asteroids (approximately 500,000 objects) and establish accurate orbits for them a minimum of 15–20 years prior to any predicted impact.
2. Spacecraft deflection systems should be designed and tested in demonstration missions that validate and provide confidence in their capability.
3. The international community must be prepared to decide on a deflection campaign in a timely manner.

Failing to provide a decision-making framework before a threatening NEO is discovered will result in lengthy argument, protracted delays, and collective paralysis. Such delays will preclude a deflection and force the world to absorb a damaging—albeit preventable—impact. With the lead time for a decision typically needed at least 10–15 years ahead of a potential impact, we should now begin to forge that vital decision-making capacity.

2.4 Impact Prevention and Decision Frequency

There are many more small asteroids than large ones. Most asteroid impacts are caused by the smallest NEOs. Earth will be struck by a 40-meter diameter object (about the minimum size that will cause surface damage) every 700 years, on average.

If damaging impacts occur an average of only once every 700 years, why should the international community deal urgently with this issue? The simple answer is that far more NEOs will *appear* to pose a threat to Earth than will actually strike it. In many instances, we won't know with certainty if an impact will occur until after it is too late to prevent the collision—whether it actually occurs or not. As a result, the decision to deflect an incoming NEO will often have to be taken when the probability of impact is 1 in 10, or even 1 in 100. For example, if the actual impact rate is 1 per 700 years, but the decision to act must be taken when the probability of impact reaches 1 in 70 (about 1.5%), then the average frequency of decision-making is once every 10 years. Over the next 10–15 years, then, the process of discovering NEOs will likely identify dozens of new objects threatening enough that they will require proactive decisions by the United Nations.

3. Toward a Decision-Making Program for Asteroid Threats

Humankind possesses the first two of the elements necessary for impact prevention: search telescopes and a proven spaceflight technology. **The missing third element is the readiness and determination of the international community to establish decision-making capacities.** This commitment to trigger timely action must be embodied in the form of a coordinated, pre-established international NEO decision-making process.

This process must include deflection criteria and campaign plans which the international community can implement rapidly and with little debate. In the absence of an agreement on a decision-making process, we may lose the opportunity to act against a NEO in time, leaving evacuation and disaster management as our only response to a pending impact. A single such missed opportunity will add painful fault-finding to the devastating physical effects of an impact. The international community must begin work now on forging all three impact prevention elements (warning, deflection technology, and a decision-making process) into an effective defense against a future collision.

The purpose of this document is to initiate a process at the United Nations level leading to the establishment of a decision-making framework for prevention of an asteroid impact. The framework should include an agreed-upon set of criteria, policies, and responsibilities, which can be applied without delay in the case of a specific asteroid threat.

The rationale for such a pre-established, international set of decision-making criteria on NEO deflection and mitigation stems from a combination of: (1) the uncertainty in the specific impact point at the time a deflection decision must be made (i.e., the potential impact zone may extend entirely across one hemisphere of the Earth), and; (2) orbital mechanics considerations which dictate that action to deflect an asteroid will temporarily raise the risk to other regions and populations in the process of eliminating the risk for all.

This temporary shift in risk from one region and population to another during NEO deflection will include a choice as to which nations will face that

heightened risk. Plainly, with a NEO impact and its proposed deflection affecting people and nations across the face of the planet, the decision criteria, policies, and practices must be determined by international agreement.

There is a strong derived benefit in having the international community grapple with these issues now, in the brief period before the incidence of specific NEO threats increases. Once a potential NEO threat arises, with a particular risk corridor and/or identified impact point, the discussions concerning deflection actions, and which nations should bear the temporary increase in risk during the campaign, will inevitably become more political and difficult. We make our recommendations for the decision-making process on the basis of the value of human life and property, independent of national political power or influence. It is critical that the decision-making process be thoroughly deliberated and agreed upon prior to the advent of a specific threat.

That process should begin now and reach a conclusion at the earliest possible time. Based on this reasoning, the ASE and its international Panel on Asteroid Threat Mitigation have submitted the present report for consideration and decision by the intergovernmental processes of the United Nations.

4. Recommendations on a Decision-Making Program for a Global Response to Asteroid Threats

The need for a NEO decision-making program leads the Association of Space Explorers and its international Panel on Asteroid Threat Mitigation to make the following recommendations to the international community, represented by the United Nations.

Recognizing that near-Earth Object impacts represent a global, long-term threat to our collective welfare, we recommend that international preparations, under the umbrella of the United Nations, are the only way our society can identify a specific impact threat and decide on effective prevention or disaster response measures.

A global, coordinated response by the United Nations to the NEO impact hazard should ensure that three logical, necessary functions are performed:

1. An Information, Analysis, and Warning Network should be established. This network would operate a global system of ground- and/or space-based telescopes to detect and track potentially hazardous NEOs. The network, using existing or new research institutions, should analyze NEO orbits to identify potential impacts. The network should establish criteria for issuing NEO impact warnings.

   Information, analysis, and warning encompass a logical flow of information beginning with basic telescopic observations of NEOs, both new and known, and progressing through orbit analyses enabling, in rare but critical cases, a hierarchy of warnings of an impending NEO threat.

2. A Mission Planning and Operations "Group," drawing on the expertise of the spacefaring nations, should be established and mandated

to outline the most likely options for NEO deflection missions. This group should assess the current, global capacity to deflect a hazardous NEO by gathering necessary NEO information, identifying required technologies, and surveying the NEO-related capabilities of interested space agencies. In response to a specific warning, the group should use these mission plans to prepare for a deflection campaign to prevent the threatened impact.

Whenever the probability of a NEO impact is high enough, and the projected impact is sufficiently far in the future, the international community should initiate preparations for a deflection campaign. Alternative mission designs, specific information needs, and coordination among the spacefaring nations (SFN) must proceed in an orderly way to achieve a deflection capability. This group should develop a set of coordinated threat responses (e.g. planning for threat verification missions) as well as plans for full deflection campaigns.

3. The United Nations should exercise oversight of the above functions through an intergovernmental Mission Authorization and Oversight "Group." This group would develop the policies and guidelines that represent the international will to respond to the global impact hazard. The Mission Authorization and Oversight Group should establish impact risk thresholds and criteria to determine when to execute a NEO deflection campaign. The Mission Authorization and Oversight Group would submit recommendations to the United Nations Security Council for appropriate action.

The above functions encompass a myriad of judgments, criteria, thresholds and policies which ultimately should represent the collective will of the international community in responding to the global threat of NEO impacts.

To safeguard humankind from future NEO impact threats, the United Nations, with its existing framework for international cooperation and decision-making, offers the best path toward implementing recommendations 1 through 3. . . .

5. Conclusion

As previously pointed out, humankind now possesses the technology to provide the first two essential elements necessary to protect the planet from asteroid impacts. Early impact warning is already underway for the largest objects of concern and new telescopes will soon increase the capability to provide impact warning for more numerous smaller objects of concern. Asteroid deflection capability, while not yet proven, is possible with current spaceflight technology and is being actively investigated by several of the world's space agencies.

The missing third element is the readiness and determination of the international community to take concerted action in response to a perceived threat to the planet.

An adequate global action program must include deflection criteria and campaign plans which, can be implemented rapidly and with little debate by the

international community. In the absence of an agreed-upon decision-making process, we may lose the opportunity to act against a NEO in time, leaving evacuation and disaster management as our only response to a pending impact. A single such missed opportunity will add painful fault-finding to the devastating physical effects of an impact. The international community should begin work now on forging its warning, technology, and decision-making capacities into an effective shield against a future collision.

Now that humankind has the scientific, technical and operational capabilities *both* to predict whether an asteroid will come too close for comfort, *and* to launch operational missions to deflect a potential impact, it is time for the international community to identify the decision-making institutions and begin the development of a coordinated decision-making process. This decision-making program proposed by the international Panel on Asteroid Threat Mitigation is only the first step in that direction.

> We are no longer passive victims of the impact process. We cannot shirk the responsibility to prevent or mitigate impacts wherever possible. . . .

EXPLORING THE ISSUE

Are We Doing Enough to Protect the Earth from Asteroid and Comet Impacts?

Critical Thinking and Reflection

1. Suppose that astronomers announce that an asteroid big enough to destroy the United States will strike Ohio in 10 years. What could we do about it?
2. Make that 25 years. What could we do about it?
3. Given the inevitability of an eventual asteroid impact, how important is it that we plan ahead? How much should we spend per year on preparations for warding off the impact or recovering afterward?
4. What factors must be considered in setting a minimum size limit (100, 300, and 1000 m) on the search for near-Earth objects?

Is There Common Ground?

No one thinks that if an asteroid or a comet struck the Earth, the consequences would be trivial. But because such impacts are rare events, many people are inclined to think they do not need to worry *now*, there is nothing that could be done to stop them, and besides, there are a great many other problems—from malaria to global hunger to climate change—that deserve funding more immediately. As the essays for this issue point out, however, it does not take huge amounts of funding to maintain a watch on the skies, inventory potential threats, and plan ahead. There are other potential disasters for which a similar precautionary approach is appropriate. Look up the following terms (begin with the listed URLs) and discuss how people are preparing for future problems.

1. Volcanoes (www.scientificamerican.com/article.cfm?id=volcano-monitoring-jindal).
2. Supervolcanoes (www.nasca.org.uk/supervolcano/supervolcano.html).
3. Tsunamis (www.ess.washington.edu/tsunami/general/warning/warning.html).
4. Earthquakes (http://earthquake.usgs.gov/).

ISSUE 13

Will the Search for Extraterrestrial Life Ever Succeed?

YES: **Seth Shostak,** from "When Will We Detect the Extraterrestrials?" *Acta Astronautica* (August 2004)

NO: **Peter Schenkel,** from "SETI Requires a Skeptical Reappraisal," *Skeptical Inquirer* (May/June 2006)

Learning Outcomes

After studying this issue, students will be able to:

1. Explain why it ever seemed reasonable to use radio telescopes to search for extraterrestrial intelligence.
2. Explain why some people think, despite the lack of success to date, that it remains worthwhile to search for extraterrestrial intelligence.
3. Explain why some people think the search for extraterrestrial intelligence (SETI) is not a worthwhile endeavor.
4. Discuss the likely consequences of successful SETI.

ISSUE SUMMARY

YES: Radio astronomer and SETI (search for extraterrestrial intelligence) researcher Seth Shostak argues that if the assumptions behind the SETI are well grounded, signals of extraterrestrial origin will be detected soon, perhaps within the next generation.

NO: Peter Schenkel argues that SETI's lack of success to date, coupled with the apparent uniqueness of Earth, suggests that intelligent life is probably rare in our galaxy and that the enthusiastic optimism of SETI proponents should be reined in.

$\mathbf{I}$n the 1960s and early 1970s, the business of listening to the radio whispers of the stars and hoping to pick up signals emanating from some alien civilization was still new. Few scientists held visions equal to Frank Drake, one of

the pioneers of the search for extraterrestrial intelligence (SETI) field. Drake and scientists like him utilize radio telescopes—large, dish-like radio receiver–antenna combinations—to scan radio frequencies (channels) for signal patterns that would indicate that the signal was transmitted by an intelligent being. In his early days, Drake worked with relatively small and weak telescopes out of listening posts that he had established in Green Bank, West Virginia, and Arecibo, Puerto Rico. See Carl Sagan and Frank Drake, "The Search for Extraterrestrial Intelligence," *Scientific American* (May 1975), and Frank Drake and Dava Sobel, *Is Anyone Out There? The Scientific Search for Extraterrestrial Intelligence* (Delacorte Press, 1992).

There have been more than 50 searches for extraterrestrial (ET) radio signals since 1960. The earliest ones were very limited. Later searches have been more ambitious, using multiple radio telescopes and powerful computers to scan millions of radio frequencies per second. New technologies and techniques continue to make the search more efficient. See Seth Shostak, "SETI's Prospects Are Bright," *Mercury* (September/October 2002), and Monte Ross, "The New Search for E.T.," *IEEE Spectrum* (November 2006).

At the outset, many people thought—and many still think—that SETI has about as much scientific relevance as searches for Loch Ness Monsters and Abominable Snowmen. However, to Drake and his colleagues, it seems inevitable that with so many stars in the sky, there must be other worlds with life upon them, and some of that life must be intelligent and have a suitable technology and the desire to search for alien life too.

Writing about SETI in the September–October 1991 issue of *The Humanist,* physicist Shawn Carlson compares visiting the National Shrine of the Immaculate Conception in Washington, D.C., to looking up at the stars and "wondering if, in all [the] vastness [of the starry sky], there is anybody out there looking in our direction. . . . [A]re there planets like ours peopled with creatures like us staring into their skies and wondering about the possibilities of life on other worlds, perhaps even trying to contact it?" That is, SETI arouses in its devotees an almost religious sense of mystery and awe, a craving for contact with the *other.* Success would open up a universe of possibilities, add immensely to human knowledge, and perhaps even provide solutions to problems that our interstellar neighbors have already defeated.

SETI also arouses strong objections, partly because it challenges human uniqueness. Many scientists have objected that life-bearing worlds such as Earth must be exceedingly rare because the conditions that make them suitable for life as we know it—composition and temperature—are so narrowly defined. Others have objected that there is no reason whatsoever to expect that evolution would produce intelligence more than once or that, if it did, the species would be similar enough to humans to allow communication. Still others say that even if intelligent life is common, technology may not be so common, or technology may occupy such a brief period in the life of an intelligent species that there is virtually no chance that it would coincide with Earth scientists' current search. Whatever their reasons, SETI detractors agree that listening for ET signals is futile. Ben Zuckerman, "Why SETI Will Fail," *Mercury* (September/October 2002), argues that the simple fact that we have

232

not been visited by ETs indicates that there are probably very few ET civilizations, and SETI is therefore futile.

Are we in fact alone? Or first? Are the conditions that lead to life and intelligence rare? Are there aliens living in disguise among us? Or are we quarantined? Reservationed? Zooed? Or maybe there is nobody there at all—not even us! (Sure, that could be it—if we are just simulations in some cosmic computer.) In *Where Is Everybody? Fifty Solutions to the Fermi Paradox and the Problem of Extraterrestrial Life* (Copernicus Books, 2002), Stephen Webb describes Fermi and his paradox in detail and offers a variety of answers that have been suggested—most seriously, some a bit tongue-in-cheek—for why the search has not succeeded. His own opinion is on the pessimistic side.

The SETI community, however, remains convinced that their effort is worthwhile. *SETI 2020: A Roadmap for the Search for Extraterrestrial Intelligence* (SETI Press, SETI Institute, 2002) is the report of the SETI Science and Technology Working Group, which between 1997 and 1999 developed a plan for the SETI effort through 2020, which will center on multi-antenna arrays, improved multichannel scanning, and initial efforts to look for infrared and optical signals. The book provides plentiful details, as well as a brief survey of SETI history, the science that backs up the idea that SETI is worth attempting, and the technology that makes SETI even remotely possible. The question of whether life even exists off Earth is surveyed by Brian Vastag, "Will We Soon Find Life in the Heavens?" *U.S. News and World Report* (August 4, 2008).

Steve Nadis, "How Many Civilizations Lurk in the Cosmos?" *Astronomy* (April 2010), discusses how the latest data have improved estimates of the various terms in the Drake equation, which has long guided estimates of how many ET civilizations might exist in the galaxy. Nadis quotes Frank Drake as saying that early estimates may have been much too low. There may be 10,000 such civilizations, and detecting even one may require that we examine 20 million stars. There is, however, an even larger obstacle to success. Paul Davies, *The Eerie Silence* (Houghton Mifflin Harcourt, 2010), notes that our efforts at detection are severely limited by the communications technologies we are familiar with, and ET civilizations may use those technologies for only a brief period in their history, moving on to others that we have not yet thought of and have no way to detect. We need new thinking, meaning that we must look for signals in neutrinos from space, embedded in the genes of viruses, and much more. See also Elizabeth Quill, "Can You Hear Me Now?" *Science News* (April 24, 2010).

What if SETI succeeds? Frank Drake noted in *Is Anyone Out There? The Scientific Search for Extraterrestrial Intelligence* (Delacorte Press, 1992) that positive results would have to be reported to everyone, at once, in order to prevent attempts to suppress or monopolize the discovery. Albert A. Harrison, "Confirmation of ETI: Initial Organizational Response," *Acta Astronautica* (August 2003), focuses on the need for a response to success, but he is skeptical that an effective response is possible; he says, "Foresight and advance preparation are among the steps that organizations may take to prepare for contact, but conservative values, skepticism towards SETI, and competing organizational priorities make serious preparation unlikely." Should our

response include sending an answer back to the source of whatever radio signals we detect? H. Paul Schuch, "The Search for Extraterrestrial Intelligence," *Futurist* (May/June 2003), suggests that there may be dangers in such a move. Those dangers are addressed by Ivan Almar and H. Paul Schuch in "The San Marino Scale: A New Analytical Tool for Assessing Transmission Risk," *Acta Astronautica* (January 2007). A few nonscientists have also begun to consider the implications of successful contact. See, for instance, Thomas Hoffman, "Exomissiology: The Launching of Exotheology," *Dialog: A Journal of Theology* (Winter 2004). David Brin, "The Dangers of First Contact," *Skeptic* (vol. 15, no. 3, 2010), argues that because the idea of free and open exchange of information is a historical anomaly here on Earth, any attempts to reply to a signal should not include our most valuable assets—our art, music, science, and other information. Instead, we should seek equal exchange, *quid pro quo*. He does not agree that those scientists are necessarily right who say that ETs must be highly advanced ethically and thus likely to treat us benignly. At the same time, he argues that we should not count on ET messages to solve our problems; it is better that we rely on ourselves.

Have the results of SETI to date been totally blank? Researchers have found nothing that justified any claim of success, but there have been a few "tantalizing signals." T. Joseph W. Lazio and Robert Naeye discuss them in "Hello? Are You Still There?" *Mercury* (May/June 2003).

In the YES selection, Seth Shostak defends SETI and argues that if the assumptions behind the search are reasonable, the search will succeed, perhaps within the next generation. In the NO selection, Peter Schenkel, a retired political scientist, argues that SETI's lack of success to date, coupled with the apparent uniqueness of Earth's history and suitability for life, suggests that intelligent life is probably rare in our galaxy. It is time, he says, "to dampen excessive SETI euphoria and to adopt a . . . stand, compatible with facts."

YES

Seth Shostak

When Will We Detect the Extraterrestrials?

Abstract

It has been more than four decades since the first, modern SETI experiment. Many hundreds of star systems have been observed in the radio over wide bandwidth and with impressive sensitivity, and the entire sky has been surveyed in a more restricted mode several times. Optical SETI experiments are underway, and have already scrutinized several thousand nearby stars, looking for nanosecond light pulses.

Still, there is no confirmed signal detection. Given the anticipated improvement in both telescopes and digital electronics applied to SETI, what is the time scale for making such a discovery? In this paper we investigate the rate of stellar surveillance by targeted radio SETI experiments for the foreseeable future, and conclude that it is likely that—if the principal assumptions underlying modern SETI are reasonable—a detection will occur within a single generation.

Introduction

When will SETI succeed is a perennial question which does not, and some would say, cannot, engender reliable answers.* The search has a long history compared with historical exploration efforts, which were typically a decade or so in length—Columbus' four voyages extended over a dozen years, and Cook's reconnaissance of the South Pacific (three voyages) spanned eleven years. In contrast, the first SETI experiment was more than forty years ago (Project Ozma). As has been pointed out, the searches since 1960 have been quite intermittent, and amount to less than two years of continuous observation at sensitivities and spectral coverage comparable to today's experiments. Nonetheless, many SETI researchers are inclined to make the Copernican assumption that our temporal location in the search for signals is mediocre, and that another few decades, or thereabouts, will be necessary for success.

---

*To avoid the ambiguity which some researchers ascribe to the word "success" in SETI, we define it as the unambiguous detection of an artificial, extraterrestrial signal.

As seen in *Acta Astronautica*, August 2004. Copyright © 2004 by Seth Shostak. Reprinted by permission. References omitted.

Others speak of SETI as a multi-generational project, and encourage a mind-set sympathetic to the "long haul." It is the author's own experience that the most common response by scientists engaged in SETI, when queried as to how long success will take, is to answer with the approximate number of years until their own retirement.

Given the myriad uncertainties of the SETI enterprise, is there any reason to believe that a better prediction could be made, or are such "gut feelings" the best we can hope for? It is the purpose of this brief paper to offer a somewhat more quantitative estimate of when SETI might succeed, based on typical assumptions made by the SETI researchers themselves. Of course, these assumptions could be grossly in error, but the merit of this approach is that the timescales presented here are congruent with SETI's own postulates. To the extent that the arguments made for conducting today's SETI experiments are credible, then the sort of predictions presented here of when a signal might be found are similarly worthy of consideration.

Approach

As for any discovery enterprise, the time required to find a sought-for phenomenon depends on (a) the frequency with which it occurs, and (b) the speed of the reconnaissance. For SETI searches, the first is, crudely, the number of contemporaneous signal generators (transmitters, if you will), and the second is the rapidity with which our telescopes can survey the sky (or, for targeted search strategies, likely locations on the sky) using spectral coverage and sensitivity adequate to find one of these transmitters.

Since the inception of modern SETI, reckoning the number of celestial transmitters has been done using the Drake Equation. The equation computes N, the number of contemporaneous, galactic transmitting sites, as the product of the rate at which intelligent societies arise and the length of time they remain in the transmitting state. As noted, these computations are restricted to our own Galaxy, on the assumption that intelligence in other galaxies would not have the incentive to send signals (or provoke replies) that would be millions of years in transit. In addition, some note that intergalactic messaging, even from nearby nebulae, would require untenable power levels: hundreds to millions of times higher than required for communication over typical intragalactic distances. These arguments have not been considered overly persuasive however, since a number of searches for extragalactic transmitters have been made.

Of possibly greater consequence is the Drake Equation's assumption that searches should be directed to stellar systems capable of hosting Earth-like worlds. Interstellar travel is difficult but not impossible, and it's unclear whether truly advanced intelligences would remain exclusively, or even principally, confined to the solar system of their birth. If migration away from the home star is common to technological intelligence, then targeted SETI searches, which are the most sensitive, could miss the most advanced (and possibly the most easily detected) transmitters.

Number of Stars to Search

With these caveats in mind, we begin by taking a conservative position, and consider the number of (galactic) transmitters predicted by Drake's Equation. It is not the provenance of this paper to evaluate the individual terms of this equation; we are only interested in their product, N. A compilation of published estimates assembled by Dick yields a (logarithmic) average of N ~ 10^5–10^6. (We note that one of Dick's compiled estimates is N = 0.003, which, if correct, would mean that it is overwhelmingly likely that there is nothing and no one to find. Among the SETI research community, this is obviously a minority view.) Drake himself is more conservative, and suggests N ~ 10^4. In the discussion that follows, we adopt a range of values for N of 10^4 to 10^6.

With this range estimate for N, and assuming a disk galaxy with diameter of ~90,000 light-years and half-power disk thickness (locally) of ~1,000 light-years, we can conclude that the nearest transmitter is 200–1,000 light-years away.

How many suitable targets lie within this distance? There are ~10^{11} stars in the galaxy. Traditionally, 5–10% of these have been considered preferred candidates for harboring intelligence: these comprise, roughly speaking, single F, G or K-type stars at least a few billion years old. The major groups excluded by this historical choice include multiple stars (approximately half of all stars) and M-dwarfs (about 90% of stars). However, recent research has shown that both close double stars and those that are widely separated (tens of AU or more) could host planets in stable orbits. M-dwarfs are presently being reconsidered as SETI targets. It might soon be concluded that only short-lived, massive stars (types A and earlier) can be reliably excluded *ab initio* as SETI targets. Since these comprise only ~1% of all stars, this would mean that virtually the entire stellar complement of the Milky Way would qualify for SETI scrutiny.

However, foreseeable astronomical discoveries may once again narrow the range of interesting stars. The current search for extrasolar planets has shown that ~10% of solar-type stars have detectable worlds, but these are skewed in favor of stars that have higher metallicities. This suggests an obvious target selection criterion. In addition, new space-based interferometers (e.g., NASA's Terrestrial Planet Finder and ESA's Darwin) proposed for deployment in a decade's time will allow not only the direct imaging of Earth-sized worlds, but spectral analyses of their atmospheres. Such techniques could tell us not only which star systems host suitable planets, but could pinpoint worlds that evidence the spectral signatures of life. And, of course, it's still possible that a deeper investigation of the conditions of planets around M-dwarfs could serve to reliably eliminate this very numerous stellar class from consideration.

Consequently, and mindful of this expected progress in our understanding of extrasolar planets, we assume that: (1) for the present decade, all galactic stars remain qualified SETI targets. (2) In the following decade, half of all unobserved stars can be eliminated *a priori* from our SETI target lists, and (3) in the third decade, 90% of unobserved stars can be eliminated. This is, we propose, a conservative projection of progress in choosing which star systems to observe.

Indeed, today's experiments often have more restrictive target lists than we are projecting for 2020 and beyond.

Rate of Target Scrutiny

Having estimated (a) the number of galactic transmitters, and (b) the fraction of star systems that need to be searched, we need only consider the rate at which the search is conducted in order to arrive at our goal: an estimate for when a signal will be found.

We first consider radio searches. Note that large swaths of the celestial sphere have been examined in so-called Sky Survey SETI experiments. The failure (so far) of these experiments to discover a signal, assuming such signals exist, could be due to (a) insufficient sensitivity (note that such sky surveys are typically at least an order-of-magnitude less sensitive than targeted searches, which means that the volume of sky sampled at any given sensitivity level is less by a factor of >60), (b) inadequate spectral coverage, or (c) an inability to monitor specific locations for more than a few seconds, with no facility for making immediate follow-up observations. This precludes detection of all but fully continuous signals.

Targeted searches moderate these shortcomings, but have the disadvantage of being a very slow reconnaissance. This is principally due to the fact that the large telescopes favored for SETI research are only intermittently available. The total number of star systems surveyed to date by the SETI Institute's premier radio search, Project Phoenix (which uses the Arecibo radio telescope), is ~500.

This slow pace of targeted radio searches is about to change. The Allen Telescope Array (ATA), a joint project of the SETI Institute and the University of California at Berkeley, will be a highly sophisticated radio antenna that can be used full-time to make SETI observations. It is anticipated that this instrument will be completed within the current decade. This immediately increases by an order of magnitude the amount of telescope time available for the Institute's targeted searches. In addition, an international consortium is planning the construction of an even larger telescope, the Square Kilometer Array (SKA). If built, this instrument could also be partially dedicated to SETI observations. For the purposes of this paper, we assume that this instrument will double the speed of SETI reconnaissance beginning in the (rather uncertain) year of 2015.

Project Phoenix surveys approximately 50–60 stellar systems annually. The ATA will not only have the benefit of ten times as much observing time as this effort, but will also incorporate multiple beams that allow the simultaneous observation of at least three star systems. In addition, efficiencies in follow-up and wider instantaneous spectral coverage will add at least another factor of 2–3 speed improvement. At a minimum, we can say that, once completed, the ATA will increase the rapidity with which nearby stars are checked for signals by at least two orders of magnitude. In its first year, it will observe considerably more stellar systems than the total investigated by Project Phoenix. We will (conservatively) assume this number to be 1,000 systems, applicable to the year 2006.

The ATA is conceived as an instrument whose capabilities can be expanded as the cost of digital computation continues to decline. According to Moore's Law, a fact-of-life in the field of computing hardware for three decades, the density of transistors on commercially available chips doubles every 18 months. In more practical terms, this means that the cost of computing is halved each 1-1/2 years. The speed (not necessarily the efficacy) of SETI experiments has historically followed this law. . . .

We can expect, therefore, that at least the speed of stellar scrutiny using the ATA will grow at this exponential rate, at least so long as Moore's Law continues to hold. How long might that be? Various pundits, including Moore himself, point to the fact that the further exploitation of silicon technology will likely hit a physical "wall" at which the dimensions of the transistors become nearly molecular in size. An additional (and perhaps more formidable) barrier to the continued reign of this law is the economic cost of new fabrication facilities and even of the chips themselves. On the other hand, foreseeing this technological barrier has stimulated research into optical and quantum computing, and these approaches are expected by many to not only sustain the pace of improvement, but perhaps to accelerate it.

For the purposes of this paper, we adopt widespread industry predictions that Moore's Law in its current form will continue to hold until 2015. Thereafter, we conservatively assume a decrease by half: doubling of computational power per dollar will take 36 months, rather than 18. The speed of SETI reconnaissance is postulated to follow this technological growth.

Having considered at some length the speed and expected improvements in radio SETI searches, we note that several optical SETI experiments are also underway. These look for short ($\leq 10^{-9}$ sec) bursts of photons that could be produced by, for example, a pulsed laser deliberately targeting our solar system. While optical SETI experiments are still relatively new, several thousand star systems have already been observed, and an instrument dedicated to an optical sky survey of the two-thirds of the sky visible from the northern hemisphere is currently under construction.

Despite these encouraging developments, we will not incorporate them into our estimate of when extraterrestrial intelligence will be found. This is because of the very real possibility that optical signals might be either highly intermittent or sent to only small numbers of targets. However, with not-unreasonable assumptions, optical SETI might succeed very soon. Consider a simple example: suppose that an extraterrestrial beacon is set up to serially target all $\sim 10^{11}$ galactic star systems, briefly illuminating their inner solar systems with a burst of nanosecond pulses once every 24 hours. (This brute-force approach would provide each star with a daily kilobit of data, which might be adequate to serve as a "pointer" to other information being served up by this transmitting society.) The observation time per beam for the planned Harvard-Princeton optical sky survey is ≥ 48 seconds, so that the chance of a detection for every sweep of the northern sky (estimated to take 150 days) is $\sim 3 \times 10^{-4}$ N, or >1 for all our estimates for N.

This sunny assessment assumes that all transmitters are detectable by the sky survey. In fact, optical searches for signals from star systems at great

distance need to be sensitive in the infrared to defeat the attenuating effect of interstellar dust. Such systems are not yet operational, as they must be space-based. However, there is no technical reason to doubt that they could be deployed within a decade or two. On the other hand, very low transmitter duty cycles may dictate that an effective optical SETI search will require the use of multiple, or possibly all-sky, detectors. Given the newness of optical SETI, and the lack of a body of historical "assumptions" regarding optical signaling, we will not factor such searches into our estimate of when a SETI detection will be made. This is obviously a conservative approach, assuming that optical SETI has any chance at all to succeed.

When a Detection Will Take Place

We now have in hand the requisite parameters to estimate the likely date of a (radio) SETI detection. . . . [We can plot] the number of targeted star systems observed using the ATA with, eventually, the addition of the SKA. . . . [We can then calculate] the volume of space (specified by a maximum distance) in which we've observed all suitable target star systems [and date when we will have observed enough star systems to expect successful SETI. If $N = 10^6$, the date will be about 2015. If $N = 10^4$, the date will be about 2027.] . . .

We remark that this span of dates for a predicted SETI detection extends less than two dozen years forward. Although SETI searches are sometimes referred to as multigenerational projects, our estimate suggests that this isn't the case: success is within the foreseeable future. Among other things, this justifies the efforts being made to plan for a detection, as well as to consider society's likely reaction and what would be a suitable response (if any).

We have tried to make conservative assumptions in this presentation. In particular, a reconnaissance of extrasolar planets, which would chart out their size, orbit, and whether or not they evidence spectral biomarkers, will eventually tightly focus the interest of SETI researchers, reducing (substantially, one assumes) the number of suitable target systems. We have only made a crude correction for this highly likely development. We have also made no assumption that SETI observations, particularly those that reach beyond a few hundred light-years, will concentrate their attentions on the galactic plane, thereby increasing the efficiency of the search.

While we have reckoned on an exponential improvement in technology that governs SETI search speed over the next two-and-a-half decades, this extrapolation is based on four decades in which this has been demonstrably true. To be on the safe side, we have assumed a slowing of this growth beginning in 2015. Finally, we have taken no account of the likelihood that a detection will be made with radio sky surveys, or using optical SETI techniques.

On the other hand, there are many possible reasons why our assessment that a detection will be made within a generation might be wrong. We have not considered the luminosity function or duty cycle of extraterrestrial transmitters, but have instead assumed that the N transmitters estimated by the Drake Equation are all detectable by the ATA and SKA. We have not speculated on the possibility that the frequency coverage of our telescopes is inadequate,

nor that the signal types to which they are sensitive are the wrong ones. And, indeed, we do not consider that physical laws of which we are still unaware might dictate a completely different approach to interstellar signaling. And, of course, our range of estimates for N are only considered opinion—and some of that opinion [states] that *no* other contemporary, sentient galactic societies exist.

Nonetheless, we reiterate that the intention of this exercise is to improve upon existing "gut feeling" speculation as to when SETI might expect a detection. While there are a myriad uncertainties attendant upon our estimate that this will occur within two dozen years, we have made this prediction using the assumptions adopted by the SETI research community itself. This community builds equipment and uses strategies that it reckons are adequate to find an extraterrestrial signal. It does this based on more than four decades of thought as to how best to prove the presence of extraterrestrial sentience. If such analyses are well grounded, then such proof will not be long in coming.

Peter Schenkel

 **NO**

SETI Requires a Skeptical Reappraisal

T he possible existence of extraterrestrial intelligence (ETI) has always stirred the imagination of man. Greek philosophers speculated about it. Giordano Bruno was burnt on the stake in Rome in 1600, mainly [for] positing the likelihood of other inhabited worlds in the universe. Kant and Laplace were also convinced of the multiplicity of worlds similar to ours. In the latter part of the nineteenth century Flammarion charmed vast circles with his books on the plurality of habitable worlds. But all these ideas were mainly philosophical considerations or pure speculations. It was only in the second half of the twentieth century that the Search for Extraterrestrial Intelligence (SETI) became a scientifically underpinned endeavor. Since the late 1950s distinguished scientists have conducted research, attempting to receive intelligent signals or messages from space via radio-telescopes. Hundreds of amateur astronomers, members of the SETI-League in dozens of countries, are scanning the sky, trying to detect evidence of intelligent life elsewhere in our galaxy. SETI pioneers, such as Frank Drake and Carl Sagan, held the stance that the Milky Way is teeming with a large number of advanced civilizations. However, the many search projects to date have not succeeded, and this daring prediction remains unverified. New scientific insights suggest the need for a more cautious approach and a revision of the overly optimistic considerations.

The standard argument for the existence of a multiplicity of intelligent life runs like this: There are about 200 to 300 billion stars in our galaxy and probably hundreds of millions, maybe even billions of planets in our galaxy. Many of these planets are likely to be located in the so-called "habitable zone" in relation [to] their star, enjoying Earth-favorable conditions for the evolution of life. The physical laws, known to us, apply also to the cosmos, and far-away stellar formations are composed of the same elements as our solar system. Therefore, it is assumed, many should possess water and a stable atmosphere, considered to be basic requisites for the development of life. Such planets must have experienced geological and biological processes similar to those on Earth, leading to the development of primitive life organisms. Then, in the course of time, following a similar course of Darwin's theory of natural selection, these evolved into more complex forms, some eventually developing cognitive capacities and—as in our case—higher intelligence.

From *Skeptical Inquirer,* vol. 30, no. 3, May/June 2006. Copyright © 2006. Used by permission of the Skeptical Inquirer Magazine. www.csicop.org.

In other words, it is maintained, our solar system, Earth, and its evolution are not exceptional cases, but something very common in our Milky Way galaxy. Consequently it must be populated by a huge number of extraterrestrial civilizations, many of them older and more advanced than ours.

Considering the enormous number of stars and planets, these seem like fair and legitimate assumptions. It indeed appears unlikely that intelligence should have evolved only on our planet. If many of these civilizations are scientifically and technologically superior to us, contact with them would give mankind a boost in many ways.

These optimistic views are based mainly on the famous Drake formula. . . . It considers the formation of stars in the galaxy, the fraction of stars with planetary systems, the number of planets ecologically suited for life, the fraction of these planets on which life and intelligent life evolves, and those reaching a communicative stage and the length of time of technical civilizations. On the basis of this formula it was estimated that a million advanced civilizations probably exist in the galaxy. The nearest one should be at a distance of about 200 to 300 light-years from Earth. German astronomer Sebastian von Hoerner estimated a number between ten thousand and ten million such civilizations.

But because of many new insights and results of research in a number of scientific fields, ranging from paleontology, geology, biology to astronomy, I believe this formula is incomplete and must be revised. The early optimistic estimates are no longer tenable. A more realistic and sober view is required.

I by no means intend to discredit SETI; the search for extraterrestrial intelligent life is a legitimate scientific endeavor. But it seems prudent to demystify this interesting subject, and to reformulate its claims on a new level, free of the romantic flair that adorns it.

Years ago, I readily admit, I myself was quite taken in by the allegations that intelligence is a very common phenomenon in the galaxy. In books, articles, and on radio and television I advocated the idea that our world, beset by problems, could learn a lot from a civilization more advanced than ours. But, in the meantime, I became convinced that a more skeptical attitude would do reality better justice. There are probably only a few such civilizations in the galaxy, if any at all. The following considerations buttress this rather pessimistic appraisal.

First of all, since project OZMA I in 1959 by Frank Drake, about a hundred radio-magnetic and other searches were conducted in the U.S. and in other countries, and a considerable part of our sky was scanned thoroughly and repeatedly, but it remained disappointingly silent. In forty-six years not a single artificial intelligent signal or message from outer space was received. Some specialists try to downplay this negative result, arguing that so far only a small part of the entire spectrum has been covered, and that more time and more sophisticated equipment is required for arriving at a definite conclusion. Technological and economic criteria may thwart the possibility of extraterrestrial civilizations beaming signals into space over long stretches of time, without knowing where to direct their signals. Or, they may use communication methods unknown to us. Another explanation is that advanced ETI may lack interest in contacting other intelligences, especially those less developed. The

argument of the Russian rocket expert Konstantin Tsiolkovski is often quoted: "Absence of evidence is not evidence of absence."

But neither of these arguments, which attempt to explain why we have not received a single intelligent signal from space, is convincing. True, future search projects may strike pay dirt and register the reception of a signal of verified artificial origin. But as long as no such evidence is forthcoming, the possibility of achieving success must be considered remote. If a hundred searches were unsuccessful, it is fair to deduce that estimates of a million or many thousands ETI are unsustainable propositions. As long as no breakthrough occurs, the probability of contact with ETI is near to zero. The argument that advanced extraterrestrials may not be interested in contact with other intelligences is also—as I will show—highly implausible.

Second, as recent research results demonstrate, many more factors and conditions than those considered by the Drake formula need to be taken into account. The geologist Peter D. Ward and the astronomer Donald Brownlee present in their book *Rare Earth* a series of such aspects, which turn the optimistic estimates of ETI upside down.

According to their reasoning, the old assumption that our solar system and Earth are quite common phenomena in the galaxy needs profound revision. On the contrary, the new insights suggest, we are much more special than thought. The evolution of life forms and eventually of intelligent life on Earth was due to a large number of very special conditions and developments, many of a coincidental nature. I'll mention only some that seem particularly important: The age, size, and composition of our sun, the location of Earth and inclination of its axis to it, the existence of water, a stable oxygen-rich atmosphere and temperature over long periods of time—factors considered essential for the evolution of life—and the development of a carbon-based chemistry. Furthermore an active interior and the existence of plate tectonics form the majestic mountain ridges like the Alps, the Himalayas and the Andes, creating different ecological conditions, propitious for the proliferation of a great variety of species. Also the existence of the Moon, Jupiter, and Saturn (as shields for the bombardment of comets and meteorites during the early stages of Earth). Also the repeated climatic changes, long ice ages, and especially the numerous and quite fortuitous catastrophes, causing the extinction of many species, like the one 65 million years ago, which led to the disappearance of dinosaurs but opened the way for more diversified and complex life forms.

Though first primitive life forms on Earth, the prokaryotic bacteria, evolved relatively rapidly, only about 500 million years after the cooling off of Earth's crust and the end of the dense bombardment of meteorites and comets, they were the only life forms during the first two billion years of Earth's 4.6-billion-year history. Mammals—including apes and man—developed much later, only after the extinction of the dinosaurs 65 million years ago. The first human-like being, the Proconsul, emerged in the Miocene Period, just about 18 million years ago. The Australopithecus, our antecessor, dates only 5 to 6 million years. In other words, it took almost 4 billion years, or more than 96 percent of the age of Earth, for intelligence to evolve—an awfully long time, even on the cosmic clock.

In this regard we should note also the caveat of the distinguished biologist Ernst Mayr, who underscored the enormous complexity of human DNA and RNA and their functions for the production of proteins, the basic building blocks of life. He estimated that the likelihood that similar biological developments may have occurred elsewhere in the universe was nil.

The upshot of these considerations is the following: Because of the very special geological, biological, and other conditions which propitiated the evolution of life and intelligence on Earth, similar developments in our galaxy are probably very rare. Primitive life forms, Ward and Brownlee conclude, may exist on planets of other stellar systems, but intelligent life, as ours, is probably very rare, if it exists at all.

Third is the so-called "Fermi Paradox," another powerful reason suggesting a skeptical evaluation of the multiplicity of intelligence in the galaxy. Italian physicist Enrico Fermi posed the annoying question, "If so many highly developed ETIs are out there, as SETI specialists claim, why haven't they contacted us?" I already expressed great doubt about some of the explanations given [for] this paradox. Here I need to focus on two more. The first refers to the supposed lack of interest of advanced aliens to establish contact with other intelligent beings. This argument seems to me particularly untrustworthy. I refer to a Norwegian book, which explains why the Vikings undertook dangerous voyages to far-away coasts in precarious vessels. "One reason," it says, "is fame, another curiosity, and a third, gain!" If the Vikings, driven by the desire to discover the unknown, reached America a thousand years ago with a primitive technology, if we—furthermore—a still scientifically and technically young civilization, search for primitive life on other planets of the solar system and their moons, it is incredible that higher developed extraterrestrial intelligences would not be spurred by likewise interests and yearnings. One of the fundamental traits of intelligence is its unquenchable intellectual curiosity and urge to penetrate the unknown. Elder civilizations, our peers in every respect, must be imbued by the same daring and scrutinizing spirit, because if they are not, they could not have achieved their advanced standards.

A second argument often posited is that distances between stars are too great for interstellar travel. But this explanation also stands on shaky ground. Even our scientifically and technically adolescent civilization is exploring space and sending probes—the Voyager crafts—which someday may reach other stellar systems. We are still far from achieving velocities, near the velocity of light, necessary for interstellar travel. But some scientists predict that in 200 or 300 years, maybe even earlier, we are likely to master low "c" velocities, and once we reach them, our civilization will send manned exploratory expeditions to the nearest stars. Automatic unmanned craft may be the initial attempts. But I am convinced that nothing will impede the desire of man to see other worlds with his own eyes, to touch their soil and to perform research that unmanned probes would not be able to perform. Evidently, civilizations tens of thousands or millions of years in our advance will have reached near c velocities, and they will be able to explore a considerable part of the galaxy. Advanced ETI civilizations would engage in such explorations not only out

of scientific curiosity, but in their own interest, for instance for spreading out and finding new habitats for their growing population, or because of the need to abandon their planet due to hazards from their star, and also because with the help of other civilizations it may confront dangers, lurking in the universe, more successfully than alone. The Fermi Paradox should therefore put us on guard, and foster a sound skepticism. Lack of interest in meeting a civilization such as ours is the least plausible reason why we have not heard from ETI.

A little mental experiment illustrates this point. Carl Sagan held once that intelligent aliens would visit Earth at least once every thousand years. But such visits have not taken place. Even extending this period to a million years, we fare no better. Let us assume an extraterrestrial craft landed on Earth any time during the era of the dinosaurs, lasting about 140 million years. It is only logical to assume the aliens would have returned at reasonable intervals to study our world and these fascinating animals, but also to find out if any one of them evolved the capability of reasoning, higher math, and building a civilization. There would have been reason for much surmise. According to paleontologists, Drake stresses, the dinosaur sauronithoides was endowed with such a potential. It was a dinosaur resembling a bird of our size and weight and possessing a mass of brain well above average, and, Drake speculates, if it had survived for an additional ten or twenty million years, it might have evolved into the first intelligent being on Earth. But it didn't happen, because the dinosaurs went extinct due to a cosmic catastrophe. When *Homo australopithecus,* then *Homo faber* and *habilis,* and lastly *Homo sapiens* evolved, shouldn't that have provoked on the part of visiting extraterrestrials a high level of interest? But no such visits are recorded. Only a few mythological, undocumented and highly suspect accounts of alleged visiting aliens exist. It is fair to assume, if advanced aliens had visited Earth during the past 200 million or, at least, during the past 16 million years, they would have left some durable, indestructible and recognizable mark, probably on the moon. But nothing has been detected. The most likely explanation? No such visits took place! There are no advanced extraterrestrial civilizations anywhere in our vicinity. If they existed, they already would have responded to our world's television signals, reaching some 60 light-years into space—another reason invalidating the claim that our galaxy is teeming with intelligence.

Another argument supporting the skeptical point of view sustained here is the fact that none of the detected planets around other stars comes close to having conditions apt for creating and sustaining life. Since Michel Mayor's Swiss group discovered the first planet outside our solar system around the star 51 Pegasi ten years ago, about 130 other planets have been identified within a distance of 200 light-years. Research results show that most are of gaseous composition, some many times the size of Jupiter, some very close to their stars, very hot and with extremely rapid orbital cycles. So far, not one presents conditions favorable for the development of even the most primitive forms of life, not to speak of more complex species. Again it may be argued that only a very tiny fraction of planets were surveyed and future research might strike upon a suitable candidate. This may well be, and I would certainly welcome

it. But so far the evidence fails to nourish optimistic expectations. The conditions in our universe are not as favorable for the evolution of life as optimists like to think.

Even if water or fossils of microorganisms should be found underneath the surface of Mars, the importance of such a finding for the theory of a multiplicity of inhabited worlds would be insignificant. Some astronomers think that Titan, the famous moon of Saturn, may have an ocean, possibly of methane. Primitive life forms may exist in it, but this remains to be seen. Even if it does, the evolutionary path from such primitive forms to complex life as human beings is—as we have seen—a long one, studded with a unique sequence of chance and catastrophes.

I am not claiming that we are probably the only intelligent species in our galaxy. Nor do I suggest that SETI activities are a waste of time and money. Though, so far, they have failed to obtain evidence for the existence of ETI, they enrich man's knowledge about the cosmos in many ways. They helped develop sophisticated search techniques, and they contribute decisively to the perception of man's cosmic destiny. Carl Sagan and Frank Drake, the two most distinguished pioneers of SETI, did groundbreaking work. That their efforts and those of other dedicated SETI experts on behalf of this great cause are tinged with a dash of too optimistic expectation is understandable and profoundly human.

However, in the interest of science and sound skepticism, I believe it is time to take the new findings and insights into account, to dampen excessive SETI euphoria and to adopt a more pragmatic and down-to-earth stand, compatible with facts. We should quietly admit that the early estimates—that there may be a million, a hundred thousand, or ten thousand advanced extraterrestrial civilizations in our galaxy—may no longer be tenable. There might not be a hundred, not even ten such civilizations. The optimistic estimates were fraught with too many imponderables and speculative appraisals. What is required is to make contact with a single extraterrestrial intelligence, obtaining irrefutable, thoroughly verified evidence, either via electromagnetic or optical waves or via physical contact, that we are not the only intelligent species in the cosmos. Maybe an alien spacecraft, attracted by our signals, will decide to visit us some day, as I surmised in my novel *Contact: Are We Ready for It?* I would be the first one to react to such a contact event with great delight and satisfaction. The knowledge that we are not alone in the vast realm of the cosmos, and that it will be possible to establish a fruitful dialogue with other, possibly more advanced intelligent beings would mark the biggest event in human history. It would open the door to fantastic perspectives.

But SETI activities so far do not justify this hope. They recommend a more realistic and sober view. Considering the negative search results, the creation of excessive expectations is only grist to the mill of the naysayers—for instance, members of Congress who question the scientific standing of SETI, imputing to it wishful thinking, and denying it financial support. This absolutely negative approach to SETI is certainly wrong, because contrary to the UFO hoax, SETI (as UCLA space scientist Mark Moldwin stressed in a recent issue of this magazine) is based on solid scientific premises and considerations.

But exaggerated estimates fail to conform to realities, as they are seen today, tending to backfire and create disappointment and a turning away from this fascinating scientific endeavor. The dream of mankind to find brethren in space may yet be fulfilled. If it is not, man should not feel sorry for his uniqueness. Rather that circumstance should boost the gratitude for his existence and his sense of responsibility for making the most of it.

EXPLORING THE ISSUE

Will the Search for Extraterrestrial Life Ever Succeed?

Critical Thinking and Reflection

1. Why do SETI fans think searching for extraterrestrial signals is worth the effort?
2. Why do SETI critics think the effort is wasted?
3. If SETI researchers ever detect extraterrestrial signals, should they reply? If so, what should they say?
4. Why are not real-life extraterrestrials likely to be much like the ones on TV and in the movies?

Is There Common Ground?

In the debate over this issue, there seems to be little common ground. One side thinks it worth continuing SETI. The other side says, "Forget it." But there are related areas of research, such as the search by astronomers for planets circling other stars, which to many have the ultimate goal of finding life-bearing worlds.

1. What are "exoplanets" and why do astronomers search for them? (http://planetquest.jpl.nasa.gov/; www.superwasp.org/exoplanets.htm)
2. One recent exoplanet discovery was briefly dubbed the "Goldilocks planet." Look up the term and discuss why both the astronomers and the media were excited.
3. To many people, the "Fermi Paradox" is no paradox at all. It posits that we have not been visited by aliens, but what about UFOs, the Roswell incident, alien abductions, and so on? Why don't SETI researchers take such things seriously?

ISSUE 14

Do Humans Belong in Space?

YES: Jeff Foust, from "The Future of Human Spaceflight: Are Astronauts Close to Extinction?" *Technology Review* (January/February 2010)

NO: Neil deGrasse Tyson, from "Delusions of Space Enthusiasts," *Natural History* (November 2006)

Learning Outcomes

After studying this issue, students will be able to:

1. Explain the potential benefits of space exploration.
2. Argue both in favor of and against sending human beings on space missions.
3. Use the threat of asteroid or comet impacts to justify expanded space exploration.
4. Explain how political realities make it difficult to justify manned space exploration.

ISSUE SUMMARY

YES: Jeff Foust, editor and publisher of *The Space Review*, argues that the ultimate goal of manned space exploration is to "chart a path for human expansion into the solar system." To support that goal will require extending the life of the International Space Station (ISS), providing more funding for mission development and encouraging the private sector to take over transportation to and from the ISS. At present, human spaceflight is not sustainable.

NO: Astronomer Neil deGrasse Tyson argues that large, expensive projects such as space exploration are driven only by war, greed, and the celebration of power. The dream of colonizing space became a delusion as soon as we beat the Russians to the moon, and it remains so.

The dream of conquering space has a long history. The Russian Konstantin Tsiolkovsky (1857–1935) and the American Robert H. Goddard (1882–1945), the pioneers of rocketry, dreamed of exploring other worlds, although neither lived long enough to see the first artificial satellite, the Soviet *Sputnik,* go up in 1957. That success sparked a race between the United States and the Soviet Union to be the first to achieve each step in the progression of space exploration. The next steps were to put dogs (the Soviet Laika was the first), monkeys, chimps, and finally human beings into orbit. Communications, weather, and spy satellites were designed and launched. And on July 20, 1969, the U.S. Project Apollo program landed the first men on the moon.

There were a few more *Apollo* landings, but not many. The United States had achieved its main political goal of beating the Soviets to the moon and, in the minds of the government, demonstrating the U.S. superiority. Thereafter, the United States was content to send automated spacecraft (computer-operated robots) to observe Venus, Mars, and the rings of Saturn; to land on Mars and study its soil; and even to carry recordings of Earth's sights and sounds past the distant edge of the solar system, perhaps to be retrieved in the distant future by intelligent life from some other world. (Those recordings are attached to the *Voyager* spacecraft, launched in 1977; published as a combination of CD, CD-ROM, and book, *Murmurs of Earth: The Voyager Interstellar Record,* it is now long out of print.) Humans have not left near-Earth orbit for two decades, even though space technology has continued to develop. The results of this development include communications satellites, space shuttles, space stations, and independent robotic explorers such as the *Mariners* and *Vikings,* the rovers *Spirit* and *Opportunity,* and the polar lander *Phoenix*, which finally found water on Mars in July 2008.

Why has human space exploration gone no further to date? One reason is that robots are now extremely capable. Although some robot spacecraft have failed partially or completely, there have been many grand successes that have added enormously to humanity's knowledge of Earth and other planets. Another is money: Lifting robotic explorers into space is expensive, but lifting people into space—along with all the food, water, air, and other supplies necessary to keep them alive for the duration of a mission—is much more expensive. And there are many people in government and elsewhere who cry that there are many better ways to spend the money on Earth.

Still another reason for the reduction in human space travel seems to be the fear that astronauts will die in space. This point was emphasized by the explosion on takeoff of the space shuttle *Challenger* in January 1986, which killed seven astronauts and froze the entire shuttle program for over two and a half years. The point was reinforced by the breakup of *Columbia* on entry on February 1, 2003. After the latter event, the public reaction included many calls for an end to such risky, expensive enterprises. See Jerry Grey, "*Columbia*—Aftermath of a Tragedy," *Aerospace America* (March 2003); John Byron, "Is Manned Space Flight Worth It?" *Proceedings* (of the U.S. Naval Institute) (March 2003) (and Richard H. Truly's response in the May issue); and "Manned or Unmanned into Space?" *USA Today* (February 26, 2003), among many others.

In 2004 when the then president George W. Bush announced his plan to send humans to the moon and Mars, beginning as soon as 2015, the reaction was immediate. James A. Van Allen asked, "Is Human Spaceflight Obsolete?" in *Issues in Science and Technology* (Summer 2004). Andrew Lawler asked, "How Much Space for Science?" in *Science* (January 30, 2004). Physicist and Nobel laureate Steven Weinberg, "The Wrong Stuff," *New York Review of Books* (April 8, 2004), argues that nothing needs doing in space that cannot be done without human presence. Until we find something that does need humans on the scene, there is no particular reason to send humans—at great expense—into space. Indeed, the president's Mars initiative may prove to be no more than a ploy to look visionary and force later presidents to face financial realities. John Derbyshire, "Space Is for Science," *National Review* (June 5, 2006), argues that the expense and hazards of putting humans in space do not justify the benefits when much cheaper automated spacecraft (robots) can make all necessary observations. Paul D. Spudis, "Who Should Explore Space? Astronaut Explorers Can Perform Science in Space That Robots Cannot," *Scientific American* (Special ed., January 2008), argues that there is no substitute for human astronauts in installing and maintaining equipment and in conducting field exploration because humans provide skills that are unlikely to be automated in the foreseeable future. Francis Slakey, "Who Should Explore Space? Unmanned Spacecraft Are Exploring the Solar System More Cheaply and Effectively Than Astronauts Are," *Scientific American* (Special ed., January 2008), argues that NASA sends humans into space chiefly for public relations purposes. Unmanned probes are much cheaper and more effective than astronauts, and many scientific organizations have recommended that space science should instead be done through robotic and telescopic missions. See also Louis D. Friedman and G. Scott Hubbard, "Examining the Vision," *American Scientist* (July/August 2008).

The question of whether robots can do the job is particularly relevant because of the success of the Mars rovers, *Spirit* and *Opportunity,* and the *Phoenix* lander. If robots continue to be successful, it seems likely that efforts to promote manned space travel will meet resistance. Funding for space exploration remains low largely because problems on Earth (environmental and other) seem to need money more urgently than space exploration projects do. The prospects for manned space expeditions to the moon, Mars, or other worlds seem very dim, although Paul D. Spudis, "Harvest the Moon," *Astronomy* (June 2003), asserts that there are four good reasons for putting people at least on the moon: "The first motivation to revisit the Moon is that its rocks hold the early history of our own planet and the solar system. Next, its unique environment and properties make it an ideal vantage point for observing the universe. The Moon is also a natural space station where we can learn how to live off-planet. And finally, it gives us an extraterrestrial filling station, with resources to use both locally and in near-Earth space." See also Paul D. Spudis, "The New Moon," *Scientific American* (December 2003). Nader Elhefnawy, "Beyond *Columbia:* Is There a Future for Humanity in Space?" *The Humanist* (September/October 2003), says that we cannot ignore the wealth of resources in space. Alex Ellery, "Humans versus Robots for Space Exploration and Development," *Space Policy* (May 2003), maintains that although "robotics

and artificial intelligence are becoming more sophisticated, they will not be able to deal with 'thinking-on-one's-feet' tasks that require generalisations from past experience. . . . [T]here will be a critical role for humans in space for the foreseeable future." Carl Gethmann, "Manned Space Travel as a Cultural Mission," *Poiesis & Praxis* (December 2006), argues that costs should not be used to reject manned space travel as a pointless option. The dream and the effort are part of our culture, and we should pursue them as far as we can afford to. Arthur Woods, "The Space Option," *Leonardo* (vol. 41, no. 4, 2008), argues that space resources are the most realistic way to ensure future human survival and success. However, an important question is whether the necessary effort and expenditure can be sustained; see David A. Broniatowski and Annalisa L. Weigel, "The Political Sustainability of Space Exploration," *Space Policy* (August 2008). George Whitesides, "The Coming Debate," *Ad Astra* (Summer 2008), argues that the most potent argument for sending humans into space is the role NASA can play in fighting global warming.

Early in 2010, President Barack Obama announced cancellation of the existing plans for a new launch system that would replace the present space shuttle, shifting support missions for the International Space Station (ISS) to commercial space flight companies, and starting work on a new system that would be able to support missions to asteroids and even Mars; see Andrew Lawler, "Obama Backs New Launcher and Bigger NASA Budget," *Science* (January 1, 2010). On June 28, 2010, Obama announced a National Space Policy that set 2025 for a human mission to an asteroid and the 2030s for a human landing on Mars, saying the policy "is about the boundless possibilities of the future." These plans have encountered considerable resistance in Congress so far (see Reid Wilson, "The New Space Race," *National Journal* (April 10, 2010)) and will surely continue to do so. Meanwhile, other countries—notably India and China—are mounting their own manned space programs.

In the YES selection, Jeff Foust, editor and publisher of *The Space Review*, summarizes the report of the Augustine Commission (*Seeking a Human Space- flight Program Worthy of a Great Nation*, www.nasa.gov/pdf/396093main_HSF_ Cmte_FinalReport.pdf (October 2009)) and argues that the ultimate goal of manned space exploration is to "chart a path for human expansion into the solar system." To support that goal will require extending the life of the ISS, providing more funding for mission development, and encouraging the private sector to take over transportation to and from the ISS. At present, human spaceflight is not sustainable. In the NO selection, astronomer Neil deGrasse Tyson argues that large, expensive projects such as space exploration are driven only by war, greed, and the celebration of power. The dream of colonizing space became a delusion as soon as we beat the Russians to the moon, and it remains so. The Apollo program was the end of an era, not the beginning that many hoped it would prove.

YES

Jeff Foust

The Future of Human Spaceflight: Are Astronauts Close to Extinction?

The International Space Station (ISS) is one of the most complex and expensive engineering projects ever undertaken. When it is completed in 2011, it will have cost nearly $100 billion. And then, just five years later, the space station will be destroyed when NASA deliberately takes it out of orbit and plunges it into Earth's atmosphere.

That, at least, is NASA's current plan. The agency would like to keep the station running, but funding for it is projected only through 2015, much to the consternation of researchers who are just beginning to use it and international partners who have invested billions of dollars in the project. Extending the life of the station would cost $2 billion to $3 billion a year. Even "deorbiting" it—dumping its remains safely into the ocean—will not be cheap, costing at least $2 billion.

The 2015 deadline means that after decades of largely directionless space policy, Congress will be forced to make at least one clear decision: it must allocate funds for either the space station's continued operation or its destruction. And that is just one of a number of urgent issues facing the country's human spaceflight program. The space shuttle is due to be retired by late 2010 or early 2011, leaving NASA without a means of sending astronauts anywhere for several years. And the key elements of NASA's exploration program, the Ares I rocket that will launch astronauts into orbit and the Orion capsule that will ferry them around in space, are several years behind schedule.

In October, the Augustine Committee, a panel chartered by the White House and chaired by former Lockheed Martin CEO Norman Augustine, issued its report on the future of space travel. The committee examined NASA's plans and explored alternatives. Much of the report discussed the merits of different destinations in space and the rocket and spacecraft technologies that could be used to reach those destinations. But embedded in the report is a rationale for why there should be a human spaceflight program at all. "The Committee concluded that the ultimate goal of human exploration is to chart a path for human expansion into the solar system," it states.

Over the years, NASA and space advocates have put forward many reasons to justify sending astronauts into space. They have garnered support by

From *Technology Review*, January/February 2010. Copyright © 2010 by Technology Review. Reprinted by permission via Copyright Clearance Center.

offering something for everybody, especially the military and scientific communities; scientific progress, strategic superiority, and international prestige have been foremost among the promised benefits. On closer inspection, though, these justifications don't hold up or are no longer relevant. For example, robotic missions are increasingly capable of scientific work in space, and they cost far less than human crews. Satellites launched on expendable boosters allowed the United States to achieve strategic dominance in space. And Cold War motives disappeared with the collapse of the Soviet Union.

Consequently, some have concluded that there is no longer any reason for human space exploration. A longtime critic of human spaceflight was the late James Van Allen, who in 1958 made the first major scientific discovery of the space age: the radiation belts around Earth that bear his name. In a 2004 essay, Van Allen wondered whether robotic spacecraft had made human spaceflight "obsolete." "At the end of the day," he wrote, "I ask myself whether the huge national commitment of technical talent to human spaceflight and the ever-present potential for the loss of precious human life are really justifiable."

But for most of the engineers and astronauts involved in the space program, astronauts can never be rendered obsolete by robots, because human spaceflight is an end in itself. They share the committee's belief that the purpose of these manned missions is to allow people to expand into, and ultimately settle, outer space.

For taxpayers who may well consider that prospect a pipe dream or the stuff of science fiction, the question is why their money should be spent to support it. The argument for funding human space exploration becomes similar to the argument for funding fundamental research: that doing so sometimes pays off big, usually in unexpected ways. By definition, high-risk ventures such as space exploration or curiosity-driven science seem unlikely to succeed and have unpredictable outcomes, but just such ventures have led to many inventions and discoveries with vast economic and historic significance.

Those who want a consistent long-term policy must reconcile their agendas, either supporting the rationale of settling space or coming up with an even better unifying purpose of their own. This must happen soon, or NASA's human space program will sputter to a halt. The committee put it bluntly: "The U.S. human spaceflight program appears to be on an unsustainable trajectory."

That has been true for some time. In early 2004, President Bush unveiled his strategy for continuing the U.S. space program. Key milestones included completing the ISS and retiring the space shuttle by 2010, developing what would become known as the Orion and Ares I by 2014, and returning humans to the moon by 2020, with long-term but undefined plans beyond that for human missions to Mars.

But Bush failed to provide a clear, unifying rationale for these plans, and they never received full funding. Under a constrained budget, the projects outlined by Bush will take years longer than originally planned. An example is the Ares V heavy-lift rocket needed for human missions to the moon. The current plan calls for it to be ready in the late 2010s, but the committee found that it could not be completed before the late 2020s—and even then there would be no money to develop the necessary lander spacecraft.

Using the Augustine Committee's rationale, however, we can make a reasonable plan based on the fundamental goal of human expansion into the solar system. With the goal of the space program clarified, money can be better spent and performance can be measured in concrete terms; Congress is far more likely to provide sufficient funding over the long term if it can see along the way that judiciously spent money is yielding tangible results. One of the first, and easiest, decisions to make is to extend the life of the ISS until 2020. If people are going to live and work in space for prolonged periods, we must test technologies and evaluate human performance under those conditions, and the ISS would be the ideal laboratory. Moreover, keeping the station operating will preserve an important international partnership for future missions.

One of the challenges in extending the life of the space station is that once the shuttle is retired, the Russian Soyuz spacecraft will be the only means of transporting crews to and from orbit until Ares I and Orion are ready, theoretically in 2015 (the committee believes that 2017 is more likely). The Augustine report suggests that NASA should get out of the business of shuttling astronauts back and forth and let the commercial sector provide transport to the station. The hope is that companies, serving NASA and other customers (such as space tourists and even other governments), can replace the shuttle sooner and at lower cost than NASA could, freeing up money for exploration.

The report also strongly endorses technology that NASA has largely overlooked to date: in-space refueling. With that capability, we wouldn't have to develop extremely expensive rockets, like the Ares V, that would be large enough to carry all the propellant needed for a trip to the moon. Fuel tanks—and thus the rockets themselves—could be smaller. Commercial operators could transport propellant and even maintain in-orbit fuel depots. The necessary technologies, the committee found, could be demonstrated in space within a few years.

If America's space community can't agree on this approach and thus secure the needed funding, the Augustine Committee concludes, it would be better to stop sending humans into space rather than wasting money and perhaps lives on a program that has no chance of success: "The human spaceflight program . . . is at a tipping point where either additional funds must be provided or the exploration program first instituted by President Kennedy must be abandoned, at least for the time being."

Neil deGrasse Tyson  **NO**

Delusions of Space Enthusiasts

Sometimes innovation gets interrupted.

Human ingenuity seldom fails to improve on the fruits of human invention. Whatever may have dazzled everyone on its debut is almost guaranteed to be superseded and, someday, to look quaint.

In 2000 B.C. a pair of ice skates made of polished animal bone and leather thongs was a transportation breakthrough. In 1610 Galileo's eight-power telescope was an astonishing tool of detection, capable of giving the senators of Venice a sneak peek at hostile ships before they could enter the lagoon. In 1887 the one-horsepower Benz Patent Motorwagen was the first commercially produced car powered by an internal combustion engine. In 1946 the thirty-ton, showroom-size ENIAC, with its 18,000 vacuum tubes and 6,000 manual switches, pioneered electronic computing. Today you can glide across roadways on in-line skates, gaze at images of faraway galaxies brought to you by the Hubble Space Telescope, cruise the autobahn in a 600-horsepower roadster, and carry your three-pound laptop to an outdoor café.

Of course, such advances don't just fall from the sky. Clever people think them up. Problem is, to turn a clever idea into reality, somebody has to write the check. And when market forces shift, those somebodies may lose interest and the checks may stop coming. If computer companies had stopped innovating in 1978, your desk might still sport a hundred-pound IBM 5110. If communications companies had stopped innovating in 1973, you might still be schlepping a two-pound, nine-inch-long cell phone. And if in 1968 the U.S. space industry had stopped developing bigger and better rockets to launch humans beyond the Moon, we'd never have surpassed the Saturn V rocket.

Oops!

Sorry about that. We haven't surpassed the Saturn V. The largest, most powerful rocket ever flown by anybody, ever, the thirty-six-story-tall Saturn V was the first and only rocket to launch people from Earth to someplace else in the universe. It enabled every Apollo mission to the Moon from 1969 through 1972, as well as the 1973 launch of Skylab I, the first U.S. space station.

Inspired in part by the successes of the Saturn V and the momentum of the Apollo program, visionaries of the day foretold a future that never came to be: space habitats, Moon bases, and Mars colonies up and running by the 1990s. But funding for the Saturn V evaporated as the Moon missions wound down. Additional production runs were canceled, the manufacturers' specialized

From *Natural History,* vol. 115, issue 9, November 2006. Copyright © 2006 by Natural History Magazine. Reprinted by permission.

machine tools were destroyed, and skilled personnel had to find work on other projects. Today U.S. engineers can't even build a Saturn V clone. . . .

What cultural forces froze the Saturn V rocket in time and space?

What misconceptions led to the gap between expectation and reality?

Soothsaying tends to come in two flavors: doubt and delirium. It was doubt that led skeptics to declare that the atom would never be split, the sound barrier would never be broken, and people would never want or need computers in their homes. But in the case of the Saturn V rocket, it was delirium that misled futurists into assuming the Saturn V was an auspicious beginning—never considering that it could, instead, be an end.

On December 30, 1900, for its last Sunday paper of the nineteenth century, the *Brooklyn Daily Eagle* published a sixteen-page supplement headlined "THINGS WILL BE SO DIFFERENT A HUNDRED YEARS HENCE." The contributors—business leaders, military men, pastors, politicians, and experts of every persuasion—imagined what housework, poverty, religion, sanitation, and war would be like in the year 2000. They enthused about the potential of electricity and the automobile. There was even a map of the world-to-be, showing an American Federation comprising most of the Western Hemisphere from the lands above the Arctic Circle down to the archipelago of Tierra del Fuego—plus sub-Saharan Africa, the southern half of Australia, and all of New Zealand.

Most of the writers portrayed an expansive future. But not all. George H. Daniels, a man of authority at the New York Central and Hudson River Railroad, peered into his crystal ball and, boneheadedly predicted:

> It is scarcely possible that the twentieth century will witness improvements in transportation that will be as great as were those of the nineteenth century.

Elsewhere in his article, Daniels envisioned affordable global tourism and the diffusion of white bread to China and Japan. Yet he simply couldn't imagine what might replace steam as the power source for ground transportation, let alone a vehicle moving through the air. Even though he stood on the doorstep of the twentieth century, this manager of the world's biggest railroad system could not see beyond the automobile, the locomotive, and the steamship. . . .

Three years later, almost to the day, Wilbur and Orville Wright made the first-ever series of powered, controlled, heavier-than-air flights. By 1957 the U.S.S.R. launched the first satellite into Earth orbit. And in 1969 two Americans became the first human beings to walk on the Moon.

Daniels is hardly the only person to have misread the technological future. Even experts who aren't totally deluded can have tunnel vision. On page 13 of the *Eagle's* Sunday supplement, the principal examiner at the U.S. Patent Office, W.W. Townsend, wrote, "The automobile may be the vehicle of the decade, but the air ship is the conveyance of the century." Sounds visionary, until you read further. What he was talking about were blimps and zeppelins. Both Daniels and Townsend, otherwise well-informed citizens of a changing world, were clueless about what tomorrow's technology would bring. . . .

Even the Wrights were guilty of doubt about the future of aviation. In 1901, discouraged by a summer's worth of unsuccessful tests with a glider, Wilbur told Orville it would take another fifty years for someone to fly. Nope: the birth of aviation was just two years away. On the windy, chilly morning of December 17, 1903, starting from a North Carolina sand dune called Kill Devil Hill, Orville was the first to fly the brothers' 600-pound plane through the air. His epochal journey lasted twelve seconds and covered 120 feet—a distance just shy of the wingspan of a Boeing 757.

Judging by what the mathematician, astronomer, and Royal Society gold medalist Simon Newcomb had published just two months earlier, the flights from Kill Devil Hill should never have taken place when they did:

> Quite likely the twentieth century is destined to see the natural forces which will enable us to fly from continent to continent with a speed far exceeding that of the bird.
>
> But when we inquire whether aerial flight is possible in the present state of our knowledge; whether, with such materials as we possess, a combination of steel, cloth and wire can be made which, moved by the power of electricity or steam, shall form a successful flying machine, the outlook may be altogether different.

. . . Some representatives of informed public opinion went even further. The *New York Times* was steeped in doubt just one week before the Wright brothers went aloft in the original Wright Flyer. Writing on December 10, 1903—not about the Wrights but about their illustrious and publicly funded competitor, Samuel E. Langley, an astronomer, physicist, and chief administrator of the Smithsonian Institution—the *Times* declared:

> We hope that Professor Langley will not put his substantial greatness as a scientist in further peril by continuing to waste his time, and the money involved, in further airship experiments. Life is short, and he is capable of services to humanity incomparably greater than can be expected to result from trying to fly.

. . . You might think attitudes would have changed as soon as people from several countries had made their first flights. But no. Wilbur Wright wrote in 1909 that no flying machine would ever make the journey from New York to Paris. Richard Burdon Haldane, the British secretary of war, told Parliament in 1909 that even though the airplane might one day be capable of great things, "from the war point of view, it is not so at present." Ferdinand Foch, a highly regarded French military strategist and the supreme commander of the Allied forces near the end of the First World War, opined in 1911 that airplanes were interesting toys but had no military value. Late that same year, near Tripoli, an Italian plane became the first to drop a bomb.

Early attitudes about flight beyond Earth's atmosphere followed a similar trajectory. True, plenty of philosophers, scientists, and sci-fi writers had thought long and hard about outer space. The sixteenth-century philosopher-friar Giordano Bruno proposed that intelligent beings inhabited an infinitude

of worlds. The seventeenth-century soldier-writer Savinien de Cyrano de Bergerac portrayed the Moon as a world with forests, violets, and people.

But those writings were fantasies, not blueprints for action. By the early twentieth century, electricity, telephones, automobiles, radios, airplanes, and countless other engineering marvels were all becoming basic features of modern life. So couldn't earthlings build machines capable of space travel? Many people who should have known better said it couldn't be done, even after the successful 1942 test launch of the world's first long-range ballistic missile: Germany's deadly V-2 rocket. Capable of punching through Earth's atmosphere, it was a crucial step toward reaching the Moon.

Richard van der Riet Woolley, the eleventh British Astronomer Royal, is the source of a particularly woolly remark. When he landed in London after a thirty-six-hour flight from Australia, some reporters asked him about space travel. "It's utter bilge," he answered. That was in early 1956. In early 1957 Lee De Forest, a prolific American inventor who helped birth the age of electronics, declared, "Man will never reach the moon, regardless of all future scientific advances." Remember what happened in late 1957? Not just one but two Soviet Sputniks entered Earth orbit. The space race had begun.

Whenever someone says an idea is "bilge" (British for "baloney"), you must first ask whether it violates any well-tested laws of physics. If so, the idea is likely to be bilge. If not, the only challenge is to find a clever engineer—and, of course, a committed source of funding.

The day the Soviet Union launched Sputnik 1, a chapter of science fiction became science fact, and the future became the present. All of a sudden, futurists went overboard with their enthusiasm. The delusion that technology would advance at lightning speed replaced the delusion that it would barely advance at all. Experts went from having much too little confidence in the pace of technology to having much too much. And the guiltiest people of all were the space enthusiasts.

Commentators became fond of twenty-year intervals, within which some previously inconceivable goal would supposedly be accomplished. On January 6, 1967, in a front-page story, *The Wall Street Journal* announced: "The most ambitious U.S. space endeavor in the years ahead will be the campaign to land men on neighboring Mars. Most experts estimate the task can be accomplished by 1985." The very next month, in its debut issue, *The Futurist* magazine announced that according to long-range forecasts by the RAND Corporation, a pioneer think-tank, there was a 60 percent probability that a manned lunar base would exist by 1986. In *The Book of Predictions,* published in 1980, the rocket pioneer Robert C. Truax forecast that 50,000 people would be living and working in space by the year 2000. When that benchmark year arrived, people were indeed living and working in space. But the tally was not 50,000. It was three: the first crew of the International Space Station. . . .

All those visionaries (and countless others) never really grasped the forces that drive technological progress. In Wilbur and Orville's day, you could tinker your way into major engineering advances. Their first airplane did not require a grant from the National Science Foundation: they funded it through their bicycle business. The brothers constructed the wings and fuselage themselves,

with tools they already owned, and got their resourceful bicycle mechanic, Charles E. Taylor, to design and hand-build the engine. The operation was basically two guys and a garage.

Space exploration unfolds on an entirely different scale. The first moon-walkers were two guys, too—Neil Armstrong and Buzz Aldrin—but behind them loomed the force of a mandate from an assassinated president, 10,000 engineers, $100 billion, and a Saturn V rocket.

Notwithstanding the sanitized memories so many of us have of the Apollo era, Americans were not first on the Moon because we're explorers by nature or because our country is committed to the pursuit of knowledge. We got to the Moon first because the United States was out to beat the Soviet Union, to win the Cold War any way we could. John F. Kennedy made that clear when he complained to top NASA officials in November 1962:

> I'm not that interested in space. I think it's good, I think we ought to know about it, we're ready to spend reasonable amounts of money. But we're talking about these fantastic expenditures which wreck our budget and all these other domestic programs and the only justification for it in my opinion to do it in this time or fashion is because we hope to beat them [the Soviet Union] and demonstrate that starting behind, as we did by a couple of years, by God, we passed them.

Like it or not, war (cold or hot) is the most powerful funding driver in the public arsenal. When a country wages war, money flows like floodwaters. Lofty goals—such as curiosity, discovery, exploration, and science—can get you money for modest-size projects, provided they resonate with the political and cultural views of the moment. But big, expensive activities are inherently long term, and require sustained investment that must survive economic fluctuations and changes in the political winds.

In all eras, across time and culture, only three drivers have fulfilled that funding requirement: war, greed, and the celebration of royal or religious power. The Great Wall of China; the pyramids of Egypt; the Gothic cathedrals of Europe; the U.S. interstate highway system; the voyages of Columbus and Cook—nearly every major undertaking owes its existence to one or more of those three drivers. Today, as the power of kings is supplanted by elected governments, and the power of religion is often expressed in non-architectural undertakings, that third driver has lost much of its sway, leaving war and greed to run the show. Sometimes those two drivers work hand in hand, as in the art of profiteering from the art of war. But war itself remains the ultimate and most compelling rationale.

Having been born the same week NASA was founded, I was eleven years old during the voyage of Apollo 11, and had already identified the universe as my life's passion. Unlike so many other people who watched Neil Armstrong's first steps on the Moon, I wasn't jubilant. I was simply relieved that someone was finally exploring another world. To me, Apollo 11 was clearly the beginning of an era.

But I, too, was delirious. The lunar landings continued for three and a half years. Then they stopped. The Apollo program became the end of an era,

not the beginning. And as the Moon voyages receded in time and memory, they seemed ever more unreal in the history of human projects.

Unlike the first ice skates or the first airplane or the first desktop computer—artifacts that make us all chuckle when we see them today—the first rocket to the Moon, the 364-foot-tall Saturn V, elicits awe, even reverence. Three Saturn V relics lie in state at the Johnson Space Center in Texas, the Kennedy Space Center in Florida, and the U.S. Space and Rocket Center in Alabama. Streams of worshippers walk the length of each rocket. They touch the mighty rocket nozzles at the base and wonder how something so large could ever have bested Earth's gravity. To transform their awe into chuckles, our country will have to resume the effort to "boldly go where no man has gone before." Only then will the Saturn V look as quaint as every other invention that human ingenuity has paid the compliment of improving upon.

EXPLORING THE ISSUE

Do Humans Belong in Space?

Critical Thinking and Reflection

1. Exploring space is a great idea—but what is in it for us?
2. In a space program dominated by robotic spacecraft and landers, what role remains for human beings?
3. How does the prospect of an asteroid impact on Earth help to justify manned space exploration?
4. How will the U.S. government respond if China puts an astronaut on the moon?

Is There Common Ground?

Those who argue over the merits of manned space exploration tend to agree that space is worth exploring. They disagree on whether it is necessary to send people into space when robots are already very capable and likely to be much more capable in a few years.

1. Just how capable are robots today? (There is a great deal of material on this question.)
2. Look up "telepresence" (see Tom Simonite, "The New, More Awkward You," *Technology Review* (January/February 2011), www.technologyreview .com/computing/26941/?a=f). Does this technology offer a compromise on the question of using either robots or humans in space?

Internet References . . .

Center for Democracy & Technology

The Center for Democracy & Technology works to promote democratic values and constitutional liberties in the digital age.

http://www.cdt.org/

Electronic Frontier Foundation

The Electronic Frontier Foundation is concerned with protecting individual freedoms and rights such as privacy as new communications technologies emerge.

http://www.eff.org

MIT Computer Science and Artificial Intelligence Laboratory

In hundreds of diverse projects, the MIT Computer Science and Artificial Intelligence Laboratory works to unlock the secrets of human intelligence, extend the functional capabilities of machines, and explore human/machine interactions.

http://www.csail.mit.edu/

Sourceforge

Sourceforge is a comprehensive guide to available open source software.

http://sourceforge.net/

Open Source Initiative

The Open Source Initiative (OSI) advocates for the benefits of open source and builds bridges among different constituencies in the open-source community.

http://www.opensource.org/

The Computer Revolution

*F*ans of computers have long been sure that the electronic wonders offer
untold benefits to society. When the first personal computers appeared
in the early 1970s, they immediately brought unheard-of capabilities
to their users. Ever since, those capabilities have been increasing. Today
children command more sheer computing power that major corporations
did in the 1950s and 1960s. Computer users are in direct contact with
their fellow users around the world. Information is instantly available
and infinitely malleable.

Some observers wonder about the purported untold benefits of computers. Specifically, will such benefits be outweighed by threats to children
(by free access to pornography and by online predators), civil order (by
free access to sites that advocate racism and violence), traditional institutions (will books, e.g., become an endangered species?), or human pride
(computers have already outplayed human champions at chess, checkers,
and go)? If computers can outthink humans at games, how long will it
be before they are as intelligent and even as conscious as we are? Should
government be allowed to monitor what we do online? And must all software be produced as proprietary product?

- Can Machines Be Conscious?
- Do Government Internet Surveillance Efforts Threaten Privacy and
  Civil Rights?
- Does Endorsing Open Source Software Fail to Respect Intellectual
  Property?

ISSUE 15

Can Machines Be Conscious?

YES: Christof Koch and Giulio Tononi, from "Can Machines Be Conscious?" *IEEE Spectrum* (June 2008)

NO: John Horgan, from "The Consciousness Conundrum," *IEEE Spectrum* (June 2008)

Learning Outcomes

After studying this issue, students will be able to:

1. Explain one method for telling whether a computer is truly intelligent.
2. Define "mental uploading" and discuss its likelihood.
3. Explain what is meant by "the singularity."
4. Explain why conscious computers may be essential to the singularity.
5. Make an attempt at explaining what is needed for a being to be "conscious."

ISSUE SUMMARY

YES: Christof Koch and Giulio Tononi argue that because consciousness is a natural phenomenon, it will eventually be artificially created. To test for such consciousness, however, will require something other than the classic Turing test.

NO: John Horgan argues that no one has the foggiest idea of what consciousness really is, and it seems highly unlikely that we will ever be able to create an artificial consciousness. "Engineers and scientists should be helping us face the world's problems and find solutions to them, rather than indulging in escapist, pseudoscientific fantasies like the singularity."

The first primitive digital computers were instantly dubbed "thinking machines" because they were able to perform functions—initially only arithmetic—that had always been considered part of the uniquely human ability to think. Some critics of the "thinking machine" label, however, objected that

arithmetic is so much simpler than, say, poetry or philosophy (after all, it is only a matter of following a few simple rules) that computers were not thinking at all. Thinking, they said, is for humans only. In fact, if a machine can do it, then it cannot possibly be real thinking. Philosopher John R. Searle, "Is the Brain's Mind a Computer Program?" *Scientific American* (January 1990), argues that mind and consciousness are special. They are what brains—not computers—do. Computers, he says, do no more than manipulate symbols. They do not know what the symbols mean.

In 1950, Alan Turing, an English mathematician and logician, devised a test to determine whether or not a machine was intelligent. The "imitation game" or "Turing test" considered whether or not one could converse with a person and with a computer (through a teletype so that neither could be seen and the human could not be heard) and, after a suitable period, tell which was which. If the computer could pass for an intelligent conversationalist, Turing felt, then it would have to be considered intelligent.

Over the next two decades, computer scientists learned how to program their machines to play games such as chess, solve mathematical theorems, analyze grammar, and perform a number of other tasks that had once been thought doable by thinking humans only. In most cases the machines were not as good at these tasks as humans, but many artificial intelligence (AI) researchers believed it was only a matter of time before the machines matched and even exceeded their creators.

Any machine that has come closest to passing the Turing test may have been in the early 1970s, when the late Kenneth Mark Colby, then a Stanford University psychiatrist and computer scientist, programmed a computer to imitate the conversational style of paranoid humans. This was much easier than programming a computer to imitate a nonparanoid human's conversational style because paranoid individuals tend to be very rigid and predictable in their responses. When Colby had psychiatrists interview the programmed computer and a human paranoid (through a teletype, per Turing's criteria), only half could correctly distinguish between computer and human. That is, the computer did, indeed, come close to passing the Turing test. On the other hand, it was not trying to pass as a normal human being, whose thought processes are far freer, more flexible, and more capable.

Will a computer ever be able to imitate a normal human being? And if it can, will that mean it is really "thinking" or really "intelligent" or really "conscious?" Many computer scientists believe that it is still just a matter of time before a computer passes the Turing test with flying colors and that that machine will be truly intelligent. Indeed, many even say that the human mind is nothing more than a program that runs on a biological machine.

Others argue that machines cannot have emotions or appreciate beauty and that computers cannot be self-aware or conscious, no matter how intelligent they may seem to an interrogator. They therefore can never be intelligent or conscious in a human way. However, research in this area has been extraordinarily fruitful. Jean-Pierre Dupuy, *The Mechanization of the Mind* (Princeton University Press, 2000), notes that in the 1940s a small group of mathematicians, engineers, and neurobiologists, working under the rubric of what

Norbert Weiner called cybernetics, began to pursue the idea that thinking is a form of computation and thus to be understood as an essentially mechanical or material process. Therefore, everything once taken as uniquely human or spiritual—meaning, purpose, and direction—should be accepted as a matter of physical law, and thus by no means restricted to the humans. That is, it became possible to think of machines that thought. Besides AI, the consequences include conceptual innovations in economics, political science, sociology, and cognitive science. It has also become a major component of the concept of the "singularity," the moment when progress accelerates to the point where we can no longer predict what the next year—or even the next week!—will be like. This may happen when artificially intelligent computers become able to design, improve, and build themselves.

Science fiction has played with the idea of "thinking machines" for decades. But is this idea nothing but science fiction? Some scientists do not think so, although they are quick to grant that the technology is not yet nearly ready to produce a convincing example. Still, they are trying, at least in restricted subsets of human intelligence such as game-playing. In February 1996, IBM's "Deep Blue," a chess-playing supercomputer, won and drew games against the human world champion, Garry Kasparov. It lost the six-game match, but it still demonstrated a skill at something most people are willing to call "thinking" that leaves us breathless. See Monty Newborn, *Kasparov versus Deep Blue: Computer Chess Comes of Age* (Springer-Verlag, 1996).

In May 1997, an improved Deep Blue topped its own performance by trouncing Kasparov 2-1, with three draws, and sent the news media into a frenzy. We are, wrote Charles Krauthammer in *The Weekly Standard*, "creating a new and different form of being. And infinitely more monstrous: creatures sharing our planet who not only imitate and surpass us in logic, who have even achieved consciousness and free will, but are utterly devoid of the kind of feelings and emotions that, literally, humanize human beings. Be afraid." Deep Blue's success seems to have many people afraid that chess-playing is real thinking and that human primacy in a very fundamental area—in fact, human identity—is now seriously threatened.

Hans Moravec does not feel threatened at all. In *Mind Children* (Harvard University Press, 1988) and its successor, *Robot: Mere Machine to Transcendent Mind* (Oxford University Press, 1998), he forecasts the transfer of human minds into immensely capable machines and speculates on the replacement of biological intelligence by machine intelligence. Ray Kurzweil, in *The Age of Spiritual Machines: When Computers Exceed Human Intelligence* (Viking, 1999), also says that he expects robots to surpass humans.

Not everyone is willing to go so far. Paul M. Churchland and Patricia Smith Churchland, "Could a Machine Think?" *Scientific American* (January 1990), "reject the Turing test as a sufficient condition for conscious intelligence [because it is] very important . . . that the right sorts of things be going on inside the artificial machine." In *The Emperor's New Mind: Concerning Computers, Minds, and the Laws of Physics* (Penguin Books, 1991), Roger Penrose, a renowned physicist and mathematician at the University of Oxford in England, concludes, "Is it not 'obvious' that mere computation cannot evoke

pleasure or pain; that it cannot perceive poetry or the beauty of an evening sky or the magic of sounds; that it cannot hope or love or despair; that it cannot have a genuine autonomous purpose? . . . Perhaps when computations become extraordinarily complicated they can begin to take on the more poetic or subjective qualities that we associate with the term 'mind.' Yet it is hard to avoid an uncomfortable feeling that there must always be something missing from such a picture."

Most definitions of artificial intelligence do not require that a computer be capable of pleasure, pain, and other feelings, but rather that it be able to do things otherwise reserved to human beings. One prospect for the near future is cars that drive themselves, thanks to advances in sensors and software; see W. Wayt Gibbs, "Innovations from a Robot Rally," *Scientific American* (Special ed., January 2008), and David Kiley, "The Coming of the Car-Bot," *Business Week Online* (July 7, 2008).

Artificial intelligence is currently a very active area of research. See David Gamez, "Progress in Machine Consciousness," *Consciousness & Cognition* (September 2008). Celeste Biever, "Will We Ever Build a Sentient Machine?" *New Scientist* (April 3, 2010), describes a number of steps toward the ultimate goal. Jon Brodkin, "IBM Brain Simulations Exceed Scale of Cat's Cortex," *Network World* (November 18, 2009), discusses IBM's multi-decade effort to simulate, neuron by neuron, a human brain. The current simulation corresponds to less than 5 percent of a human brain, but that is enough to provoke projections that within a few decades human beings may be falling in love with—and perhaps even marrying—robots. See Fred Hapgood, "Deus ex Machina," *Discover* (June 2008), and David Levy, *Love and Sex with Robots: The Evolution of Human–Robot Relationships* (Harper, 2007).

In the YES selection, Christof Koch and Giulio Tononi argue that because consciousness is a natural phenomenon, it will eventually be artificially created. To test for such consciousness, however, will require something other than the classic Turing test. John Horgan argues that since no one has the foggiest idea of what consciousness really is, it seems highly unlikely that we will ever be able to create an artificial consciousness. "Engineers and scientists should be helping us face the world's problems and find solutions to them, rather than indulging in escapist, pseudoscientific fantasies like the singularity."

YES

**Christof Koch and
Giulio Tononi**

Can Machines Be Conscious?

Would you sell your soul on eBay? Right now, of course, you can't. But in some quarters it is taken for granted that within a generation, human beings—including you, if you can hang on for another 30 years or so—will have an alternative to death: being a ghost in a machine. You'll be able to upload your mind—your thoughts, memories, and personality—to a computer. And once you've reduced your consciousness to patterns of electrons, others will be able to copy it, edit it, sell it, or pirate it. It might be bundled with other electronic minds. And, of course, it could be deleted.

That's quite a scenario, considering that at the moment, nobody really knows exactly what consciousness is. Pressed for a pithy definition, we might call it the ineffable and enigmatic inner life of the mind. But that hardly captures the whirl of thought and sensation that blossoms when you see a loved one after a long absence, hear an exquisite violin solo, or relish an incredible meal. Some of the most brilliant minds in human history have pondered consciousness, and after a few thousand years we still can't say for sure if it is an intangible phenomenon or maybe even a kind of substance different from matter. We know it arises in the brain, but we don't know how or where in the brain. We don't even know if it requires specialized brain cells (or neurons) or some sort of special circuit arrangement of them.

Nevertheless, some in the singularity crowd are confident that we are within a few decades of building a computer, a simulacrum, that can experience the color red, savor the smell of a rose, feel pain and pleasure, and fall in love. It might be a robot with a "body." Or it might just be software—a huge, ever-changing cloud of bits that inhabit an immensely complicated and elaborately constructed virtual domain.

We are among the few neuroscientists who have devoted a substantial part of their careers to studying consciousness. Our work has given us a unique perspective on what is arguably the most momentous issue in all of technology: whether consciousness will ever be artificially created.

We think it will—eventually. But perhaps not in the way that the most popular scenarios have envisioned it.

Consciousness is part of the natural world. It depends, we believe, only on mathematics and logic and on the imperfectly known laws of physics, chemistry, and biology; it does not arise from some magical or otherworldly quality. That's good news, because it means there's no reason why consciousness can't be reproduced in a machine—in theory, anyway.

In humans and animals, we know that the specific content of any conscious experience—the deep blue of an alpine sky, say, or the fragrance of jasmine redolent in the night air—is furnished by parts of the cerebral cortex, the outer layer of gray matter associated with thought, action, and other higher brain functions. If a sector of the cortex is destroyed by stroke or some other calamity, the person will no longer be conscious of whatever aspect of the world that part of the brain represents. For instance, a person whose visual cortex is partially damaged may be unable to recognize faces, even though he can still see eyes, mouths, ears, and other discrete facial features. Consciousness can be lost entirely if injuries permanently damage most of the cerebral cortex, as seen in patients like Terri Schiavo, who suffered from persistent vegetative state. Lesions of the cortical white matter, containing the fibers through which parts of the brain communicate, also cause unconsciousness. And small lesions deep within the brain along the midline of the thalamus and the midbrain can inactivate the cerebral cortex and indirectly lead to a coma—and a lack of consciousness.

To be conscious also requires the cortex and thalamus—the corticothalamic system—to be constantly suffused in a bath of substances known as neuromodulators, which aid or inhibit the transmission of nerve impulses. Finally, whatever the mechanisms necessary for consciousness, we know they must exist in both cortical hemispheres independently.

Much of what goes on in the brain has nothing to do with being conscious, however. Widespread damage to the cerebellum, the small structure at the base of the brain, has no effect on consciousness, despite the fact that more neurons reside there than in any other part of the brain. Neural activity obviously plays some essential role in consciousness but in itself is not enough to sustain a conscious state. We know that at the beginning of a deep sleep, consciousness fades, even though the neurons in the corticothalamic system continue to fire at a level of activity similar to that of quiet wakefulness.

Data from clinical studies and from basic research laboratories, made possible by the use of sophisticated instruments that detect and record neuronal activity, have given us a complex if still rudimentary understanding of the myriad processes that give rise to consciousness. We are still a very long way from being able to use this knowledge to build a conscious machine. Yet we can already take the first step in that long journey: we can list some aspects of consciousness that are not strictly necessary for building such an artifact.

Remarkably, consciousness does not seem to require many of the things we associate most deeply with being human: emotions, memory, self-reflection, language, sensing the world, and acting in it. Let's start with sensory input and motor output: *being conscious requires neither.* We humans are generally aware of what goes on around us and occasionally of what goes on within our own bodies. It's only natural to infer that consciousness is linked to our interaction with the world and with ourselves.

Yet when we dream, for instance, we are virtually disconnected from the environment—we acknowledge almost nothing of what happens around us, and our muscles are largely paralyzed. Nevertheless, we are conscious, sometimes vividly and grippingly so. This mental activity is reflected in electrical

recordings of the dreaming brain showing that the corticothalamic system, intimately involved with sensory perception, continues to function more or less as it does in wakefulness.

Neurological evidence points to the same conclusion. People who have lost their eyesight can both imagine and dream in images, provided they had sight earlier in their lives. Patients with locked-in syndrome, which renders them almost completely paralyzed, are just as conscious as healthy subjects. Following a debilitating stroke, the French editor Jean-Dominique Bauby dictated his memoir, *The Diving Bell and the Butterfly*, by blinking his left eye. Stephen Hawking is a world-renowned physicist, best-selling author, and occasional guest star on "The Simpsons," despite being immobilized from a degenerative neurological disorder.

So although being conscious depends on brain activity, it does not require any interaction with the environment. Whether the development of consciousness requires such interactions in early childhood, though, is a different matter.

How about emotions? Does a conscious being need to feel and display them? No: *being conscious does not require emotion*. People who've suffered damage to the frontal area of the brain, for instance, may exhibit a flat, emotionless affect; they are as dispassionate about their own predicament as they are about the problems of people around them. But even though their behavior is impaired and their judgment may be unsound, they still experience the sights and sounds of the world much the way normal people do.

Primal emotions like anger, fear, surprise, and joy are useful and perhaps even essential for the survival of a conscious organism. Likewise, a conscious machine might rely on emotions to make choices and deal with the complexities of the world. But it could be just a cold, calculating engine—and yet still be conscious.

Psychologists argue that consciousness requires selective attention—that is, the ability to focus on a given object, thought, or activity. Some have even argued that consciousness is selective attention. After all, when you pay attention to something, you become conscious of that thing and its properties; when your attention shifts, the object fades from consciousness.

Nevertheless, recent evidence favors the idea that a person can consciously perceive an event or object without paying attention to it. When you're focused on a riveting movie, your surroundings aren't reduced to a tunnel. You may not hear the phone ringing or your spouse calling your name, but you remain aware of certain aspects of the world around you. And here's a surprise: the converse is also true. People can attend to events or objects—that is, their brains can preferentially process them—without consciously perceiving them. This fact suggests that being conscious does not require attention.

One experiment that supported this conclusion found that, as strange as it sounds, people could pay attention to an object that they never "saw." Test subjects were shown static images of male and female nudes in one eye and rapidly flashing colored squares in the other eye. The flashing color rendered the nudes invisible—the subjects couldn't even say where the nudes were in

the image. Yet the psychologists showed that subjects nevertheless registered the unseen image if it was of the opposite sex.

What of memory? Most of us vividly remember our first kiss, our first car, or the images of the crumbling Twin Towers on 9/11. This kind of episodic memory would seem to be an integral part of consciousness. But the clinic tells us otherwise: *being conscious does not require either explicit or working memory.*

In 1953, an epileptic man known to the public only as H.M. had most of his hippocampus and neighboring regions on both sides of the brain surgically removed as an experimental treatment for his condition. From that day on, he couldn't acquire any new long-term memories—not of the nurses and doctors who treated him, his room at the hospital, or any unfamiliar well-wishers who dropped by. He could recall only events that happened before his surgery. Such impairments, though, didn't turn H.M. into a zombie. He is still alive today, and even if he can't remember events from one day to the next, he is without doubt conscious.

The same holds true for the sort of working memory you need to perform any number of daily activities—to dial a phone number you just looked up or measure out the correct amount of crushed thyme given in the cookbook you just consulted. This memory is called dynamic because it lasts only as long as neuronal circuits remain active. But as with long-term memory, you don't need it to be conscious.

Self-reflection is another human trait that seems deeply linked to consciousness. To assess consciousness, psychologists and other scientists often rely on verbal reports from their subjects. They ask questions like "What did you see?" To answer, a subject conjures up an image by "looking inside" and recalling whatever it was that was just viewed. So it is only natural to suggest that consciousness arises through your ability to reflect on your perception.

As it turns out, though, *being conscious does not require self-reflection.* When we become absorbed in some intense perceptual task—such as playing a fast-paced video game, swerving on a motorcycle through moving traffic, or running along a mountain trail—we are vividly conscious of the external world, without any need for reflection or introspection.

Neuroimaging studies suggest that we can be vividly conscious even when the front of the cerebral cortex, involved in judgment and self-representation, is relatively inactive. Patients with widespread injury to the front of the brain demonstrate serious deficits in their cognitive, executive, emotional, and planning abilities. But they appear to have nearly intact perceptual abilities.

Finally, *being conscious does not require language.* We humans affirm our consciousness through speech, describing and discussing our experiences with one another. So it's natural to think that speech and consciousness are inextricably linked. They're not. There are many patients who lose the ability to understand or use words and yet remain conscious. And infants, monkeys, dogs, and mice cannot speak, but they are conscious and can report their experiences in other ways.

So what about a machine? We're going to assume that a machine does not require anything to be conscious that a naturally evolved organism—you or me, for example—doesn't require. If that's the case, then, to be conscious a

machine does not need to engage with its environment, nor does it need long-term memory or working memory; it does not require attention, self-reflection, language, or emotion. Those things may help the machine survive in the real world. But to simply have subjective experience—being pleased at the sight of wispy white clouds scurrying across a perfectly blue sky—those traits are probably not necessary.

So what is necessary? What are the essential properties of consciousness, those without which there is no experience whatsoever?

We think the answer to that question has to do with the amount of *integrated information* that an organism, or a machine, can generate. Let's say you are facing a blank screen that is alternately on or off, and you have been instructed to say "light" when the screen turns on and "dark" when it turns off. Next to you, a photodiode—one of the very simplest of machines—is set up to beep when the screen emits light and to stay silent when the screen is dark. The first problem that consciousness poses boils down to this: both you and the photodiode can differentiate between the screen being on or off, but while you can see light or dark, the photodiode does not consciously "see" anything. It merely responds to photons.

The key difference between you and the photodiode has to do with how much information is generated when the differentiation between light and dark is made. Information is classically defined as the reduction of uncertainty that occurs when one among many possible outcomes is chosen. So when the screen turns dark, the photodiode enters one of its two possible states; here, a state corresponds to one bit of information. But when you see the screen turn dark, you enter one out of a huge number of states: seeing a dark screen means you aren't seeing a blue, red, or green screen, the Statue of Liberty, a picture of your child's piano recital, or any of the other uncountable things that you have ever seen or could ever see. To you, "dark" means not just the opposite of light but also, and simultaneously, something different from colors, shapes, sounds, smells, or any mixture of the above.

So when you look at the dark screen, you rule out not just "light" but countless other possibilities. You don't think of the stupefying number of possibilities, of course, but their mere existence corresponds to a huge amount of information.

Conscious experience consists of more than just differentiating among many states, however. Consider an idealized 1-megapixel digital camera. Even if each photodiode in the imager were just binary, the number of different patterns that imager could record is $2^{1\,000\,000}$. Indeed, the camera could easily enter a different state for every frame from every movie that was or could ever be produced. It's a staggering amount of information. Yet the camera is obviously not conscious. Why not?

We think that the difference between you and the camera has to do with integrated information. The camera can indeed be in any one of an absurdly large number of different states. However, the 1-megapixel sensor chip isn't a single integrated system but rather a collection of one million individual, completely independent photodiodes, each with a repertoire of two states. And a million photodiodes are collectively no smarter than one photodiode.

By contrast, the repertoire of states available to you cannot be subdivided. You know this from experience: when you consciously see a certain image, you experience that image as an integrated whole. No matter how hard you try, you cannot divvy it up into smaller thumbprint images, and you cannot experience its colors independently of the shapes, or the left half of your field of view independently of the right half. Underlying this unity is a multitude of causal interactions among the relevant parts of your brain. And unlike chopping up the photodiodes in a camera sensor, disconnecting the elements of your brain that feed into consciousness would have profoundly detrimental effects.

To be conscious, then, you need to be a single integrated entity with a large repertoire of states. Let's take this one step further: your level of consciousness has to do with how much integrated information you can generate. That's why you have a higher *level* of consciousness than a tree frog or a supercomputer.

It is possible to work out a theoretical framework for gauging how effective different neural architectures would be at generating integrated information and therefore attaining a conscious state. This framework, the integrated information theory of consciousness, or IIT, is grounded in the mathematics of information and complexity theory and provides a specific measure of the amount of integrated information generated by any system comprising interacting parts. We call that measure Φ and express it in bits. The larger the value of Φ, the larger the entity's conscious repertoire. (For students of information theory, Φ is an intrinsic property of the system, and so it is different from the Shannon information that can be sent through a channel.)

IIT suggests a way of assessing consciousness in a machine—a Turing Test for consciousness, if you will. Other attempts at gauging machine consciousness, or at least intelligence, have fallen short. Carrying on an engaging conversation in natural language or playing strategy games were at various times thought to be uniquely human attributes. Any machine that had those capabilities would also have a human intellect, researchers once thought. But subsequent events proved them wrong—computer programs such as the chatterbot ALICE and the chess-playing supercomputer Deep Blue, which famously bested Garry Kasparov in 1997, demonstrated that machines can display human-level performance in narrow tasks. Yet none of those inventions displayed evidence of consciousness.

Scientists have also proposed that displaying emotion, self-recognition, or purposeful behavior are suitable criteria for machine consciousness. However, as we mentioned earlier, there are people who are clearly conscious but do not exhibit those traits.

What, then, would be a better test for machine consciousness? According to IIT, consciousness implies the availability of a large repertoire of states belonging to a single integrated system. To be useful, those internal states should also be highly informative about the world.

One test would be to ask the machine to describe a scene in a way that efficiently differentiates the scene's key features from the immense range of other possible scenes. Humans are fantastically good at this: presented with a

photo, a painting, or a frame from a movie, a normal adult can describe what's going on, no matter how bizarre or novel the image is.

Consider the following response to a particular image: "It's a robbery—there's a man holding a gun and pointing it at another man, maybe a store clerk." Asked to elaborate, the person could go on to say that it's probably in a liquor store, given the bottles on the shelves, and that it may be in the United States, given the English-language newspaper and signs. Note that the exercise here is not to spot as many details as one can but to discriminate the scene, as a whole, from countless others.

So this is how we can test for machine consciousness: show it a picture and ask it for a concise description. . . . The machine should be able to extract the gist of the image (it's a liquor store) and what's happening (it's a robbery). The machine should also be able to describe which objects are in the picture and which are not (where's the getaway car?), as well as the spatial relationships among the objects (the robber is holding a gun) and the causal relationships (the other man is holding up his hands because the bad guy is pointing a gun at him).

The machine would have to do as well as any of us to be considered as conscious as we humans are—so that a human judge could not tell the difference—and not only for the robbery scene but for any and all other scenes presented to it.

No machine or program comes close to pulling off such a feat today. In fact, image understanding remains one of the great unsolved problems of artificial intelligence. Machine-vision algorithms do a reasonable job of recognizing ZIP codes on envelopes or signatures on checks and at picking out pedestrians in street scenes. But deviate slightly from these well-constrained tasks and the algorithms fail utterly.

Very soon, computer scientists will no doubt create a program that can automatically label thousands of common objects in an image—a person, a building, a gun. But that software will still be far from conscious. Unless the program is explicitly written to conclude that the combination of man, gun, building, and terrified customer implies "robbery," the program won't realize that something dangerous is going on. And even if it were so written, it might sound a false alarm if a 5-year-old boy walked into view holding a toy pistol. A sufficiently conscious machine would not make such a mistake.

What is the best way to build a conscious machine? Two complementary strategies come to mind: either copying the mammalian brain or evolving a machine. Research groups worldwide are already pursuing both strategies, though not necessarily with the explicit goal of creating machine consciousness.

Though both of us work with detailed biophysical computer simulations of the cortex, we are not optimistic that modeling the brain will provide the insights needed to construct a conscious machine in the next few decades. Consider this sobering lesson: the roundworm *Caenorhabditis elegans* is a tiny creature whose brain has 302 nerve cells. Back in 1986, scientists used electron microscopy to painstakingly map its roughly 6000 chemical synapses and its complete wiring diagram. Yet more than two decades later, there is still no working model of how this minimal nervous system functions.

Now scale that up to a human brain with its 100 billion or so neurons and a couple hundred trillion synapses. Tracing all those synapses one by one is close to impossible, and it is not even clear whether it would be particularly useful, because the brain is astoundingly plastic, and the connection strengths of synapses are in constant flux. Simulating such a gigantic neural network model in the hope of seeing consciousness emerge, with millions of parameters whose values are only vaguely known, will not happen in the foreseeable future.

A more plausible alternative is to start with a suitably abstracted mammal-like architecture and evolve it into a conscious entity. Sony's robotic dog, Aibo, and its humanoid, Qrio, were rudimentary attempts; they operated under a large number of fixed but flexible rules. Those rules yielded some impressive, lifelike behavior—chasing balls, dancing, climbing stairs—but such robots have no chance of passing our consciousness test.

So let's try another tack. At MIT, computational neuroscientist Tomaso Poggio has shown that vision systems based on hierarchical, multilayered maps of neuronlike elements perform admirably at learning to categorize real-world images. In fact, they rival the performance of state-of-the-art machine-vision systems. Yet such systems are still very brittle. Move the test setup from cloudy New England to the brighter skies of Southern California and the system's performance suffers. To begin to approach human behavior, such systems must become vastly more robust; likewise, the range of what they can recognize must increase considerably to encompass essentially all possible scenes.

Contemplating how to build such a machine will inevitably shed light on scientists' understanding of our own consciousness. And just as we ourselves have evolved to experience and appreciate the infinite richness of the world, so too will we evolve constructs that share with us and other sentient animals the most ineffable, the most subjective of all features of life: consciousness itself.

John Horgan  **NO**

The Consciousness Conundrum

I'm 54, with all that entails. Gray hair, trick knee, trickier memory. I still play a mean game of hockey, and my love life requires no pharmaceutical enhancement. But entropy looms ever larger. Suffice it to say, I would love to believe that we are rapidly approaching "the singularity." Like paradise, technological singularity comes in many versions, but most involve bionic brain boosting. At first, we'll become cyborgs, as stupendously powerful brain chips soup up our perception, memory, and intelligence and maybe even eliminate the need for annoying TV remotes. Eventually, we will abandon our flesh-and-blood selves entirely and upload our digitized psyches into computers. We will then dwell happily forever in cyberspace where, to paraphrase Woody Allen, we'll never need to look for a parking space. Sounds good to me!

Notably, singularity enthusiasts tend to be computer specialists, such as the author and retired computer scientist Vernor Vinge, the roboticist Hans Moravec, and the entrepreneur Ray Kurzweil. Intoxicated by the explosive progress of information technologies captured by Moore's Law, such singularitarians foresee a "merger of biological and nonbiological intelligence," as Kurzweil puts it, that will culminate in "immortal software-based humans." It will happen not within a millennium, or a century, but no later than 2030, according to Vinge. These guys—and, yes, they're all men—are serious. Kurzweil says he has adopted an antiaging regimen so that he'll "live long enough to live forever."

Specialists in real rather than artificial brains find such bionic convergence scenarios naive, often laughably so. Gerald Edelman, a Nobel laureate and director of the Neurosciences Institute, in San Diego, says singularitarians vastly underestimate the brain's complexity. Not only is each brain unique, but each also constantly changes in response to new experiences. Stimulate a brain with exactly the same input, Edelman notes, and you'll never see the same signal set twice in response.

"This is a wonderful project—that we're going to have a spiritual bar mitzvah in some galaxy," Edelman says of the singularity. "But it's a very unlikely idea."

Neuroscience is indeed thriving. Membership in the Society for Neuroscience has surged from 500, when it was founded in Washington, D.C., in 1970, to almost 40 000 today. New brain journals seem to spring up daily, crammed with data from ever-more-powerful brain probes such as magnetic-resonance imaging and transcranial magnetic stimulation. In addition to such

From *IEEE Spectrum,* June 2008, part of Special Report: The Singularity. Copyright © 2008 by IEEE Spectrum. Reprinted by permission.

noninvasive methods, scientists can stick electrodes in brains to monitor and stimulate individual neurons. Researchers are also devising electrode-based "neural prostheses" to help people with nervous-system disorders such as deafness, blindness, paralysis, and memory loss.

In spite of all those advances, neuroscientists still do not understand at all how a brain (the squishy agglomeration of tissue and neurons) makes a conscious mind (the intangible entity that enables you to fall in love, find irony in a novel, and appreciate the elegance of a circuit design). "No one has the foggiest notion," says the neuroscientist Eric Kandel of Columbia University Medical Center, in New York City. "At the moment all you can get are informed, intelligent opinions." Neuroscientists lack an overarching, unifying theory to make sense of their sprawling and disjointed findings, such as Kandel's Nobel Prize–winning discovery of the chemical and genetic processes that underpin memory formation in sea slugs.

The brain, it seems, is complex enough to conjure fantasies of techno-transcendence and also to foil their fulfillment.

A healthy adult brain contains about 100 billion nerve cells, or neurons. A single neuron can be linked via axons (output wires) and dendrites (input wires) across synapses (gaps between axons and dendrites) to as many as 100 000 other neurons. Crank the numbers and you find that a typical human brain has quadrillions of connections among its neurons. A quadrillion is a one followed by 15 zeroes; a stack of a quadrillion U.S. pennies would go from the sun out past the orbit of Jupiter.

Adding to the complexity, synaptic connections constantly form, strengthen, weaken, and dissolve. Old neurons die and—evidence now indicates, overturning decades of dogma—new ones are born.

Far from being stamped from a common mold, neurons display an astounding variety of forms and functions. Researchers have discovered scores of distinct types just in the optical system. Neurotransmitters, which carry signals across the synapse between two neurons, also come in many different varieties. In addition to neurotransmitters, neural-growth factors, hormones, and other chemicals ebb and flow through the brain, modulating cognition in ways both profound and subtle.

Indeed, the more you learn about brains, the more you may wonder how the damn things work. And in fact, sometimes they don't. They succumb to schizophrenia, bipolar disorder, depression, Alzheimer's disease, and many other disorders that resist explanation and treatment.

Nevertheless, the brain is a computer, singularitarians insist. It just has an extremely messy wiring diagram. According to this perspective, neurons resemble transistors, absorbing, processing, and reemitting the electrochemical pulses known as action potentials. With an amplitude of one-tenth of a volt and a duration of one millisecond, action potentials are remarkably uniform, and they do not dissipate even when zipping down axons a meter long (yes, a full meter). Also called spikes, to reflect their appearance on oscilloscopes, action potentials supposedly serve as the brain's basic units of information.

Within a decade or so, computers will surpass the computational power of brains, many singularitarians say. They base this claim on the assumption

that those spikes represent the brain's total computational capacity. If the brain contains one quadrillion synapses processing on average 10 action potentials per second, then the brain performs 10 quadrillion operations per second. At some point in the near future, some singularitarians say, computers will surpass that processing rate and leave us in their cognitive dust unless we embrace them through bionic convergence or uploading.

We've heard such prophesies before. A half century ago, artificial-intelligence pioneers such as Marvin Minsky of MIT and Herbert Simon of Carnegie Mellon University predicted that computers would exceed human intelligence within a generation. Their prophesies inspired sci-fi writers like Arthur C. Clarke—creator of the cybervillain HAL—as well as younger AI visionaries like Kurzweil, Moravec, and Vinge.

But even Minsky admits that computers are still idiot savants. "I wish I could tell you that we have intelligent machines, but we don't," he says. The world's most powerful computers, he acknowledges, lack the common sense of a toddler; they can't even distinguish cats from dogs unless they are explicitly and painstakingly programmed to do so.

Nevertheless, singularitarians are quite right that, if current trends continue, supercomputers will exceed 10 quadrillion operations per second within a decade. IBM's Blue Gene/P supercomputer, introduced nearly a year ago, can be configured to process up to 3 quadrillion operations per second, although no customer has yet ordered one with the full complement of 884 736 processors that would be needed to get that kind of a processing rate. Argonne National Laboratory, in Illinois, is now completing the upgrade of a Blue Gene/P that should be good for around half a quadrillion operations per second.

So would a fully configured Blue Gene/P be cognitive, perhaps like a monkey or a tree frog, if not like us? Of course not. As any singularitarian would agree, intelligence requires software at least as much as hardware. And that software will soon be available, the singularitarians say, because scientists will in the next couple of decades reverse engineer the brain's software, yielding all sorts of benefits. First, the brain's programming tricks will be transferred to computers to make them smarter. Moreover, given the right interface, our brains and computers will communicate as readily as Macs and PCs. And eventually, of course, our personal software will be extracted from our frail flesh and blood and uploaded into advanced robots or computers. (Don't forget to back yourself up on a hard drive!) We'll walk the earth in impervious titanium-boned bodies. Or we'll inhabit impossibly lush virtual paradises specifically created to please and stimulate our disembodied, digital psyches.

Many neuroscientists do assume that, just as computers operate according to a machine code, the brain's performance must depend on a "neural code," a set of rules or algorithms that transforms those spikes into perceptions, memories, meanings, sensations, and intentions. If such a neural code exists, however, neuroscientists still have no idea what that code is. Or, more accurately, like voters in a U.S. presidential primary, researchers have a surfeit of candidates, each seriously flawed.

The first neural code was discovered more than 70 years ago by the British electrophysiologist Edgar Adrian, who found that when he increased the

pressure on neurons involved in the sense of touch, they fired at an increased rate. That so-called rate code has now been demonstrated in many different animals, including *Homo sapiens*. But a rate code is a crude, inefficient way to convey information; imagine trying to communicate solely by humming at different pitches.

Neuroscientists have long suspected that the brain employs subtler codes. One of them might be a temporal code, in which information is represented not just in a cell's rate of firing but also in the precise timing between spikes. For example, a rate code would treat the spike sequences 010101 and 100011 as identical because they have the same number of 0 and 1 bits. But a temporal code would assign different meanings to the two strings because the bit sequences are different. That's a vital distinction: the biophysicist William Bialek of Princeton University calculates that temporal coding would boost the brain's information-processing capacity close to the Shannon limit, the theoretical maximum that information theory allows for a given physical system.

Some neuroscientists suspect that temporal codes predominate in the prefrontal cortex and other brain structures associated with "higher" cognitive functions, such as decision making. In these regions, neurons tend to fire on average only one or two times per second, compared with the 100 or more times of sensory and motor neurons.

Other neural-coding theories abound. On a more macro level, researchers are seeking "population codes" involving the correlated firing of many neurons. Edelman, at the Neurosciences Institute, has advocated a scheme called neural Darwinism, in which our recognition of, say, an animal emerges from competition between large populations of neurons representing different memories: Dog? Cat? Weasel? Rat? The brain quickly settles on the population that most closely matches the incoming stimulus. Perhaps because Edelman has cloaked it in impenetrable jargon, neural Darwinism has not caught on.

Wolf Singer of the Max Planck Institute for Brain Research, in Frankfurt, has won more support for a code involving many neurons firing at the same rate and time. Do such synchronous oscillations play a crucial role in cognition and perhaps even underpin consciousness? Singer thinks they might.

Consciousness is not easy to define, let alone create in a machine. The psychologist William James described it succinctly as attention plus short-term memory. It's what you possess right now as you read this article, and what you lack when you are asleep and between dreams, or under anesthesia.

In 1990, the late Nobel laureate Francis Crick and his colleague Christof Koch proposed that the 40-hertz synchronized oscillations found a year earlier by Singer and his collaborator were one of the neuronal signatures of consciousness. But Singer says the brain probably employs many different codes in addition to oscillations. He also emphasizes that researchers are "only at the beginning of understanding" how neural processes "bring forth higher cognitive and executive functions." And bear in mind that it's still a very long way from grasping those functions to understanding how they give rise to consciousness. And yet without that understanding, it's hard to imagine how anyone could build an artificial brain sophisticated enough to sustain and nurture an individual human consciousness indefinitely.

Given our ignorance about the brain, Singer calls the idea of an imminent singularity "science fiction."

Koch shares Singer's skepticism. A neuroscientist at Caltech, Koch was a close friend and collaborator of Crick, who together with James Watson unraveled the structure of DNA in 1953. During the following decade or so, Crick and other researchers established that the double helix mediates an astonishingly simple genetic code governing the heredity of all organisms. Koch says, "It is very unlikely that the neural code will be anything as simple and as universal as the genetic code."

Neural codes seem to vary in different species, Koch notes, and even in different sensory modes within the same species. "The code for hearing is not the same as that for smelling," he explains, "in part because the phonemes that make up words change within a tiny fraction of a second, while smells wax and wane much more slowly."

Evidence from research on neural prostheses suggests that brains even devise entirely new codes in response to new experiences. "There may be no universal principle" governing neural-information processing, Koch says, "above and beyond the insight that brains are amazingly adaptive and can extract every bit of information possible, inventing new codes as necessary."

Theoretical quibbles notwithstanding, singularitarians insist that neural prostheses are already leading us toward bionic convergence. By far the most successful prosthesis is the cochlear implant. During the past few decades, about 100 000 hearing-impaired people around the world have been equipped with the devices, which restore hearing by feeding signals from an external microphone to the auditory nerve via electrodes. But as the deaf memoirist Michael Chorost points out, cochlear implants are far from perfect.

In his 2005 book, *Rebuilt: How Becoming Part Computer Made Me More Human*, Chorost recounts how he learned to live with an implant after losing his hearing in 2001. Although thrilled by the device, which restored his social life, he also recognizes its limitations. Because a cochlear implant provides a crude simulacrum of our innate auditory system, it generally requires a breaking-in period, during which technicians tweak the device's settings to optimize its performance. With that assistance, the brain—perhaps by devising a brand-new coding scheme—learns how to exploit the peculiar, artificial signals. Even then, the sound quality is often poor, especially in noisy settings. Chorost says he still occasionally relies on lip reading and contextual guessing to decipher what someone is saying to him. Cochlear implants do not work at all in some people, for reasons that are not well understood.

By far the most ambitious neural-prosthesis program involves computer chips that can restore or augment memory. Researchers at the University of Southern California, in Los Angeles, have designed chips that mimic the firing patterns of tissue in the hippocampus, a minute seahorse-shaped neural structure thought to underpin memory. Biomedical engineering professor Theodore Berger, a leader of the USC program, has suggested that one day brain chips might allow us to instantly upload expertise. But the memory chips are years away from testing. In rats.

Discussions of memory chips leave Andrew Schwartz cold. A neural-prosthesis researcher at the University of Pittsburgh, Schwartz has shown that monkeys can learn to control robotic arms by means of chips embedded in the brain's motor cortex. But no one has any idea how memories are encoded, Schwartz says. "We know so little about the higher functions of the brain that it seems ridiculous to talk about enhancing things like intelligence and memory," he says. Moreover, he says, downloading complex knowledge directly into the brain would require not just stimulating millions of specific neurons but also altering synaptic connections throughout the brain.

That brings us to the interface problem, the most practical obstacle to bionic convergence and uploading. For now, electrodes implanted into the brain remain the only way to precisely observe and fiddle with neurons. It is a much messier, more difficult, and more dangerous interface than most people realize. The electrodes must be inserted into the brain through holes drilled in the skull, posing the risk of infection and brain damage. They often lose contact with neurons; at any one moment an array of 100 electrodes might make contact with only half that many cells. Scar tissue or blood can encrust the electrode, cells around it might shift their position or die, and electrodes have been known to corrode.

Researchers are testing various strategies for improving contact between neurons and electronics. They are making electrodes out of conducting polymers, which are more compatible with neural tissue than silicon or metal; coating electrodes with naturally occurring glues, called cell-adhesion molecules, which helps cells in the brain and elsewhere stick together; and designing electrode arrays that automatically adjust the position of the electrodes to maximize the reception of neural signals.

At Caltech and elsewhere, engineers have designed hollow electrodes that can inject fluids into the surrounding tissue. The fluids could consist of nerve-growth factors, neurotransmitters, and other substances. The nerve-growth factors encourage cells to grow around electrodes, while the neurotransmitters enhance or supplement electrical-stimulation treatment. Neuroscientists are also testing optical devices that can monitor and stimulate neurons, as well as genetic switches that turn neurons on or off.

To be sure, it's promising work. Terry Sejnowski, a neuroscientist at the Salk Institute for Biological Studies, in San Diego, says the new technologies will make it possible "to selectively activate and inactivate specific types of neurons and synapses as well as record from all the neurons in a volume of tissue." That, in turn, might make it possible to build more effective and reliable neural prostheses.

But again, it's a fantastically long way from there to consciousness uploading. Even singularitarians concede that no existing interface can provide what is required for bionic convergence and uploading: the precise, targeted communication, command, and control of billions of neurons. So they sidestep the issue, predicting that all current interfaces will soon yield to very small robots, or "nanobots." Remember the 1966 motion picture *Fantastic Voyage*? That's the basic idea. But try to imagine, in place of Raquel Welch in a form-fitting wet suit, robotic submarines the size of blood cells. They infiltrate the

entire brain, then record all neural activity and manipulate it by zapping neurons, tinkering with synaptic links, and so on. The nanobots will be equipped with some sort of Wi-Fi so that they can communicate with one another as well as with electronic systems inside and outside the body.

Nanobots have inspired some terrific "X-Files" episodes as well as the Michael Crichton novel *Prey*. But they have as much basis in current research as fairy dust.

Steven Rose has nothing against technoenhancement. The neurobiologist at England's Open University wears eyeglasses and is proud of his titanium knee and dental implants. He says a lot can be done to improve the brain's performance through improved drugs, neural prostheses, and perhaps genetic engineering. But he calls the claims about imminent consciousness uploading "pretty much crap."

Rose disputes the singularitarians' contention that computers will soon surpass the brain's computational capacity. He suspects that computation occurs at scales above and below the level of individual neurons and synapses, via genetic, hormonal, and other processes. So the brain's total computational power may be many orders of magnitude greater than what singularitarians profess.

Rose also rejects the basic premise of uploading, that our psyches consist of nothing more than algorithms that can be transferred from our bodies to entirely different substrates, whether silicon or glass fibers or as-yet-unimaginable quantum computers. The information processing that constitutes our selves, Rose asserts, evolved within—and may not work in any medium other than—a social, crafty, emotional, sex-obsessed flesh-and-blood primate.

To dramatize that point, Rose poses a thought experiment involving a "cerebroscope," which can record everything that happens in a brain, at micro and macro levels, in real time. Let's say the cerebroscope (hey, maybe it's based on nanobots!) records all of Rose's neural activity as he watches a red bus coming down a street. Could the cerebroscope reconstruct Rose's perception? No, he says, because his neural response to even that simple stimulus grows out of his brain's entire previous history, including the incident in his childhood when a bus almost ran him over.

To interpret the neural activity corresponding to any moment, Rose elaborates, scientists would need "access to my entire neural and hormonal life history" as well as to all his corresponding experiences. Scientists would also need detailed knowledge of the changing social context within which Rose has lived; his attitude toward buses would be different if terrorists recently had attacked one. The implication of his thought experiment is that our psyches will never be totally reducible, computable, predictable, and explainable. Or, disappointingly enough, downloadable into everlasting new containers.

Perhaps the old joke is right after all: If the brain were simple enough for us to understand, we wouldn't be smart enough to understand it.

Let's face it. The singularity is a religious rather than a scientific vision. The science-fiction writer Ken MacLeod has dubbed it "the rapture for nerds," an allusion to the end-time, when Jesus whisks the faithful to heaven and leaves us sinners behind.

Such yearning for transcendence, whether spiritual or technological, is all too understandable. Both as individuals and as a species, we face deadly serious problems, including terrorism, nuclear proliferation, overpopulation, poverty, famine, environmental degradation, climate change, resource depletion, and AIDS. Engineers and scientists should be helping us face the world's problems and find solutions to them, rather than indulging in escapist, pseudoscientific fantasies like the singularity.

EXPLORING THE ISSUE

Can Machines Be Conscious?

Critical Thinking and Reflection

1. How might pleasure, pain, and beauty be expressed in ways that a computer could "compute?"
2. Can the Turing test really tell whether a machine is intelligent?
3. What is "mental uploading?" Will it ever be more than science fiction?
4. Is emotion needed for consciousness? Why or why not?

Is There Common Ground?

Many people who do not believe true computer consciousness or intelligence is possible nevertheless work hard at creating software that at least gives the impression of being intelligent. The annual Loebner Prize competition assesses the results of this work; see http://www.loebner.net/Prizef/loebner-prize.html.

1. One consequence of the work on artificial intelligence has been better and better chatbots. Visit http://www.jabberwacky.com/ and http://alice.pandorabots.com/ to compare two examples. How convincing are they?
2. Recall the discussion of Kenneth Mark Colby's work. Does this help you understand how chatbots fall short (if they do)?

ISSUE 16

Do Government Internet Surveillance Efforts Threaten Privacy and Civil Rights?

YES: James A. Lewis, from "Cybersecurity: Next Steps to Protect Critical Infrastructure," testimony before Senate Committee on Commerce, Science, and Transportation hearing (February 23, 2010)

NO: Amitai Etzioni, from "Are New Technologies the Enemy of Privacy?" *Knowledge Technology & Policy* (Summer 2007)

Learning Outcomes

After studying this issue, students will be able to:

1. Explain the reasons for expanded government surveillance of electronic communications.
2. Explain why many people do not trust government agencies to be responsible in their use of surveillance technologies.
3. Explain how modern communications technology (including the Internet) makes surveillance difficult.
4. Discuss the trade-offs involved when the need for surveillance conflicts with the need for privacy.

ISSUE SUMMARY

YES: James A. Lewis of the Center for Strategic and International Studies argues that proposed legislation, The Cybersecurity Act of 2009, which calls for Internet surveillance without regard to other legal restrictions, is needed "to bring law to the Wild West" of the Internet and enhance Internet security.

NO: Amitai Etzioni argues that new technologies such as those that enable Internet monitoring pose new threats, in particular to privacy. If there must be government surveillance programs, there must also be mechanisms for oversight and accountability. However, the mechanisms of accountability must not lie solely in the hands of government.

The Fourth Amendment to the U.S. Constitution established the right of private citizens to be secure against unreasonable searches and seizures. "Unreasonable" has come to mean "without a search warrant" for physical searches of homes and offices, and "without a court order" for interceptions of mail and wiretappings of phone conversations.

Private citizens who—for whatever reason—do not wish to have their communications with others shared with law enforcement and security agencies have long sought ways to preserve their privacy. They therefore welcomed changes in communications technology, from easily tappable copper wires to fiber optics, from analog (which mimics voice vibrations) to digital (which encodes them). But the U.S. Department of Justice sought legislation to require that the makers and providers of communications products and services ensure that their products remain tappable, and in September 1992, the Clinton Administration submitted to Congress the Digital Telephony Act, a piece of legislation designed to prevent advancing technology from limiting the government's ability legally to intercept communications. For a defense of this measure, see Dorothy Denning, "To Tap or Not to Tap," *Communications of the ACM* (March 1993). Whitfield Diffie and Susan Landau warn of the associated risks to privacy, security, and innovation in "Brave New World of Wiretapping," *Scientific American* (September 2008), and "Communications Surveillance: Privacy and Security at Risk," *Communications of the ACM* (November 2009). Many others have also objected, noting that government surveillance programs smack of Orwell's Big Brother (in the novel *1984*) and warning that they pose severe threats to our traditional concepts of liberty.

Yet, government is hardly the only threat. Privacy is under attack by both hackers and commercial interests (such as Facebook). Pornography abounds. Children are enticed on social networking sites by sex criminals. Identity theft has become common. E-mail advertisements (spam) and fraudulent offers (scams) are sent out to the millions by computers taken over by malware. And governments everywhere worry that attacks by freelance hackers and enemy "cyberwar" agencies could cripple financial, communication, and energy systems. In response to the obvious threats—especially after the "War on Terror" began in the aftermath of September 11, 2001—the U.S. government has advanced a series of ever more ambitious proposals to monitor Internet traffic, including e-mails, e-commerce transactions, and even Google searches with the intent of detecting misbehavior before it happens and—of course—intervening.

At the same Senate hearing where James A. Lewis provided the testimony, reprinted in the YES selection, Mike McConnell, executive vice president, National Security Business, Booz Allen Hamilton, and a former director of the National Security Agency warned that "cyberwar" is a serious and growing threat. The hearing was being held to discuss the Cybersecurity Act of 2009, which (among other things) "calls on the Department of Commerce to establish and maintain a clearinghouse on information related to cybersecurity threat and vulnerability to public and private infrastructure deemed 'critical' by the president. The Secretary of Commerce would be given access to this information without

regard to any provision of law, regulation, rule, or policy restricting such access." The bill would also give the president new authority to "declare a cybersecurity emergency and order the limitation or shutdown of Internet traffic to and from any compromised Federal Government or United States critical infrastructure information system or network" (www.opencongress.org/bill/111-s773/show). The Electronic Frontier Foundation (EFF) (see Jennifer Granick's "Federal Authority over the Internet? The Cybersecurity Act of 2009" (April 10, 2009), www.eff.org/deeplinks/2009/04/cybersecurity-act) sees this bill as posing a serious threat to both privacy and security while providing no more than a nod to protecting privacy and civil liberties. In June 2010, Janet Napolitano, head of the Department of Homeland Security, spoke to the American Constitution Society for Law and Policy, saying that enhancing security by monitoring Internet communications does not necessarily weaken civil liberties: "We can significantly advance security without having a deleterious impact on individual rights in most instances. At the same time, there are situations where trade-offs are inevitable." Stuart Taylor, Jr., "How Civil-Libertarian Hysteria May Endanger Us All," *National Journal* (February 22, 2003), contends that those who object to such government surveillance have their priorities wrong. Curbing "government powers in the name of civil liberties [exacts] too high a price in terms of endangered lives."

In July 2008, President Bush signed the revised Foreign Intelligence Surveillance Act, designed to expand the government's warrantless electronic spying activities and ensure retroactive immunity for cooperative telecommunications firms. "According to Bush, the law will be a critical factor in preventing another attack on U.S. soil and vital in securing the safety of the citizens." The American Civil Liberties Union (ACLU) and other groups have objected that the bill is unconstitutional, but without effect on its implementation.

The basic shape of the debate is simple: surveillance and data collection are useful. The issue gained fresh importance in 2005, when the PATRIOT Act came up for renewal (see "'Trust Me' Just Doesn't Fly," *USA Today* (April 13, 2005)), and the federal 2006 budget for surveillance technology and manpower increased greatly (see www.epic.org/privacy/budget/fy2006/). Private businesses have very similar attitudes toward employees and even customers; see Stephanie Armour, "Employers Look Closely at What Workers Do on the Job," *USA Today* (November 8, 2006). The EFF, the Electronic Privacy Information Center (EPIC), and numerous other groups and individuals insist equally strenuously that the right to privacy must come first.

Government surveillance programs reflect many fears about the Internet—that it is a place where evil lurks, where technically skilled criminals use their skills to fleece the unsuspecting public, where terrorists plot unseen, and where technology lends immunity to detection, apprehension, and prosecution. David Talbot, "Moore's Outlaws," *Technology Review* (July/August 2010), notes that the threat is growing rapidly, and sooner or later an attack will bring a city or major corporation to its knees. Former Homeland Security official Stewart Baker compared the potential impact to that of the BP oil spill in the Gulf of Mexico; see Pam Benson, "U.S. Vulnerable to Cyber Threats, Experts Warn" (June 17, 2010), www.cnn.com/2010/US/06/16/cyber.threats.report/index.html?hpt+C2). Does this amount to a real "cyberwar" threat?

A few days after McConnell testified that it does, he said in an opinion piece ("Mike McConnell on How to Win the Cyberwar We're Losing," *Washington Post* (February 28, 2010)), "The United States is fighting a cyber-war today, and we are losing." General Keith Alexander, head of the Defense Department's U.S. Cyber Command (www.defense.gov/home/features/2010/0410_cybersec/), is preparing as if he is right. However, Howard Schmidt, the Obama administration's cybersecurity chief, says, "There is no cyberwar" (see Ryan Singel, "White House Cyber Czar: 'There Is No Cyberwar,'" *Wired Online* (March 4, 2010), www.wired.com/threatlevel/2010/03/Schmidt-cyberwar/). Robert Graham of Errata Security insists, "Cyberwar Is Fiction" (June 7, 2010), http://erratasec.blogspot.com/search?q=cyberwar+is+fiction. In a debate over whether the cyberwar threat is being exaggerated (Tim Wilson, "In Debate, Audience Finds that the Cyberwar Threat Is Not Exaggerated," *Dark Reading* (June 10, 2010), www.darkreading.com/story/showArticle.jhtml?articleID=225600193), participants—including Mike McConnell—agreed that there has been a great deal of hype about the topic. But the threat is real.

Many people, however, worry that the worse threat is that posed by efforts to enhance security by monitoring and regulating the Internet to civil rights and privacy. Yves Poullet, "The Fight against Crime and/or the Protection of Privacy: A Thorny Debate!" *International Review of Law Computers & Technology* (July 2004), discusses the issue from the European standpoint and notes that "there is no worse danger than this cyber-surveillance, which hunts a man down in his most intimate space and raises within him a perpetual and haunting fear of exposure." Concerns over the use of surveillance cameras and RFID chips are expressed by Patrick Tucker, "Fun with Surveillance," *The Futurist* (November–December 2006). James Harkin, "You're Being Watched," *New Statesman* (January 15, 2007), thinks that digital tracking technologies may, overall, be a force for good. Julian Sanchez, "The Pinpoint Search," *Reason* (January 2007), argues that new surveillance technologies pose serious threats to ordinary expectations of privacy. Mark O'Brien, "Law, Privacy and Information Technology: A Sleepwalk Through the Surveillance Society?" *Information & Communications Technology Law* (March 2008), contends that new surveillance technologies can result in an inappropriate imbalance between the society's need for surveillance and the individual's need for privacy.

In the YES selection, James A. Lewis of the Center for Strategic and International Studies argues that The Cybersecurity Act of 2009, which calls for Internet surveillance without regard to other legal restrictions, is needed "to bring law to the Wild West" of the Internet and enhance Internet security. In the NO selection, Amitai Etzioni argues that new technologies, such as those that enable Internet monitoring, pose new threats, in particular, to privacy. If there must be government surveillance programs, there must also be mechanisms for oversight and accountability. However, the mechanisms of accountability must not lie solely in the hands of government.

YES

James A. Lewis

Cybersecurity: Next Steps to Protect Critical Infrastructure

[T]he] comprehensive "Cybersecurity Act of 2009" . . . is important because it is a broad step to rethinking our approach to the internet, to cyberspace, and to the role of government.

The pioneers of cyberspace wanted governments to have a very limited role. They expected a self-governing global commons to emerge, and argued that there were no borders, that technology moved to fast, that old rules of business and security did not apply. They expected a global commons; instead they got the wild west. The internet was not designed to be secure; the rules and contracts put in place when it was commercialized were not written with security in mind. The result is Hobbesian, that is to say nasty and brutish, if not short. So the issue for the nation is how to bring law to the Wild West, how to move from a do-it-yourself homebrew approach to cybersecurity, and how to secure a global digital infrastructure upon which we now depend. Legislation like the Cybersecurity Act of 2010 can play a crucial role.

Cybersecurity has become an important issue over the last decade as the internet changed to become a significant global infrastructure. The U.S. in particular has woven computer networks into so many of its economic activities that we are as reliant on the internet as we are on any other critical infrastructure. Networked activities can be cheaper and more efficient, so companies large and small have migrated to the internet because it can provide competitive advantage. Our national defense relies heavily upon networks. Networks reinforced existing trends in military the realization that intangible factors—greater knowledge, faster decision making increased certainty—would increase effectiveness of our military force.

That technologies designed in the early 1970s have worked so well and have so cleanly scaled to support more than a billion users is an amazing triumph, but anyone with malicious intent can easily exploit these networks. The internet was not designed to be a global infrastructure upon which hundreds of millions of people would depend. It was never designed to be secure. The early architects and thinkers of cyberspace in the first flush of commercialization downplayed the role of government. The vision was that cyberspace would be a global commons led and shaped by private action, where a self-organizing community could invent and create. This ideology of a self-organizing global commons has shaped internet policy and cybersecurity, but we must now recognize that this pioneer approach is now inadequate.

U.S. Senate, February 23, 2010.

There are two reasons for this inadequacy. First, private efforts to secure networks will always be overwhelmed by professional military and criminal action. The private sector does not have the capability to defeat an advanced opponent like the SRV or the PLA, organizations that invest hundreds of millions of dollars and employ thousands of people to defeat any defense. We do not expect airlines to defend our airspace against enemy fighter planes and we should not expect private companies to defend cyberspace against foreign governments.

Second, absent government intervention, security may be unachievable. Two ideas borrowed from economics help explain this—public goods and market failure. Public goods are those that benefit all of society but whose returns are difficult for any individual to capture. Basic research is one public good that the market would not adequately supply if government did not create incentives. Cybersecurity is another such public good where market forces are inadequate.

We talk about cyber attack and cyber war when we really should be saying cyber espionage and cybercrime. Espionage and crime are not acts of war. They are, however, daily occurrences on the internet, with the U.S. being the chief victim, and they have become a major source of harm to national security. The greatest damage to the U.S. comes from espionage, including economic espionage. We have lost more as a nation to espionage than at any time since the 1940s. The damage is usually not visible, but of course, the whole purpose of espionage is not to be detected.

This is not cyberwar, Russia, China, and cybercriminals of all types have no interest in disrupting Wall Street, the internet, or the American economy. There is too much to steal, so why would anyone close off this gold mine. As with any good espionage exploit or mafia racket, the perpetrators want stability, a low profile, and smooth operations going so they can continue to reap the benefits.

There is a potential for cyber attack, but it is so far constrained by political and technological barriers. Terrorists likely do not yet have the advanced cyber capabilities needed to launch crippling strikes. The alternative, that they have these capabilities but have chosen for some reason not to use them, is ridiculous. There are nations that could launch a crippling strike, but they are likely to do soon only as part of a larger armed conflict with the United States. These nations do not love jihadis any more than we do, so they are unlikely in the near future to transfer advanced cyber capabilities to terrorists. Presumably, in the case of Russia and China their cyber criminal proxies are also instructed not to take jihadi clients (although there is one incident where it is alleged that Russian hackers served as mercenaries for Hezbollah, against Israel). Should any of these conditions change—the technological constraints that limit terrorists and the political constraints that limit states and advanced cyber criminals— the U.S. is in no position to defend itself against cyber attack.

Short of armed conflict (over Taiwan or Georgia), China or Russia is unlikely to use cyber strikes against the U.S. The political risk is too high—it would be like sending a bomber or a missile against a power plant, and the U.S. response would be vigorous. Our opponents, however, have reportedly

conducted reconnaissance missions against critical infrastructure—the electrical grid, for example—to allow them to strike if necessary in the event of conflict. Cyber attack is cheaper and faster than a missile or plane, there is some chance that the attacker can deny responsibility (because of the weak authentication on the internet). Right now, our opponents have the advantage but it is within our capabilities to change this.

Getting this change requires a new approach. Many of the solutions to the problem of cybersecurity our nation has tried are well past their sell-by date. Public–private partnerships, information sharing, government-lead-by-example, self-regulation, and market-based solutions are remedies we have tried for more than a decade without success. These policies overestimate incentives for private action and misalign government and private sector responsibilities.

Like other new technologies in the past—airplanes, cars, steam engines—the appeal and the benefits are so great that we have rushed to adopt the internet despite serious safety problems. These problems are amplified by the global connectivity of the new infrastructure, as the speed of internet connections means that geographical distance provides little in the way of protection. For those earlier technologies, safety came about through innovation driven by government mandates, and by agreements among nations. The same process of development is necessary to secure cyberspace. The Cybersecurity Act of 2009 could play a vital role in this improvement.

This will not be an easy task. The United States does not like to deal with market failure. This has been true since the earliest days of the republic. Steam engines, although notoriously unsafe, had to wait forty years until a series of savage accidents costing hundreds of live led Congress to impose safety regulations. Automobile safety rules took more than half a century and initially faced strong opposition from manufacturers. The initial air safety regulations appeared only twenty-three years after the first flight. There is the recurring hope that "intellect and practical science," to quote a 19th Century Congressional report explaining why regulation was unnecessary for steamboats put it, will lead to improvement via some automatic and self-correcting market process and without government intervention.

Just as cars were not built to be safe until government pressure changed auto manufacturers' behavior, cyberspace will not be secure until government forces improvement. Twelve years of reliance on voluntary efforts and self-regulation have put us in an untenable situation. Some may argue that a move away from the market or a greater emphasis on security or a larger role for government will damage innovation in cyberspace. This argument is in part a reflection of competition among various bureaucracies, advanced to protect turf, but is also reflects a misunderstanding of the nature of innovation. There are grounds to be concerned about the ability of the U.S. to innovate when compared to other nations, but the real obstacles are a weak education system, poorly designed tax policies, damaging immigration rules, and misinvestment that makes it hard to develop new technologies and competitors. Removing these obstacles would be politically difficult and face strong opposition. It is easier to insist instead that keeping the internet open and anonymous or bringing broadband to undeserving areas will somehow generate

growth. Greater security is more likely to increase innovation, by reducing the loss of intellectual property and by increasing demand for more valuable internet services.

Another reason put forward for not taking action is the supposedly border-less nature of cyberspace. The pioneers of cyberspace wanted their new creation to be a global commons, a shared space that no one owns. The designers of the internet built the network to reflect their values, which were nonhierarchical and to a degree, antiauthoritarian and anti-government. One of the original cyberspace theorists was also a songwriter for the Grateful Dead, and it was he who issued the famous Declaration of Independence of cyberspace, saying there was no room or need for governments. Cyberspace would be a global commons where a self-organizing community could invent and create.

This is an ill-conceived notion that continues to distort our thinking. Cyberspace is an artificial construct produced by machines. Those machines are all owned by individuals or organizations and all exist in some physi-cal location that is subject to the sovereign control of some nation. Cyber-space is like the public space in a shopping mall, a "pseudo commons" or a condominium.

In some instances, of course, such as the Internet Engineering Task Force or the Open Source Software Movement, this vision of an open, nonhierarchi-cal community has worked exceptionally well. But to use a historical analogy, many of the pioneers of the internet expected Woodstock and the "Summer of Love," instead they got Altamont and the Hells Angels. The combination of unplanned global access, porous technologies, and weak governance makes this newly critical infrastructure exceptionally vulnerable. As our reliance as a nation increases, so does our vulnerability to remote exploitation and perhaps attack.

Cyberspace is not a global commons. It is a shared global infrastructure. There is rarely a moment when a collection of bits moving from one computer to another is not actually on a network that someone owns and that is physi-cally located in a sovereign state. The exceptions might be undersea cables or satellite transmissions, but the action still takes place on an owned facility where the owner is subject to some country and its laws. At best, this could be a "pseudo commons." It looks like a commons but actually is not, as someone owns the resources in question and that someone is subject to the laws of some nation. Cyberspace is in fact a more like a condominium, where there are many contiguous owners.

Governance of this condominium is both weak and fragmented. There are no agreed rules, other than business contracts, and no "condominium board," no process to develop rules. Action in cyberspace takes place in a context defined by commercial law and business contracts. When the United States commercialized the internet, it chose this legal construct accommodate business activity, but it is inadequate for security, particularly as the Internet spread to countries around the world and to nations with very different values and laws.

The proposed legislation would go a long way to correct these problems. To put the problem in a larger perspective, it is time to move from the policies

created in the pioneer phase of the internet. It is time to close the Wild West. This will require a broad rethinking of American law and policy, and will require adapting to the technologies we now depend on. It will need new kinds of international agreements, new standards and rules for industry, and new approaches to the professionalization of those who operate networks. This is no small task but, judging from experience, it is inevitable. This process has occurred before, often with help from the government. The Commerce Department of the 1920s, for example, encouraged several major industries, including the automotive and radio industries, to standardize, to professionalize, and to create associations and rules that serve the public interest.

A "one size fits all" strategy will not work. We will need to manage international engagement, critical infrastructure regulation, and economic stability all at the same time. Progress faces significant obstacles. There are legitimate concerns over civil liberties. There are strong business interests in avoiding regulation. And there are the tattered remnants of a vision of cyberspace as some kind of utopian frontier. Governance is a central issue for each of these. Governance is the process for creating rules, resolving disputes, and ensuring compliance. Our beliefs about the nature of cyberspace have downplayed the role of formal governance and now we are paying the price. Changing this, as we did for steamboats, cars and airplanes, is part of the long-term process to adjust to new environment created by technological change.

This bill contains many of the essential elements of the new approach we need. A comprehensive national strategy that considers all aspects of national security and puts forward a long-term vision for cyberspace is an essential starting point for making this new infrastructure secure. It will be essential, of course, to avoid merely repeating the formulas of 1998 or 2003 in a new strategy. We've heard repeatedly that there is a shortfall of individuals with the requisite skills for cybersecurity. The scholarships, competitions and workforce plans outlined in this bill would go a long way to repair this. The legal review and the intelligence assessment are long overdue. The call for the creations of a response and restoration developed with the private sector that the president could implement in a crisis is crucial for national defense.

As with any major piece of legislation, there will be considerable criticism. Some of this criticism is ideological, some reflects self-interest, and some is the result of a healthy skepticism as to our ability to carry out some of the ambitious measures contained in the bill. There was initially concern that emphasizing the authority the President already has to intervene in network operations during a crisis would somehow give the ability to shut off the internet. This stemmed mainly from an inaccurate reading of the bill and perhaps from the desire to preserve the notion of cyberspace as an untrammeled commons where government has little or no role. Frankly, efforts to deny the President adequate authority in a crisis are like expressing a preference for Katrina-like disaster management. I hope we can do better.

No one ever disagrees with the notion of more education, but the more contentious aspect of the workforce development is the requirement for certification and training. Being able to certify that someone has the necessary skill and knowledge is a requisite part of professionalization. We do this for

doctors, lawyers, pilots, barbers, plumbers and real estate agents. Some certification requirements are Federal, many are developed by states. Many in the IT industry believe that they are not ready for this step. Certification requires knowing what is useful and necessary and being able teach it and test it. It is on the former that there is disagreement—that we do not know what is necessary for security.

This may have been true at one time but I believe it is changing. In the last few years, as people have been able to collect more data on security problems, to develop metrics, and to identify steps that will reduce risk, it is possible to think of a training program for cybersecurity. This is part of a larger move from compliance drive security, which has largely failed, to performance driven security. The concept of a cybersecurity dashboard found in Section 203 reflects this shift to a data driven approach to cybersecurity. The Act, if passed, will accelerate the development and professionalization of those parts of cyberspace that provide critical services to the nation.

These are all politically difficult issues, but this situation is not new. Every time a new technology has reshaped business, warfare and society, there has been a lag in developing the rules—law, judicial precedents, regulations—needed to safeguard society. Cyberspace is different in its global scope and in the immediate nature of the damage America suffers. Waiting for some natural process or perfect solution not only puts our nation at risk, it gives our opponents an advantage. We would be well served if Congress passed this bill.

Amitai Etzioni  **NO**

Are New Technologies the Enemy of Privacy?

Abstract Privacy is one good among other goods and should be weighed as such. The relationship between technology and privacy is best viewed as an arms race between advancements that diminish privacy and those that better protect it, rather than the semi-Luddite view which sees technology as one-sided development enabling those who seek to invade privacy to overrun those who seek to protect it. The merits or defects of particular technologies are not inherent to the technologies, but rather, depend on how they are used and above all, on how closely their use is monitored and accounted for by the parties involved. In order to reassure the public and to ensure accountability and oversight, a civilian review board should be created to monitor the government's use of surveillance and related technologies. Proper accountability requires multiple layers of oversight, and should not be left solely in the hands of the government.

An Arms Race versus a Luddite Imagery

The relationship between privacy and technology should be viewed as akin to the relationship between security and technology or prosperity and technology rather than approached from a Luddite perspective. However, much of the literature on privacy follows this second track. It depicts various technological developments, such as electronic databases, computerized searches, and surveillance instruments, as attacks on privacy. Indeed, the more alarmist accounts speak of a 'surveillance society' and the 'death of privacy.' Although these alarmist critics recognize that there is no way to turn back the clock to a pre-digital age, they bemoan the rise of privacy-invading technologies—criticisms similar in tone and terms to the complaints that the Luddites lodged against the development of industrial equipment, from the loom to the steam engine, in the nineteenth century. And like the Luddites, today's critics have, thus, sought to curb these technological advancements if they cannot be eliminated altogether.

Before showing that such critics misunderstand the relationship between privacy and the new technological developments of the digital age, I should reiterate a point that I have spelled out elsewhere: Privacy is merely one good

From *Knowledge Technology & Policy,* Summer 2007, pp. 115–119 (notes omitted). Copyright © 2007 by MetaPress. Reprinted by permission of Springer Science and Business Media.

among many others. It always has been and needs to be weighed against other goods, without an a priori assumption that privacy should trump all other considerations. If a child is brought to the emergency room with cigarette burns on his body and X-rays reveal that his arm has been broken twice before, ER attendants will suspect that the child has been subject to abuse. And they are required by law (and by all that is decent) to ask various privacy-violating questions of the child and of those who attend to him, including his parents. Here, the wellbeing of the child trumps both his and his parents' right to privacy. Moreover, historical developments, for instance, the rise of the threat of terrorism, change the relative weight one ought to accord to the privacy of those who seek to enter one's country. More generally, it follows that one ought not to consider every privacy reduction as a social or human loss.

As far as the relationship between technology and privacy is concerned, it is best viewed as an arms race between advancements that diminish privacy and those that better protect it—as opposed to a one-sided develop-ment in which those who invade privacy overrun those who seek to protect it. Although several new privacy-diminishing technologies exist or are being created, they are countered by other developments designed to better protect privacy. At any given point in time, new devices of both kinds are created, sometimes altering the balance in favor of privacy and sometimes tipping it in favor of the invaders. Moreover, every new mode of attack tends to invite a quest for a new mode of defense—for example, the way in which new computer viruses invite the formation of new security patches.

True, the balance between privacy-invading and privacy-securing tech-nology is changing all of the time. However, if one compares routine com-munications today to those of say 1975, one finds a significant net *increase* in privacy, largely due to the development of high-powered encryption. In 1975, the routine communications of an ordinary citizen might have included phone calls (easily 'bugged' or listened to on another extension by a jealous spouse) and letters (readily intercepted and steamed open by the authorities or a jealous lover or employee). Other means of routine communications—postcards and cables—were even less secure and private. In contrast, many of today's routine communications are sent electronically, secured by high-powered encryption capabilities programmatically built into many computers—capabilities sure to be found on more PCs in the future. As a result, nowadays, when a person sends a routine email via the Internet, it cannot be easily read, even if inter-cepted, because not only does it travel in divided packets but it also is likely to be encrypted. In short, it is much more difficult today to violate someone's privacy by accessing and reading a routine communication than it was in the pre-digital era.

Turning to non-routine communications, in the past, some senders were willing to engage in extra measures to ensure privacy, such as using a courier or primitive devices like invisible ink and simple code systems, when deal-ing with highly sensitive or personal communiqués. Today, all of these mea-sures are still available but so is the high-powered encryption discussed above. Granted, it is true that new developments have occurred, enabling those with the knowledge and means to crack such encryption codes and read messages

sent from thousands of miles away, say between bin Laden and his mother in Saudi Arabia. However, such technologies are highly specialized and costly. In short, when scrutinizing the security of today's communications, one must acknowledge that, in general, the current methods of sending routine and non-routine communications prove much more secure than the avenues used in the past, such as the wire or traditional mail.

The same holds true for the storage of information. Medical and financial records are much more secure in encrypted databases than they ever were in locked cabinets, places where such information has historically been stored. This newfound security also applies to other types of information, as long as it is properly encrypted. The absence of such measures reveals more about the extent to which those involved are not seriously privacy-minded, at least for the data at issue, than it does about a threat from new technologies.

All in all, privacy is challenged but far from dead, and various technological developments will continue to enhance it even as others attack it.

Accountability

Advancements in technology are frequently characterized either as boons or anathemas. The same holds true for those technologies that directly impact privacy. However, like most technological developments, those concerning the invasion of privacy cannot be easily lumped into simple categories of good or bad per se, although they are often treated in this manner. Instead, their merits or defects depend on how they are used and, above all, on how closely their use is monitored and accounted for by the parties involved. For example, it makes no sense to seek a ban on cameras in public spaces because someone in London used one to violate the privacy of a couple making out in a car (assuming that they had an expectation of privacy in a car parked in a public space in the first place).

To highlight the point, a simple example will serve: Take the case of electronic toll systems, such as the E-ZPass program used in several parts of the USA. Once an individual enrolls in E-ZPass, he receives an electronic device to place in his car. Each time that he travels through a toll, an antenna picks up on the device, and the appropriate amount is deducted from a prepaid toll account. Proponents of such systems see them as a necessity in the face of ever-increasing traffic and argue that they will revolutionize toll collection by minimizing bottlenecks and the need to build additional booths. But privacy advocates, like Jordana Beebe of Privacy Rights Clearinghouse, assert that such toll collections could encroach on individual liberties and worry over how data will be used. Of E-ZPass, Beebe said, "The primary thing to keep in mind with an E-ZPass is basically you're enabling a tracking system."

Yet one should note first of all that, like many technologies cited by civil liberty groups as sources of privacy violations, such as programs enabling credit card orders over the Internet, E-ZPass participation is voluntary. No one is required to use it. However, millions of Americans find they would rather have the convenience of using these technologies than concern themselves unduly with matters of privacy. Indeed, noted privacy expert Alan Westin

divides people into three groups. On one end of the spectrum is a minority of the population (25%) that are 'privacy fundamentalists,' deeply concerned about privacy rights, and on the other end is one-fifth that are 'privacy unconcerned.' The majority (55%) are people that Westin identifies as 'privacy pragmatists,' individuals who tend not to mind personal data collection as long as they feel informed about the solicitor, the possible gains or repercussions of releasing the information, and the safety measures put into place. The comments of the chief executive of the Intelligent Transportation Systems, Neal Schuster, suggest that drivers' reasons for choosing E-ZPass prove consistent with Westin's findings: "We do it because of the convenience and we do it because there are laws that protect us."

In any event, the main issue with E-ZPass is not the technology itself but the ways in which it is used—and that use supervised. As with other technologies, E-ZPass can be employed both in ways that most would find unproblematic and quite beneficial and in a manner that many would find very troubling indeed. Suppose, for example, that a car is recorded going through a designated E-ZPass lane. After it is confirmed that the driver prepaid the toll, that record is immediately erased. Few would mind. However, the response would be vastly different if the record in question were filed away and added to other information about us in some comprehensive government dossier in which information about our travels would be kept for years and would be easily accessed by the police, the media, divorce lawyers, and others.

Clearly, for the issue at hand of privacy invasion and protection, the same technology can be used in very different ways. Still, one more crucial step must be undertaken when analyzing technologies involving privacy (and many others) and that is to move beyond assessing each technology on its own merits. The key question is how much accountability and oversight exists for the use to which the technology is put. To return to the example at hand, assume we are told that E-ZPass is used merely in the minimal way described above—information is immediately erased after verification that the toll has been paid, and the information about who traveled when and where is not otherwise available. Still, we might wonder whether these limitations on the use of the information are observed and, if so, who enforces such curbs and how. One major reason we have laws, policing, and oversight is that we do not automatically trust the authorities to do what is right.

How Can Accountability Be Provided?

To some extent, the needed accountability is already built into the government, and it should not be dismissed. For instance, the Inspector General of the Department of Justice issued two highly critical reports of the FBI in 2003. These reports alerted Congress and the public to the FBI's wrongdoings and pressured it to modify its practices. Furthermore, congressional committees have oversight power. And they correctly demanded more specific information about the usage of various powers provided by certain sections of the Patriot Act in an effort to render the uses of the technologies involved, e.g., wiretapping, more legitimate. However, the record shows that, on their own,

these committees cannot provide the needed countervailing force to government agencies hell bent on following their own course in the name of national security.

The press, the next line of defense, has been doing a sound job of regularly reporting about a variety of abuses and about programs with absurd designs, leading the government to send many ideas back to the drawing board and to greatly reform aspects of the no-fly lists, the tracking of foreign students, and airport scanning methods, among others.

Many citizens (me included) find these layers of oversight of value but still insufficient. Such people have an inherently healthy distrust of the government and fear that it would conceal information (the way that the CIA kept some detainees off the books), would doctor it, or would refuse to disclose it—even to Congress. To further strengthen oversight for law enforcement authorities and to reassure the public that they are not running amok, we need a civilian review board. It would be composed of the kind of people who served on the 9/11 Commission: bipartisan, highly respected by the public, able to work together, not in the running for public office, and patriotic. These individuals would need the proper level of security clearance to review detailed records to ensure that nobody is pulling the wool over their eyes. The board would issue regular reports about its generalized findings without revealing specifics about sources and methods. Such oversight would allow one and all to determine whether, in most cases, the search of databases, delayed disclosure, and other new security measures have been employed legitimately and used for good purposes or whether the opposite is the case. Such reports should lead to internal reforms in government agencies, as they will have to expect future rounds of similar audits.

Reliable E-ID

To close, I point to a new technological development that would greatly enhance privacy. New technologies are now being developed and introduced that would allow people to present proof of their identity when communicating via the Internet, much like presenting a passport when crossing national borders. Sometimes referred to as 'digital certificates,' such E-IDs can be provided through a 'certificate authority' or CA, such as GeoTrust or VeriSign. Once established, these digital certificates consist of a variety of information that enables those on the other end of a business transaction to confirm that an individual is who he says he is. The electronic postmark (EPM) extension launched by the US Post Office in partnership with Microsoft and Authenti-Date in October of 2003 is just one example of a technological development that seeks to provide reliable E-IDs. Overall, such E-IDs make it much more difficult for unauthorized persons to gain access to a variety of information, and they will help to minimize identity theft.

The technology behind E-IDs is complex and in flux, and it is not my purpose in this paper to enter into an explanation of its intricacies, especially considering the many different options offered by various vendors. I simply wish to outline the basic concepts of E-IDs as a means by which to provide

another example of how some advancements in technology *are helping to safeguard privacy as others infringe upon it.*

Conclusion

In conclusion, privacy is under attack by new technologies, but it is also benefiting from new technologies. Those concerned about privacy should work to improve the regulations controlling the use of these technologies rather than adopt a semi-Luddite position, hoping these technologies will go away or be suppressed. How carefully the use of various technologies is monitored is, as a rule, more important than the capabilities of the technologies themselves. Proper accountability requires multiple layers of oversight. And for that accountability to be fully effective in limiting abuse and building public trust, it cannot be left solely in the hands of the government.

EXPLORING THE ISSUE

Do Government Internet Surveillance Efforts Threaten Privacy and Civil Rights?

Critical Thinking and Reflection

1. Are you uncomfortable with the idea that government agencies may be watching every move you make on the Internet? Why?
2. Can you trust law enforcement and security agencies to be reasonable in their suspicions about your behavior?
3. Is the nature of the Internet essentially antiauthoritarian?
4. Is protecting national security more important than protecting individual liberties?

Is There Common Ground?

There is much agreement that the Internet makes available a great deal of objectionable material and that criminals and terrorists use modern communications technology (including the Internet) in support of their nefarious activities. The question is what to do about it. A related question is whether those entrusted with doing something about it can be trusted not to abuse their powers.

1. Has government ever abused its surveillance powers? (Start your research with the Wikipedia article on "surveillance abuse"; it has a number of useful references. Also search on "wiretap abuse.")
2. *Quis custodiet ipsos custodes* is an old Latin saying. What does it mean, and what is its relevance to this issue?
3. In 2010, Wikileaks received a great deal of attention for releasing thousands of classified documents, some of which proved embarrassing to people in government. Research the story and discuss whether Wikileaks was justified in its actions.

ISSUE 17

Does Endorsing Open Source Software Fail to Respect Intellectual Property?

YES: International Intellectual Property Alliance (IIPA), from *Indonesia: 2010 Special 301 Report on Copyright Protection and Enforcement* (February 12, 2010)

NO: Michael Tiemann, from "The OSI Categorically Rejects IIPA's Special Pleadings Against Open Source," *Open Source Initiative* (May 3, 2010)

Learning Outcomes

After studying this issue, students will be able to:

1. Explain the concept of "open source."
2. Explain the purpose of copyright and patent law.
3. Discuss whether the International Intellectual Property Alliance (IIPA) is more interested in protecting intellectual property or income.
4. Explain how copyright protections are essential to open source products.

ISSUE SUMMARY

YES: The International Intellectual Property Alliance (IIPA) argues that Indonesia should be put on the United States Trade Representative's "Special 301" watchlist because, in part, Indonesia's attempt to promote open source solutions "encourages a mindset that does not give due consideration to the value of intellectual creations."

NO: Michael Tiemann of Open Source Initiative objects strenuously, arguing that open source software is just as much an intellectual creation as proprietary software, it depends just as much on copyright protections, and because open source preferences have been promoted in several states, as well as portions of the federal government, the IIPA's position amounts to an attack on the United States itself.

T o understand the open source movement and the opposition toward it, understanding a bit of the history of the computer industry helps. It had its roots in academia at a time when the reward structure was *not* the same as in the corporate world. Historically, academics have not seen their score in the game of life in terms of money, but rather in terms of respect or prestige. To gain such respect or prestige, they made their ideas, investigations, discoveries, and conclusions freely available (much as described in this book's *Introduction*, under the "Communication" part of the scientific method). In the last few decades, academics have found numerous opportunities to patent their discoveries and start up businesses, and the profit motive has entered academia. To some, it has polluted the purity of the older reward system.

The first computers were built with government money for government (often military) purposes. Corporations such as IBM played an important role in developing large commercial computers (mainframes) and their software. During the 1950s and 1960s, computers became common on college and university campuses, and programming languages became easier to use. A great many students graduated with computer experience, programming skills, and the then-standard academic value system. Many became computer hobbyists and played a major part in the development of the personal computer. Since they were hobbyists, money was not always the point. From the beginning, some PC software were commercial, but by the 1970s and 1980s, "shareware" (pay if you like it) and "freeware" (it's free!) were common. Some software still fit this model, to a degree; AVG antivirus software (http://free.avg.com/us-en/226285?cmpid=fs_hp_testb_226285), for instance, provides a free version that does the basic job and a pay version that adds bells and whistles.

To oversimplify, in the beginning the corporate world just did not see how big the computer revolution was going to be. But that changed. "Payware" became much more common, moving as it did so through a number of copy-protection schemes (some of which were as simple as saying, "Cheat, and your computer will stop working!"). There were some efforts to tarnish the image of freeware and shareware, but they were not successful. In time the open source movement took form. Some open source software are free (think of the Firefox browser and the OpenOffice productivity suite). Some ask for donations. Some are packaged for sale with manuals, consulting, and support (various Linux distributions). The defining feature is that the source code for the software is available for users to modify, with good modifications feeding back into the distributed software (see Chris DiBona and Sam Ockman, *Open Sources* (O'Reilly, 1999)). In other words, open source software is community-built and community-supported software. Its proponents argue that this gives open source software immense advantages even beyond the low up-front cost.

There are of course opponents as well as proponents of open source. Many are opponents because they see the advantages of open source costing them sales. In 2010, one of those opponents, the International Intellectual Property Alliance (IIPA), made headlines by seeking to have the United States Trade Representative put several countries on its "Special 301" watchlist— which is used to pressure countries into handling international trade in ways

more satisfactory to the U.S. interests—in part because of their approval of open source software.

Michael Tiemann of Open Source Initiative wrote the response to the IIPA, which is reprinted in the NO selection. But this essay was by no means the only objection. He also wrote "OSFA Refutes IIPA's Attack on Open Source Software" for *Open Source for America* (http://opensourceforamerica.org/opensource-attack). The title of Bobbie Johnson's *Guardian* blogpost, "When Using Open Source Makes You an Enemy of the State" (www.guardian.co.uk/technology/blog/2010/fed/23/opensource-intellectual-property), says it all. Under the headline "Encouraging Open Source Could Land You in Trouble" (www.technollama.co.uk/encouraging-open-source-could-land-you-in-trouble), Andres Guadamuz, lecturer of law at the University of Edinburgh, concluded, "It is nice to know where the IIPA stands. Only commercial intellectual property is worthy of protection, everything else is as bad as piracy." (Is piracy that bad? On April 12, 2010, the U.S. Government Accountability Office released *Intellectual Property: Observations on Efforts to Quantify the Economic Effects of Counterfeit and Pirated Goods* [GAO-10-423]. The basic point is that the numbers often cited by the IIPA and other groups "cannot be substantiated due to the absence of underlying studies." Piracy is a sizeable problem, but we do not have the numbers to say how bad it really is.)

Despite the objections, the IIPA's position apparently swayed the United States Trade Representative, which on April 30, 2010, released the 2010 Watchlist. According to the press release (www.ustr.gov/about-us/press-office/press-releases/2010/april/ustr-releases-2010-special-301-report-intellectual-p), "Trading partners on the Priority Watch List do not provide an adequate level of IPR protection or enforcement, or market access for persons relying on intellectual property protection. China, Russia, Algeria, Argentina, Canada, Chile, India, Indonesia, Pakistan, Thailand, and Venezuela are on the Priority Watch List. These countries will be the subject of particularly intense engagement through bilateral discussion during the coming year."

It is worth noting that the open source approach is by no means limited to computer software. Kate Greene, "Open Up and Say Eureka," *Technology Review* (November/December 2008), describes a number of efforts to make gadgets as hackable as software and notes that "technology companies . . . are recognizing that embracing openness doesn't amount to giving away the store. If they aim to provide a platform for other designers rather than trying to design the best product for everyone . . . they are freed to focus on what large companies are uniquely equipped to do: namely, high-volume production, customer service, and brand marketing."

Both open source software and hardware play important parts in the development of home 3D printers such as Fab@Home (http://fabathome.org/) and RepRap (http://reprap.org/wiki/Main_Page), which proponents say is roughly where the home PC was in the mid-1970s. In two decades, the PC created an economic and social revolution, and they expect 3D printing will do the same. See Thomas A. Easton, "The Design Economy: A Brave New World for Businesses and Consumers," *The Futurist* (January–February 2009).

In related news, in June 2010, the American Society of Composers, Authors and Publishers (ASCAP) and National Music Publishers Association (NMPA)

attacked the "Free Culture Movement," as represented by organizations such as Creative Commons, the Electronic Frontier Foundation, and Public Knowledge, on the grounds that they support a different version of copyright that would permit artists to free access to their work. This is the same version of copyright that supports open source software, and its proponents have fired back at ASCAP and NMPA with vigor. See Drew Wilson, "Copyright War Escalates with NMPA Joining ASCAP's Attack on Free Culture," (June 29, 2010) (www.zeropaid.com/news/89600/copyright-war-escalates-with-nmpa-joining-ascaps-attack-on-free-culture/).

In the YES selection, the IIPA's discussion of Indonesia in its appeal to the United States Trade Representative makes explicit its view that open source software and intellectual property are incompatible concepts. It argues that Indonesia's attempt to promote open source solutions "encourages a mindset that does not give due consideration to the value of intellectual creations." In the NO selection, Michael Tiemann of Open Source Initiative objects strenuously, arguing that open source software is just as much an intellectual creation as proprietary software, it depends just as much on copyright protections, and because open source preferences have been promoted in several states, as well as portions of the federal government, the IIPA's position amounts to an attack on the United States itself.

YES

International Intellectual Property Alliance (IIPA)

Indonesia: 2010 Special 301 Report on Copyright Protection and Enforcement

Special 301 Recommendation

IIPA recommends that Indonesia remain on the Priority Watch List.

Executive Summary

IIPA congratulates Indonesian President Susilo Bambang Yudhoyono, his Vice President, and his new Cabinet on re-election in July 2009 for a second term (running until 2014). As a result of this election, IIPA hopes that the momentum of May 2009 Trade and Investment Framework Agreement (TIFA) discussions between USTR Ambassador Kirk and Indonesian Trade Minister Mari Pangestu, which included intellectual property rights issues, can be carried forward into 2010. With the establishment of a new Cabinet in October 2009, IIPA also hopes the Indonesian government can follow through on the promise to protect copyright and open the copyright market in Indonesia. WIPO reports that a study is under way to evaluate the contribution of creativity to Indonesia's economy. Other studies in the region have shown high output by creative industries both in terms of contribution to gross domestic product and good jobs. Those studies support the proposition that adequate and effective protection of intellectual property in a country, as well as adequate market access to foreign companies, are vital to ensure continued positive contributions to real and human capital in the country.

Unfortunately, in Indonesia, piracy problems, including end-user piracy of business software, mall piracy including mobile device piracy and CD-R and DVD-R burning, book piracy, illegal camcording, pay TV piracy, some factory optical disc piracy, and emerging Internet-based piracy cause serious economic harm to right holders. In many instances, organized criminal groups engaged in other criminal behavior are suspected of or have been detected engaging in piracy. Piracy levels in Indonesia remained among the highest in the world in 2009. In terms of enforcement, key government enforcement agencies assisted industry in certain respects, for example, with several raids as part of a National IP Campaign instituted against those engaged in end-user piracy of business

software. In September 2009, the Task Force extended this National IP Campaign to other sectors, making visits to mall owners and warning them that distribution or fostering distribution of infringing goods could lead to actions against them in 2010. However, IIPA members do not report that this increased focus of attention on piracy problems has led to significant deterrent enforcement actions against all kinds of piracy, increased prosecutions, improvements to the court system, or fighting corruption.

Worse yet, instead of focusing attention on piracy and solutions to the problem, the government retained onerous market access barriers, including the requirement to locally manufacture film prints and home videos in Indonesia (which had been suspended throughout 2009) and added new restrictions. For example, in March 2009, the Ministry of Administrative Reform (MenPAN) issued Circular Letter No. 1 of 2009 to all central and provincial government offices including State-owned enterprises, endorsing the use and adoption of open source software within government organizations. While the government issued this circular in part with the stated goal to "reduc[e] software copyright violation[s]," in fact, by denying technology choice, the measure will create additional trade barriers and deny fair and equitable market access to software companies. In September 2009, a new Film Law was enacted which would impose a local film quota and strict censorship requirements on local and foreign films. The Film Law is so badly conceived that no one in the film industry to our knowledge, including local and foreign industry, has come out in its support.

Priority Actions Requested in 2010

IIPA requests that the government of Indonesia take the following actions, which would result in the most significant near term commercial benefits to the copyright industries:

Market Access and Related Issues

- Rescind March 2009 MenPAN circular letter endorsing the use and adoption of open source software which threatens to create additional trade barriers and deny fair and equitable market access to software companies.
- Repeal Film Law that imposes a local film quota and strict censorship requirements on local and foreign films.
- Immediately lift market access restrictions on the 1) requirement to locally replicate all theatrical prints and home video titles released in Indonesia; 2) direct distribution of audiovisual products; and 3) ban on the broadcast of most foreign programming in Indonesia.

Enforcement Issues

- Follow through on the National IP Task Force's "Campaign" to take deterrent action against piracy, including:
  - Corporate end-user piracy, to protect the local and international business software industry from the use of unlicensed business software for any commercial purpose.

- Retail and mall piracy, including imposition of landlord liability for mall owners.
- Mobile device piracy.
- Illegal camcording of movies in cinemas.
- Signal theft, i.e., those who engage in decrypting encrypted television or cable/satellite signals, or those that transmit or retransmit signals (whether decrypted with or without authorization).
- Book piracy, to address and bring enforcement actions against illegal photocopying on and near university campuses, print piracy, and unauthorized translations.
- Bring and conclude more high-profile deterrent criminal piracy cases, including distributors, warehouses, factories, and high-profile cases involving end-user piracy of business software.
- Commit to expand Commercial Courts in Medan, Jakarta, Semarang, Surabaya, and Makassar to adjudicate copyright cases, establish special IP courts for criminal cases, and take steps to improve judicial processes by developing a cadre of well-qualified, IP-literate judges and prosecutors.
- Address corruption and transparency issues, for example, by creating a database viewable by right holders on all commenced raid actions and status reports on such cases.
- Expedite the establishment by the Directorate General of IPR (DGIPR) of a "Directorate of Investigation" so that Civil Servant Investigators are authorized to enforce all IP laws.

Legislative Issues

- Enact a modern copyright law fully implementing the WIPO Copyright Treaty (WCT) and WIPO Performances and Phonograms Treaty (WPPT) and providing for effective enforcement, including, among other necessary changes:
  - maintaining *ex officio* powers to raid upon suspicion of infringement;
  - codifying in the copyright law explicit liability against mall landlords;
  - providing minimum criminal penalties for all kinds of copyright infringement, including sellers of pirate goods and pirate end-users of business software;
  - ensuring appropriate cybercrime provisions are in place against Internet-based infringements, and creating incentives for service providers to help enforce against Internet and mobile copyright piracy;
  - criminalizing the act of camcording in cinemas;
  - properly protecting sound recordings under the law;
  - extending term of protection.
- Ensure copyright infringement is included in larger fight against organized criminal behavior (i.e., that infringement is a predicate ground for broader criminal investigation, seizure/freezing of assets, etc.).
- Make optical disc regulations more effective by 1) making inspections routine, unannounced and off-hours; 2) enforcing against SID Code violations, including gouging off or non-use of source identification codes; 3) providing transparency in raids and results; and 4) ensuring that the Department of Industry collects exemplars.

Market Access and Related Issues

In 2009, the government of Indonesia took backward steps by further closing a market already considered to be one of the least open in the world for copyright businesses. As of 2008, the government had already essentially closed the market to entertainment companies, severely limiting investment in media businesses, and imposing strict restrictions on the kind of foreign content that could be broadcast in the country. The situation considerably worsened in 2008 due to the imposition of a local manufacturing requirement for the replication of film prints and home video/DVDs released in Indonesia. In 2009, the government issued a Circular announcing a government procurement policy for public sector software usage that would if implemented deny software companies of a level-playing field with the public sector and set a very poor example in terms of technology choice and procurement practices for the private sector, and enacted an ill-conceived Film Law which imposes an onerous quota for local film production and strict censorship restrictions that foreign and even local film companies oppose.

Government Procurement Preference Denies U.S. Software Companies a Level Playing Field: The government of Indonesia, under its Ministry of Administrative Reform (MenPAN), officially sent to all central and provincial government offices, including state-owned enterprises in Indonesia, Circular Letter No. 1 of 2009 issued on March 30, 2009, endorsing the use and adoption of open source software within government organizations. More specifically, the MenPAN letter, concerning the "Utilization of Legal Software and Open Source Software (OSS)," encourages government agencies to use "FOSS" (Free Open Source Software) with a view toward implementation by the end of 2011, which the Circular states will result in the use of legitimate open source and FOSS software and a reduction in overall costs of software. The letter was followed by subsequent clarification documents, including an April 2009 State Ministry of Research & Technology (RISTEK) document regarding the "Migration to Open Source in Government Agencies."

While IIPA has no issue with one of the stated goals of the circular, namely, "reducing software copyright violation," the Indonesian government's policy as indicated in the circular letter instead simply weakens the software industry and undermines its long-term competitiveness by creating an artificial preference for companies offering open source software and related services, even as it denies many legitimate companies access to the government market. Rather than fostering a system that will allow users to benefit from the best solution available in the market, irrespective of the development model, it encourages a mindset that does not give due consideration to the value to intellectual creations. As such, it fails to build respect for intellectual property rights and also limits the ability of government or public-sector customers (e.g., State-owned enterprise) to choose the best solutions to meet the needs of their organizations and the Indonesian people. It also amounts to a significant market access barrier for the software industry. The "Principles for Technology Choice Pathfinder," adopted by APEC in 2006 (furthering the 2002 "Statement to Implement APEC Policies on Trade and the Digital Economy," to which Indonesia was a participant), recognize that

procurement preferences can close markets and stifle innovation and economic development. By implementing this government procurement preference policy, the Indonesian government is not adopting an effective approach to drive down piracy rates, but rather, is creating an additional trade barrier and denying fair and equitable market access to software companies worldwide, which is inconsistent with the APEC Principles.

Rather than start down this path away from innovation and to further promote respect for copyright, the government should abandon the Circular's approach and follow a realistic policy framework that includes adequate education and effective enforcement of IP rights and non-discrimination in business choice, software development, and licensing models. The government of Indonesia promised to legalize the public sector's use of software, e.g., in the January 13, 2006 Indonesian Ministry of Communication and Information (MOCI) and Microsoft Memorandum of Understanding (MOU) in which the government undertakes to legalize government use of its products on government computers. We strongly urge USTR to consider the implications that Indonesia's open source preference policy has on IP protection and access to Indonesia's market for U.S. goods and services. . . .

Piracy and Enforcement Challenges in Indonesia

Indonesia Ranks in World's Top 12 Highest Business Software End-User Piracy Rates, But Enforcement Cooperation Remains Generally Good: The willful use of unlicensed or pirate software in the workplace continues to cause the greatest losses to business software companies in Indonesia. The software piracy rate in Indonesia rose slightly, from 85% to 86%, between 2008 and 2009 and still exceeds the Asia regional average (which was 61% in 2008). For 2008, Indonesia ranked 12th highest in the world in terms of global piracy rate, and 19th highest in the world in terms of global losses. Failure to deal with software piracy harms not only U.S. (and other foreign) software companies but harms Indonesia's local economy. A January 2008 study done by the International Data Corporation (IDC) with the Business Software Alliance (BSA) concluded that decreasing Indonesia's software piracy rate by ten percent over a four year period to 2011 would add US$1.8 billion to Indonesia's economy, create 2,200 new high-wage high-tech jobs and generate an additional $90 million in tax revenue.

Overall, enforcement against end-user software infringements in businesses did not improve much in 2009. Some police commands who signed memoranda of understanding (MOUs) have been very cooperative when identifying and following through on cases of end-user infringement. The police are normally taking *ex officio* actions, although in many cases the police take these actions without notifying right holders and administer fines without consulting the industry. This lack of transparency raises obvious concerns and also diminishes the deterrent value of such actions. In 2009, there were 42 overall actions against end-user piracy of business software, with police

initiating 13 corporate end-user raids based on BSA complaints, and 29 police-initiated raids.

Further exacerbating the end-user software piracy problem in Indonesia has been a generally ineffective judicial system to combat piracy. It often takes an unusually lengthy period for a case to be finalized and there is no indication that IPR cases (especially criminal prosecutions) are being prioritized. In 2009, we understand that criminal trials against corporate end-user piracy in the country were concluded (one decided by the Semarang District Court in Central Java, and two others decided by the South Jakarta District Court). This follows seven criminal convictions in 2008. In the South Jakarta cases, the police successfully investigated and prosecuted two IT managers for using unlicensed software for business purposes. In November 2009, these two defendants were found guilty for end-user piracy by the South Jakarta District Court. They were both sentenced to six months imprisonment, suspended for 10 months probation, and fined IDR10 million (about US$1,050), which may be substituted with 2 months imprisonment. This sentence was shocking to the local software industry due to the extremely low, non-deterrent fines imposed. . . .

Training and Public Awareness

Various Industry Trainings Provide Capacity Building Assistance in 2009: In 2009, as in previous years, the copyright industries conducted and participated in various training and public awareness activities in Indonesia. Training has been carried out with police, although more needs to be done. For example, in October 2009, BSA spoke to about a dozen police officers from West Java Regional Police and about 100 students from the Faculty of Law, University of Padjajaran in Bandung, West Java, about legal aspects of corporate end-user piracy. In addition, BSA and the U.S. Commercial Services hosted a mini "software asset management" (SAM) seminar targeting 63 companies in Jakarta in May 2009. IIPA understands that some enforcement seminars have taken place in Lampung, Medan and Bali as part of the National IP Campaign in February 2009. The Motion Picture Association provided training throughout the year for approximately 180 theater employees on anti-camcording investigation and enforcement techniques.

U.S. Department of Justice Program Lends Positive Support to Industry: IIPA members continue to support the training program from the United States, the "International Criminal Investigative Training Assistance Program" (ICITAP) which commenced in October 2006. This program, comprising an anti-piracy enforcement initiative and an optical disc piracy initiative, has led in the past to some concrete positive results in terms of facilitating better enforcement against copyright infringements. It also helped build capacity, mentored, and provided technical assistance to optical disc factory inspection teams that include officials from the Department of Industry (DOI), Police, Customs, the Department of Trade and the Directorate General of Intellectual Property Rights in implementing the provisions of the optical disc regulations.

Copyright Law and Related Issues

Copyright Law Implementing Regulations Still Have Not Been Issued: Copyright protection in Indonesia is governed by the Law of the Republic of Indonesia, Number 19 Year 2002 Regarding Copyright (Copyright Law) (effective July 29, 2003) (Undang-Undang RI No. 19 Thn 2002 Tentang Hak Cipta). Regulations dealing with "rights management information" (RMI) were finalized in 2005, but implementing regulations regarding technological protection measures (TPMs) (as covered in Article 27 of the Copyright Law) are still missing and are needed to fully implement the WCT and the WPPT. Indonesia joined the WCT on June 5, 1997 (in force March 6, 2002), and the WPPT on February 15, 2005.

Copyright Law Amendments Needed to Modernize Protection: Reform of the Copyright Law has been in the works for a several years, and IIPA understands that a draft set of amendments emerged in 2008 and is currently in the legislative queue. IIPA encourages the Indonesian government to ensure that any proposed changes are open for public consultation and comment. The following issues should be dealt with in any amendment, to ensure that the law meets the needs of the modern copyright system and keeps abreast of the latest in international and WCT and WPPT obligations:

- **Provide Minimum Criminal Penalties for All Kinds of Copyright Infringement:** There is a continuing need to provide a minimum criminal penalty clause as to all copyright infringements. The current Copyright Law provides minimum criminal penalties only for the production or manufacture of pirate goods (see Article 72(1) of the Copyright Law). For future amendments, it would be vital to provide minimum criminal penalties for sellers of pirate goods as well as those who engage in corporate end-user piracy, especially in view of the low fines we have seen imposed by the courts. The law should also maintain current maximum sentencing provisions. We understand there is a draft criminal code being considered, but IIPA has not been given an opportunity to review such a draft (and it may be that the minimum penalties will be dealt with directly in the copyright law).
- **Maintain Ex Officio Powers to Raid Upon Suspicion of Infringement:** It is important that, for the next amendment of the Copyright Law, copyright infringement must remain a state offense. Any change from this could result in a significant decrease in the numbers of raids and decrease the efficacy of enforcement in Indonesia.
- **Provide for Landlord Liability:** Landlords that do not directly infringe but control infringement of tenants and financially benefit from such infringement should be held liable in Indonesia. This would ensure that all mall owners would be responsible for ridding their premises of piracy. Articles 55 and 56 of the Penal Code provide for criminal liability for one who forces others to commit or jointly commits a criminal act (Article 55(1)) or one who providing "opportunity" or "intentionally 'persuades' others" to commit a criminal act. We understand the government is considering codifying such liability for criminal copyright infringements as to mall landlords who have infringing activity occurring on their premises. IIPA supports this move.

- **Cover Copyright Infringement Under Cybercrime Law, and Provide Incentives for Service Providers to Cooperate, Including Notice and Takedown:** With Internet piracy, including P2P downloading, increasing in Indonesia, it is imperative that the laws adequately address computer-based infringements. The government of Indonesia has reportedly just enacted a new Cyber Law. IIPA has not had an opportunity to review this law, but looks forward to doing so to compare it against the Council of Europe Cybercrime Convention. Reportedly, the law requires some technical implementing regulations including those related to ISP liability, although it is already apparently being employed to prosecute cases involving online pornography or distribution of false information through Internet media, although unfortunately not involving copyright piracy. The law should be used to combat IP-related cybercrime including copyright infringements. It is also very important to ensure that proper incentives are put into place to ensure service providers cooperate with right holders to curtail such infringing activities. Service providers need to be reminded of potential liability for infringements occurring over their networks, and mechanisms need to be available to ensure removal of infringing content, including notice and takedown as well as effective and fair policies in place by ISPs as to potential termination of repeat infringers, and to ensure assistance to right holders in identifying and removing infringing content and P2P piracy. . . .

Generalized System of Preferences

Indonesia currently participates in the Generalized System of Preferences (GSP) program, a U.S. trade program, which offers preferential trade benefits to eligible beneficiary countries. One of the discretionary criteria of this program is that the country provides "adequate and effective protection for intellectual property rights." In 2008, almost $2.2 billion worth of Indonesian goods entered the U.S. under the duty-free GSP code, accounting for almost 13.8% of its total imports to the U.S. During 2009, almost $1.5 billion worth of Indonesian goods, or almost 11.3% of Indonesia's total imports to the U.S., entered the U.S. under the duty-free GSP code. Indonesia needs to continue to endeavor to meet the adequate and effective test under the statute to remain eligible to continue to receive favorable treatment under the GSP program.

Michael Tiemann  **NO**

The OSI Categorically Rejects IIPA's Special Pleadings Against Open Source

Introduction

Moore's Law, Disk Law, and Fiber Law have created an economic engine for growth, promising exponentially improving computing, storage, and networking performance for the foreseeable future. And yet according to a 2003 UNCTAD report, "there has been no Moore's Law for software," and indeed it is because of software that computer systems have become more expensive, more complex, and less reliable. The global economy spent $3.4T USD on Information and Communication Technologies in 2008, of which we estimate $1T USD was wasted on "bad software." And reconfirming the 2003 report and our own numbers updated for 2010, others have estimated losses of at least $500B and as much as $6T USD (meaning that for every dollar spent on ICT, that dollar and almost one more went down the drain). Whether the annual loss number is $500B, $1T, or $6T, all represent an unsustainable cost and undeniable evidence that something in the dominant design of the proprietary software industry is deeply flawed.

Open source software is an alternative approach to software development that allows, rather than prohibits, users and developers to collaborate and innovate together. It encourages, rather than threatens, transparency and accountability. It rewards meritorious behavior and it routes around bottlenecks caused by concentration of power and control. Open source software was the catalyst that helped effect the revolution of the World Wide Web, where for the first time in history, the promise of the freedom of the press was available to anybody with a computer and an Internet connection. Indeed, open source software was, and remains, the technology of the whole Internet itself. When Thomas Friedman claimed that open source is the most powerful and disruptive of the ten flattening forces described in the best-selling book *The World Is Flat*, it was no surprise to us. But now a consortium of industry trade associations, the International Intellectual Property Alliance (IIPA), has launched an attack against open source, and so we must stand up, defend our position, and explain how the use of open source leads to the continued progress of the 21st century economy.

The successes of open source software are too numerous to mention in a single article. A few examples establish that open source has become the most reliable and sustainable software with virtually unlimited upside potential. The interests of the State, be they security, accountability, transparency, or economic opportunity, are advanced by open source. The NSA's SE Linux project single-handedly restored the economic viability of a highly secure platform able to securely run a growing range of innovative applications. Its protections have resulted in an operating system kernel that has suffered zero critical security vulnerabilities in more than four years of commercial availability. The US Department of Defense issued a memo in 2009 stating "To effectively achieve its missions, the Department of Defense must develop and update its software-based capabilities faster than ever, to anticipate new threats and respond to continuously changing requirements. The use of Open Source Software (OSS) can provide advantages in this regard . . ." The Executive Office of the President has been collaborating with the Sunlight Foundation and others to provide greater transparency into US Federal spending, using open source software to collect, index, and publish hundreds of billions of dollars worth of Federal procurements and contracts. And open source software is the fastest growing segment of the software industry, registering double-digit organic growth compared to zero-to-negative growth of the industry as a whole. It is little wonder that in the State of California, considered by most to be the epicenter of America's technology industry, Chief Information Officer Terri Takai published ITPL-10-01, which serves to "formally establish the use of Open Source Software (OSS) in California state government as an acceptable practice."

Other nations, seeing the success of open source in US and State governments, industry, and R&D, have initiated their own investigations into open source software, and many have liked what they have found. The CSIS Open Source Policy report documents the progress of hundreds of open source policies around the world, and open source policy research studies . . . show that open source adoption positively correlates with the Human Development Index. By contrast, rates of software piracy have no correlation whatsoever with that index. Moreover, objective quality metrics (published in reports sponsored by the Department of Homeland Security) show not only that Open Source Software has achieved a hundredfold higher quality than typical proprietary software (as measured by defect density per 1000 lines of source code), but open source continues to improve its quality metrics by double digits per year while proprietary software remains static in its (not very good) defect density. The fact that open source software has achieved such a quality differential should be sufficient for open source to win in a neutral competitive bidding process—and it does as shown by its revenue and market share growth. But software is not merely a commodity to be consumed, it is an investment whose value can increase with proper stewardship. Customers who buy software with the rights and community necessary to effect continuous improvement get good value for their money. Governments who seek those rights are being smart about the dollars they spend today without artificially limiting the adaptations they may need to make tomorrow. This is one reason why governments are not only seeking best value for today's dollar, but the freedoms to

make today's investment more valuable tomorrow, and why open source has become an explicit consideration in policies, procurements, and discussions of best practices.

Open Source Provides Long-Term Value Beyond Proprietary Alternatives

Unlike proprietary software, whose value diminishes over time as it become obsolete (if it was ever useful in the first place), open source software, as a knowledge commons, permits a kind of compound interest to accrue to its intellectual capital base. (The theory underlying this discovery won a Nobel Prize in economics for 2009.) It should therefore be no surprise that open source software should be one of the key drivers in advancing national technology objectives among all nations, whether developing or developed. Anyone who has seen the progress and the potential of open source software, should be surprised by an information infrastructure built on software that prohibits independent improvement, frustrates interoperabilty, criminalizes collaboration, and defeats Moore's Law. And yet this is the heart of the IIPA's recommendation. But it is not only the heart of that recommendation that is rotten.

Attacks by the IIPA Are Unjust

A recent blog posting at *The Guardian* about the IIPA's recommendation, and its influence over US "Special 301" rules, suggests that there is something well hidden from review: a secret trial to which neither the accused nor any jury are invited to attend. Andres Guadamuz has done the digging to reveal that guilt has been read out in a Star Chamber. Orders have been handed down that are not only unjust, but entirely arbitrary. An excerpt from Wikipedia provides the following definition and explanation of the term "Selective Enforcement" as follows:

> Selective enforcement is the ability that executors of the law (such as police officers or administrative agencies, in some cases) have to arbitrarily select choice individuals as being outside of the law. The use of enforcement discretion in an arbitrary way is referred to as selective enforcement or selective prosecution.
>
> Historically, selective enforcement is recognized as a sign of tyranny, and an abuse of power, because it violates rule of law, allowing men to apply justice only when they choose. Aside from this being inherently unjust, it almost inevitably must lead to favoritism and extortion, with those empowered to choose being able to help their friends, take bribes, and threaten those they desire favors from.

Singling out a single country like Indonesia for policies that can be found across the European Union (not to mention within US civilian, academic, military, and intelligence communities) is a blatant case of selective enforcement, one which hides the absurdity of the claims by the narrowness of their

application. The sheer hypocrisy of the claims made by the IIPA should cause anybody to doubt the merits of those claims, such as this:

> While IIPA has no issue with one of the stated goals of [the Ministry of Administrative Reform (MenPAN) . . . Circular Letter No. 1 of 2009 issued on March 30, 2009, endorsing the use and adoption of open source software within government organizations], namely, "reducing software copyright violation," the Indonesian government's policy as indicated in the circular letter instead simply weakens the software industry and undermines its long-term competitiveness by creating an artificial preference for companies offering open source software and related services, even as it denies many legitimate companies access to the government market. Rather than fostering a system that will allow users to benefit from the best solution available in the market, irrespective of the development model, it encourages a mindset that does not give due consideration to the value to intellectual creations. As such, it fails to build respect for intellectual property rights and also limits the ability of government or public-sector customers (e.g., State-owned enterprise) to choose the best solutions to meet the needs of their organizations and the Indonesian people. It also amounts to a significant market access barrier for the software industry.

The IIPA complains that the open source community does not respect intellectual property. "Intellectual property" conflates trade secrets, patents, copyrights, and trademarks. By pretending as if these separate domains are all one common thing, and then arguing by analogy how all should be understood, the concept of "intellectual property" has taken on a meaning that has no actual basis in law. Worse, this meaning has been construed to actually contradict the original purpose that was enshrined into the US Constitution, which was "To promote the Progress of Science and useful Arts, by securing for limited Times to Authors and Inventors the exclusive Right to their respective Writings and Discoveries." The copyright clause speaks not at all to any natural rights of Authors and Inventors, but only to the goal of progress. If there were any invention worthy of protection by law, it would be the invention of how to make more progress in science and the useful arts. Which is precisely what open source software now appears to be doing.

But even if one does not believe that open source is a better way of doing things, there is no question that open source is equally dependent—no more, no less—than proprietary software on the strong protections of copyright law. Open source depends on the strong ability to grant rights to those who wish to copy our work—a true copy right!—and thus we respect copyright at least as much as those who don't trust it enough to call it by its real name. If anything, the ones guilty of not respecting copyright are those who invent new terms like "intellectual property" and then write up and promote their own legal theories: as to how such stuff is supposed to work, who should be rewarded for buying into their system, and who should be punished if they do not.

Open source software is today a part of every commercial software solution. IIPA's assertion that expecting use of open source software "denies many legitimate companies access to the government market" is a desperate distortion of

the truth. It requires a suspension of belief in core suppliers like IBM, Oracle, Red Hat, Microsoft, HP—and most others—all of whom have already integrated open source into their business in one of the ways Gartner describes. To say it "undermines [the software market's] long-term competitiveness" beggars belief, given the enormous competitive impetus the industry has received from the relaxation of lock-in and the introduction of new competitive innovation from open source. Far from being "a significant market access barrier," an open source requirement corrects the power a small number of suppliers have been able to derive from lock-in and the exercise of monopoly—in some cases illegally and unremedied.

Further, IIPA's position represents a direct attack on the very government to which it is making a recommendation. If expecting the presence of open source did indeed "simply weaken the software industry," the US government itself would be culpable since the Department of Defence has issued and clari-fied clear guidance preferring open source software for most purposes. By their logic, it would be justifiable for foreign governments to embargo the USA.

The greatest outrage arose from the assertion that "it fails to build respect for intellectual property rights," which compresses into a few words both an inversion of the truth and a dishonest, self-serving conceptual framing. Open source software has no impact on the use of trademarks, patents or trade secrets, so the stew of "intellectual property" here actually refers only to copy-right. To say that open source fails to build respect for copyright is ridiculous. Open source licensing is copyright licensing and thus depends upon and pro-motes the greatest possible respect for copyright. Without that respect, open source software would be impossible. One suspects the comment is derived more from a desire to mislead government for commercial purposes by associ-ating open source with file sharing in order to smear and discredit it from the worldview of the RIAA (Recording Industry Association of America).

Open Source Supports Business

Open Source was not parachuted in from an alternate universe. It is a result of the ordinary business decision to build versus buy. Businesses purchase some software and write some other software themselves. They have found that they can reduce their cost of writing software by sharing it with the public. They turn the software into a commodity, available at minimal cost. Inevitably, this is going to annoy the people who would rather that software be a scarce eco-nomic good only available through certain vendors (themselves). Of course they have the right to make their case, as they have. But their case must be clearly identified as special pleading designed to advance their own ends, not a general defense of business interests.

Conclusion

The entire position taken by IIPA is unbalanced. It relies on outdated defi-nitions, special interests, and a fear of innovation and new business model opportunities. It blends them together to abuse an outdated mechanism of the

US government with a condemnation that applies to the US itself. America has a role in defending free markets around the world. The IIPA's stance does not support that role, and should not be respected.

We call on national organizations, such as Open Source for America, to take action by representing the large and growing open source community.

EXPLORING THE ISSUE

Does Endorsing Open Source Software Fail to Respect Intellectual Property?

Critical Thinking and Reflection

1. What does "open source" mean?
2. Does any business or other institution have a right to continue its operations as it is accustomed to doing?
3. What is the purpose of copyright and patent law?
4. In what sense does endorsing the use of open source software help to prevent copyright infringement?

Is There Common Ground?

Both sides of this debate agree that copyright law is important. The Open Source and Free Culture movements, however, use it differently from the IIPA. There are many different open source "licenses"; see http://www.opensource.org/docs/osd and http://www.opensource.org/licenses/index.html. After studying the definitions here, answer the following questions:

1. Does any open source license permit piracy or theft of software?
2. Does any open source license fail to permit software buyers to share the software with others?
3. Does any open source license fail to permit for-profit distribution of software?

Internet References . . .

Foundation for Biomedical Research

The Foundation for Biomedical Research promotes public understanding and support of the ethical use of animals in scientific and medical research.

http://www.fbresearch.org

Bioethics.net and The American Journal of Bioethics

Bioethics.net, founded in 1993, was the first bioethics Web site. Together with *The American Journal of Bioethics* (AJOB), it has grown to become the most read source of information about bioethics.

http://bioethics.net

National Human Genome Research Institute

The National Human Genome Research Institute directs the Human Genome Project for the National Institutes of Health (NIH).

http://www.genome.gov/

The U.S. Department of Energy Human Genome Project

This site offers a huge amount of information and links on genetics and cloning research.

**http://www.ornl.gov/techresources/
Human_Genome/elsi/Cloning.html**

Humanity+

Humanity+ is the leading transhumanist association, dedicated to promoting understanding, interest, and participation in the field of human enhancement.

http://humanityplus.org/

Center for Alternatives to Animal Testing

The Johns Hopkins Center for Alternatives to Animal Testing (CAAT) promotes humane science by supporting the creation, development, validation, and use of alternatives to animals in research, product safety testing, and education.

http://caat.jhsph.edu/

Ethics

*S*ociety's standards of right and wrong have been hammered out over millennia of trial, error, and (sometimes violent) debate. Accordingly, when science and technology offer society new choices to make and new things to do, debates are renewed over whether or not these choices and actions are ethically acceptable. Today there is vigorous debate over such topics as the use of animals in research; cloning of both stem cells and whole organisms; and enhancing the human form with genetic engineering, electronic accessories, and even mechanical aids.

- Is "Animal Rights" Just Another Excuse for Terrorism?
- Should We Reject the "Transhumanist" Goal of the Genetically, Electronically, and Mechanically Enhanced Human Being?

ISSUE 18

Is "Animal Rights" Just Another Excuse for Terrorism?

YES: John J. Miller, from "In the Name of the Animals: America Faces a New Kind of Terrorism," *National Review* (July 3, 2006)

NO: Steven Best, from "Dispatches from a Police State: Animal Rights in the Crosshairs of State Repression," *International Journal of Inclusive Democracy* (January 2007)

Learning Outcomes

After studying this issue, students will be able to:

1. Explain why animals are used in research.
2. Explain why alternatives to the use of animals in research are sought.
3. Describe the difference between "animal welfare" and "animal rights."
4. Explain why society chooses to restrain extreme protests.

ISSUE SUMMARY

YES: Journalist John Miller argues that animal rights extremists have adopted terrorist tactics in their effort to stop the use of animals in scientific research. Because of the benefits of such research, if the terrorists win, everyone loses.

NO: Professor Steven Best argues that the new Animal Enterprise Protection Act is excessively broad and vague, imposes disproportionate penalties, endangers free speech, and detracts from prosecution of real terrorism. The animal liberation movement, on the other hand, is both a necessary effort to emancipate animals from human exploitation, and part of a larger resistance movement opposed to exploitation and hierarchies of any and all kinds.

Modern biologists and physicians know a great deal about how the human body works. Some of that knowledge has been gained by studying human

cadavers and tissue samples acquired during surgery and through "experiments of nature." Some knowledge of human biology has also been gained from experiments on humans, such as when patients agree to let their surgeons and doctors try experimental treatments.

The key word here is *agree*. Today it is widely accepted that people have the right to consent or not to consent to whatever is done to them in the name of research or treatment. In fact, society has determined that research done on humans without their free and informed consent is a form of scientific misconduct. However, this standard does not apply to animals, experimentation on which has produced the most knowledge of the human body.

Although animals have been used in research for at least the last 2000 years, during most of that time, physicians who thought they had a workable treatment for some illness commonly tried it on their patients before they had any idea whether or not it worked or was even safe. Many patients, of course, died during these untested treatments. In the mid-nineteenth century, the French physiologist Claude Bernard argued that it was sensible to try such treatments first on animals to avoid some human suffering and death. No one then questioned whether or not human lives were more valuable than animal lives. In the twentieth century, Elizabeth Baldwin, in "The Case for Animal Research in Psychology," *Journal of Social Issues* (vol. 49, no. 1, 1993), argued that animals are of immense value in medical, veterinary, and psychological research, and they do not have the same moral rights as humans. Our obligation, she maintains, is to treat them humanely.

Today geneticists generally study fruit flies, roundworms, and zebra fish. Physiologists study mammals, mostly mice and rats but also rabbits, cats, dogs, pigs, sheep, goats, monkeys, and chimpanzees. Experimental animals are often kept in confined quarters, cut open, infected with disease organisms, fed unhealthy diets, and injected with assorted chemicals. Sometimes the animals suffer. Sometimes the animals die. And sometimes they are healed, albeit often of diseases or injuries induced by the researchers in the first place.

Not surprisingly, some observers have reacted with extreme sympathy and have called for better treatment of animals used in research. This "animal welfare" movement has, in turn, spawned the more extreme "animal rights" movement, which asserts that animals—especially mammals—have rights as important and as deserving of regard as those of humans. Thus, to kill an animal, whether for research, food, or fur, is the moral equivalent of murder. See Steven M. Wise and Jane Golmoodall, *Rattling the Cage: Toward Legal Rights for Animals* (Perseus, 2000) and Roger Scruton and Andrew Tayler, "Do Animals Have Rights?" *The Ecologist* (March 2001).

As the idea that people must give informed consent to what is done to them in the name of research gained currency, along with the related idea that whatever is done should aim to benefit them, some people have tried to extend these ideas to animals. They say that just as scientists cannot do whatever they wish to humans, they cannot do whatever they wish to animals. Harriet Ritvo, "Toward a More Peaceable Kingdom," *Technology Review* (April 1992), says that the animal rights movement "challenges the ideology of science itself . . . forcing experimenters to recognize that they are not necessarily carrying out an independent

exercise in the pursuit of truth—that their enterprise, in its intellectual as well as its social and financial dimensions, is circumscribed and defined by the culture of which it is an integral part." The continuing debate is driven by the periodic discovery of researchers who seem quite callous (at least to the layperson's eye) in their treatment of animals (see Kathy Snow Guillermo, *Monkey Business: The Disturbing Case That Launched the Animal Rights Movement* [National Press, 1993]), by the charge that animal rights advocates just do not understand nature or research, and by the countercharge that animal research is irrelevant (see Peter Tatchell, "Why Animal Research Is Bad Science," *New Statesman* (August 9, 2004)).

Among books that are pertinent to this issue are F. Barbara Orlans, *In the Name of Science: Issues in Responsible Animal Experimentation* (Oxford University Press, 1993); Rod Strand and Patti Strand, *The Hijacking of the Humane Movement* (Doral, 1993); Deborah Blum, *The Monkey Wars* (Oxford University Press, 1994); and Tom Regan, *Empty Cages: Facing the Challenge of Animal Rights* (Rowman and Littlefield, 2005). Adrian R. Morrison provides a guide to responsible animal use in "Ethical Principles Guiding the Use of Animals in Research," *American Biology Teacher* (February 2003). Barry Yeoman, "Can We Trust Research Done with Lab Mice," *Discover* (July 2003), notes that the conditions in which animals are kept can make a huge difference in their behavior and in their responses to experimental treatments.

Reviewing recent developments in the animal rights movement, Damon Linker, in "Rights for Rodents," *Commentary* (April 2001), concludes, "Can anyone really doubt that, were the misanthropic agenda of the animal-rights movement actually to succeed, the result would be an increase in man's inhumanity, to man and animal alike? In the end, fostering our age-old 'prejudice' in favor of human dignity may be the best thing we can do for animals, not to mention for ourselves." An editorial in *Lancet*, "Animal Research Is a Source of Human Compassion, Not Shame," (September 4, 2004), insists that the use of animals in biomedical research is both an essentially humanistic endeavor and necessary. Assistant professor of anesthesiology and radiology at the University of Pittsburgh Stuart Derbyshire writes in "Vivisection: Put Human Welfare First," *Spiked-Online* (June 1, 2004), that the use of animals in research is justified by the search for knowledge, not just the search for medical treatments, and reflects a moral choice to put humans first. Josie Appleton, "Speciesism: A Beastly Concept: Why It Is Morally Right to Use Animals to Our Ends," *Spiked-Online* (February 23, 2006), contends that the development of human civilization has been marked by increasing separation from animals. Humans come first, and it is entirely moral to use animals for our own ends. Torturing animals is wrong, but mostly because it reflects badly upon the torturer. Wesley J. Smith, *A Rat Is a Pig Is a Dog Is a Boy: The Human Cost of the Animal Rights Movement* (Encounter, 2010), defends the stance that human interests must come before those of animals; granting rights to animals is an attack on human dignity. Animal-rights extremists defend the opposing view vigorously, even going so far as to firebomb researchers' homes and cars; see Greg Miller, "Scientists Targeted in California Firebombings," *Science* (August 8, 2008). John Hadley, "Animal Rights Extremism and the Terrorism Question," *Journal of Social Philosophy* (Fall 2009), questions whether such

extremist actions really fall under the "terrorism" label, but most people seem to have no trouble using the label. P. Michael Conn and James V. Parker of the Oregon National Primate Research Center describe in *The Animal Research War* (Palgrave Macmillan, 2008) how animals are used and protected in research and the benefits of their use, while also detailing the movement of terrorist tactics from the United Kingdom to the United States. In their view, "It is extremely important that an informed public know what is really going on and how it impacts on the future of health care and medical advances."

Yet the idea that animals have rights too continues to gain ground. Steven M. Wise finds in *Drawing the Line: Science and the Case for Animal Rights* (Perseus, 2002) that there is a spectrum of mental capacities for different species, which supports the argument for rights. Niall Shanks, in "Animal Rights in the Light of Animal Cognition," *Social Alternatives* (Summer 2003) considers the moral/philosophical justifications for animal rights and stresses the question of consciousness. Jim Motavalli, in "Rights from Wrongs," *E Magazine* (March/April 2003), describes with approval the movement toward giving animals legal rights (though not necessarily human rights). Jeffrey Stinson, "Activists Pursue Basic Legal Rights for Great Apes," *USA Today* (July 15, 2008), describes current efforts to grant such rights to the great apes. Paul Starobin, "Animal Rights on the March," *National Journal* (May 22, 2010), notes that the animal rights movement is shifting toward legislative efforts to meet their goals.

You can find the benefits of the use of animals discussed on a number of Web sites. Begin with Americans for Medical Progress (www.amprogress.org). For a list of specific benefits, visit the Pennsylvania Society for Biomedical Research at http://www.psbr.org/about.htm.

The animal welfare movement has led to important reforms in the treatment of animals, to the development of several alternatives to using animals in research, and to a considerable reduction in the number of animals used in research. See Alan M. Goldberg and John M. Frazier, "Alternatives to Animals in Toxicity Testing," *Scientific American* (August 1989); Wade Roush, "Hunting for Animal Alternatives," *Science* (October 11, 1996); and Erik Stokstad, "Humane Science Finds Sharper and Kinder Tools," *Science* (November 5, 1999); there is also a scientific journal, *ALTEX: Alternatives to Animal Experimentation* (http://altweb.jhsph.edu/altex/index.html). However, it has also led to hysterical objections to in-class animal dissections, terrorist attacks on laboratories, the destruction of research records, and the theft of research materials (including animals).

In the YES selection, journalist John Miller argues that animal rights extremists have adopted terrorist tactics in their effort to stop the use of animals in scientific research. Because of the benefits of such research, if the terrorists win, everyone loses. In the NO selection, professor Steven Best argues that new laws against animal rights "terrorism" represent the efforts of animal exploitation industries that seek immunity from criticism. The new Animal Enterprise Protection Act is excessively broad and vague, imposes disproportionate penalties, endangers free speech, and detracts from prosecution of real terrorism. The animal liberation movement, on the other hand, is both a necessary effort to emancipate animals from human exploitation, and part of a larger resistance movement opposed to exploitation and hierarchies of any and all kinds.

YES

John J. Miller

In the Name of the Animals: America Faces a New Kind of Terrorism

Six days after the World Trade Center was destroyed, the New York Stock Exchange rang its opening bell and traders sang "God Bless America" from the floor: They wanted to send a loud-and-clear message to the world that al-Qaeda could not shut down the U.S. economy. Even though the Dow suffered its biggest one-day point-loss in history, the mere fact that buying and selling could resume so quickly marked an inspiring day for capitalism and against terrorism.

On September 7, 2005, however, terrorists struck again, and the NYSE still hasn't recovered. This time, they didn't target a couple of skyscrapers near the exchange, but rather a company called Life Sciences Research (LSR). It had recently qualified for a NYSE listing and its senior management had gathered on Wall Street to celebrate the occasion. Just a few minutes before the first trades were set to occur, NYSE president Catherine Kinney informed her guests that their listing would be postponed. It was immediately obvious to everyone from LSR what had happened: "A handful of animal extremists had succeeded where Osama bin Laden had failed," Mark Bibi, the company's general counsel, would say in congressional testimony the next month.

LSR is better known by the name of its operating subsidiary, Huntingdon Life Sciences (HLS), which is in the business of testing products on animals to assess their safety and comply with government regulations. Most people probably don't like to think about what goes on in these labs—vivisections of monkeys, for instance—but they also appreciate the importance of research whose ultimate goal is the protection and enhancement of human health. About 95 percent of all lab animals are rats and mice, but for animal-rights extremists who believe that "a rat is a pig is a dog is a boy" (as Ingrid Newkirk of People for the Ethical Treatment of Animals once said), the whole endeavor is deeply immoral. And some of them have decided that because the traditional practices of honest persuasion and civil disobedience haven't changed many hearts or minds, they must now adopt a different strategy—something they euphemistically call "direct action." These are efforts to intimidate and harass animal researchers and everyone who comes into contact with them. In recent years, hardcore activists have embraced property destruction and physical

From *The National Review,* July 3, 2006, pp. 38–40. Copyright © 2006 by National Review, Inc., 215 Lexington Avenue, New York, NY 10016. Reprinted by permission.

assaults. "This is the number-one domestic terrorist threat in America," says Sen. James Inhofe, an Oklahoma Republican. Keeping LSR off the Big Board probably represents their greatest achievement yet.

Red in Tooth and Claw

The animal-rights movement may be wrongheaded, but there's no denying that most of its members are motivated by genuine compassion for animals and a sincere commitment to preventing cruelty. There's also no denying that violence in their name has become a significant problem. Just as the pro-life movement is haunted by the murderers of abortion doctors, the environmental and animal-rights movements are cursed by their own packs of fierce radicals. A year ago, the FBI said that 35 of its offices were conducting more than 150 investigations into "animal rights/ecoterrorist activities." The number of illegal incidents involving these activities has risen sharply, from 220 in the 1980s and 1990s to 363 in just the last five years, according to a recent report by the Foundation for Biomedical Research, an association of businesses and universities that conduct animal research. (By contrast, abortion-clinic violence appears to be subsiding.)

"Other groups don't come close in terms of the financial damage they've done," says John Lewis, an FBI agent who until recently coordinated federal efforts against domestic terrorism. Not even militants in the mold of Timothy McVeigh, the man behind the Oklahoma City bombing in 1995? "We have an acute interest in all of these groups, but when the rubber meets the road, the eco- and animal-rights terrorists lately have been way out in front." Lewis estimates that they've caused around $100 million in damage, mostly property destruction affecting businesses, much of it from arson. This fall, eleven defendants will face trial in Oregon for causing an estimated $20 million in damage in five states.

Although animal-rights terrorism is fundamentally barbaric, its execution has assumed increasingly sophisticated forms. The campaign against Huntingdon Life Sciences began in the United Kingdom seven years ago with the formation of a group called Stop Huntingdon Animal Cruelty, or SHAC. Soon after, SHAC recruited members in the United States to focus on an HLS facility in New Jersey, using methods that were deployed to great effect in the U.K. A federal trial earlier this year—perhaps the most important trial ever held involving animal-rights extremism—put the group's methods on full display.

Many of SHAC's efforts targeted HLS directly. An electronic attack in 2002, for instance, caused the HLS server to overload. But other confrontations involved HLS employees away from work: cars vandalized in driveways, rocks tossed through the windows of homes, and graffiti messages such as "PUPPY KILLER" spray-painted on houses. Descriptions of these incidents were dutifully posted on SHAC's own website, often with an unnerving sense of glee. After a tire-slashing visit to the home of one HLS employee, for example, the SHACtivists seemed pleased that "his wife is reportedly on the brink of a nervous breakdown and divorce." These messages were meant to generate publicity, build a sense of momentum, and serve as models for activists spread across

the country. In Britain, one top HLS employee was attacked by a group of hooded men wielding ax handles. "It's only a matter of time before it happens in the United States," warns Frankie Trull, head of the Foundation for Biomedical Research. "Everything they do over there eventually comes over here."

Intimidating employees in their private lives places pressure on HLS itself. But SHAC's harassment didn't stop with HLS employees. They also engaged in "tertiary targeting"—i.e., taking aim at companies with ties to HLS, plus their workers. Dozens of firms decided that doing business with HLS simply wasn't worth it. Deloitte & Touche, which had audited the HLS books, ended its relationship. Lawn gardeners quit. Even a security company that provided services to HLS succumbed to the abuse.

SHAC's methods certainly can be menacing, as transcripts from the trial make clear. One of SHAC's main targets was Marsh, a company that sold insurance to HLS. There was a smoke-bomb attack at an office in Seattle, forcing the evacuation of a high-rise building. In San Antonio, SHAC members glued the locks to a Marsh office and plastered the windows and doors of the building with pictures of a mutilated dog. Once they even stormed inside, screaming threats: "You have the blood of death on your hands! . . . We know where you live! You cannot sleep at night! We will find you!"

And they made good on these threats. Marsh employees were repeatedly harassed at home. There were late-night phone calls: "Are you scared? Do you think the puppies should be scared?" Other calls were more menacing: "We know where you live. You shouldn't sleep at night. You shouldn't rest until the puppies rest." Marion Harlos, who was managing director for Marsh in San Antonio, said that people went through her mail, ordered magazine subscriptions in her name, and rang her doorbell and dashed off in a kind of never-ending Devil's Night. Sometimes protesters would gather in front of her house, banging drums and hollering into megaphones. "They proceeded to parade the neighborhood, shout my name, that of my children," she said. "I was petrified. I was petrified for my children." The kids were kept indoors: "We did not know what was going to take place. Would someone be in the front yard? Would someone be in the back yard? Would someone come up and talk to them? Would someone try and take them?" To make a bad situation even worse, a neighbor threatened to sue Harlos, claiming that the ongoing presence of protesters was hurting property values. Harlos eventually moved.

Sally Dillenback, a Marsh employee in Dallas, had a similarly harrowing experience. A SHAC website published private information, some of it probably obtained by going through her trash: her home address, her car's license-plate number, and even her auto-insurance policy number. Most unsettling, however, was the information about her children: their names, the names of their schools and teachers, and descriptions of their after-school activities. "I felt that my family might be threatened with that kind of information being posted," she testified. The activists certainly didn't leave her alone; they plastered pictures on the side of her house, her mailbox, and her sidewalk. A SHAC website described the strategy: "Let the stickers serve to remind Marsh employees and their neighbors that their homes are paid for in the blood, the blood of innocent animals." On other occasions, animal-rights radicals held protests

outside her home with drums and bullhorns. They followed her to church. The scariest moment may have been when Dillenback read an e-mail: "It asked how I would feel if they cut open my son . . . and filled him with poison the way that they, Huntingdon, [were] doing to animals." Her husband bought a semi-automatic shotgun, even though Mrs. Dillenback doesn't like guns: "He was wanting to protect the family."

Pundits in Black Ski Masks

Marsh employees were by no means the only tertiary victims of abuse. Two bombs went off at a California office of Chiron, a biotech company. Nobody was hurt, but the second explosion was delayed—a tactic sometimes used by terrorists to kill first responders. Workers at GlaxoSmithKline, a pharmaceutical company, also had their windows smashed and mail stolen. In one case, SHAC posted information about the spouse of a GSK employee who was undergoing treatment for alcoholism. Another employee was summoned to the Baltimore morgue to identify a dead relative—but when she arrived, she learned the call was a hoax.

Sometimes, the connections between SHAC targets and HLS were so tenuous as to be almost nonexistent. Elaine Perna, a housewife who is married to an executive who retired from the Bank of New York—another company with ties to HLS—confronted SHAC when protesters appeared on her porch. "When I opened the door, they were yelling at me through the bullhorn. One spat at my face through the screen and yelled obscenities at me, about me, about my husband." A defense lawyer's attempt to minimize the incident—"All Ms. Gazzola did was she screamed through the bullhorn, didn't she?"—irritated Perna: "They were yelling at me through a bullhorn, they were calling me effing this and my husband effing that and spitting in my face through a screen. Now, if you think that 'that's all,' you know, you can call it 'that's all.' But to me, it wasn't 'that's all.'" The mayhem didn't stop until the police arrived.

On March 2, a jury convicted six members of SHAC (at press time, sentencing had not yet occurred). This is an important victory, but animal-rights extremism isn't going away—groups such as Hugs for Puppies and Win Animal Rights are now on the scene, continuing their perverse crusade. They certainly don't lack for true believers. In Senate testimony last fall, Jerry Vlasak of the North American Animal Liberation Press Office announced that violence against HLS was "extensional self-defense" in behalf of "non-human animals." Recently, a mysterious full-page advertisement appeared in the *New York Times* and the *Wall Street Journal*. It featured the image of a man in a black ski mask, alongside the words "I Control Wall Street" and a short account of the NYSE fiasco. "Nobody knows who paid for it," says Trull. One theory proposes that a group of institutional investors are responsible; another claims that it's a backhanded attempt by animal-rights activists to raise anxieties even further. HLS still isn't listed.

Several members of Congress have tried to address this species of domestic terrorism by proposing legislation that would toughen the Animal Enterprise Protection Act, a law that was passed before the advent of "tertiary targeting."

At the recent trial, prosecutors secured convictions against SHAC only because they were able to rely on anti-stalking laws. "They had to scour the federal code, looking for violations," says Brent McIntosh, a deputy assistant attorney general at the Department of Justice. "This is an enormous, surreptitious, and interstate conspiracy. We need to strengthen laws against it." Bills to do so have been introduced in both the House and the Senate, but a crowded legislative calendar probably means they won't be debated until a new Congress convenes next year.

The stakes are high. "Five years from now, we don't want to count up another $100 million in losses," says the FBI's Lewis. That's true, although the real costs of animal-rights terrorism aren't really quantifiable: They come in the form of medical discoveries that are delayed or never made, products that aren't approved, and careers that aren't started. Whatever the real price tag, one thing is certain: Each time an animal-rights terrorist wins, people lose.

Steven Best    **NO**

Dispatches from a Police State: Animal Rights in the Crosshairs of State Repression

Welcome to the post-constitutional America, where defense of animal rights and the earth is a terrorist crime.

In the wake of 9/11, and in the midst [of] the neoliberal attack on social democracies, efforts to grab dwindling resources, and crush dissent of any kind, the US has entered a neo-McCarthyist period rooted in witch-hunts and political persecution. The terms and players have changed, but the situation is much the same as the 1950s: the terrorist threat has replaced the communist threat, Attorney General Alfred [*sic*] Gonzalez dons the garb of Sen. Joseph McCarthy, and the Congressional Meetings on Eco-Terrorism stand in for the House Un-American Activities Committee. The Red Scare of communism has morphed into the *Green Scare* of ecoterrorism, where the bad guy today is not a commie but an animal, environmental, or peace activist. In a nightmare replay of the 1950s, activists of all kinds today are surveilled, hassled, threatened, jailed, and stripped of their rights. As before, the state conjures up dangerous enemies in our midst and instills fear in the public, so that people willingly forfeit liberties for an alleged security that demands secrecy, non-accountability, and centralized power. . . .

The bogus "war on terror" has served as a highly-effective propaganda and bullying device to ram through Congress and the courts a pro-corporate, anti-environmental, authoritarian agenda. Using vague, catch-all phrases such as "enemy combatants" and "domestic terrorists," the Bush administration has rounded up and tortured thousands of non-citizens (detaining them indefinitely in military tribunals without right to a fair trial) and surveilled, harassed, and imprisoned citizens who dare to challenge the government or corporate system it protects and represents.

"The Animal Enterprise Protection Act"

While dissent in general has become ever-more criminalized in the dark days of the Bush Reich, animal rights activists especially have been caught in the crosshairs of state repression, targeted by "anti-terrorist" legislation that subverts First Amendment rights to protect the blood money of corporate

From *International Journal of Inclusive Democracy*, vol.3, no.1, January 2007 (excerpts). Copyright © 2007 by Steven Best. Reprinted by permission of the author.

exploiters. This is because the animal rights/liberation movement is not only one of the most dramatic forms of resistance alive today (such as [is] evident in the dramatic raids, rescues, sabotage, and arson attacks of the Animal Liberation Front, a global movement), but also is an economic threat to postindustrial capital which is heavily rooted in science and research, and therefore dependent upon (it believes) animal experimentation.

In 1992, a decade before the passage of the USA PATRIOT Act, animal exploitation groups such as the National Association for Biomedical Research successfully lobbied Congress to pass a federal law called the Animal Enterprise Protection Act (AEPA). This legislation created the new crime of "animal enterprise terrorism," and laid out hefty sentences and fines for any infringement. The law applies to anyone who "intentionally damages or causes the loss of any property" of an "animal enterprise" (research facilities, pet stores, breeders, zoos, rodeos, circuses, furriers, animal shelters, and the like), or who causes an *economic loss* of any kind. The AEPA defines an "animal rights or ecological terrorist organization" as "two or more persons organized for the purpose of supporting any politically motivated activity intended to obstruct or deter any person from participating in any activity involving animals or an activity involving natural resources." The act criminalizes actions that obstruct "any lawful activity involving the use of natural resources with an economic value."

Like the category of "domestic terrorism" that is a keystone in the USA PATRIOT Act attack on civil liberties, the frightening thing about the AEPA is its strategic vagueness that subsumes any and every form of protest and demonstration against exploitative industries to a criminal act, specifically, to a *terrorist* act. Thus, the actions of two or more people can be labeled terrorist if they leaflet a circus, protest an experimental lab, block a road to protect a forest, do a tree-sit, or block the doors of a fur store. Since, under the purview of the AEPA, any action that interferes with the profits and operations of animal and environmental industries, even boycotts and whistle-blowing could be criminalized and denounced as terrorism. On the sweeping interpretations of such legislation, Martin Luther King, Mahatma Gandhi, and Cesar Chavez would today be vilified and imprisoned as terrorists, since the intent of their principled boycott campaigns was precisely to cause "economic damage" to unethical businesses. And since the AETA, like the legal system in general, classifies animals as "property," their "theft" (read: *liberation*) is unequivocally defined as a terrorist offense.

There already are laws against sabotage and property destruction, so isn't the AEPA just a redundant piece of legislation? No—not once [one] understands its hidden agenda which strikes at the heart of the Bill of Rights. The real purpose of the AEPA is to protect animal and earth exploitation industries from protest and criticism, not property destruction and "terrorism." The AEPA redefines vandalism as ecoterrorism, petty lawbreakers as societal menaces, protestors and demonstrators as domestic terrorists, and threats to their blood money as threats to national security. Powerful economic and lobbying forces, they seek immunity from criticism, to intimidate anyone contemplating protest against them, and to dispatch their opponents to prison.

Free Speech on Trial: The SHAC 7

Hovering over activists' heads like the sword of Damocles for over a decade, the AEPA dropped in March, 2006, with the persecution and conviction of seven members of a direct action group dedicated to closing down the world's largest animal-testing company, Huntingdon Life Sciences (HLS). Exercising their First Amendment rights, activists from the Stop Huntingdon Animal Cruelty (SHAC) campaign ran a completely legal and highly effective campaign against HLS, driving them to the brink of bankruptcy. Since 1999, SHAC activists in the UK and US have waged an aggressive direct action campaign against HLS, notorious for extreme animal abuse (torturing and killing 500 animals a day) and manipulated research data. SHAC roared onto the historical stage by combining a shrewd knowledge of the law, no non-sense direct action tactics, and a singular focus on one corporation that represents the evils of the entire vivisection industry. From email and phone blockades to raucous home demonstrations, SHACtivists have attacked HLS and pressured over 100 companies to abandon financial ties to the vivisection firm. By 2001, the SHAC movement drove down HLS stock values from $15/share to less than $1/share. Smelling profit emanating from animal bloodshed, investment banking firm Stephens Inc. stepped in to save HLS from bankruptcy. But, as happened to so many companies before them, eventually Stephens too could not withstand the intense political heat and so fled the SHAC kitchen. Today, as HLS struggles for solvency, SHAC predicts its imminent demise.

Growing increasingly powerful through high-pressure tactics that take the fight to HLS and their supporters rather than to corrupt legislatures, the SHAC movement poses a clear and present danger to animal exploitation industries and the state that serves them. Staggered and driven into the ropes, it was certain that SHAC's opponents would fight back. Throwing futile jabs here and there, the vivisection industry and the state recently teamed up to mount a major counterattack.

Alarmed indeed by the new form of animal rights militancy, HLS and the biomedical research lobby commanded special sessions with Congress to ban SHAC campaigns. On May 26, 2004, a police dragnet rounded up seven prominent animal rights activists in New Jersey, New York, Washington, and California. Hordes of agents from the FBI, Secret Service, and other law agencies stormed into the activists' homes at the crack of dawn, guns drawn and helicopters hovering above. Handcuffing those struggling for a better world, the state claimed another victory in its phony "war against terror." Using the AEPA, HLS successfully prosecuted the "SHAC 7," who currently are serving prison sentences up to six years.

After the SHAC 7 conviction, David Martosko, the noxious research director of the Center for Consumer Freedom and a fierce opponent of animal rights, joyously declared: "This is just the starting gun." Indeed, corporations and legislators continue to press for even stronger laws against animal rights and environmental activism, as the Bush administration encloses the nation within a vast web of surveillance and a militarized garrison.

In September 2006, the US senate unanimously passed a new version of the AEPA (S3990), significantly renamed the "Animal Enterprise *Terrorism* Act" (AETA). To prevent critical discussion, the Senate fast-tracked the bill without hearings or debate, and just before adjourning for the election recess. In November 2006, the House approved the bill (HR 4239), and President Bush obligingly signed it into law. Beyond the portentous change in name, the new and improved version extends the range of legal prosecution of activists, updates the law to cover Internet campaigns, and enforces stiffer penalties for "terrorist" actions. Created to stop the effectiveness of the SHAC-style tactics that biomedical companies had habitually complained about to Congress, the AETA makes it a criminal offense to interfere not only with so-called "animal enterprises" directly, but also with third-party organizations such as insurance companies, law firms, and investment houses that do business with them.

Thus, the Senate version of the bill expands the law to include "any property of a person or entity having a connection to, relationship with, or transactions with an animal enterprise." The chain of relations, like the application of the law, extends possibly to the point of infinity. As journalist Will Potter notes, "The clause broadens the scope of legislation that is already overly broad." This problem is compounded further with additional vague concepts such as criminalize actions that create "reasonable fear" in the targets of protest, making actions like peaceful home demonstrations likely candidates for "ecoterrorism."

As the Equal Justice Alliance aptly summarizes the main problems with the AETA:

- "It is excessively broad and vague.
- It imposes disproportionately harsh penalties.
- It effectively brands animal advocates as 'terrorists' and denies them equal protection.
- It effectively brands civil disobedience as 'terrorism' and imposes severe penalties.
- It has a chilling effect on all forms of protest by endangering free speech and assembly.
- It interferes with investigation of animal enterprises that violate federal laws.
- It detracts from prosecution of real terrorism against the American people."

ACLU Betrayal

A sole voice of dissent in Congress, Representative Dennis Kucinich (D-Ohio) stated that the bill compromises civil rights and threatens to "chill" free speech. Virtually alone in examining the issue from the perspective of the victims rather than victimizers, Kucinich said: "Just as we need to protect people's right to conduct their work without fear of assault, so too this Congress has yet to address some fundamental ethical principles with respect to animals. How should animals be treated humanely? This is a debate that hasn't come here."

One of the most unfortunate aspects of the passing of this bill was the failure of the American Civil Liberties Union to challenge it. The ACLU did indeed write a letter to Congress about the passing of the AETA, to caution against conflating illegal and legal protest, but the organization failed to challenge the real terrorism perpetuated by animal and earth exploitation industries, and ultimately consented to their worldview and validity.

In an October 30, 2006, letter to Chairman of the House Judiciary Committee F. James Sensenbrenner and Ranking Member John Conyers, the ACLU writes that it "does not oppose this bill, but believes that these minor changes are necessary to make the bill less likely to chill or threaten freedom of speech." Beyond proposed semantic clarifications, the ACLU mainly warns against broadening the law to include legal activities such as boycotts: "Legitimate expressive activity may result in economic damage. . . . Care must therefore be taken in penalizing economic damage to avoid infringing upon legitimate activity."

Thus, unlike dozens of animal protection groups who adamantly reject the AETA *en toto*, the ACLU "does not oppose the bill." In agreement with corporate interests, the ACLU assures the government it "does not condone violence or threats." It thereby dodges the complex question of the legitimacy of sabotage against exploitative industries. The ACLU uncritically accepts (1) the corporate–state definition of "violence" as intentional harm to *property*, (2) the legal definition of animals as "property," and (3) the use of the T-word to demonize animal liberationists rather than animal exploiters. Ultimately, the ACLU sides with the government against activists involved in illegal forms of liberation or sabotage, a problematic alliance in times of global ecocide. The ACLU thereby defends *the property rights* of industries to torture and slaughter billions of animals over the *moral rights* of animals to bodily integrity and a life free from exploitation and gratuitous violence.

The ACLU failed to ask the tough questions journalist Will Potter raised during his May 23, 2006 testimony before the House Committee holding a hearing on the AETA, and to follow Potter in identifying key inconsistencies in bill. Does the ACLU really think that their proposed modifications would be adequate to guarantee that the AETA doesn't trample on legal rights to protest? Are they completely ignorant and indifferent to the fact that the AEPA was just used to send the SHAC 7 to jail for the crime of protesting fraudulent research and heinous killing? And just where was the ACLU during the SHAC 7 trial, one of the most significant First Amendment cases in recent history? Why does the ACLU only recognize violations of the Constitution against human rights advocates? Do they think that animal rights activists are not citizens? Do they not recognize that tyrannical measures used against animal advocates today will be used against all citizens tomorrow? How can the world's premier civil rights institution [be] blatantly speciesist and bigoted toward animals? *Why will they come to the defense of the Ku Klux Klan but not the SHAC 7?* The ACLU's silence in the face of persecution of animal rights activists unfortunately is typical of most civil rights organizations that are too bigoted and myopic to grasp the implications of state repression of animal rights activists for human rights activists and all forms of dissent.

Animal Liberation as a New Social Movement

Corporate exploiters and Congress have taken the US down a perilous slippery slope, where it becomes difficult to distinguish between illegal and legal forms of dissent, between civil disobedience and terrorism, between PETA and Al Qaeda, and between liberating chickens from a factory farm and flying passenger planes into skyscrapers. The state protects the corporate exploiters who pull their purse strings and stuff their pockets with favors and cash.

The right to free speech ends as soon as you begin to exercise it. As the politics of nature—the struggle for liberation of animals and the earth—is the most dynamic fight today, one that poses a serious threat to corporate interests, animal and earth liberationists are under ferocious attack. The growing effectiveness of direct action anti-vivisection struggles will inevitably bring a reactionary and retaliatory response by the corporate–state complex to crack down on democratic political freedoms to protest, as well as new Draconian laws that represent a concerted effort by power brokers to crush the movement for animal liberation.

In the "home of the brave, land of the free," activists are followed by federal agents; their phone conversations and computer activity [are] monitored, their homes are raided, they are forced to testify before grand juries and pressured to "name names," they are targets of federal round ups, they are jailed for exercising constitutionally protected rights and liberties. Saboteurs receive stiffer prison sentences than rapists, bank robbers, and murderers. There has never been freedom of speech or action in the US, but in the post-9/11 climate, where the USA PATRIOT Act is the law of the land, not the Constitution and Bill of Rights, activists are demonized as terrorists—not just the Animal Liberation Front (ALF), Earth Liberation Front (ELF), and SHAC, but also completely legal and peaceful groups like Food Not Bombs and vegan outreach organizations.

The massive police resources of the US state are being used far more to thwart domestic dissent than to improve homeland insecurity. While Big Brother is obsessed with the email, conversations, and meetings of people who know a thing or two about the duties of citizenship, the airlines, railways, subways, city centers, and nuclear power plants remain completely vulnerable to an attack, which, according to the elites, is imminent.

The contemporary animal liberation movement is an *extension of the new social movements,* and as such issues "post-materialist" demands that are not about higher wages but the end to hierarchy and violence, and a new relation with the natural world.

Second, it is a *postindustrial movement,* operating within a global postindustrial society where the primary aspects of the economy no longer center on processing of physical materials as much as information, knowledge, science, and research. Transnational corporations such as Monsanto, pharmaceutical industries such as GlaxoSmithKline, AstraZeneca, Novartis, and Pfizer, and drug testing corporations such as Huntingdon Life Sciences show the importance of science and research for the postindustrial economy, and thus the relevance of the animal liberation movement.

This movement also is an *anti-globalization* movement in that the corporations it attacks often are transnational and global in scope, part of what I call the Global Vivisection Complex (GVC). The GVC is comprised of pharmaceutical industries, biotechnology industries, medical research industries, universities, and testing laboratories, all using animal experimentation to test and market their drugs. As animals are the gas and oil for these corporate science machines, the animal liberation movement has disrupted corporate supply chains, thwarted laboratory procedures, liberated captive slaves, and attacked the legitimacy of biomedical research as an effective scientific paradigm.

Fourth, the animal liberation movement is an *abolitionist movement,* seeking empty cages not bigger cages, demanding rights not "humane treatment" of the slaves, opposing the greatest institution of domination and slavery ever created—the empire of human supremacy over millions of species and billions of animal slaves.

To an important degree, the historical and socio-economic context for the emergence of the animal advocacy movement (in all its diverse tendencies and aspects) is the industrialization of animal exploitation and killing. This is dramatically evident with the growth of slaughterhouses at the turn of the 20th century, the emergence and globalization of factory farming after World War II, and the subsequent growth of research capital and animal experimentation. To this, one would have to add expanding human population numbers, the social construction of carnivorous appetites, and the rise of fast food industries which demand the exploitation and massacre of ever-growing numbers of animals, now in the tens of billions on a global scale. Along with other horrors and modes of animal exploitation, the industrialization, mechanization, and globalization of animal exploitation called into being an increasingly broad, growing, and powerful animal liberation movement.

Animal liberation builds on the great abolitionist struggle of past centuries and is the abolitionist movement of our day. Animal liberationists are waging war against the oldest and last form of slavery to be formally abolished—the exploitation of nonhuman animals. Just as the modern economy of Europe, the British colonies in America, and the United States after the Revolutionary War were once entirely dependent on the trafficking in human slaves, so now the current global economy would crash if all animal slaves were freed from every lab, cage and other mode of exploitation. Animal liberation is in fact the anti-slavery movement of the present age and its moral and economic ramifications are as world-shaking, possible more so, than the abolition of the human slavery movement (which of course itself still exists in some sectors of the world in the form of sweatshops, child sex slavery, forced female prostitution, and the like).

The animal liberation movement is a profound threat to the corporate–state complex and hierarchical society in two ways.

First, it is a serious economic threat, as the planetary capitalist system thrives off animal exploitation with the meat/dairy and biomedical research industries. In the UK, for instance, where the animal rights movement has been particularly effective, drug-makers are the third most important contributor to the economy after power generation and oil industries. The

animal rights movement has emerged as a powerful anti-capitalist and anti-(corporate) globalization force in its ability to monkeywrench the planetary vivisection machine and challenge transnational corporations such as HLS, GlaxoSmithKline, and Novartis.

Second, the animal rights movement is a potent ideological and psychological threat. The fight for animal liberation demands radical transformations in the habits, practices, values, and mindset of all human beings as it also entails a fundamental restructuring of social institutions and economic systems predicated on exploitative practices. The philosophy of animal liberation assaults the identities and worldviews that portray humans as conquering Lords and Masters of nature, and it requires entirely new ways of relating to animals and the earth. Animal liberation is a direct attack on the power human beings—whether in premodern or modern, non-Western or Western societies—have claimed over animals, since at least the dawn of agricultural society ten thousand years ago.

Total Liberation

As the dynamics that brought about global warming, rainforest destruction, species extinction, and poisoning of communities are not reducible to any single factor or cause—be it agricultural society, the rise of states, anthropocentrism, speciesism, patriarchy, racism, colonialism, industrialism, technocracy, or capitalism—all radical groups and orientations that can effectively challenge the ideologies and institutions implicated in domination and ecological destruction have a relevant role to play in the global social-environmental struggle. While standpoints such as deep ecology, social ecology, ecofeminism, animal liberation, Black liberation, and the Earth Liberation Front are all important, none can accomplish systemic social transformation by itself. Working together, however, through a diversity of critiques and tactics that mobilize different communities, a flank of militant groups and positions can drive a battering ram into the structures of power and domination and open the door to a new future.

Although there is diversity in unity, there must also be unity in diversity. Solidarity can emerge in recognition of the fact that all forms of oppression are directly or indirectly related to the values, institutions, and *system* of global capitalism and related hierarchical structures. To be unified and effective, however, anti-capitalist and anti-imperialist alliances require mutual sharing, respectful learning, and psychological growth, such that, for instance, black liberationists, ecofeminists, and animal liberationists can help one another overcome racism, sexism, and speciesism.

The larger context for current dynamics in the animal liberation movement involves the emergence of the neoliberal project (as a response to the opening of the markets that was made necessary by the continuous expansion of transnational corporations in the post-war period) which was crucial in the elites' effort to destroy socialism and social democracy of any kind, to privatize all social structures, to gain total control of all resource markets and dwindling resources, and to snuff out all resistance. The animal rights/liberation

movement has come under such intense fire because it has emerged as a threat to operations and profits of postindustrial capital (heavily rooted in research and therefore animal experimentation) and as a significant form of resistance. The transnational elite want the fire crushed before its example of resistance becomes a conflagration.

Conversely, the animal liberation movement is most effective not only as a single-issue focus to emancipate animals from human exploitation, but to join a larger resistance movement opposed to exploitation and hierarchies of any and all kinds. Clearly, SHAC and the ALF alone are not going to bring down transnational capitalism, pressuring HLS and raiding fur farms and laboratories will not themselves ignite revolutionary change, and are more rear-guard, defensive actions. The project to emancipate animals, in other words, is integrally related to the struggle to emancipate humans and the battle for a viable natural world. To the extent that the animal liberation movement grasps the big picture that links animal and human oppression struggles as one, and seeks to uncover the roots of hierarchy including that of humans over nature, they can be viewed as a profound new liberation movement that has a crucial place in the planetary struggles against injustice, oppression, exploitation, war, violence, capitalist neo-liberalism, and the destruction of the natural world and biodiversity.

Yet, given the profound relation between the human domination of animals and the crisis—social, ethical, and environmental—in the human world and its relation to the natural world, the animal liberation movement is in a unique position to articulate the importance of new relations between human and human, human and animal, and human and nature.

New social movements and Greens have failed to realize their radical potential. They have abandoned their original demands for radical social change and become integrated into capitalist structures that have eliminated "existing socialist countries" as well as social democracies within the present neoliberal globalization which has become dominant. A new revolutionary force must therefore emerge, one that will build on the achievements of classical democratic, libertarian socialist, and anarchist traditions; incorporate radical green, feminist, and indigenous struggles; synthesize animal, Earth, and human liberation standpoints; and build a global social-ecological revolution capable of abolishing transnational capitalism so that just and ecological societies can be constructed in its place.

Notes

For Feinstein's pathetic capitulation to the Green Scare and her sordid alliance with neo-McCarthyite Senator James "Global Warming is a Myth" Inhofe (R-Okla.), see her press release. . . .

The text of the "Animal Enterprise Protection Act of 1992" is available online.

In states such as Oregon and California, related legislation has already passed which declares it a felony terrorist offense to enter any animal facility with a camera or video recorder "with the intent to defame the facility or facility's owner." See Steven Best, "It's War: The Escalating Battle Between Activists and the Corporate-State Complex," in *Terrorists or Freedom*

Fighters? Reflections on the Liberation of Animals (Lantern Books, 2004), pp. 300–339 (eds. Steven Best and Anthony J. Nocella II).

For a more detailed analysis of the SHAC struggle in the context of political economy, see Steven Best and Richard Kahn, "Trial By Fire: The SHAC 7, Globalization, and the Future of Democracy," *Animal Liberation Philosophy and Policy Journal,* Volume II, Issue 2, 2004 . . .

On the SHAC 7 trial, see Steven Best and Richard Kahn, "Trial By Fire: The SHAC7, Globalization, and the Future of Democracy."

For the text of S3880, the final bill that passed in both houses, see . . .

Will Potter, "Analysis of Animal Enterprise Terrorism Act."

"Why Oppose AETA."

. . . Kucinich also challenged the AETA as being redundant and created a "specific classification" to repress legitimate dissent.

The ACLU letter to Congress is available at . . .

For a list of animal advocacy groups opposed to the AETA, see . . .

For Potter's testimony before the House Committee on the Judiciary Subcommittee on Crime, Terrorism, and Homeland Security see . . .

EXPLORING THE ISSUE

Is "Animal Rights" Just Another Excuse for Terrorism?

Critical Thinking and Reflection

1. What is the difference between the "animal rights" and the "animal welfare" movements?
2. Why must drugs be tested for safety and efficacy?
3. Should extreme forms of protest be restrained for the good of society?
4. Do all animals (including cockroaches, for instance) have rights? If not, where do we draw the line?

Is There Common Ground?

Both the animal welfare and animal rights movements are rooted in awareness of past abuses of animals. Unfortunately, animal abuse is not just in the past. It shows up far too often in the daily news.

1. Check your local paper (or favorite news site) for stories on animal abuse. They may involve puppy mills, farms, dog tracks, dog or cock fighting, and more. Discuss what is being done about these cases, and by whom (animal welfare or animal rights groups).
2. Do some animals seem more deserving of "rights" than others? Does intelligence matter? Or, how closely are they related to us? (There have been proposals to grant great apes legal rights very similar to human rights; in Spain, in 2008, such rights were actually granted; see http://www.time.com/time/world/article/0,8599,1824206,00.html.)
3. How is animal welfare protected in your state? (See http://www.animallaw.com/.)

ISSUE 19

Should We Reject the "Transhumanist" Goal of the Genetically, Electronically, and Mechanically Enhanced Human Being?

YES: M. J. McNamee and S. D. Edwards, from "Transhumanism, Medical Technology, and Slippery Slopes," *Journal of Medical Ethics* (September 2006)

NO: Maxwell J. Mehlman, from "Biomedical Enhancements: Entering a New Era," *Issues in Science and Technology* (Spring 2009)

Learning Outcomes

After studying this issue, students will be able to:

1. Explain what transhumanism is.
2. Explain why ethicists worry about "slippery slopes."
3. Discuss why some people find the idea of enhancing the human body and mind objectionable.
4. Discuss whether government should subsidize technologies that hold the potential to exacerbate differences among people.

ISSUE SUMMARY

YES: M. J. McNamee and S. D. Edwards argue that the difficulty of showing that the human body *should* (rather than *can*) be enhanced in ways espoused by the transhumanists amounts to an objection to transhumanism.

NO: Maxwell J. Mehlman argues that the era of routine biomedical enhancements is coming. Since the technology cannot be banned, it must be regulated and even subsidized to ensure that it does not create an unfair society.

In the early 1970s, scientists first discovered that it was technically possible to move genes—biological material that determines a living organism's physical makeup—from one organism to another and thus (in principle) to give bacteria, plants, and animals new features and correct genetic defects of the sort that cause many diseases, such as cystic fibrosis. Most researchers in molecular genetics were excited by the potentialities that suddenly seemed within their grasp. However, a few researchers—as well as many people outside the field— were disturbed by the idea. Among other things, they feared that we were on the verge of an era when people would be so modified that they would no longer be human. Some critics were also suspicious of the researchers' motives. Andrew Kimbrell, *The Human Body Shop: The Engineering and Marketing of Life* (HarperSanFrancisco, 1993), thought the development of genetic engineering was so marked by scandal, ambition, and moral blindness that society should be deeply suspicious of its purported benefits.

Since then the idea that human beings will one day be enhanced has grown. The idea now encompasses genetic changes to cure or prevent disease and modify height, muscle strength, and cognitive capabilities; the use of chemicals to improve performance in sports; and even the incorporation of electronic and robotic elements in the human body to add senses and enhance memory, thinking abilities, strength, and a great deal more. In fact, the idea has become a movement known as transhumanism that "promotes an interdisciplinary approach to understanding and evaluating the opportunities for enhancing the human condition and the human organism opened up by the advancement of technology" (see the Humanity+ site at http://humanityplus .org/). The goal is to eliminate aging, disease, and suffering. The transhumanist vision extends to "posthumanism," when what human beings become will make present-day humans look like chimpanzees by comparison. It even includes the possibility of uploading human minds into computers! See George Dvorsky, "Better Living Through Transhumanism," *Journal of Evolution & Technology* (September 2008).

Some people find this vision frightening. Francis Fukuyama, "Transhumanism," *Foreign Policy* (September/October 2004), has called transhumanism "the world's most dangerous idea." Critics find changing human form and capability objectionable because they believe the result is in some sense unnatural. They believe that making some people more capable will exacerbate social distinctions and put those who can afford the changes in the position of old-fashioned aristocracies. Life will be even more unfair than it is today.

Michael Bess, "Icarus 2.0: A Historian's Perspective on Human Biological Enhancement," *Technology and Culture* (January 2008), finds transhumanism in essence dehumanizing: "The technologies of enhancement threaten human dignity precisely because they tempt us to think of a person as an entity that can be 'improved.' To take this step is to break down human personhood into a series of quantifiable traits—resistance to disease, intelligence, and so forth— that are subject to augmentation or alteration. The danger in doing this lies in reducing individuals to the status of products, artifacts to be modified and reshaped according to our own preferences, like any other commodity. In this

act, inevitably, we risk losing touch with the quality of intrinsic value that all humans share equally, no matter what their traits may be. In this sense, the well-intentioned effort to enhance a person can result in treating them as a mere *thing*."

Josh Fischman, "A Better Life with Bionics," *National Geographic* (January 2010), describes current work in developing prostheses controlled by nerve signals from nerves that have been surgically rerouted to communicate more effectively with the artificial limb's circuitry, a clear example of "improvement" of the human being. He also discusses electronic cochlear implants and artificial retinas. An accompanying editorial comment says, "Bionics is technology at its most ingenious and humane."

Among those who favor transhumanism, few come through more strongly than James Hughes, executive director of the Institute for Ethics & Emerging Technologies (http://ieet.org/). He has argued vigorously that enhancement technologies such as genetic engineering offer "such good that the risks are dwarfed" and finds "faith in the potential unlimited improvability of human nature and expansion of human powers far more satisfying than a resignation to our current limits." See his "Embracing Change with All Four Arms: A Post-Humanist Defense of Genetic Engineering," *Eubios Journal of Asian and International Bioethics* (June 1996). Nicholas Agar, "Whereto Transhumanism? The Literature Reaches Critical Mass," *Hastings Center Report* (May–June 2007), finds that "transhumanism is a movement brimming with fresh ideas. Transhumanists succeed in making the intuitive appeal of posthumanity obvious even if they don't yet have the arguments to compel everybody else to accept their vision." Julian Savalescu and Nick Bostrom (a prominent founder of the transhumanism movement) provide a very positive overview in *Human Enhancement* (Oxford University Press, 2009). Susan Schneider, "Future Minds: Transhumanism, Cognitive Enhancement and the Nature of Persons," in Vardit Ravitsky, Autumn Fiester, and Arthur L. Caplan, eds., *The Penn Center Guide to Bioethics* (Springer, 2009), considers the question of whether people who have undergone extreme modifications are still the people they were before. Is personhood affected? Is the soul affected? "There are," she writes, "some serious issues which require working out." James Wilson, "Transhumanism and Moral Equality," *Bioethics* (October, 2007), finds that objections to transhumanism on the grounds that enhanced humans will be considered morally superior to unenhanced humans are groundless, for "once we understand the basis for human equality, it is clear that anyone who now has sufficient capacities to count as a person from the moral point of view will continue to count as one even if others are fundamentally enhanced; and it is [a mistake] to think that a creature which had even far greater capacities than an unenhanced human being should count as more than an equal from the moral point of view." David Gelles, "Immortality 2.0," *The Futurist* (January–February 2009), concludes that "skepticism of transhumanism is, arguably, natural. At the deepest level, living forever interferes with everything we understand about the world. . . . But such concerns may not matter any more." The change is already under way, and we may be underestimating how far it will go. See also Jonathan Weiner, *Long for This World: The Strange Science of Immortality* (Ecco,

2010). However, A. Rajczi, "One Danger of Biomedical Enhancements," *Bioethics* (July 2008), cautions, "By spending too much time, energy, and resources on enhancements, we could set back our pursuit of our deepest goals such as living happily and leading ethical lives." Philippe Verdoux, "Transhumanism, Progress and the Future," *Journal of Evolution & Technology* (July 2009), finds pursuing the transhumanist dream the safest route into the future. Philip Hefner, "The Animal That Aspires to Be an Angel: The Challenge of Transhumanism," *Dialog: A Journal of Theology* (Summer 2009), finds that transhumanism "represents a fundamental challenge to our understanding of human nature, and in particular [with] what God has created us to become." Joanna Zylinska, "Playing God, Playing Adam: The Politics and Ethics of Enhancement," *Journal of Bioethical Inquiry* (June 2010), takes a different view of humanity's deepest goals and nature, for humanity coevolves with technology.

One way in which the change is already upon us appears in the realm of sports. With "Drugs in Sport," J. C. McGrath and D. A. Cowan introduce a special issue of the *British Journal of Pharmacology* (June 2008), containing 11 articles covering the major groups of drugs used illicitly in sports work and making the case that using drugs to enhance performance "undermines the [fair play] ethos of sport." Steven Kotler, "Juicing 3.0," *Popular Science* (August 2008), notes that athletes are not just abusing steroids. Many enhancement techniques—using reaction time stimulants, hormones that affect muscle, and gene replacement—are going to become commonplace in the next few years. Researchers are already working on ways to detect gene doping and other enhancements; see Ronald Bailey, "Testing Your Strength," *Reason* (April 2007), and Theodore Friedmann, Olivier Rabin, and Mark S. Frankel, "Gene Doping and Sport," *Science* (February 5, 2010). However, it seems likely that future enhancement techniques may be very difficult to detect. It may be necessary to accept enhancements as a legitimate part of athletics and other realms of endeavor.

In the YES selection, M. J. McNamee and S. D. Edwards discuss the idea that even to start on the transhumanist agenda is to set humanity on a "slippery slope" leading to disaster. They argue that of the several types of slippery slope, the one most threatening to transhumanism is the "arbitrary" slippery slope, meaning that the progression from the first change to the last is not based on any sense of the moral good, but only on subjective preference. They argue that this poses a challenge to transhumanists, to show that the changes they embrace *should* be embraced rather than just *can* be embraced. In the NO selection, professor of bioethics Maxwell J. Mehlman argues that the era of routine biomedical enhancements is coming. Since the technology cannot be banned, it must be regulated and even subsidized to ensure that it does not create an unfair society.

**M. J. McNamee and
S. D. Edwards**

Transhumanism, Medical Technology, and Slippery Slopes

No less a figure than Francis Fukuyama recently labelled transhumanism as "the world's most dangerous idea." Such an eye-catching condemnation almost certainly denotes an issue worthy of serious consideration, especially given the centrality of biomedical technology to its aims. In this article, we consider transhumanism as an ideology that seeks to evangelise its human-enhancing aims. Given that transhumanism covers a broad range of ideas, we distinguish moderate conceptions from strong ones and find the strong conceptions more problematic than the moderate ones. We also offer a critique of Boström's position published in this journal. We discuss various forms of slippery slope arguments that may be used for and against transhumanism and highlight one particular criticism, moral arbitrariness, which undermines both forms of transhumanism.

What Is Transhumanism?

At the beginning of the 21st century, we find ourselves in strange times; facts and fantasy find their way together in ethics, medicine and philosophy journals and websites. Key sites of contestation include the very idea of human nature, the place of embodiment within medical ethics and, more specifically, the systematic reflections on the place of medical and other technologies in conceptions of the good life. A reflection of this situation is captured by Dyens who writes,

> What we are witnessing today is the very convergence of environments, systems, bodies, and ontology toward and into the intelligent matter. We can no longer speak of the human condition or even of the posthuman condition. We must now refer to the intelligent condition.

We wish to evaluate the contents of such dialogue and to discuss, if not the death of human nature, then at least its dislocation and derogation in the thinkers who label themselves transhumanists.

One difficulty for critics of transhumanism is that a wide range of views fall under its label. Not merely are there idiosyncrasies of individual academics, but there does not seem to exist an absolutely agreed on definition of

From *Journal of Medical Ethics*, volume 32, 2006, pp. 513–518. Copyright © 2006 by Institute of Medical Ethics. Reprinted by permission of BMJ Publishing Group via Rightslink.

transhumanism. One can find not only substantial differences between key authors and the disparate disciplinary nuances of their exhortations, but also subtle variations of its chief representatives in the offerings of people. It is to be expected that any ideology transforms over time and not least of all in response to internal and external criticism. Yet, the transhumanism critic faces a further problem of identifying a robust target that stays still sufficiently long to locate it properly in these web-driven days without constructing a "straw man" to knock over with the slightest philosophical breeze. For the purposes of targeting a sufficiently substantial target, we identify the writings of one of its clearest and intellectually robust proponents, the Oxford philosopher and cofounder of the World Transhumanist Association, Nick Boström, who has written recently in these pages of transhumanism's desire to make good the "half-baked" project that is human nature.

Before specifically evaluating Boström's position, it is best first to offer a global definition for transhumanism and then to locate it among the range of views that fall under the heading. One of the most celebrated advocates of transhumanism is Max More, whose website reads "no more gods, nor more faith, no more timid holding back. The future belongs to posthumanity." We will have a clearer idea then of the kinds of position transhumanism stands in direct opposition to. Specifically, More asserts,

> "Transhumanism" is a blanket term given to the school of thought that refuses to accept traditional human limitations such as death, disease and other biological frailties. Transhumans are typically interested in a variety of futurist topics, including space migration, mind upload- ing and cryonic suspension. Transhumans are also extremely interested in more immediate subjects such as bio- and nano-technology, com- puters and neurology. Transhumans deplore the standard paradigms that attempt to render our world comfortable at the sake of human fulfilment.

Strong transhumanism advocates see themselves engaged in a project, the purpose of which is to overcome the limits of human nature. Whether this is the foundational claim, or merely the central claim, is not clear. These limitations—one may describe them simply as features of human nature, as the idea of labelling them as limitations is itself to take up a negative stance towards them—concern appearance, human sensory capacities, intelligence, lifespan and vulnerability to harm. According to the extreme transhumanism programme, technology can be used to vastly enhance a person's intelligence; to tailor their appearance to what they desire; to lengthen their lifespan, per- haps to immortality; and to reduce vastly their vulnerability to harm. This can be done by exploitation of various kinds of technology, including genetic engi- neering, cybernetics, computation and nanotechnology. Whether technology will continue to progress sufficiently, and sufficiently predictably, is of course quite another matter.

Advocates of transhumanism argue that recruitment or deployment of these various types of technology can produce people who are intelligent and immortal, but who are not members of the species *Homo sapiens*. Their species

type will be ambiguous—for example, if they are cyborgs (part human, part machine)—or, if they are wholly machines, they will lack any common genetic features with human beings. A legion of labels covers this possibility; we find in Dyen's recently translated book a variety of cultural bodies, perhaps the most extreme being cyberpunks:

> . . . a profound misalignment between existence and its manifestation. This misalignment produces bodies so transformed, so dissociated, and so asynchronized, that their only outcome is gross mutation. Cyberpunk bodies are horrible, strange and mysterious (think of *Alien*, *Robocop*, *Terminator*, etc.), for they have no real attachment to any biological structure.

Perhaps a reasonable claim is encapsulated in the idea that such entities will be posthuman. The extent to which posthuman might be synonymous with transhumanism is not clear. Extreme transhumanists strongly support such developments.

At the other end of transhumanism is a much less radical project, which is simply the project to use technology to enhance human characteristics—for example, beauty, lifespan and resistance to disease. In this less extreme project, there is no necessary aspiration to shed human nature or human genetic constitution, just to augment it with technology where possible and where desired by the person.

Who Is for Transhumanism?

At present it seems to be a movement based mostly in North America, although there are some adherents from the UK. Among its most intellectually sophisticated proponents is Nick Boström. Perhaps the most outspoken supporters of transhumanism are people who see it simply as an issue of free choice. It may simply be the case that moderate transhumanists are libertarians at the core. In that case, transhumanism merely supplies an overt technological dimension to libertarianism. If certain technological developments are possible, which they as competent choosers desire, then they should not be prevented from acquiring the technologically driven enhancements they desire. One obvious line of criticism here may be in relation to the inequality that necessarily arises with respect to scarce goods and services distributed by market mechanisms. We will elaborate this point in the Transhumanism and slippery slopes section.

So, one group of people for the transhumanism project sees it simply as a way of improving their own life by their own standards of what counts as an improvement. For example, they may choose to purchase an intervention, which will make them more intelligent or even extend their life by 200 years. (Of course it is not self-evident that everyone would regard this as an improvement.) A less vociferous group sees the transhumanism project as not so much bound to the expansion of autonomy (notwithstanding our criticism that will necessarily be effected only in the sphere of economic consumer choice) as one that has the potential to improve the quality of life for humans in general.

For this group, the relationship between transhumanism and the general good is what makes transhumanism worthy of support. For the other group, the worth of transhumanism is in its connection with their own conception of what is good for them, with the extension of their personal life choices.

What Can Be Said in Its Favour?

Of the many points for transhumanism, we note three. Firstly, transhumanism seems to facilitate two aims that have commanded much support. The use of technology to improve humans is something we pretty much take for granted. Much good has been achieved with low-level technology in the promotion of public health. The construction of sewage systems, clean water supplies, etc, is all work to facilitate this aim and is surely good work, work which aims at, and in this case achieves, a good. Moreover, a large portion of the modern biomedical enterprise is another example of a project that aims at generating this good too.

Secondly, proponents of transhumanism say it presents an opportunity to plan the future development of human beings, the species *Homo sapiens*. Instead of this being left to the evolutionary process and its exploitation of random mutations, transhumanism presents a hitherto unavailable option: tailoring the development of human beings to an ideal blueprint. Precisely whose ideal gets blueprinted is a point that we deal with later.

Thirdly, in the spirit of work in ethics that makes use of a technical idea of personhood, the view that moral status is independent of membership of a particular species (or indeed any biological species), transhumanism presents a way in which moral status can be shown to be bound to intellectual capacity rather than to human embodiment as such or human vulnerability in the capacity of embodiment.

What Can Be Said Against It?

Critics point to consequences of transhumanism, which they find unpalatable. One possible consequence feared by some commentators is that, in effect, transhumanism will lead to the existence of two distinct types of being, the human and the posthuman. The human may be incapable of breeding with the posthuman and will be seen as having a much lower moral standing. Given that, as Buchanan *et al.* note, much moral progress, in the West at least, is founded on the category of the human in terms of rights claims, if we no longer have a common humanity, what rights, if any, ought to be enjoyed by transhumans? This can be viewed either as a criticism (we poor humans are no longer at the top of the evolutionary tree) or simply as a critical concern that invites further argumentation. We shall return to this idea in the final section, by way of identifying a deeper problem with the open-endedness of transhumanism that builds on this recognition.

In the same vein, critics may argue that transhumanism will increase inequalities between the rich and the poor. The rich can afford to make use of transhumanism, but the poor will not be able to. Indeed, we may come to

think of such people as deficient, failing to achieve a new heightened level of normal functioning. In the opposing direction, critical observers may say that transhumanism is, in reality, an irrelevance, as very few will be able to use the technological developments even if they ever manifest themselves. A further possibility is that transhumanism could lead to the extinction of humans and posthumans, for things are just as likely to turn out for the worse as for the better (e.g., those for precautionary principle).

One of the deeper philosophical objections comes from a very traditional source. Like all such utopian visions, transhumanism rests on some conception of good. So just as humanism is founded on the idea that humans are the measure of all things and that their fulfilment is to be found in the powers of reason extolled and extended in culture and education, so too transhumanism has a vision of the good, albeit one loosely shared. For one group of transhumanists, the good is the expansion of personal choice. Given that autonomy is so widely valued, why not remove the barriers to enhanced autonomy by various technological interventions? Theological critics especially, but not exclusively, object to what they see as the imperialising of autonomy. Elshtain lists the three c's: choice, consent and control. These, she asserts, are the dominant motifs of modern American culture. And there is, of course, an army of communitarians ready to provide support in general moral and political matters to this line of criticism. One extension of this line of transhumanism thinking is to align the valorisation of autonomy with economic rationality, for we may as well be motivated by economic concerns as by moral ones where the market is concerned. As noted earlier, only a small minority may be able to access this technology (despite Boström's naive disclaimer for democratic transhumanism), so the technology necessary for transhumanist transformations is unlikely to be prioritised in the context of artificially scarce public health resources. One other population attracted to transhumanism will be the elite sports world, fuelled by the media commercialisation complex—where mere mortals will get no more than a glimpse of the transhuman in competitive physical contexts. There may be something of a double-binding character to this consumerism. The poor, at once removed from the possibility of such augmentation, pay (per view) for the pleasure of their envy.

If we argue against the idea that the good cannot be equated with what people choose simpliciter, it does not follow that we need to reject the requisite medical technology outright. Against the more moderate transhumanists, who see transhumanism as an opportunity to enhance the general quality of life for humans, it is nevertheless true that their position presupposes some conception of the good. What kind of traits is best engineered into humans: disease resistance or parabolic hearing? And unsurprisingly, transhumanists disagree about precisely what "objective goods" to select for installation into humans or posthumans.

Some radical critics of transhumanism see it as a threat to morality itself. This is because they see morality as necessarily connected to the kind of vulnerability that accompanies human nature. Think of the idea of human rights and the power this has had in voicing concern about the plight of especially vulnerable human beings. As noted earlier a transhumanist may be thought

to be beyond humanity and as neither enjoying its rights nor its obligations. Why would a transhuman be moved by appeals to human solidarity? Once the prospect of posthumanism emerges, the whole of morality is thus threatened because the existence of human nature itself is under threat.

One further objection voiced by Habermas is that interfering with the process of human conception, and by implication human constitution, deprives humans of the "naturalness which so far has been a part of the taken-for-granted background of our self-understanding as a species" and "Getting used to having human life biotechnologically at the disposal of our contingent preferences cannot help but change our normative self-understanding."

On this account, our self-understanding would include, for example, our essential vulnerability to disease, ageing and death. Suppose the strong trans-humanism project is realised. We are no longer thus vulnerable: immortality is a real prospect. Nevertheless, conceptual caution must be exercised here—even transhumanists will be susceptible in the manner that Hobbes noted. Even the strongest are vulnerable in their sleep. But the kind of vulnerability transhumanism seeks to overcome is of the internal kind (not Hobbes's external threats). We are reminded of Woody Allen's famous remark that he wanted to become immortal, not by doing great deeds but simply by not dying. This will result in a radical change in our self-understanding, which has inescapably normative elements to it that need to be challenged. Most radically, this change in self-understanding may take the form of a change in what we view as a good life. Hitherto a human life, this would have been assumed to be finite. Transhumanists suggest that even now this may change with appropriate technology and the "right" motivation.

Do the changes in self-understanding presented by transhumanists (and genetic manipulation) necessarily have to represent a change for the worse? As discussed earlier, it may be that the technology that generates the possibility of transhumanism can be used for the good of humans—for example, to promote immunity to disease or to increase quality of life. Is there really an intrinsic connection between acquisition of the capacity to bring about transhumanism and moral decline? Perhaps Habermas's point is that moral decline is simply more likely to occur once radical enhancement technologies are adopted as a practice that is not intrinsically evil or morally objectionable. But how can this be known in advance? This raises the spectre of slippery slope arguments.

But before we discuss such slopes, let us note that the kind of approach (whether characterised as closed-minded or sceptical) Boström seems to dislike is one he calls speculative. He dismisses as speculative the idea that offspring may think themselves lesser beings, commodifications of their parents' egoistic desires (or some such). None the less, having pointed out the lack of epistemological standing of such speculation, he invites us to his own apparently more congenial position:

> We might speculate, instead, that germ-line enhancements will lead to more love and parental dedication. Some mothers and fathers might find it easier to love a child who, thanks to enhancements, is bright, beautiful, healthy, and happy. The practice of germ-line enhancement might

lead to better treatment of people with disabilities, because a general demystification of the genetic contributions to human traits could make it clearer that people with disabilities are not to blame for their disabilities and a decreased incidence of some disabilities could lead to more assistance being available for the remaining affected people to enable them to live full, unrestricted lives through various technological and social supports. Speculating about possible psychological or cultural effects of germ-line engineering can therefore cut both ways. Good consequences no less than bad ones are possible. In the absence of sound arguments for the view that the negative consequences would predominate, such speculations provide no reason against moving forward with the technology. Ruminations over hypothetical side effects may serve to make us aware of things that could go wrong so that we can be on the lookout for untoward developments. By being aware of the perils in advance, we will be in a better position to take preventive countermeasures.

Following Boström's speculation then, what grounds for hope exist? Beyond speculation, what kinds of arguments does Boström offer? Well, most people may think that the burden of proof should fall to the transhumanists. Not so, according to Boström. Assuming the likely enormous benefits, he turns the tables on this intuition—not by argument but by skilful rhetorical speculation. We quote for accuracy of representation (emphasis added):

> Only after a fair comparison of the risks with the likely positive consequences can any conclusion based on a cost-benefit analysis be reached. In the case of germ-line enhancements, the potential gains are enormous. Only rarely, however, are the potential gains discussed, perhaps because they are too obvious to be of much theoretical interest. By contrast, uncovering subtle and non-trivial ways in which manipulating our genome could undermine deep values is philosophically a lot more challenging. But if we think about it, we recognize that the promise of genetic enhancements is anything but insignificant. Being free from severe genetic diseases would be good, as would having a mind that can learn more quickly, or having a more robust immune system. Healthier, wittier, happier people may be able to reach new levels culturally. To achieve a significant enhancement of human capacities would be to embark on the transhuman journey of exploration of some of the modes of being that are not accessible to us as we are currently constituted, possibly to discover and to instantiate important new values. On an even more basic level, genetic engineering holds great potential for alleviating unnecessary human suffering. Every day that the introduction of effective human genetic enhancement is delayed is a day of lost individual and cultural potential, and a day of torment for many unfortunate sufferers of diseases that could have been prevented. Seen in this light, *proponents of a ban or a moratorium on human genetic modification must take on a heavy burden of proof* in order to have the balance of reason tilt in their favor.

Now one way in which such a balance of reason may be had is in the idea of a slippery slope argument. We now turn to that.

Transhumanism and Slippery Slopes

A proper assessment of transhumanism requires consideration of the objection that acceptance of the main claims of transhumanism will place us on a slippery slope. Yet, paradoxically, both proponents and detractors of transhumanism may exploit slippery slope arguments in support of their position. It is necessary therefore to set out the various arguments that fall under this title so that we can better characterise arguments for and against transhumanism. We shall therefore examine three such attempts but argue that the arbitrary slippery slope may undermine all versions of transhumanists, although not every enhancement proposed by them.

Schauer offers the following essentialist analysis of slippery slope arguments. A "pure" slippery slope is one where a "particular act, seemingly innocuous when taken in isolation, may yet lead to a future host of similar but increasingly pernicious events." Abortion and euthanasia are classic candidates for slippery slope arguments in public discussion and policy making. Against this, however, there is no reason to suppose that the future events (acts or policies) down the slope need to display similarities—indeed we may propose that they will lead to a whole range of different, although equally unwished for, consequences. The vast array of enhancements proposed by transhumanists would not be captured under this conception of a slippery slope because of their heterogeneity. Moreover, as Sternglantz notes, Schauer undermines his case when arguing that greater linguistic precision undermines the slippery slope and that indirect consequences often bolster slippery slope arguments. It is as if the slippery slopes would cease in a world with greater linguistic precision or when applied only to direct consequences. These views do not find support in the later literature. Schauer does, however, identify three non-slippery slope arguments where the advocate's aim is (a) to show that the bottom of a proposed slope has been arrived at; (b) to show that a principle is excessively broad; (c) to highlight how granting authority to X will make it more likely that an undesirable outcome will be achieved. Clearly (a) cannot properly be called a slippery slope argument in itself, while (b) and (c) often have some role in slippery slope arguments.

The excessive breadth principle can be subsumed under Bernard Williams's distinction between slippery slope arguments with (a) horrible results and (b) arbitrary results. According to Williams, the nature of the bottom of the slope allows us to determine which category a particular argument falls under. Clearly, the most common form is the slippery slope to a horrible result argument. Walton goes further in distinguishing three types: (a) thin end of the wedge or precedent arguments; (b) Sorites arguments; and (c) domino-effect arguments. Importantly, these arguments may be used both by antagonists and also by advocates of transhumanism. We shall consider the advocates of transhumanism first.

In the thin end of the wedge slippery slopes, allowing P will set a precedent that will allow further precedents (Pn) taken to an unspecified problematic terminus. Is it necessary that the end point has to be bad? Of course this is the typical linguistic meaning of the phrase "slippery slopes." Nevertheless, we may turn the tables here and argue that [the] slopes may be viewed positively

too. Perhaps a new phrase will be required to capture ineluctable slides (ascents?) to such end points. This would be somewhat analogous to the ideas of vicious and virtuous cycles. So transhumanists could argue that, once the artificial generation of life through technologies of in vitro fertilisation was thought permissible, the slope was foreseeable, and transhumanists are doing no more than extending that life-creating and fashioning impulse.

In Sorites arguments, the inability to draw clear distinctions has the effect that allowing P will not allow us to consistently deny Pn. This slope follows the form of the Sorites paradox, where taking a grain of sand from a heap does not prevent our recognising or describing the heap as such, even though it is not identical with its former state. At the heart of the problem with such arguments is the idea of conceptual vagueness. Yet the logical distinctions used by philosophers are often inapplicable in the real world. Transhumanists may well seize on this vagueness and apply a Sorites argument as follows: as therapeutic interventions are currently morally permissible, and there is no clear distinction between treatment and enhancement, enhancement interventions are morally permissible too. They may ask whether we can really distinguish categorically between the added functionality of certain prosthetic devices and sonar senses.

In domino-effect arguments, the domino conception of the slippery slope, we have what others often refer to as a causal slippery slope. Once P is allowed, a causal chain will be effected allowing Pn and so on to follow, which will precipitate increasingly bad consequences.

In what ways can slippery slope arguments be used against transhumanism? What is wrong with transhumanism? Or, better, is there a point at which we can say transhumanism is objectionable? One particular strategy adopted by proponents of transhumanism falls clearly under the aspect of the thin end of the wedge conception of the slippery slope. Although some aspects of their ideology seem aimed at unqualified goods, there seems to be no limit to the aspirations of transhumanism as they cite the powers of other animals and substances as potential modifications for the transhumanist. Although we can admire the sonic capacities of the bat, the elastic strength of lizards' tongues and the endurability of Kevlar in contrast with traditional construction materials used in the body, their transplantation into humans is, to coin Kass's celebrated label, "repugnant."

Although not all transhumanists would support such extreme enhancements (if that is indeed what they are), less radical advocates use justifications that are based on therapeutic lines up front with the more Promethean aims less explicitly advertised. We can find many examples of this manoeuvre. Take, for example, the Cognitive Enhancement Research Institute in California. Prominently displayed on its website front page . . . we read, "Do you know somebody with Alzheimer's disease? Click to see the latest research breakthrough." The mode is simple: treatment by front entrance, enhancement by the back door. Borgmann, in his discussion of the uses of technology in modern society, observed precisely this argumentative strategy more than 20 years ago:

> The main goal of these programs seems to be the domination of nature. But we must be more precise. The desire to dominate does

not just spring from a lust of power, from sheer human imperialism. It is from the start connected with the aim of liberating humanity from disease, hunger, and toil and enriching life with learning, art and athletics.

Who would want to deny the powers of viral diseases that can be genetically treated? Would we want to draw the line at the transplantation of non-human capacities (sonar path finding)? Or at in vivo fibre optic communications backbone or anti-degeneration powers? (These would have to be non-human by hypothesis). Or should we consider the scope of technological enhancements that one chief transhumanist, Natasha Vita More, propounds:

> A transhuman is an evolutionary stage from being exclusively biological to becoming post-biological. Post-biological means a continuous shedding of our biology and merging with machines. (. . .) The body, as we transform ourselves over time, will take on different types of appearances and designs and materials. (. . .)
>
> For hiking a mountain, I'd like extended leg strength, stamina, a skin-sheath to protect me from damaging environmental aspects, self-moisturizing, cool-down capability, extended hearing and augmented vision (Network of sonar sensors depicts data through solid mass and map images onto visual field. Overlay window shifts spectrum frequencies. Visual scratch pad relays mental ideas to visual recognition bots. Global Satellite interface at micro-zoom range).
>
> For a party, I'd like an eclectic look—a glistening bronze skin with emerald green highlights, enhanced height to tower above other people, a sophisticated internal sound system so that I could alter the music to suit my own taste, memory enhance device, emotional-select for feel-good people so I wouldn't get dragged into anyone's inappropriate conversations. And parabolic hearing so that I could listen in on conversations across the room if the one I was currently in started winding down.

Notwithstanding the difficulty of bringing together transhumanism under one movement, the sheer variety of proposals merely contained within Vita More's catalogue means that we cannot determinately point to a precise station at which we can say, "Here, this is the end we said things would naturally progress to." But does this pose a problem? Well, it certainly makes it difficult to specify exactly a "horrible result" that is supposed to be at the bottom of the slope. Equally, it is extremely difficult to say that if we allow precedent X, it will allow practices Y or Z to follow as it is not clear how these practices Y or Z are (if at all) connected with the precedent X. So it is not clear that a form of precedent-setting slippery slope can be strictly used in every case against transhumanism, although it may be applicable in some.

Nevertheless, we contend, in contrast with Boström that the burden of proof would fall to the transhumanist. Consider in this light, a Sorites-type slope. The transhumanist would have to show how the relationship

between the therapeutic practices and the enhancements are indeed transitive. We know night from day without being able to specify exactly when this occurs. So simply because we cannot determine a precise distinction between, say, genetic treatments G1, G2 and G3, and transhumanism enhancements T1, T2 and so on, it does not follow that there are no important moral distinctions between G1 and T20. According to Williams, this kind of indeterminacy arises because of the conceptual vagueness of certain terms. Yet, the indeterminacy of so open a predicate "heap" is not equally true of "therapy" or "enhancement." The latitude they permit is nowhere near so wide.

Instead of objecting to Pn on the grounds that Pn is morally objectionable (i.e., to depict a horrible result), we may instead, after Williams, object that the slide from P to Pn is simply morally arbitrary, when it ought not to be. Here, we may say, without specifying a horrible result, that it would be difficult to know what, in principle, can ever be objected to. And this is, quite literally, what is troublesome. It seems to us that this criticism applies to all categories of transhumanism, although not necessarily to all enhancements proposed by them. Clearly, the somewhat loose identity of the movement— and the variations between strong and moderate versions—makes it difficult to sustain this argument unequivocally. Still the transhumanist may be justified in asking, "What is wrong with arbitrariness?" Let us consider one brief example. In aspects of our lives, as a widely shared intuition, we may think that in the absence of good reasons, we ought not to discriminate among people arbitrarily. Healthcare may be considered to be precisely one such case. Given the ever-increasing demand for public healthcare services and products, it may be argued that access to them typically ought to be governed by publicly disputable criteria such as clinical need or potential benefit, as opposed to individual choices of an arbitrary or subjective nature. And nothing in transhumanism seems to allow for such objective dispute, let alone prioritisation. Of course, transhumanists such as More find no such disquietude. His phrase "No more timidity" is a typical token of transhumanist slogans. We applaud advances in therapeutic medical technologies such as those from new genetically based organ regeneration to more familiar prosthetic devices. Here the ends of the interventions are clearly medically defined and the means regulated closely. This is what prevents transhumanists from adopting a Sorites-type slippery slope. But in the absence of a telos, of clearly and substantively specified ends (beyond the mere banner of enhancement), we suggest that the public, medical professionals and bioethicists alike ought to resist the potentially open-ended transformations of human nature. For if all transformations are in principle enhancements, then surely none are. The very application of the word may become redundant. Thus it seems that one strong argument against transhumanism generally—the arbitrary slippery slope—presents a challenge to transhumanism, to show that all of what are described as transhumanist enhancements are imbued with positive normative force and are not merely technological extensions of libertarianism, whose conception of the good is merely an extension of individual choice and consumption.

Limits of Transhumanist Arguments for Medical Technology and Practice

Already, we have seen the misuse of a host of therapeutically designed drugs used by non-therapeutic populations for enhancements. Consider the non-therapeutic use of human growth hormone in non-clinical populations. Such is the present perception of height as a positional good in society that Cuttler *et al.* report that the proportion of doctors who recommended human growth hormone treatment of short non-growth hormone deficient children ranged from 1% to 74%. This is despite its contrary indication in professional literature, such as that of the Pediatric Endocrine Society, and considerable doubt about its efficacy. Moreover, evidence supports the view that recreational body builders will use the technology, given the evidence of their use or misuse of steroids and other biotechnological products. Finally, in the sphere of elite sport, which so valorises embodied capacities that may be found elsewhere in greater degree, precision and sophistication in the animal kingdom or in the computer laboratory, biomedical enhancers may latch onto the genetically determined capacities and adopt or adapt them for their own commercially driven ends.

The arguments and examples presented here do no more than to warn us of the enhancement ideologies, such as transhumanism, which seek to predicate their futuristic agendas on the bedrock of medical technological progress aimed at therapeutic ends and are secondarily extended to loosely defined enhancement ends. In discussion and in bioethical literatures, the future of genetic engineering is often challenged by slippery slope arguments that lead policy and practice to a horrible result. Instead of pointing to the undesirability of the ends to which transhumanism leads, we have pointed out the failure to specify their telos beyond the slogans of "overcoming timidity" or Boström's exhortation that the passive acceptance of ageing is an example of "reckless and dangerous barriers to urgently needed action in the biomedical sphere."

We propose that greater care be taken to distinguish the slippery slope arguments that are used in the emotionally loaded exhortations of transhumanism to come to a more judicious perspective on the technologically driven agenda for biomedical enhancement. Perhaps we would do better to consider those other all-too-human frailties such as violent aggression, wanton self-harming and so on, before we turn too readily to the richer imaginations of biomedical technologists.

Maxwell J. Mehlman  **NO**

Biomedical Enhancements:
Entering a New Era

Recently, the Food and Drug Administration (FDA) approved a drug to lengthen and darken eyelashes. Botox and other wrinkle-reducing injections have joined facelifts, tummy tucks, and vaginal reconstruction to combat the effects of aging. To gain a competitive edge, athletes use everything from steroids and blood transfusions to recombinant-DNA–manufactured hormones, Lasik surgery, and artificial atmospheres. Students supplement caffeine-containing energy drinks with Ritalin and the new alertness drug modafinil. The military spends millions of dollars every year on biological research to increase the warfighting abilities of our soldiers. Parents perform genetic tests on their children to determine whether they have a genetic predisposition to excel at explosive or endurance sports. All of these are examples of biomedical enhancements: interventions that use medical and biological technology to improve performance, appearance, or capability in addition to what is necessary to achieve, sustain, or restore health.

The use of biomedical enhancements, of course, is not new. Amphetamines were doled out to troops during World War II. Athletes at the turn of the 20th century ingested narcotics. The cognitive benefits of caffeine have been known for at least a millennium. Ancient Greek athletes swallowed herbal infusions before competitions. The Egyptians brewed a drink containing a relative of Viagra at least 1,000 years before Christ. But modern drug development and improvements in surgical technique are yielding biomedical enhancements that achieve safer, larger, and more targeted enhancement effects than their predecessors, and more extraordinary technologies are expected to emerge from ongoing discoveries in human genetics. (In addition, there are biomechanical enhancements that involve the use of computer implants and nanotechnology, which are beyond the scope of this article.)

What is new is that biomedical enhancements have become controversial. Some commentators want to outlaw them altogether. Others are concerned about their use by athletes and children. Still others fret that only the well-off will be able to afford them, thereby exacerbating social inequality.

Banning enhancements, however, is misguided. Still, it is important to try to ensure that they are as safe and effective as possible, that vulnerable populations such as children are not forced into using them, and that they are not available only to the well-off. This will require effective government and private action.

A Misguided View

Despite the long history of enhancement use, there recently has emerged a view that it is wrong. The first manifestation of this hostility resulted from the use of performance enhancements in sports in the 1950s, especially steroids and amphetamines. European nations began adopting anti-doping laws in the mid-1960s, and the Olympic Games began testing athletes in 1968. In 1980, Congress amended the Federal Food, Drug, and Cosmetic Act (FFDCA) to make it a felony to distribute anabolic steroids for nonmedical purposes. Two years later, Congress made steroids a Schedule III controlled substance and substituted human growth hormone in the steroid provision of the FFDCA. Between 2003 and 2005, Congress held hearings lambasting professional sports for not imposing adequate testing regimens. Drug testing has also been instituted in high-school and collegiate sports.

The antipathy toward biomedical enhancements extends well beyond sports, however. Officially, at least, the National Institutes of Health (NIH) will not fund research to develop genetic technologies for human enhancement purposes, although it has funded studies in animals that the researchers tout as a step toward developing human enhancements. It is a federal crime to use steroids to increase strength even if the user is not an athlete. Human growth hormone is in a unique regulatory category in that it is a felony to prescribe it for any purpose other than a specific use approved by the FDA. (For example, the FDA has not approved it for anti-aging purposes.) There is an ongoing controversy about whether musicians, especially string players, should be allowed to use beta blockers to steady their hands. And who hasn't heard of objections to the use of mood-altering drugs to make "normal" people happier? There's even a campaign against caffeine.

If the critics had their way, the government would ban the use of biomedical enhancements. It might seem that this would merely entail extending the War on Drugs to a larger number of drugs. But remember that enhancements include not just drugs, but cosmetic surgery and information technologies, such as genetic testing to identify nondisease traits. So a War on Enhancements would have to extend to a broader range of technologies, and because many are delivered within the patient-physician relationship, the government would have to intrude into that relationship in significant new ways. Moreover, the FDA is likely to have approved many enhancement drugs for legitimate medical purposes, with enhancement use taking place on an "off-label" basis. So there would have to be some way for the enhancement police to identify people for whom the drugs had been legally prescribed to treat illness, but who were misusing them for enhancement purposes.

This leads to a far more profound difficulty. The War on Drugs targets only manufacture, distribution, and possession. There is virtually no effort to punish people merely for using an illegal substance. But a successful ban on biomedical enhancement would have to prevent people from obtaining benefits from enhancements that persisted after they no longer possessed the enhancements themselves, such as the muscles built with the aid of steroids or the cognitive improvement that lasts for several weeks after normal people

stop taking a certain medicine that treats memory loss in Alzheimer's patients. In short, a ban on enhancements would have to aim at use as well as possession and sale.

To imagine what this would be like, think about the campaign against doping in elite sports, where athletes must notify anti-doping officials of their whereabouts at all times and are subject to unannounced, intrusive, and often indecent drug tests at any hour of the day or night. Even in the improbable event that regular citizens were willing to endure such an unprecedented loss of privacy, the economic cost of maintaining such a regime, given how widespread the use of highly effective biomedical enhancements might be, would be prohibitive.

A ban on biomedical enhancements would be not only unworkable but unjustifiable. Consider the objections to enhancement in sports. Why are enhancements against the rules? Is it because they are unsafe? Not all of them are: Anti-doping rules in sports go after many substances that pose no significant health risks, such as caffeine and Sudafed. (A Romanian gymnast forfeited her Olympic gold medal after she accidentally took a couple of Sudafed to treat a cold.) Even in the case of vilified products such as steroids, safety concerns stem largely from the fact that athletes are forced to use the drugs covertly, without medical supervision. Do enhancements give athletes an "unfair" advantage? They do so only if the enhancements are hard to obtain, so that only a few competitors obtain the edge. But the opposite seems to be true: Enhancements are everywhere. Besides, athletes are also tested for substances that have no known performance-enhancing effects, such as marijuana. Are the rewards from enhancements "unearned"? Not necessarily. Athletes still need to train hard. Indeed, the benefit from steroids comes chiefly from allowing athletes to train harder without injuring themselves. In any event, success in sports comes from factors that athletes have done nothing to deserve, such as natural talent and the good luck to have been born to encouraging parents or to avoid getting hurt. Would the use of enhancements confound recordkeeping? This doesn't seem to have stopped the adoption of new equipment that improves performance, such as carbon-fiber vaulting poles, metal skis, and oversized tennis racquets. If one athlete used enhancements, would every athlete have to, so that the benefit would be nullified? No, there would still be the benefit of improved performance across the board—bigger lifts, faster times, higher jumps. In any case, the same thing happens whenever an advance takes place that improves performance.

The final objection to athletic enhancement, in the words of the international Olympic movement, is that it is against the "spirit of sport." It is hard to know what this means. It certainly can't mean that enhancements destroy an earlier idyll in which sports were enhancement-free; as we saw before, this never was the case. Nor can it stand for the proposition that a physical competition played with the aid of enhancements necessarily is not a "sport." There are many sporting events in which the organizers do not bother to test participants, from certain types of "strong-man" and powerlifting meets to your neighborhood pickup basketball game. There are several interesting historical explanations for why athletic enhancement has gained such a bad rap, but

ultimately, the objection about "the spirit of sport" boils down to the fact that some people simply don't like the idea of athletes using enhancements. Well, not exactly. You see, many biomedical enhancements are perfectly permissible, including dietary supplements, sports psychology, carbohydrate loading, electrolyte-containing beverages, and sleeping at altitude (or in artificial environments that simulate it). Despite the labor of innumerable philosophers of sport, no one has ever come up with a rational explanation for why these things are legal and others aren't. In the end, they are just arbitrary distinctions.

But that's perfectly okay. Lots of rules in sports are arbitrary, like how many players are on a team or how far the boundary lines stretch. If you don't like being all alone in the outfield, don't play baseball. If you are bothered by midnight drug tests, don't become an Olympian.

The problem comes when the opponents of enhancement use in sports try to impose their arbitrary dislikes on the wider world. We already have observed how intrusive and expensive this would be. Beyond that, there are strong constitutional objections to using the power of the law to enforce arbitrary rules. But most important, a ban on the use of enhancements outside of sports would sacrifice an enormous amount of societal benefit. Wouldn't we want automobile drivers to use alertness drugs if doing so could prevent accidents? Shouldn't surgeons be allowed to use beta blockers to steady their hands? Why not let medical researchers take cognitive enhancers if it would lead to faster cures, or let workers take them to be more productive? Why stop soldiers from achieving greater combat effectiveness, rescue workers from lifting heavier objects, and men and women from leading better sex lives? Competent adults who want to use enhancements should be permitted to. In some instances, such as in combat or when performing dangerous jobs, they should even be required to.

Protecting the Vulnerable

Rejecting the idea of banning enhancements doesn't mean that their use should be unregulated. The government has several crucial roles to play in helping to ensure that the benefits from enhancement use outweigh the costs.

In the first place, the government needs to protect people who are incapable of making rational decisions about whether to use enhancements. In the language of biomedical ethics, these are populations that are "vulnerable," and a number of them are well recognized. One such group, of course, is people with severe mental disabilities. The law requires surrogates to make decisions for these individuals based on what is in their best interests.

Another vulnerable population is children. There can be little disagreement that kids should not be allowed to decide on their own to consume powerful, potentially dangerous enhancement substances. Not only do they lack decisionmaking capacity, but they may be much more susceptible than adults to harm. This is clearly the case with steroids, which can interfere with bone growth in children and adolescents.

The more difficult question is whether parents should be free to give enhancements to their children. Parents face powerful social pressures to help

their children excel. Some parents may be willing to improve their children's academic or athletic performance even at a substantial risk of injury to the child. There are many stories of parents who allow their adolescent daughters to have cosmetic surgery, including breast augmentation. In general, the law gives parents considerable discretion in determining how to raise their children. The basic legal constraint on parental discretion is the prohibition in state law against abuse or neglect, and this generally is interpreted to defer to parental decisionmaking so long as the child does not suffer serious net harm. There are no reported instances in which parents have been sanctioned for giving their children biomedical enhancements, and the authorities might conclude that the benefits conferred by the use of an enhancement outweighed even a fairly significant risk of injury.

Beyond the actions of parents, there remains the question of whether some biomedical enhancements are so benign that children should be allowed to purchase them themselves. At present, for instance, there is no law in the United States against children purchasing coffee, caffeinated soft drinks, and even high-caffeine–containing energy drinks. (Laws prohibiting children from buying energy drinks have been enacted in some other countries.)

At the same time, it may be a mistake to lump youngsters together with older adolescents into one category of children. Older adolescents, although still under the legal age of majority, have greater cognitive and judgmental capacities than younger children. The law recognizes this by allowing certain adolescents, deemed "mature" or "emancipated" minors, to make legally binding decisions, such as decisions to receive medical treatment. Older adolescents similarly may deserve some degree of latitude in making decisions about using biomedical enhancements.

Children may be vulnerable to pressure to use enhancements not only from their parents, but from their educators. Under programs such as No Child Left Behind, public school teachers and administrators are rewarded and punished based on student performance on standardized tests. Private schools compete with one another in terms of where their graduates are accepted for further education. There is also intense competition in school athletics, especially at the collegiate level. Students in these environments may be bull-dozed into using enhancements to increase their academic and athletic abilities. Numerous anecdotes, for example, tell of parents who are informed by teachers that their children need medication to "help them focus"; the medication class in question typically is the cognition-enhancing amphetamines, and many of these children do not have diagnoses that would warrant the use of these drugs.

Beyond students, athletes in general are vulnerable to pressure from coaches, sponsors, family, and teammates to use hazardous enhancements. For example, at the 2005 congressional hearings on steroid use in baseball, a father testified that his son committed suicide after using steroids, when in fact he killed himself after his family caught him using steroids, which the boy had turned to in an effort to meet his family's athletic aspirations.

Another group that could be vulnerable to coercion is workers. Employers might condition employment or promotion on the use of enhancements that increased productivity. For example, an employer might require its nighttime

work force to take the alertness drug modafinil, which is now approved for use by sleep-deprived swing-shift workers. Current labor law does not clearly forbid this so long as the drug is relatively safe. From an era in which employees are tested to make sure they aren't taking drugs, we might see a new approach in which employers test them to make sure they are.

Members of the military may also be forced to use enhancements. The military now conducts the largest known biomedical enhancement research project. Under battlefield conditions, superiors may order the use of enhancements, leaving soldiers no lawful option to refuse. A notorious example is the use of amphetamines by combat pilots. Technically, the pilots are required to give their consent to the use of the pep pills, but if they refuse, they are barred from flying the missions.

The ability of government regulation to protect vulnerable groups varies depending on the group. It is important that educators not be allowed to give students dangerous enhancements without parental permission and that parents not be pressured into making unreasonable decisions by fearful, overzealous, or inadequate educators. The law can mandate the former, but not easily prevent the latter. Coaches and trainers who cause injury to athletes by giving them dangerous enhancements or by unduly encouraging their use should be subject to criminal and civil liability. The same goes for employers. But the realities of military life make it extremely difficult to protect soldiers from the orders of their superiors.

Moreover, individuals may feel pressure to use enhancements not only from outside sources, but from within. Students may be driven to do well in order to satisfy parents, gain admittance to more prestigious schools, or establish better careers. Athletes take all sorts of risks to increase their chances of winning. Workers may be desperate to save their jobs or bring in a bigger paycheck, especially in economically uncertain times. Soldiers better able to complete their missions are likely to live longer.

Surprisingly, while acknowledging the need to protect people from outside pressures, bioethicists generally maintain that we do not need to protect them from harmful decisions motivated by internal pressures. This position stems, it seems, from the recognition that, with the exception of decisions that are purely random, everything we decide to do is dictated at least in part by internal pressures, and in many cases, these pressures can be so strong that the decisions may no longer appear to be voluntary. Take, for example, seriously ill cancer patients contemplating whether or not to undergo harsh chemotherapy regimens. Bioethicists worry that, if we focused on the pressures and lack of options created by the patients' dire condition, we might not let the patients receive the treatment, or, in the guise of protecting the patients from harm, might create procedural hurdles that would rob them of their decision-making autonomy. Similarly, these bioethicists might object to restricting the ability of workers, say, to use biomedical enhancements merely because their choices are highly constrained by their fear of losing their jobs. But even if we accept this argument, that doesn't mean that we must be indifferent to the dangers posed by overwhelming internal pressure. As we will see, the government still must take steps to minimize the harm that could result.

Individuals may be vulnerable to harm not only from using enhancements, but from participating in experiments to see if an enhancement is safe and effective. Research subjects are protected by a fairly elaborate set of rules, collectively known as the "Common Rule," that are designed to ensure that the risks of the research are outweighed by the potential benefits and that the subjects have given their informed consent to their participation. But there are many weaknesses in this regulatory scheme. For one thing, these rules apply only to experiments conducted by government-funded institutions or that are submitted to the FDA in support of licensing applications, and therefore they do not cover a great deal of research performed by private industry. Moreover, the rules were written with medically oriented research in mind, and it is not clear how they should be interpreted and applied to enhancement research. For example, the rules permit children to be enrolled as experimental subjects in trials that present "more than minimal risk" if, among other things, the research offers the possibility of "direct benefit" to the subject, but the rules do not say whether an enhancement benefit can count as a direct benefit. Specific research protections extend to other vulnerable populations besides children, such as prisoners and pregnant women, but do not explicitly cover students, workers, or athletes. In reports of a project several colleagues and I recently completed for the NIH, we suggest a number of changes to current regulations that would provide better protection for these populations.

Ensuring Safety and Effectiveness

Beginning with the enactment of the Pure Food and Drug Act in 1906, we have turned to the government to protect us from unsafe, ineffective, and fraudulent biomedical products and services. Regardless of how much freedom individuals should have to decide whether or not to use biomedical enhancements, they cannot make good decisions without accurate information about how well enhancements work. In regard to enhancements in the form of drugs and medical devices, the FDA has the legal responsibility to make sure that this information exists.

The FDA's ability to discharge this responsibility, however, is limited. In the first place, the FDA has tended to rely on information from highly stylized clinical trials that do not reflect the conditions under which enhancements would be used by the general public. Moreover, the deficiencies of clinical trials are becoming more apparent as we learn about pharmacogenetics—the degree to which individual responses to medical interventions vary depending on the individual's genes. The FDA is beginning to revise its rules to require manufacturers to take pharmacogenetics into consideration in studying safety and efficacy, but it will be many years, if ever, before robust pharmacogenetic information is publicly available. The solution is to rely more on data from actual use. Recently the agency has become more adamant about monitoring real-world experience after products reach the market, but this information comes from self-reports by physicians and manufacturers who have little incentive to cooperate. The agency needs to be able to conduct its own surveillance of actual use, with the costs borne by the manufacturers.

Many biomedical enhancements fall outside the scope of FDA authority. They include dietary supplements, many of which are used for enhancement purposes rather than to promote health. You only have to turn on late-night TV to be bombarded with claims for substances to make you stronger or more virile. Occasionally the Federal Trade Commission cracks down on hucksters, but it needs far greater resources to do an effective job. The FDA needs to exert greater authority to regulate dietary supplements, including those used for enhancement.

The FDA also lacks jurisdiction over the "practice of medicine." Consequently, it has no oversight over cosmetic surgery, except when the surgeon employs a new medical device. This limitation also complicates the agency's efforts to exert authority over reproductive and genetic practices. This would include the genetic modification of embryos to improve their traits, which promises to be one of the most effective enhancement techniques. Because organized medicine fiercely protects this limit on the FDA, consumers will have to continue to rely on physicians and other health care professionals to provide them with the information they need to make decisions about these types of enhancements. Medical experts need to stay on top of advances in enhancement technology.

Even with regard to drugs and devices that are clearly within the FDA's jurisdiction, its regulatory oversight only goes so far. Once the agency approves a product for a particular use, physicians are free to use it for any other purpose, subject only to liability for malpractice and, in the case of controlled substances, a requirement that the use must comprise legitimate medical practice. Only a handful of products, such as Botox, have received FDA approval for enhancement use; as noted earlier, enhancements predominantly are unapproved, off-label uses of products approved for health-related purposes. Modafinil, for example, one of the most popular drugs for enhancing cognitive performance, is approved only for the treatment of narcolepsy and sleepiness associated with obstructive sleep apnea/hypopnea syndrome and shift-work sleep disorder. Erythropoietin, which athletes use to improve performance, is approved to treat anemias. The FDA needs to be able to require manufacturers of products such as these to pay for the agency to collect and disseminate data on off-label experience. The agency also has to continue to limit the ability of manufacturers to promote drugs for off-label uses, in order to give them an incentive to obtain FDA approval for enhancement labeling.

An enhancement technology that will increase in use is testing to identify genes that are associated with nondisease characteristics. People can use this information to make lifestyle choices, such as playing sports at which they have the genes to excel, or in reproduction, such as deciding which of a number of embryos fertilized in vitro will be implanted in the uterus. An area of special concern is genetic tests that consumers can use at home without the involvement of physicians or genetic counselors to help them interpret the results. Regulatory authority over genetic testing is widely believed to be inadequate, in part because it is split among the FDA and several other federal agencies, and there are growing calls for revamping this regulatory scheme that need to be heeded.

Any attempt to regulate biomedical enhancement will be undercut by people who obtain enhancements abroad. The best hope for protecting these "enhancement tourists" against unsafe or ineffective products and services lies in international cooperation, but this is costly and subject to varying degrees of compliance.

To make intelligent decisions about enhancement use, consumers need information not only about safety and effectiveness, but about whether they are worth the money. Should they pay for Botox injections, for example, or try to get rid of facial wrinkles with cheaper creams and lotions? When the FDA approved Botox for cosmetic use, it ignored this question of cost-effectiveness because it has no statutory authority to consider it. In the case of medical care, consumers may get some help in making efficient spending decisions from their health insurers, who have an incentive to avoid paying for unnecessarily costly products or services. But insurance does not cover enhancements. The new administration is proposing to create a federal commission to conduct health care cost-effectiveness analyses, among other things, and it is important that such a body pay attention to enhancements as well as other biomedical interventions.

Subsidizing Enhancement

In these times of economic distress, when we already question whether the nation can afford to increase spending on health care, infrastructure, and other basic necessities, it may seem foolish to consider whether the government has an obligation to make biomedical enhancements available to all. Yet if enhancements enable people to enjoy a significantly better life, this may not be so outlandish, and if universal access avoids a degree of inequality so great that it undermines our democratic way of life, it may be inescapable.

There is no need for everyone to have access to all available enhancements. Some may add little to an individual's abilities. Others may be so hazardous that they offer little net benefit to the user. But imagine that a pill is discovered that substantially improves a person's cognitive facility, not just their memory but abilities such as executive function—the highest form of problem-solving capacity—or creativity. Now imagine if this pill were available only to those who already were well-off and could afford to purchase it with personal funds. If such a pill were sufficiently effective, so that those who took it had a lock on the best schools, careers, and mates, wealth-based access could drive an insurmountable wedge between the haves and have-nots, a gap so wide and deep that we could no longer pretend that there is equality of opportunity in our society. At that point, it is doubtful that a liberal democratic state could survive.

So it may be necessary for the government to regard such a success-determining enhancement as a basic necessity, and, after driving the cost down to the lowest amount possible, subsidize access for those unable to purchase it themselves. Even if this merely maintained preexisting differences in cognitive ability, it would be justified in order to prevent further erosion of equality of opportunity.

The need for effective regulation of biomedical enhancement is only going to increase as we enter an era of increasingly sophisticated technologies. Existing schemes, such as the rules governing human subjects research, must be reviewed to determine whether additions or changes are needed to accommodate this class of interventions. Government agencies and private organizations need to be aware of both the promise and the peril of enhancements and devote an appropriate amount of resources in order to regulate, rather than stop, their use.

EXPLORING THE ISSUE

Should We Reject the "Transhumanist" Goal of the Genetically, Electronically, and Mechanically Enhanced Human Being?

Critical Thinking and Reflection

1. What is transhumanism?
2. What is a "slippery slope" argument?
3. What bodily or mental enhancements would you find desirable? Why?
4. Should government subsidize biomedical enhancements for those who cannot afford them? Why or why not?

Is There Common Ground?

"Common ground" is difficult to find here, for many of those who object to enhancing the human mind and body seem to draw rather arbitrary lines to distinguish between enhancements they find acceptable and those they do not.

1. Is the line between internal and external enhancements, or between new and old? Consider eyeglasses versus lens implants (done when cataracts must be removed), hearing aids versus cochlear implants, crutches and canes versus artificial hips and knees.
2. Do computers give us fundamentally new abilities for communication and memory expansion? Do we accept these abilities? Will it make a difference when we can implant our computers inside our heads?
3. What other technological enhancements of the human body and mind do most of us accept readily?
4. Does the list of acceptable enhancements expand as time goes on and technology progresses?

Internet References . . .

The J. Craig Venter Institute

The J. Craig Venter Institute, formed in October 2006, is a world leader in genomics research, including the effort to create synthetic cells.

www.jcvi.org

United States Department of Defense, U.S. Cyber Command

The U.S. Cyber Command is a unit of the Department of Defense (DoD) that defends information networks and prepares to conduct military cyberspace operations to ensure US/Allied freedom of action in cyberspace and deny the same to adversaries.

www.defense.gov/home/features/2010/0410_cybersec/

Bonus Issues

*T*he three debates presented in this unit represent issues that are new to the expanded edition.

- Should Society Impose a Moratorium on the Use and Release of "Synthetic Biology" Organisms?
- Is Cyber-War or Cyber-Terrorism a Genuine Threat?
- Will Robots Take Your Job?

ISSUE 20

Should Society Impose a Moratorium on the Use and Release of "Synthetic Biology" Organisms?

YES: Jim Thomas, Eric Hoffman, and Jaydee Hanson, from *Offering Testimony from Civil Society on the Environmental and Societal Implications of Synthetic Biology* (May 27, 2010)

NO: Gregory E. Kaebnick, from *Written Testimony of Gregory E. Kaebnick to the House Committee on Energy and Commerce* (May 27, 2010)

Learning Outcomes

After studying this issue, students will be able to:

1. Explain what "dual-use" technologies are and why they warrant special regulation.
2. Discuss the impact of the ability to make "synthetic cells" on traditional views of life.
3. Discuss the difficulty of preventing all the potential risks of a new technology.
4. Make a reasonable forecast of future developments of synthetic biology technology.

ISSUE SUMMARY

YES: Jim Thomas, Eric Hoffman, and Jaydee Hanson, representing the Civil Society on the Environmental and Societal Implications of Synthetic Biology, argue that the risks posed by synthetic biology to human health, the environment, and natural ecosystems are so great that Congress should declare an immediate moratorium on releases to the environment and commercial uses of synthetic organisms and require comprehensive environmental and social impact reviews of all federally funded synthetic biology research.

NO: Gregory E. Kaebnick of the Hastings Center argues that although synthetic biology is surrounded by genuine ethical and moral concerns—including risks to health and environment—

which warrant discussion, the potential benefits are too great to call for a general moratorium.

In the past century, biologists have learned an enormous amount of knowledge about how the cell—the basic functional unit of all living things—works. By the early 1970s, they had begun to move genes from one organism to another and dream of designing plants and animals (including human beings) with novel combinations of features. By 2002, with Defense Department funding, Jeronimo Cello, Aniko Paul, and Eckard Wimmer were able to construct a live poliovirus from raw laboratory chemicals. This feat was a long way from constructing a bacterium or animal from raw chemicals, but it was enough to set alarm bells of many kinds ringing. Some people thought this work challenged the divine monopoly on creation. Others feared that if one could construct one virus from scratch, one could construct others, such as the smallpox virus, or even tailor entirely new viruses with which natural immune systems and medical facilities could not cope. Some even thought that the paper was irresponsible and should not have been published because it pointed the way toward new kinds of terrorism. See Michael J. Selgelid and Lorna Weir, "Reflections on the Synthetic Production of Poliovirus," *Bulletin of the Atomic Scientists* (May/June 2010).

In 2010, the next step was taken. Craig Venter's research group announced that they had successfully synthesized a bacterial chromosome (the set of genes that specifies the function and form of the bacterium) and implanted it in a bacterium of a different species whose chromosome had been removed. The result was the conversion of the recipient bacterium into the synthesized chromosome's species. See Daniel G. Gibson et al., "Creation of a Bacterial Cell Controlled by a Chemically Synthesized Genome," *Science* (July 2, 2010). The report received a great deal of media attention, much of it saying that Venter's group had created a living cell, even though only the chromosome had been synthesized. The chromosome's biochemically complex container— a cell minus its chromosome—had *not* been synthesized.

The goal of this work is not the creation of life, but rather the ability to exert unprecedented control over what cells do. In testimony before the House Committee on Energy and Commerce Hearing on Developments in Synthetic Genomics and Implications for Health and Energy (May 27, 2010), Venter said "The ability to routinely write the 'software of life' will usher in a new era in science, and with it, new products and applications such as advanced biofuels, clean water technology, food products, and new vaccines and medicines. The field is already having an impact in some of these areas and will continue to do so as long as this powerful new area of science is used wisely." See also Pamela Weintraub, "J. Craig Venter on Biology's Next Leap: Digitally Designed Life-Forms that Could Produce Novel Drugs, Renewable Fuels, and Plentiful Food for Tomorrow's World," *Discover* (January/February 2010); and Michael A. Peters and Priya Venkatesan, "Bioeconomy and Third Industrial Revolution in the Age of Synthetic Life," *Contemporary Readings in Law and Social Justice* (vol. 2, no. 2, 2010). However, the ETC Group, which anticipated a synthetic organism in

2007, condemns the lack of rules governing synthetic biology, calls it "a quintessential Pandora's box moment," and calls for a global moratorium on further work; see "Synthia Is Alive . . . and Breeding: Panacea or Pandora's Box?" *ETC Group News Release* (May 20, 2010), (www.etcgroup.org/content/synthia-alive-%E2%80%A6-and-breeding-panacea-or-pandoras-box). A number of artists have also joined the debate; see Sara Reardon, "Visions of Synthetic Biology," *Science* (September 2, 2011). Some biologists have already established do-it-yourself "community labs," looking ahead to the day when synthetic biology is something anyone can do; see Sam Kean, "A Lab of Their Own," *Science* (September 2, 2011). And the FBI's Weapons of Mass Destruction Directorate's Biological Countermeasures Unit encourages "a kind of neighborhood watch" among the do-it-yourselfers; see Delthia Ricks, "Bio Hackers," *Discover* (October 2011).

Researchers had been working on synthetic biology for a number of years, and well before Craig Venter's group announced their accomplishment, prospects and consequences were already being discussed. Michael Specter, "A Life of Its Own," *New Yorker* (September 28, 2009), describes progress to date and notes "the ultimate goal is to create a synthetic organism made solely from chemical parts and blueprints of DNA." If this sounds rather like manipulating living things the way children manipulate Legos, Drew Endy of MIT and colleagues created in 2005 the BioBricks Foundation to make that metaphor explicit. See also Rob Carlson, *Biology Is Technology: The Promise, Peril, and Business of Engineering Life* (Harvard University Press, 2010). David Deamer, "First Life and Next Life," *Technology Review* (May/June 2009), notes that the next step is to create entire cells, not just a single bacterial chromosome. Charles Petit, "Life from Scratch," *Science News* (July 3, 2010), describes the even more ambitious work of Harvard's Jack Szostak, who is trying to understand how life began by constructing a pre-cell just sophisticated enough to take in components, grow, divide, and start evolving. Szostak expects to succeed within a few years. Such efforts, say Steven A. Benner, Zunyi Yang, and Fei Chen, "Synthetic Biology, Tinkering Biology, and Artificial Biology: What Are We Learning?" *Comptes Rendus Chimie* (April 2011), will drive a better understanding of biology in ways that mere analysis cannot.

Immediately after the Venter group's announcement of their accomplishment, Vatican representatives declared that synthetic biology was "a potential time bomb, a dangerous double-edged sword for which it is impossible to imagine the consequences" and "Pretending to be God and parroting his power of creation is an enormous risk that can plunge men into barbarity"; see "Vatican Greets First Synthetic Cell with Caution," *America* (June 7–14, 2010). Chuck Colson, "Synthetic Life: The Danger of God-Like Pretensions," *Christian Post* (June 16, 2010), says "God-like control [of risks] isn't only hubris, it's pure fantasy. The only real way to avoid the unthinkable is not to try and play God in the first place. But that would require the kind of humility that Venter and company reject out-of-hand." Nancy Gibbs, "Creation Myths," *Time* (June 28, 2010), says "The path of progress cuts through the four-way intersection of the moral, medical, religious and political—and whichever way you turn, you are likely to run over someone's deeply held beliefs. Venter's bombshell revived the oldest of ethical debates, over whether scientists were playing God or proving he does not exist because someone re-enacted Genesis in suburban Maryland." The "playing God"

objection seems likely to grow louder as synthetic biology matures, but it is also likely to fade just as it has done after previous advances such as in vitro fertilization and surrogate mothering. Henk van den Belt, "Playing God in Frankenstein's Footsteps: Synthetic Biology and the Meaning of Life," *NanoEthics* (December 2009), notes that "While syntheses of artificial life forms cause some vague uneasiness that life may lose its special meaning, most concerns turn out to be narrowly anthropocentric. As long as synthetic biology creates only new microbial life and does not directly affect human life, it will in all likelihood be considered acceptable."

What will be more significant will be discussions such as Gautam Mukunda, Kenneth A. Oye, and Scott C. Mohr, "What Rough Beast? Synthetic Biology, Uncertainty, and the Future of Biosecurity," *Politics and the Life Sciences* (September 2009). Mukunda et al. see synthetic biology as seeking "to create modular biological parts that can be assembled into useful devices, allowing the modification of biological systems with greater reliability, at lower cost, with greater speed, and by a larger pool of people than has been the case with traditional genetic engineering." It is thus a "dual-use" technology, meaning that it has both benign and malign applications. This has clear implications for national security, both offensive and defensive, but they find those implications least alarming in the short term. In the long term, the defensive implications are most important. Because the offensive implications are there, regulation and surveillance of research and development will be necessary in order to forestall terrorists and criminals. Jonathan B. Tucker, "Could Terrorists Exploit Synthetic Biology?" *New Atlantis: A Journal of Technology & Society* (Spring 2011), sees potential problems. Mildred K. Cho and David A. Relman, "Synthetic 'Life,' Ethics, National Security, and Public Discourse," *Science* (July 2, 2010), caution that some concerns about biosecurity and ethics are real but some are imagined; being realistic and avoiding exaggeration are essential if the science is not to become a victim of public mistrust. Meera Lee Sethi and Adam Briggle, "Making Stories Visible: The Task for Bioethics Commissions," *Issues in Science and Technology* (Winter 2011), caution that the stories we tell ourselves about technology (such as "synthetic biology is like computers") may hide issues that warrant deep and careful thought. The Biotechnology Industry Organization's Brent Erickson, Rina Singh, and Paul Winters, "Synthetic Biology: Regulating Industry Uses of New Biotechnologies," *Science* (September 2, 2011), think it crucial that regulation does not impede innovation and development of new products.

In the YES selection Jim Thomas, Eric Hoffman, and Jaydee Hanson, representing the Civil Society on the Environmental and Societal Implications of Synthetic Biology, argue that the risks posed by synthetic biology to human health, the environment, and natural ecosystems are so great that Congress should declare an immediate moratorium on releases to the environment and commercial uses of synthetic organisms and require comprehensive environmental and social impact reviews of all federally funded synthetic biology research. In the NO selection, Gregory E. Kaebnick of the Hastings Center argues that although synthetic biology is surrounded by genuine ethical and moral concerns—including risks to health and environment—which warrant discussion, the potential benefits are too great to call for a general moratorium.

YES ↵

**Jim Thomas, Eric
Hoffman, and Jaydee Hanson**

Offering Testimony from Civil Society on the Environmental and Societal Implications of Synthetic Biology

. . . **L**ast week, the J. Craig Venter Institute announced the creation of the first living organism with a synthetic genome claiming that this technology would be used in applications as diverse as next generation biofuels, vaccine production and the clean up of oil spills. We agree that this is a significant technical feat however; we believe it should be received as a wake-up call to governments around the world that this technology must now be accountably regulated. While attention this week has been on the activities of a team from Synthetic Genomics Inc, the broader field of synthetic biology has in fact quickly and quietly grown into a multi-billion dollar industry with over seventy DNA foundries and dozens of "pure play" synthetic biology companies entering the marketplace supported by large investments from Fortune 500 energy, forestry, chemical and agribusiness companies. That industry already has at least one product in the marketplace (Du Pont's 'Sorona' bioplastic), and another recently cleared for market entry in 2011 (Amyris Biotechnology's 'No Compromise' biofuel) as well as several dozen near to market applications. We believe the committee should consider the implications of this new industry as a whole in its deliberations not just the technical breakthrough reported last week. Without proper safeguards in place, we risk introducing synthetically constructed living organisms into the environment, intentionally or inadvertently through accident and worker error, that have the potential to destroy ecosystems and threaten human health. We will see the widespread commercial application of techniques with grave dual-use implications. We further risk licensing their use in industrial applications that will unsustainably increase the pressure of human activities on both land and marine ecologies through the increased take of biomass, food resources, water and fertilizer or displacement of wild lands to grow feedstocks for bio-based fuel and chemical production.

We call on Congress to:

1. Implement a moratorium on the release of synthetic organisms into the environment and also their use in commercial settings. This

U.S. House of Representatives Committee on Energy and Commerce, May 27, 2010.

moratorium should remain in place until there is an adequate scientific basis on which to justify such activities, and until due consideration of the associated risks for the environment, biodiversity, and human health, and all associated socio-economic repercussions, are fully and transparently considered.

2. As an immediate step, all federally funded synthetic biology research should be subject to a comprehensive environmental and societal impact review carried out with input from civil society, also considering indirect impacts on biodiversity of moving synthetic organisms into commercial use for fuel, chemicals and medicines. This should include the projects that received $305 million from the Department of Energy in 2009 alone.

3. All synthetic biology projects should also be reviewed by the Recombinant DNA Advisory Committee.

On Synthetic Biology for Biofuels—Time for a Reality Check

Much of the purported promise of the emerging Synthetic Biology industry resides in the notion of transforming biomass into next generation biofuels or bio-based chemicals where synthetic organisms work as bio-factories transforming sugars to high value products. On examination much of this promise is unrealistic and unsustainable and if allowed to proceed could hamper ongoing efforts to conserve biological diversity, ensure food security and prevent dangerous climate change. The sobering reality is that a switch to a bio-based industrial economy could exert much more pressure on land, water, soil, fertilizer, forest resources and conservation areas. It may also do little to address greenhouse gas emissions, potentially worsening climate change.

By way of an example, the team associated with Synthetic Genomics Inc who have recently announced the creation of a synthetic cell have specifically claimed that they would use the same technology to develop an algal species that efficiently converts atmospheric carbon dioxide into hydrocarbon fuel, supposedly addressing both the climate crisis and peak oil concerns in one fell swoop. Yet, contrary to the impression put forth by these researchers in the press, algae, synthetic or otherwise, requires much more than just carbon dioxide to grow—It also requires water, nutrients for fertilizer and also sunlight (which therefore means one needs land or open ocean—this can't be done in a vat without also consuming vast quantities of sugar).

In order for Synthetic Genomics or their partners to scale up algal biofuel production to make a dent in the fuel supply, the process would likely exert a massive drain on both water and on fertilizers. Both fresh water and fertilizer (especially phosphate-based fertilizers) are in short supply, both are already prioritized for agricultural food production and both require a large amount of energy either to produce (in the case of fertilizers) or to pump to arid sunlight-rich regions (in the case of water). In a recent life-cycle assessment of algal biofuels published in the journal *Environmental Science and Technology*

researchers concluded that algae production consumes more water and energy than other biofuel sources like corn, canola, and switch grass, and also has higher greenhouse gas emissions. "Given what we know about algae production pilot projects over the past 10 to 15 years, we've found that algae's environmental footprint is larger than other terrestrial crops," said Andres Clarens, an assistant professor in U.Virginia's Civil and Environmental Department and lead author on the paper. Moreover scaling-up this technology in the least energy-intensive manner will likely need large open ponds sited in deserts, displacing desert ecosystems. Indeed the federally appointed Invasive Species Advisory Committee has recently warned that non-native algal species employed for such biofuel production could prove ecologically harmful and is currently preparing a fuller report on the matter.

Meanwhile it is not clear that the yield from algal biofuels would go far to meeting our energy needs. MIT inventor Saul Griffiths has recently calculated that even if an algae strain can be made 4 times as efficient as an energy source than it is today it would still be necessary to fill one Olympic-size swimming pool of algae every second for the next twenty five years to offset only half a terawatt of our current energy consumption (which is expected to rise to 16 TW in that time period). That amounts to massive land use change. Emissions from land use change are recognized as one of the biggest contributors to anthropogenic climate change.

Moving Forward—Time for New Regulation

The rapid adoption of synthetic biology is moving the biotechnology industry into the driving seat of industrial production across many previously disparate sectors with downstream consequences for monopoly policy. Meanwhile its application in commercial settings uses a set of new and extreme techniques whose proper oversight and limits has not yet been debated. It also enables many more diverse living organisms to be produced using genetic science at a speed and volume that will challenge and ultimately overwhelm the capacity of existing biosafety regulations. For example, Craig Venter has claimed in press and in his patent applications that when combined with robotic techniques the technology for producing a synthetic cell can be perfected to make millions of new species per day. Neither the US government nor any other country has the capacity to assess such an outpouring of new synthetic species in a timely or detailed manner. The Energy and Commerce Committee urgently needs to suggest provisions for regulating these new organisms and chemicals derived from them under the Toxic Substances Control Act, Climate Change legislation and other legislation under its purview before allowing their release into the environment. It also needs to identify how it intends to ensure that the use of such organisms whether in biorefineries, open ponds or marine settings does not impinge on agriculture, forestry, desert and marine protection, the preservation of conservation lands, rural jobs or livelihoods.

To conclude, Congress must receive this announcement of a significant new lifeform as a warning bell, signifying that the time has come for governments to fully regulate all synthetic biology experiments and products.

It is imperative that in the pursuit of scientific experimentation and wealth creation, we do not sacrifice human health, the environment, and natural ecosystems. These technologies could have powerful and unpredictable consequences. These are life forms never seen on the planet before now. Before they are unleashed into the environment and commercial use, we need to understand the consequences, evaluate alternatives properly, and be able to prevent the problems that may arise from them.

Gregory E. Kaebnick  **NO**

Written Testimony of Gregory E. Kaebnick to the House Committee on Energy and Commerce

. . . The ethical issues raised by synthetic biology are familiar themes in an ongoing conversation this nation has been having about biotechnologies for several decades. . . .

The concerns fall into two general categories. One has to do with whether the creation of synthetic organisms is a good or a bad thing in and of itself, aside from the consequences. These are thought of as intrinsic concerns. Many people had similar intrinsic concerns about reproductive cloning, for example; they just felt it was wrong to do, regardless of benefits. Another has to do with potential consequences—that is, with risks and benefits. The distinction between these categories can be difficult to maintain in practice, but it provides a useful organizational structure.

1. Intrinsic Concerns

I will start with the more philosophical, maybe more baffling, kind of concern—the intrinsic concerns. They are an appropriate place to start because the work just published by researchers at Synthetic Genomics, Inc., has been billed as advancing our understanding of these issues in addition to making a scientific advance.

This announcement is not the first time we have had a debate about whether biotechnology challenges deeply held views about the status of life and the power that biotechnology and medicine give us over it. There was a similar debate about gene transfer research in the 1970s and 1980s, about cloning and stem cell research in the 1990s, and—particularly in the last decade but also earlier—about various tools for enhancing human beings. They have been addressed by the President's Commission for the Study of Ethical Problems in Medicine and Biomedical and Behavioral Research in 1983, by President Clinton's National Bioethics Advisory Council, and by President Bush's President's Council on Bioethics. These concerns are related to even older concerns in medicine about decisions to withhold or withdraw medical treatment at the end of life.

U.S. House of Representatives Committee on Energy and Commerce, May 27, 2010.

The fact that we have had this debate before speaks to its importance. I believe the intrinsic concerns deserve respect, and with some kinds of biotechnology I think they are very important, but for synthetic biology, I do not think they provide a basis for decisions about governance.

A. Religious or Metaphysical Concerns

The classic concern about synthetic biology is that it puts human beings in a role properly held by God—that scientists who do it are "playing God," as people say. Some may also believe that life is sacred, and that scientists are violating its sacredness. Prince Charles had this in mind in a famous polemic some years ago when he lamented that biotechnology was leading to "the industrialisation of Life."

To object to synthetic biology along these lines is to see a serious moral mistake in it. This kind of objection may be grounded in deeply held beliefs about God's goals in creating the world and the proper role of human beings within God's plan. But these views would belong to particular faiths—not everybody would share them. Moreover, there is a range of opinions even within religious traditions about what human beings may and may not do. Some people celebrate human creativity and science. They may see science as a gift from God that God intends human beings to develop and use.

The announcement that Synthetic Genomics, Inc., has created a synthetic cell appears to some to disprove the view that life is sacred, but I do not agree. Arguably, what has been created is a synthetic genome, not a completely synthetic cell. Even if scientists manage to create a fully synthetic cell, however, people who believe that life is sacred, that it is something more than interacting chemicals, could continue to defend that belief. A similar question arises about the existence of souls in cloned people: If people have souls, then surely they would have souls even if they were created in the laboratory by means of cloning techniques. By the same reasoning, if microbial life is more than a combination of chemicals, then even microbial life created in the laboratory would be more than just chemicals. In general, beliefs about the sacredness of life are not undermined by science. Moreover, even the creation of a truly synthetic cell would still start with existing materials. It would not be the kind of creating with which God is credited, which is creating something from nothing—creation ex nihilo.

B. Concerns that Synthetic Biology Will Undermine Morally Significant Concepts

A related but different kind of concern is that synthetic biology will simply undermine our shared understanding of important moral concepts. For example, perhaps it will lead us to think that life does not have the specialness we have often found in it, or that we humans are more powerful than we have thought in the past. This kind of concern can be expressed without talking about God's plan.

Synthetic biology need not change our understanding of the value of life, however. The fact that living things are created naturally, rather than by people, would be only one reason for seeing them as valuable, and we could continue

to see them as valuable when they are created by people. Further, in its current form, synthetic biology is almost exclusively about engineering single-celled organisms, which may be less troubling to people than engineering more complex organisms. If the work is contained within the laboratory and the factory, then it might not end up broadly changing humans' views of the value of life.

Also, of course, the fact that the work challenges our ideas may not really be a moral problem. It would not be the first time that science has challenged our views of life or our place in the cosmos, and we have weathered these challenges in the past.

C. Concerns about the Human Relationship to Nature

Another way of saying that there's something intrinsically troubling about synthetic biology, again without necessarily talking about the possibility that people are treading on God's turf, is to see it as a kind of environmentalist concern. Many environmentalists want to do more than make the environment good for humans; they also want to save nature from humans—they want to save endangered species, wildernesses, "wild rivers," old-growth forests, and mountains, canyons, and caves, for example. We should approach the natural world, many feel, with a kind of reverence or gratitude, and some worry that synthetic biology—perhaps along with many other kinds of biotechnology—does not square with this value.

Of course, human beings have been altering nature throughout human history. They have been altering ecosystems, affecting the survival of species, affecting the evolution of species, and even creating new species. Most agricultural crop species, for example, are dramatically different from their ancestral forebears. The issue, then, is where to draw the line. Even people who want to preserve nature accept that there is a balance to be struck between saving trees and harvesting them for wood. There might also be a balance when it comes to biotechnology. The misgiving is that synthetic biology goes too far—it takes human control over nature to the ultimate level, where we are not merely altering existing life forms but creating new forms.

Another environmentalist perspective, however, is that synthetic biology could be developed so that it is beneficial to the environment. Synthetic Genomics, Inc. recently contracted with Exxon Mobil to engineer algae that produce gasoline in ways that not only eliminate some of the usual environmental costs of producing and transporting fuel but simultaneously absorb large amounts of carbon dioxide, thereby offsetting some of the environmental costs of burning fuel (no matter how it is produced). If that could be achieved, many who feel deeply that we should tread more lightly on the natural world might well find synthetic biology attractive. In order to achieve this benefit, however, we must be confident that synthetic organisms will not escape into the environment and cause harms there.

Concerns Involving Consequences

The second category of moral concerns is about consequences—that is, risks and benefits. The promise of synthetic biology includes, for example, better ways of producing medicine, environmentally friendlier ways of producing

fuel and other substances, and remediation of past environmental damage. These are not morally trivial considerations. There are also, however, morally serious risks. These, too, fall into three categories.

Concerns about Social Justice

Synthetic biology is sometimes heralded as the start of a new industrial age. Not only will it lead to new products, but it will lead to new modes of production and distribution; instead of pumping oil out of the ground and shipping it around the world, we might be able to produce it from algae in places closer to where it will be used. Inevitably, then, it would have all sorts of large-scale economic and social consequences, some of which could be harmful and unjust. Some commentators hold, for example, that if synthetic biology generates effective ways of producing biofuels from feedstocks such as sugar cane, then farmland in poor countries would be converted from food production to sugar cane production. Another set of concerns arises over the intellectual property rights in synthetic biology. If synthetic biology is the beginning of a new industrial age, and a handful of companies received patents giving them broad control over it, the results could be unjust.

Surely we ought to avoid these consequences. It is my belief that we can do so without avoiding the technology. Also, traditional industrial methods themselves seem to be leading to disastrous long-term social consequences; if so, synthetic biology might provide a way toward better social outcomes.

Concerns about Biosafety

Another concern is about biosafety—about mechanisms for containing and controlling synthetic organisms, both during research and development and in industrial applications. The concern is that organisms will escape, turn out to have properties, at least in their new environment, different from what was intended and predicted, or maybe mutate to acquire them, and then pose a threat to public health, agriculture, or the environment. Alternatively, some of their genes might be transferred to other, wild microbes, producing wild microbes with new properties.

Controlling this risk means controlling the organisms—trying to prevent industrial or laboratory accidents, and then trying to make sure that, when organisms do escape, they are not dangerous. Many synthetic biologists argue that an organism that devotes most of its energy to producing jet fuel or medicine, that is greatly simplified (so that it lacks the genetic complexity and therefore the adaptability of a wild form), and that is designed to work in a controlled, contained environment, will simply be too weak to survive in the wild. For added assurance, perhaps engineering them with failsafe mechanisms will *ensure* that they are incapable of surviving in the wild.

Concerns about Deliberate Misuse

I once heard a well-respected microbiologist say that he was very enthusiastic about synthetic biology, and that the only thing that worries him is the

possibility of catastrophe. The kind of thing that worries him is certainly possible. The 1918 flu virus has been recreated in the laboratory. In 2002, a scientist in New York stitched together stretches of nucleotides to produce a string of DNA that was equivalent to RNA polio virus and eventually produced the RNA virus using the DNA string. More recently, the SARS virus was also created in the laboratory. Eventually, it will almost certainly be possible to recreate bacterial pathogens like smallpox. We might also be able to enhance these pathogens. Some work in Australia on mousepox suggests ways of making smallpox more potent, for example. In theory, entirely new pathogens could be created. Pathogens that target crops or livestock are also possible.

Controlling this risk means controlling the people and companies who have access to DNA synthesis or the tools they could use to synthesize DNA themselves. There are some reasons to think that the worst will never actually happen. To be wielded effectively, destructive synthetic organisms would also have to be weaponized; for example, methods must be found to disperse pathogens in forms that will lead to epidemic infection in the target population while sparing one's own population. Arguably, terrorists have better forms of attacking their enemies than with bioweapons, which are still comparatively hard to make and are very hard to control. However, our policy should amount to more than hoping for the best.

Governance

In assessing these risks and establishing oversight over synthetic biology, we do not start from square one. There is an existing framework of laws and regulations, put into action by various agencies and oversight bodies, that will apply to R&D and to different applications. The NIH is extending its guidelines for research on genetic engineering to ensure that they are applicable to research on synthetic biology. These Guidelines are enforced by the NIH's Recombinant DNA Advisory Committee and a network of Institutional Biosafety Committees at research institutions receiving federal funding. Many applications would fall under the purview of various federal laws and the agencies that enforce them. For example, a plan to release synthetic organisms into the sea to produce nutrients that would help rebuild ocean food chains would have to pass muster with the EPA. The USDA and FDA also have regulatory authority over applications. The FBI and the NIH's National Science Advisory Board for Biosecurity are formulating policy to regulate the sale of synthetic DNA sequences that might pose a threat to biosecurity.

At the same time, the current regulatory framework may need to be augmented. First, there are questions about whether the existing laws leave gaps. Research conducted by entirely privately funded laboratory might not [be] covered by the NIH's Guidelines, for example. Field testing of a synthetic organism—that is, release into the environment as part of basic research— might not be covered by the existing regulations of the EPA or the USDA. Questions about the adequacy of existing regulations are even more pointed when it comes to concerns about biosecurity, particularly if or when powerful benchtop synthesizers are available in every lab.

The other big question is whether the regulatory bodies' ability to do risk assessment of synthetic biology is adequate. Synthetic biology differs from older forms of genetic engineering in that a synthetic organism could combine DNA sequences found originally in many different organisms, or might even contain entirely novel genetic code. The eventual behavior of these organisms in new environments, should they accidentally end up in one, may therefore be hard to predict.

The synthetic biologists' goal of simplicity is crucial. One of the themes of traditional biology is that living things are usually more complex than they first appear. We should not assume at the outset that synthetic organisms will shed the unpredictability inherent to life. Life tends to find a way. As a starting assumption, we should expect that artificial life will try to find a way as well.

Another difficulty in assessing concerns about both biosafety and deliberate misuse is that, if the field evolves so that important and even innovative work could be done in small, private labs, even in homes, then it could be very difficult to monitor and regulate. The threats of biosafety and deliberate misuse would have to be taken yet more seriously.

Concluding Comments

I take seriously concerns that synthetic biology is bad in and of itself, and I believe that they warrant a thorough public airing, but I do not believe that they provide a good basis for restraining the technology, at least if we can be confident that the organisms will not lead to environmental damage. Better yet would be to get out in front of the technology and ensure that it benefits the environment. Possibly, some potential applications of synthetic biology are more troubling than others and should be treated differently.

Ultimately, I think the field should be assessed on its possible outcomes. At the moment, we do not understand the possible outcomes well enough. We need, I believe:

- more study of the emergence, plausibility, and impact of potential risks;
- a strategy for studying the risks that is multidisciplinary, rather than one conducted entirely within the field;
- a strategy that is grounded in good science rather than sheer speculation, yet flexible enough to look for the unexpected; and
- an analysis of whether our current regulatory framework is adequate to deal with these risks and how the framework should be augmented.

Different kinds of applications pose different risks and may call for different responses. Microbes intended for release into the environment, for example, would pose a different set of concerns than microbes designed to be kept in specialized, contained settings. Overall, however, while the risks of synthetic biology are too significant to leave the field alone, its potential benefits are too great to call for a general moratorium.

EXPLORING THE ISSUE

Should Society Impose a Moratorium on the Use and Release of "Synthetic Biology" Organisms?

Critical Thinking and Reflection

1. What are "dual-use" technologies?
2. Does creating a synthetic cell disprove the idea that life is sacred?
3. How long do you think it will be before synthetic biology can be done at home? Is the prospect frightening?
4. Can all risks be prevented?

Is There Common Ground?

As with many technologies, some people see mostly risks and would, if they could, stop the development of the technology. Others see mostly benefits and think that those benefits are worth putting up with the risks. A more nuanced approach is to determine which risks and benefits seem most likely and then to carefully weigh them against each other. This approach is known as risk–benefit or cost–benefit analysis, and it is used in medicine, engineering, business, and other areas.

1. What seem to be the most likely or worrisome risks associated with synthetic biology technology?
2. What seem to be the most likely benefits associated with synthetic biology technology?
3. Do you think the benefits are worth the risks?

ISSUE 21

Is Cyber-War or Cyber-Terrorism a Genuine Threat?

YES: **Mike McConnell**, from "Mike McConnell on How to Win the Cyber-War We're Losing," *The Washington Post* (February 28, 2010)

NO: **Maura Conway**, from "Privacy and Security Against Cyberterrorism," *Communications of the ACM* (February 2011)

Learning Outcomes
After studying this issue, students will be able to:
1. Describe the potential impact of a cyber-war attack on the United States.
2. Explain what measures might be taken to prevent cyber-war or cyber-terrorism attacks.
3. Explain why cyber-war or cyber-terrorism attacks may be unlikely.

ISSUE SUMMARY

YES: Mike McConnell argues that the United States is already under attack by cyber-warriors, and we are losing. We need to upgrade cyber-defenses and be prepared to counter-attack. This may include requiring the private sector to share more information with government agencies.

NO: Maura Conway argues that even though various cyber-based attacks have been called "cyber-war" and "cyber-terrorism," definitions are crucial. In particular, "cyber-terrorism" fails to qualify as terrorism because it lacks the spectacular public impact of destroying buildings with airliners. "Cyberterrorism . . . is not in our near future."

In June 2010, the Stuxnet worm attacked Iranian nuclear facilities. It used stolen digital certificates to take over control software and interfere with the normal function of nuclear power plants, electrical distribution systems, and oil pipelines. Early reports said the Stuxnet worm was so complex that it must have taken large teams of programmers, millions of dollars in funding, and many months of work to produce it. Iran insisted it had to be an Israeli-American

cyber-attack, and on June 1, 2012, David E. Sanger reported in "Obama Order Sped up Wave of Cyberattacks against Iran," *New York Times*, that interviews with European, U.S., and Israeli officials have revealed that in 2006, President George W. Bush initiated the development of the Stuxnet worm under the code-name Olympic Games. Samuel Greengard, "The New Face of War," *Communications of the ACM* (December 2010), considers this a sign of the way wars will be fought in the future. "The risk of cyber-warfare is growing, and many . . . warn that political leaders aren't entirely tuned into the severity of the threat." It must be taken seriously, for it is only a matter of time before cyber-war is real. Richard A. Clarke and Richard K. Knake, *Cyber War: The Next Threat to National Security and What to Do about It* (HarperCollins, 2010), stress that because society is now totally dependent on telecommunications networks, it is also vulnerable to widespread, long-lasting damage. James P. Farwell and Rafal Rohozinski, "Stuxnet and the Future of Cyber War," *Survival* (February/March 2011), note that cyber-war "offers great potential for striking at enemies with less risk than using traditional means." They also note that many cyber-war techniques are rooted in cyber-crime (viruses, worms, bot-nets, identity theft, hacking, fraud, and more), which has been with us since the dawn of the Internet.

The methods of defending against cyber-war and cyber-terrorism are also rooted in the fight against cyber-crime. Few people today do not have antivirus and/or anti-malware software on their computers. The U.S. government has long sought extensions to digital telephony and the Internet of traditional wiretapping laws that permitted law-enforcement agencies to listen in on the conversations of criminal suspects (see Declan McCullagh, "FBI: We Need Wiretap-Ready Web Sites—Now," *CNET News* (May 4, 2012), http://news.cnet.com/8301-1009_3-57428067-83/fbi-we-need-wiretap-ready-web-sites-now/). After September 11, 2001, the War on Terrorism began and every tool that promised to help identify terrorists before or catch them after they committed their dreadful acts was seen as desirable. However, when the Department of Defense's Defense Advanced Research Projects Agency (DARPA) proposed a massive computer system capable of sifting through purchases, tax data, court records, Google searches, e-mails, and other information from government and commercial databases to seek suspicious patterns of behavior, many people objected that this amounted to a massive assault on privacy and was surely in violation of the Fourth Amendment to the U.S. Constitution (which established the right of private citizens to be secure against unreasonable searches and seizures; "unreasonable" has come to mean "without a search warrant" for physical searches of homes and offices and "without a court order" for interceptions of mail and wiretappings of phone conversations). This Total or Terrorism Information Awareness (TIA) program soon died although many of its components continued under other names; see Shane Harris, "TIA Lives On," *National Journal* (February 25, 2006). Simon Cooper, "Who's Spying on You?" *Popular Mechanics* (January 2005), argues that we are now subject to massively increased routine surveillance and the collection of personal data by both government and business with very few restrictions on how the data are used. Peter Brown, "Privacy in an Age of Terabytes and Terror," *Scientific American* (September 2008), says, "A cold wind is blowing across the landscape of privacy. The twin imperatives of technological advancement and

counter-terrorism have led to dramatic and possibly irreversible changes in what people can expect to remain of private life." See also Hina Shamsi and Alex Abdo, "Privacy and Surveillance Post-9/11," *Human Rights* (Winter 2011).

Fears of government intrusion were not eased when in July 2008 President Bush signed the revised Foreign Intelligence Surveillance Act, designed to expand the government's warrantless electronic spying activities and ensure retroactive immunity for cooperative telecommunications firms. Nor in 2011 when Congress reapproved the Patriot Act and President Obama signed the bill. Government surveillance programs such as these reflect many fears about the Internet—that it is a place where evil lurks, where technically skilled criminals use their skills to fleece the unsuspecting public, where terrorists plot unseen, where enemy nations plot to destroy industrial infrastructure and bring the nation to its knees, and where technology lends immunity to detection, apprehension, and prosecution. David Talbot, "Moore's Outlaws," *Technology Review* (July/August 2010), notes that the threat is growing rapidly, and sooner or later a cyber-war or cyber-terrorist attack will bring a city or major corporation to its knees. Former Homeland Security official Stewart Baker compared the potential impact to that of the BP oil spill in the Gulf of Mexico; see Pam Benson, "U.S. Vulnerable to Cyber Threats, Experts Warn," *CNN.com* (June 17, 2010), www.cnn.com/2010/ US/06/16/cyber.threats.report/index.html?hpt+C2. Austin Wright, "The Unseen Cyber-War," *National Defense* (December 2009), describes numerous efforts to penetrate the computers of government and defense contractors to steal defense secrets. However, notes Seymour M. Hersh, "The Online Threat," *New Yorker* (November 1, 2010), cyber-espionage is not the same thing as cyber-war.

Does this amount to a real "cyber-terrorism" or "cyber-war" threat? General Keith Alexander, head of the Defense Department's U.S. Cyber Command (www.defense.gov/home/features/2010/0410_cybersec/), is preparing as if it does. However, Howard Schmidt, the Obama administration's cybersecurity chief, says "There is no cyberwar" (see Ryan Singel, "White House Cyber Czar: 'There Is No Cyberwar,'" *Wired Online* (March 4, 2010), www.wired.com/threatlevel/2010/03/ Schmidt-cyberwar/. Robert Graham of Errata Security insists "Cyberwar Is Fiction" (June 7, 2010), http://erratasec.blogspot.com/2010/06/cyberwar-is-fiction.html. Peter Sommer and Ian Brown, "Reducing Systemic Cybersecurity Risk" OECD (Organization for Economic Co-operation and Development)/IFP (International Futures Programme) Project on "Future Global Shocks," 2011), conclude "that very few single cyber-related events have the capacity to cause a global shock. Governments nevertheless need to make detailed preparations to withstand and recover from a wide range of unwanted cyber events, both accidental and deliberate. There are significant and growing risks of localised misery and loss as a result of compromise of computer and telecommunications services." Robert A. Miller, Daniel T. Kuehl, and Irving Lachow, "Cyber War: Issues in Attack and Defense," *Joint Force Quarterly* (2nd Quarter, 2011), say that some sort of cyber-war is an inevitable component of future conflicts, and dealing with it will not be easy. Ellen Nakashima, "With Plan X, Pentagon Seeks to Spread U.S. Military Might to Cyberspace," *Washington Post* (May 31, 2012), reports that the DARPA is now working on developing techniques to launch cyberstrikes against computer-based attacks, as well as survive those attacks.

In a debate over whether the cyber-war threat is being exaggerated (Tim Wilson, "In Debate, Audience Finds that the Cyberwar Threat Is Not Exaggerated," *DarkReading* (June 10, 2010), www.darkreading.com/story/showArticle .jhtml?articleID=225600193, participants agreed that there has been a great deal of hype about the topic, but the threat is real. On the other hand, many people worry that the worse threat is that posed to civil rights and privacy by efforts to enhance security by monitoring and regulating the Internet. Stephen J. Lukasik, "Protecting Users of the Cyber Commons," *Communications of the ACM* (September 2011), suggests that the best approach may be a bottom-up, community-based threat identification and response system and notes that similar community-based approaches have served the Internet very well in other areas. Others note the need for international treaties; see Scott W. Beidleman, "Defining and Deterring Cyber War," *Military Technology* (2011), and Seung Hyun Kim et al., "A Comparative Study of Cyber Attacks," *Communications of the ACM* (March 2012).

In May 2011, two security researchers demonstrated that it was possible to create a Stuxnet-type threat with very limited resources—at home, on a laptop computer, and in just a couple of months. According to Shaun Waterman, "Homemade Cyberweapon Worries Federal Officials," *Washington Times* (May 24, 2011), "Officials at the Department of Homeland Security were so distressed by the researchers' findings that they asked the two men to cancel a planned presentation at a computer security conference." They obliged, but the incident raises concerns about how easy it would be for nations, terrorists, or criminals to attack major components of society's infrastructure. In June 2011, the U.S. Department of Defense announced that it was prepared to retaliate against cyber-attacks with conventional weaponry; see David Talbot, "U.S. Aims Missiles at Hackers," *Technology Review Online* (June 2, 2011), www.technologyreview.com/web/37692/?a=f. However, Jerry Brito and Tate Wilkins recall the Bush administration lies about Iraq's nuclear threat in "Wired Opinion: Cyberwar Is the New Yellowcake," *Wired Online* (February 14, 2012), www.wired.com/threatlevel/2012/02/yellowcake-and-cyberwar/. R. Scott Kemp, "Cyberweapons: Bold Steps in a Digital Darkness?" *Bulletin of the Atomic Scientists* (June 7, 2012), www.thebulletin.org/web-edition/op-eds/cyberweapons-bold-steps-digital-darkness, argues that "We are at a key turning point . . . in which a nation must decide what role cyberweapons will play in its national defense. . . . for the United States and other highly developed nations whose societies are critically and deeply reliant on computers, the safe approach is to direct cyber research at purely defensive applications."

In the YES selection, Mike McConnell, director of the National Security Agency in the Clinton administration and director of national intelligence during President George W. Bush's second term, argues that the United States is already under attack by cyber-warriors, and we are losing. We need to upgrade cyber-defenses and be prepared to counter-attack. This may include requiring the private sector to share more information with government agencies. In the NO selection, Maura Conway argues that even though various cyber-based attacks have been called "cyber-war" and "cyber-terrorism," definitions are crucial. In particular, "cyber-terrorism" fails to qualify as terrorism because it lacks the spectacular public impact of destroying buildings with airliners. "Cyberterrorism . . . is not in our near future."

YES

Mike McConnell

Mike McConnell on How to Win the Cyber-War We're Losing

The United States is fighting a cyber-war today, and we are losing. It's that simple. As the most wired nation on Earth, we offer the most targets of significance, yet our cyber-defenses are woefully lacking.

The problem is not one of resources; even in our current fiscal straits, we can afford to upgrade our defenses. The problem is that we lack a cohesive strategy to meet this challenge.

The stakes are enormous. To the extent that the sprawling U.S. economy inhabits a common physical space, it is in our communications networks. If an enemy disrupted our financial and accounting transactions, our equities and bond markets or our retail commerce—or created confusion about the legitimacy of those transactions—chaos would result. Our power grids, air and ground transportation, telecommunications, and water-filtration systems are in jeopardy as well.

These battles are not hypothetical. Google's networks were hacked in an attack that began in December and that the company said emanated from China. And recently the security firm NetWitness reported that more than 2,500 companies worldwide were compromised in a sophisticated attack launched in 2008 and aimed at proprietary corporate data. Indeed, the recent Cyber Shock Wave simulation revealed what those of us involved in national security policy have long feared: For all our war games and strategy documents focused on traditional warfare, we have yet to address the most basic questions about cyber-conflicts.

What is the right strategy for this most modern of wars? Look to history. During the Cold War, when the United States faced an existential threat from the Soviet Union, we relied on deterrence to protect ourselves from nuclear attack. Later, as the East-West stalemate ended and nuclear weapons proliferated, some argued that preemption made more sense in an age of global terrorism.

The cyber-war mirrors the nuclear challenge in terms of the potential economic and psychological effects. So, should our strategy be deterrence or preemption? The answer: both. Depending on the nature of the threat, we can deploy aspects of either approach to defend America in cyberspace.

During the Cold War, deterrence was based on a few key elements: attribution (understanding who attacked us), location (knowing where a strike came from), response (being able to respond, even if attacked first) and transparency (the enemy's knowledge of our capability and intent to counter with massive force).

Against the Soviets, we dealt with the attribution and location challenges by developing human intelligence behind the Iron Curtain and by fielding early-warning radar systems, reconnaissance satellites and undersea listening posts to monitor threats. We invested heavily in our response capabilities with intercontinental ballistic missiles, submarines and long-range bombers, as well as command-and-control systems and specialized staffs to run them. The resources available were commensurate with the challenge at hand—as must be the case in cyberspace.

Just as important was the softer side of our national security strategy: the policies, treaties and diplomatic efforts that underpinned containment and deterrence. Our alliances, such as NATO, made clear that a strike on one would be a strike on all and would be met with massive retaliation. This unambiguous intent, together with our ability to monitor and respond, provided a credible nuclear deterrent that served us well.

How do we apply deterrence in the cyber-age? For one, we must clearly express our intent. Secretary of State Hillary Rodham Clinton offered a succinct statement to that effect last month in Washington, in a speech on Internet freedom. "Countries or individuals that engage in cyber-attacks should face consequences and international condemnation," she said. "In an Internet-connected world, an attack on one nation's networks can be an attack on all."

That was a promising move, but it means little unless we back it up with practical policies and international legal agreements to define norms and identify consequences for destructive behavior in cyberspace. We began examining these issues through the Comprehensive National Cybersecurity Initiative, launched during the George W. Bush administration, but more work is needed on outlining how, when and where we would respond to an attack. For now, we have a response mechanism in name only.

The United States must also translate our intent into capabilities. We need to develop an early-warning system to monitor cyberspace, identify intrusions and locate the source of attacks with a trail of evidence that can support diplomatic, military and legal options—and we must be able to do this in milliseconds. More specifically, we need to reengineer the Internet to make attribution, geolocation, intelligence analysis and impact assessment—who did it, from where, why and what was the result—more manageable. The technologies are already available from public and private sources and can be further developed if we have the will to build them into our systems and to work with our allies and trading partners so they will do the same.

Of course, deterrence can be effective when the enemy is a state with an easily identifiable government and location. It is less successful against criminal groups or extremists who cannot be readily traced, let alone deterred through sanctions or military action.

There are many organizations (including al-Qaeda) that are not motivated by greed, as with criminal organizations, or a desire for geopolitical advantage, as with many states. Rather, their worldview seeks to destroy the systems of global commerce, trade and travel that are undergirded by our cyber-infrastructure. So deterrence is not enough; preemptive strategies might be required before such adversaries launch a devastating cyber-attack.

We preempt such groups by degrading, interdicting and eliminating their leadership and capabilities to mount cyber-attacks, and by creating a more resilient cyberspace that can absorb attacks and quickly recover. To this end, we must hammer out a consensus on how to best harness the capabilities of the National Security Agency, which I had the privilege to lead from 1992 to 1996. The NSA is the only agency in the United States with the legal authority, oversight and budget dedicated to breaking the codes and understanding the capabilities and intentions of potential enemies. The challenge is to shape an effective partnership with the private sector so information can move quickly back and forth from public to private—and classified to unclassified—to protect the nation's critical infrastructure.

We must give key private-sector leaders (from the transportation, utility and financial arenas) access to information on emerging threats so they can take countermeasures. For this to work, the private sector needs to be able to share network information—on a controlled basis—without inviting lawsuits from shareholders and others.

Obviously, such measures must be contemplated very carefully. But the reality is that while the lion's share of cybersecurity expertise lies in the federal government, more than 90 percent of the physical infrastructure of the Web is owned by private industry. Neither side on its own can mount the cyber-defense we need; some collaboration is inevitable. Recent reports of a possible partnership between Google and the government point to the kind of joint efforts—and shared challenges—that we are likely to see in the future.

No doubt, such arrangements will muddy the waters between the traditional roles of the government and the private sector. We must define the parameters of such interactions, but we should not dismiss them. Cyberspace knows no borders, and our defensive efforts must be similarly seamless.

Ultimately, to build the right strategy to defend cyberspace, we need the equivalent of President Dwight D. Eisenhower's Project Solarium. That 1953 initiative brought together teams of experts with opposing views to develop alternative strategies on how to wage the Cold War. The teams presented their views to the president, and Eisenhower chose his preferred approach—deterrence. We now need a dialogue among business, civil society and government on the challenges we face in cyberspace—spanning international law, privacy and civil liberties, security, and the architecture of the Internet. The results should shape our cybersecurity strategy.

We prevailed in the Cold War through strong leadership, clear policies, solid alliances and close integration of our diplomatic, economic and military efforts. We backed all this up with robust investments—security never comes cheap. It worked, because we had to make it work.

Let's do the same with cybersecurity. The time to start was yesterday.

Maura Conway  **NO**

Privacy and Security Against Cyberterrorism

Like the 2007 cyber attacks on Estonia, the October 2010 Stuxnet botnet attack on Iranian nuclear facilities made cyber-based attacks global news. The Estonian attacks were largely labeled a cyberwar by journalists, although some did invoke the concept of cyberterrorism. The Stuxnet attack, on the other hand, has been very widely described as cyberterrorism, including by the Iranian government.

Cyberterrorism is a concept that appears recurrently in contemporary media. It is not just reported upon in newspapers and on television, but is also the subject of movies (such as 1990's *Die Hard II* and 2007's *Die Hard IV: Live Free or Die Hard*) and popular fiction books (for example, Winn Schwartau's 2002 novel *Pearl Harbor Dot Com*). This coverage is particularly interesting if one believes, as I do, that no act of cyberterrorism has ever yet occurred and is unlikely to at any time in the near future. Having said that, it is almost always portrayed in the press as either having already occurred or being just around the corner. As an academic, I'm not alone in arguing that no act of cyberterrorism has yet occurred and, indeed, some journalists agree; most, however, seem convinced as to the salience of this threat. Why?

I can only surmise that, just as a large amount of social psychological research has shown, the uncertain and the unknown generally produce fear and anxiety. This is the psychological basis of an effective movie thriller: the fear is greatest when you suspect something, but you're not certain what it is. The term "cyberterrorism" unites two significant modern fears: fear of technology and fear of terrorism. Fear of terrorism, though the likelihood of any one of us being the victim of terrorism is statistically insignificant, has become perhaps normalized; but fear of technology? In fact, for those unfamiliar with the workings of complex technologies, these are perceived as arcane, unknowable, abstract, and yet increasingly powerful and ubiquitous. Many people therefore fear that technology will become the master and humankind the servant. Couple this relatively new anxiety with age-old fears associated with apparently random violence and the result is a truly heightened state of alarm. Many journalists—although fewer technology journalists than others—have succumbed, like members of the general population, to these fears, to which the journalists have then added further fuel with their reporting.

From *Communications of the ACM*, February 2011, pp. 26–28. Copyright © 2011 by Association for Computing Machinery. Reprinted by permission.

The Definition Issue

The second stumbling block for journalists is that just as the definition of terrorism is fraught, so too is the definition of cyberterrorism. My preference is to distinguish between cyberterrorism and terrorist use of the Net. This is the distinction FBI Director Robert Mueller seemed implicitly to be drawing in a March 2010 speech in which he stated that "the Internet is not only used to plan and execute attacks; it is a target in and of itself . . . We in the FBI, with our partners in the intelligence community, believe the cyber terrorism threat is real, and it is rapidly expanding." Where the FBI Director and I diverge is in the efficacy of the cyberterrorist threat as opposed to that of everyday terrorist use of the Net (that is, for radicalization, researching and planning, financing, and other purposes).

Dorothy Denning's definitions of cyberterrorism are probably the most well known and respected. Her most recent attempt at defining cyberterrorism is: ". . . [H]ighly damaging computer-based attacks or threats of attack by non-state actors against information systems when conducted to intimidate or coerce governments or societies in pursuit of goals that are political or social. It is the convergence of terrorism with cyberspace, where cyberspace becomes the means of conducting the terrorist act. Rather than committing acts of violence against persons or physical property, the cyberterrorist commits acts of destruction or disruption against digital property."

Analyses of cyberterrorism can be divided into two broad categories on the basis of where the producers stand on the definition issue: those who agree broadly with Denning versus those who wish to incorporate not just use, but a host of other activities into the definition. The literature can also be divided on the basis of where the authors stand on the magnitude of the cyberterrorism threat. Dunn-Cavelty uses the term "Hypers" to describe those who believe a cyberterrorist attack is not just likely, but imminent, and the term "De-Hypers" to describe those who believe such an attack is unlikely. Most journalists are hypers, on the other hand I'm emphatically a de-hyper. In this column, I lay out the three major reasons why.

Three Arguments Against Cyberterrorism

In my opinion, the three most compelling arguments against cyberterrorism are:

- The argument of Technological Complexity;
- The argument regarding 9/11 and the Image Factor; and
- The argument regarding 9/11 and the Accident Issue.

The first argument is treated in the academic literature; the second and third arguments are not, but ought to be. None of these are angles to which journalists appear to have devoted a lot of thought or given adequate consideration.

In the speech mentioned earlier, FBI Director Mueller observed "Terrorists have shown a clear interest in pursuing hacking skills. And they will either train their own recruits or hire outsiders, with an eye toward combining

physical attacks with cyber attacks." That may very well be true, but the argument from Technological Complexity underlines that "wanting" to do something is quite different from having the ability to do the same. Here's why:

Violent jihadis' IT knowledge is not superior. For example, in research carried out in 2007, it was found that of a random sampling of 404 members of violent Islamist groups, 196 (48.5%) had a higher education, with information about subject areas available for 178 individuals. Of these 178, some 8 (4.5%) had trained in computing, which means that out of the entire sample, less than 2% of the jihadis came from a computing background. And not even these few could be assumed to have mastery of the complex systems necessary to carry out a successful cyberterrorist attack.

Real-world attacks are difficult enough. What are often viewed as relatively unsophisticated real-world attacks undertaken by highly educated individuals are routinely unsuccessful. One only has to consider the failed car bomb attacks planned and carried out by medical doctors in central London and at Glasgow airport in June 2007.

Hiring hackers would compromise operational security. The only remaining option is to retain "outsiders" to undertake such an attack. This is very operationally risky. It would force the terrorists to operate outside their own circles and thus leave them ripe for infiltration. Even if they successfully got in contact with "real" hackers, they would be in no position to gauge their competency accurately; they would simply have to trust in same. This would be very risky.

So on the basis of technical know-how alone cyberterror attack is not imminent, but this is not the only factor one must take into account. The events of Sept. 11, 2001 underscore that for a true terrorist event spectacular moving images are crucial. The attacks on the World Trade Center were a fantastic piece of performance violence; look back on any recent roundup of the decade and mention of 9/11 will not just be prominent, but pictures will always be provided.

The problem with respect to cyberterrorism is that many of the attack scenarios put forward, from shutting down the electric power grid to contaminating a major water supply, fail on this account: they are unlikely to have easily captured, spectacular (live, moving) images associated with them, something we—as an audience—have been primed for by the attack on the World Trade Center on 9/11.

The only cyberterrorism scenario that would fall into this category is interfering with air traffic control systems to crash planes, but haven't we seen that planes can much more easily be employed in spectacular "real-world" terrorism? And besides, aren't all the infrastructures just mentioned much easier and more spectacular to simply blow up? It doesn't end there, however. For me, the third argument against cyberterrorism is perhaps the most compelling; yet it is very rarely mentioned.

In 2004, Howard Schmidt, former White House Cybersecurity Coordinator, remarked to the U.S. Senate Committee on the Judiciary regarding Nimda and Code Red that "we to this day don't know the source of that. It could have very easily been a terrorist." This observation betrays a fundamental

misunderstanding of the nature and purposes of terrorism, particularly its attention-getting and communicative functions.

A terrorist attack with the potential to be hidden, portrayed as an accident, or otherwise remain unknown is unlikely to be viewed positively by any terrorist group. In fact, one of the most important aspects of the 9/11 attacks in New York from the perpetrators viewpoint was surely the fact that while the first plane to crash into the World Trade Center could have been accidental, the appearance of the second plane confirmed the incident as a terrorist attack in real time. Moreover, the crash of the first plane ensured a large audience for the second plane as it hit the second tower.

Alternatively, think about the massive electric failure that took place in the northeastern U.S. in August 2003: if it was a terrorist attack—and I'm not suggesting that it was—but *if it was*, it would have been a spectacular failure.

Conclusion

Given the high cost—not just in terms of money, but also time, commitment, and effort—and the high possibility of failure on the basis of manpower issues, timing, and complexity of a potential cyberterrorist attack, the costs appear to me to still very largely outweigh the potential publicity benefits. The publicity aspect is crucial for potential perpetrators of terrorism and so the possibility that an attack may be apprehended or portrayed as an accident, which would be highly likely with regard to cyberterrorism, is detrimental. Add the lack of spectacular moving images and it is my belief that cyberterrorism, regardless of what you may read in newspapers, see on television, or obtain via other media sources, is not in our near future.

So why then the persistent treatment of cyberterrorism on the part of journalists? Well, in this instance, science fiction-type fears appear to trump rational calculation almost every time. And I haven't even begun to discuss how the media discourse has clearly influenced the pronouncements of policymakers.

EXPLORING THE ISSUE

Is Cyber-War or Cyber-Terrorism a Genuine Threat?

Critical Thinking and Reflection

1. Is there a difference between "cyber-war" and "cyber-terrorism"?
2. Is all the talk of "cyber-war" and "cyber-terrorism" just hype?
3. The Defense Department is talking of retaliating against cyber-attackers with conventional weapons. Why will it be difficult to find the cyber-attackers?

Is There Common Ground?

There are many reasons to keep intruders out of computer networks. Criminal hackers use malware to take control of home (and other) computers to steal private information—usernames and passwords, in particular—so they can steal from bank accounts, use credit cards, and steal identity. Spies want to steal secret files. Cyber-warriors may wish to disrupt electricity generation, shut down factories, shut down the Internet, or perhaps just mess with a city's traffic lights to cause traffic jams (among other things). In other words, it may be less about cyber-war than about cyber-security.

1. How do you protect your own computer (passwords, firewalls, encryption, etc.)?
2. Visit your campus IT department and ask how it protects the campus network from intruders.
3. Do you think similar measures would work against a cyber-war or cyber-terrorist attack?

Internet References

United States Department of Defense, U.S. Cyber Command

The U.S. Cyber Command is a unit of the Department of Defense (DoD) that defends information networks and prepares to conduct military cyberspace operations to ensure US/Allied freedom of action in cyberspace and deny the same to adversaries.

www.defense.gov/home/features/2010/0410_cybersec/

ISSUE 22

Will Robots Take Your Job?

YES: Marshall Brain, from "Robotic Nation" (Summer 2003), http://marshallbrain.com/robotic-nation.htm

NO: Peter Gorle and Andrew Clive, from "Positive Impact of Industrial Robots on Employment," *Metra Martech* (February 21, 2011)

Learning Outcomes
After studying this issue, students will be able to:
1. Explain what kinds of jobs are now and may soon be suitable for robots.
2. Discuss the impact of robotics on their future job prospects.
3. Apply their understanding of how robots will affect future jobs in a discussion of career choices.

ISSUE SUMMARY

YES: Marshall Brain argues that by the middle of the twenty-first century, robots will be able to perform nearly any normal job that a human performs today. They will eliminate a huge portion of the jobs currently held by humans. Those humans will be unemployed and—if welfare systems cannot keep up with need—destitute. He insists that "It is time to start rethinking our economy."

NO: Peter Gorle and Andrew Clive argue that robots are not a threat to human employment. Historically, increases in the use of automation almost always increase both productivity and employment. Over the next few years, the use of robotics will generate 700,000–1,000,000 new jobs.

T he idea that technology threatens jobs is not new. In the early 1800s, the "Luddites" were textile workers who destroyed new weaving machinery that could be operated by unskilled labor. The movement faded away with the end of the Napoleonic Wars, but its name has continued to be applied to those

who oppose industrialization, automation, computerization, and even any new technology. See, for example, Steven E. Jones, *Against Technology: From the Luddites to Neo-Luddism* (CRC Press, 2006).

Not surprisingly, modern computer technology arouses many job-related fears, for computers seem to be growing ever more capable. When IBM's "Watson" won a dramatic victory in the game of "Jeopardy," many wondered if we were finally seeing true artificial intelligence. Kirk L. Kroeker, "Weighing Watson's Impact," *Communications of the ACM* (July 2011), notes that despite many dismissive comments, Watson is an excellent demonstration of the power of machine learning. Future applications of the technology will soon play important roles in medicine (extracting information from vast numbers of medical books and journals), law, education, and the financial industry. Many of these applications do not require that a robot look and act like a human being, but researchers are working on that, too; see Alex Wright, "Robots Like Us," *Communications of the ACM* (May 2012).

"Robocars"—cars that drive themselves, with no human hand at the wheel—have already been demonstrated and their capabilities are improving rapidly; see Sebastian Thrun, "Toward Robotic Cars," *Communications of the ACM* (April 2010), and Alex Wright, "Automotive Autonomy," *Communications of the ACM* (July 2011). Before they can be broadly used, there must be changes in legislation (can you be guilty of OUI if the car drives itself?) and insurance, among other things; see "The Future of the Self-Driving Automobile," *Trends E-Magazine* (December 2010), and John Markoff, "Collision in the Making Between Self-Driving Cars and How the World Works," *New York Times* (January 23, 2012). Given such changes, we can expect to see job losses among taxi drivers and truckers, among others.

Robots may also cost other people their jobs. Jason Borenstein, "Robots and the Changing Workforce," *AI & Society* (2011), notes that robotic workers are going to become ever more common, and though new job opportunities are bound to arise from this, many jobs will disappear and the human workforce will change in many ways—including necessary education and worker income. Judith Aquino, "Nine Jobs that Humans May Lose to Robots," *Business Insider* (March 22, 2011), says the endangered list includes not only drivers, but also pharmacists, lawyers and paralegals, astronauts, store clerks, soldiers, babysitters, rescuers, and sportswriters and other reporters. John Sepulvado asks "Could a Computer Write This Story?" (CNN, May 11, 2012) (http://edition. cnn.com/2012/05/11/tech/innovation/computer-assisted-writing/index.html), and points to a company, Narrative Science (www.narrativescience.com/), that is working on making the answer yes. Farhad Manjoo asks (and answers) "Will Robots Steal Your Job? If You're Highly Educated, You Should Still Be Afraid," *Slate* (September 26, 2011) (www.slate.com/articles/technology/robot_invasion/2011/09/ will_robots_steal_your_job.html). "Robots to Take 500,000 Human Jobs . . . for Now," *The Fiscal Times* (December 29, 2011), notes that every industry, from agriculture to the military, will be affected. Martin Ford, "Google's Cloud Robotics Strategy—and How It Could Soon Threaten Jobs," *Huffington Post* (January 3, 2012), says that "nearly any type of work that is on some level routine in nature—regardless of the skill level or educational requirements—is likely to

someday be impacted by [robotic] technologies. The only real question is how soon it will happen." This foreboding thought is echoed by Dan Lyons, "Who Needs Humans?" *Newsweek* (July 25, 2011). David J. Lynch is more optimistic: in "It's a Man vs. Machine Recovery," *Bloomberg Businessweek* (January 5, 2012), he notes that businesses are buying machines more than hiring people, but "there's nothing wrong with the labor market that resurgent demand wouldn't fix." There may also be a need to consider the ethics involved, for as more robots enter the workplace, they will bring with them changed expectations (robots are tireless, and they don't need health insurance, retirement plans, vacations, and even pay; will employers expect the same of humans?); this may even mean restricting the use of robots; see Jason Borenstein, "Computing Ethics: Work Life in the Robotic Age," *Communications of the ACM* (July 2010).

How bad is it going to be? In the YES selection, Marshall Brain argues that by the middle of the twenty-first century, robots will be able to perform nearly any normal job that a human performs today. They will eliminate a huge portion of the jobs currently held by humans. Those humans will be unemployed and—if welfare systems cannot keep up with need—destitute. Brain insists that "It is time to start rethinking our economy." (His ideas are also discussed by Joanna Glasner, "How Robots Will Steal Your Job," *Wired* (August 5, 2003).) In the NO selection, Peter Gorle and Andrew Clive argue that robots are not a threat to human employment. Historically, increases in the use of automation almost always increase both productivity and employment. Over the next few years, the use of robotics will generate 700,000–1,000,000 new jobs.

Robotic Nation

I went to McDonald's this weekend with the kids. We go to McDonald's to eat about once a week because it is a mile from the house and has an indoor play area. Our normal routine is to walk in to McDonald's, stand in line, order, stand around waiting for the order, sit down, eat and play.

On Sunday, this decades-old routine changed forever. When we walked in to McDonald's, an attractive woman in a suit greeted us and said, "Are you planning to visit the play area tonight?" The kids screamed, "Yeah!" "McDonald's has a new system that you can use to order your food right in the play area. Would you like to try it?" The kids screamed, "Yeah!"

The woman walks us over to a pair of kiosks in the play area. She starts to show me how the kiosks work and the kids scream, "We want to do it!" So I pull up a chair and the kids stand on it while the (extremely patient) woman in a suit walks the kids through the screens. David ordered his food, Irena ordered her food, I ordered my food. It's a simple system. Then it was time to pay. Interestingly, the kiosk only took cash in the form of bills. So I fed my bills into the machine. Then you take a little plastic number to set on your table and type the number in. The transaction is complete.

We sat down at a table. We put our number in the center of the table and waited. In about 10 seconds the kids screamed, "When is our food going to get here???" I said, "Let's count." In less than two minutes a woman in an apron put a tray with our food on the table, handed us our change, took the plastic number and left.

You know what? It is a nice system. It works. It is much nicer than standing in line. The only improvement I would request is the ability to use a credit card.

As nice as this system is, however, I think that it represents the tip of an iceberg that we do not understand. This iceberg is going to change the American economy in ways that are very hard to imagine.

The Iceberg

The iceberg looks like this. On that same day, I interacted with five different automated systems like the kiosks in McDonald's:

- I got money in the morning from the ATM.
- I bought gas from an automated pump.

- I bought groceries at BJ's (a warehouse club) using an extremely well-designed self-service check out line.
- I bought some stuff for the house at Home Depot using their not-as-well-designed-as-BJ's self-service check out line.
- I bought my food at McDonald's at the kiosk, as described above.

All of these systems are very easy-to-use from a customer standpoint, they are fast, and they lower the cost of doing business and should therefore lead to lower prices. All of that is good, so these automated systems will proliferate rapidly.

The problem is that these systems will also eliminate jobs in massive numbers. In fact, we are about to see a seismic shift in the American workforce. As a nation, we have no way to understand or handle the level of unemployment that we will see in our economy over the next several decades.

These kiosks and self-service systems are the beginning of the robotic revolution. When most people think about robots, they think about independent, autonomous, talking robots like the ones we see in science fiction films. C-3PO and R2-D2 are powerful robotic images that have been around for decades. Robots like these will come into our lives much more quickly than we imagine—self-service checkout systems are the first primitive signs of the trend. Here is one view from the future to show you where we are headed:

> Automated retail systems like ATMs, kiosks and self-service checkout lines marked the beginning of the robotic revolution. Over the course of fifteen years starting in 2001, these systems proliferated and evolved until nearly every retail transaction could be handled in an automated way. Five million jobs in the retail sector were lost as a result of these systems.
>
> The next step was autonomous, humanoid robots. The mechanics of walking were not simple, but Honda had proven that those problems could be solved with the creation of its ASIMO robot at the turn of the century. Sony and other manufacturers followed Honda's lead. Over the course of two decades, engineers refined this hardware and the software controlling it to the point where they could create humanoid bodyforms with the grace and precision of a ballerina or the mass and sheer strength of the Incredible Hulk.
>
> Decades of research and development work on autonomous robotic intelligence finally started to pay off. By 2025, the first machines that could see, hear, move and manipulate objects at a level roughly equivalent to human beings were making their way from research labs into the marketplace. These robots could not "think" creatively like human beings, but that did not matter. Massive AI systems evolved rapidly and allowed machines to perform in ways that seemed very human.
>
> Humanoid robots soon cost less than the average car, and prices kept falling. A typical model had two arms, two legs and the normal human-type sensors like vision, hearing and touch. Power came from small, easily recharged fuel cells. The humanoid form was preferred, as opposed to something odd like R2-D2, because a humanoid shape fit easily into an environment designed around the human body.

A humanoid robot could ride an escalator, climb stairs, drive a car, and so on without any trouble.

Once the humanoid robot became a commodity item, robots began to move in and replace humans in the workplace in a significant way. The first wave of replacement began around 2030, starting with jobs in the fast food industry. Robots also filled janitorial and house-keeping positions in hotels, motels, malls, airports, amusement parks and so on.

The economics of one of these humanoid robots made the decision to buy them almost automatic. In 2030 you could buy a humanoid robot for about $10,000. That robot could clean bathrooms, take out trash, wipe down tables, mop floors, sweep parking lots, mow grass and so on. One robot replaced three six-hour-a-day employees. The owner fired the three employees and in just four months the owner recovered the cost of the robot. The robot would last for many years and would happily work 24 hours a day. The robot also did a far bet-ter job—for example, the bathrooms were absolutely spotless. It was impossible to pass up a deal like that, so corporations began buying armies of humanoid robots to replace human employees.

The first completely robotic fast food restaurant opened in 2031. It had some rough edges, but by 2035 the rough edges were gone and by 2040 most restaurants were completely robotic. By 2055 the robots were everywhere. The changeover was that fast. It was a startling, amaz-ing transformation and the whole thing happened in only 25 years or so starting in 2030.

In 2055 the nation hit a big milestone—over half of the American workforce was unemployed, and the number was still rising. Nearly every "normal" job that had been filled by a human being in 2001 was filled by a robot instead. At restaurants, robots did all the cooking, cleaning and order taking. At construction sites, robots did everything— Robots poured the concrete, laid brick, built the home's frame, put in the windows and doors, sided the house, roofed it, plumbed it, wired it, hung the drywall, painted it, etc. At the airport, robots flew the planes, sold the tickets, moved the luggage, handled security, kept the building clean and managed air traffic control. At the hospital robots cared for the patients, cooked and delivered the food, cleaned every-thing and handled many of the administrative tasks. At the mall, stores were stocked, cleaned and clerked by robots. At the amusement park, hundreds of robots ran the rides, cleaned the park and sold the conces-sions. On the roads, robots drove all the cars and trucks. Companies like Fedex, UPS and the post office had huge numbers of robots instead of people sorting packages, driving trucks and making deliveries.

By 2055 robots had taken over the workplace and there was no turning back.

I know what you are thinking. You are thinking, "This is *impossible*— there will not be humanoid robots in 2055. It is a ridiculous suggestion." But they will be here. Humanoid robots are as inevitable as airplanes.

Imagine this. Imagine that you could travel back in time to the year 1900. Imagine that you stand on a soap box on a city street corner in 1900 and you say to the gathering crowd, "By 1955, people will be flying at supersonic

speeds in sleek aircraft and traveling coast to coast in just a few hours." In 1900, it would have been insane to suggest that. In 1900, *airplanes did not even exist*. Orville and Wilbur did not make the first flight until 1903. The Model T Ford did not appear until 1909.

Yet, by 1947, Chuck Yeager flew the X1 at supersonic speeds. In 1954, the B-52 bomber made its maiden flight. It took only 51 years to go from a rickety wooden airplane flying at 10 MPH, to a gigantic aluminum jet-powered Stratofortress carrying 70,000 pounds of bombs halfway around the world at 550 MPH. In 1958, Pan Am started non-stop jet flights between New York and Paris in the Boeing 707. In 1969, Americans set foot on the moon. It is unbelievable what engineers and corporations can accomplish in 50 or 60 short years.

There were millions of people in 1900 who believed that humans would never fly. They were completely wrong. However, I don't think *anyone* in 1900 could imagine the B-52 happening in 54 years.

Over the next 55 years, the same thing will happen to us with robots. In the process, the entire employment landscape in America will change. Here is why that will happen.

Moore's Law

You have probably heard about Moore's law. It says that CPU power doubles every 18 to 24 months or so. History shows Moore's law very clearly. You can see it, for example, by charting the course of Intel microprocessor chips starting with Intel's first single-chip microprocessor in 1971:

- In 1971, Intel released the 4004 microprocessor. It was a 4-bit chip running at 108 kilohertz. It had about 2,300 transistors. By today's standards it was extremely simple, but it was powerful enough to make one of the first electronic calculators possible.
- In 1981, IBM released the first IBM PC. The original PC was based on the Intel 8088 processor. The 8088 ran at 4.7 megahertz (43 times faster clock speed than the 4004) and had nearly 30,000 transistors (10 times more).
- In 1993, Intel released the first Pentium processor. This chip ran at 60 megahertz (13 times faster clock speed than the 8088) and had over three million transistors (10 times more).
- In 2000 the Pentium 4 appeared. It had a clock speed of 1.5 gigahertz (25 times faster clock speed than the Pentium) and it had 42 million transistors (13 times more). [ref]

You can see that there are two trends that combine to make computer chips more and more powerful. First there is the increasing clock speed. If you take any chip and double its clock speed, then it can perform twice as many operations per second. Then there is the increasing number of transistors per chip. More transistors let you get more done per clock cycle. For example, with the 8088 processor it took approximately 80 clock cycles to multiply two 16-bit integers together. Today you can multiply two 32-bit floating point

numbers every clock cycle. Some chips today even allow you to get more than one floating point operation done per clock cycle.

Taking Moore's law literally, you would expect processor power to increase by a factor of 1,000 every 15 or 20 years. Between 1981 and 2001, that was definitely the case. Clock speed improved by a factor of over 300 during that time, and the number of transistors per chip increased by a factor of 1,400. A processor in 2002 is 10,000 times faster than a processor in 1982 was. This trend has been in place for decades, and there is nothing to indicate that it will slow down any time soon. Scientists and engineers always get around the limitations that threaten Moore's law by developing new technologies. [ref]

The same thing happens with RAM chips and hard disk space. A 10 megabyte hard disk cost about $1,000 in 1982. Today you can buy a 250 gigabyte drive that is twice as fast for $350. Today's drive is 25,000 times bigger and costs one-third the price of the 1982 model because of Moore's law. In the same time period—1982 to 2002—standard RAM (Random Access Memory) available in a home machine has gone from 64 kilobytes to 128 megabytes—it improved by of factor of 2,000.

What if we simply extrapolate out, taking the idea that every 20 years things improve by a factor of 1,000 or 10,000? What we get is a machine in 2020 that has a processor running at something like 10 trillion operations per second. It has a terabyte of RAM and one or two petabytes of storage space (a petabyte is one quadrillion bytes). A machine with this kind of power is nearly incomprehensible—there are only two or three machines on the planet with this kind of power today (the monstrous NEC Earth Simulator, with 5,000 separate processor chips working together, is one example). In 2020, every kid will be running their video games on a $500 machine that has that kind of power.

What if we extrapolate another 20 years after that, to 2040? A typical home machine at that point will be 1,000 times faster than the 2020 machine. Human brains are thought to be able to process at a rate of approximately one quadrillion operations per second. A CPU in the 2040 time frame could have the processing power of a human brain, and it will cost $1,000. It will have a petabyte (one quadrillion bytes) of RAM. It will have one exabyte of storage space. An exabyte is 1,000 quadrillion bytes. That's what Moore's law predicts.

The computer power we will have in a home machine around 2050 will be utterly amazing. A typical home computer will have processing power and memory capacity that exceeds that of a human brain. What we will have in 2100 is anyone's guess. The power of a million human brains on the desktop? It is impossible to imagine, but not unlikely.

We need to start thinking about that future today. People are talking optimistically about fielding a team of humanoid robotic soccer players able to beat the best human players in 2050. Imagine a team of C-3POs running and kicking as well as or better than the best human soccer stars, but never getting tired or injured. Imagine that same sort of robot taking 50% of America's jobs. This Honda ad for ASIMO, and the fact that Honda is running it, are telling:

Between 1981 and 2002, the Processing Power, Hard Disk Space and RAM in a Typical Desktop Computer Increased Dramatically Because of Moore's Law. Extrapolating Out to the Years 2021 and 2041 Shows a Startling Increase in Computer Power. The Point Where Small, Inexpensive Computers Have Power Approaching That of the Human Brain Is Just a Few Decades Away.

	1981	2001	2021	2041
Processor	330 thousand ops/sec	1 billion ops/sec	10 trillion ops/sec	10 quadrillion ops/sec
Disk space	10 megabytes	250 gigabytes	1 petabyte	1 exabyte
Memory (RAM)	64 kilobytes	256 megabytes	1 terabyte	1 petabyte

As the ad says, "ASIMO could be quite useful in some very important tasks." One of those very important tasks will be to take your job.

The point is simple. In the 2050 time frame, you can expect to buy a $1,000 home computer that has the computing power and memory of the human brain. Manufacturers will marry that computer with a humanoid robotic chassis like ASIMO, a fuel cell and advanced AI software to create autonomous humanoid robots with startling capabilities. It is not really hard to imagine that we will have robots like C-3PO walking around and filling jobs as early as the 2030 time frame. What's missing from robots right now is brainpower, and by 2030 we will start to have more silicon brainpower than we know what to do with.

The New Employment Landscape

We have no way to understand what is coming or how it will affect us. Keep this fact in mind: the workplace of today is not really that much different from the workplace of 100 years ago. Humans do almost all of the work today, just like they did in 1900. A restaurant today is nearly identical to a restaurant in 1900. An airport, hotel or amusement park today is nearly identical to any airport, hotel or amusement park seen decades ago. Humans do nearly everything today in the workplace, just like they always have. That's because humans, unlike robots, can see, hear and understand language. Robots have never really competed with humans for real jobs because computers have never had the vision systems needed to drive cars, work in restaurants or deliver packages. All that will change very quickly by the middle of the 21st century. As CPU chips and memory systems finally reach parity with the human brain, and then surpass it, robots will be able to perform nearly any normal job that a human performs today. The self-service checkout lines that are springing up everywhere are the first sign of the trend.

The problem, of course, is that all of these robots will eliminate a huge portion of the jobs currently held by human beings. For example, there are 3.5 million jobs in the fast food industry alone. Many of those will be lost to kiosks. Many more will be lost to robots that can flip burgers and clean bathrooms. Eventually they will all be lost. The only people who will still have jobs in the fast food industry will be the senior management team at corporate headquarters.

The same sort of thing will happen in retail stores, hotels, airports, factories, construction sites, delivery companies and so on. All of these jobs will evaporate at approximately the same time, leaving all of those workers unemployed. The Post Office, FedEx and UPS together employed over a million workers in 2002. Once robots can drive the trucks and deliver the packages at a much lower cost than human workers can, those 1,000,000 or so employees will be out on the street.

If you look at the 2000 census figures, you can see the magnitude of the problem. According to the census, there were 114 million employees working for 7 million companies in 2000. The employees brought home almost $4 trillion in wages that year. Here's the breakdown by industry:

U.S. Jobs by Industry According to the 2000 Census.

NAICS	Industry	Employees	Wages ($1,000)
11	Forestry, fishing, hunting, and agriculture supp	183,565	4,682,533
21	Mining	456,128	22,091,246
22	Utilities	655,230	40,650,836
23	Construction	6,572,800	239,910,149
31–33	Manufacturing	16,473,994	643,953,798
42	Wholesale trade	6,112,029	270,122,206
44–45	Retail trade	14,840,775	302,552,506
48–49	Transportation & warehousing	3,790,002	125,592,421
51	Information	3,545,731	209,393,800
52	Finance & insurance	5,963,426	346,805,452
53	Real estate & rental & leasing	1,942,046	59,212,092
54	Professional, scientific & technical services	6,816,216	362,008,229
55	Management of companies & enterprises	2,873,521	211,361,063
56	Admin, support, waste mgt, remediation services	9,138,100	210,281,063
61	Educational services	2,532,324	61,923,347
71	Arts, entertainment & recreation	1,741,497	43,203,906
72	Accommodation & food services	9,880,923	125,581,836
81	Other services (except public administration)	5,293,399	109,876,770
	Total	114,064,976	3,879,430,052

When you look at this chart, it is easy to understand that there will be huge job losses by 2040 or 2050 as robots move into the workplace. For example:

- Nearly every construction job will go to a robot. That's about 6 million jobs lost.
- Nearly every manufacturing job will go to a robot. That's 16 million jobs lost.
- Nearly every transportation job will go to a robot. That's 3 million jobs lost.
- Many wholesale and retail jobs will go to robots. That's at least 15 million lost jobs.
- Nearly every hotel and restaurant job will go to a robot. That's 10 million jobs lost.

If you add that all up, it's over 50 million jobs lost to robots. That is a conservative estimate. By 2050 or so, it is very likely that over half the jobs in the United States will be held by robots.

All the people who are holding jobs like those today will be unemployed.

American society has no way to deal with a situation where half of the workers are unemployed. During the Great Depression at its very worst, 25% of the population was unemployed. In the robotic future, where 50 million jobs are lost, there is the potential for 50% unemployment. The conventional wisdom says that the economy will create 50 million new jobs to absorb all the unemployed people, but that raises two important questions:

- What will those new jobs be? They won't be in manufacturing—robots will hold all the manufacturing jobs. They won't be in the service sector (where most new jobs are now)—robots will work in all the restaurants and retail stores. They won't be in transportation—robots will be driving everything. They won't be in security (robotic police, robotic firefighters), the military (robotic soldiers), entertainment (robotic actors), medicine (robotic doctors, nurses, pharmacists, counselors), construction (robotic construction workers), aviation (robotic pilots, robotic air traffic controllers), office work (robotic receptionists, call centers and managers), research (robotic scientists), education (robotic teachers and computer-based training), programming or engineering (outsourced to India at one-tenth the cost), farming (robotic agricultural machinery), etc. We are assuming that the economy is going to invent an entirely new category of employment that will absorb half of the working population.
- Why isn't the economy creating those new jobs now? Today there are millions of unemployed people. There are also tens of millions of people who would gladly abandon their minimum wage jobs scrubbing toilets, flipping burgers, driving trucks and shelving inventory for something better. This imaginary new category of employment does not hinge on technology—it is going to employ people, after all, in massive numbers—it is going to employ half of today's working population. Why don't we see any evidence of this new category of jobs today?

Labor = Money

Right now, a majority of people in America trade their labor for money, and then they use the money to participate in the economy. Our entire society is built around a simple equation: *labor = money*. This equation explains why any new labor-saving technology is disruptive—it threatens a group of people with joblessness and welfare.

Autonomous humanoid robots will take disruption to a whole new level. Once fully-autonomous, general-purpose humanoid robots are as easy to buy as an automobile, most people in the economy will not be able to make the *labor = money* trade anymore. They will have no way to earn money, and that means they end up homeless and on welfare.

With that many people on welfare, cost control becomes a big issue. We are already seeing the first signs of it today. The January 20, 2003 issue of *Time* magazine notes the trend:

> "Cities have lost patience, concentrating on getting the homeless out of sight. In New York City, where shelter space can't be created fast enough, Mayor Mike Bloomberg has proposed using old cruise ships for housing."

This is not science fiction—this is today's news. What we are talking about here are massive, government-controlled welfare dormitories keeping everyone who is unemployed "out of sight." Homelessness is increasing because millions of people are living on the edge. Millions of working adults and families are trying to make a living from millions of low-paying jobs at places like Wal-Mart and McDonald's. Most of those low-paying jobs are about to evaporate.

This article from the NYTimes sums up our current situation with this quote:

> Jobs have not followed growth, the committee wrote, because of increases in workers' productivity. In fact, Ms. Reaser said, the unemployment rate is unlikely to fall until the economy expands at an annual rate of 3.5 percent or 4 percent, the sort of pace attained in only two quarters since the recovery supposedly began.
>
> With productivity growing at more than 2 percent a year, and the labor force growing about 1 percent a year, she said, the "hurdle rate" of growth for increasing the share of Americans with jobs cannot be less than 3 percent.

The term "worker productivity" in this quote means "robots." We are seeing the tip of the iceberg right now, because robotic replacement of human workers in every employment sector is about to accelerate rapidly. Combine that with a powerful trend pushing high-paying IT jobs to India. Combine it with the rapid loss of call-center jobs to India. When the first wave of robots and offshore production cut in to the factory workforce in the 20th century, the slack was picked up by service sector jobs. Now we are about to see the

combined loss of massive numbers of service-sector jobs, most of the remaining jobs in factories, and many white collar jobs, all at the same time.

When a significant portion of the normal American population is permanently living in government welfare dormitories because of unemployment, what we will have is a third-world nation. These citizens will be imprisoned by unemployment in their own society. If you are an adult in America and you do not have a job, you are flat out of luck. That is how our economy is structured today—you cannot live your life unless you have a job. Many people—perhaps a majority of Americans—will find themselves out of luck in the coming decades.

The arrival of humanoid robots should be a cause for celebration. With the robots doing most of the work, it should be possible for everyone to go on perpetual vacation. Instead, robots will displace millions of employees, leaving them unable to find work and therefore destitute. I believe that it is time to start rethinking our economy and understanding how we will allow people to live their lives in a robotic nation.

Peter Gorle and Andrew Clive  **NO**

Positive Impact of Industrial Robots on Employment

Introduction

Study Aim

The study analyses the impact of the use of robots in the industrialized production of goods on employment. The study covers years 2000 to 2016.

Project Scope

The sectors considered are:

1. The large automotive players as well as the component suppliers.
2. Electronics and its interface with specialist plastics [solar cells, photovoltaics etc or other advanced materials], particularly clean rooms [but not the very specialised microchip manufacturing application].
3. Food and beverage, [health, cleanliness and safety*]
4. Plastics [and Rubber] Industry as such, not only in combination with Electronics, Chemicals and Pharmaceuticals, . . .

Other than the automotive sector, the brief specified that SMEs (Small and Medium Enterprises) up to 250 employees were specified as the target where possible. By agreement, this has been given less emphasis in the project as there is little available information on the use of robots specifically by smaller companies.

Industrial Robots Are the Target

Global markets are covered by the economic background data. The study then focused on six key countries. Brazil, China, Germany, Japan, Republic of Korea and USA.

Method

The project is based largely on analyses of economic data on the six selected countries.This has been combined with the data on Robot use provided by IFR [International Federation of Robotics].

Conclusions were drawn by the Metra Martech team based on economic and industry knowledge. There are considerable gaps in the information available and the main quantifications show orders of magnitude rather than precise numbers. These conclusions have been tested on IFR members in the countries. The testing process involved a two stage set of questions which were responded to by eighteen of these experts. The first question set established the validity of the main assumptions made by Metra Martech; the second was a more detailed set of questions, sent by IFR to selected experts. . . .

The Economic Factors: And Their Effects on the Use of Robotics

Displacement and Re-Employment

Where automation displaces people in manufacturing it almost always increases output. In some cases it allows such an increase in production and related decrease in unit price that it creates a whole new market and generates the need for downstream jobs to get the product to the consumer. It releases employees for other, often new jobs outside manufacturing. Historically, this has always been the case.

An alternative view is that this displacement in the future will be more difficult to place, as service robotics may take over many of the new job opportunities in human tasks such as in banking, fast food chains, and retailing petrol forecourts.

What is likely is that the growth of the production, marketing, selling and maintaining service robots will create the next wave of employment.

The USA has provided a good example, where the total number of people in employment has grown, driven by increase in population, increased participation by women and increased immigrant labour. The long downward trend in manufacturing as a proportion of total employment has been caused by failure to remain competitive in manufacturing as the industrialising countries have grown capacity. . . .

What is driving this trend to fewer employees in manufacturing is that manufacturers have steadily improved manufacturing productivity, largely by increasing the size of production units, automating tasks and sourcing components globally.

. . . [D]oubling use of robots in the past ten years in USA has not affected the trend. By contrast, Germany, which has proportionately many more robots, also doubled the number of robots and has achieved slightly higher growth with almost no reduction in manufacturing employment.

Pressure to increase productivity in the developed countries, has been precipitated by greatly increased competition from overseas manufacturers, and passing of high labour content production to the low labour cost areas.

Pressure to use robotics in the developing countries has been that, despite availability of low cost labour, consistency and accuracy required to compete

with or meet the requirements of the developed markets, can sometimes only be achieved by robotics.

Five other economic factors have to be considered:

- Globalisation
- Increasing speed of technology development
- Age and skills profiles
- Wage levels
- Health and safety legislation levels

Globalisation of the Market

There has been very rapid growth of the very large developing markets of China and India.

These are low labour cost countries and while labour costs can be expected to level up around the world, these two countries are likely to be relatively low cost areas for at least 20 years. The markets are so large that they encourage the development of locally grown research and technology. This means the phase when China, for example, largely produced goods to western specifications is passing.

Two defences that the developed countries have to maintain their wealth creating production capacity [without putting up trade barriers] are:

1. To put more money into research and development. The success of the Frauenhofer Institutes in Germany, and the new 150bn Yen FIRST projects [Funding program for world leading Innovative R&D on Science and Technology] in Japan are examples of this.
2. To reduce dependence on high cost labour by introducing automation when it offers an economic alternative.

Increasing Speed of Technology Development

This is about the pace of technological development, and the opportunity which this provides for those who can introduce the new technologies. It results in the shortening of product life cycles. Shorter cycles call for more flexible robotics. The product sectors which are the target for this report are not all affected to the same degree by shortening life cycles. Length of production run is an allied factor. Increasing customisation of products, and the flexibility needed by smaller companies are likely to be met by the next generation of robots.

Age and Skills Profiles

The ageing populations in, for example China, Japan and Germany are often cited as an added reason for adoption of robotics. USA is also affected but to a lesser degree.

A very significant ageing is forecast, but if we consider the workforce, within the timescale of the survey, only Japan is significantly affected, with a projected 5% loss of people of employable age. The German situation will

become critical in the following years, but is projected to be less than 2% loss in workforce because of ageing, between now and 2016. Our discussions with robotics experts identify specific problems with ageing workforce in the aerospace sector in USA, but this is outside the scope of the present study.

The existence of skills gaps is reported to be a problem, but this is more a question of education and training regimes than the effect of population ageing.

Several factors are involved in addition to age, the change in population as a whole, the change in people of [currently] employable age, the overall number of people employed and the success of skills training in the country. . . .

Skills Gaps

Even with increasing levels of technology training around the world, reports on the subject show that skills gaps are occurring. The recession has accelerated this. The idea of a jobless recovery [see extract below] favours investment in productivity rather than people. There is another factor connected to this which is the much greater computer and electronic interface skills of the up and coming generation. They also have higher expectations about the type of work they would like to do.

The problem is more of skills mismatch than overall skills availability. This is a structural training problem rather than a consequence of the ageing population.

- jobs are changing
- educational attainment is lagging. . . .

Wage Costs and Availability of Low Cost Labour

One of the arguments against robots, contested by the suppliers, is that they are less flexible in operation and demand more up-front investment than the employment of low cost [often immigrant in the developed countries] labour.

The high labour cost sectors are more likely to use robots.

The differences between the countries are large too, although the interpretation of comparative data is often difficult. . . .

Low Cost Labour

China, and to some extent Brazil, have had access to low cost indigenous labour.

Japan and to a lesser extent Korea have restricted incoming workers.

USA and parts of Europe have until recently allowed this inflow, and both areas have used fewer robots proportionately as a partial result of this, with the exception of Germany. The table shows very large differences in immigration. . . .

Health, Safety [H&S] and Environment

The increasing attention to these factors adds impetus to the employment of robotics in hazardous environments, or those involving great monotony. In the developed countries, H&S is a steadily advancing area; in the developing countries, progress is very sporadic.

According to the International Labor Organization (ILO), 270 million workers fall victim to occupational injuries and illnesses, leading to 2.3 million deaths annually, showing that the problem is significant.

There is pressure from consumer groups to force manufacturers in developing countries to look after their workers to a standard approaching that achieved by the developed world manufacturers, but progress is slow.

However, no specific new initiatives have been identified in the study so far, which would cause a ***step change*** in the current trend to gradual improvement of health and safety practices in the six countries being studied. . . .

Summary

Overall Rise in Employment

Overall paid employment has risen in most countries. In the six considered here, only Japan has seen a decline.

This is driven by increasing participation of women, and increases in population, including immigration in some cases. It is also caused by the increasing demand for services, and the creation of completely new products and markets, often related to the application of electronics to communication.

The statistics mainly point to reduction in employment in manufacturing in the developed countries, but this is often a small reduction. It coincides with an increase in output and an increase in robotics use except in the case of Japan.

The extra number that have gained employment in the years 2000 to 2008 is far greater than the small numbers losing their jobs in manufacturing.

The new jobs have been in:

1. distribution and services, some of the distribution jobs are the result of manufacturers outsourcing their distribution. In the past these jobs would have been classified as part of manufacturing.
2. and also in new manufacturing applications, particularly using technology advances to create new consumer products [mobile phones, computers, games etc].

In the industrialising countries, as could be expected, there has been a sharp rise in employment in manufacturing, as well as increase in output.

Productivity increases are not just caused by automation and robotics, but it is one of three main factors, along with increased size of manufacturing plants and the globalisation of sourcing. *Note: while the IFR numbers provide a*

clear basis from which to work, it has not always been possible to separate robotics from automation in our analyses.

Individual countries differ greatly, the importance of manufacturing is only 11% of employment in USA . . . but 24% in Germany and as high as 27% in more recently industrialising countries such as The Republic of Korea.

The level of robotics use has almost always doubled, in all of the six countries [except Japan] in the eight years covered by the study. The proportion of the workforce that is unemployed has hardly changed in this period. . . .

Employment *Directly* Due to the Use of Robotics [World]

The robot industry itself generates on the order of 150,000 jobs worldwide, to which can be added the support staff and operators, another 150,000 people.

There are three other types of application where robotics create or preserve jobs. These are jobs which can only be done by robots.

I Where the product cannot be made to satisfactory precision, consistency and cost, without Robotics.

II Where the conditions under which the current work is done are unsatisfactory [may be illegal in the developed countries], but where a robot will operate.

III Where [particularly] a developed country manufacturing unit with high labour costs is threatened by a unit in a low labour cost area.

Employment *Indirectly* Due to the Use of Robotics

A much larger source of employment, at least partly due to robotics, is the newly created downstream activity necessary to support manufacturing which can only be done by robots. We have been conservative in what we have chosen to include here. Some of the people we have spoken to, for example, would have liked us to have included large parts of the automotive sector sales and distribution employment. Our conclusion was that much of this infrastructure was in place before robots were widely used, and so not resulting from the use of robots.

The best example is the communication and leisure equipment business, from distribution to retailing. In the USA, this part of retailing is of the order of 1 million. In world terms this accounts for 3 to 5 million of jobs which would not exist if automation and robotics had not been developed to allow production of millions of electronic products, from phones to Playstations. . . .

Note that China now produces more cars than USA, but the number of robots used in vehicle manufacture in China is estimated at 28,000 compared with 77,000 in USA.

Robot density in a sector only provides a partial view of employment which is dependent on robotics. For example, use of robotics in the automotive sector does not cover all parts of the industry. However, large parts of the motor vehicle assembly sector would be lost to a country if it did not employ robotics. Probably not the components side, this is often highly automated but less likely to depend on robotics.

In the electronics sector some components could not be made without robotics, or could not be made at a cost which would sell, which would cause job losses not just in manufacture but downstream as well.

Potential for New Job Creation in the Years up to 2016

There are five main areas where new jobs may be created in the next five years by the use of robotics.

I. Continued development of new products based on the development of electronics and communication technology. One of the new areas identified, for example, is the manufacture of service robots. Another is the development and mass adoption of renewable energy technologies.

II. Expansion of existing economies and industries, notably automotive.

III. Greater use of robotics in the SME [small and medium enterprises] sectors, particularly in the developed countries, to protect or win back manufacture from the low cost countries, or to win back production which had been seen as hazardous, but which had been taken up by the developing countries.

IV. Greater use of robotics in the food sector [where current use is low] as processed meals develop, to meet more stringent hygiene conditions.

V. Expansion of the robotics sector itself, to cope with the growth in demand. We have assumed a 15% growth which adds 45,000 people.

Overall Effect

Direct employment due to robotics:

2 to 3 million jobs created in world manufacturing

Considering the world population of industrial robots at just over 1 million, **that is 2 to 3 jobs per robot in use.**

Indirect employment downstream of this more than doubles this number.

For the future, 700,000 to 1 million new jobs to be created by robots in the next five years.

EXPLORING THE ISSUE

Will Robots Take Your Job?

Critical Thinking and Reflection

1. What are "industrial" robots?
2. What kinds of jobs now held by humans may robots be able to do in the near future?
3. Why do robots threaten more than just industrial jobs?
4. In what ways might robots create jobs?
5. If robots take all the jobs, what will people do?

Is There Common Ground?

Computer technology (including robotics) is a rapidly growing field. Indeed, in the past whenever someone would say "Computers can't do X!" someone else would add "Yet!" They'd be right, too, for computers can now do a great many things their predecessors could not. Surely this applies to robotics as well, and robots have been expanding their presence in the workplace for decades. They will continue to do so, and Marshall Brain and Peter Gorle and Andrew Clive may well agree that there is a fine line between robots taking jobs and—in a faltering economy—robots keeping companies alive without hiring more humans. It is also worth stressing that the YES and NO selections differ in their timelines. Marshall Brain says job loss will be severe by the middle of the twenty-first century. Peter Gorle and Andrew Clive say many (up to 1 million) jobs will be created in the next five years. If they had tried to project further into the future, perhaps they would have agreed with Marshall Brain.

1. Why have employers welcomed robots in the workplace?
2. What jobs seem to you to be out of reach for robots (so far!)?
3. Marshall Brain suggests that it is time to rethink our economy. Where would you begin?

Contributors to This Volume

EDITOR

THOMAS A. EASTON is a professor of science at Thomas College in Waterville, Maine, where he has been teaching environmental science; science, technology, and society; and computer science since 1983. He received a BA in biology from Colby College in 1966 and a PhD in theoretical biology from the University of Chicago in 1971. He writes and speaks frequently on scientific and futuristic issues. His books include *Focus on Human Biology*, 2nd ed., coauthored with Carl E. Rischer (HarperCollins, 1995), *Careers in Science*, 4th ed. (VGM Career Horizons, 2004), *Classic Edition Sources: Environmental Studies*, 4th ed. (McGraw-Hill, 2011), *Taking Sides: Clashing Views on Controversial Issues in Science, Technology, and Society* (McGraw-Hill, 10th ed., 2011), and *Taking Sides: Clashing Views on Controversial Environmental Issues* (McGraw-Hill, 14th ed., 2011). Dr. Easton is also a well-known writer and critic of science fiction.

AUTHORS

STEVEN BEST is an associate professor of philosophy at the University of Texas, El Paso. His most recent book (coauthored with Anthony J. Nocella) is *Igniting a Revolution: Voices in Defense of the Earth* (AK Press, 2006). According to his Web site (www.drstevebest.org/), "He has come under fire for his uncompromising advocacy of 'total liberation' (humans, animals, and the earth) and has been banned from the UK for the power of his thoughts."

MARSHALL BRAIN is a writer, national speaker, consultant, and business coach, best known as the founder of "How Stuff Works," a website he started in 1998. In 2007 Discovery Communications purchased HowStuffWorks.com for $250 million. He is also well known as the host of the show "Factory Floor," which appeared on the National Geographic channel.

KEVIN BULLIS is the energy editor of *Technology Review.*

ANDRWE CLIVE is a senior consultant with Metra Martech, a firm specializing in industrial and economic analyses for governments and international organizations.

GREGORY CONKO is a senior fellow at the Competitive Enterprise Institute. He is the coauthor, with Henry I. Miller, of *The Frankenfood Myth: How Protest and Politics Threaten the Biotech Revolution* (Praeger, 2004).

MAURA CONWAY is a lecturer in international security in the School of Law and Government at Dublin City University in Dublin, Ireland.

SUSAN E. DUDLEY is the administrator of the Office of Management and Budget's (OMB) Office of Information and Regulatory Affairs.

LINDA S. ERDREICH is a senior managing scientist in Exponent's Health Sciences Center for Epidemiology, Biostatistics, and Computational Biology, and has 30 years of experience in environmental epidemiology and health risk assessment.

AMITAI ETZIONI is university professor and professor of international affairs, George Washington University, where he is the director of the Institute for Communitarian Policy Studies. His latest book is *How Patriotic Is the Patriot Act? Freedom Versus Security in the Age of Terrorism* (Routledge, 2008).

JAMES R. FLEMING, professor of science, technology, and society at Colby College in Waterville, Maine, is a public policy scholar at the Wilson Center and holds the American Association for the Advancement of Science's Roger Revelle Fellowship in Global Environmental Stewardship.

DAVE FOREMAN is the director and senior fellow of the Rewilding Institute. He has been active in wildlife conservation for more than 30 years. His books include *Confessions of an Eco-Warrior* (Harmony, 1991) and *Rewilding North America* (Island Press, 2004).

JEFF FOUST is the editor and publisher of *The Space Review* (www.thespacereview.com/).

JULIUS GENACHOWSKI is the chair of the Federal Communications Commission.

PETER GORLE is the managing director of Metra Martech, a firm specializing in industrial and economic analyses for governments and international organizations.

FRANCESCA T. GRIFO is the director of the Union of Concerned Scientists' Scientific Integrity Program.

JAYDEE HANSON is the policy director at the International Center for Technology Assessment (/www.icta.org).

ERIC HOFFMAN is a genetic technology policy campaigner with Friends of the Earth (www.foe.org/healthy-people/biofuels-synthetic-biology).

JOHN HORGAN is an award-winning science journalist and director of the Center for Science Writings at the Stevens Institute of Technology, Hoboken, New Jersey. His latest book is *Rational Mysticism: Dispatches from the Border Between Science and Spirituality* (Houghton Mifflin, 2003).

MICHAEL HORN is a retired aerospace scientist.

THE INSTITUTE OF MEDICINE has since its creation in 1970 served as the component of the National Academies that deals with health-related issues.

INTERNATIONAL INTELLECTUAL PROPERTY ALLIANCE (IIPA) is a coalition of trade associations (the Association of American Publishers, the Business Software Alliance, the Entertainment Software Association, the Independent Film & Television Alliance, the Motion Picture Association of America, the National Music Publishers' Association, and the Recording Industry Association of America). It works to improve international protection and enforcement of copyrighted materials and open up foreign markets closed by piracy and other market access barriers.

HEATHER D. JOSEPH is the executive director of the Scholarly Publishing and Academic Resources Coalition Committee.

GREGORY E. KAEBNICK is a research scholar at The Hastings Center and editor of the Hastings Center Report.

BRUCE KNIGHT spent several years as the Undersecretary for Marketing and Regulatory Programs at the U.S. Department of Agriculture. He is now a consultant focusing on conservation and environmental issues related to agriculture.

CHRISTOF KOCH is a professor of cognitive and behavioral biology at California Institute of Technology.

JAMES A. LEWIS is director and senior fellow, Technology and Public Policy Program, at the Center for Strategic and International Studies.

ALLISON MacFARLANE is an associate professor of environmental science and policy at George Mason University and a member of the U.S. Energy Department's Blue Ribbon Commission on America's Nuclear Future. She

is the coauthor, with Rod Ewing, of *Uncertainty Underground: Yucca Mountain and High-Level Nuclear Waste Disposal* (MIT Press, 2006).

MIKE McCONNELL was the director of the National Security Agency in the Clinton administration and the director of national intelligence during President George W. Bush's second term. A retired Navy vice admiral, he is executive vice president of Booz Allen Hamilton, which consults on cyber-security for the private and public sector.

ANNE PLATT McGINN is a senior researcher at the Worldwatch Institute and the author of "Why Poison Ourselves? A Precautionary Approach to Synthetic Chemicals," *Worldwatch Paper 153* (November 2000).

M. J. McNAMEE is a reader in philosophy at the Centre for Philosophy, Humanities and Law in Healthcare, School of Health Science, University of Wales, Swansea, United Kingdom.

MAXWELL J. MEHLMAN is the Arthur E. Petersilge Professor of Law, director of the Law-Medicine Center, and professor of Bioethics at Case Western Reserve University. His latest book is *The Price of Perfection: The Individual and Society in the Era of Biomedical Enhancement* (Johns Hopkins University Press, 2009).

KYLE McSLARROW is the president and chief executive officer of the National Cable & Telecommunications Association.

MICHAEL MEYER, the European editor for *Newsweek International,* is a member of the New York Council on Foreign Relations and was an Inaugural Fellow at the American Academy in Berlin. He won the Overseas Press Club's Morton Frank Award for business/economic reporting from abroad in 1986 and 1988 and was a member of the *Newsweek* team that won a 1993 National Magazine Award for its coverage of the Los Angeles riots. He is the author of *The Alexander Complex* (Times Books, 1989), an examination of the psychology of American empire builders.

HENRY I. MILLER is a research fellow at Stanford University's Hoover Institution. His research focuses on public policy toward science and technology, especially biotechnology. He is the coauthor, with Gregory Conko, of *The Frankenfood Myth: How Protest and Politics Threaten the Biotech Revolution* (Praeger, 2004).

JOHN J. MILLER is *National Review*'s national political reporter. His latest book is *A Gift of Freedom: How the John M. Olin Foundation Changed America* (Encounter Books, 2005).

OLGA V. NAIDENKO is a senior scientist at Environmental Working Group (EWG), a nonprofit research and advocacy organization based in Washington, District of Columbia; Ames, Iowa; and Oakland, California.

THE NATIONAL ACADEMY OF SCIENCES (NAS), part of the National Academies (www.nationalacademies.org/), is a society of distinguished scholars that analyzes and reports on scientific and technological issues when called upon by government agencies.

RICK NEWMAN is chief business correspondent for *U.S. News and World Report* and the author of *Firefight: Inside the Battle to Save the Pentagon on 9/11* (Presidio, 2008) and *Bury Us Upside Down: The Misty Pilots and the Secret Battle for the Ho Chi Minh Trail* (Presidio, 2006).

RALPH OMAN is Pravel Professorial Lecturer in Intellectual Property Law and Fellow of the Creative and Innovative Economy Center, The George Washington University Law School. He is counsel for the intellectual property practice group of the firm Dechert, LLP, and has served as Register of Copyrights of the United States and as chief counsel of the Senate Subcommittee on Patents, Copyrights, and Trademarks.

DONALD R. ROBERTS is a professor in the Division of Tropical Public Health, Department of Preventive Medicine and Biometrics, Uniformed Services University of the Health Sciences.

PETER SCHENKEL is a retired political scientist interested in the question of what contact with advanced aliens would mean to humanity.

RUSSELL L. SCHWEICKART is the chairman of the B612 Foundation, whose goal is "to significantly alter the orbit of an asteroid, in a controlled manner, by 2015." As an astronaut, he served as the lunar module pilot for *Apollo 9*, March 3–13, 1969.

SETH SHOSTAK is a senior astronomer at the SETI Institute and the author of *Sharing the Universe: Perspectives on Extraterrestrial Life* (Berkeley Hills Books, 1998).

KRISTIN SHRADER-FRECHETTE is the O'Neill Family Professor, Department of Biological Sciences and Department of Philosophy, at the University of Notre Dame. She is the author of *Taking Action, Saving Lives: Our Duties to Protect Environmental and Public Health* (Oxford University Press, 2007).

FRANCIS SLAKEY is Upjohn Professor of Physics and Biology at Georgetown University and associate director of public affairs for the American Physical Society.

JEFFREY M. SMITH is the director of the Institute for Responsible Technology and the Campaign for Healthier Eating in America. He is the author of the International bestseller *Seeds of Deception* (Yes! Books, 2003). His latest book is *Genetic Roulette: The Documented Health Risks of Genetically Engineered Foods* (Yes! Books, 2007).

PAUL D. SPUDIS is a staff scientist at the Lunar and Planetary Institute in Houston. He has served on numerous committees advising NASA on exploration strategies. With Ben Bussey, he coauthored *The Clementine Atlas of the Moon* (Cambridge University Press, 2004).

JIM THOMAS is a program manager at ETC Group (Action Group on Erosion, Technology and Concentration) (http://eee.etcgroup.org/issues/synthetic_biology).

MICHAEL TIEMANN is vice-president of Open Source Affairs at Red Hat, Inc., as well as president of the Open Source Initiative.

GIULIO TONONI is a professor of psychiatry at the University of Wisconsin, Madison.

J. SCOTT TURNER is an associate professor of biology at the SUNY College of Environmental Science and Forestry in Syracuse, New York. His latest book is *The Tinkerer's Accomplice: How Design Emerges from Life Itself* (Harvard University Press, 2007).

J. ANTHONY TYSON is an astrophysicist and professor of physics at the University of California, Davis, and the director of the Large Synoptic Survey Telescope (LSST) project.

NEIL deGRASSE TYSON is the director of the Hayden Planetarium at the American Museum of Natural History. His latest book is *Death by Black Hole and Other Cosmic Quandaries* (Norton, 2007).

JULIA WHITTY is a former documentary filmmaker and the author of *Deep Blue Home: An Intimate Ecology of Our Wild Ocean* (Houghton Mifflin Harcourt, 2010).

RAY L. WULF is an Oklahoma farmer and rancher. Until 2009, he was the president and CEO of American Farmers and Ranchers Mutual Insurance Company in Oklahoma City.